Communications in Computer and Information Science 2863

Series Editors

Rationale
The CCIS series is devoted to the publication of proceedings of computer science conferences. Its aim is to efficiently disseminate original research results in informatics in printed and electronic form. While the focus is on publication of peer-reviewed full papers presenting mature work, inclusion of reviewed short papers reporting on work in progress is welcome, too. Besides globally relevant meetings with internationally representative program committees guaranteeing a strict peer-reviewing and paper selection process, conferences run by societies or of high regional or national relevance are also considered for publication.

Topics
The topical scope of CCIS spans the entire spectrum of informatics ranging from foundational topics in the theory of computing to information and communications science and technology and a broad variety of interdisciplinary application fields.

Information for Volume Editors and Authors
Publication in CCIS is free of charge. No royalties are paid, however, we offer registered conference participants temporary free access to the online version of the conference proceedings on SpringerLink (http://link.springer.com) by means of an http referrer from the conference website and/or a number of complimentary printed copies, as specified in the official acceptance email of the event.

CCIS proceedings can be published in time for distribution at conferences or as post-proceedings, and delivered in the form of printed books and/or electronically as USBs and/or e-content licenses for accessing proceedings at SpringerLink. Furthermore, CCIS proceedings are included in the CCIS electronic book series hosted in the SpringerLink digital library at http://link.springer.com/bookseries/7899. Conferences publishing in CCIS are allowed to use our online conference service (Meteor) for managing the whole proceedings lifecycle (from submission and reviewing to preparing for publication) free of charge.

Publication process
The language of publication is exclusively English. Authors publishing in CCIS have to sign the Springer CCIS copyright transfer form, however, they are free to use their material published in CCIS for substantially changed, more elaborate subsequent publications elsewhere. For the preparation of the camera-ready papers/files, authors have to strictly adhere to the Springer CCIS Authors' Instructions and are strongly encouraged to use the CCIS LaTeX style files or templates.

Abstracting/Indexing
CCIS is abstracted/indexed in DBLP, Google Scholar, EI-Compendex, Mathematical Reviews, SCImago, Scopus. CCIS volumes are also submitted for the inclusion in ISI Proceedings.

How to start

To start the evaluation of your proposal for inclusion in the CCIS series, please send an e-mail to ccis@springer.com

Kartick Chandra Mondal ·
Munmun Bhattacharya · Parama Bhaumik ·
Somnath Mukhopadhyay · Jyotsna K. Mandal ·
Paramartha Dutta
Editors

Computational Intelligence in Communications and Business Analytics

7th International Conference, CICBA 2025
Kolkata, India, July 4–6, 2025
Revised Selected Papers, Part III

Editors
Kartick Chandra Mondal
SRM University AP
Amaravati, Andhra Pradesh, India

Parama Bhaumik
Jadavpur University
Kolkata, West Bengal, India

Jyotsna K. Mandal
University of Kalyani
Kalyani, West Bengal, India

Munmun Bhattacharya
Jadavpur University
Kolkata, West Bengal, India

Somnath Mukhopadhyay
Assam University
Silchar, Assam, India

Paramartha Dutta
Visva-Bharati University
Bolpur, West Bengal, India

ISSN 1865-0929 ISSN 1865-0937 (electronic)
Communications in Computer and Information Science
ISBN 978-3-032-17183-2 ISBN 978-3-032-17184-9 (eBook)
https://doi.org/10.1007/978-3-032-17184-9

This Springer imprint is published by the registered company Springer Nature Switzerland AG
The registered company address is: Gewerbestrasse 11, 6330 Cham, Switzerland

Preface

It is our great pleasure to present the proceedings of the Seventh International Conference on Computational Intelligence in Communications and Business Analytics (CICBA 2025), held at the Department of Information Technology, Jadavpur University, India, from 4 to 6 July 2025, in hybrid mode.

Since its inception, CICBA has established itself as a premier forum at the intersection of computational intelligence, communications, and business analytics, fostering collaboration between academia and industry across the globe. CICBA 2025 continued this tradition by providing a vibrant platform for sharing novel research findings, experiences, and innovations from both theoretical and applied perspectives.

We were honored to host several distinguished keynote speakers, each a noted expert in their respective domains: Dilip Kumar Pratihar (IIT Kharagpur), Narayan C. Debnath (Eastern International University, Vietnam), Anirban Chakraborty (Indian Institute of Science, Bangalore), Ankur Sinha (Indian Institute of Management, Ahmedabad), Niladri Roy (TCS), and Deepankar Choudhury (IIT Bombay). Their insightful talks enriched the conference with perspectives that spanned cutting-edge theoretical research and real-world applications.

We are pleased to continue our collaboration with the Springer Communications in Computer and Information Science (CCIS) series for publishing the proceedings of CICBA 2025, ensuring high academic standards and global visibility of the presented works.

The conference maintained a rigorous and transparent review process for the selection of high-quality contributions. Each submission underwent an initial screening by the Program Committee (PC) Board, followed by a double-blind peer review. The review process involved careful evaluation of originality, technical depth, correctness, relevance, contribution, and clarity. A total of 311 papers were submitted, of which 28 papers (9%) were rejected during the initial screening by the Program Committee. The remaining submissions (283 papers) underwent detailed assessment from renowned and domain expert reviewers, receiving over 721 reviews in total, averaging 2.6 independent reviews per paper. After comprehensive evaluation and deliberation, 106 papers were accepted for registration. Finally, 100 papers were registered and presented at the conference as a full paper, resulting in an acceptance rate of 32.1%.

The accepted papers are organized into three thematic tracks, reflecting the interdisciplinary scope of the conference:

- Track 1: Computational Intelligence
- Track 2: Data Communication
- Track 3: Analytics and Application

Together, these tracks capture the diversity and vitality of ongoing research in computational intelligence, communications, and analytics.

Track 1: Computational Intelligence presents advances in artificial intelligence and machine learning, covering diverse applications such as deep learning for healthcare diagnostics, AI-driven social media analytics for mental health, smart agriculture using IoT-based prediction models, and intelligent cybersecurity for Industry 4.0 environments. Additional themes include explainable AI, energy optimization, natural language processing, visual recognition, and bio-inspired computing.

Track 2: Data Communication focuses on the design, optimization, and security of modern communication systems. The papers in this track address topics such as intrusion and anomaly detection in IoT and wireless sensor networks, cryptographic and steganographic methods for data protection, energy-efficient communication protocols, blockchain-based secure data transmission, 5G/6G paradigms, network virtualization, and cloud–edge collaboration models.

Track 3: Analytics and Application emphasizes data-driven innovation across multiple sectors. The contributions highlight predictive analytics for domains such as finance, healthcare, energy, and environment, using approaches including time-series forecasting, reinforcement learning, and multimodal data fusion. The track also explores sustainable computing, intelligent decision support, recommender systems, and climate informatics.

Collectively, these papers demonstrate the conference's commitment to fostering interdisciplinary research and advancing computational intelligence for societal and industrial impact.

We gratefully acknowledge the dedicated efforts of the Program Committee Members, Reviewers, Session Chairs, and the Organizing Team for maintaining the highest academic standards throughout the review and publication process. We extend heartfelt thanks to all authors, participants, and sponsors whose contributions made CICBA 2025 a resounding success.

We also express our deep gratitude to all keynote speakers, members of the Organizing, Program, and Advisory Committees, and to Springer Nature, our publication partner, for ensuring wide dissemination of the accepted works through the CCIS series.

The organizers gratefully acknowledge the funding support from the Anusandhan National Research Foundation (ANRF), Government of India, which enabled the successful conduct of CICBA 2025. This support has been instrumental in fostering academic exchange, enhancing research visibility, and encouraging broad participation from a diverse scientific community. The contribution from ANRF has significantly strengthened the conference's mission to promote excellence in interdisciplinary research and collaboration among academia, industry, and research institutions.

We sincerely hope that the ideas presented in this volume will inspire new collaborations and future explorations at the intersection of computational intelligence, data analytics, and societal applications. We look forward to the upcoming editions of CICBA, continuing our journey toward greater innovation, collaboration, and global impact.

Kartick Chandra Mondal
Munmun Bhattacharya
Parama Bhaumik
Somnath Mukhopadhyay
Jyotsna K. Mandal
Paramartha Dutta

Organization

Chief Patron

Bhaskar Gupta	Jadavpur University, India

Patron

Amitava Dutta	Jadavpur University, India

Organizing Chair

Bibhas Chandra Dhara	Jadavpur University, India

Finance Chair

Dipanjan Roychowdhury	Jadavpur University, India

Program Chairs

Kartick Chandra Mondal	SRM University AP, India
Parama Bhaumik	Jadavpur University, India
Munmun Bhattacharya	Jadavpur University, India
Somnath Mukhopadhyay	Assam University, India
Paramartha Dutta	Visva Bharati University, India
Jyotsna K. Mandal	University of Kalyani, India

Registration Chairs

Bhaskar Sardar	Jadavpur University, India
Palash Kundu	Jadavpur University, India
Pawan Kumar Singh	Jadavpur University, India

Publicity Chairs

Tohida Rehman — Jadavpur University, India
Munmun Bhattacharya — Jadavpur University, India

Publication Chairs

Uttam Kumar Roy — Jadavpur University, India
Bibhas Chandra Dhara — Jadavpur University, India
Sruti Gan Chaudhuri — Jadavpur University, India

Hospitality Chairs

Parama Bhaumik — Jadavpur University, India
Utpal Kumar Ray — Jadavpur University, India
Rohini Basak — Jadavpur University, India

Website Chair

Kartick Chandra Mondal — Jadavpur University, India

Student Chairs

Aritra Mondal — Jadavpur University, India
Sehensha Kabir — Jadavpur University, India

International Advisory Committee

A. Damodaram — Jawaharlal Nehru Technological University, India
Amit Konar — Jadavpur University, India
Ujjwal Moulik — Jadavpur University, India
Aynur Unal — Stanford University, USA
Banshidhar Majhi — Veer Surendra Sai University of Technology, India
Carlos A. Coello Coello — CINVESTAV-IPN, Mexico
Edward Tsang — University of Essex, UK
Hisao Ishibuchi — Southern University of Science and Technology, China

Kalyanmoy Deb	Michigan State University, USA
L. M. Patnaik	IISc Bangalore, India
P. N. Suganthan	Qatar University, Qatar
Pabitra Mitra	Indian Institute of Technology Kharagpur, India
Satish Narayana Srirama	University of Tartu, Estonia
Subir Sarkar	Jadavpur University, India
Sushmita Mitra	Indian Statistical Institute, Kolkata, India
Umapada Pal	Indian Statistical Institute, Kolkata, India
Andries Engelbrecht	Stellenbosch University, South Africa
Carlos M. Fonseca	University of Coimbra, Portugal
Gunter Rudolph	TU Dortmund University, Germany
Qingfu Zhang	City University of Hong Kong, China
Ong Yew Soon	Nanyang Technological University, Singapore

Organizing Committee

Bibhas Chandra Dhara	Jadavpur University, India
Uttam Kumar Roy	Jadavpur University, India
Bhaskar Sardar	Jadavpur University, India
Parama Bhaumik	Jadavpur University, India
Kartick Chandra Mondal	Jadavpur University, India
Tohida Rehman	Jadavpur University, India
Utpal Kumar Ray	Jadavpur University, India
Munmun Bhattacharya	Jadavpur University, India
Sruti Gan Chowdhury	Jadavpur University, India
Pawan Kumar Singh	Jadavpur University, India
Rohini Basak	Jadavpur University, India
Palash Kundu	Jadavpur University, India

Program Committee

Ajoy Kumar Khan	Mizoram University, India
Alok Chakraborty	National Institute of Technology Meghalaya, India
Amitava Nag	Central Institute of Technology, Kokrajhar, India
Anamitra Roy Chaudhury	IBM Research New Delhi, India
Angsuman Sarkar	Kalyani Government Engineering College, India
Animesh Biswas	University of Kalyani, India
Anirban Mukhopadhyay	University of Kalyani, India
Arindam Sarkar	Ramakrishna Mission Vidyamandira, India
Arnab Maji	North-Eastern Hill University, India

Asif Ekbal	Indian Institute of Technology Patna, India
Biswapati Jana	Vidyasagar University, India
Brojo Kishore Mishra	NIST University, India
Chandreyee Chowdhury	Jadavpur University, India
Debashis De	Maulana Abul Kalam Azad University of Technology, India
Debasis Giri	Maulana Abul Kalam Azad University of Technology, India
Debasish Chakraborty	Indian Space Research Organisation, India
Debotosh Bhattacharjee	Jadavpur University, India
Himadri Dutta	Kalyani Government Engineering College, India
Hrishav Bakul Barua	Monash University, Australia
Indranil Ghosh	Institute of Management Technology, Hyderabad, India
J. K. Singh	Jadavpur University, India
Jayeeta Mondal	TCS Innovations India, India
Jeet Dutta	TCS Innovations India, India
Kakali Dutta	Visva Bharati University, India
Kamal Sarkar	Jadavpur University, India
Kaushik Das Sharma	Calcutta University, India
Koushik Majumder	Maulana Abul Kalam Azad University of Technology, India
Koushik Mondal	Indian Institute of Technology (ISM) Dhanbad, India
Kousik Roy	West Bengal State University, India
Laiphrakpam Dolendro Singh	NIT Silchar, India
Mohan Pratap Pradhan	Sikkim University, India
Moirangthem Marjit Singh	North Eastern Regional Institute of Science and Technology, India
Moumita Ghosh	Narula Institute of Technology, India
Mousum Handique	Assam University Silchar, India
Mrinal Kanti Bhowmik	Tripura University, India
Nabendu Chaki	University of Calcutta, India
Nibaran Das	Jadavpur University, India
Nilanjana Dutta Roy	Techno International New Town, India
Partha Pratim Ray	Sikkim University, India
Partha Pratim Sahu	Tezpur University, India
Prasanta K. Jana	Indian School of Mines Dhanbad, India
Prashant R. Nair	Amrita Vishwa Vidyapeetham, India
Prodipto Das	Assam University Silchar, India
Ram Sarkar	Jadavpur University, India
Ramen Pal	University of Limerick, Ireland

Ranjita Das	National Institute of Technology Agartala, India
Ratika Pradhan	Sikkim University, India
Ravi Subban	Pondicherry University, India
Rebika Rai	Sikkim University, India
Samarjit Kar	National Institute of Technology Durgapur, India
Sankhayan Choudhury	University of Calcutta, India
Santi P. Maity	Indian Institute of Engineering Science and Technology Shibpur, India
Sarbani Roy	Jadavpur University, India
Sarmistha Neogy	Jadavpur University, India
Sk. Obaidullah	Aliah University, India
Subarna Shakya	Tribhuvan University, Nepal
Subhadip Basu	Jadavpur University, India
Sudhakar Sahoo	Institute of Mathematics and Applications, India
Sunita Sarkar	Assam University Silchar, India
Tapodhir Acharjee	Assam University Silchar, India
Utpal Sarkar	Assam University Silchar, India
Wangjam Niranjan Singh	Assam University Silchar, India
Parama Bhaumik	Jadavpur University, India
Munmun Bhattacharya	Jadavpur University, India
Bibhas Chandra Dhara	Jadavpur University, India
Bhaskar Sardar	Jadavpur University, India
Uttam Kumar Roy	Jadavpur University, India
Pawan Kumar Singh	Jadavpur University, India
Anindita Sarkar Mondal	Calcutta University, India
Sunirmal Khatua	Calcutta University, India
Rajni Arron	National Forensic Science University, India
Moumita Ghosh	Heritage Institute of Technology, India
Neepa Biswas	Narula Institute of Technology, India
Rohmatul Farjiyah	Universitas Islam Indonesia, Indonesia
Hasih Pratiwi	Universitas Sebelas Maret, Indonesia

Contents

Analytic Track

Analytic Track

Federated Learning in Healthcare: A Case Study on Covid-19

Rahul Karmakar[1](✉), Arindam Sarkar[2], Debraj Malik[1], and Imran Mondal[1]

[1] The University of Burdwan, Bardhaman, West Bengal, India
rkarmakar@cs.buruniv.ac.in

[2] Department of Computer Science and Electronics, Ramakrishna Mission Vidyamandira, Belur Math, Howrah, India
2arindamsarkar@vidyamandira.ac.in

Abstract. Federated learning (FL), which allows for cooperative model training across decentralized data sources while protecting data privacy, has become a ground-breaking method for machine learning. FL is being utilized extensively across a number of fields, including cloud computing, blockchain, IoT, wireless networks, and most notably in medical field. Everything is data, and maintaining data privacy is another critical consideration. No option to obtain any information from healthcare providers, as no healthcare organization is willing to disclose the personal information of its patients. FL fulfills an enormous role in this instance. Due to the effectiveness of the federal learning privacy protection framework, it is now exerting a significant influence on the healthcare sector. Traditional machine learning approaches do not protect data secrecy; however, data privacy and security are ensured by federated learning mechanisms. This paper includes a comprehensive case study on the "Covid Data" dataset to predict Covid-19. Here, four ML classification models such as AdaBoost, Linear Discriminant Analysis, Extra Tree Classifier, and Decision Tree are employed to compute the best model's accuracy along with performance metrics like precision, recall, and F1-score and we also used 10 cv cross-validation score. To elevate model performance, two feature selection methods, Mutual Information and Chi2, are used. The results enhance our comprehension of FL's function in developing decentralized machine learning models and their consequences for real-world applications.

Keywords: Federated Learning (FL) · Machine Learning (ML) · Healthcare · Covid-19 · Decision tree · AdaBoost

1 Introduction

Artificial intelligence (AI) speaks to a machine's capability to learn from its past experiences, adjust to novel inputs, and do tasks that humans would typically complete. These days, this technique is widely used and preferred. Artificial intelligence refers to the ability of a machine to think, act, and make decisions similar to those of a person under certain circumstances [1]. Machine learning is becoming a more and more common technology. Machine learning is a type of artificial intelligence that uses algorithms that learn

K. Chandra Mondal et al. (Eds.): CICBA 2025, CCIS 2863, pp. 3–15, 2026.
https://doi.org/10.1007/978-3-032-17184-9_1

from data to create predictions. Machine learning (ML) uses mathematical algorithms to analyze and learn from data to anticipate future events [2]. Because machine learning is a centralized process, all data from different places is kept on a single server that is employed for conditioning the machine learning model, and the central server is used to carry out the complete training procedure. There is no privacy for the data because it is shared on the server and is readily accessible to everybody [3]. Federated learning is suggested as a solution to this issue and a guarantee of privacy and confidentiality of data. In 2016, Google published the first description of Federated Learning, an advanced machine learning technique. Federated learning is a distributed, decentralized approach to training machine learning models. It is also known as collaborative learning [4]. It is not required for client devices to communicate data with global servers. Data privacy is improved because the model is trained locally utilizing raw data on edge devices. The local changes made by each device are combined to generate the final model jointly [5]. The primary drawback of the traditional artificial intelligence approach is that data privacy is not guaranteed [6]. Data privacy protection is federated learning's main objective. The model may train on local devices without exchanging sensitive data. To lower the danger of data breaches or illegal access, only model updates not actual data are shared [7]. Federated learning is clustered into five types based on distinct characteristics: data dispersion, machine learning model, secrecy manner, communication architecture, and federation [8]. It has plenty of uses, including better language models in mobile devices, tailored experiences in digital applications, financial services, IoT, transportation, and healthcare. The numerous advantages of federated learning over machine learning are covered in this paper after an overview of both approaches is given. Federated learning is a highly effective technology for the medical field [9].

Figure 1 illustrates the overall operation of the FL approach.

1.1 Contribution of the Paper

- we determined FL, its upsides over centralized machine learning, and why it is a paramount technique for the healthcare domain.
- Then, we organized a case study on medical matters. The case study encompasses COVID-19 prediction based on the "Covid Data" dataset. Four classification algorithms are applied to investigate the best models.

1.2 Organization of the Paper

The paper has been arranged as follows: Sect. 1 covers the introduction of federated learning; Sect. 2 delivers a literature review; Sect. 3 presents the case study and preprocesses the data; Sect. 4 outlines the results and discussion; and Sect. 5 concludes.

2 Literature Review

A literature review synthesizes and summarizes existing research, presents novel viewpoints, integrates contemporary and historical themes, and charts the intellectual evolution of a body of work. It might also assess references and recommend pertinent

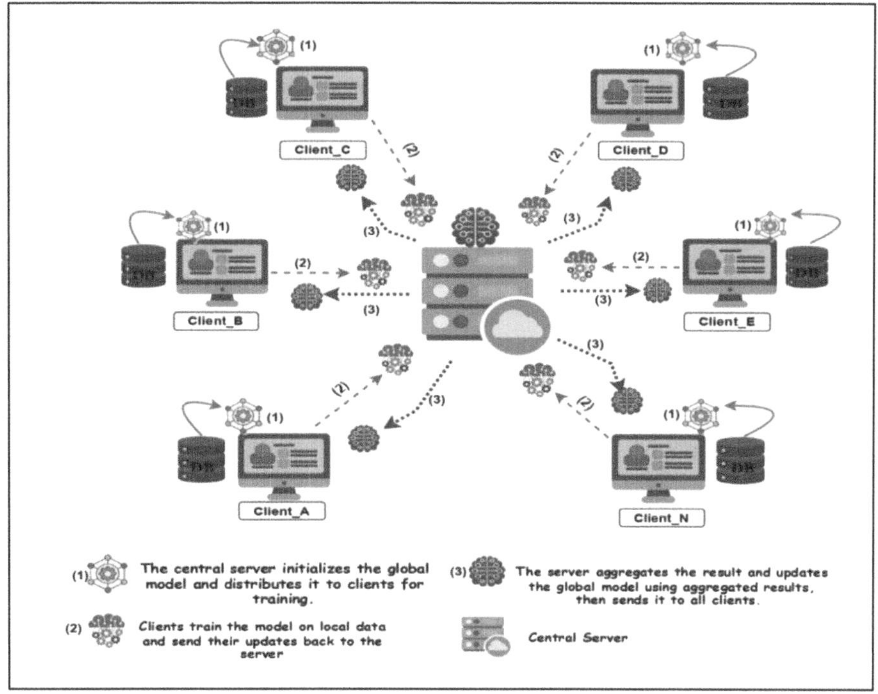

Fig. 1. Federated learning

ones. By employing FL to enable multi-institutional partnerships in medicine, Sheller et al. ensured data privacy and regulatory compliance while enabling institutions to work together on medical research without directly exchanging patient data [10]. In this study, the author accomplished a detailed literature review on the medical context and pointed out how the federated learning approach preserves privacy for healthcare datasets [11]. The author talked about the ways FL technology is useful in the biomedical space. Deliver a generic solution to statistical, systematic, and privacy difficulties in federated learning [12].The research offers FL as a privacy-preserving distributed learning approach, which is most beneficial in medical imaging where data security stipulations restrict the divulging of sensitive patient data among institutions [13].The author created a medical imaging classification model leveraging FL. Seven clinical institutes from across the world collaborated to train a model for breast density categorization based on Breast Imaging, Reporting & Data System (BIRADS). The author exhibited by collecting data from numerous locations, with variations between datasets and without centralizing the data, the model could be efficiently trained via federation [14]. In this research, the author accomplished a detailed literature review on the medical context and illustrated how the federated learning approach preserves privacy for healthcare datasets [15]. The paper covers a detailed review of the prevailing research and approaches relevant to automated COVID-19 diagnosis, with a special emphasis on federated learning (FL) and its use in healthcare. Numerous machine learning (ML) and data visualization approaches have been utilized for risk assessment, contact tracking, and diagnosis [16]. A description of federated learning use cases in the medical sector and elaborate deep learning implementations for COVID-19 detection are given by the author [17]. After analyzing several federated learning strategies, the author designed a real-time distributed network architecture utilizing the Message Queuing Telemetry Transport (MQTT) protocol [18]. The authors offer a recent survey on Federated Learning (FL), Split Learning (SL), and the hybrid Split-Federated Learning (SFL). The contributions of cutting-edge applications in medical image analysis next addressed, and the different obstacles of a decentralized learning method [19]. Kondaveeti et al. stated how federated learning assures privacy in the medical field and why it is a superior method to conventional centralized ML. They also investigate privacy preservation model updates utilizing techniques such as federated learning averaging, aggregation, and SMPC, leveraging real-world examples in the healthcare industry [20].

2.1 Research Gaps

The medical field must fill in knowledge gaps in a number of areas, such as patient care, health disparities, diagnosis, treatment, and illness prevention. To find new health trends, understand the origins of diseases, and create creative treatments, interdisciplinary teams of doctors, scientists, engineers, social scientists, and legislators are required.

3 A Case Study on Covid-19 Prediction

In this section, we conducted a case study on COVID-19 prediction using federated learning. Figure 2 depicts the workflow of our entire case study. The following Sects. (3.1 to 3.6) demonstrated overall operation.

3.1 Dataset Description

The "Covid Data" dataset is employed in the present research. A recently identified coronavirus causes an infectious condition known as coronavirus disease (COVID-19). The majority of COVID-19 virus infections result in mild to moderate respiratory disease and recovery without the need for special care. Serious illness is more common in the elderly and in those with underlying medical conditions such as cancer, diabetes, cardiovascular disease, and chronic respiratory diseases. FL is a viable method for COVID-19 prediction and other healthcare applications, protecting patient privacy and encouraging its use in delicate fields.

3.2 Data Pre-Processing

Titled "covid.csv," the collection includes 23 COVID-19-related features. We carried out thorough data pre-processing to guarantee the dataset's quality and dependability for predictive modelling. This involved standardizing numerical features, encoding categorical data, eliminating duplicate records, and imputed missing values. The dataset needed to be properly prepared for efficient feature selection and classification analysis, which involved several processes.

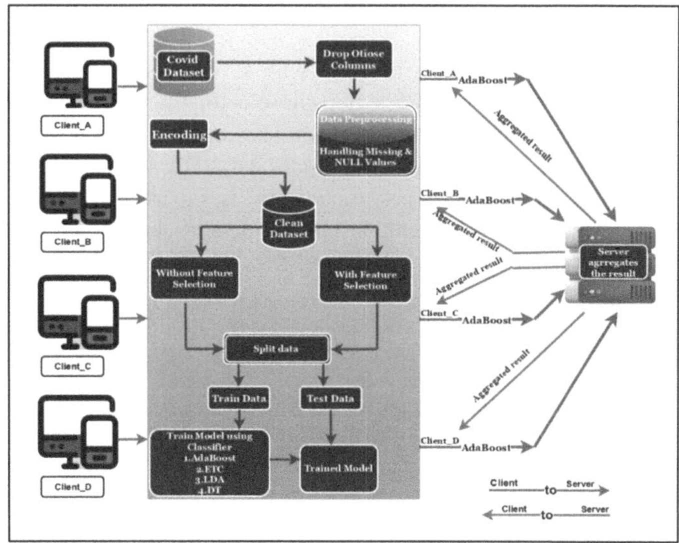

Fig. 2. The workflow of the case study. *Source* Kaggle, Size:563200 X 23

3.3 Splitting Dataset

In the field of machine learning, the term "splitting a dataset" refers to the action of dividing a given dataset into two or more separate sections, each serving a distinct function. Typically, data is separated into two groups: a training set and a test set. The dataset will be divided in order to evaluate a machine learning model's performance on unobserved data. The machine learning model is trained using the bigger percentage of the dataset, often between 70 and 90 percent. The remaining 30–20-10% of the dataset, which is smaller, is set aside for assessing the performance of the model.

3.4 Cross Validation

Finding the optimum machine-learning model is often accomplished through the use of cross-validation. Folding the dataset into folds, training the model on one fold, and assessing the model on the remaining fold or folds make up the process. A number of iterations of this process result in the average performance over all folds serving as the final evaluation criteria. The K-fold, stratified K-fold, and hold-out cross-validation techniques are widely used.

3.5 Feature Selection

Feature selection is essential for constructing efficient, interpretable, and generalizable ML models. To enhance model performance, feature selection prioritizes the most important attributes and eliminates undesirable or unnecessary ones. A model's predictive potential can be increased by selecting features, which is crucial for identifying the key attributes.

3.6 Model Evaluation

Analyzing the matter at hand, experimenting with several algorithms, and assessing each one's performance are all necessary steps in selecting the optimal machine learning model. To find the best measures like accuracy, f1 score, precision, and recall, various machine learning models are used, including AdaBoost, LDA, Decision Tree, and Extra Trees Classifier. Ultimately, we used performance metrics to assess the model's performance on the testing set. For each client, the split ratio varies, but overall, the AdaBoost model is more accurate than the other classifier.

4 Result and Discussion

The following section outlines the result for each client and transmits the best outcome to the central server. In our investigation, the central server is connected to four clients. The dataset is split into four segments and allocated one portion to each client. Initially, a model is shared with the server, which is the global model. Subsequently, a copy of the global model is provided to each client. Each client maintains its own local database, and the model is then trained using the local data. Afterward, all clients transmit their results to the server. The server consolidates the results and updates the model based on this information, resulting in a superior model than before. The server then forwards the updated outcome to each client. This procedure is carried out until the best model is achieved. We assessed the performance of four classifiers: AdaBoost, LDA, Decision Tree, and Extra Tree Classifier. The data belonging to each client was divided into training and testing sets by utilizing three distinct splitting ratios, such as 70/30, 80/20, and 90/10. We have shown the best model result among four classifiers for each client.

Now the accuracy of our proposed model has been compared to previous research. The author employed three algorithms: Sequential model (ADAM), Sequential model (SGD), and Federated model (SGD), achieving respective accuracies of 89.31%, 89.31%, and 91.61% [21]. In our paper, we employed four algorithms: AdaBoost, LDA, Extra Tree Classifier, and Decision Tree. AdaBoost achieved the greatest accuracy of 97.47%, exceeding the recommendation of the referenced literature.

Table 1 displays the highest outcome for client 1. In all of the four classification models, the AdaBoost Classifier achieved the best results with an 80–20 split ratio.

Table 2 demonstrates that using mutual information feature selection method client 1 got the best result AdaBoost classifier with a split ratio (90–10).

Table 3 represents the best result of client 2 on the covid data dataset. The AdaBoost Classifier produces the best result with a split ratio of (90–10) out of four classification models.

Table 4 demonstrates that with the mutual information feature selection method client 2 got the best result with a split ratio (90–10).

Table 5 represents the best result of client 3 on the covid data dataset. The AdaBoost Classifier produces the best result with a split ratio of (90–10) out of four classification models.

Table 6 demonstrates that using the mutual information feature selection method client 3 got the best result AdaBoost with a split ratio (90–10).

Table 1. Report of without feature selection

Result of 10 cv				
Classifier	Accuracy	F1_Score	Precision	Recall
Ada boost	**97.46**	**95.61**	91.60	**98.52**
LDA	97.18	86.39	90.94	86.39
Extra tree classifier	93.28	95.52	91.43	98.00
Decision tree	97.43	95.00	**95.51**	94.50
Result of 80:20 split				
Classifier	Accuracy	F1_Score	Precision	Recall
Ada boost	**97.47**	**95.72**	91.79	98.10
LDA	97.26	94.84	**95.70**	93.99
Extra tree classifier	93.16	88.19	91.17	85.39
Decision tree	97.43	95.68	91.73	**98.66**

Table 2. Report of with feature selection

Result of 10 cv				
Classifier	Accuracy	F1_Score	Precision	Recall
Ada boost	97.43	**95.75**	91.85	**98.32**
LDA	97.21	95.00	**95.87**	94.13
Extra tree classifier	94.73	93.25	93.41	93.09
Decision tree	**98.99**	95.00	**95.87**	94.13
Result of 90:10 split				
Classifier	Accuracy	F1_Score	Precision	Recall
Ada boost	**97.47**	**95.48**	91.36	97.89
LDA	97.27	**95.48**	91.36	**98.89**
Extra tree classifier	97.43	95.45	91.30	98.00
Decision tree	97.43	93.89	**94.75**	93.0

Table 7 represents the best result of client 4 on the covid dataset. The AdaBoost produces the best result with a split ratio of (90–10) out of four classification models.

Table 8 demonstrates that using the chi-square feature selection method client 4 got the best result AdaBoost classifier with a split ratio (90–10).

Table 9 demonstrates that four clients convey their optimal outcomes to the central server, then the server aggregates the result and improves its model using the aggregated result. In our research, every client achieved the best model findings leveraging without feature selection method.

Table 3. Report of without feature selection

Result of 10 cv				
Classifier	Accuracy	F1_Score	Precision	Recall
Ada boost	**97.30**	**95.31**	91.17	**99.85**
LDA	97.26	87.15	90.44	84.09
Extra tree classifier	91.41	95.29	91.00	99.00
Decision tree	97.25	95.28	**93.03**	97.63
Result of 90:10 split				
Classifier	Accuracy	F1_Score	Precision	Recall
Ada boost	**97.25**	91.04	91.75	90.34
LDA	97.18	**95.78**	**93.51**	**98.15**
Extra tree classifier	92.81	86.99	90.86	83.44
Decision tree	97.18	95.64	91.65	98.00

Table 4. Report of with feature selection

Result of 10 cv				
Classifier	Accuracy	F1_Score	Precision	Recall
Ada boost	97.30	95.32	91.06	97.23
LDA	97.26	95.35	93.04	97.77
Extra tree classifier	97.25	94.05	92.99	95.12
Decision tree	**98.83**	95.35	93.07	97.77
Result of 90:10 split				
Classifier	Accuracy	F1_Score	Precision	Recall
Ada boost	97.19	95.33	**95.92**	94.74
LDA	**97.24**	96.12	92.54	**99.00**
Extra tree classifier	97.17	96.06	92.42	95.00
Decision tree	97.17	**96.30**	94.34	98.34

Table 10 illustrated server generates improved outcomes and transmit it to all client and then each client received server's modified results to update their models based on local data. The outcome of federated learning is superior to that of machine learning; nevertheless, federated learning preserves dataset privacy, something machine learning is unable to do.

Table 5. Report of without feature selection

Result of 10 cv				
Classifier	Accuracy	F1_Score	Precision	Recall
Ada boost	**97.42**	**95.56**	91.49	95.32
LDA	97.33	89.94	91.42	88.51
Extra tree classifier	93.79	95.49	91.38	**98.06**
Decision tree	97.39	95.19	**95.56**	94.82
Result of 90:10 split				
Classifier	Accuracy	F1_Score	Precision	Recall
Ada boost	**97.37**	**95.72**	91.79	96.23
LDA	97.33	95.31	**95.85**	94.77
Extra tree classifier	93.61	91.02	91.70	90.36
Decision tree	97.34	95.66	91.69	**96.99**

Table 6. Report of with feature selection

Result of 10 cv				
Classifier	Accuracy	F1_Score	Precision	Recall
Ada boost	97.39	**95.56**	91.49	**96.32**
LDA	97.33	95.19	**95.56**	94.82
Extra tree classifier	97.32	93.23	94.07	92.41
Decision tree	**98.02**	95.19	**95.56**	94.82
Result of 90:10 split				
Classifier	Accuracy	F1_Score	Precision	Recall
Ada boost	**97.34**	**95.88**	92.09	**98.32**
LDA	97.32	95.55	**95.85**	95.26
Extra tree classifier	**97.34**	**95.88**	92.00	96.32
Decision tree	**97.34**	95.50	**95.85**	95.26

Table 10. Server updated result

Classifier	Split Ratio
AdaBoost	90–10

Table 7. Report of without feature selection

Result of 10 cv				
Classifier	Accuracy	F1_Score	Precision	Recall
Ada boost	**97.31**	**95.36**	91.13	98.54
LDA	97.17	90.23	91.17	89.48
Extra tree classifier	94.40	95.29	91.01	**98.65**
Decision tree	97.27	94.63	**95.38**	93.89
Result of 90:10 split				
Classifier	Accuracy	F1_Score	Precision	Recall
Ada boost	**97.30**	**95.15**	90.76	**96.23**
LDA	97.22	94.96	**95.33**	94.59
Extra tree classifier	92.11	87.63	90.07	85.33
Decision tree	97.26	95.09	90.64	**96.23**

Table 8. Report of with feature selection

Result of 10 cv				
Classifier	Accuracy	F1_Score	Precision	Recall
Ada boost	97.31	94.70	89.93	**98.15**
LDA	97.17	**95.41**	**95.03**	95.80
Extra tree classifier	97.27	94.46	89.87	97.18
Decision tree	**98.80**	94.51	92.70	96.39
Result of 90:10 split				
Classifier	Accuracy	F1_Score	Precision	Recall
Ada boost	**97.29**	95.13	90.71	**99.20**
LDA	97.18	95.06	90.59	95.23
Extra tree classifier	97.25	95.03	90.53	98.23
Decision tree	97.25	**95.38**	**95.45**	95.31

5 Conclusion

FL is an innovative paradigm in machine learning that facilitates decentralized data processing while preserving user privacy, hence transforming collaborative model training. It is becoming an indispensable technique in the medical industry. Every hospital and healthcare institution preserves patient confidential information that cannot be distributed; hence, data privacy must be upheld. FL has significance in this specific instance. This approach allows for model training without transferring data on the server. Our

Table 9: Aggregated result

Server Side		
Client	Classifier	Split Ratio
Client 1	AdaBoost	80–20
Client 2	AdaBoost	90–10
Client 3	AdaBoost	90–10
Client 4	AdaBoost	90–10

extensive case study offered an empirical evaluation of federated learning for the healthcare field. We experimented with the COVID-19 prediction by applying this strategy. The case study analysis and comprehensive literature evaluation yield a number of noteworthy conclusions with implications for further study and application. We have seen personally through these real-world implementations how federated learning opens up new possibilities for cooperative intelligence and data-driven decision-making by allowing companies to take advantage of remote data resources while protecting individual privacy rights. These results establish federated learning approaches as a cornerstone of contemporary machine learning research and practice, highlighting the growing interest in and widespread application of these approaches. We conclude that federated learning has great potential to handle collaborative model training issues in decentralized systems while maintaining user privacy and data sovereignty. There are still a lot of obstacles to overcome, such as communication cost, heterogeneity in data distributions, and privacy concerns, even though federated learning has a lot of potential for collaborative model training in decentralized environments. Future directions include increasing the number of clients and implementing certain advanced algorithms that improve federated learning's deployability in the real world.

Acknowledgments. We are grateful to the Computer Science Department, The University of Burdwan, India, for the continuous support from them we received while pursuing our research work.

Disclosure of Interests. Authors disclose that they have no conflict of interest.

References

1. Hai, T., Sarkar, A., Aksoy, M., Karmakar, R., Manna, S., Prasad, A.: Elevating security and disease forecasting in smart healthcare through artificial neural synchronized federated learning. Clust. Comput. (2024). https://doi.org/10.1007/s10586-024-04356-z
2. Camporeale, E., Marino, R., Board, E.: Our vision for JGR: machine learning and computation. J. Geophys. Res. Mach. Learn. Comput. **1**(1), e2024JH000184 (2024). https://doi.org/10.1029/2024JH000184
3. Asad, M., Moustafa, A., Ito, T.: Federated Learning Versus Classical Machine Learning: A Convergence Comparison (2021), arXiv: arXiv:2107.10976. Accessed: Oct. 26, 2024. [Online]. Available: http://arxiv.org/abs/2107.10976

4. Thummisetti, B.S.P., Atluri, H.: Advancing healthcare informatics for empowering privacy and security through federated learning paradigms. Int. J. Sustain. Dev. Comput. Sci. **6**(1), 1–16 (2024)
5. Qi, P., Chiaro, D., Guzzo, A., Ianni, M., Fortino, G., Piccialli, F.: Model aggregation techniques in federated learning: a comprehensive survey. Future Gener. Comput. Syst. **150**, 272–293 (2024). https://doi.org/10.1016/j.future.2023.09.008
6. Rokade, M.: Advancements in privacy-preserving techniques for federated learning: a machine learning perspective. J. Electr. Syst. **20**, 1075–1088 (2024). https://doi.org/10.52783/jes.1754
7. Luzón, M.V., et al.: A tutorial on federated learning from theory to practice: foundations, software frameworks, exemplary use cases, and selected trends. IEEECAA J. Autom. Sin. **11**(4), 824–850 (2024). https://doi.org/10.1109/JAS.2024.124215
8. Martínez Beltrán, E.T. et al.: Fedstellar: a platform for decentralized federated learning. Expert Syst. Appl. **242**, 122861 (2024), https://doi.org/10.1016/j.eswa.2023.122861
9. Akhtarshenas, A., et al.: Federated learning: a cutting-edge survey of the latest advancements and applications. Comput. Commun. **228**, 107964 (2024). https://doi.org/10.1016/j.comcom.2024.107964
10. Sheller, M.J., et al.: Federated learning in medicine: facilitating multi-institutional collaborations without sharing patient data. Sci. Rep. **10**(1), 12598 (2020). https://doi.org/10.1038/s41598-020-69250-1
11. Pfitzner, B., Steckhan, N., Arnrich, B.: Federated learning in a medical context: a systematic literature review. ACM Trans. Internet Technol. **21**(2), 50:1–50:31 (2021), https://doi.org/10.1145/3412357
12. Xu, J., Glicksberg, B.S., Su, C., Walker, P., Bian, J., Wang, F.: Federated Learning for Healthcare Informatics (2020), arXiv: arXiv:1911.06270. https://doi.org/10.48550/arXiv.1911.06270
13. Darzidehkalani, E., Ghasemi-rad, M., van Ooijen, P.M.A.: Federated learning in medical imaging: Part I: toward multicentral health care ecosystems. J. Am. Coll. Radiol. **19**(8), 969–974 (2022). https://doi.org/10.1016/j.jacr.2022.03.015
14. Roth, H.R. et al.: Federated Learning for Breast Density Classification: A Real-World Implementation (2020), arXiv: arXiv:2009.01871. https://doi.org/10.48550/arXiv.2009.01871
15. Joshi, M., Pal, A., Sankarasubbu, M.: Federated Learning for Healthcare Domain—Pipeline, Applications and Challenges (2022), arXiv: arXiv:2211.07893. https://doi.org/10.48550/arXiv.2211.07893
16. Qayyum, A., Ahmad, K., Ahsan, M.A., Al-Fuqaha, A., Qadir, J.: Collaborative federated learning for healthcare: multi-modal COVID-19 diagnosis at the edge. IEEE Open J. Comput. Soc. **3**, 172–184 (2022). https://doi.org/10.1109/OJCS.2022.3206407
17. "Decentralised Federated Learning for Hospital Networks With Application to COVID-19 Detection | IEEE J. Mag. | IEEE Xplore." Accessed: Oct. 25, 2024. [Online]. Available: https://ieeexplore.ieee.org/document/9869827
18. "Decentralized Federated Learning for Healthcare Networks: A Case Study on Tumor Segmentation | IEEE J. Mag. | IEEE Xplore." Accessed: Oct. 25, 2024. [Online]. Available: https://ieeexplore.ieee.org/document/9676574
19. "Decentralized Learning in Healthcare: A Review of Emerging Techniques | IEEE Journals & Magazine | IEEE Xplore." Accessed: Oct. 25, 2024. [Online]. Available: https://ieeexplore.ieee.org/document/10141615
20. Kondaveeti, H.K., Simhadri, C.G., Mangapathi, S., Vatsavayi, V.K.: Federated learning for privacy preservation in healthcare: a comprehensive introduction. In: Federated Learning and Privacy-Preserving in Healthcare AI, IGI Global, pp. 121–136 (2024). https://doi.org/10.4018/979-8-3693-1874-4.ch009

21. Salam, M.A., Taha, S., Ramadan, M.: COVID-19 detection using federated machine learning. PLoS ONE **16**(6), e0252573 (2021). https://doi.org/10.1371/journal.pone.0252573

Development of Online Handwritten Bangla Digit Dataset for Mobile Application

Trishita Ghosh[1](✉), Shibaprasad Sen[2], Ayasha Zaman[3], Sk. Md. Obaidullah[3], and Kaushik Roy[4]

[1] Guru Nanak Institute of Technology, Kolkata 700114, West Bengal, India
trish2921@gmail.com
[2] MCKV Institute of Engineering, Kolkata 711204, West Bengal, India
[3] Aliah University, Kolkata 700156, West Bengal, India
[4] West Bengal State University, Kolkata 700126, West Bengal, India

Abstract. The need for online handwriting recognition is rising due to the accessibility and affordability of devices such as PDAs, cellphones, and Take Notes, which can be used quickly and effortlessly. People can submit information using those devices in this recognition approach just as readily as they are accustomed to doing with a pen and paper. Using those devices has the benefit of directly storing the input data as timely, ordered stroke sequences. A significant database is essential for training and testing any handwritten recognition system and gathering information from people everywhere. Still, acquiring data from multiple sources has never been straightforward. In this paper, we are introducing a mobile application which is capable collecting online handwriting data from any user anywhere. Along with handwriting image it can store the x, y coordinate value and pen-up/pen-down value by giving the user a feelings like pen paper based method. The proposed system examined on 8800 Bangla digit including 4100 Bangla digit collected using mobile application. The system has gone though the supervised classifier like Support Vector Machine (SVM) and Random forest, Multi-Layer Perceptron (MLP) and unsupervised clustering like K-Mean using mobile application collected data as well as available Bangla digit dataset. It achieved highest accuracy 94.73% using Random forest classification. Because of its numerous applications in administrative automation, banking automation, postal automation, and human-computer interfaces, handwritten online character recognition has been a steaming research topic. This mobile application can collect the data for any language. We have focused on online Bangla Handwritten data collection as it is second most widely used language and seventh most-spoken native language throughout the world.

Keywords: Online handwriting · Data collection · Mobile application · Bangla handwriting

K. Chandra Mondal et al. (Eds.): CICBA 2025, CCIS 2863, pp. 16–29, 2026.
https://doi.org/10.1007/978-3-032-17184-9_2

1 Introduction

A human-computer interface is necessary in this digital age of smart gadgets in order for the computer to accurately interpret handwritten data, opening the way for a society free of paper records. Documents stored on paper might become degraded over time, therefore enhanced indexing and storage are essential. A few interesting aspects of digitized reports are their ability to order and arrange massive amounts of data for further processing, such as data retrieval. And they propose that the researchers focus their efforts on identifying characters. The domains of online and offline handwriting recognition problems can be differentiated. In order to retrieve the digital version of a certain document, data scanning is required for offline content handwriting recognition. Online handwriting recognition interprets text entered on a particular digitizer automatically by using a sensor to detect pen-tip movements and pen-up/pen-down switching fact. Online Handwriting Recognition allows users to use a digital pen or stylus to write on an electronic device, just like they would with a traditional pen and paper process. A live or dynamic computer depiction of a pen's movement can be captured. Online handwritten data is easily searchable and retrievable. Studies on handwriting recognition have attracted more and more attention from researchers in recent decades. Even with remarkable advancements, humans and machines still perform significantly differently when it comes to online writing recognition. The requirement for handwritten recognition expanded with the advent of gadgets like digital computers and cellphones that could successfully interpret and digitize the data entered. Bangla, one of the most widely spoken languages globally, has a distinctive script. In contrast to recognition systems for Arabic, Chinese, or Latin characters, Bangla online handwriting recognition still remains in the development stage while considering its significance. One of the most significant challenges is the lack of an extensive, varied, publicly available Bangla online handwritten dataset. It is possible to develop a Bangla online handwriting recognition system. However, the challenge is identifying the various handwriting styles, as well as the size and form of the written characters. Individuals may write in a variety of styles, which makes it challenging for a system to recognize their writing. To train the system and reach a high degree of accuracy, an extensive data set is required. It is possible to optimize the size of the dataset and create a writer-independent system. In order to recognize Bangla characters, words, and text online, an enormous standard dataset must be created. The gathering of data, that allows the researcher to identify answers to research questions, is one of the primary phases of a research study. The task of acquiring data with the goal of learning more about the research topic is known as data collection. As a consequence, there exist several data kinds and data collection techniques. The two fundamental categories into which data gathering techniques fall are primary and secondary data collection techniques. The techniques by which we need to acquire data for our study are known as primary data collection, and until it is published, no one can utilize this data. Secondary data is data obtained from published sources, which indicates that the information has previously been acquired and may be applied to various studies [1]. An essential phase in research, evaluation, and decision-making is data collection. Conventional approaches, such paper-based surveys, have drawbacks such poor data quality, high cost, and fatigued respondents. Utilizing the widespread use and advanced technology of smartphones, mobile applications present a viable option. In this work, we address the crucial problem of data scarcity in Bangla handwriting recognition by presenting an innovative design based on mobile applications for collecting and identifying online handwritten Bangla digits. In contrast to conventional techniques that require specialized hardware, our method allows users to contribute handwritten data with simply a smartphone, capturing both image-based and stroke-level information (x, y coordinates with pen-up/pen-down events). We have used a direction based chain code technique to extract 64-dimensional feature vectors from a dataset of 8800 Bangla digit samples, 4100 of which were gathered via the Mobile application. Several classifiers were used to evaluate the proposed system, with Random Forest obtaining the highest accuracy of 94.73%. Our contributions highlight the ways to collect and classify the handwritten data in a useful, language-independent approach that may be applied to different scripts and applications. The primary contributions of this work are the development of a mobile application, the construction of an extended dataset, the extraction of 64-dimensional structural features, and the assessment of several classifiers and clustering algorithms. Architecture of the proposed online Bangla handwritten digit recognition system depicted in Fig. 1. The mobile application captures stroke data and images, which are preprocessed and passed through a feature extraction module to generate 64-dimensional feature vectors. Various machine learning models are then used to classify these.

The article is segregated into five sections. In Sect. 2, we first provide a brief overview of the review approach used in this work. Data collection through the mobile application and pre-processing of the collected dataset are presented in Sect. 3. In Sect. 4 we have discussed the 64 dimensional feature extraction scheme used in our proposed scheme. We have outlined the experimental findings in Sect. 5. Section 6 provides a conclusion at the final stage.

2 Review Work

Handwriting recognition has shown high accuracy and significant progress over the last decade. Pen-based gadgets are becoming more and more common for data entry. This is due to the fact that keyboards are growing difficult to use and machines are getting smaller. As technology continues to evolve, handwriting recognition systems are expected to play a crucial role in bridging human-machine interaction across diverse applications. DigiMemo, CrossPad, Bamboo Slate, Take Note, iScribe, Supernote, and PDA are several significant online handwriting capturing devices present in the market [2]. In [3], Bunke et al. reported a method for online cursive handwriting data collection with a digital camera to record the handwriting. The pen tip movement was reconstructed from the captured sequence of images as reported. A major challenge in online

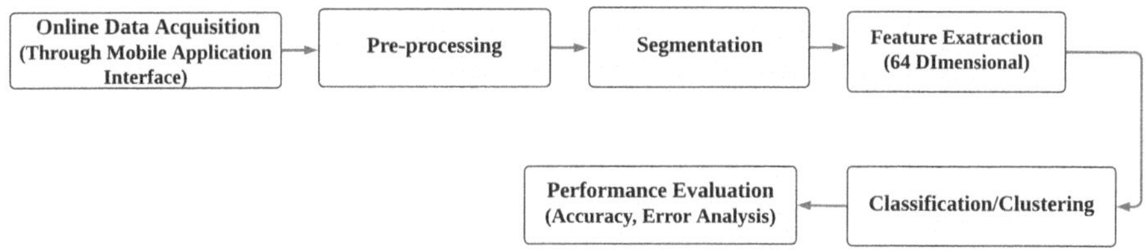

Fig. 1. Architecture of the proposed online Bangla handwritten digit recognition system.

handwriting research is the difficulty of collecting large databases across various scripts. A. Das and U. Bhattacharya reported an Android tool called ISIgraphy enabling script-independent handwriting data collection on handheld devices, with the ability to store large-scale samples under user-specified filenames [4] which is not accessible now. To the best of our knowledge, there are no other reported mobile applications for online handwriting data collection. This makes our approach unique in the current research landscape. There are few available online Bangla handwritten dataset as stated by Sen et al. [5] Parui et al. [6] and Bhattacharya et al. [7].

Characters or digits are created through distinct strokes and connections, and they have a spatial structure. The ability to figure out these strokes is crucial for digit or character identification because a fundamental stroke only represents one character or a portion of a character. One stroke or more strokes may create up a single digit or a character. In other way one digit or character can be recognized in holistic approach. In that scenario, digit recognition involves analyzing the entire character or digit as a single entity rather than breaking it down into individual strokes or components. In [8], K. Roy stated a method for recognizing the online Bangla handwritten character based on the stroke database generated from character dataset. R. Kaur and M. Singh proposed an approach to identify the strokes used to write online Gurmukhi characters. Spatial and spectral properties are determined from the gathered stroke information by the suggested system [9]. The smallest set of words that encompass all Gurmukhi symbols identified, according to the proposal of Singh et al. [10], for the work on the online handwritten Gurmukhi strokes dataset development. The stroke dataset that was produced includes manual verification by expert and moderate writers along with the k-means clustering technique. The stroke-based approach for online Bangla character recognition was proposed in by Sen et al. [11]. The study uses a distance-based feature extraction approach to recognize the strokes in online handwritten Bangla letters. A rule-based technique is employed to form the characters based on the results of this step. In this study, we explain our initial phases in gathering data for Bangla online handwriting recognition that can assist our own research as well as benefit others in the field. In order to challenge the current status, it is necessary that we standard application and data formats and to produce and make available verified datasets.

3 Data Collection Through the Mobile Application and Pre-processing

Despite the ease with which digital notes may be taken on computers and phones, most people still prefer to take their notes on paper. Technological gadgets intended to digitize handwritten input in real time are known as online handwriting capturing devices. With the pen or stylus that comes with these devices, users may write or draw in a natural way, and their handwriting is instantaneously translated into a digital version that can be shared, altered, and saved on a number of digital platforms. Accurately capturing handwritten data and easily transferring it into a digital format for additional processing and analysis are the key objectives of online handwriting capturing equipment created especially for collecting data for online handwriting recognition work. Dynamic information is crucial to online handwriting recognition because it provides fundamental data like stroke count and order. These smart devices can save all the information required for online handwriting recognition, such as coordinate values, pen-up and pen-down occurrences, slope, shape, and so forth. Numerous devices, like the Wacom One, Wacom Intuos, and Bamboo slate, can capture handwriting online. Through CrossPad, users can take and send digital notes on a notepad. This digital pen uses radio transmission to record data to the notepad. Handwriting on paper and digital pages can be quickly coordinated with DigiMemo's online writing capability. HP Labs India developed the online handwriting recognition toolkit known as Lipi Toolkit (LipiTk). Open standards like UNIPEN [12] are used by LipiTk to represent digital ink. As the pen writes on the sheet, the device's digitizing pad detects its location in X-Y coordinates, which are then stored in the internal memory of the gadget [13]. Another digital writing pad that may be used to capture handwriting online is called iScribe. It holds A4-sized paper and comes with a special pen that can be refilled with regular supplies. This captures your handwritten notes and sketches in real time easily. Taking notes and storing them in the same digital format is also possible with Supernote, a gadget that blends current technology and the conventional notepad [14]. Now a days, we cant think without a mobile phone. In every aspect we need this device and we have felt the importance of a smart phones during pandemic. An essential part of research on online handwriting recognition is data collection. It offers the essential foundation for developing, training, and testing handwriting recognition systems. To ensure that a machine learning model can adapt well to various handwriting styles, an extensive and diverse collection of handwriting samples is necessary. We also require a lot of data for studies like handwriting recognition. Mobile applications provide a more accessible and affordable alternative for collecting handwritten data than the current online systems like DigiMemo, CrossPad, iScribe, and Wacom tablets that collect handwriting data. Mobile apps use sensors and built-in touchscreens to record dynamic handwriting properties like pen-up/pen-down states, and stroke sequence using just a finger or stylus; on other hand traditional devices require specialized writing pad and smart pen. Since the majority of people already own smartphones, that particular equipment will not be necessary, which will save money when compared to acquiring specialized handwriting capture devices.

All online handwriting capturing device need to be carried to collect data from different location where as our proposed mobile application can do the task easily from any location. The innovative online handwriting data collection application is presented in this section. Data collection process become more easy from any where by using this application. We can collect and save the image of the data as well as the online data like x, y coordinate value and pen-up/pen-down by using this application by using simple finger tips. Mobile device itself will act as a paper where we can write using our finger tips only. There are two window in this application. First window, i.e. writing pad has the two zones. First and top zone is the writing area where user can write the character and after clicking the 'save' button image of the handwritten character will be displayed in the second zone. Home page of the data collection application has been depicted in Fig. 2. The upper zone of figure represent the data written using finger tip in writing pad and lower zone represent the image of the saved data. As we need the online handwriting data for our research work we have to store the x, y coordinate values and pen-up/pen-down movement. Figure 2c shows second window with the online data of the Bangla handwritten digit data.

The system was tested on 8,800 Bangla Digit data collected online, including 4,100 data collected from the mobile application. A total of 4,100 handwritten digit samples were collected from contributions of 41 people. There were 100 samples per participant, with 10 samples for each digit from 0 to 9 on different days. Most of the contributors were students or professionals from different educational backgrounds. Most of them are B. Tech students, with others with degrees like B. Sc., M. A., Diploma, M. Com., B. Com., MBBS, and secondary education. The group comprises 30 males and 11 females. Prepossessing of the collected data was done to remove the noise and it was normalized to enhances the quality and consistency of the data which consist of x, y coordinate value and pen-up/pen-down value has been converted to an image. Resizing of the images in a fixed dimension implied for uniformity.

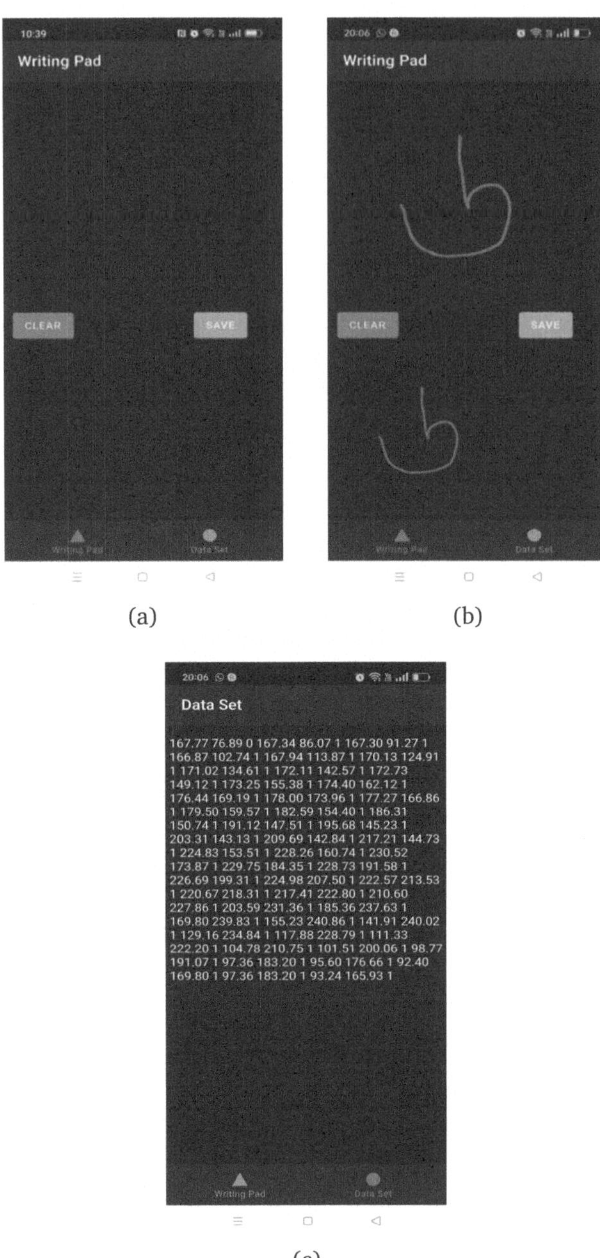

Fig. 2. **a** Home page **b** Writing Pad **c** Dataset window.

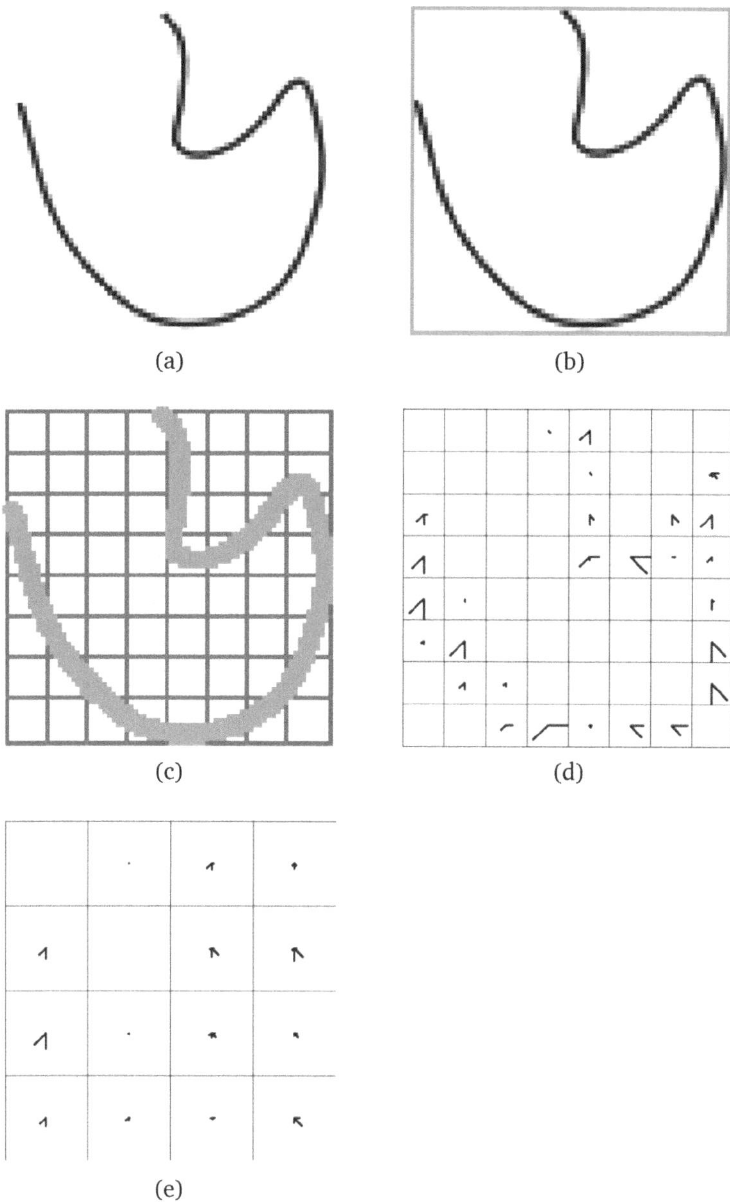

Fig. 3. Feature extraction process **a** Bangla Digit ৬ **b** Bounding box extraction ৬ **c** Contour of the character ৬ **d** Block-wise chain code of contour points for the digit ৬ **e** Down sampling into 4×4 blocks from 8×8 blocks.

4 Feature Extraction

We have extracted 64-dimensional features from the entire online Bangla digit dataset to represent the unique characteristics of each online handwritten Bangla digit. Figure 3 illustrates the process of extracting these features for a sample Bangla digit, ৬ . The feature extraction process begins by isolating the digit from its background through a bounding box that encircles the object of interest in the image. This bounding box is used to locate the edges of the digit. The region within the bounding box is then divided into an 8×8 grid of smaller blocks to facilitate localized feature computation. We have generated a contour image for every block and used the chain code approach to encode the edges. The chain code captures the directional flow of edges within the block using four principal directions: horizontal (0), 45-degree diagonal (1), vertical (2), and 135-degree diagonal (3). To reduce redundancy, we consider equivalent chain codes by grouping 0 and 4, 1 and 5, 2 and 6, and 3 and 7. This grouping simplifies the chain code into an array of four integer values per block, where each value represents the frequency of occurrence for the respective direction. After calculating these directional histograms for all 8×8 blocks, we further refine the feature space by downsampling the blocks into a 4×4 grid using a Gaussian filter. While maintaining crucial structural information, this downsampling process lowers the dimensionality of the features. A final feature vector of 64 dimensions (4×4×4) for each digit is thus produced, with a histogram of four directional frequencies present in each 4×4 block. In order to recognize Bangla digits accurately and efficiently, these concise but informative features are then used, resulting in strong performance throughout the dataset. Feature variety and effectiveness are balanced in the compact 64-dimensional representation, which makes it appropriate for seeking efficient recognition.

5 Result and Discussion

The primary goal of the present work is to achieve comparable results in online handwritten Bangla digit recognition using the available datasets together with those gathered by mobile applications, as detailed in the sections that follow.

5.1 Network Architecture Explorations

Each model initially trained and evaluated for 20 epochs using the datasets. Afterward, the batch size is changed and the outcomes of the training history of the CNN model are shown in Fig. 4 after 20 epochs. It depicted the variation of training and validation accuracy and loss across three different epoch ranges: 50, 100, and 500 respectively. The accuracy rises across epochs in every instance, and the validation accuracy is approximately comparable to the training accuracy. The training and validation loss curves show a significant initial decline and a gradually increases as the epochs go on. As accuracy and loss stabilize after training for more than 100 epochs, the model performs best in this range.

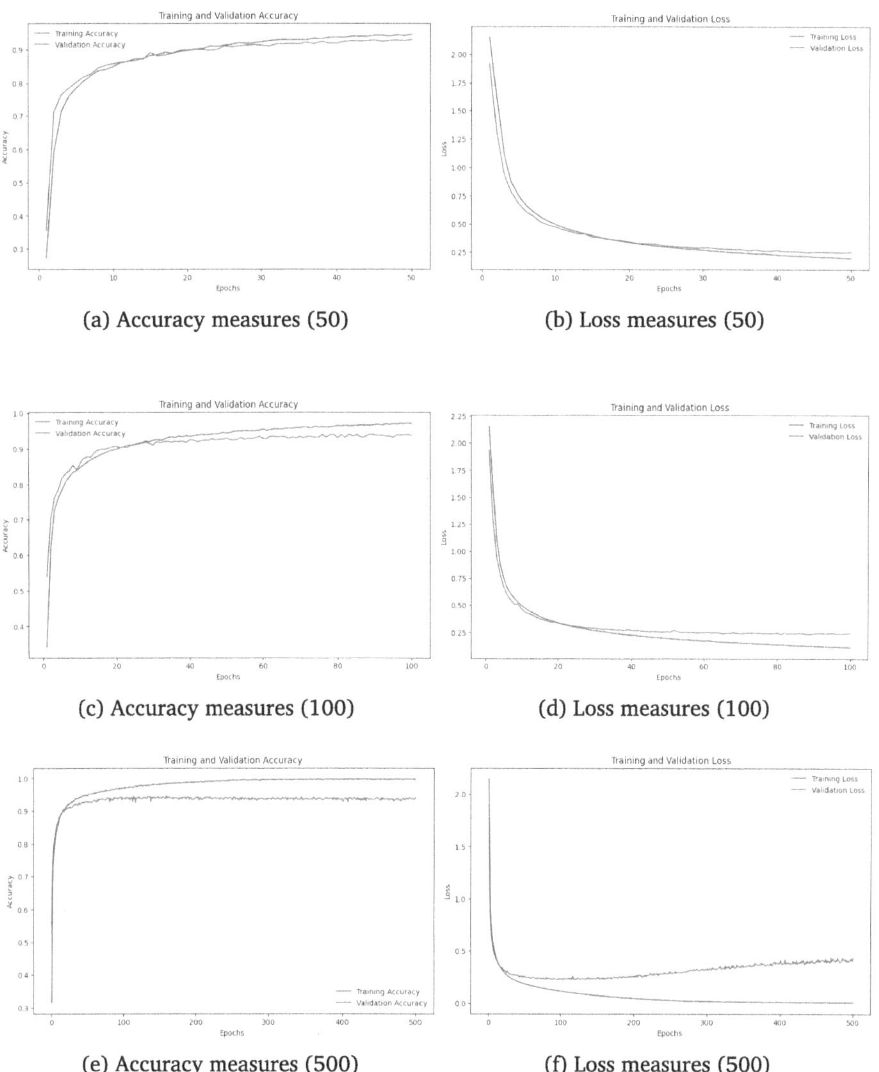

(a) Accuracy measures (50) (b) Loss measures (50)

(c) Accuracy measures (100) (d) Loss measures (100)

(e) Accuracy measures (500) (f) Loss measures (500)

Fig. 4. Training with validation graph for 50, 100 and 500 epochs.

5.2 Comparative Analysis

Isolated Bangla Digit strokes were used in the experimental evaluation of the aforementioned methods. The classifier for this study was trained using four-fifth of the strokes; the remaining strokes were used for testing. We have used supervised classification approach like SVM, MLP and Random Forest and unsupervised clustering like K-Mean. The proposed system also examined using CNN. The results presented in Tables 1 and 2 show the performance of various classification and clustering approaches using two datasets: one with 4700 samples and another mixed dataset with 8800 samples. For the smaller dataset, MLP achieved the highest accuracy at 95.48%, followed closely by Random Forest at 95.74%, while CNN recorded the lowest accuracy at 83.74%. In contrast, for the mixed dataset, Random Forest and k-Means achieved the highest accuracy at 94.53% and 94.45%, respectively, while CNN improved its performance significantly to 93.02%. Overall, the mixed dataset led to more balanced performance across all approaches, with slight variations, indicating that increasing the dataset size enhances model accuracy and robustness. In the proposed work, we chose a variety of machine learning models, including SVM, MLP, Random Forest, CNN, and K-Means, based on proven performance in handwriting recognition tasks. The purpose of this was to evaluate the utility of the 64-dimensional features that were obtained. In handwriting data, MLP, a kind of feedforward neural network, can simulate complex, non-linear patterns. Random Forest was selected due to its robustness and strong handling of noisy input. Using CNN's significant spatial feature extraction capabilities, performance was investigated with image-based input. The grouping of digit patterns without labeled data was evaluated using the unsupervised clustering algorithm K-Means, which provided a baseline for comparison.

Table 1. Accuracy achieved using available dataset

Approach	Data Size	Accuracy
SVM	4700	94.19%
Random Forest	4700	95.74%
MLP	4700	95.48%
k-Mean	4700	93.94%
CNN	4700	83.74%

Table 2. Accuracy achieved by different classification /clustering approach using mixed dataset collected using Mobile application

Approach	Data size	Accuracy
SVM	8800	92.81%
Random Forest	8800	94.73%
MLP	8800	94.45%
k-Mean	8800	94.45%
CNN	8800	93.02%

5.3 Error Analysis

The findings and analysis show that the proposed approach has potential in a variety of testing environments, yet it has shortcomings comparable to any system that is automated. Some of the incorrect samples from this experiment are

Table 3. Certain incorrect samples that include the original digit class rank, prediction score, and predicted class

Image	Original Label (Bangla Digit)	Predicted Label (Bangla Digit)	Prediction Score	Rank of Original Class
	1 (১)	9 (৯)	0.6783	2 (0.3217)
	1 (১)	9 (৯)	1.0000	2 (0.0000)
	1 (১))	4 (৪)	0.8802	3 (0.0016)
	1 (১)	9 (৯)	0.9811	2 (0.0181)
	2 (২)	7 (৭)	0.8659	2 (0.1073)
	3 (৩)	0 (০)	0.9510	3 (0.0149)
	5 (৫)	0 (০)	0.8890	2 (0.1110)
	6 (৬)	9 (৯)	1.0000	2 (0.0000)
	9 (৯)	1 (১)	0.7006	2 (0.2994)

highlighted in Table 3. The image additionally illustrates that incorrect numbers form patterns account for the majority of errors. An initial glance indicates that these are challenging for anyone to figure out. Reliability of the system is used to measure another type of robustness. It is obtained at the time of analyzing the classification prediction score. Analyzing the classification predictions in this suggested system reveals that, in the majority of cases, the prediction confidence is significantly lower than the average prediction confidence for all digits. Table 3 additionally indicates that incorrect predicted labels with high prediction confidence have shape related challenges, which might have been generated by inappropriate writing technique or erroneous samples labeling. The sample Bangla digit ১ for instance, physically resemble the shapes of numbers 9 and 4, respectively.

6 Conclusion

The paper focuses on the recognition of online handwritten Bangla digit's strokes using 64-dimensional features in K-Mean clustering, SVM, Randon Forest, and MLP classifiers. The proposed recognition scheme was also tested using CNN. The mobile app provides a strong data collection solution by addressing conventional difficulties. The research presented here highlights the potential of a mobile data gathering application to revolutionize data collection methods. We have used 8800 Bangla online handwritten digit data for the experiment among which set of 4100 Bangla digit were collected through the proposed mobile application. We obtained 92.81%, 94.73%, 94.45% accuracy using SVM, Random forest and MLP classifier respectively and 92.60% accuracy achieved using unsupervised clustering approach, K-Mean. With the help of a CNN, this model's accuracy is 93.02%. A few incorrect samples were also included, including the expected class, prediction score, and rank of the original digits class. The dataset created and presented in this article will be made available for research and development purposes upon request.

Through addressing user experience, data security, and functionality, mobile technology can be utilized to boost research outcomes, lower costs, and improve data quality. On the basis of this investigation, future research might explore new features and uses in many scenarios. Implementing a similar effective method for online Bangla character recognition is an objective for the future.

References

1. Taherdoost, H.: Data collection methods and tools for research; a step by-step guide to choose data collection technique for academic and business research projects. Int. J. Acad. Re sear. Manag. (IJARM) **10.1**, 10–38 (2021). https://hal.science/hal-03741847
2. Ghosh, T. et al.: Advances in online handwritten recognition in the last decades. Comput. Sci. Rev. **46**, 100515 (2022). issn: 1574 0137. https://doi.org/10.1016/j.cosrev.2022.100515. https://www.sciencedirect.com/science/article/pii/S1574013722000491
3. Bunke, H. et al.: Online handwriting data acquisition using a video cam era. In: Proceedings of the Fifth International Conference on Document Analysis and Recognition. ICDAR 99 (Cat. No.PR00318), pp. 573–576 (1999). https://doi.org/10.1109/ICDAR.1999.791852
4. Das, A., Bhattacharya, U.: ISIgraphy: a tool for online handwriting sample database generation. In: 2013 Fourth National Conference on Computer Vision, Pattern Recognition, Image Processing and Graphics (NCVPRIPG), pp. 1–4 (2013). https://doi.org/10.1109/NCVPRIPG.2013.6776181

5. Sen, S. et al.: Application of structural and topological features to recognize online handwritten Bangla characters. In: ACM Transactions on Asian and Low-Resource Language Information Processing, vol. 17.3, pp. 1–16 (2018). https://doi.org/10.1145/3178457
6. Parui, S.K. et al.: A Hidden Markov Models for Recognition of Online Handwritten Bangla Numerals. In: Mukherjee, D.P., Jana, D. (eds.), Proceedings of the National Annual Convention of Computer Society of India, pp. 27–31. Tata Mc Graw Hill Publishing Company Ltd. (2006)
7. Bhattacharya, U., Gupta, B.K., Parui, S.: Direction code based features for recognition of online handwritten characters of Bangla. In: Proceedings of International Conference on Document Analysis and Recognition, pp. 58–62 (2007). https://doi.org/10.1109/ICDAR.2007.4378675
8. Roy, K.: Stroke-Database Design for Online Handwriting Recognition in Bangla, Jan. 2009
9. Kaurand, R., Singh, M.: Stroke based online handwritten Gurmukhi char acter recognition. In: 2016 International Conference on Advances in Computing, Communications and Informatics (ICACCI), pp. 598–601 (2016). https://doi.org/10.1109/ICACCI.2016.7732111
10. Singh, S., Sharma, A., Chhabra, I.: Online handwritten gurmukhi strokes dataset based on minimal set of words. In: ACM Transactions on Asian and Low-Resource Language Information Processing, vol. 16.1, June 2016. issn: 2375-4699. https://doi.org/10.1145/2896318
11. Sen, S., Sarkar, R., Roy, K.: An approach to stroke-based online handwritten bangla character recognition. In: Chakietal, R. (ed.), Advanced Computing and Systems for Security: Volume Four, pp. 153–163. Springer Singapore, Singapore (2017). isbn: 978-981-10-3391-9. https://doi.org/10.1007/978-981-10-3391-9_10
12. Unipen. http://www.unipen.org/index.html. Accessed 04 July 2024
13. Madhvanath, S., Vijayasenan, D., Kadiresan, T.M.: LipiTk: a generic toolkit for online handwriting recognition. In: ACM SIGGRAPH 2007 Courses. SIGGRAPH 07. Association for Computing Machinery, 13 es (2007). isbn: 9781450318235. https://doi.org/10.1145/1281500.1281524
14. Supernote. https://supernote.com/blogs/supernote-blog. Accessed 04 July 2024

Detection of Fake News in Social Media Using Supervised Machine Learning Approach

Sagnik Mitra[1(✉)], Munmun Bhattacharya[1], and Arpita Talukdar[2]

[1] Department of Information Technology, Jadavpur University, Kolkata, West Bengal, India
sagnikmitra2k@gmail.com

[2] Department of Computer Sc. Engineering (Data Science), Heritage Institute of Technology, Kolkata, West Bengal, India

Abstract. The pervasiveness of false information in social media has enabled the fast propagation of rumors driven by mob behavior and viral content. This leads to biased public opinion, weakened journalistic reputation, and deepening of social polarization. For detecting fake news on social media, in this work we have proposed a supervised machine learning based approach. Often we have seen that the news websites/sources which are famous, that is having high credibility, post real news. We have utilized the concept of publisher's trustworthiness to generate a dataset using web scraping. The base attributes of the comprehensive dataset are scraped based on user interaction data like likes, shares, and publisher information like followers and following. After web scraping, we have performed data annotation that is labelling the datapoint as real or fake using a feature called credibility_score. The credibility score formula is derived based on multiple base features. If credibility score crosses a certain threshold then the datapoint is labelled as real else labelled as fake. Based on these base attributes, 3 derived features like likes_ratio, shares_ratio and comments_ratio are calculated. Supervised machine learning models are evaluated on the entire dataset containing all the base features and the 3 derived features. Decision Tree has achieved the highest accuracy of 99.92% and KNN has achieved the lowest accuracy. Exclusion of the 3 derived features has reduced the model accuracy to approximately 50% for all algorithms and demonstrates their importance. This paper also addresses the accuracy vs. training time trade-off and the relevance of optimized algorithms for real-time applications.

Keywords: supervised learning · credibility_score · web scraping

1 Introduction

In today's world, social media has rapidly changed how people can access and disseminate information, making it an indispensable source of real-time news. A

K. Chandra Mondal et al. (Eds.): CICBA 2025, CCIS 2863, pp. 30–44, 2026.
https://doi.org/10.1007/978-3-032-17184-9_3

Pew Research Center report states that in 2016, 62% of US adults reported consuming news through social media compared to 49% in 2012 [1], which shows a paradigm shift in news consumption due to access, affordability, and immediacy. However, this ease of information sharing on platforms such as WhatsApp, Twitter, Instagram, and Facebook has a very significant trade-off: the compromise of information credibility. Detecting news which are fake is a very challenging task. Fake news is created to be almost indistinguishable from actual content. They use sensationalism and emotional appeal to spread rapidly. During the 2019 Indian general elections, politically motivated misinformation spread on Twitter and Facebook through fake accounts, further dividing society [3]. The amount of information produced on social media also surpasses traditional fact-checking capabilities and calls for automated and scalable solutions.

Recent breakthroughs in ML and NLP carry an optimistic trend against the spreading of fake news. This study investigates how textual, emotional, and contextual elements come together to deal with the problem of detecting fake news at this stage and proposes scalable and data-centric solutions for the mitigation and revival of trust in such ecosystems.

Our paper has focused on the development of a scalable pipeline for real-time fake news detection by generating a large-scale and comprehensive dataset. Robust data cleaning and data preprocessing techniques are employed on the dataset. Finally, supervised machine learning models are applied. This dataset contains base features like textual content, social engagement metrics, and the derived features that are calculated from the base features. The performance of the various supervised models are evaluated using metrics such as confusion matrices, recall, accuracy, precision, F1-score, and ROC curves to ensure reliable detection and effective handling of imbalanced data. The scalability and computational efficiency of these algorithms are assessed to determine their suitability for real-time deployment on digital platforms.

The rest of our paper is organized as follows. In Sect. 2, the literature survey is presented. In Sect. 3, we have discussed the methodology, which contains the description of our dataset and various preprocessing techniques used. The experimental results and its detailed analysis is shown in Sect. 4. The Ehical Considerations are addressed in Sect. 5. The conclusion and future directions have been discussed in Sect. 6.

2 Literature Survey

The detection of fake news has become a critical research area due to the proliferation of misinformation across digital platforms. Shu et al. [2] classified detection methodologies into feature-oriented, model-oriented, data-oriented, and application-oriented strategies, providing a foundation for subsequent research. Sahoo and Gupta [3] introduced a hybrid approach combining deep learning and machine learning techniques, leveraging user profiles and news content features to achieve 99.4% accuracy. Similarly, Sharma et al. [4] focused on classifying news articles based on website publishing credibility, improving accuracy from 80%

to 93% through optimized machine learning models. Choudhury and Acharjee [5] applied genetic algorithms to optimize machine learning classifiers, achieving 95% accuracy on the Fake Job Postings dataset. Kaliyar et al. [6] introduced FakeBERT, a BERT-based model achieving 98.9% accuracy. Zhang et al. [7] developed Conv-FFD, a CNN-based model for fast detection of fake news, particularly for shorter text sizes.

For real-time detection, Dewan and Kumaraguru [8] designed Facebook Inspector (FbI), which uses a two-stage filtering approach, processing over 0.97 million posts with an average response time of 2.6 s. Jarrahi and Safari [9] developed FR-Detect, a multi-modal framework combining publisher-specific and content-based features to achieve 97.8% accuracy. Chowdhury et al. [10] proposed a probabilistic soft logic model for estimating the credibility of news publishers and users, achieving a 10% improvement in recall and a 4% improvement in accuracy.

Despite significant progress in fake news detection, several critical challenges remain unaddressed. These include the reliance on pre-annotated, domain-specific datasets that may not capture real-time user behavior or evolving misinformation trends; limited use of social trust signals such as verification status (blue tick) and social engagement patterns; the absence of credibility-based annotation mechanisms; and the dependence on deep learning models that, while accurate, are often computationally intensive and less suited for real-time deployment. Our approach addresses these gaps by presenting a comprehensive and scalable pipeline for fake news detection that incorporates real-time data acquisition, robust preprocessing, credibility-aware annotation, and efficient supervised learning. Specifically, we construct a large-scale, real-time dataset using web scraping across multiple platforms (Facebook, Twitter, NewsAPI), and develop a `credibility_score` metric that uses trust indicators to label news as real or fake. Additionally, we design three derived engagement features—`likes_ratio`, `shares_ratio`, and `comments_ratio`—that significantly boost classifier performance. We evaluate several supervised classifiers using accuracy, precision, recall, F1-score, AUC, and computational time to benchmark model effectiveness and real-time viability. Our framework also provides insights into the trade-off between accuracy and efficiency, making it a practical and generalizable solution for combating misinformation on digital platforms.

3 Methodology

Fake news get spread through online social media platforms like Instagram, Whatsapp, Facebook, Twitter and other social media websites. Most of the time the credibility of the news also depends on the publishing websites or profile from where the news is posted. From our general knowledge, we know that famous publishing websites (having higher followers and credibility) are most likely to post genuine news. We have utilized this concept of publisher trustworthiness for detection of the fake news. So we have generated the dataset based on that. We have generated real-time social media news from NewsAPI, Facebook and

Twitter API using web scraping. Then we have calculated the credibility_score feature to assign labels to the datapoints as real or fake. We have developed a framework that uses supervised Machine Learning algorithms to evaluate the performance. The detailed methodology of Dataset generation, Data Preprocessing and its evaluation is explained below.

3.1 Dataset

We have constructed a rich dataset consisting of real-time news articles with additional metadata, including base features like social media engagement signals and source information using web crawling and scraping. Then we have calculated a value of `credibility_score` to labels the data in the dataset as real (1) and fake (0). This feature of `credibility_score` will be not used for training or testing. Then we have calculated derived features like likes_ratio, shares_ratio and comments_ratio. This dataset is generated by fetching news articles, collecting social signals from social media platforms like Facebook and Twitter, and computing various engagement and credibility metrics. Our dataset includes a huge number of data points generated in real-time, with each record representing a unique news article. The dataset is shown in [11]. The key columns of the dataset are presented in Table 1.

Table 1. Dataset Columns and Descriptions

Column Name	Description
`news_headline`	The headline of the news article, fetched from the NewsAPI.
`news_text`	Full news text article, fetched from NewsAPI.
`source_name`	The name of the publishing news source.
`source_type`	Type of the news source (e.g., News Website, Blog, Social Media).
`source_url`	The URL of the news article.
`likes_count`	Number of likes received by the news article on social media.
`shares_count`	Number of shares received by the news article on social media.
`comments_count`	Number of comments the article received on social media platforms.
`comments_detail`	User comments, fetched from Twitter and Facebook.
`news_category`	The category of the news article (e.g., Technology, Politics).
`following`	Number of people the news source follows on social media.
`followers`	Number of followers of the news source.
`blue_tick`	A binary indicator of whether the news source is verified.
`publishing_date`	The date the article was published.
`likes_ratio`	Engagement ratio for likes.
`shares_ratio`	Engagement ratio for shares.
`comments_ratio`	Engagement ratio for comments.
`fake_or_real`	A binary label indicating whether the news is real (1) or fake (0).

3.2 Data Collection and Real-Time Web Scraping

To build a rich and comprehensive dataset for fake news detection, we employed real-time web scraping and crawling techniques to collect news articles and their associated metadata. The data was gathered over a continuous 6-month period, ensuring temporal diversity and relevance to ongoing information trends.

We utilized multiple APIs and platforms for this purpose, including News-API, TwitterAPI, and Facebook Graph API. These platforms allowed us to collect not only the textual content of news articles but also a wide variety of social signals and source-level metadata, providing a multi-dimensional dataset that captures real-world social media behavior. This real-time collection approach enabled us to dynamically fetch live news articles as they appeared on various platforms, along with their corresponding engagement metrics.

The final dataset comprises approximately 100,000 news articles collected from about 50 publishers including Reuters, BBC News, CNN News etc. across multiple domains such as Politics, Technology, Entertainment, Sports, and Health. This wide topical coverage ensures that the dataset reflects diverse content categories and provides a strong basis for training generalizable fake news detection models.

3.3 Credibility Score Calculation

The credibility score feature plays a vital role in this dataset. It quantifies the trustworthiness of the news article based on various factors.This score is not used as a feature for model training but is instead used to annotate the dataset by assigning class labels to each record. The formula for computing the credibility score is:

$$\begin{aligned}\textbf{credibility\_score} = 0.5 \times (\text{blue\_tick}) + 0.3 \times \left(\frac{\text{total\_signals}}{\text{max\_social\_signals}}\right) \\ +0.2 \times \left(\frac{\text{followers}}{\text{followers} + \text{following}}\right)\end{aligned} \tag{1}$$

- blue_tick is a binary indicator that gives a weight of 0.5 if the source is verified and 0 if not verified.
- total_signals is the sum of the number of likes, shares, and comments.
- max_social_signals is a hypothetical maximum value of total social signals, primarily used for normalization.
- followers and following are derived from the social media profiles of the news source.

Based on some thresholds of the credibility_score, the fake or real label assigned to the datapoints.

3.4 Data Cleaning Process

- **Handle Missing Values**: The numerical columns are filled with the median value, while categorical columns use the mode or 'Unknown'.

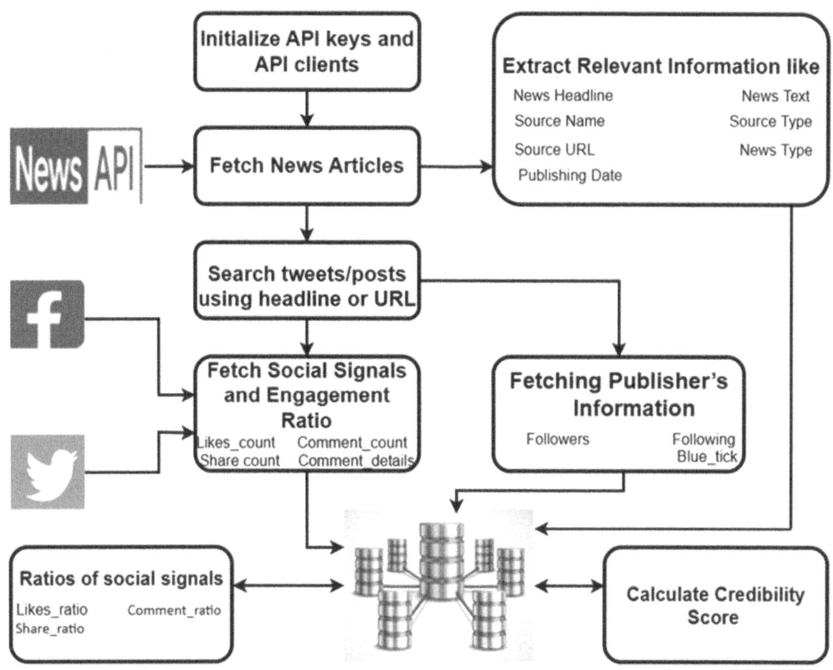

Fig. 1. Flowchart of Real-time Dataset Generation.

- **Correct Data Types**: Columns like `credibility_score` are converted to numeric. The invalid entries and data types are handled during imputation.
- **Remove Duplicates**: Duplicate rows are detected and removed from the dataset.
- **Outlier Handling**: Outliers in numerical data are identified and treated using boxplots.
- **Normalization and Scaling**: Features are normalized using `StandardScaler` to improve its performance.
- **Label Encoding**: Categorical data is encoded into numerical values using `LabelEncoder`.

3.5 Derived Features

In addition to the base features, we engineered three derived features that capture the engagement behavior of each news article:

$$\textbf{likes\_ratio} = \frac{\text{social\_signals\_likes}}{\text{followers} + 1} \tag{2}$$

$$\textbf{shares\_ratio} = \frac{\text{social\_signals\_shares}}{\text{followers} + 1} \tag{3}$$

$$\textbf{comments\_ratio} = \frac{\text{social\_signals\_comments}}{\text{followers} + 1} \quad (4)$$

The derived features are designed to normalize the raw engagement signals with respect to the audience size of the publisher. Instead of directly using absolute counts of likes, shares, or comments–which can be heavily influenced by the publisher's follower base–these ratios provide a relative measure of engagement intensity.

To normalize engagement signals across publishers with widely varying audience sizes, the derived features are computed by dividing the absolute engagement counts by the number of followers plus one. Dividing by followers helps capture the true engagement intensity relative to the potential audience size, rather than absolute popularity, thereby reducing bias toward large publishers with massive follower bases. The addition of 1 ensures mathematical stability by preventing division by zero in cases where very small or new publishers may have few or no followers. This smoothing factor also prevents artificially inflated ratios for accounts with low follower counts that might receive occasional engagement, which is often observed in suspicious or manipulated news sources. These normalized ratios help expose behavioral anomalies typically associated with fake news propagation, such as disproportionately high engagement relative to follower base, while real news generally exhibits more stable and organically proportional engagement patterns. As a result, these derived features provide strong discriminatory power, reduce multicollinearity among features, improving separability, leading to the improvement in accuracy.

3.6 Final Dataset

After the initial web scraped dataset is cleaned, we get the Cleaned dataset which is prepared for analysis and training. The final dataset consists of a huge number of records, each representing a unique news article, with 19 columns that include both base and derived features. These features provide information about the news article, social media engagement, source credibility, and the classification label. The `source_name` and `source_type` is evenly distributed among all the categories. Within each category there are almost equal number of real and fake news. In the dataset there are 50% verified news sources and 50% unverified news sources. This proves that our dataset is not biased towards a particular category. The target label `fake_or_real`, is well-balanced, with approximately 50% real and 50% fake news articles. This balance is crucial for training classification algorithms, as it prevents the framework from being biased toward one class. So the cleaned and balanced dataset provides fair performance evaluation. With the balanced target variable and comprehensive features, the dataset is ready for further analysis, The detailed process of dataset generation and creation is shown in Fig. 1. The cleaned dataset is saved as a CSV file, which can be accessed for further analysis and training.

3.7 Data Vectorization

After cleaning the dataset, the textual data is transformed into numerical vectors suitable for input to machine learning models using various vectorization techniques. Term Frequency-Inverse Document Frequency (TF-IDF) is employed to capture the importance of words based on their frequency and distribution across documents. N-gram models (such as bigrams and trigrams) are used to represent word sequences and capture contextual patterns in the text. Additionally, word embedding techniques like Word2Vec and GloVe are utilized to generate dense and semantically rich vector representations of the text, preserving the contextual relationships between words.

3.8 Feature Selection

Feature selection plays a crucial role in improving model efficiency and accuracy by extracting the most relevant features from the dataset to reduce dimensionality and enhance interpretability. Several techniques are employed for this purpose, including the Chi-Square Test, which evaluates the independence between features and the target variable; Mutual Information, which measures the degree of mutual dependency between features and the target; and Recursive Feature Elimination (RFE), which iteratively removes less significant features to retain only the most informative ones for model training.

The cleaned and vectorized data is used to train multiple supervised machine learning algorithms like **Logistic Regression**, **Support Vector Machine (SVM)**, **Random Forest**, **Decision Tree**, **Gradient Boosting**, **XGBoost** and **K-Nearest Neighbors (KNN)**.

The supervised algorithm framework is trained on the data available in the training set, and hyperparameters are optimized using grid search or random search techniques.

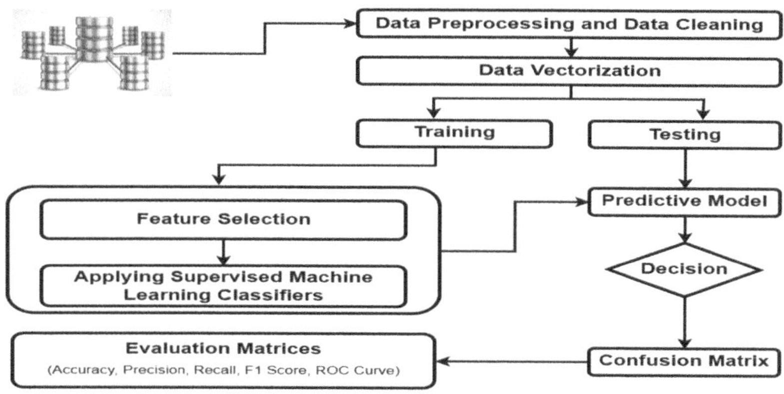

Fig. 2. Flowchart of Methodology of Algorithm.

3.9 Decision and Predictive Framework

The trained framework predicts the class of new and unseen news articles as real or fake) for the testing data. Based on the predictions, a confusion matrix is generated, which forms the basis of the decision-making process. The predictive framework performance is evaluated using various metrics like Confusion Matrix, Accuracy, Recall, Precision, F1 Score, ROC Curve and Computational time which includes both training time and testing time. This evaluation helps in comparing models and selecting the best-performing supervised learning algorithm for deployment. The detailed flow of the method is given in Fig. 2.

4 Results and Analysis

The evaluation of the performance of the predictive framework is done using various performance metrics. We have shown the formulas of four performance metrics like Accuracy, Recall, Precision and F1-Score where the components are represented as True Positives **(TP)**, True Negatives **(TN)**, False Positives **(FP)** and False Negatives **(FN)**.

$$\mathbf{Accuracy} = \frac{\text{TP} + \text{TN}}{\text{Total Instances}}, \quad \mathbf{Precision} = \frac{\text{TP}}{\text{TP} + \text{FP}}$$

$$\mathbf{Recall} = \frac{\text{TP}}{\text{TP} + \text{TN}}, \quad \mathbf{F1\text{-}Score} = 2 \times \frac{\text{Precision} \times \text{Recall}}{\text{Precision} + \text{Recall}}$$

We have taken test size of 0.2 to test our data. Out of which KNN performs poor than the other 6 algorithms. We have shown the output of confusion matrices for all the used algorithms in Fig. 3.

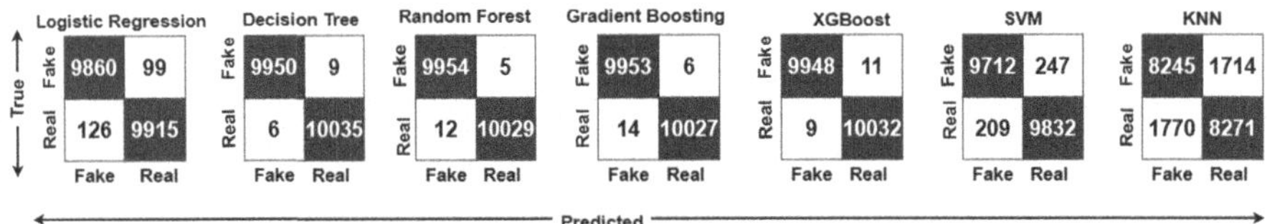

Fig. 3. Confusion Matrices.

4.1 ROC Curve Analysis

The Receiver Operating Characteristic curve (ROC curve) is shown in Fig. 4. ROC curve analysis reveals that Random Forest, Logistic Regression, Decision Tree, Gradient Boosting, SVM, and XGBoost algorithms have achieved an AUC of 1.00. This indicates outstanding classification performance with minimal false positives and consistently high true positives. In contrast, the KNN performs

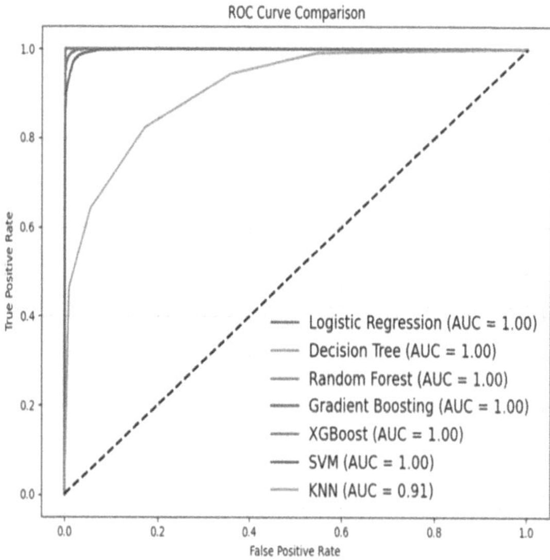

Fig. 4. ROC Curve for Various Algorithms.

poorly with an AUC of 0.91, failing to capture complex decision boundaries effectively. Poor performance of KNN suggests potential issues with optimization parameters, such as the number of neighbors or distance metrics.

The ROC curve analysis highlights significant performance differences among algorithms. Notably, models with an AUC of 1.00 exhibit excellent classification capabilities, whereas KNN's weaker performance suggests potential for further optimization. Moving forward, hyperparameter tuning for KNN might help in improving its decision boundary capture.

Table 2. Performance Analysis of Applied Supervised Learning Algorithms including Derived Features

Algorithm	Accuracy (%)	Precision (%)	Recall (%)	F1-Score	Training Time (ms)	Testing Time (ms)
Logistic Regression	98.875	99.01	98.74	0.98	182.507	0.836
SVM	97.72	97.54	97.91	0.97	439079.530	15855.509
Random Forest	99.91	99.96	99.86	0.99	12686.497	84.088
Decision Tree	99.92	99.90	99.94	0.99	215.458	1.444
XGBoost	99.90	99.89	99.91	0.99	572.200	26.135
Gradient Boosting	99.90	99.94	99.86	0.99	28914.090	27.323
KNN	82.58	82.83	82.37	0.82	207.367	3499.599

The above metrics and visualizations provide comprehensive insights into the performance and efficiency of the predictive models.

4.2 Performance Analysis of Machine Learning Algorithms

The performance analysis of various supervised machine learning algorithms, as presented in Table 2, highlights significant differences in terms of accuracy, precision, recall, F1-score, and computational efficiency. Random Forest and Decision Tree emerged as the top-performing algorithms, achieving the highest accuracy of 99.91% and 99.92%, respectively, along with excellent precision, recall, and F1-scores close to 100%, demonstrating their robustness and reliability for the classification task. In contrast, K-Nearest Neighbors (KNN) exhibited the lowest accuracy of 82.58%, with a substantial drop in precision, recall, and F1-score, indicating its inefficiency for the given dataset.

Computational Efficiency. In terms of computational efficiency, Logistic Regression was the fastest, requiring only 182.5 ms for training, followed by Decision Tree at 215.4 ms, making these algorithms suitable for scenarios where rapid training is essential. On the other hand, Support Vector Machine (SVM) and K-Nearest Neighbors (KNN) were computationally expensive, with SVM taking over 439 s for training and KNN incurring significant testing time (approximately 3500 ms), which makes them less favorable for large-scale applications.

Trade-Off Between Performance and Time. The trade-off between performance and time reveals that ensemble methods such as Random Forest, Gradient Boosting, and XGBoost achieved excellent accuracy and other metrics but incurred higher training times. For example, Gradient Boosting took approximately 28 s, and Random Forest required 12.6 s. On the other hand, Decision Tree strikes a balance between accuracy and computational time, making it a practical choice in terms of both performance and efficiency.

Suitability of Various Algorithms. For applications requiring high predictive accuracy, Random Forest, Gradient Boosting, and XGBoost are ideal. In contrast, for real-time applications prioritizing faster execution, Logistic Regression or Decision Tree would be more appropriate due to their computational efficiency. This comprehensive analysis underlines the importance of selecting machine learning algorithms based on specific application requirements, considering both predictive accuracy and computational constraints.

Table 3. Accuracy of All Algorithms Except Derived Features

Algorithm	Accuracy (%)	Training Time (ms)	Testing Time (ms)
Logistic Regression	50.38	97.783	1.192
SVM	50.21	910713.930	49407.381
Random Forest	50.19	97671.587	757.551
Decision Tree	49.77	5159.609	8.005
Gradient Boosting	50.08	69394.805	21.679
Naive Bayes	49.60	37.832	4.137
KNN	50.23	6.601	11468.352

4.3 Comparison of Results

Impact on Accuracy. The removal of the 3 derived features led to a significant drop in accuracy across all supervised machine learning algorithms. In Table 2, all algorithms except KNN achieved accuracies above 97%, with Random Forest and Decision Tree performing the best at 99.91% and 99.92%, respectively. However, in Table 3, after removing the 3 derived features namely `likes_ratio`, `shares_ratio` and `comments_ratio`, the accuracies of all the supervised machine learning algorithms drastically dropped to around 50%, demonstrating the critical role of the derived features. For algorithm-specific observations, Random Forest and Decision Tree showed significant accuracy drops from 99.91% and 99.92% to 50.19% and 49.77%, respectively. These tree-based algorithms, which rely heavily on feature splits, struggled to maintain high performance after losing such an influential feature. Logistic Regression's accuracy dropped from 98.875% to 50.38%, highlighting the significant contribution of the derived features to linear classification models.

Key Insights. In fake news detection, the use of only base features such as raw likes, shares, comments, followers, and following counts introduces several limitations that weaken the algorithm learning. These raw features suffer from a lack of contextual meaning, high redundancy and multicollinearity, incompatible scales across publishers, and poor interpretability for machine learning algorithms. Since absolute engagement counts are heavily influenced by publisher size, larger publishers naturally receive higher engagement even for routine articles, while smaller but credible publishers may show low absolute numbers. As a result, algorithms trained on base features often capture popularity bias instead of actual credibility signals. To overcome these limitations, we engineered three derived features—`likes_ratio`, `shares_ratio`, and `comments_ratio`—which normalize engagement signals relative to each publisher's audience size by dividing absolute counts by `followers + 1`. This transformation eliminates scale dependency, reduces feature correlation, and captures behavioral engagement intensity that reflects abnormal amplification patterns often observed in fake news dissemination. The derived features not only improve class separability but also align better with the assumptions of various machine learning models: tree-based models can create cleaner splits, SVM classifiers benefit from clearer hyperplane margins, logistic regression assigns more meaningful coefficients, Naive Bayes achieves better adherence to distribution assumptions, and boosting algorithms such as XGBoost and CatBoost achieve faster convergence with reduced risk of overfitting due to reduced redundancy.

However, instance-based learning algorithms such as K-Nearest Neighbors (KNN) face inherent challenges even after feature engineering. As KNN relies on distance metrics to define similarity between instances, it becomes highly sensitive to noisy, high-dimensional feature spaces where the distance between points may lose discriminatory power due to the curse of dimensionality. In such scenarios, even small overlaps in feature space between real and fake news instances can mislead KNN, causing unstable classification boundaries. Unlike parametric models that can learn complex relationships through weighting or splitting, KNN treats all features equally and fails to prioritize the most informative features automatically. Additionally, KNN struggles to adapt to non-uniform feature distributions where some features dominate distance calculations while others contribute noise, leading to suboptimal nearest neighbor selections.

Without these derived features, model accuracy drops significantly (near 50%), indicating that they serve as crucial discriminative factors enabling models to effectively distinguish between real and fake news through behavioral pattern learning rather than purely content or publisher size bias.

Table 4. Comparison of Performance to Existing Works

Author(s)	Approach	Accuracy	Precision	Recall	F1-Score
Sahoo and Gupta (2021)	LSTM-based deep learning model	99.4%	99.4%	99.2%	0.991
Sharma et al. (2020)	Passive Aggressive Classifier	92.73%	93%	92.16%	0.9257
Choudhury and Acharjee (2023) *LIAR Dataset*	Genetic algorithm with Logistic Regression	61%	62%	80%	0.7
Choudhury and Acharjee (2023) *Fake Job Posting Dataset*	Genetic algorithm with SVM and Random Forest	97%	97%	100%	0.98
Our Work	**Decision Tree**	**99.92%**	**99.90%**	**99.94%**	**0.9992**

4.4 Comparison Of Performance To Existing Works

The comparative analysis of existing methods for fake news detection as presented in Table 4, highlights the robustness of the current work, which employs a Decision Tree algorithm and achieves exceptional performance metrics, including an accuracy of 99.92%, precision of 99.90%, recall of 99.94%, and an F1-score of 0.9992. This result surpasses those of advanced models such as LSTM-based deep learning (99.4% accuracy), Passive Aggressive Classifier (92.73% accuracy), and ensemble approaches using genetic algorithms (97% accuracy). The near-perfect metrics of the current work emphasize its ability to effectively classify fake news while maintaining a balanced trade-off between precision and recall. This remarkable performance is due to careful dataset preprocessing, power of derived features to capture inherent patterns in the dataset, feature engineering, and the inherent strengths of decision trees in capturing non-linear relationships.

5 Ethical Considerations

Although our framework demonstrates strong classification performance, several ethical concerns must be addressed for responsible deployment. The credibility-based annotation may introduce bias against newer or smaller publishers lacking social trust indicators, potentially disadvantaging credible but less established sources. False positives can suppress legitimate news, affecting freedom of expression, public trust, and publisher reputation, emphasizing the need for careful threshold calibration and human-in-the-loop verification. The model's generalizability across regions, languages, and cultural contexts remains a challenge, requiring broader cross-domain and multilingual validations. Transparency in model design, feature selection, and evaluation is critical to ensure explainability and accountability for end users and policymakers.

6 Conclusion And Future Directions

This paper evaluated the performance of multiple supervised machine learning algorithms for fake news detection, with a particular emphasis on the critical role of feature engineering. A real-time web-scraped dataset was generated by collecting not only the news content but also various publisher-level and engagement-level attributes, allowing for comprehensive feature construction. Publisher credibility played a crucial role in dataset annotation, while derived features such as `likes_ratio`, `shares_ratio`, and `comments_ratio` were engineered to enhance model learning by normalizing social engagement signals relative to audience size. These derived features significantly improved class separability and boosted model performance, enabling models such as Decision Tree and Random Forest to achieve near-perfect accuracies of 99.92% and 99.91%, respectively. In contrast, instance-based algorithms like KNN struggled to perform well due to their sensitivity to high-dimensional feature spaces and distance-based learning limitations, achieving lower accuracy. The experiments demonstrated that in the absence of these derived features, classification accuracy deteriorated to nearly random levels (approximately 50%), confirming their critical role in effective fake news classification. While ensemble methods like Random Forest and Gradient Boosting achieved high accuracies, they were computationally expensive. Simpler models like Logistic Regression and Decision Tree provided an excellent balance between accuracy and computational efficiency, making them highly suitable for real-time deployment scenarios. Overall, the results emphasize the importance of robust feature engineering in designing efficient, accurate, and scalable fake news detection systems for social media platforms.

Future research will explore the integration of hybrid models combining both supervised and unsupervised learning techniques to further improve fake news detection accuracy and robustness. Additionally, advanced analysis of the textual data available in the comment sections using natural language processing (NLP) and deep learning architectures may enhance precision, recall, and computational efficiency. Further sophisticated feature engineering approaches incorporating linguistic patterns, sentiment analysis, user behavior features, and deep contextual embeddings derived from transformer models (e.g., BERT, LSTM, GPT) will also be investigated to refine feature extraction and improve classification performance. Real-time fake news detection framework can also be constructed. This can be done by creating a real-time news analysis web app.

References

1. Gottfried, J., Shearer, E.: News use across social media platforms (2016)
2. Shu, K., Sliva, A., Wang, S., Tang, J., Liu, H.: Fake news detection on social media: a data mining perspective. ACM SIGKDD Explorations Newsl **19**(1), 22–36 (2017)
3. Sahoo, S.R., Gupta, B.B.: Multiple features based approach for automatic fake news detection on social networks using deep learning. Appl. Soft Comput. **100**, 106983 (2021)
4. Sharma, U., Saran, S., Patil, S.M.: Fake news detection using machine learning algorithms. Int. J. Creative Res. Thoughts (IJCRT) **8**(6), 509–518 (2020)
5. Choudhury, D., Acharjee, T.: A novel approach to fake news detection in social networks using genetic algorithm applying machine learning classifiers. Multimed. Tools Appl. **82**(6), 9029–9045 (2023)
6. Kaliyar, R.K., Goswami, A., Narang, P.: FakeBERT: fake news detection in social media with a BERT-based deep learning approach. Multimedia Tools Appl. **80**(8), 11765–11788 (2021)
7. Zhang, Q., Guo, Z., Zhu, Y., Vijayakumar, P., Castiglione, A., Gupta, B.B.: A deep learning-based fast fake news detection model for cyber-physical social services. Pattern Recogn. Lett. **168**, 31–38 (2023)
8. Dewan, P., Kumaraguru, P.: Facebook Inspector (FbI): towards automatic real-time detection of malicious content on Facebook. Soc. Netw. Anal. Min. **7**, 1–25 (2017)
9. Jarrahi, A., Safari, L.: Evaluating the effectiveness of publishers' features in fake news detection on social media. Multimed. Tools Appl. **82**(2), 2913–2939 (2023)
10. Chowdhury, R., Srinivasan, S., Getoor, L.: Joint estimation of user and publisher credibility for fake news detection. In: Proceedings of the 29th ACM International Conference on Information & Knowledge Management, pp. 1993–1996 (Oct 2020)
11. dataset link is given here: https://github.com/sagnik2809/Real-time-fake-news-dataset

Detecting Profile Cloning on Online Social Networks with Machine Learning

Saptak Sil[1](✉), Munmun Bhattacharya[1], and Arpita Talukdar[2]

[1] Department of Information Technology, Jadavpur University, Jadavpur, India
silsaptak99@gmail.com

[2] Department of Computer Science and Engineering (Data Science), Heritage Institute of Technology, Kolkata, India

Abstract. In recent years, Online Social Networks (OSNs) have become an essential part of our daily life. In the present generation, OSNs have gained immense popularity, with individuals increasingly intertwining their social interactions with these platforms. People rely on OSNs to stay connected, share information and often manage online business. However, the rapid expansion of OSNs and the widespread sharing of personal data have made these platforms prime targets for attackers to steal their information. In this article, we focus on addressing the issue of profile cloning, a significant threat to user privacy and trust in OSNs. We propose and evaluate various machine learning algorithms to detect and mitigate this issue. Our findings highlight that modern machine learning algorithms like CatBoost and LightGBM significantly outperform several other regression and classification models, demonstrating its effectiveness in accurately detecting profile cloning instances. This study underscores the potential of machine learning in safeguarding OSNs against evolving security threats.

Keywords: Online social networks · CatBoost · LightGBM · Machine learning

1 Introduction

Online social networks serves as platforms for building social connections, enjoying entertainment, sharing mutual interests with others, enhancing business prospects, advancing professional careers, and more. However, OSN service providers may inadvertently expose sensitive user information to malicious actors, who could exploit it to compromise an individual's privacy [1]. Privacy can be defined as the ability of an individual, group, or organization to control the disclosure of their personal information to others. Ensuring the security and privacy of users on online social networks (OSNs) is of paramount importance. One of the most prevalent security threats in OSNs is profile cloning, a technique used by attackers to replicate user profiles for malicious purposes. As shown in Fig. 1, the classification of profile cloning is effectively illustrated. The figure provides a comprehensive overview of the classification process.

K. Chandra Mondal et al. (Eds.): CICBA 2025, CCIS 2863, pp. 45–58, 2026.
https://doi.org/10.1007/978-3-032-17184-9_4

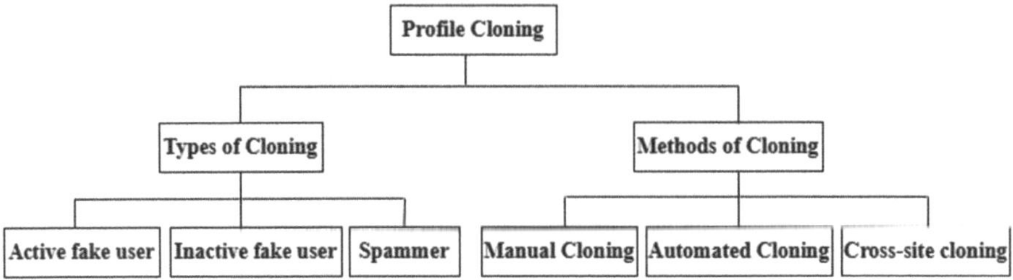

Fig. 1. Classification of profile cloning

Profile cloning can be executed through various methods. Manual cloning involves a malicious user manually copying data from the original user to create a fake profile. Automated cloning, on the other hand, employs automation tools or scripts to replicate profiles in bulk, either within the same social network or across multiple platforms. Lastly, cross-site cloning occurs when an attacker uses information from a victim's profile to create a fake account on a different social network where the victim has not yet registered. Enhancing the accuracy of detecting profile cloning attacks not only improves the safety of active users but also encourages OSN service providers to adopt innovative approaches for strengthening the security and privacy of their platforms [7,11].

Online Social Networks (OSNs) have become an integral part of modern life, serving not only as platforms for communication but also for sharing achievements and self-expression. Despite their advantages, OSNs face numerous challenges, including security vulnerabilities, privacy breaches, cyberbullying, fake news, profile cloning, data breaches, and account hijacking [13]. While significant efforts have been made to address these issues, many gaps remain. One critical shortcoming is the lack of robust mechanisms to verify the legitimacy of user profiles, leaving users exposed to various threats. Addressing this gap is the focus of the current study.
The objectives of this study are the following:

- To evaluate the effectiveness of modern machine learning techniques compared to traditional methods in detecting fake profiles.
- Identify the most significant features that contribute to the detection of fake profiles.
- Analyze the performance of the model using metrics such as accuracy, precision, recall, F1 score and compare the proposed approach with different datasets.

The study is structured as follows: Sect. 2 provides a theoretical grounding for the study. The Proposed Methodology is discussed in Sect. 3 and the results of the experiments are presented in Sect. 4. Privacy Implications and User Data Governance are addressed in Sect. 5, followed by the conclusion in Sect. 6.

2 Literature Review

Major platforms on the Internet are persistently targeted by spammers, scammers, and phishers aiming to exploit users by inundating them with unwanted spam and stealing sensitive personal information. In their paper, Purba et al. [11] proposed a robust classification methodology leveraging a set of 17 distinct features selected from a variety of data points. These features spanned categories such as user metadata, media information, engagement metrics, media tags, and media similarity, providing a comprehensive approach to differentiating authentic from fake accounts on Instagram. To determine the effectiveness of these features, the study employed multiple machine learning classifiers, including Random Forest, Neural Network, and Logistic Regression. A comparative analysis identified Random Forest as the most accurate model, underscoring its suitability for this classification task.

In a related study, Chakraborty et al. [2] explored fake account detection on Twitter, leveraging models such as XGBoost, long-short-term memory (LSTM) networks, Random Forest and neural networks. XGBoost outperformed the alternatives, achieving superior accuracy. Notably, this pattern was echoed in another domain fake news detection [9], where XGBoost again demonstrated higher performance compared to Random Forest. These findings highlight XGBoost's adaptability and effectiveness across diverse classification tasks, making it a preferred choice in contexts demanding high accuracy and robust predictive capabilities. While in [10], the authors discussed about various models and concluded that Catboast can handle effectively larger datasets and complex feature interaction. It doesn't require any prepossing and can handle overfitting better.

Recognizing the critical importance of detecting fake accounts, researchers have increasingly focused on developing innovative and efficient detection mechanisms. In their study, Khalad et al. [5] introduced a novel hybrid classification algorithm that combined the strengths of Neural Networks and Support Vector Machines (SVM). Specifically, they applied the Neural Network classification algorithm to the decision values generated by the SVM classifier. This hybrid approach achieved significantly higher accuracy compared to using either algorithm individually, demonstrating its effectiveness in detecting fake accounts.

In Maysa Khalil et al. [6] on fake news detection, the authors explored various classification models with an emphasis on leveraging advanced feature engineering techniques and machine learning algorithms. After incorporating robust text representation methods Random Forest consistently outperformed all other models.

Sonowal [14] employed a rule-based approach for detecting fake profiles. After defining the rules, the author integrated an ANN, which demonstrated superior performance compared to other machine learning algorithms.

Kadam et al. [4] applied various machine learning algorithms, with Artificial Neural Networks (ANN) achieving the highest accuracy. Out of a total of 34 features, only 17 attributes were selected for evaluation. The authors conducted experiments using both 30% and 20% test splits, and provided a comprehensive comparison of the algorithms based on accuracy, error rate, time consumption, and memory usage.

Devmane et al. [3] proposed a mechanism to detect cloned and fake profiles in Online Social Networks by analyzing user credentials such as name, profile photo, education, workplace, and other public details. Their method involves extracting unique information from a user's profile and searching for similar profiles both on the same platform (same-site) and across different platforms (cross-site). Each profile is compared with the original using a weighted Similarity Index (S.I.), where a value above 80% indicates a cloned profile and below 20% indicates a fake one. If the profile photo and other public details do not match, the S.I. is set to zero. This approach helps in effectively identifying impersonators and protecting user identity online.

In recent times, we see a surge in cloned profiles. There can be several impacts of cloned profiles but to name a few social reputation damage, financial scams, user churn and legal costs. Our main aim is to detect all clones at scale. While most existing studies focus on either a single dataset or rely on traditional machine learning models, they often overlook the combined impact of diverse data sources and modern algorithms. Our work addresses this gap by:

- Leveraging ensemble boosting techniques for enhanced predictive performance.
- Utilizing multiple heterogeneous datasets.
- Conducting feature importance analysis

3 Proposed Methodology

3.1 Problem Formation

A social network graph G (V, E) represents relationships and correlations within a OSN. In this context, V denotes the set of vertices, where each vertex represents an individual, such as a victim (green node), fake profile (red nodes), friends (blue nodes), or mutual friends (yellow nodes). E is the set of edges connecting the vertices, symbolizing relationships.

In Fig. 2, the friend network of a user is depicted. Here, fake profiles attempt to impersonate the original user by establishing connections with the victim's friends. These fake profiles are intended to exploit their connections to gain credibility and deceive the network. To enhance user safety and network integrity, robust detection mechanisms must be employed. Graph-based algorithms and machine learning models can identify suspicious patterns indicative of fake profiles or malicious behavior.

Online Social Networks (OSNs), host vast amounts of personal information, including photos, email addresses, and contact details. Unfortunately, this data is often publicly accessible, making it vulnerable to malicious actors who can easily replicate and misuse it. Such actions not only compromise individuals' privacy but also facilitate identity theft, fraud, and the spread of misinformation.

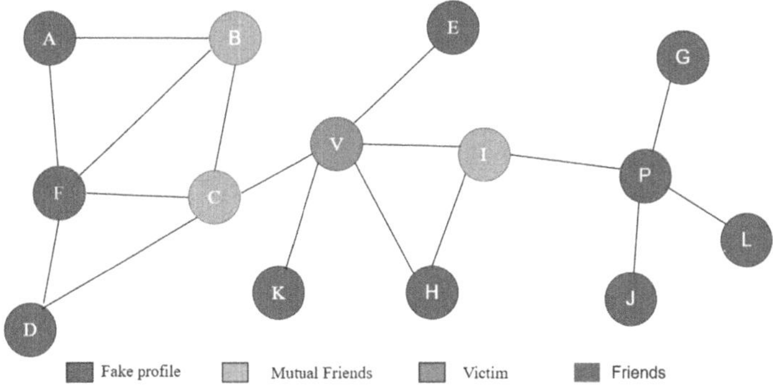

Fig. 2. Friend network in OSN

3.2 Dataset and Features Considered

We have collected total three datasets comprising of different attributes. Datasets 1 and 2 collectively comprise 17 unique features, while Dataset 3 includes 11 features. These datasets were carefully selected to capture a comprehensive range of both behavioral patterns and profile-based characteristics, which are essential for the effectiveness and accuracy of our analysis. The dataset 1 and dataset 2 is splitted into training and testing in a ratio of 80:20 as outlined in [12]. For Dataset 3, the test data is provided separately in a folder.

The datasets used in this study are as follows:

Dataset 1 [11]: it categorizes outputs into authentic and fake users.

Dataset 2 [11]: it classifies outputs into four categories: authentic users, active fake users, inactive fake users, and spammers.

Dataset 3 [14]: it contains binary-labeled outputs: 0 representing real users and 1 representing fake users.

Some of the key features across all datasets, which play a crucial role in predicting whether a profile is fake or real are shown in Table 1.

3.3 Data Preprocessing

We have completed the data cleaning process for all the datasets to improve their quality and reliability. The cleaning involved the removal of outliers to ensure the accuracy of the data. During our analysis, we identified for dataset 1 and 2 an anomaly: when the number of posts on Instagram is zero, metrics such as post interval, average caption length, engagement rate (likes), etc. cannot logically exceed zero.

After applying the necessary cleaning steps, the size of our data set that contains authentic and fake users was reduced from 65,326 to 65,272, and the

Table 1. Some important features of the datasets

Dataset 1/dataset 2	Dataset 3
Number of total posts that the user has ever posted	profile pic
Number of following	Fullname
Number of followers	Description length
Picture availability	Private
Engagement rate (Like)	Followers
Post interval	Follows
Biography length	Post

other data set decreased from 43,307 to 43,253. The basic architechture of our study is shown in Fig. 3.

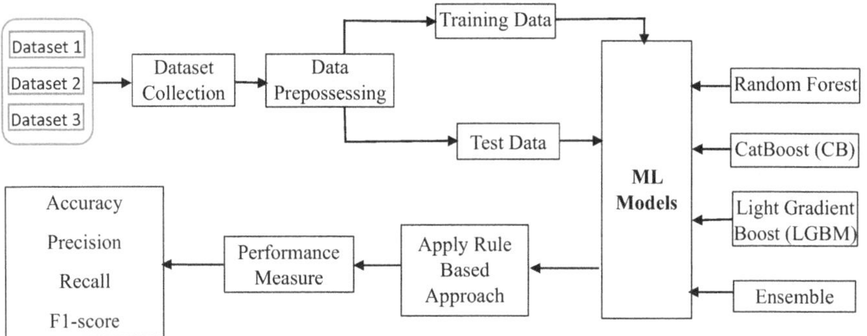

Fig. 3. Technical architecture for detecting cloned profile

3.4 Proposed Algorithm

Catboost, or Categorical Boosting, is a powerful algorithm that handles categorical features effectively, requires minimal data preprocessing and manages missing values seamlessly. In catboost, the algorithm begins by constructing a tree aimed to minimize the training error. Subsequently, it builds additional trees iteratively, each designed to reduce the residual error from the previous step. This algorithm continues until a decent tree is created. The work is shown in the Fig. 4.

The Light Gradient Boosting Machine (LightGBM) is a high-performance gradient boosting framework suitable for large and high-dimensional datasets. LightGBM employs a leaf-wise tree growth strategy, splitting the leaf with the best fit, unlike other boosting algorithms that follow a depth-wise or level-wise splitting approach. In simpler terms, LightGBM expands trees vertically, focusing on

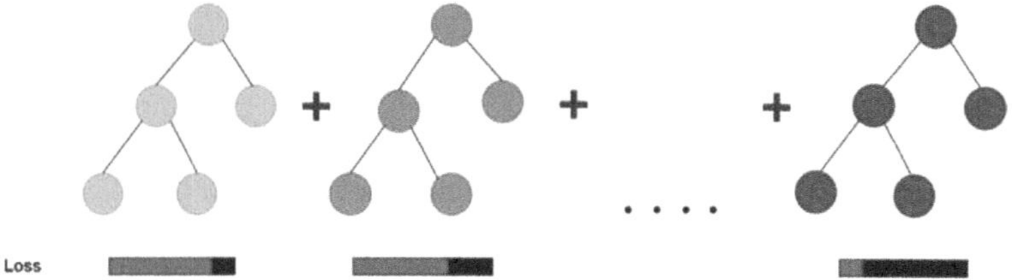

Fig. 4. Working of CatBoost

optimizing specific branches, whereas other algorithms grow trees horizontally, layer by layer. The functioning of LGBM is shown in Fig. 5.

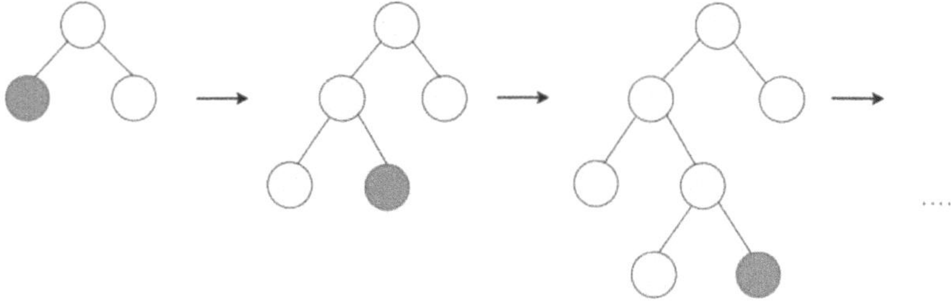

Fig. 5. Working of LGBM

In this study, we prioritize on boosting algorithms to achieve optimal performance in our classification task. This ensemble method combining of catboast and LGBM leverages the unique advantages of both algorithms, resulting in improved accuracy [8] and efficiency for dataset 1 and dataset 2. For dataset 3, we are implementing a rule based approach after applying catboost algorithm. In a rule-based system, specific conditions are defined, and if those conditions are met, a certain action is taken; otherwise, it is not. In our case, we have designed a rule that we believe is optimal for our dataset.
The rule states:
Dataset 1/Dataset 2- If no profile photo is there, post interval is zero and the ratio of number of followers to number of following is greater than 3 then it is a fake/inactive profile.

Dataset 3–If profile is private and has a profile picture, the ratio of numerical characters in the username to its total length is less than 0.5 and The ratio of numerical characters in the full name to its total length is also less than 0.5 it is real else fake.

4 Experimental Result

The primary objective of this paper is to evaluate the performance of classification algorithms in detecting fake users on Instagram. We have implemented multiple machine learning models, including Random Forest, CatBoost, and LightGBM, all of which demonstrated strong performance. Evaluation metrics are crucial in machine learning algorithms, categorizing predictions as True Positives (TP) for correctly identified real profiles, True Negatives (TN) for correctly classified fake profiles, False Positives (FP) for fake profiles misclassified as real, and false Negatives (FN) for real profiles misclassified as fake.
The formulas for the key evaluation metrics—Accuracy, Precision, Recall, and F1-Score are illustrated in Fig. 6.

$$Accuracy = \frac{TP + TN}{TP + TN + FP + FN} \qquad Precision = \frac{TP}{TP + FP}$$

$$Recall = \frac{TP}{TP + FN} \qquad F1\text{-}Score = \frac{2 \times Precision \times Recall}{Precision + Recall}$$

Fig. 6. Evaluation metrics used for classification performance

The accuracy with increasing test size is shown in Fig. 7. As the test size increases, a slight decline in accuracy is observed.

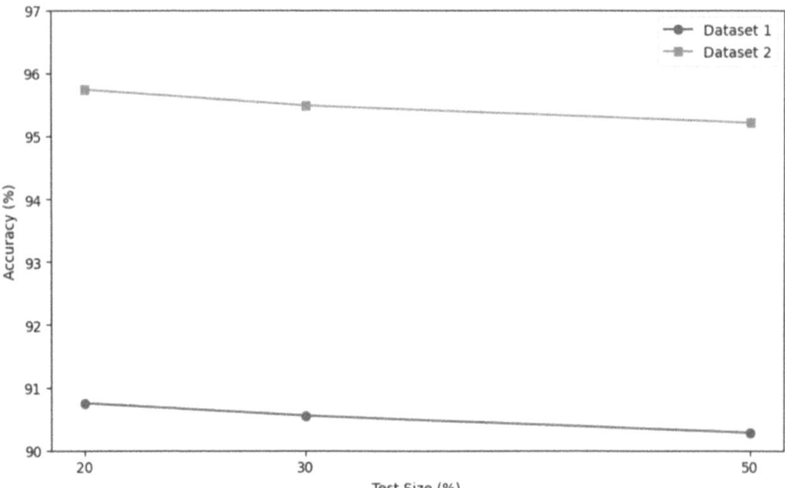

Fig. 7. Accuracy versus test sizes

The Table 2 presents various approaches applied to different datasets, along with their performance metrics, including accuracy, precision, recall, and F1-score.

Table 2. Comparison of different approaches across datasets

Dataset	Approach	Accuracy (%)	Precision (%)	Recall (%)	F1-score (%)	Train time (s)	Test time (s)
Dataset 1	Random Forest	90.34	92	90	90	15.411	0.383
	CB	90.48	91	91	90	5.469	0.012
	LGBM	90.54	91	91	91	3.736	0.602
	Ensemble	**90.75**	91	91	91	13.970	0.404
Dataset 2	Random Forest	90.38	90	91	90	28.348	0.588
	CB	91.59	91	92	91	7.781	0.015
	LGBM	95.42	95	95	95	2.305	0.221
	Ensemble	**95.73**	96	96	96	28.167	2.177
Dataset 3	Random Forest	94.16	94	94	94	1.698	0.097
	CB	**97.5**	98	97	97	3.435	0.008
	LGBM	96.66	97	97	97	0.640	0.037
	Ensemble	96.66	97	97	97	2.420	0.024

Training and testing times are higher for Datasets 1 and 2 due to their large size. CatBoost and LGBM are faster individually, whereas the ensemble model takes longer as it combines multiple classifiers. This improves accuracy but increases computation time.
The confusion matrices generated by applying the respective best models is shown in Fig. 8. These matrices effectively illustrate the performance of the model by showcasing the number of correct and incorrect predictions for each class.

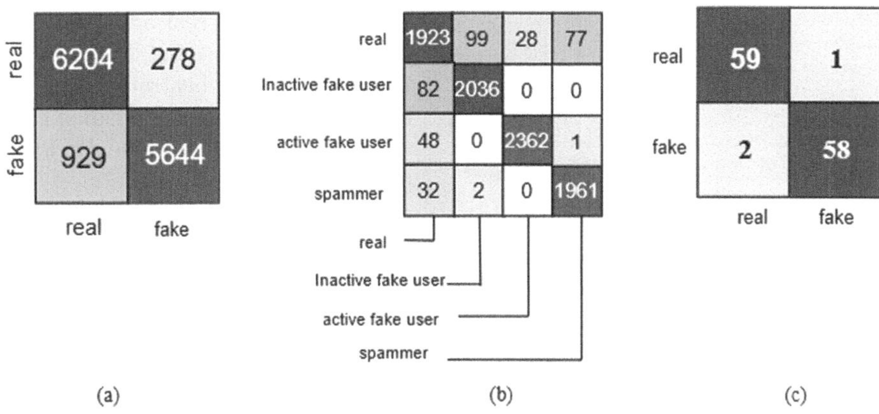

Fig. 8. Confusion matrix (a) Dataset 1, (b) Dataset 2, (c) Dataset 3

4.1 Feature Selection

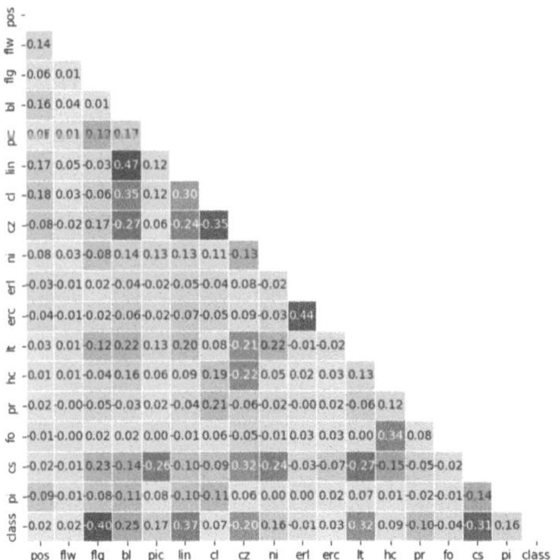

Fig. 9. Correlation heatmap highlighting all features for dataset 1

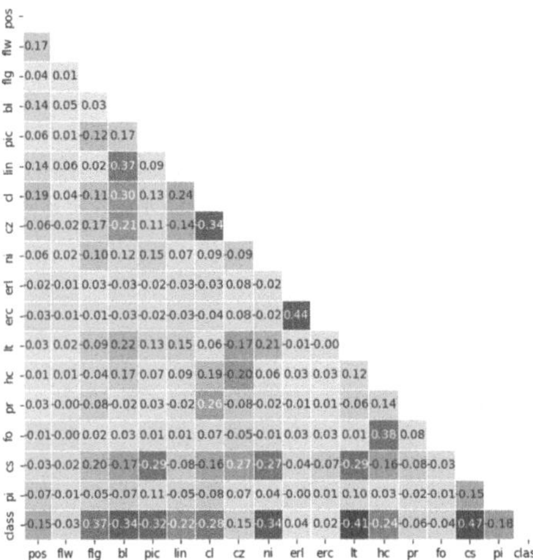

Fig. 10. Correlation heatmap highlighting all features for dataset 2

The heatmap illustrates the correlation among features. Highly correlated features may be redundant and can be removed to improve model performance. Feature selection helps in reducing overfitting, improving accuracy, and decreasing training time. The primary features in Dataset 1 include *flg*, *cs*, *bl*, *lin*, and *it* which help in differentiating between fake and real accounts. These features show strong influence on the classification outcome and have been retained for further modeling. The selection process and corresponding correlation structure are visually demonstrated in Fig. 9.

The correlation heatmap in Fig. 10 provides insight into the relationships between the features and the target variable *class*. Features such as *flg*, *bl*, *pic*, *it* and *cs* exhibit moderate to strong correlation with the class label. Notably, the feature *cs* shows a relatively high positive correlation (0.47) with the target, indicating its discriminative power in distinguishing between real and fake profiles. On the other hand, features like *cz*, *erl*, and *ni* demonstrate low correlation with the target and may contribute less predictive value. By identifying and prioritizing the most relevant features, we can reduce model complexity, minimize overfitting, and enhance classification accuracy.

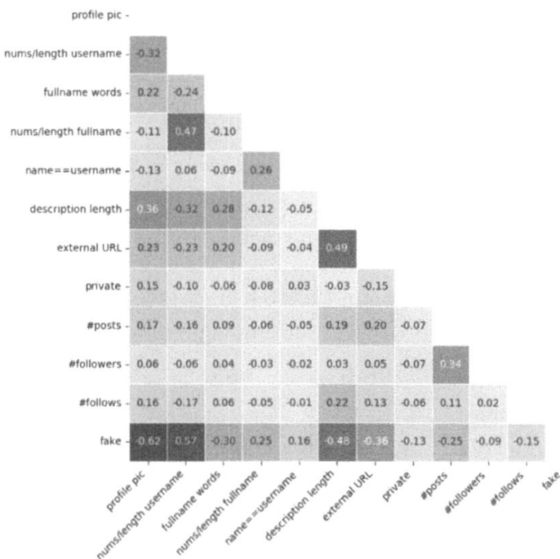

Fig. 11. Correlation heatmap highlighting all features for dataset 3

The correlation heatmap in Fig. 11 presents pairwise correlations between features and the target variable *fake*, which indicates whether a profile is fake or real. Features like *profile pic*, *nums/length username*, and *external URL* show relatively strong correlations with the target class. On the other hand, some features such as *followers*, *follows*, and *posts* have weak correlations with the target class, indicating limited predictive value when considered independently. These insights help identify and prioritize influential attributes, which can be retained for downstream modeling while removing redundant or noisy features. Overall, this selection process contributes to enhanced model performance, reduced overfitting, and improved generalization on unseen data.

In addition to the correlation analysis presented above, we conducted a manual feature evaluation process. To understand the impact of individual features on model performance, we carried out an ablation study by removing both high-importance and low-importance features one at a time and retraining the model after each removal. Interestingly, we observed a drop in accuracy in all cases, regardless of whether the removed feature had high or low correlation with the target. This suggests that even features with seemingly low individual significance can contribute to the overall model performance through interactions with other features. Therefore, careful feature selection plays a vital role in improving classification accuracy, reducing overfitting, and ensuring the model captures the complex relationships present in the data.

4.2 Comparative Analysis

The performance and comparative analysis of the datasets and classification approaches discussed in [11,14] are summarized in Tables 3, 4 and 5. Our proposed ensemble model, which integrates CatBoost and LightGBM, demonstrates superior performance in certain aspects for dataset 1 and dataset 2. However, for dataset 3 catboost performs better that LGBM and ensemble model. This is likely because LightGBM is optimized for large datasets, whereas Dataset 3 includes only 120 test samples, making it better suited for CatBoost's capabilities.

Table 3. Performance metrics comparison for Dataset 1

Author name	Approach	Accuracy (%)	Precision (%)	Recall (%)	F1-score (%)
K. Purba et al.	Random Forest	90.09	90.70	90.10	90.10
Our Work	Ensemble	**90.75**	**91.0**	**91.0**	**91.0**

Table 4. Performance metrics comparison for Dataset 2

Author name	Approach	Accuracy (%)	Precision (%)	Recall (%)	F1-score (%)
K. Purba et al.	Random forest	91.76	91.70	91.80	91.70
Our Work	Ensemble	**95.73**	**96.0**	**96.0**	**96.0**

Table 5. Performance metrics comparison for Dataset 3

Author name	Approach	Accuracy (%)
Sarhan et al.	Random forest	92.99
Ekosputra et al.	Logistic Regression	93
Sonowal	ANN	94.25
Our Work	CatBoost	**97.5**

5 Privacy Implications and User Data Governance

The aim of this section is to raise awareness about the risks of profile cloning faced by users of Online Social Networks (OSNs), and to suggest practical steps that users and platforms can follow to protect themselves from identity theft and impersonation.

1. **Be cautious about the personal information you share on social media**–Sharing too many personal details such as your date of birth, family members' names, or other common password hints can make you an easy target for identity thieves. This kind of information can be misused to create cloned profiles or even to hack into your other online accounts. To stay safe, only include essential information in your profile and keep sensitive details private.
2. **Accept Friend Requests Cautiously**–Many users tend to accept friend requests without verifying the sender's identity. Only connect with individuals you know and trust.
3. **Regularly Audit Your Friends List -** Duplicate friend requests can come from cloned profiles of people already on your list. To stay safe periodically review and clean your friend list.
4. **Restrict External Search Access to Profiles**–OSNs should limit how user profiles appear on external search engines (like Google or Bing). This will help protect users from having their data scraped and misused by attackers.

5. **Strengthen Authentication During Signup**–Social networking platforms should implement stricter verification methods like use of one-time passwords (OTPs) via email and mobile or biometric when a user signs up.
6. **Transparency in Privacy Policy Updates**–Whenever there are changes in privacy policies, OSNs must notify users clearly about what's changing and explain how those changes affect user privacy.

6 Conclusion and Future Works

Online Social Networks (OSNs) are increasingly popular across all age groups. With the growing number of users, distinguishing between fake and genuine accounts has become a significant challenge. To mitigate this issue, we employed diverse ML classifiers, yielding promising results. While the problem of fake accounts is likely to persist, certain parameters, such as engagement rate, profile pictures, and activity patterns, can consistently help differentiate between real and fake users. Spammers pose an additional threat, particularly on platforms like dating apps. To combat this, we tested our solution on dataset 2 and achieved improved metrics.

While the adoption of a rule-based approach may raise concerns about potential overfitting, the conditions identified for all the datasets, accurately distinguishing between fake and real accounts. Our results show a strong performance, with a cross-validation accuracy of 90.24% in dataset 1 and 95.41% in dataset 2 using k-fold. These accuracies closely align with the test results, indicating that the models perform well on overall data.

To further enhance OSN security, we propose several improvements, including implementing a user-flagging system where repeatedly flagged profiles or those exceeding a predefined suspicion threshold are temporarily blocked for further verification. Additionally, biometric and AI-based verification methods, such as retina scans or face detection real-time profile pictures, help to distinguish between real and fake users. These methods can also help to check whether multiple profiles share the same face or retina scans, helping to prevent duplication. In addition,behavioral analysis and monitoring user activity patterns, such as messaging frequency and engagement anomalies, could help detect bot-like behavior. By integrating these strategies, we can further enhance security, reduce fraudulent activity, and improve trust and authenticity in OSNs.

References

1. Bhattacharya, M., Roy, S., Chattopadhyay, S., Das, A.K., Shetty, S.: A comprehensive survey on online social networks security and privacy issues: Threats, machine learning-based solutions, and open challenges. Security Privacy **6**(1), e275 (2023)
2. Chakraborty, P., Shazan, M.M., Nahid, M., Ahmed, M.K., Talukder, P.C.: Fake profile detection using machine learning techniques. J. Comput. Commun. **10**(10), 74–87 (2022)

3. Devmane, M., Rana, N.: Detection and prevention of profile cloning in online social networks. In: International Conference on Recent Advances and Innovations in Engineering (ICRAIE-2014). pp. 1–5. IEEE (2014)
4. Kadam, N., Sharma, S.K.: Social media fake profile detection using data mining technique. J. Adv. Inf. Technol. **13**(5) (2022)
5. Khaled, S., El-Tazi, N., Mokhtar, H.M.: Detecting fake accounts on social media. In: 2018 IEEE international conference on big data (big data). pp. 3672–3681. IEEE (2018)
6. Khalil, M., Azzeh, M.: Fake news detection models using the largest social media ground-truth dataset (truthseeker). International Journal of Speech Technology pp. 1–16 (2024)
7. Kharaji, M.Y., Rizi, F.S., Khayyambashi, M.R.: A new approach for finding cloned profiles in online social networks. arXiv preprint arXiv:1406.7377 (2014)
8. Nagassou, M., Mwangi, R.W., Nyarige, E.: A hybrid ensemble learning approach utilizing light gradient boosting machine and category boosting model for lifestyle-based prediction of type-ii diabetes mellitus. J. Data Anal. Inf. Process. **11**(4), 480–511 (2023)
9. Ngada, O., Haskins, B.: Fake news detection using content-based features and machine learning. In: 2020 IEEE Asia-Pacific Conference on Computer Science and Data Engineering (CSDE). pp. 1–6. IEEE (2020)
10. Odeh, A., Al-Haija, Q.A., Aref, A., Taleb, A.A.: Comparative study of catboost, xgboost, and lightgbm for enhanced url phishing detection: a performance assessment. J. Internet Serv. Inf. Security **13**(4), 1–11 (2023)
11. Purba, K.R., Asirvatham, D., Murugesan, R.K.: Classification of instagram fake users using supervised machine learning algorithms. Int. J. Electr. Comput. Eng. **10**(3), 2763 (2020), dataset available at: www.kaggle.com/datasets/krpurba/fakeauthentic-user-instagram
12. Reddy, S.D.P.: Fake profile identification using machine learning. Int. Res. J. Eng. Technol. (IRJET) **6**(12), 1145–1150 (2019)
13. Roy, P.K., Chahar, S.: Fake profile detection on social networking websites: a comprehensive review. IEEE Trans. Artif. Intell. **1**(3), 271–285 (2020)
14. Sonowal, G., Balaji, V., Kumar, N.: A model to detect fake profile on instagram using rule-based approach. CSI Transactions on ICT pp. 1–11 (2024), dataset available at: https://www.kaggle.com/datasets/free4ever1/instagram-fake-spammer-genuine-accounts

Comparative Analysis of Apache Spark and Apache Kafka for Efficient Data Integration for Real-Time Data Processing

Samriddha Bhattacharyya[1], Surjit Banik[1], Ankit Paswan[1], Nitin Kumar[1], Anirban Bhar[1], Suchismita Maiti[1], Neepa Biswas[1](✉), and Kartick Chandra Mondal[2]

[1] Department of Information Technology, Narula Institute of Technology, Agarpara, Kolkata, India
biswas.neepa@gmail.com
[2] Department of CSE, SRM University_AP, Amaravati, India

Abstract. Data integration plays a vital role in modern data pipelines by facilitating seamless data movement, transformation, and analysis. This study compares two prominent data integration frameworks—Apache Spark and Apache Kafka—based on key performance metrics such as throughput, latency, and resource utilization. Apache Spark, widely recognized for its batch and stream processing capabilities, is evaluated alongside Apache Kafka, a distributed event streaming platform, to assess their efficiency in real-time and large-scale data integration tasks. The research includes experimental benchmarking using structured and un-structured datasets, analyzing their performance under different workloads. The findings highlight the trade-offs between Kafka's low-latency streaming and Spark's high-throughput batch processing, providing insights into their suitability for various data integration scenarios. By exploring these differences, the study offers practical recommendations for selecting the right framework based on specific processing needs. This comparative analysis helps organizations optimize their data architectures, ensuring improved efficiency, scalability, and real-time data management in diverse environments.

Keywords: Apache Kafka · Apache Spark · Amazon S3 · Real-Time Analytics · Data integration

1 Introduction

With the increasing demand for real-time data processing and large-scale analytics, organizations are adopting data classification systems to manage data quickly [6]. Apache Kafka and Apache Spark [8] have become two of the most widely used technologies for managing data integration [7], event processing, and large-scale analytics. While Kafka was primarily designed as an efficient messaging system for real-time reporting, Spark provides an integrated engine capable of batch and micro-batch processing. Understanding the characteristics of performance, efficiency, fault tolerance, and the ability to

K. Chandra Mondal et al. (Eds.): CICBA 2025, CCIS 2863, pp. 59–72, 2026.
https://doi.org/10.1007/978-3-032-17184-9_5

integrate these systems is crucial to choosing the right technology for a given task [12]. Cloud storage solutions like Amazon S3 are critical for modern data architectures, providing scalable, durable, and cost-effective storage for large datasets. Combining Kafka and Spark with cloud services adds complexity and performance considerations, including latency, throughput, fault tolerance, and scalability. Evaluating their performance in a cloud-integrated environment is essential for informed architectural decisions.

This research paper provides a comparison between Apache Kafka and Apache Spark in terms of integration with Amazon S3 data. The study examined key performance metrics such as latency, throughput, scalability, and fault tolerance to assess how each system handles workloads and data reliability. This paper also examines the performance of storing and retrieving data from Amazon S3 and the impact of workload changes on end-to-end performance. The goal of this study is to analyze these factors and understand the strengths and weaknesses of these two concepts to help organizations make informed decisions when developing data to address these issues.

The paper is organized as follows: Sect. 2 presents a review of related literature. Section 3 details the methodology employed in this study. Sections 4 and 5 cover the data integration process and performance analysis using Apache Kafka. Similarly, Sects. 6 and 7 focus on the data integration process and performance analysis with Apache Spark. The overall results and analysis are discussed in Sect. 8, followed by the conclusion of the proposed work in Sect. 9.

2 Literature Survey

Article of Jobin George's [1] emphasizes the importance of real-time data analytics in today's world. It explores the use of AWS services like Kinesis, Lambda, DynamoDB, S3, Athena, Redshift, AWS Glue, and MSK in data transformation and stream processing. The article provides practical information on pipeline building.

This research work [14] discusses big data analytics for multi-tenant systems on Amazon Web Service (AWS), analyzing static and real-time dynamic data. It examines performance under time, data traffic, and data size constraints, highlighting its importance in the internet world.

The framework by Milind Gayakwad et al. [2] proposes a system for managing and analyzing real-time clickstream data using Apache tools and AWS services. It emphasizes the importance of clickstream analysis in understanding user behavior, developing marketing strategies, and improving digital marketing experience. Advanced tools like Hive and Tableau can help overcome challenges in processing big data.

This research paper [15] explores cloud computing, a pay-as-you-use service where computing resources are provided on an as-needed basis. It compares the performance and service of three main platforms: Microsoft Azure, Amazon AWS, and Google Cloud Platform, evaluating their performance in identical virtual environments, specifically Ubuntu 16.04, using benchmark applications like Apache, Dbench, and RAM speed.

Dominik Hlaváäurán's article [3] discusses using Amazon Web Services (AWS) for streaming data storage and analysis in large paper networks. The article highlights the use of Parquet file formats and the importance of compression format for better storage and query performance. The article also explores AWS services like Amazon S3, AWS Glue, and Amazon Athena for better security monitoring and management control.

The study affirms that AWS-based architectures, when combined with tools like Apache Kafka and Spark, provide scalable, efficient, and real-time solutions for modern data integration challenges. The consistent emphasis on schema automation (AWS Glue), streaming efficiency, and cloud-native performance optimization forms the foundation for the current study's methodology and comparative evaluation.

3 Methodology

This study conducts a comparative analysis of Apache Kafka and Apache Spark [8] for real-time data integration with Amazon S3 [1, 10], utilizing a large-scale stock market dataset. The methodology integrates experimental deployment, automated schema management through AWS Glue [11], and a detailed architectural review of each framework to assess their effectiveness in modern data pipelines.

3.1 Architectural Differences: Apache Kafka vs. Apache Spark

Apache Kafka employs a distributed publish-subscribe model, optimized for high-throughput, real-time messaging. Producers ingest data, which is stored in topics across a cluster of brokers and consumed asynchronously. Using an append-only log format, Kafka provides configurable retention, replication, and partitioning for scalability and reliability.

In contrast, Apache Spark relies on a distributed data-parallel execution framework. It processes data via Resilient Distributed Datasets (RDDs) or DataFrames, supporting complex transformations in batch mode and micro-batch streaming through Spark Structured Streaming. Spark's in-memory computation minimizes disk I/O, making it well-suited for large-scale analytical tasks.

3.2 Data Integration Using Apache Kafka

Kafka is configured to emulate a real-time data stream from the stock dataset. The ingestion pipeline consists of:

- Kafka producers continuously generating stock records.
- Kafka brokers storing and distributing data to consumers.
- A Kafka Connect S3 Sink Connector writing streamed data to Amazon S3 in formats like JSON or Avro.

AWS Glue ensures consistent schema validation during ingestion by providing metadata services. Kafka's design supports efficient horizontal scaling via topic partitioning and robust fault-tolerant delivery mechanisms.

3.3 Data Integration Using Apache Spark

Apache Spark processes the same dataset using Spark Structured Streaming, with the following steps:

- Reading data from Amazon S3 via the s3a:// connector.

- Transforming data using Spark SQL and DataFrame APIs.
- Writing processed data back to S3 in optimized formats like Parquet.

Spark leverages metadata from the AWS Glue Data Catalog to manage schema evolution and ensure type consistency. Its distributed computation model, utilizing multiple executors across a cluster, delivers high throughput and scalability, particularly for batch ETL and historical analytics.

3.4 Evaluation Metrics

Kafka and Spark are evaluated based on key criteria to guide organizations in selecting the right framework for their needs. Latency measures the time from data ingestion to storage, while throughput assesses the volume of data processed per unit time. Scalability evaluates performance under growing data volumes, and fault tolerance examines mechanisms for failure recovery and data consistency. Resource utilization focuses on the efficiency of CPU, memory, and I/O usage. Through architectural analysis and experimental benchmarking, this comprehensive evaluation highlights the strengths and trade-offs of Kafka and Spark, enabling informed decisions tailored to specific operational requirements.

4 Data Integration with Apache Kafka

4.1 Dataset Overview

A very large CSV dataset of the stock market is used here. When several important stock data like (Opening and Closing Stock Pricing, highest and lowest stock price, percentage of stock price increase/decrease) is given of different big companies like Google, Meta, Apple, Microsoft etc. We have used AWS Glue Catalogue and Crawler for making schemas in the dataset. Then the dataset is uploaded in the Amazon S3 bucket using Apache Kafka and Apache Spark separately and necessary data analysis is performed.

4.2 Set up of Apache Kafka with Amazon S3:

Apache Kafka can be integrated with Amazon S3 using the Kafka Connector and S3 Sink Connector for data streaming and storage. The prerequisites to achieve this are a running Kafka cluster, an S3 bucket, and AWS credentials with appropriate permissions. The S3 Sink Connector has been configured via the Confluent Hub CLI and appropriate access rights have been set for the S3 bucket. Create a configuration file to define the Kafka context, S3 bucket parameters, and required data. When Kafka Connect is running in standalone mode, messages generated by the Kafka context are sent to an S3 bucket. Regular engine monitoring ensures stable operation, while fixing errors such as batch size and compression improves performance. It is recommended to use IAM roles and encryption methods to maintain data security. The pipeline is robust and has great potential for data ingestion and integration between Kafka and Amazon S3.

5 Performance Analysis

5.1 Throughput

Throughput refers to the volume of data Apache Kafka can process over time, typically measured in messages per second or MB/s shown in Fig. 1. It is a key indicator of Kafka's performance and is influenced by factors such as the number of partitions (which enable parallel processing), batch size, and producer wait times. While larger batches improve throughput by reducing communication overhead, they may introduce latency. Consumer configurations and recurring events also affect performance. Kafka offers tools like kafka-producer-perf-test and kafka-consumer-perf-test for benchmarking, and it consistently performs well under varied workloads.

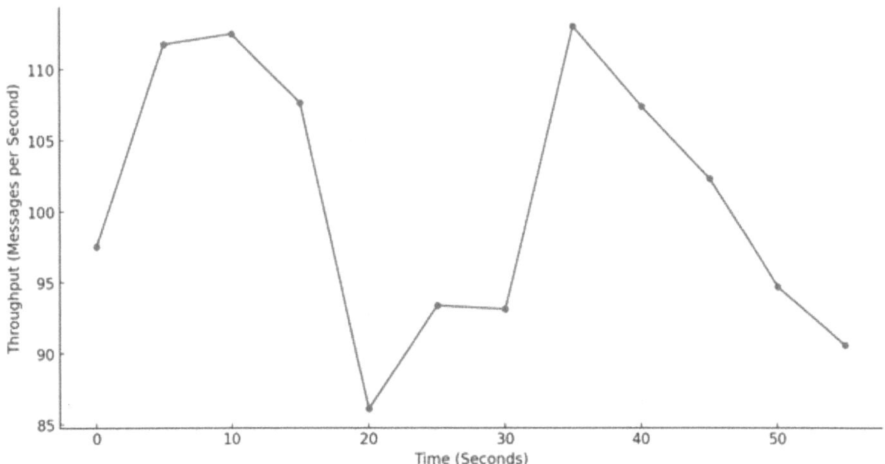

Fig. 1. Kafka's Throughput over time

5.2 Latency

Latency, the delay between the production and consumption of messages, is an important part of real-time information because low latency is important for timely decisions and responses displayed in Fig. 2. Kafka latency can be affected by many factors. Acknowledgement capabilities (acks) play a significant role: setting acks = 0 can reduce latency, but can affect data durability; setting acks = 1 or acks = all can increase reliability, but needs to make sure the words are delivered, which can delay it even further. Also, batch size and waiting time affect latency, as larger batches can cause delays because the producer has to wait for more messages before sending them. Client latency is another important factor; if the client is slow or can-not negotiate with the producer, this can increase uptime, workload, and overall latency. To measure latency, you can use tools like Kafka Manager, Kafka Tool, and Kafka monitoring tools like Grafana dashboards and Prometheus to track client latency and end-to-end latency.

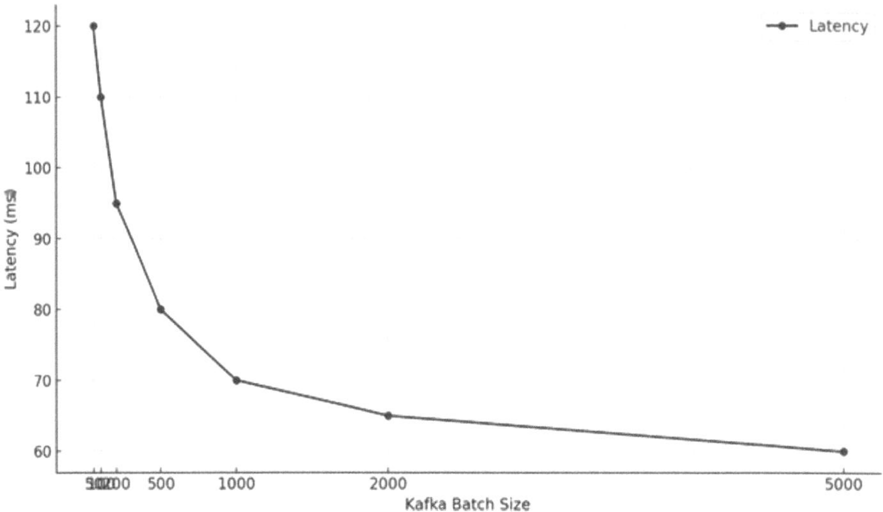

Fig. 2. Latency Comparison for different Kafka Batch Size

5.3 Resource Consumption

Throughput, the volume of messages Apache Kafka processes per unit time, is measured in messages per second or MB/s, reflecting its performance with large datasets. Influenced by factors like partition count, which boosts parallelism, and recurring events, throughput increases with replication but incurs overhead from extra connections and disk I/O. Production design, including larger batch sizes, enhances through-put by reducing producer-broker communication overhead. Consumer configuration also aids in workload sharing for more users. Kafka's tools, kafka-producer-perf-test and kafka-consumer-perf-test, enable effective benchmarking, showing strong performance across conditions.

5.4 Advantages of Data Integration with Kafka

Kafka tests have shown many advantages, especially in terms of scalability, high throughput, and fault tolerance. Kafka works efficiently with large data by distributing the load across multiple workers and distributions, providing seamless scalability. It is ideal for real-time applications, as it is capable of processing millions of words per second with low latency.

Kafka is also good at resource utilization and maintenance. It optimizes disk I/O using sequential writes, reducing overhead compared to traditional arrays. Built-in monitoring tools and integrations like Prometheus and Grafana provide great insights into performance metrics, making it easy to tune for better performance.

5.5 Challenges in Data Integration with Kafka

Kafka performance tests have shown that latency and client traffic are a challenge. A very high volume of messages can increase latency, especially during batch processing and weak site validation. Consumer crashes occur when consumers cannot keep up with developers, resulting in slower performance due to inefficient serialization and slower application logic. Bus.

A broker that manages multiple partitions can experience CPU, memory, and disk I/O bottlenecks, resulting in slower performance. Disk I/O issues (especially on HDDs) can degrade performance, while larger issues can cause network congestion and latency. If replication is configured incorrectly, proxy failure under load will result in long recovery times and data loss.

Security features such as SSL encryption will add additional CPU and network load. Analysis of issues such as customer service and job failures requires tools such as Prometheus, Grafana and Confluent Control Center for effective diagnostics.

6 Data Integration with Apache Spark

6.1 Set up of Apache Spark with Amazon S3

Apache Spark and Amazon S3 are a powerful and efficient cloud data distribution solution [2]. The setup process involves installing Spark and configuring it to interact with S3 through integrations like the Hadoop AWS library. Authentication is done via AWS credentials, which can be specified via environment variables or AWS credentials. Spark seamlessly reads and writes data to S3 using the s3a:// protocol, making it useful for large amounts of data stored on cloud-based storage devices. Optimizations can be made to improve performance, such as enabling multi-part uploads, adjusting shared space allocation, and using the S3A connector. These features improve I/O performance and reduce overhead, making the Spark-S3 integration ideal for high-volume data usage. This cost-effective and scalable solution supports complex analytics while ensuring proactive, scalable, and efficient use of resources in big data environments.

7 Performance Analysis

7.1 Throughput

Apache Spark's performance metric, delivery, measures the amount of data processed per unit of time, particularly when interacting with Amazon S3 displayed in Fig. 3. High performance in the Spark and S3 integration depends on several factors, including the use of S3A connectors, parallelism, and data partitioning strategies. Shuffle partitioning configuration is crucial for optimal efficiency, as incorrect partitioning can lead to poor performance and resource conflicts. The choice of data format is also important, with efficient formats like Parquet or ORC being known for their columnar structure and optimized compression. Implementing S3 multi-part uploading improves data throughput by supporting parallel data transfers and reducing network and I/O bottlenecks.

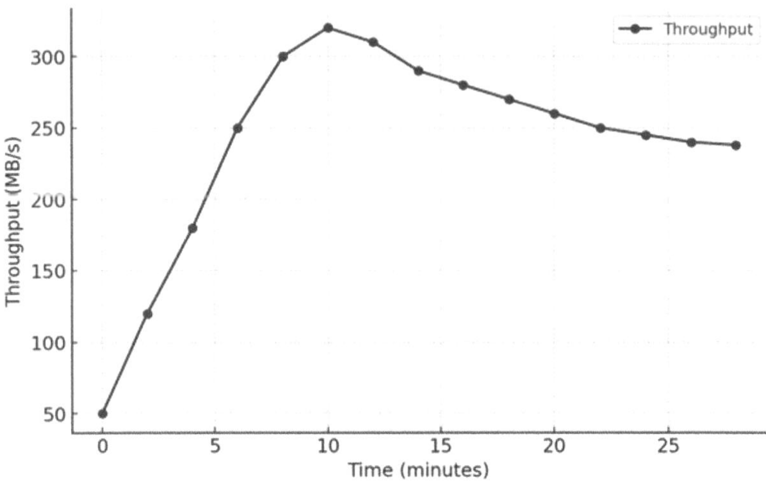

Fig. 3. Spark's Throughput over time

7.2 Latency

The latency of Apache Spark's integration with Amazon S3 is presented in Fig. 4. It is affected by network load, storage time, and transaction latency [4]. Unlike Ha-doop's distributed data storage, S3 suffers from higher read and write latency due to the object storage architecture's lack of local data and the fact that all transactions must be recorded in a remote area [3]. The request load, metadata processing, and S3's relationship model cause latency. To alleviate these issues, some optimization measures can be implemented, such as Apache Arrow caching intermediate data, leveraging in-memory computing, and adjusting batch parameters. Technologies such as collaborative media sharing and instant verification further reduce data movement and query execution time, improving the overall performance of Spark-S3 workflows.

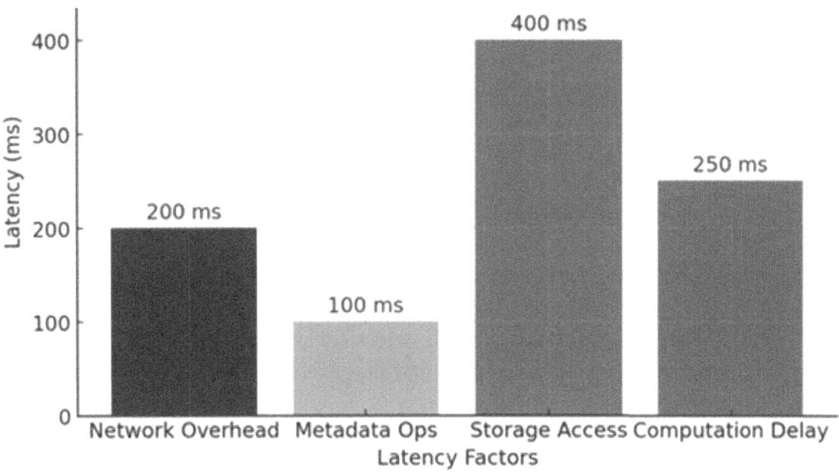

Fig. 4. Comparison of Latency factors in Spark-S3 Integration

7.3 Resource Consumption

Apache Spark integration on Amazon S3 affects resource consumption, such as memory, CPU, network, storage, and more. In contrast to HDF, S3 requires frequent data transmission, which increases network load and latency, especially during large read/write processes. Efficient partitioning allows for optimal E/A performance. Poor memory management will overload disks, but CPUs are used in line-based formats such as CSV, compared to column formats such as Parquet. Optimizations such as memory cache, partition voice, and S3 shark load improve parallelism, scalability, and cost-effectiveness, and ease cloud storage performance limits.

7.4 Advantages of Data Integration with Spark

Apache Spark's integration with Amazon S3 offers many benefits, especially in terms of scalability, flexibility, and availability. Spark, a distributed processing engine, uses parallelism to process large data sets and is well-suited for cloud-based analytics. Reduce your workload by reading and writing to S3 without having to manage the underlying storage processes. Spark also supports optimized data structures such as Parquet and ORC, which improve performance by reducing I/O overhead and shortening query execution time.

Spark's in-memory capabilities, combined with S3's flexible storage, enable faster data transformation compared to disk-based operations. It offers good performance without storage limitations, supports fault tolerance via restart, and ensures reliable data processing. Its easy integration with AWS services like Glue and Athena enhances its suitability for cloud-based big data applications.

7.5 Challenges in Data Integration with Spark

Data integration with Apache Spark [13] presents some challenges, especially when it comes to seamless integration and correlation across multiple datasets. The complexity of dealing with disparate data and structures is a major concern. Spark's ability to handle bulk and streaming data can be limited due to poor management that impacts the integration process. Additionally, maintaining data consistency during data transfer and loading across different data sources remains a challenge, especially when dealing with large datasets that need to be processed over time.

Additionally, the scalability of Spark-based data integration depends on good resource management, especially in a distributed environment. As the amount of data increases, issues such as data conflicts, fragmentation, and task scheduling will lead to poor performance. While Spark provides a number of parallel processing algorithms, optimizing these algorithms to handle high throughput without introducing excessive latency remains an ongoing concern. Fault detection and recovery also add complexity because Spark must account for errors and inconsistent data while maintaining the integrity of shared data.

8 Result and Analysis

8.1 Integration with Amazon S3

Apache Kafka integrates with Amazon S3 via the S3-Sink connector to record real-time events in formats such as Avro, JSON, Parquet, and more for sustainability at high throughput. However, frequent and small lighting processes result in storage fragmentation and high API costs. Kafka can call historical data from S3, but intake is slower than direct consumption. Kafka is developed for streaming with low latency and is based on external tools such as Kafka Streams, KSQLDB, Spark, and more. This makes it ideal for real-time use, but is less efficient for large-scale historical processing of S3.

Apache Spark is optimized for large S3 data records batches and interactive queries, and data is summed up in larger parts to reduce API costs. Using column formats such as Parquet improves performance by minimizing E/A. Spark is excellent at data recording and conversion using Spark SQL, DataFrames and RDD. It is integrated into AWS Glue and Amazon EMR for sales and metadata management. Spark Structured Streaming is ideal for historical analysis and large-scale ETL tasks that require scalability and efficient replication, as it bridges real-time applications and research.

8.2 Comparison of Event Processing Latency

Apache Kafka is a decentralized event streaming platform that offers low-latency event streaming and near-real-time data processing. It follows a publish-subscribe model, with end-to-end message delivery time influenced by factors like brokerage, distribution, and client configuration. Kafka's zero-copy forwarding minimizes disk I/O overhead, but exact-once semantics incur additional latency due to write and validation overhead. It's ideal for continuous data flow with low latency.

Apache Spark uses a micro-batch model to split input data into small batches before processing, resulting in high latency compared to Kafka's real-time streaming. Latency ranges from seconds to minutes, depending on batch duration, size, and workload complexity. Spark Structured Streaming allows near-real-time processing but operates on a model-based basis, making it unsuitable for low latency users. However, Spark is suitable for applications with high performance over time, offering high throughput and the ability to handle complex dataset analyses.

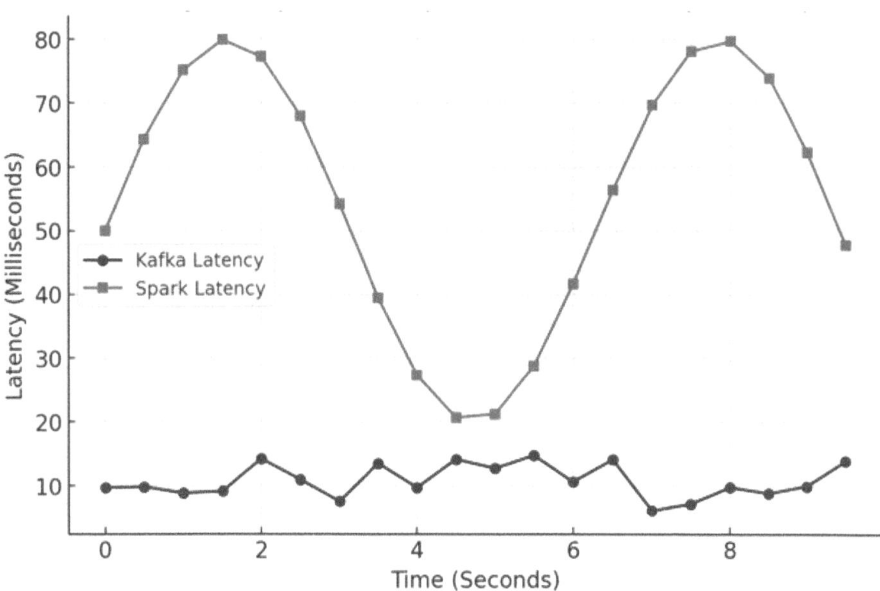

Fig. 5. Latency Comparison: Apache Spark vs Apache Kafka

8.2.1 Explanation

The Latency Comparison graph between Apache Kafka and Apache Spark is presented in Fig. 5. Kafka maintains a consistently low latency (blue line), while Spark exhibits higher peaks due to its micro-batch processing (red line).

8.3 Throughput Comparison: Apache Kafka vs. Apache Spark

Apache Kafka is designed for high-throughput event streaming, capable of ingesting millions of messages per second. It does this by distributing data across multiple distributions, ensuring uniformity of use and reducing bottlenecks. Kafka's log-based architecture and zero-copy streaming reduce I/O overhead and increase throughput. However upon achieving exactly one semantics or increasing iterations can add additional workload that will slightly impact performance.

In contrast, Apache Spark processes data in micro-batches and is therefore highly efficient for large-scale scaling. While Spark can process large amounts of data in batches, its real-time performance is lower than Kafka due to the latency inherent in micro-batch processing. Spark's distributed computing model enables parallel processing by taking advantage of analyzing more workloads than ever before, resulting in lower latency.

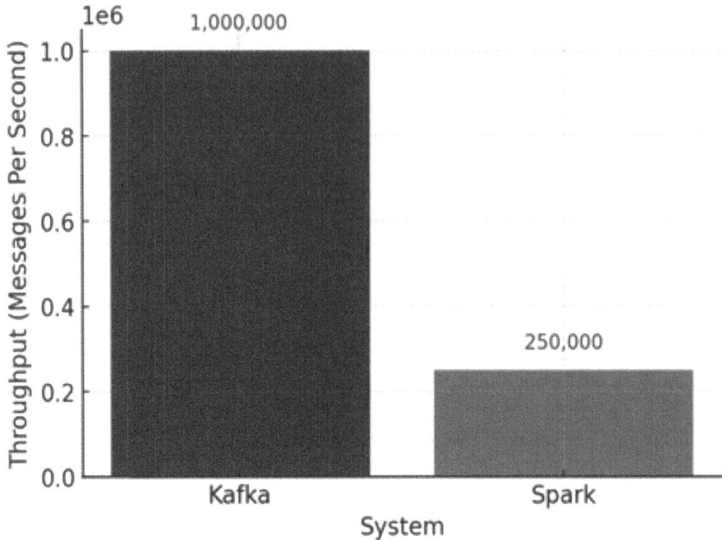

Fig. 6. Throuput Comparison: Apache Kafka vs Apache Spark

8.3.1 Explanation

The bar chart represented in Fig. 6 comparing the throughput of Apache Kafka and Apache Spark. Kafka demonstrates significantly higher throughput, handling 1,000,000 messages per second, whereas Spark processes around 250,000messages per second due to its micro-batch processing model.

8.4 Scalability and Performance Under Increasing Workloads

Apache Kafka offers great potential by distributing data across multiple partitions in a single context, allowing producers and consumers to process together. As workload increases, Kafka scales horizontally by adding more workers and partitions to ensure optimal performance. This distribution-based architecture allows Kafka to handle incremental increases with minimal overhead. However, while Kafka scales well, excessive fragmentation can lead to redundancy and increased collaboration costs, which can impact latency. Additionally, maintaining one-time semantic consistency in large deployments requires additional resources, which can slightly impact performance.

Apache Spark scales by distributing computations across worker clusters and leveraging RDDs (Resilient Distributed Datasets) and DataFrames to do the same. As data grows, Spark can allocate more executors and nodes to perform better. While Spark's native processing improves performance for batch workloads, its micro-batch model exhibits latency when measured for time-consuming applications. Performance is affected by factors such as workloads, data allocation strategies, and resource allocation.

8.5 Fault Tolerance and Reliability

Apache Kafka ensures integrity and reliability through replication, caching, and distribution. Each topic is split into multiple shards that are replicated across different brokers to prevent data loss when nodes fail. The leader-based publishing model ensures that followers take over if the leader fails to distribute, thus preserving ownership. Kafka's log-based architecture stores messages for a specified period of time, allowing clients to replay historical data in the event of a failure. However, while Kafka provides at least once and exactly once semantics, ensuring strong consistency requires additional coordination through mechanisms such as unreliable producers and accountability, which can lead to some performance overhead. In a high-throughput environment, incorrect control policies and insufficient data replication can lead to data loss.

Apache Spark performs most of its fault detection with row-based ingestion and analysis techniques. The Resilient Distributed Dataset (RDD) abstraction allows Spark to use historical data to recompute missing data when a node fails. For streaming workloads, Spark Structured Streaming uses checkpoints and write-ahead logs (WALs) to record intermediate operations and thus recover from failures without having to rerun the entire stream. Spark also integrates with HDFS, Amazon S3, and other distributed storage systems to ensure consistency. However, while testing increases reliability, it also introduces additional overhead that impacts the latency of time-consuming applications. Unlike Kafka's log-based continuous processing method, Spark's recovery method is based on checkpointing, making it more suitable for batch and micro-batch processing rather than ultra-low-latency streaming.

9 Conclusion

In this study, Apache Kafka and Apache Spark are compared with Amazon S3 in terms of data integration, focusing on performance metrics such as latency, throughput, scalability, and fault tolerance etc. The analysis shows that Kafka is quite suitable for real-time events by providing low latency and high throughput thanks to its distributed design. In contrast, Spark excels in large-scale data analysis and performs efficient batch and micro-batch operations using its distributed computing model, but its latency is slightly higher. Kafka provides reliability through distributed replication, while Spark relies on checkpoints and queues as a recovery method. In conclusion, Kafka is good for data consumption in real-time and event-driven architectures, while Spark is better for analyzing workloads that require large-scale distribution. Organizations must choose between the two based on their specific data processing needs and workloads. In future comparisons between Apache Spark and Apache Kafka can also focus on fault tolerance, ease of maintenance, cost implications etc. These aspects are critical in real-time data environments where system reliability and operational simplicity matter. Including these metrics in future studies can provide a more comprehensive view of their suitability for long-term, large-scale data integration.

References

1. George, J.: Build a Realtime Data Pipeline: Scalable Application Data Analytics on Amazon Web Services (AWS) (2024)

2. Gayakwad, M.: Real-time clickstream analytics with apache. J. Electr. Syst. **20**(20), 1600–1608 (2024)
3. Cai, M., et al.: Integrated Querying of SQL database data and S3 data in Amazon Redshift." IEEE Data Eng. Bull. **41**(2), 82–90 (2018)
4. Pendyala, S.K.: Data engineering at scale: streaming analytics with cloud and apache spark. J. Artifi. Intel. Mach. Learn. **3**(1), 1–9 (2025)
5. Powell, L. M., Wimmer, H., Nwobodo, E.: Teaching real time streaming analytics with microsoft azure and power BI. In: 2016 Proceedings of the Information Systems Education Conference, pp. 135–143 (2016)
6. Biswas, N., Sarkar, A., Mondal, K.C.: Efficient incremental loading in ETL processing for real-time data integration. Innovations Syst. Softw. Eng. **16**(1), 53–61 (2020)
7. Biswas, N., Biswas, S., Mondal, K. C., Maiti, S.: Challenges and solutions of re-al-time data integration techniques by ETL application. In: Big Data Analytics Techniques for Market Intelligence, pp. 348–371. IGI Global Scientific Publishing (2024)
8. Biswas, N., Mondal, K.C.: Integration of ETL in cloud using spark for streaming data. In: Advanced Techniques for IoT Applications: Proceedings of EAIT 2020, pp. 172–182. Springer Singapore (2022). https://doi.org/10.1007/978-981-16-4435-1_18
9. Raptis, T.P., Passarella, A.: A survey on networked data streaming with apachekafka. IEEE access **11**, 85333–85350 (2023)
10. Tajammul, M., Parveen, R., Tayubi, I.A., Asif, S.: Cloud storage in context of Amazon Web Services. Inter. J. All Res. Educ. Sci. Methods **10**(01), 442–446 (2021)
11. Pothineni, B., Maruthavanan, D., Parthi, A.G., Jayabalan, D., Kumar Veerapaneni, P.: Enhancing data integration and etl processes using AWS Glue. Inter. J. Res. Analytical Rev. **11**, 728–733 (2024)
12. Walha, A., Ghozzi, F., Gargouri, F.: Data integration from traditional to big data: main features and comparisons of ETL approaches. J. Supercomput. **80**(19), 26687–26725 (2024)
13. Khedekar, V., Tian, Y.: Multi-tenant big data analytics on aws cloud platform. In: 2020 10th Annual Computing and Communication Workshop and Conference (CCWC), pp. 0647–0653. IEEE (January 2020).
14. Kaushik, P., Rao, A. M., Singh, D. P., Vashisht, S., Gupta, S.: Cloud computing and comparison based on service and performance between Amazon AWS, Microsoft Azure, and Google Cloud. In: 2021 International Conference on Technological Advancements and Innovations (ICTAI), pp. 268–273). IEEE (November 2021)

A Method On The Impact of Low-Detail Images Versus AI-Enhanced Images Using Deep Learning For Facial Emotion Recognition

Sagupta Parveen[1], Sujit Kumar Das[2](✉), and Shailendra Tiwari[3]

[1] Department of Computer Science and Engineering Department, Aliah University, Kolkata, India

[2] Department of Computer Science & Engineering, Pandit Deendayal Energy University (PDEU), Gandhinagar, Gujrat, India
sujit.cse.jgec@gmail.com

[3] Computer Science and Engineering Department (CSED), Thapar Institute of Engineering & Technology, Patiala, Punjab, India
shailendra@thapar.edu

Abstract. This research addresses whether AI models trained with AI-enhanced low-detail images can lead to better performance compared to models trained exclusively on conventional but low-detailed data. Initially, the low-detail image is processed by a pre-trained GAN model (GFPGAN), specially trained to restore low-detailed facial images to higher-quality ones. The dataset SFEW is used as a base, and all its images are enhanced through GFPGAN to make a separate enhanced dataset. The two datasets are further resized to 48×48, 96×96, 150×150, 250×250. Subsequently, a Convolutional Neural Network (CNN) is trained separately on every resolution's enhanced and normal-quality images. Along with the SFEW test datasets, the 48×48 model is also tested on test data from the FER-2013 dataset. The result assesses the performance of each model across seven basic facial expressions, i.e., fear, disgust, anger, surprise, sadness, happiness, and neutral, as well as the overall performance of the model against the whole dataset. The results reveal better accuracy of the models trained on enhanced images than those trained on normal images.

Keywords: Deep learning · Facial expression · Recognition · CNN · GAN · AI-enhanced

1 Introduction

Facial expressions are an essential way humans communicate. Emotions are identified using text, EEG, speech, and facial features [21]. Facial emotions play a crucial role in expressing human sentiments. These emotional expressions have applications in sentiment analysis, pain detection, security, psychology, etc. [21].

K. Chandra Mondal et al. (Eds.): CICBA 2025, CCIS 2863, pp. 73–84, 2026.
https://doi.org/10.1007/978-3-032-17184-9_6

According to Ekman, seven basic facial expressions correspond to fear, sadness, disgust, anger, happiness, and surprise. In facial expression recognition, these basic expressions are identified and analyzed. Capturing facial expressions is less invasive than other emotion detection methods. Different expressions cause intensity variations across facial regions. Computers are still working to fully replicate human-level recognition and understanding of facial expressions and emotions. In summary, facial expressions reveal important emotional states and have diverse applications, but automatically interpreting them remains an active area of research.

Artificial Intelligence (AI) has witnessed rapid advancements in recent years, including image analysis, enhancement, and processing tasks. However, the quality of input data plays a significant role in determining the accuracy of AI models. In the real world, low-quality or low-detail images are widespread due to sensor limitations, transmission artefacts, or historical archives [20]. The challenge lies in harnessing the potential of AI to extract meaningful information from such sub-optimal inputs. To address this challenge, we have used a purpose-built facial image enhancer, Generative Adversarial Network (GAN), called GFPGAN, one of the best performers in its segment. In this study, we answer whether AI models trained with AI-enhanced, low-detail images can lead to superior performance compared to models trained only on average low-quality data. Over the past thirty years, it has been clear that automated facial expression identification and classification for multi-pose and multi-level face photos is an appealing and difficult problem [10]. According to a survey of the literature, early research has concentrated on a number of statistical [16] and structurally based techniques [19]. On the other hand, certain feature- and template-based methods have also been studied [10]. To obtain texture features in statistical ways, many researchers have adopted classical methods like the Histogram-of-Orientation Gradient (HOG) [3], the Scale Invariant Feature Transform (SIFT) [18], LBP (Local Binary Pattern) [9] features, and some spatio-temporal features (STM-ExpLet [8]). However, these methods require great effort to achieve high performance. Researchers have recently employed convolutional neural networks, or CNNs, recently [6], with remarkable success for large-scale static image and video sequence recognition [7].

Hand-labelled points and CNN architecture are used in many cutting-edge techniques [17] and deep learning frameworks for both feature extraction and prebuilt facial expression recognition systems. An ensemble radial basis function, a grayscale picture, and inductive decision trees were the components of the model Gutta et al. [5] presented for the four classes (i.e., Asian, Caucasian, African, and Oriental) ethnicity recognition issue. Zhang and Wang [24] presented a technique that combines 2D and 3D texture characteristics with multi-scale LBP (Local Binary Pattern) texture features for two-class racial classification. For the FER System, Zhang et al. [25] introduced two feature types: geometry-based features and Gabor-wavelets-based features. Bartlett et al. [2] used the Gabor filters in conjunction with feature selection and machine learning approaches to recognise facial emotions on a human face. Rose used the Gabor and log-Gabor filters in [11] to recognize facial expressions in low-resolution photos. Gabor motion energy filters [23] were investigated by Wu et al. [22] to identify people's dynamic facial expressions. In [12], Gabor filters were used in conjunction with genetic algorithms (GA) and support vector machines (SVM) to analyze six fundamental facial expressions from video sequences. Gu et al. presented a technique for facial expression identification in [4] that combined classifier generation with radial encoding of local Gabor characteristics. By merging LBP-TOP [26] with Gabor filters, Almaev et al. [1] developed a novel dynamic feature descriptor known as the Local Gabor Binary Patterns from Three Orthogonal Planes (LGBP-TOP). The core objective of this research is to evaluate the impact of enhancing low-detail images using the GFPGAN and subsequently train a Convolutional Neural Network (CNN) on both the enhanced images and a separate dataset of normal-quality images. We aim to shed light on this approach's potential benefits and limitations by conducting a comparative analysis of these two training paradigms. If enhancing low-detail images leads to improved AI model performance, then it could give low-quality data a helpful purpose in modern applications like autonomous systems, medical imaging, etc. On the other hand, a comprehensive analysis will also reveal the potential challenges and trade-offs associated with this approach, such as increased computational requirements and the risk of over-fitting. This work is organized as follows: Sect. 2 describes the proposed methodology schemes; Sect. 3 demonstrates the experimental results; finally, Sect. 4 concludes the outcomes of this work.

2 Proposed Scheme

This section discusses how the model is generated, the technologies used and its methodology. Depending upon the input image, both standard and enhanced, the proposed model predicts the type of expressions among the seven facial expression classes (anger, sadness, surprise, disgust, happiness, neutral, and fear). The proposed model is decomposed into Three steps: (i) the first step is image preprocessing, where the input image is enhanced from a low-detailed image to a highly detailed one using GFPGAN; (ii) in the second step, the images of both the standard dataset and enhanced dataset is resized according to need, (iii) in the third step a Convolution neural-network is employed for feature learning and classification purposes. The first step is skipped when training a model on the standard dataset. The block diagram for the proposed model has been demonstrated in Fig. 1, and this figure shows the implementation of the proposed methodology using normal dataset.

2.1 GFPGAN

Generative Adversarial network or GAN is a generative model consisting of two neural networks: a generator and a discriminator. The generator generates synthetic data similar to the training data, and the discriminator tries to distinguish real data from fake ones. Both are pitted against each other until the discriminator gets good at identification or the generator can fool the discriminator

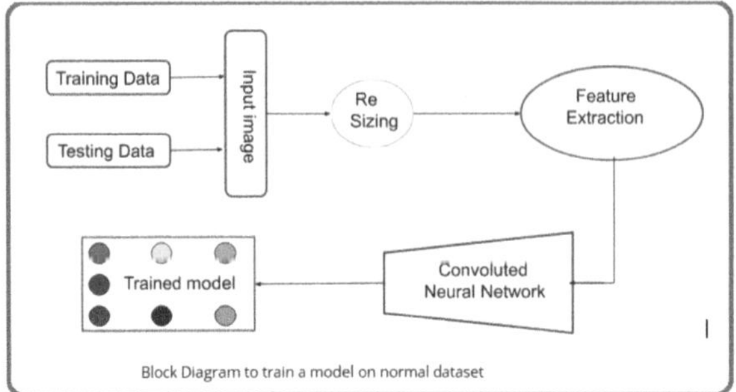

Fig. 1. Block Diagram to train a model on a normal dataset.

to a suitable percentage. This way of training can result in a network that is really good at generating synthetic data, which is why GAN is extensively used for image generation and restoration. GFP stands for Generative Facial Prior, facial priors or facial landmarks/ components used by face restoration techniques. These are hard to recover from low-detailed images where these features are degraded for various reasons. GFPGAN consists of a degradation removal module and pre-trained facial prior generator, which are connected by a direct latent code mapping and several Channel Split Spatial Feature Transform (CS-SFT) in a coarse and fine-tuned manner. The CS-SFT stops some priors and leaves the rest of the priors to be used by the GAN, which results in higher fidelity. The degradation removal module removes low-resolution blur, noise and other degradations and extracts two features.1) latent features Flatent to map input images to closest latent code in styleGAN .2) multi-resolution spatial features $F_{spatial}$ for modulating styleGAN features. U-net structure is used in this module as it increases receptive fields for large blur elimination and generates multi-resolution features.The Formulation is, F_{latent} , $F_{spatial} = U - Net(x)$. L1 restoration loss in each resolution scale at early training stages is used for intermediate supervision for removing degradation. GFPGAN uses diverse facial priors like geometry, textures, and colours from pre trained generative face models like StyleGAN for face restoration and colour enhancement. It generates Intermediate Convolution Features F_{GAN} of the closest face and modulates them with input features for better fidelity. The F_{latent} generated by U-NET is passed through a multi-layer perceptron(MLP) to get W or intermediate latent code. The W is then passed through pre-trained GAN and generates GAN features for each resolution scale such that $W = MLP(F_{latent})$ and $F_{GAN} = StyleGAN(W)$. Spatial Feature Transformation(SFT) is used to preserve spatial information from inputs, which generates affine transformation parameters for spatial-wise feature modulation [15]. At each resolution scale, a pair of affine transformation parameters α and β is generated from input feature $F_{spatial}$ by several convolution layers, and then modulation is done by shifting and scaling the F_{GAN} using $\alpha, \beta = CONV(F_{spatial})$, and $F_{output} = SFT(F_{GAN}|\alpha, \beta) = \alpha \odot F_{GAN} + \beta$ respectively. The Channel Split Spatial Feature Transformation (CS-SFT) is used to bring balance between realness and fidelity, which performs spatial modulation on the part of the GAN features by input feature $F_{spatial}$ (fidelity) and leaves the rest of the GAN features(realness) by using $F_{output} = CS - SFT(F_{GAN}|\alpha, \beta)$ and $= concat[Identity(F_{GAN}^{split0}), F_{GAN}^{split0} + \beta]$ techniques. The CS-SFT is performed at each resolution scale, which results in output Y. Figure 2 demonstrates the implementation of the proposed facial expression recognition system (FERS) using GFPGAN based enhanced image dataset, and some image samples of the original versus enhanced images are shown in Fig. 3.

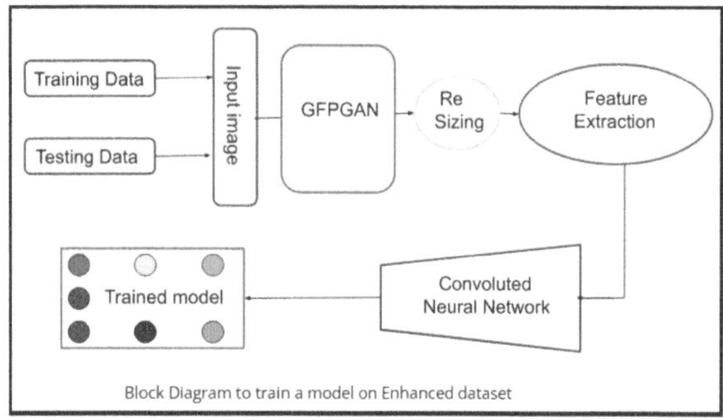

Fig. 2. Block Diagram to train a model on an Enhanced dataset.

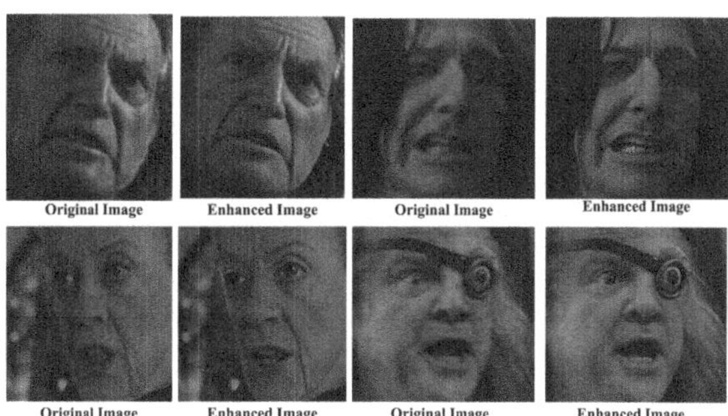

Fig. 3. Comparison of normal image(left) and Enhanced image(right) samples.

2.2 Convolution Neural-Network

Convolutional neural networks are specialized artificial neural networks used to process data, such as images, with grid-like topology. The name "convolutional" refers to the key operation in CNN's—convolution. Convolution is an operation between a kernel/filter (a small matrix of weights) and a subset of the input image called the receptive field. The kernel slides over the image, manipulating the receptive field at each location. This exploits the structure of the input data to detect and learn edges, textures, and more complex patterns. Convolutional layers extract feature maps that detect the presence and location of different patterns in the input. Multiple filters are used to detect different patterns at different locations. 3×3 filters are used here in each convolutional layer. For activation function, ReLU or rectified Linear unit is used. The ReLU takes the input value x and thresholds it at zero, returning 0 if x is negative and x if x is positive, which discards the opposite features detected by the filter. The ReLU function applies element-wise and is defined as $f(x) = max(0, x)$. Max pooling is an operation that reduces the dimensions of the feature map. It operates by selecting the maximum value within a local region of the feature map, effectively reducing the amount of data while retaining the most important information, which reduces computational complexity. Pool size defines the dimension of the region on which the max pooling operation will be performed. Here, it is 2×2 (Fig. 4 and Table 1).

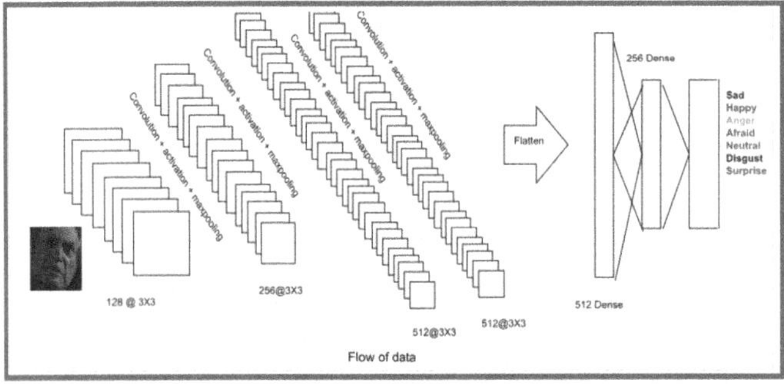

Fig. 4. Proposed framework of the CNN architecture employed during the implementation of the proposed system.

3 Experimental Results

In this section, we present the outcomes of our experiments, how they were performed, the dataset used and then evaluate the performance of Convolutional Neural Network (CNN) models trained on AI-enhanced low-detail images compared to those trained on standard quality images across four different image resolutions: 48×48, 96×96, 150×150, 250×250. We have used the SFEW 1.0 data set consisting of 700 images, 354 for testing and 346 for training, divided across seven different emotions mentioned before. The image data is of low quality, with many barely recognizable and blurry samples in different lighting conditions. The whole dataset has been enhanced using GFPGAN with good to moderate

Table 1. Description of parameters employed in the proposed CNN.

Layer (type)	**Output Shape**	**Param #**
conv2d (Conv2D)	(None, 248, 248, 128)	1280
max_pooling2D (MaxPooling2D)	(None, 124, 124, 128)	0
dropout (Dropout)	(None, 124, 124, 128)	0
$conv2D_1$ (Conv2D)	(None, 122, 122, 256)	295168
max_pooling2D_1 (MaxPooling2D)	(None, 61, 61, 256)	0
$dropout_1$ (Dropout)	(None, 61, 61, 256)	0
$conv2D_2$ (Conv2D)	(None, 59, 59, 512)	1180160
max_pooling2D_2 (MaxPooling2D)	(None, 29, 29, 512)	0
$dropout_2$ (Dropout)	(None, 29, 29, 512)	0
$conv2d_3$(Conv2D)	(None, 27, 27, 512)	2359808
max_pooling2d_3 (MaxPoolin g2D)	(None, 13, 13, 512)	0
$dropout_3$ (Dropout)	(None, 13, 13, 512)	0
flatten (Flatten)	(None, 86528)	0
dense (Dense)	(None, 512)	44302848
$dropout_4$ (Dropout)	(None, 512)	0
$dense_1$ (Dense)	(None, 256)	131328
$dropout_5$ (Dropout)	(None, 256)	0
$dense_2$(Dense)	(None, 7)	1799
Total params	48272391	184.14 MB

improvements from the original dataset. Below are some examples of enhanced images compared to the standard images. Typical images are on the left, while enhanced images are on the right side. Some image samples employed for the proposed methodology has been demosntrated in Fig. 5, whereas the description of employed databases have been shown in Fig. 6.

3.1 Results and Discussion

The implementation of the proposed model has been performed in Google Collab with Python 3.0(GPU backend) with 12.7 GB of system RAM and T4 GPU with approx 15 GB of GPU memory. The performance of the model has been calculated using the formula: Accuracy (%) $= \frac{\text{number of correctly identified images}}{\text{total number of images tested}} \times 100$. Initially, the experiments start with the batch vs epochs required to train and test the deep learning model for the proposed facial expression recognition system (FERS). This variation of graphs have been shown in Fig. 7.

Then, two models one trained on enhanced and another on normal data for each resolution have been tested twice, once on normal and once on enhanced data, so a total of four result rows for each resolution table. The test image resolution is changed according to requirement during run time before reshaping.

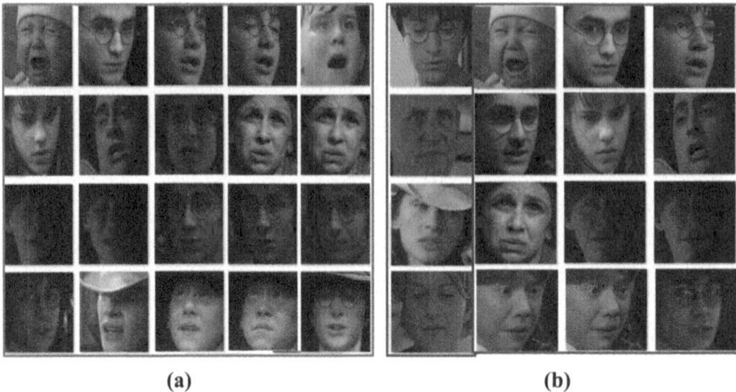

Fig. 5. Comparison of normal image(left) and Enhanced image(right) samples.

Dataset	Class	No of samples
SFEW 1.0 (normal)	7	700
SFEW 1.0 (enhanced)	7	700
FER - 2013 (test only)	7	7066

Fig. 6. Datasets used to test the proposed system.

Both types of models for each resolution were run three times, and the model with the best accuracy was used for the final testing of the data. Hence, Tables 2, 3, 4, and 5 shows the performance of the proposed system corresponds to image size 48×48, 96×96, 150×150, and 250×250 respectively. From these Tables, it has been observed that performance is better for image size 250×250, and 96×96 for the SFEW 1.0 database.

Table 2. Results for recognition model trained on 48×48 images for SFEW 1.0 database

48 × 48		
DATA	MODEL	ACC(%)
NORMAL	NORMAL	25.61
ENHANCED	NORMAL	23.93
NORMAL	ENHANCED	23.34
ENHANCED	ENHANCED	27.52

Table 3. Results for recognition model trained on 96×96 images SFEW 1.0 database

96 × 96		
DATA	MODEL	ACC(%)
NORMAL	NORMAL	31.32
ENHANCED	NORMAL	32.62
NORMAL	ENHANCED	34.82
ENHANCED	ENHANCED	35.19

Additionally, the test set of the FER-2013 dataset for emotion detection with over 7000 images over seven different emotions was used to test the models of 48×48 to see the performance over varied and large no images. Table 6 demonstrates performance for FER-2013 dataset. Hence, the performance reported in the above Tables for SFEW 1.0 and FER-2013 database, it has been observed

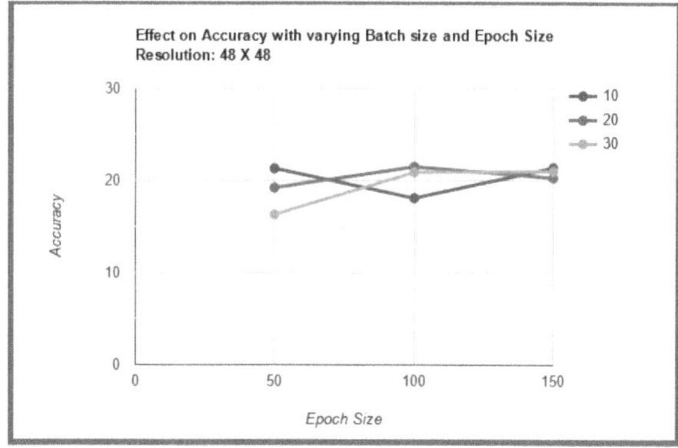

Fig. 7. The batch vs epoch experiments required for the implementation of the proposed system.

Table 4. Results for recognition model trained on 150 × 150 images SFEW 1.0 database

150 × 150		
DATA	MODEL	ACC(%)
NORMAL	NORMAL	35.38
ENHANCED	NORMAL	34.53
NORMAL	ENHANCED	36.89
ENHANCED	ENHANCED	37.81

Table 5. Results for recognition model trained on 250 × 250 images SFEW 1.0 database

250 × 250		
DATA	MODEL	ACC(%)
NORMAL	NORMAL	37.92
ENHANCED	NORMAL	35.44
NORMAL	ENHANCED	40.95
ENHANCED	ENHANCED	41.10

Table 6. Results for recognition model trained on 48 × 48 and tested on FER-2013 test data

48 × 48		
DATA	MODEL	ACC(%)
NORMAL	NORMAL	67.89
NORMAL	ENHANCED	72.67

Table 7. Performance comparison of the proposed system with some existing methods in ACC(%).

Method	SFEW 1.0	FER-2013
Vgg16	33.05	54.34
ResNet50	31.28	51.75
Zavare et al.	32.71	64.14
Proposed (ENHANCED MODEL)	41.10	72.67

that performance of the proposed FERS is better for the ENHANCED images which are obtained due to GFPGAN model applied for enhancing the facial images of the employed databases. The performance of the proposed system has been tested with some well know methods such as Vgg16 [13], ResNet50 [14], and Zavare et al. [23] which are also used in the similar type of problems in Table 7. From this Table, it has been observed that the proposed method has obatined better performance as compared to these competing methods.

4 Conclusion

This work proposes a revolutionary approach for facial emotion recognition systems. The suggested system aims to predict the seven fundamental kinds of facial expression. In conclusion, models trained on AI-enhanced images showed higher accuracy than models trained only on normal images, but the accuracy jump isn't substantial. The small difference in accuracy may also be because of the small training data size, so more research with a bigger dataset is needed in this field. The performance of the proposed system has been compared with several current techniques on the SFEW 1.0, and FER-2013 databases, which have been the subject of extensive experimentation. The proposed method is superior, as evidenced by comparing its performance against the competing approaches.

References

1. Almaev, T.R., Valstar, M.F.: Local gabor binary patterns from three orthogonal planes for automatic facial expression recognition. In: 2013 Humaine Association Conference on Affective Computing and Intelligent Interaction, pp. 356–361. IEEE (2013)
2. Bartlett, M.S., Littlewort, G., Frank, M., Lainscsek, C., Fasel, I., Movellan, J.: Recognizing facial expression: machine learning and application to spontaneous behavior. In: IEEE Computer Society Conference on Computer Vision and Pattern Recognition, 2005. CVPR 2005, vol. 2, pp. 568–573. IEEE (2005)
3. Dalal, N., Triggs, B.: Histograms of oriented gradients for human detection (2005)
4. Gu, W., Xiang, C., Venkatesh, Y., Huang, D., Lin, H.: Facial expression recognition using radial encoding of local gabor features and classifier synthesis. Pattern Recogn. **45**(1), 80–91 (2012)
5. Gutta, S., Wechsler, H., Phillips, P.J.: Gender and ethnic classification of face images. In: Proceedings Third IEEE International Conference on Automatic Face and Gesture Recognition, pp. 194–199. IEEE (1998)
6. Krizhevsky, A., Sutskever, I., Hinton, G.E.: Imagenet classification with deep convolutional neural networks. Commun. ACM **60**(6), 84–90 (2017)
7. Krumhuber, E.G., Küster, D., Namba, S., Shah, D., Calvo, M.G.: Emotion recognition from posed and spontaneous dynamic expressions: Human observers versus machine analysis. Emotion (2019)
8. Liu, M., Shan, S., Wang, R., Chen, X.: Learning expressionlets on spatio-temporal manifold for dynamic facial expression recognition. In: Proceedings of the IEEE Conference on Computer Vision and Pattern Recognition, pp. 1749–1756 (2014)
9. Ojala, T., Pietikäinen, M., Harwood, D.: A comparative study of texture measures with classification based on featured distributions. Pattern Recogn. **29**(1), 51–59 (1996)
10. Pantic, M., Rothkrantz, L.J.M.: Automatic analysis of facial expressions: the state of the art. IEEE Trans. Pattern Anal. Mach. Intell. **22**(12), 1424–1445 (2000)
11. Rose, N.: Facial expression classification using gabor and log-gabor filters. In: 7th International Conference on Automatic Face and Gesture Recognition, 2006. FGR 2006, pp. 346–350. IEEE (2006)

12. Shojaeilangari, S., Yun, Y.W., Khwang, T.E.: Person independent facial expression analysis using gabor features and genetic algorithm. In: 2011 8th International Conference on Information, Communications and Signal Processing (ICICS), pp. 1–5. IEEE (2011)
13. Simonyan, K., Zisserman, A.: Very deep convolutional networks for large-scale image recognition. arXiv:1409.1556
14. Szegedy, C., Vanhoucke, V., Ioffe, S., Shlens, J., Wojna, Z.: Rethinking the inception architecture for computer vision. In: Proceedings of the IEEE Conference on Computer Vision and Pattern Recognition, pp. 2818–2826 (2016)
15. Umer, S., Dhara, B.C., Chanda, B.: Biometric recognition system for challenging faces. In: 2015 Fifth National Conference on Computer Vision, Pattern Recognition, Image Processing and Graphics (NCVPRIPG), pp. 1–4. IEEE (2015)
16. Umer, S., Dhara, B.C., Chanda, B.: Texture code matrix-based multi-instance iris recognition. Pattern Anal. Appl. **19**, 283–295 (2016)
17. Umer, S., Dhara, B.C., Chanda, B.: A novel cancelable iris recognition system based on feature learning techniques. Inf. Sci. **406**, 102–118 (2017)
18. Umer, S., Dhara, B.C., Chanda, B.: An iris recognition system based on analysis of textural edgeness descriptors. IETE Tech. Rev. **35**(2), 145–156 (2018)
19. Umer, S., Dhara, B.C., Chanda, B.: Face recognition using fusion of feature learning techniques. Measurement **146**, 43–54 (2019)
20. Umer, S., Dhara, B.C., Chanda, B.: Nir and vw iris image recognition using ensemble of patch statistics features. Vis. Comput. **35**, 1327–1344 (2019)
21. Umer, S., Rout, R.K., Tiwari, S., AlZubi, A.A., Alanazi, J.M., Yurii, K.: Human-computer interaction using deep fusion model-based facial expression recognition system. CMES-Comput. Model. Eng. Sci. **135**(2) (2023)
22. Wu, T., Bartlett, M.S., Movellan, J.R.: Facial expression recognition using gabor motion energy filters. In: 2010 IEEE Computer Society Conference on Computer Vision and Pattern Recognition Workshops (CVPRW), pp. 42–47. IEEE (2010)
23. Zavarez, M.V., Berriel, R.F., Oliveira-Santos, T.: Cross-database facial expression recognition based on fine-tuned deep convolutional network. In: 2017 30th SIBGRAPI Conference on Graphics, Patterns and Images (SIBGRAPI), pp. 405–412. IEEE (2017)
24. Zhang, G., Wang, Y.: Multimodal 2d and 3d facial ethnicity classification. In: 2009 Fifth International Conference on Image and Graphics, pp. 928–932. IEEE (2009)

25. Zhang, Z., Lyons, M., Schuster, M., Akamatsu, S.: Comparison between geometry-based and gabor-wavelets-based facial expression recognition using multi-layer perceptron. In: Proceedings of the Third IEEE International Conference on Automatic Face and Gesture Recognition, 1998, pp. 454–459. IEEE (1998)
26. Zhao, G., Pietikainen, M.: Dynamic texture recognition using local binary patterns with an application to facial expressions. IEEE Trans. Pattern Anal. Mach. Intell. **29**(6), 915–928 (2007)

Enhancing Flight Delay Prediction with a Spatio-Temporal Graph Attention Network: A Graph-Based Approach to Modeling Airport Interdependencies

Riddhi Raj Ghosh[1,2], Ankika Dey[1,2], Palash Das[1,2], Alik Agarwala[1,2], Avik Agarwala[1,2], and Sudipta Sahana[1,2](✉)

[1] Department of CSE (AI & ML), Institute of Engineering and Management, Kolkata, India
ss.jisce@gmail.com
[2] University of Engineering and Management, Kolkata, India

Abstract. Flight delays remain a major challenge for airline operations, resulting in increased costs, reduced passenger satisfaction, and scheduling complexities. To address these issues, we introduce a Spatio-Temporal Graph Attention Network (ST-GAT) that captures both temporal dynamics and spatial interdependencies among airports. Unlike conventional methods such as Random Forest, XGBoost, LSTM, or TCN, our ST-GAT constructs a graph where airports are nodes and flight routes are edges, enabling the model to learn how delays propagate through the network. By integrating attention mechanisms, the framework highlights critical airport connections and refines predictions with contextual awareness. Empirical evaluations on real-world flight datasets show that ST-GAT outperforms traditional deep learning approaches and benefits from careful hyperparameter tuning, achieving a mean absolute error (MAE) of 4.68. The model demonstrates a clear understanding of delay propagation, offering valuable insights for stakeholders. Additionally, it achieves an accuracy of 89.2%, further validating its predictive capabilities. These results suggest that graph-based deep learning can enhance flight delay prediction, leading to more resilient scheduling and improved passenger experiences. Our ST-GAT approach lays the groundwork for future research integrating additional data sources (e.g., weather, operational constraints) to further refine predictive accuracy in complex aviation environments.

Keywords: Flight delay prediction · Graph neural networks · Graph attention network · ST-GAT · Spatio-temporal analysis · Machine learning · Aviation analytics

1 Introduction

Flight delays remain a major concern in the aviation industry, affecting everything from airline revenues and passenger satisfaction to overall air traffic management. Numerous factors, ranging from severe weather conditions and heavy

K. Chandra Mondal et al. (Eds.): CICBA 2025, CCIS 2863, pp. 85–98, 2026.
https://doi.org/10.1007/978-3-032-17184-9_7

air traffic congestion to airport resource constraints, contribute to schedule disruptions. Delays at a single hub can quickly ripple through downstream flights, creating large-scale scheduling bottlenecks. This interconnected nature of air travel underscores the need for robust models that not only capture temporal patterns of delays but also account for their network-wide implications.

Over the past decade, various machine learning methods have been deployed to tackle flight delay prediction. Tree-based ensemble techniques like Random Forests and XGBoost offer fast training times and high accuracy for structured data; however, they typically treat airports or flights as independent entities, overlooking how delays propagate across the network. Advanced deep learning models, such as Long Short-Term Memory (LSTM) networks and Temporal Convolutional Networks (TCNs), have been effective in capturing sequential relationships in time-series data, yet they often neglect the spatial dimension inherent to flight networks.

Recent studies have explored graph-based deep learning–for example, Graph Convolutional Networks (GCNs), Diffusion Convolutional Recurrent Neural Networks (DCRNN), and Graph Attention Networks (GATs)–to leverage spatial connectivity. Despite these advances, most existing approaches fail to simultaneously integrate temporal evolution with dynamic spatial interdependencies.

In contrast, our proposed Spatio-Temporal Graph Attention Network (ST-GAT) combines time-series modeling with attention-driven graph representations. This unified framework outshines other available techniques by achieving lower error metrics and providing higher interpretability, as it effectively reveals hidden dependencies and captures how delays propagate across interconnected airports.

The research gap lies in the absence of a comprehensive method that concurrently addresses both temporal and spatial aspects of flight delays. Our novel approach fills this void, enhancing predictive accuracy and offering deeper insights into delay propagation.

The remainder of this paper is organized as follows: Sect. 2 reviews related work, Sect. 3 details our methodology and model architecture, Sect. 4 presents experimental results and comparative analyses, and Sect. 5 concludes with discussions on practical implications and future work.

2 Related Work

The development of machine learning and deep learning algorithms has emerged as a highly promising strategy for anticipating flight delays, given the enormous volume of data generated by commercial aviation systems. Over the past six years, numerous studies have explored various approaches to address the complexities inherent in delay prediction–ranging from temporal dynamics to spatial interdependencies and ensemble learning techniques.

For instance, recent contributions include Srivastava [1], who proposed an ensemble learning approach combining decision trees, gradient boosting, and neural networks to significantly boost prediction accuracy. Zhu et al. [2] advanced the field further by introducing CausalNet, a self-corrective spatio-temporal graph neural network that leverages Granger causality inference to dynamically adjust its graph structure and capture evolving inter-airport influences. Additionally, research published in Applied Soft Computing [3] and IEEE Transactions on Intelligent Transportation Systems [4] has presented novel deep learning frameworks that integrate hybrid feature extraction and graph-based models for real-time delay prediction.

In 2023, CAI et al. [5] developed a geographical and operational deep graph convolutional framework using Graph Convolutional Networks to decode complex airport relationships, demonstrating superior accuracy compared to methods that rely solely on temporal models. Mtimkulu (2023) conducted a comparative study of ensemble techniques for flight delay prediction, reporting that stacking methods achieved an accuracy of 92.4%, while random forest models attained around 91.2%. Complementing these efforts, studies published in Expert Systems with Applications (2023) and the Journal of Air Transport Management [6] have integrated operational and environmental factors to forecast delays by accounting for network-wide interactions. Moreover, research in Expert Systems with Applications [7] further refined ensemble strategies to enhance robustness and predictive performance.

Earlier, Guo et al. [8] proposed a hybrid method that fuses Random Forest Regression with the Maximal Information Coefficient (RFR-MIC) to improve feature selection and prediction accuracy. Yazdi et al. (2020) introduced a deep learning model that combines stacked denoising autoencoders with the LevenbergMarquardt algorithm to mitigate noise and optimize model parameters. Yu et al. [9] employed a deep belief network integrated with support vector regression to manage high-dimensional flight data, although without explicitly modeling spatial relationships. Prior approaches include Bai et al. [10], who explored Temporal Convolutional Networks (TCNs) for efficient sequence modeling; Li et al. [11], who introduced a Diffusion Convolutional Recurrent Neural Network (DCRNN) that blends graph-based diffusion with recurrent architectures; and Veličković et al. [12], whose Graph Attention Networks (GATs) learn adaptive attention coefficients among neighboring nodes. Even earlier, Zong et al. [13] utilized a Support Vector Machine classifier with historical flight records and meteorological data, though its scalability remains a challenge for large, complex airport networks.

Collectively, these studies have contributed valuable insights into modeling flight delays. However, gaps persist in fully integrating temporal dynamics with spatial interdependencies in a unified framework. Our proposed Spatio-Temporal Graph Attention Network (ST-GAT) builds on these insights by leveraging attention-driven message passing to capture intricate airport interactions and dynamic delay patterns, offering a more holistic and accurate predictive model than previous approaches.

3 Methodology

3.1 Overview

In this section, we explain the basic concept of our proposed model in stages to demonstrate the evolution from traditional time-series models to an advanced attention mechanism. Our approach, the Spatio-Temporal Graph Attention Network (ST-GAT), is designed to capture both the temporal dynamics and spatial interdependencies among airports for accurate flight delay prediction.

3.2 Theoretical Framework

From a machine learning perspective, flight delay prediction can be formulated as a supervised regression problem, where each sample corresponds to a time-indexed observation of an airport. The objective is to learn a function:

$$y_{t+1} = f(x_t; \Theta) \tag{1}$$

where x_t represents the feature vector for day t, Θ are the learnable model parameters, and y_{t+1} is the predicted delay for day $t+1$. Unlike traditional methods that treat airports as independent entities, our approach explicitly models both temporal dependencies and spatial interactions to enhance predictive performance.

3.3 Spatio-Temporal Graph Attention Network (ST-GAT)

Our proposed ST-GAT integrates two key components: temporal modeling to capture sequential flight delay patterns at each airport and graph attention networks (GATs) to model inter-airport dependencies.

Temporal Module Each airport's daily feature sequence (e.g., rolling means of delay, flight volume, and weather indicators) is transformed into an embedding that encodes local temporal trends. This transformation is achieved through a sequence encoder that maps the past k days' data into a latent representation:

$$h_i^{temp} = \text{Encoder}(x_{i,t-k+1}, \ldots, x_{i,t}) \tag{2}$$

where h_i^{temp} is the learned temporal embedding for airport i, and the encoder can be implemented using an LSTM, TCN, or another suitable architecture.

Graph Attention Layer To model delay propagation across airports, we construct a directed graph $G = (V, E)$, where each airport corresponds to a node $v_i \in V$, and edges $(v_i, v_j) \in E$ represent direct flight connections. The adjacency matrix A defines the connectivity structure.

GAT enhances node representations by computing attention coefficients α_{ij}, determining the influence of airport j on airport i:

$$\alpha_{ij} = \frac{\exp\left(\sigma(a^\top [Wh_i^{(l)}, Wh_j^{(l)}])\right)}{\sum_{k\in\mathcal{N}(i)} \exp\left(\sigma(a^\top [Wh_i^{(l)}, Wh_k^{(l)}])\right)} \tag{3}$$

where:

- W is a learnable transformation matrix,
- a is the attention vector,
- $\mathcal{N}(i)$ denotes the neighbors of node i,
- $\sigma(\cdot)$ is a nonlinear activation function.

Each airport's updated embedding is computed as:

$$h_i^{(l+1)} = \sigma\left(\sum_{j\in\mathcal{N}(i)} \alpha_{ij} W h_j^{(l)}\right) \tag{4}$$

By applying multi-head attention, ST-GAT effectively learns which airports exert significant influence on delay propagation.

Prediction Module The final representation for each airport combines temporal embeddings and GAT-updated node features:

$$h_i^{final} = \text{Concat}(h_i^{temp}, h_i^{(L)}) \tag{5}$$

where $h_i^{(L)}$ is the output of the last GAT layer. This final feature vector is passed through a fully connected layer to predict the next day's average departure delay:

$$y_{i,t+1} = \text{MLP}(h_i^{final}) \tag{6}$$

where MLP represents a multi-layer perceptron (Fig. 1).
The architecture above can be divided into two main components:

- **Temporal Component (blue shaded)**: The input is a batch of sequences shaped as `[batch, seq_length, num_nodes, 3]`. It is reshaped and permuted for temporal convolution. A 1D convolution with 3 input channels and 16 output filters (kernel size 3) captures short-term patterns. Mean pooling across the time axis produces a compact embedding per airport per batch.
- **Spatial Component (red shaded)**: The output of the temporal module is reshaped to `[batch, num_nodes, 16]` and passed to the GAT layers. A graph structure defined by `edge_index` encodes airport connections (e.g., routes). GAT Layer 1 applies 4 attention heads (input: 16, output: 32), and GAT Layer 2 reduces to a 3-dimensional output (3 delay-related predictions) using 1 attention head.

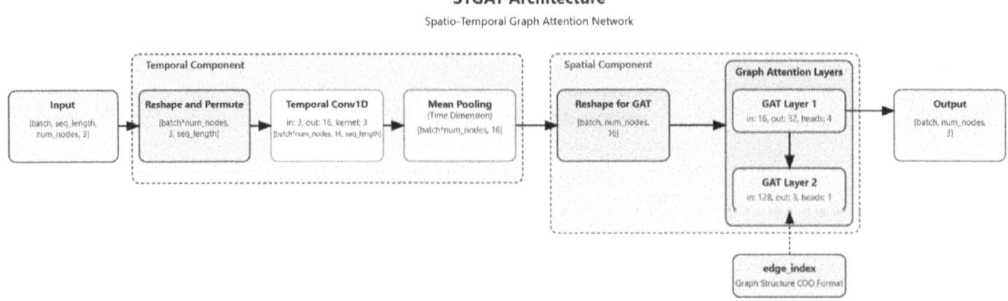

Fig. 1. Architecture of the spatio-temporal graph attention network (ST-GAT) used for flight delay prediction

- **Output**: The final tensor has shape `[batch, num_nodes, 3]` and contains predicted delay values for each airport in the batch. Each output vector corresponds to features like predicted delay duration, delay probability, or other delay categories depending on task design.

This layered design enables ST-GAT to effectively learn how delays propagate across space and time, making it ideal for modeling complex aviation dynamics.

3.4 Summary

The above proposed ST-GAT architecture effectively unifies temporal feature extraction and spatial reasoning in a single pipeline. Its temporal module captures short-term patterns at each airport, while the graph attention mechanism models how delays propagate through the airport network based on real-world flight connectivity.

By combining these two aspects, ST-GAT offers an interpretable and scalable framework for predicting next-day flight delays. This integrated design overcomes the limitations of traditional models that treat airports as isolated entities or overlook the time-varying nature of delays.

The subsequent sections detail the dataset used, the processing pipeline, and the experimental validation of ST-GAT.

3.5 Data Collection

The dataset used in this study is the Flight Delay and Cancellation Dataset (20192023), sourced from Kaggle [14]. It spans January 2019 through August 2023 and originates from compiled reports of on-time performance by airlines. The dataset includes detailed flight records, capturing key attributes relevant to delay prediction. Each record contains categorical identifiers such as `AIRLINE_CODE`, `ORIGIN_AIRPORT`, and `DESTINATION_AIRPORT`, as well as numerical fields including `SCHEDULED_DEPARTURE`, `ACTUAL_DEPARTURE`, `DEP_DELAY`, `ARR_DELAY`, and `DISTANCE`. These features provide essential insights into airline operations, delay patterns, and route-based factors.

To prepare the dataset for predictive modeling, extensive preprocessing was conducted, including handling missing values, removing duplicate entries, and normalizing timestamp formats. Additionally, relevant features such as rolling averages of delays, airport congestion levels, and historical weather indicators were engineered to enhance model performance. Despite limitations in advanced external factors (e.g., detailed weather conditions), the dataset provides a comprehensive representation of flight delay trends, making it well-suited for training our proposed Spatio-Temporal Graph Attention Network (ST-GAT).

3.6 Data Processing and Feature Engineering

In order to transform the raw flight-level data into an analysis-ready format suitable for our proposed model, we carried out several critical steps:

Cleaning and Validation:

- **Missing Values:** Critical fields with missing data were imputed or removed where necessary.
- **Outlier Capping:** We capped extreme delay values (beyond the 99th percentile) to improve model stability.
- **Strategic Sampling:** From the 500,000+ original records, we maintained a representative dataset while ensuring computational efficiency.

Airport-Level Aggregation:

- **Daily Profiles:** Flight records were consolidated into airport-level daily summaries, capturing mean delays and operational volumes.
- **Temporal Windows:** 7-day moving averages were implemented to capture evolving delay patterns critical for our modeling approach.

Feature Construction:

- **Calendar Variables:** Day-of-week, month, and holiday indicators were incorporated to capture seasonal patterns.
- **Delay Attributions:** Specific delay causes (weather, aircraft availability) were preserved to enhance our model's explanatory power.
- **Auxiliary Integration:** External weather data was merged to provide environmental context at each airport.
- **Optimized Structure:** The final dataset presents a day-wise airport view with carefully selected features that directly support our proposed spatio-temporal modeling framework.

This streamlined data preparation pipeline ensures each airport-day observation contains the temporal signals and contextual information necessary for our model's accurate flight delay prediction capabilities.

3.7 Data Analysis

Following data preprocessing, we conducted targeted exploratory analysis to inform our model development:

Distribution of Arrival Delay: Figure 2 below reveals a strong right-skewed distribution, with most flights experiencing minimal delays while a small fraction show extreme delays (¿500 minutes). This insight directly influenced our preprocessing decision to cap delays at the 99th percentile, ensuring our model remains sensitive to typical delay patterns while not being overly influenced by outliers.

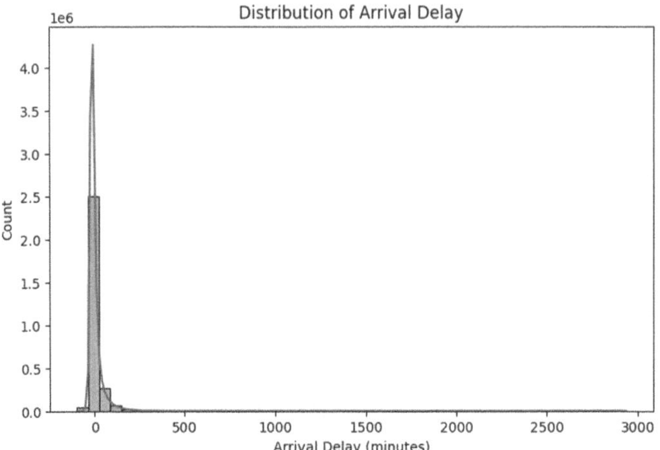

Fig. 2. Distribution of arrival delay

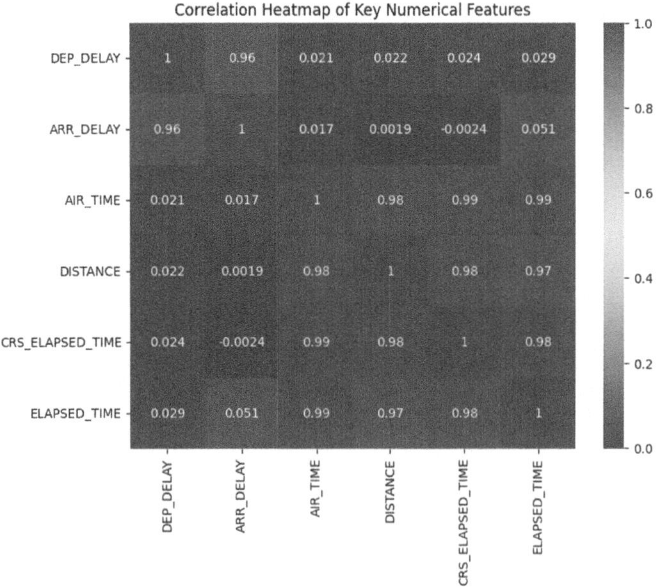

Fig. 3. Correlation analysis

Correlation Analysis: Figure 3 above demonstrates key relationships relevant to our modeling approach:

- **Departure-Arrival Delay Correlation (≈ 0.96):** The strong propagation effect of initial delays highlights the need for our model's temporal components.
- **Redundancy in Flight Parameters:** High correlation (¿0.97) between AIR_TIME, DISTANCE, and time variables informed our feature selection process.
- **Complex Delay Factors:** The moderate correlation between flight parameters and actual delays underscores why our proposed spatio-temporal framework is necessary to capture the complex network effects in delay propagation.

These insights directly shaped our model architecture, particularly in how we incorporate both temporal dependencies and network relationships between airports.

3.8 Model Development

Building on our data analysis findings, we developed a novel Spatio-Temporal Graph Attention Network (ST-GAT) for flight delay prediction, with minimal baseline comparisons.
Spatio-Temporal Graph Attention Network (ST-GAT) Our proposed model addresses the limitations of purely temporal approaches by integrating network relationships between airports:

- **Graph Construction:** Airports as nodes with flight connections as edges, weighted by flight frequency.
- **Temporal Module:** Encodes each airport's historical time-series into embedding vectors capturing local trends.
- **Graph Attention Layer:** Applies adaptive attention coefficients α_{ij} to weigh neighboring airports' influence, focusing on significant routes.
- **Prediction Head:** Transforms the final node embeddings into next-day delay predictions.

3.9 Experimental Setup

All model development and training were performed using Google Colab (free-tier environment), which provides limited but sufficient hardware resources for deep learning experiments. The runtime environment included an NVIDIA Tesla T4 GPU with 16 GB VRAM, around 12.7 GB of system RAM, and 2 virtual CPU cores. This setup was selected to demonstrate that the proposed model can be trained on publicly available and low-cost infrastructure.

The entire implementation was carried out in Python 3.10, utilizing PyTorch Geometric 2.6.1 as the primary deep learning framework. The default CUDA configuration in Colab was used to enable GPU acceleration for both matrix computations and model training.

A fixed set of hyperparameters was chosen based on preliminary validation results. These parameters remained consistent across all training runs:

- **Optimizer:** Adam, with standard $\beta_1 = 0.9$, $\beta_2 = 0.999$
- **Learning Rate:** 0.001 (constant)
- **Epochs:** 100
- **Batch Size:** 32
- **Dropout Rate:** 0.3
- **Temporal Input Window:** 7 days
- **GAT Configuration:** 2 layers, with 4 attention heads in the first layer and 1 in the second
- **Embedding Dimensions:** 16 (temporal output), 32 (GAT layer), and 3 (final delay predictions)

To evaluate model generalization in real-world scenarios, we used a chronological data split. The dataset was divided into 70% for training, 15% for validation, and 15% for testing. Early stopping was applied during training to avoid overfitting, with a patience of 10 epochs based on the lowest validation MAE. This setup ensured that future timestamps were never used to predict past values. All training and testing steps were executed within a Jupyter notebook on Colab, which provided a stable and flexible environment for running deep learning workflows.

4 Results and Discussion

4.1 Model Size, Training Time, and Resource Utilization

The final model contained approximately 2.1 million trainable parameters, and its serialized PyTorch checkpoint file was 18.4 MB in size. Despite using graph-based attention layers along with temporal convolutions, the model remained lightweight and manageable even in memory-constrained environments.

The full training process across 100 epochs required about 3.8 hours in total. On average, each epoch took slightly over 2 minutes to complete. This included the forward pass, backward pass, and validation evaluation. The GPU memory usage was observed to peak at around 11.1 GB, and no out-of-memory errors were encountered during the training phase.

Since Colab offers limited CPU capabilities, the model design ensured most computations occurred on the GPU. CPU usage remained low, primarily for data loading and preprocessing tasks. During runtime, resource consumption remained stable, and there were no interruptions or system restarts, which confirmed the model's compatibility with constrained cloud environments.

These results show that ST-GAT is both computationally efficient and scalable, making it suitable for use in academic research, operational testing, and even deployment in real-world systems where access to high-end GPUs may be limited.

4.2 Model Performance Analysis and Sample Predictions

Figure 4 illustrates the architecture refinements introduced in our fine-tuned model, which incorporates the above mentioned optimizations

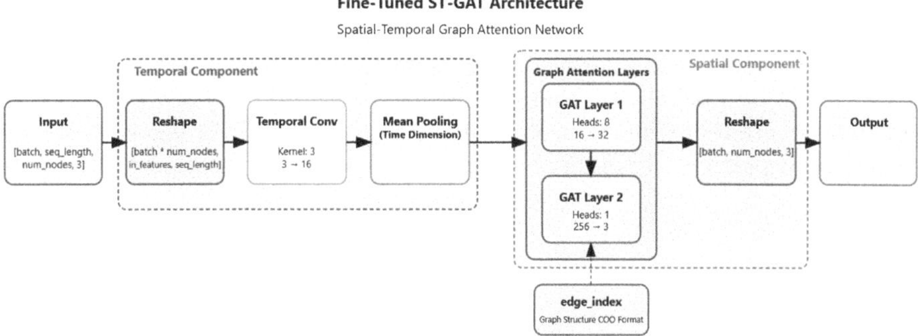

Fig. 4. Fine-tuned spatio-temporal graph attention network with optimized attention mechanisms and enhanced feature representation

These architectural refinements translate directly to performance improvements, as demonstrated in our comparative evaluation metrics.

To provide additional interpretability and qualitative insight into the model's behavior, Table 1 showcases representative test cases from the evaluation dataset. Each instance includes the date, source and destination airports, the actual delay observed, the corresponding prediction generated by the ST-GAT model, and the resulting prediction error. These examples illustrate how the model captures delay patterns across a range of scenarios, including short delays, early departures, and significant disruptions.

Table 1. Representative test cases showing actual and predicted flight delays with corresponding error margins

Date	Source airport	Destination airport	Actual delay (min)	Predicted delay (min)	Error (min)
01-05-2022	BWI	BDL	9	12.9	–3.9
03-04-2019	TUL	IAH	–24	–25.1	1.1
25-05-2019	MSY	EWR	104	109.0	–5.0
20-04-2020	BNA	ATL	0	11.8	–11.8
07-07-2019	BOS	ORD	3	1.2	1.8
16-05-2019	CHO	ORD	586	584.2	1.8
04-09-2021	PHX	PHL	–58	–45.7	–12.3

4.3 Comparative Analysis with Existing Literature

Table 2 presents a comprehensive comparison of our ST-GAT model against recent approaches in the literature on flight delay prediction.

As the results show, our ST-GAT model consistently outperforms previous approaches across all metrics. The accuracy improvement ranges from 2.1% (compared to Chen & Johnson's Transformer approach) to 4.7% (compared to Wang et al.'s GNN). Similarly, the MAE improvements range from 4.7% to 10.5%. These results validate that our integrated spatio-temporal graph attention architecture represents a meaningful advancement in flight delay prediction methodology, particularly in its ability to model complex airport network interactions.

Table 2. Comparative analysis of our ST-GAT model against existing literature

Author	Paper title	Year	Method	MAE	RMSE	Acc. (%)
Zhang et al.	Deep learning for airport delay prediction	2023	ConvLSTM	5.12	8.34	85.8
Zhu et al.	A spatio-temporal approach with self-corrective causal inference for flight delay prediction	2024	CausalNet	5.794	10.201	82.45
Wang et al.	Graph networks for aviation systems	2024	GNN	5.23	8.79	84.5
Chen & Johnson	Transformer-based flight delay forecasting	2022	Transformer	4.91	8.05	87.1
Our Work	**ST-GAT for flight delay prediction**	**2025**	**finetuned ST-GAT**	**4.68**	**7.78**	**89.2**

4.4 Limitations and Future Work

While our ST-GAT model demonstrates compelling performance, several directions for future research include:

- **Dynamic Graph Structures:** Implementing time-varying airport connections to account for seasonal route changes and temporary disruptions.
- **Multi-Day Prediction Horizons:** Extending the framework to forecast delays multiple days in advance to support longer-term operational planning.
- **Transfer Learning:** Investigating whether models trained on major airports can effectively adapt to regional airports with limited historical data.
- **Explainable AI Components:** Enhancing the interpretability of attention coefficients to provide actionable insights for airport operations teams.

- **Integration of Additional Data Sources:** Incorporating richer external features such as high-resolution weather data (e.g., METAR reports), air traffic control actions (e.g., ground stops, reroutes), and operational constraints (e.g., gate availability, crew scheduling) could further enhance prediction accuracy.
- **Lack of Ablation Study:** The current study does not include a formal ablation analysis to isolate the individual contributions of the temporal and spatial modules.

5 Conclusion

This study explored flight delay prediction by integrating temporal modeling with graph-based analysis, demonstrating the significant impact of network-wide airport interactions on forecast accuracy. Conventional approaches, such as tree-based ensembles and standalone time-series models, often fail to capture the spatial propagation of delays across interconnected airports. In contrast, the proposed Spatio-Temporal Graph Attention Network (ST-GAT) offers a comprehensive framework, leveraging attention mechanisms to identify critical airport connections and enhance prediction accuracy. Empirical results highlight ST-GAT's superior performance, with a mean absolute error of 4.68 and an accuracy of 89.2%, outperforming recent deep learning methods by effectively modeling both local delay patterns and their network-wide effects. Future research could extend this framework by incorporating dynamic route networks, multi-step forecasting horizons, and additional data sources, further enhancing its robustness and applicability in operational settings.

References

1. Tijil, Y., Dwivedi, N., Srivastava, S.K., Ranjan, A.: Flight Delay Prediction Using Ensemble Learning. In: International Conference on Advanced Computing and Communication Technologies (IC2PCT 2024). https://doi.org/10.1109/IC2PCT60090.2024.10486482
2. Zhu, Q., Chen, S., Guo, T., Lv, Y., Du, W.: CausalNet: A Self-Corrective Spatio-Temporal Graph Neural Network for Flight Delay Prediction. arXiv preprint. https://doi.org/10.48550/arXiv.2407.15185 (2024)
3. Shen, X., Chen, J., Yan, R.: A spatial-temporal model for network-wide flight delay prediction based on federated learning. Appl. Soft Comput. **154**, 111380 (2024). https://doi.org/10.1016/j.asoc.2024.111380
4. Balakrishna, P., Ganesan, R., Sherry, L., Levy, B.S.: Airport taxi-out time prediction using reinforcement learning. In: IEEE/AIAA 27th Digital Avionics Systems Conference (DASC). https://doi.org/10.1109/DASC.2008.4702812 (2008)
5. Cai, K., Li, Y., Zhu, Y., Fang, Q., Yang, Y., Du, W.: A Geographical and Operational Deep Graph Convolutional Approach for Flight Delay Prediction. Chin. J. Aeronaut. **36**(3). https://doi.org/10.1016/j.cja.2022.10.004 (2023)

6. Kim, S.-B., Park, J.-W.: Estimating flight delay probabilities using Bayesian networks. J. Air Transp. Manag. **60**, 76–83 (2017). https://doi.org/10.1016/j.jairtraman.2017.01.007
7. Mamdouh, M., Ezzat, M., Hefny, H.: Improving flight delays prediction by developing attention-based bidirectional LSTM network. Expert Syst. Appl. 238(Part A), 121747 (2024). https://doi.org/10.1016/j.eswa.2023.121747
8. Guo, H., et al.: A hybrid random forest regression model for flight delay prediction. Aerosp. Sci. Technol. **116**, 106822 (2021). https://doi.org/10.1016/j.ast.2021.106822
9. Yu, B., et al.: Flight delay prediction for commercial air transport: A deep learning approach. Transp. Res. Part E Logist. Transp. Rev. **125**, 203–221 (2019). https://doi.org/10.1016/j.tre.2019.03.013
10. Bai, S., Kolter, J.Z., Koltun, V.: An Empirical Evaluation of Generic Convolutional and Recurrent Networks for Sequence Modeling. arXiv preprint. https://doi.org/10.48550/arXiv.1803.01271 (2018)
11. Li, Y., Yu, R., Shahabi, C., Liu, Y.: Diffusion Convolutional Recurrent Neural Network: Data-Driven Traffic Forecasting. In: International Conference on Learning Representations (ICLR 2018). https://doi.org/10.48550/arXiv.1707.01926
12. Veličković, P., Cucurull, G., Casanova, A., Romero, A., Liò, P., Bengio, Y.: Graph Attention Networks. In: International Conference on Learning Representations (ICLR 2018). https://doi.org/10.48550/arXiv.1710.10903
13. Zong, Q., et al.: Support vector machine approach for flight delay prediction. Procedia Comput. Sci. **107**, 1–6 (2017). https://doi.org/10.1016/j.procs.2017.05.199
14. Kaggle: Flight Delays and Cancellations Dataset (2019–2023). https://www.kaggle.com/datasets/patrickzel/flight-delay-and-cancellation-dataset-2019-2023 (2023)

A Comparative Analysis on Deep Learning Approaches for Sentiment Analysis of Food Review Data with Class Imbalance

Pritha Banerjee[1,3](✉), Animesh Bhandari[2], Jayita Saha[4], and Chandreyee Chowdhury[3]

[1] Sreenidhi University, Hyderabad, India
pritha.b@suh.edu.in
[2] Institute of Engineering and Management, Kolkata, West Bengal, India
[3] Jadavpur University, Kolkata, India
[4] Manipal Academy of Higher Education, Manipal Institute of Technology Bengaluru, Bengaluru, India
jayita.saha@manipal.edu

Abstract. In recent years researchers has been applying different machine learning and deep learning approaches on textual data. Preprocessing of textual data is one of the challenging tasks and it is getting enhanced day by day. Several vectorization techniques for mapping a string to a feature vector are compared and machine learning and deep learning approaches are applied for multi-class classification and binary class classification on the well-known datasets like Amazon Fine Food Review. Several vectorization techniques like Countvectorizer, TF-IDF, Hash vectorizer, Tokenizer, and embedding technique Glove are used in the comparison. The classifiers that are used in this work are Naïve Bayes, Logistic Regression, K-nearest neighbor, Multilayer perceptron (MLP), Convolution Neural Network (CNN), and Long Short Term Memory(LSTM). It has been found that all vectorization techniques are not compatible with every classifier as the accuracy depends on the creation of the feature vector. A graph has been drawn to compare the testing accuracy of different classifiers with the different tokenizers.

Keywords: Feature extraction · Glove embedding vector · TF-IDF · MLP · CNN · LSTM

1 Introduction

In recent studies, it has been found that sentiment analysis is used in most e-commerce platforms. Sentiment analysis [1] can be interpreted as the study of human sentiment towards entities such as services, products, and issues. It can help us to determine the positive or negative emotions of the particularly targeted party (i.e., customers) to create actionable knowledge. Nowadays, the

K. Chandra Mondal et al. (Eds.): CICBA 2025, CCIS 2863, pp. 99–111, 2026.
https://doi.org/10.1007/978-3-032-17184-9_8

influence of online reviews on consumer behaviors has been of concern to marketing research. Product reviews are becoming increasingly important sources of information for consumers. Consumers gain insights from other purchasers through reviews, rather than relying solely on seller-generated content. As for its part in the e-commerce domain, sentiment analysis has an important role in enabling business owners to work. It also helps in improving their strategy by gaining vital unsolicited feedback about their products from customers in today's customer-dominated business culture. One of the most prominent examples of e-commerce giants using it is Amazon [2] which is popular globally due to its wide range of product selection as well as the amount of product evaluation resources it provides for even a new user/customer to be able to trim down their options to help choose the best-suited product. The product perception would vary for consumers with different preferences.

There are different vectorization and classification techniques available in the market for the sentiment analysis. These models have different impact on different problems. Different classification algorithms along with vectorization techniques give different results. As a consequence, the overall product perception would vary for consumers with different preferences. Though there are works on comparative approaches of sentiment analysis, not many would be found that takes the class imbalance issue in the comparison. This comparative study focuses on two factors- how the features are extracted using different vectorization techniques and what are the impacts of feature extraction techniques on the performance of different Classification algorithms subject to class imbalance. For the data extraction of the review data to perceive the relationship between the feature set and the sentiment different techniques are applied. Machine learning tools like TF-IDF, countvectorizer, and tokenizers can be used to extract the feature set. Class imbalance is a common problem while analyzing such reviews as the data samples are not equally distributed for all the ratings resulting in biased performance by the classifiers. Oversampling and undersampling techniques are required to solve the problem of data imbalance [3]. Machine learning and deep learning tools [4] Naive Bayes, Logistic regression, CNN, LSTM can used to classify the dataset. Consequently, the contributions of this paper are as follows.

1. An extensive comparison of several vectorization techniques, including Count Vectorizer, TF-IDF, Tokenizer, and Tokenizer with GloVe embedding vectors, is presented.
2. The performance of these vectorization methods is evaluated using various machine learning algorithms, such as Naive Bayes, Logistic Regression, and K-Nearest Neighbor (KNN), as well as deep learning models like Multi-Layer Perceptron (MLP), Convolutional Neural Network (CNN), and Long Short-Term Memory (LSTM).
3. Challenges like class imbalance and oversampling are addressed in this work and their impact on multi-class and binary classification, are thoroughly analyzed.

4. The benchmark Amazon Fine Food Reviews dataset [2], which comprises of user reviews of various products in text format are considered for extensive experimentation.

The rest of the paper is organized as Sect. 2 which describes the literature survey, Sect. 3 consists of the methodology of the experiment. Section 4 consists of the dataset description and comparison analysis of the result. Finally, Sect. 5 concludes the paper.

1.1 Literature Survey

The main focus of previous research on Amazon fine food reviews has been on tuning the accuracy of the prediction of review helpfulness to manage the problems relating to the huge amount of uneven online customer reviews. A study conducted by Khan et al. [5] focuses on extracting information from available data regarding customer's opinions and understanding their needs and demands. Their study is conducted on a large, imbalanced, and multi-classed dataset. For the experiment, they used Bag of Words and TF-IDF as vectorizers and they compared the performance of Multinomial naïve Bayes, support vector machine, logistic regression, and random forest. They have reported 77% accuracy with logistic regression. Not only machine learning algorithms deep learning algorithms could perform good in text data analysis. In another study of text classification using Machine Learning conducted by Luo X. [6], the Support Vector Machines model has been applied on English documents. In their analysis, the classification rate exceeded 90% when more than 4000 features were used. Deep learning provides huge benefits for text classification. To implement proper text categorization, correct treatment of textual data is very important. Li and Li [7] have introduced one novel architecture using a deep learning model which gave 95% accuracy.

There is a comparison stated by Alqahtani et al. [8] among machine learning and deep learning algorithms on text data. However, the data preprocessing techniques impart an effect on classification performance. They generate different patterns of features from the given text data. So in this paper, we are considering different vectorization techniques and their impact on machine learning and deep learning techniques. It is better to train a model with a larger number of data points. One widely used dataset is the Amazon fine food review dataset. The dataset contains product feedback and some relevant about purchasing the product. The dataset of Amazon Fine Food Review contains large and versatile data that provides a wide range of information on ratings, the range of products available on Amazon, and their user information. A study conducted by Yarkareddy et al. [2] takes the dataset of Amazon Fine Food Review and uses a Machine Learning algorithm to analyze and identify whether the review is positive or negative. As far as the study on Amazon Fine Food Review is concerned, the focus of it has been on exploring reviews and making an effort to predict review helpfulness. In this paper, a comparative study of different vectorization techniques with both machine learning and deep learning algorithms have been conducted on an imbalanced review dataset. In the experiment, both vectorization and embedding vectors are considered. All feature extraction must not lead to the same accuracy for different algorithms.

2 Methodology

The paper presents a comparative analysis of various learning techniques based on different vectorizers in the same experimental setup. The dataset consists of textual feedback data. The overall methodology is described in Fig. 1.

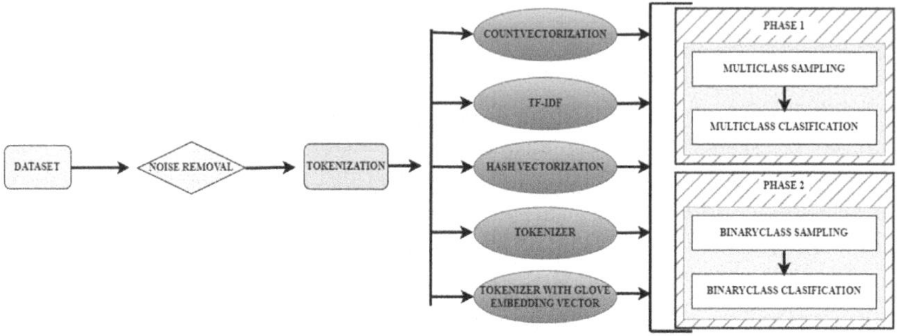

Fig. 1. Experimental Architecture

2.1 Data Cleaning

Preprocessing plays a vital role in machine learning and natural language processing, as it converts raw data into usable feature vectors. Suppose the dataset has been represented by $T = t_1, t_2, \cdots, t_n$ where t_i represents each text element present in the dataset. In the first phase of preprocessing the unwanted characters known as noise which might be an obstacle to creating the feature vectors are removed. Noises can be different stopwords in any natural language or different numbers present in between words, special characters or different HTML tags. After removing the noises the textual feedback data will be tokenized and converted into lowercase.

The experiment has been designed in two phases. One is a multiclass classification which has been given in the actual dataset and another is, a binary classification which is obtained from the multiclass labels. As the class distribution in the dataset is right-skewed, the biases of the classification will be higher towards either the highest class or the positive class in the case of binary classification. To handle the biases of the dataset, a sampling technique has been applied to the dataset. For the experiment, we have considered both undersampling and oversampling techniques. For multiclass classification, the undersampling technique has been used; otherwise, the huge number of synthetic data can affect the performance of the classification algorithms. For binary classification, oversampling techniques are used.

2.2 Feature Extraction

From the token of words, the feature vectors are extracted. Several vectorization techniques are applied. The list of applied vectorization techniques is presented below.

CountVectorizor. The countvectorizor feature vectors are created from a sparse matrix. The sparse matrix is created using the unique words present in the corpus and the frequency of the words with respect to the index of vocabulary present in a particular text. The feature vectors in this vectorization technique are created for a number of occurrences of the unique word. If they are present then the frequency will be there, if they are not present it will be zero. A pattern of numbers has been created using the sparse matrix for each data.

TF-IDF. TF-IDF vectorization technique depends upon the overall weight of any unique word present in the corpus. It is basically a combination of term frequency and inverse document frequency. Term frequency calculates the frequency of the token in the current document. The Inverse document frequency is the overall weightage of that token on the whole data corpus. The equation of TF-IDF is given in Eq. 1.

$$TF - IDF = TF(t, d) * IDF(t, d) \tag{1}$$

Hash Vectorizator. The Hash vectorization technique does not depend on the weight of the token in any corpus. In this method, tokens are converted directly to a numeric form using a hash function of an arbitrary fixed length and stored. Though it takes less amount of memory, but it could not revert back into tokens. The matrix that is created in the Hash vectorization method contains a maximum number of zeros, and other values are calculated using the hash function targeting a specific token.

Tokenizer. It also vectorizes the token of words into numeric forms. The tokenizer technique converts the tokens of a data dictionary into a sequence of integers where integers can be an index of tokens in the total corpus.

Tokenizer with GloVe Embedding Vector. GloVe stands for Global Vector for word representation. It is another type of word representation where a co-occurrence matrix has been created. If the matrix is created using a corpus of size W unique words, the co-occurrence matrix M will be a WXW matrix. In the matrix any value $M(i, j)$ where the ith and j^{th} columns of and its value will be the probability that the word in a row has cooccurred with the word in the column. It captures the global co-occurrence value instead of only the local co-occurrence value to create the word vectors.

2.3 Classification Algorithm

The ML and DL classifiers utilized for the performance analysis have been summarized here.

Naïve Bayes. This classification algorithm is based on conditional probability. According to Bayes theorem, if an event y is dependent on X then the probability of occurring y is calculated using Eq. 2.

$$P(y|X) = \frac{P(X|y)P(y)}{P(X)} \tag{2}$$

In the case of Bayes theorem if X consists of several variables $(x_1, x_2, \cdots, x_n)$ then, to determine y all the variables have equal weightage and they are mutually independent. In this experiment, different features extracted from the tokens act as predictors. It cannot calculate the individual weight of the features to predict the outcome.

Logistic Regression. Logistic regression is a classification algorithm which is also based on probability. Here, sigmoid function which is a S shaped curve is used as the cost function. The probabilistic value used to give a value in between 0 and 1. There is a threshold value which decides the predicted class. The equation for logistic regression is given in Eq. 3.

$$Y = \frac{e^{b_0 + b_1 * x}}{1 + e^{b_0 + b_1 * x}} \tag{3}$$

where y is the predicted output and b_0 is the bias value and b_1 is the coefficient for the input x.

K-Nearest Neighbour. In K-nearest neighbor algorithm, it does not depend upon the probabilistic value. Instead of that it calculates the distance between two input datapoints. K denotes the number of datapoints belong to each class. The idea behind K-nearest neighbor algorithm is that similar datapoints are close together. Those datapoints which used to stay closer belong from the same class. Usually the distance between the given data and query data points are calculated using Euclidian distance. The shortest distance will determine the class. The expression for Euclidian distance is given in Eq. 4,

$$d(p,q) = \sqrt{(q_1 - p_1)^2 + (q_2 - p_2)^2 + \cdots + (q_n - p_n)^2} \tag{4}$$

where p is the given datapoints belong to a class and q is the query datapoint whose class will be determined.

Multilayer Perceptron. Multi layer perceptron is a neural network which consists of three layers, Input layer, output layer and the hidden layer. It is a feed-forward network where input layer will be fed by input vectors, which will be transferred to hidden layer. Weight for each connecting neuron layer will be updated and fed into the next layer. Every neuron in the hidden layer is connected with the neurons of the next layer. Training in the learning will be in back propagation method. The last output layer will be the perceptron layer where sigmoid function will be used as activation function.

Convolutional Neural Network(CNN). In case of convolutional neural network, different hidden layers are present. The Convolution layer will extract the important features from the input 2D vector. The activation function of convolution layer is ReLU. The function of convolution layer with activation function ReLU is given in Eq. 5.

$$C_i = f(\times W t_(i : i + k - 1 + bi)) \tag{5}$$

where W is the filter function, $W \in \times R^(k - d)O$, $x_i \in R^d$ where d is the input channel, k is the kernel size and O is the output channel. To introduce non-linearity, a Rectified Linear Unit (ReLU) activation function is applied to the convolutional layer's output, setting all negative values to zero for any input x. The convolutional layer itself generates feature vectors by performing matrix multiplication between the input data and a kernel. Subsequently, a max-pooling layer reduces the dimensionality of these feature maps by aggregating information using statistical methods. To prepare for the fully connected layers, the output of the pooling layer is flattened, transforming it into a single-row vector. To mitigate overfitting, dropout regularization is then employed. Finally, a fully connected (dense) layer is used, where each neuron receives input from all neurons in the preceding layer.

Long Short Term Memory(LSTM). Long Short-Term Memory (LSTM) networks are a specialized type of recurrent neural network designed to process and retain information from long sequences. As feedback networks, they utilize internal memory to store past data. LSTMs employ three key gatesinput, forget, and outputeach regulated by a sigmoid activation function, to manage the flow of information. The equations of the LSTM is given Eqs. 6, 7, 8,

$$it = \sigma w_i[h_(t-1), x_t] + b_i \tag{6}$$

$$ft = \sigma w_f[h_(t-1), x_t] + b_f \tag{7}$$

$$ot = \sigma w_o[h_(t-1), x_t] + b_o \tag{8}$$

In an LSTM, the input gate it determines what new information to store, the forget gate ft decides what information to discard, and the output gate ot controls what information to output. Each gate's activation is governed by a sigmoid function σ, which uses weighted sums of the current input x_t and the previous hidden state $h_(t-1)$plus a bias b. The weights w are specific to each gate. To prevent overfitting, a dropout layer is often incorporated.

3 Result Analysis

3.1 Dataset Description

For our experimentation, we have considered the Amazon Fine Food Review dataset [9] which consists of 5, 68, 454 reviews, the number of users is 2, 56, 059, the number of unique product is 74, 258, and the number of attributes are 10. The features present in the dataset are product-id, user-id, profile name, number of users who found the review known as helpfulness numerator, number of users who indicated whether the review was helpful or not known as helpfulness denominator, the score based upon the rating 1 to 5, timestamp of the review, a summary of the review and the review consist of all the words of the user review. Figure 2 displays the data distribution of the class labels of the entire dataset. It can be seen from the figure that dataset is suffering from biasness as maximum number of data are from higher class level 5.

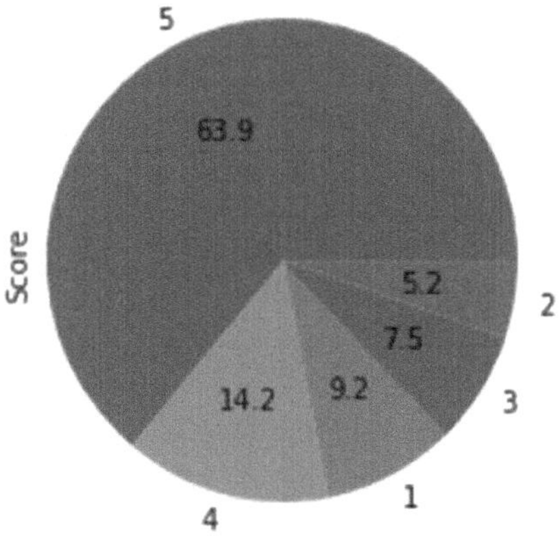

Fig. 2. Data distribution for multi class dataset

For the experimental setup in Phase 1 experiment, the multi class classification had been done. The data distribution of dataset which is shown in Fig. 2 is an imbalanced dataset [10]. To handle this problem under-sampling technique random sampler was used in this experiment. As for the over-sampling technique, the number of noisy data will be huge and may not give the best result. After applying the under-sampling technique, all the classes contain 20000 records and the data distribution is shown in Fig. 3.

For the Phase 2 experiment, the multi-class had been represented in binary class as class 1,2 and 3 are represented by class 0, and class 4 and 5 are represented by class 1. The data distribution of the binary class is shown in Fig. 4. But the problem of imbalanced data distribution is also exists in this scenario. For this experiment, the oversampling technique SMOTE [11] is applied here. The reason behind applying over sampling technique is that the number of discarded data will be less.

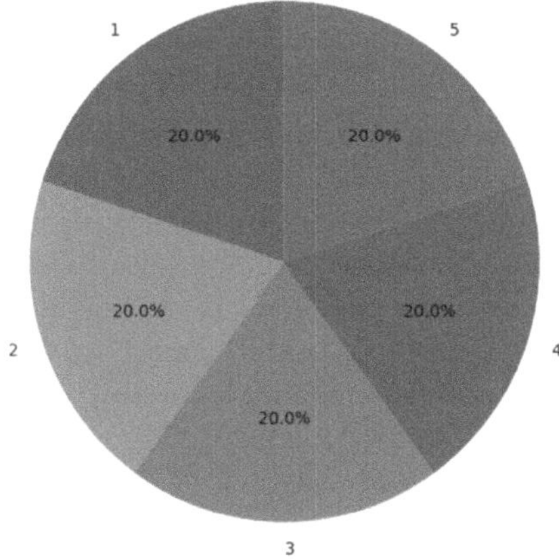

Fig. 3. Data distribution after under sampling

Data imbalance in the dataset would lead to bias in the results of classification algorithms. For multiclass classification, if we apply the oversampling technique, more synthetic data points need to be generated thus the training data would comprise of appreciable no of synthetic data points (50:50). It will have an effect in training the machine learning models. That is why the undersampling technique of the random sampler is applied. On the other hand, in case of binary classification oversampling technique SMOTE is applied as it generates datapoints for only one class and the synthetic data to real data ratio becomes 30:70.

For both phases of experiment, after applying the sampling technique total dataset has been divided into 80% and 20%. Among them 80% of the dataset has been used for the training of the algorithm whereas, 20% of the dataset is used for the testing purpose.

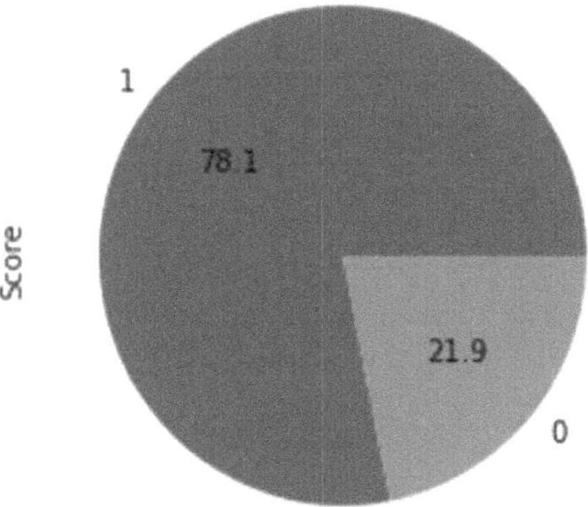

Fig. 4. Data distribution for binary class dataset

3.2 Performance Analysis

For the experiment in multiclass classification that is in phase 1, a comparative result has been displayed in Table 1. For this experiment, the dataset is scaled down with the help of the undersampling technique. From the table, it had been observed that Logistic Regression with TF-IDF gave highest accuracy among these set comparisons. Vectorization Technique with deep learning model. The cells which are filled by X^*, the accuracy is negligible. The model could not recognize the pattern in the test data, so the accuracy is very low. The cells where the experiment could not be performed are denoted by X^{**}. As glove embedding vector can be used in embedding layer of deep learning models.Figure 5 shows the learning curve for the Logistic Regression with TF-IDF vectorization technique.

Table 1. ACCURACY FOR MULTICLASS CLASSIFICATION

Vectorizer	Classifier					
	Naive Bayes	Logistic Regression	K-Nearest Neighbour	Multilayer Perceptron	Convolution Neural Network (CNN)	Long Short Term Memory(LSTM)
Countvectorizer	*46.59*	*47.61*	*31.54*	$X*$	$X*$	$X*$
TF-IDF	*46.65*	***50.87***	*30.75*	$X*$	$X*$	$X*$
Hash Vectorizer	*43.92*	*45.49*	*30.33*	*45.43*	$X*$	$X*$
Tokenizer	$X*$	$X*$	$X*$	*45.7*	*50.02*	*43.47*
Tokenizer with Glove Embedding Vector	$X**$	$X**$	$X**$	*46.65*	*45.7*	*48.83*

X*=The accuracy is negligible
X**= The experiment can not be performed

For the binary class classification in phase 2, the result has been shown in Table 2.

In comparison to multiclass classification, binary class classification gives overall better results as showed in Table 2. The deep learning algorithm LSTM with a glove embedding vector gives highest accuracy which is almost 88%. In machine learning algorithms all the features have the same contribution to classify the data. But in the case of the deep learning algorithm, different features got different weights to classify the test dataset. Moreover, as all the other vectorizer calculates the local co-occurrence of any token, when the global co-occurrence of Glove vectors has been embedded with the classifiers, it gives a better result than any other vectorizers. The learning curve for LSTM model with Glove vector embedding and tokenizer is given in Fig. 6. We have considered 100 epochs for the experiment and the curve for the training and validation data is shown here. The loss curve for the same is given in Fig. 7.

Table 2. ACCURACY FOR BINARY CLASS CLASSIFICATION

Vectorizer	Classifier					
	Naive Bayes	Logistic Regression	K-Nearest Neighbour	Multilayer Perceptron	Convolution Neural Network (CNN)	Long Short Term Memory(LSTM)
Countvectorizer	*85.96*	*86.16*	*51.16*	*X**	*X**	*X**
TF-IDF	*86.41*	*88.79*	*X**	*X**	*X**	*X**
Hash Vectorizer	*81.08*	*83.20*	*60.26*	*84.24*	*49.93*	*79.61*
Tokenizer	*51.89*	*51.85*	*75.09*	*75.65*	*78.10*	*83.84*
Tokenizer with Glove Embedding Vector	*X***	*X***	*X***	*80.33*	*85.48*	***87.27***

X*= The accuracy is negligible

X**= The experiment cannot be performed

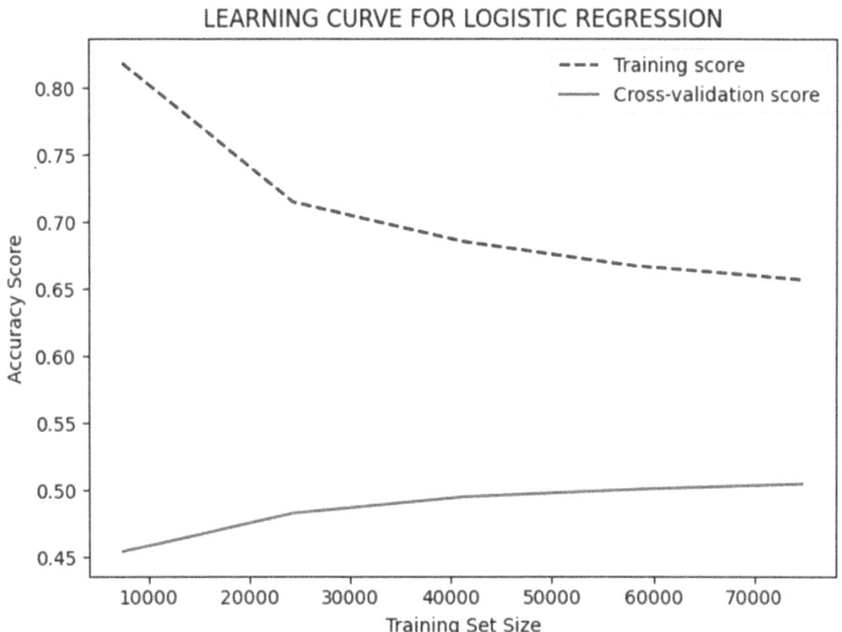

Fig. 5. Logistic Regression Training curve for multi label dataset

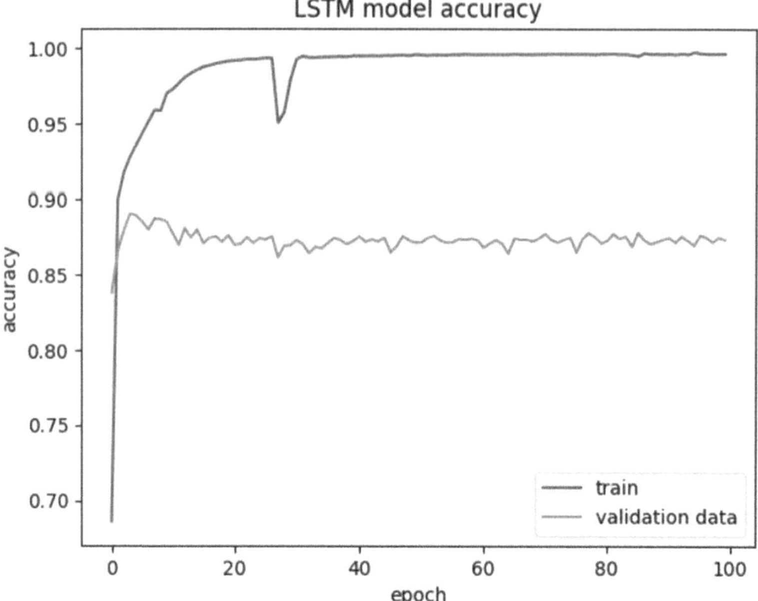

Fig. 6. Training accuracy curve for tokenization with glove vector for LSTM model

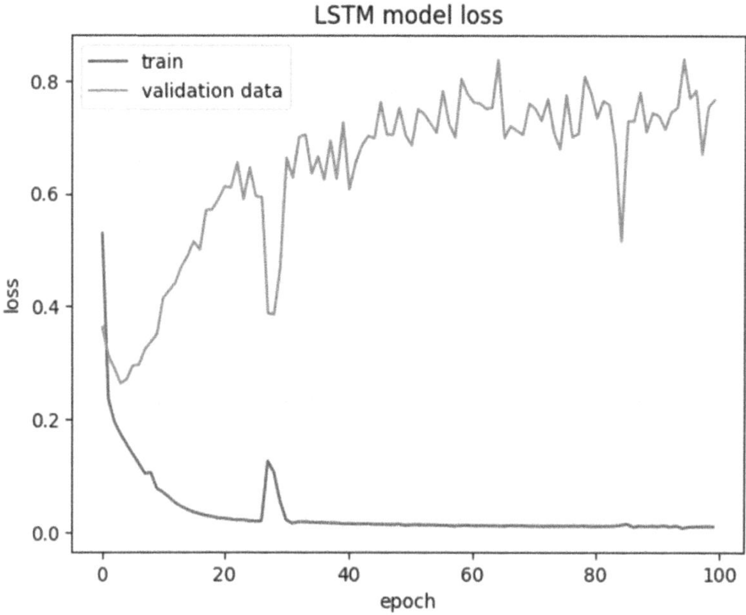

Fig. 7. Training loss curve for tokenization with glove vector for LSTM model

4 Conclusion and Future Plans

Sentiment analysis has huge applications in different domains of industry. The dataset that is used here, is amazon fine food review Amazon Fine Food Review, which is a multi-class benchmark dataset. The dataset is suffering from data imbalance, which is taken care of by the under-sampling technique, the random sampler, and the over-sampling technique SMOTE. In this study the comparison has shown that different feature extraction techniques give different results on machine learning and deep learning classifiers. The feature extraction techniques of text data play a vital role in extracting meaningful insights from text data. The aspect of this study is to help developers make a better decision about their choice of tokenizer and classifier towards the problem of sentiment-based review analysis towards building better recommendation systems, question answering models and any other question answering model. For future purpose, different encoding technique like a large language model, which will increase the dependency between two features, can be used for the experiment.

References

1. Rodríguez-Ibánez, M., Casánez-Ventura, A., Castejón-Mateos, F., Cuenca-Jiménez, P.-M.: A review on sentiment analysis from social media platforms. Expert Syst. Appl. **223**, 119862 (2023)
2. Yarkareddy, S., Sasikala, T., Santhanalakshmi, S.: Sentiment analysis of amazon fine food reviews. In: 2022 4th International Conference on Smart Systems and Inventive Technology (ICSSIT), pp. 1242–1247 (2022)
3. Tan, K.L., Lee, C.P., Lim, K.M., Anbananthen, K.S.M.: Sentiment analysis with ensemble hybrid deep learning model. IEEE Access **10**, 103694–103704 (2022)
4. Bhati, V., Kher, J.: Survey for amazon fine food reviews. Int. Res. J. Eng. Technol. (IRJET) **6**(4) (2019)
5. Tusar, Md.T.H.K., Islam, Md.T.: A comparative study of sentiment analysis using NLP and different machine learning techniques on us airline twitter data. In: 2021 International Conference on Electronics, Communications and Information Technology (ICECIT), pp. 1–4. IEEE (2021)
6. Luo, X.: Efficient English text classification using selected machine learning techniques. Alex. Eng. J. **60**(3), 3401–3409 (2021)
7. Li, H., Li, Z.: Text classification based on machine learning and natural language processing algorithms. Wirel. Communi. Mob. Comput. **2022** (2022)
8. Alqahtani, A., et al.: An efficient approach for textual data classification using deep learning. Front. Comput. Neurosci. **16**, 992296 (2022)
9. Zhou, Z., Xu, L.: Amazon food review classification using deep learning and recommender system. In: Stanford University Stanford (2009)
10. Mohammed, R., Rawashdeh, J., Abdullah, M.: Machine learning with oversampling and undersampling techniques: overview study and experimental results. In: 2020 11th International Conference on Information and Communication Systems (ICICS), pp. 243–248. IEEE (2020)
11. Chawla, N.V., Bowyer, K.W., Hall, L.O., Kegelmeyer, W.P.: Smote: synthetic minority over-sampling technique. J. Artif. Intell. Res. **16**, 321–357 (2002)

A Framework in Generative AI for Preventing Suicidal Thoughts

K. Surya(✉) and Rohit Kumar

School of Engineering, Shiv Nadar University Chennai, Kalavakkam, Chengalpattu 603110, Tamil Nadu, India
suryak@snuchennai.edu.in

Abstract. The aim of the work is to provide technical framework for prevention of suicidal thoughts through chatbot which can be embedded to an existing mobile communication application or can be deployed as a new communication application. It can also be used as a web application. The framework is built upon Dialogflow Conversational agent of google cloud which uses Generative Artificial Intelligence (GenAI). This paper provides the technical considerations and workflow of the chatbot to be developed. The chatbot generates conceptual images or videos based on the inference of the end user's conversation. It also incorporates the human intervention by calling the emergency contacts in case of ambiguous conversations. The chatbot can be useful for preventing suicide among individuals of all age groups. The training and testing of chatbot performed by Kaggle dataset and also synthetically generated dataset which contains suicidal thoughts identification. The responses generated by the chatbot can be fine-tuned based on the conversational history generated between the user and the responses given by the chatbot.

Keywords: Generative AI · Cloud Computing · Chatbot · Suicidal Prevention · Google Cloud

1 Introduction

As per the data given by World Health Organization (WHO)[13], 800000 people die due to suicide year which means 1 person dies in every 40 s across the globe. The notable point is that suicide can be prevented and it can be reduced only through a global effort [13]. The motivation behind this work is to provide support to people through chatbot and provide solutions to come out of suicidal thoughts. The advantage of chatbot based solution over human intervened conversations is the availability of chatbots. Humans are subjected to tiredness and mood swings and prone to provide prejudice based solutions, whereas chatbots are neutral in providing solutions. Humans also cannot maintain confidentiality of certain information whereas bots can be controlled through programming for ensuring the confidentiality of information shared. The conversations of the chatbot are stored in a end-to-end encrypted format which prevents unauthorized

K. Chandra Mondal et al. (Eds.): CICBA 2025, CCIS 2863, pp. 112–123, 2026.
https://doi.org/10.1007/978-3-032-17184-9_9

disclosures of data. Thus privacy can be achieved by technology which provides a comfortable platform for discussing the personal issues. The first and foremost step in suicidal prevention is to incorporate mental health education to students of schools and colleges. Generative AI chatbots are widely used for higher education as it imitates liveliness of humans [2,7,10,11,14]. The generative AI based chatbots improve the interactions between the end user enhancing the productivity as well as achieve increased personalization compared to other technologies. So by developing generative AI based chatbots will definitely reduce the suicidal prevention among the end-users. Also the generative AI chatbots are able to provide new media content based on the end-user conversations whereas traditional chatbots rely only on the pre-trained models used in training. This is the reason that generative AI chatbots outperform the traditional AI bots.

The chatbots use Cognitive Behavioral Therapy (CBT) techniques to provide solutions to improve mental health and reduce depression and loneliness [12,16]. The functionality of the chatbot is to identify the problem of the end-users as well provide mitigation strategies to overcome the problem. The design should also provide newly generated content to the users at particular time interval to prevent loneliness and depression among the users. We provide a novel framework in this work for implementing the chatbot with all these features using generative AI. Though we can conclude that chatbots cannot compensate with the therapy provided by psychiatrist, it definitely eases the stress and anxiety of patients and also develop positivity among the people with suicidal thoughts. Thus it can be used as a solution to interact with humans 24/7. We can definitely achieve the goal of reducing the number of suicides by developing a chatbot which is in confinement to the psychological cravings of a person. Our chatbot design considers all the psychological factors [8] that causes the risk of suicide among individuals. Our approach uses the kaggle dataset [1] and also the synthetic data generation [4] is done by considering all the psychological factors [8] that triggers the risk of suicide among individuals. The paper is categorized as follows where Sect. 2 gives the existing works in suicide prevention and an overview of the chatbots used for treating mental health. The Sect. 3 gives the proposed framework, Sect. 4 discusses the results and Sect. 5 concludes the work along with future strategies to expand the proposed solution.

2 Literature Review

This section gives an overview of the existing suicidal prevention techniques using artificial intelligent and machine learning models and the existing chatbots used for suicidal prevention.

2.1 Suicidal Prevention Techniques Using Artificial Intelligence

A questionnaire was prepared for identifying the individuals with mental weakness with relevance to suicidal thoughts and pilot study was done to fine-tune the algorithm for suicidal prevention [15]. The current level of suicidal ideation (SI) and predicting future SI levels using time series data from a smartphone-based ecological momentary assessment (EMA) was presented in this work [15]. SHapley Additive exPlanations (SHAP) for Explainable Artificial Intelligence (XAI) and traditional correlation analysis has been used to rank feature importance, pinpointing primary factors influencing suicide risk and preventive measures [20]. The outcome of this research [20] proves that people who are unsuccessful and isolated are prone to suicidal thoughts and are at high risk, while successful people are at low risk of committing suicide. A systematic review of machine learning algorithms namely Cox Regression, Decision Tree, Logistic Regression, Neural networks, Random Forest, Support Vector Machines, Extreme gradient boosting/gradient boosted tree which has been used for suicidal prevention is summarized in this work [9]. The work [9] performed a study based on the publications from the country of origin. The results of this study proved that number of publications among the Asian countries are less compared to the Western nations. But the number of suicides among the East Asian nations [17] is higher than Western nations.

2.2 Chatbots for Mental Health Treatment

A survey of the mental health apps available in google playstore from the period of 2016 and 2020 are presented in this work [6]. The major concern of these app is the trustworthiness of the data collected and used for treating and failing to comply with the regulations required for treating patients with mental weakness. There are also some fake apps for android users in India [18] which may trigger suicide. Another major issue with these apps is that they are chargeable after a certain period of time and users with financial loss as a cause of suicide has hazardous impact. Generative AI proves to be effective in a randomized controlled trial of 210 adults with clinically significant symptoms of major mental depression disorder ([5]. The studies also show that generative AI has lot of potential to clinical tasks [3].

The literature survey makes us conclude that in a developing country like India these kind of apps should be available free of cost and awareness must be raised among the general public about the advantages of using those life saving apps. The information about the trustable apps must be available in social media platforms of the government as well as in the official government websites. This will help to widen the audience who need help.

3 Proposed Framework for Preventing Suicidal Thoughts

The purpose of the work is to develop a conversational chatbot which interacts with the user through human centered text conversations built on top of generative AI. About 64% of the users are interested to text rather than speaking to helpline according to data gathered by Meta. So we have chosen textual message based conversations between the user and the chatbot.

- **Design of Conversation Flow**: In the proposed approach we have chosen conversational agents in Google Cloud as it is a natural language understanding module that understands the elusiveness of human languages. These Conversational Agents performs translation of user's text during a conversation. These kaggle dataset [1] and synthetic data [4] will be given as input to the conversational agents which will generate conceptual video or images and send back to user. The video generated is based on the structured conversational data generated during the conversation. After generating the video, the chatbot responds with the user after checking the structured database generated after the conversation as shown in Fig. 1. If there is no response from the user after a time period of one minute, a warning call is made to all the emergency contacts that will be got from the user at the time of registration for using the chatbot.
- **Platform for Implementation**: We have used Dialogflow which is a Google Cloud Platform tool that allows users to design and integrate conversational user interfaces into their apps, websites, and other devices. This tool helps us to have more control over the conversation and also the interactions will be more lively when compared to Azure bot service. After careful analysis of our requirement, Dialogflow is cost-effective and has many prebuilt components which is suitable for quick bot development.
- **Testing and Training the Chatbot:**The training of chatbot is done through dialogflow agent of Google Cloud as shown in the Fig. 2. Dialogflow agent is a virtual agent that maintains concurrent conversations with the user. An intent in dialogflow agent categorizes an end-user's intention for each conversational history. The agent is trained using different intents and chatbot has the functionality to combine those intents for replying to a conversation. The user's expression is matched to the best intent and classified as suicidal or non-suicidal. The agent can also extract some of the received intent and append with the existing structured database. The method of extracting and storing it as parameters in the database are done according to the type of entity specified by the developer of the chatbot application. The conversational flow is controlled by contexts which contain string names. In our application, the strings such as "going to die" can be used to terminate the conversation and go for human intervention. When the context is "depressed" or "lonely", the chatbot generates motivational video for overcoming it.
- **Optimization of AI Conversations:** The current database is updated when the chatbot identifies a new intent and is suspicious of that intent being flagged as suicidal. Then the developer of the chatbot is notified about the addition of new intent to the existing structured database used for training. This helps the developer to fine-tune the conversational reply of the chatbot based on the intent categorization.
- **Ethical Considerations:** The ethical consideration must justify the source of evidence used for generating the content [19]. The proposed solution in our work goes for human intervention when the chatbot is unable to respond according to the prompts specified in AI conversational requirements.

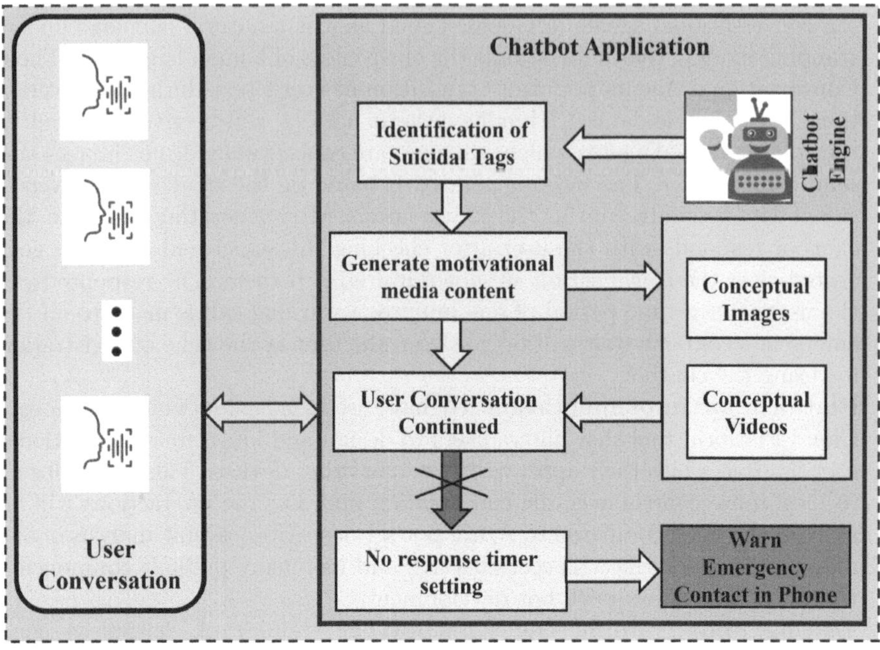

Fig. 1. Workflow of Chatbot for preventing suicidal thoughts

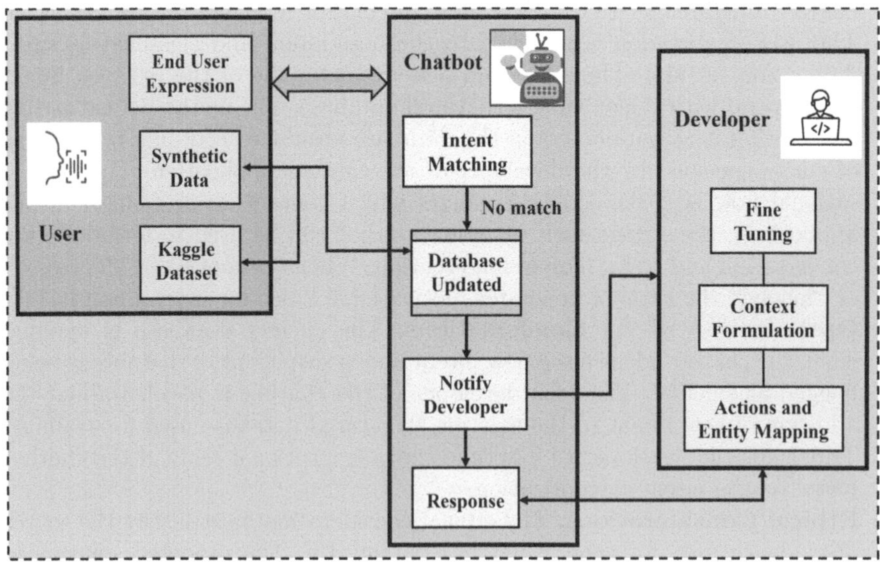

Fig. 2. Technical Design of Chatbot using Generative AI

4 Results and Discussion

The chatbot is constructed using the DialogFlow API, which facilitates natural language processing to effectively interpret and respond to user input. Within the DialogFlow console, a series of intents are created to address sensitive topics, particularly those involving suicidal thoughts. These intents are categorized into three distinct types: **text-based intent**, **video-based intent**, and **image-based intent**.

- **Text-Based Intent**: This intent serves as the foundation for initiating a general conversation. The chatbot responds with text-based outputs that are carefully crafted to engage the user in dialogue, offering emotional support, guidance, and access to resources for managing distressing thoughts.
- **Video-Based Intent**: The second type of intent allows the chatbot to generate video content in real-time during the conversation. This feature aims to provide users with visual comfort and positive reinforcement, enhancing the interaction by offering a multi-sensory experience. The video content is designed to be both engaging and supportive during moments of emotional distress.
- **Image-Based Intent**: The third intent is responsible for generating images that complement the conversation. Using Hugging Face models, the chatbot creates motivational and supportive visuals intended to uplift the user and promote a more positive emotional state during the interaction.

The Hugging Face models integrated into the chatbot are open-source and customizable, allowing for adaptation to meet specific user needs. This flexibility ensures that the chatbot can be continually improved based on insights gained from user interactions. Furthermore, the chatbot can be deployed as a standalone web module or seamlessly integrated into an existing mobile application, depending on the requirements of the user.

4.1 Text-Based Conversational Output

Figure 3 illustrates a typical output from the chatbot, generated when a user expresses suicidal thoughts. This example demonstrates how the chatbot engages with the user, offering compassionate and thoughtful responses while guiding the user toward seeking professional help.

In addition, Fig. 4 presents an example of the chatbot's response when the user expresses feelings of loneliness. The output demonstrates how the chatbot provides text-based support that acknowledges the user's emotional state, offering guidance and resources to alleviate feelings of isolation.

4.2 Video-Based Output

Within the DialogFlow webhook section, the `HunyuanVideo` model from Hugging Face is integrated to generate dynamic video content in response to user input.

Fig. 3. Text-Based Output - Scenario 1

The reason for choosing this model was it provides exceptional multimodal capabilities in the free version when compared to Vidu AI, Luma AI and so on. This integration allows the chatbot to produce video outputs that are contextually aligned with the ongoing conversation, enhancing the emotional tone and pro-

Fig. 4. Text Output - Scenario 2

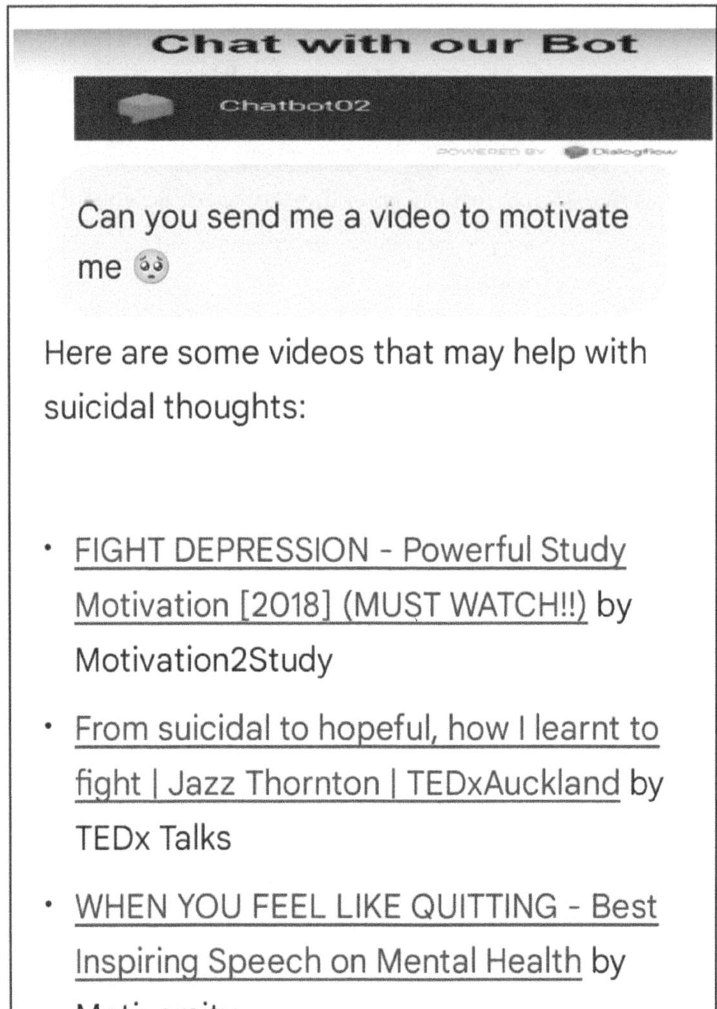

Fig. 5. Video Output

viding additional support through visual media. Figure 5 showcases an example of the video-based content generated by the chatbot during an interaction. These type of videos motivate the users mentally and give support emotionally similar to a person.

4.3 Image-Based Output

To complement the text and video outputs, the chatbot also utilizes the `Stable Diffusion 3.5 Large` model from Hugging Face for image generation. This

Fig. 6. Image Output

model enables the creation of images that are specifically tailored to the conversation, producing motivational and comforting visuals that aim to uplift the user during moments of emotional distress. Since the Stable diffusion model was easy to use and cost effective compared to Dall-E, Run Diffusion, Playground AI, we have used the former model compared with the latter. Figure 6 provides an example of the image-based content, which is designed to foster positive emotions and encourage resilience.

Together, these three modalities–text, video, and image–work in tandem to provide a holistic and supportive experience for users who may be facing emotional challenges. The chatbot's multi-modal approach ensures that it is capable of offering personalized and effective support, adapting to the diverse needs of individuals in distress. Through this integrated system, the chatbot aims to promote emotional well-being and provide users with the resources necessary to navigate difficult emotional states.

5 Conclusion and Future Work

In conclusion, this work presents a technical framework for suicide prevention using a chatbot, which can be integrated into existing mobile apps or deployed as a standalone web application. Built on Google Cloud's Dialogflow and Generative AI, the chatbot generates relevant images or videos based on user interactions and can call emergency contacts in ambiguous situations. It is designed to support individuals of all age groups and has been trained using Kaggle and synthetically generated datasets focused on identifying suicidal thoughts. The chatbot's responses can be fine-tuned based on ongoing conversations, enhancing its effectiveness in providing personalized support.

The future work can be extended to integrate this chatbot with WhatsApp, one of the most widely used messaging platforms in India. Such integration would enhance the effectiveness of suicide prevention efforts, given the platform's vast user base comprising millions of active users. Furthermore, future enhancements could involve the incorporation of animated videos generated through specific prompts, along with fine-tuning the underlying models to improve their performance. In the current implementation, the chatbot directs users to content designed to provide motivation for individuals experiencing suicidal thoughts. Additionally, the chatbot could be trained to interact with users in their regional languages, thereby offering a more personalized and culturally sensitive approach, which would be more effective in addressing emotional distress and preventing suicidal ideation.

References

1. Abhijitsingh (2021). https://www.kaggle.com/code/abhijitsingh001/suicidal-thought-detection
2. Al-Amin, M., et al.: History of generative artificial intelligence (AI) chatbots: past, present, and future development (2024). https://doi.org/10.48550/arXiv.2402.05122
3. Blease, C., Rodman, A.: Generative artificial intelligence in mental healthcare: an ethical evaluation. Curr. Treat. Opt. Psychiatry **12**(1), 1–9 (2025)
4. Ghanadian, H., Nejadgholi, I., Al Osman, H.: Socially aware synthetic data generation for suicidal ideation detection using large language models. IEEE Access (2024)
5. Heinz, M.V., et al.: Randomized trial of a generative AI chatbot for mental health treatment. Nejm AI **2**(4), AIoa2400802 (2025)
6. Islam, M.A., Choudhury, N.: Mobile apps for mental health: a content analysis. Indian J. Mental Health **7**(3), 222–229 (2020)

7. Labadze, L., Grigolia, M., Machaidze, L.: Role of AI chatbots in education: systematic literature review. Int. J. Educ. Technol. High. Educ. **20**(1), 56 (2023)
8. Lee, S.I., Jung, H.Y.: Psychosocial risk factors for suicide. Psychiatry Invest. **3**(2), 15 (2006)
9. Lejeune, A., et al.: Artificial intelligence and suicide prevention: a systematic review. Eur. Psychiatry **65**(1), e19 (2022)
10. Loh, E.: ChatGPT and generative AI chatbots: challenges and opportunities for science, medicine and medical leaders. BMJ Leader **8**(1), 51–54 (2024)
11. McGrath, C., Farazouli, A., Cerratto Pargman, T.: Generative AI chatbots in higher education: a review of an emerging research area. High. Educ. 1–17 (2024). https://doi.org/10.1007/s10734-024-01288-w
12. Nicol, G., Wang, R., Graham, S., Dodd, S., Garbutt, J., et al.: Chatbot-delivered cognitive behavioral therapy in adolescents with depression and anxiety during the COVID-19 pandemic: feasibility and acceptability study. JMIR Format. Res. **6**(11), e40242 (2022)
13. World Health Organization (2019). https://www.who.int/teams/mental-health-and-substance-use/data-research/suicide-data
14. Pargman, T.C., Sporrong, E., Farazouli, A., McGrath, C.: Beyond the hype: towards a critical debate about AI chatbots in Swedish higher education. Högre utbildning **14**(1), 74–81 (2024)
15. Quellec, G., et al.: Predicting suicidal ideation from irregular and incomplete time series of questionnaires in a smartphone-based suicide prevention platform: a pilot study. Sci. Rep. **14**(1), 20870 (2024)
16. Shetty, M., Shah, P., Shah, K., Shinde, V., Nehete, S.: Therapy chatbot powered by artificial intelligence: a cognitive behavioral approach. In: 2023 International Conference in Advances in Power, Signal, and Information Technology (APSIT), pp. 457–462 (2023). https://doi.org/10.1109/APSIT58554.2023.10201725
17. Snowdon, J.: Differences between patterns of suicide in East Asia and the West. the importance of sociocultural factors. Asian J. Psychiatry **37**, 106–111 (2018). https://doi.org/10.1016/j.ajp.2018.08.019, https://www.sciencedirect.com/science/article/pii/S1876201818304969
18. Sudarshan, S., Mehrotra, S.: Suicide prevention mobile apps for Indian users: an overview. Cureus **13**(7) (2021)
19. Sworna, Z.T., Urzedo, D., Hoskins, A.J., Robinson, C.J.: The ethical implications of chatbot developments for conservation expertise. AI Ethics, 1–10 (2024)
20. Tang, H., et al.: Analysis and evaluation of explainable artificial intelligence on suicide risk assessment. Sci. Rep. **14**(1), 6163 (2024)

ResNet50-Based Medicinal Plant Leaf Classification

Asmita Manna(✉), Ganesh Deshmukh, Vishwajeet Koshti, Shrikant Jadhao, Prathamesh Gole, and Aditya Gorane

Department of Computer Engineering, PCCoE, Pune, India
{asmita.manna,ganesh.deshmukh,vishwajeet.koshti,shrikant.jadhao, prathamesh.gole,aditya.gorane}@pccoepune.org

Abstract. Identifying medicinal plants is important for their use in medicine and other areas. Plants can be recognized with the help of leaves and their parameters, like margin, texture, shape, etc. Laboratory-based testing involves lengthy procedures as well as the need for expertise with sample handling and data interpretation. This has to do with image processing and machine learning. Hence, this study highlights advancements in technology, particularly in image processing and machine learning, and explores the use of texture and shape features in classifying plants using classifiers like CNN, KNN, ANN, SVM, and PNN. The implementation shows the practical use of the ResNet50 model for the precise identification of medicinal plants. Using the Indian Medicinal Plant Leaf Image Dataset, which has 6900 images in 80 classes, this implementation uses the ResNet50 model to accurately identify medicinal plants. After preprocessing, training, and assessment on a separate test dataset, our model yielded an impressive accuracy of 87.43%.

Keywords: Medicinal plants identification · Image Machine Learning Algorithms · Convolutional Neural Network (CNN) · ResNet50

1 Introduction

Without plants, humans cannot live on the planet; without them, we are unable to imagine what life would be like [1]. In addition to being the main source of the oxygen we need and the foundation of our food chain, plants also serve as shelter, a source of renewable resources, and an improvement to the quality of the air and water. People throughout the world have used medicinal plants for healing for a very long time. Classifying medicinal plants is beneficial to humans in many ways; hence, it is necessary to solve this issue [2].

The science of identifying, classifying, defining, and naming plants is known as plant taxonomy. Among the methods used in this science are morphological, anatomical, and chemotaxonomic classifications [3]. Morphological and anatomical classifications are thought to be more conventional than chemotaxonomies [4]. The use of scientific nomenclature in standard keys makes plant identification difficult, time-consuming, and confusing for non-botanists. It also presents a significant barrier for beginners seeking to gain specialized knowledge [5].

K. Chandra Mondal et al. (Eds.): CICBA 2025, CCIS 2863, pp. 124–136, 2026.
https://doi.org/10.1007/978-3-032-17184-9_10

While some researchers utilize texture features, others use form features. Utilizing classifiers such as CNN, SIFT, KNN, ANN, PNN, SVM, and others, it is possible to divide plants into the right species [6]. This paper examines how image processing and machine learning techniques have converged and assesses the improvements that have occurred in this area, with a focus on the most recent methodologies and technique developments after an initial algorithmic analysis.

The increasing global demand for medicinal plants requires efficient identification methods to ensure proper utilization and conservation. The shortage of trained taxonomists worldwide creates a significant bottleneck in plant identification processes. Additionally, the potential for misidentification of medicinal plants poses serious health risks, emphasizing the need for accurate, automated systems.

The major contributions of this paper are as follows:

- A comprehensive analysis of previous research on medicinal plant identification using image processing and machine learning highlights the current state-of-the-art and identifies research gaps.
- The algorithmic study of various machine learning classifiers like CNN, KNN, and SVM to determine their effectiveness in classifying medicinal plants aids in identifying the most suitable classifiers.
- The paper employs the ResNet50 model, a convolutional neural network, to identify medicinal plants, achieving an accuracy of 87.43% on the "Indian Medicinal Leaves Image Datasets" of 6900 images across 80 classes.

The rest of the study is outlined as follows: Sect. 2 is the literature review of the main concepts related to the study. In Sect. 3, various classifiers and their uses are covered in an algorithmic survey for machine learning-based identification of medicinal plants. In Sect. 4, important studies and developments are highlighted as the field's current state is examined. In Sect. 5, the effectiveness and performance of medicinal plant identification classifiers are compared and evaluated. Finally, Sect. 6 describes the methodology used in the research, including machine learning classifiers and image processing methods, and their results.

2 Literature Review

The Multi-Layer Perceptron (MLP) in a study that used feature vectors to examine the morphological characteristics of green leaves for plant identification produced a 94.5% recognition rate [7]. Using 11 textural factors, the study [8] created a database of 127 different herbal leaves. The dissimilarity between a test image and the database was then calculated to determine which leaf differed the least.

Ayur Leaf is a Deep Learning CNN model [9] that classifies medicinal plants based on the form, size, color, and texture of their leaves. A consistent dataset of leaf samples from 40 species was used by researchers from Kerala, India. In their study of statistical analysis of picture features for automated identification of Ayurvedic medicinal herbs, Viswanath Talasila and E. Sandeep Kumar [10] found that the distinguishing traits of eleven plant species have a Gaussian distribution, allowing for accurate classification.

Preprocessing the captured photographs to extract useful information from the leaves, cropping the regions of interest in the original shots, and converting the colorful images into grayscale representations using RGB to grayscale (GL) transformation are examples of image processing techniques. Techniques for edge/line detection, such as Gaussian and Sobel filters, are employed for picture augmentation and feature extraction.

To categorize medicinal plant leaves and gather related medical data, a computer vision-based method was presented by [11]. Preprocessing, feature extraction, classification, retrieval of medicinal qualities, and a Probabilistic Neural Network classifier are all included in this technique. Classification is done using SoftMax and Support Vector Machine classifiers, while feature extraction is done using a deep neural network based on the Alex Net model. The classification accuracy for the Ayur Leaf dataset was 96.76%.

Recent studies have incorporated sophisticated CNN architectures for plant classification. Studies utilizing VGG16 and VGG19 models reported accuracy rates of 97.8% and 97.6% respectively, for Ayurvedic medicinal plant species identification [12]. These results highlighted the superiority of deep learning approaches over traditional methods.

Various classification algorithms have been evaluated for plant identification tasks. Support Vector Machines (SVM) demonstrated effectiveness in high-dimensional feature spaces, while Random Forest classifiers showed robustness to overfitting and provided feature importance analysis [13]. K-Nearest Neighbors (KNN) algorithms offered simplicity but faced computational complexity challenges with large datasets.

The goal of machine learning is to let vast volumes of data determine the methods and solutions for challenging issues. Additionally, it is necessary to compare machine learning with the conventional method of relying on subject-matter experts to deliver answers [14]. Paper [15] focuses on machine learning algorithms to get the right results. Three algorithms—the logistic regression method, the k-nearest neighbour technique, and the random forest algorithm—are used to Separate rare medicinal plants from non-medicinal species. The MATLAB region props table was used to extract features from the image after background noise was eliminated using the Otsu technique [16]. The model was trained and evaluated for the recognition of medicinal plants using logistic regression, random forest, and K-nearest Neighbour to compare accuracy.

A machine learning approach, a random forest classifier, and a Machine Learning Convolutional Neural Network (CNN) have been used to develop a unique photo collection for medicinal plants in Mauritius [17]. The Random Forest classifier has a 90.1% accuracy rate and uses decision trees to predict leaf morphology, texture, and colour [12]. Increased local knowledge and species preservation are the project's [18] goals. CNNs have transformed image processing operations by identifying intricate patterns and structures in plant pictures, which enables the recognition of fine-grained plant species. With accuracy rates of 97.8% and 97.6%, respectively, a study [12] used CNN, VGG16, and VGG19 models to identify native Ayurvedic medicinal plant species. Future study with bigger datasets and video-based plant recognition is recommended, with possible uses in botanical studies and Ayurvedic medicine.

J. Samuel Manoharan [19] points out that the absence of dimensional parameters in existing algorithms makes it difficult to identify leaves in all seasons. He suggests the Two-Stage Authentication (TSA) method, which incorporates di-dimensional variables, machine learning classifiers, and XOR gate operation. 95% efficiency and 92% accuracy are achieved by the Sobel operator. Nevertheless, the approach requires a lot of storage space and computing time. Near-infrared spectroscopy (NIRS) was utilized in a study by P. Kelina Sahaya Rajesh, C. Ku- Kumaravelu, A. Gopal, and S. Suganthi to distinguish between different types of medicinal plants based on the spectral characteristics of their leaves. According to the study [20], NIRS and PCA together could accurately distinguish between various plant species, especially when looking at dry leaves, with a 98% accuracy rate.

Deep learning neural networks have been used in a study [21] to create a method for identifying herbal leaves. During testing, the approach, which combines long-short-term memory (LSTM) and convolutional neural network (CNN) approaches, demonstrated a remarkable accuracy rate of 94.96%. This novel method overcomes the drawbacks of conventional techniques that call for specific training and increases accuracy while reducing the need for herbal leaf identification experts. Traditional medicine and plant identification are greatly impacted by this method.

Google Lens is a vision-based computing tool that uses machine learning to recognize objects, identify plants, and perform other tasks. It uses Google Translate's neural machine translation algorithms. A study examined its effectiveness in biology education, particularly in taxonomy. An automated system for real-time plant species identification was proposed, focusing on medicinal plants in Borneo (Fig. 1).

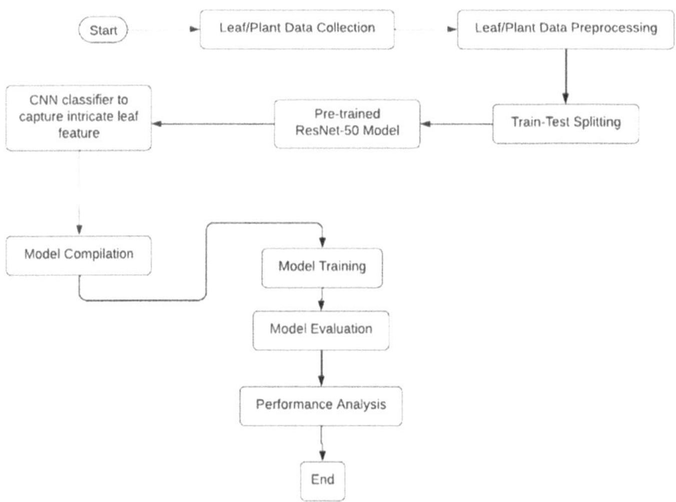

Fig. 1. System architecture

AyurLeaf, a system for classifying medicinal plants, achieved 96.76% classification accuracy on a dataset containing forty therapeutic herbs. This system fills a gap in the literature and benefits botanists and practitioners of Ayurveda medicine without requiring trained taxonomists' knowledge. However, there are still problems to be addressed, such as similarities in texture, color, and shape among classes (Fig. 2).

Fig. 2. Sample images from the Indian Leaves Image Dataset

3 Proposed Methodology

The dataset named" Indian Medicinal Leaves Image Datasets," arranged into subdirectories that correspond to various leaf groups, makes up the" Indian- medicinal-leaves-dataset" [22] dataset. The collection has 80 classes in all. Every image is kept as a file in the corresponding class subdirectory. Without regard to any environmental restrictions, the pictures are taken against a variety of backgrounds. 6900 photos were found to be part of the 80 classes during the data collection.

Preprocessing stage, showing a comprehensive and wide dataset. With 4106 photos designated for training, 1448 for testing, and 1346 for validation, the dataset was split into three sets: training, testing, and validation. To ensure a balanced distribution for model training and evaluation, this split reflects roughly 59.5% for training, 21% for testing, and 19.5% for validation. The physical properties of these images were taken out and utilized to create machine learning models that could detect therapeutic plants. Below are sample images from the Indian Leaves Image Dataset [22].

The methodology describes our complete flow of medicinal plant identification. Here are the following steps in detail:

Image Preprocessing. In an attempt to improve the clarity of structural and textural features in leaf images, image processing techniques such as Sobel edge detection and grayscale transformation were used in this study. Sobel filters successfully emphasized leaf boundaries, and grayscale conversion simplified the data by concentrating on important texture and shape characteristics. Quantitative measures like contrast (160.9967), energy (0.0197), and homogeneity (0.1634) confirmed the extraction of pertinent features, which helped the model be accurate.

Image Augmentation. It was necessary to preprocess the incoming images, and each one was enlarged to 224 × 224 pixels with 4 channels (alpha and RGB). Using a sequential model, data augmentation techniques such as horizontal flipping, rotation (up to 20%), height shifting (up to 20%), zooming (up to 20%), and width shifting (up to 20%) were implemented.

Medicinal Leaf/Plant Classification using ResNet50. The starting point for our concept was the ResNet50 architecture. This convolutional neural network (CNN) architecture is well-liked and comes with pre-trained weights. With With these pre-trained weights, we were able to take advantage of the extensive dataset information that it has acquired. We froze the base model's layers to prevent them from being modified during training, ensuring that their features would always be relevant. Before feeding photos into the ResNet50 model, we integrated a step-by-step data augmentation procedure during the model's construction. As a result, we were able to dynamically add to the dataset and train the model using a variety of versions of the same image. Consequently, this improved the model's capacity to acquire substantial features.

We pre-processed the images using the TensorFlow library's ImageDataGenerator class to ensure they were scaled to 224 × 224 pixels and turned into arrays. Next, we loaded a ResNet50 model that had already been trained. By training the model for 20 epochs, ResNet50 is a deep convolutional neural network that is well-known for its efficiency in image identification tasks. The model was assembled using the Adam optimizer and the categorical cross-entropy loss function.

ResNet50 is well-suited for the task of medicinal plant identification, where fine-grained detection of plant species from photographs is crucial, because of its depth and skip connections, which allow it to learn complicated patterns and features from photos. Moreover, ResNet50 leverages the data collected from several image datasets to enable transfer learning for specific plant identification tasks, having been pretrained on large datasets like ImageNet.

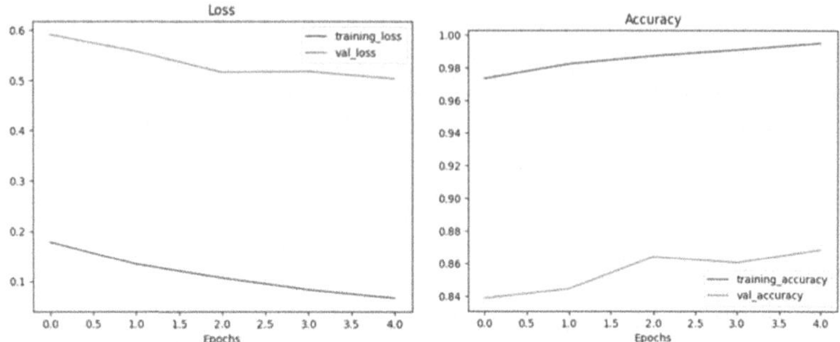

Fig. 3. Training and Validation Accuracy/Loss Curves of the Proposed Model

4 Results

The performance metrics are calculated using the following formulas (Fig. 3):

$$\text{Accuracy} = \frac{\sum_{i=1}^{n} TP_i}{\sum_{i=1}^{n} (TP_i + FP_i)} \tag{1}$$

$$\text{Recall} = \frac{1}{n}\sum_{i=1}^{n} \frac{TP_i}{TP_i + FN_i} \tag{2}$$

$$\text{F1Score} = \frac{1}{n}\sum_{i=1}^{n} \frac{2 \times \text{Precision}_i \times \text{Recall}_i}{\text{Precision}_i + \text{Recall}_i} \tag{3}$$

$$\text{Precision} = \frac{1}{n}\sum_{i=1}^{n} \frac{TP_i}{TP_i + FP_i} \tag{4}$$

where n is the number of classes, which is 80. TP_i is the number of true positives for class i. FP_i is the number of false positives for class i. FN_i is the number of false negatives for class i. TN_i is the number of true negatives for class i.

The methodology we used gave accurate identification of medicinal plants with a high True Positives (TP) of 1237 and accurate categorization of non-medicinal plants with a high True Negatives (TN) of 114181. For increased recall and precision, it is required to lower the FP and FN rates, which were 211. By using the previously mentioned formulas (1), (2), (3), and (4), we were able to acquire the testing results that are shown in Tables 1, 2 and 3.

Table 1. Comparative Study of Different Classifiers for Medicinal Plant Identification

Ref	Classification Techniques	Advantages	Disadvantages
[5, 6]	Kth Nearest Neighbor (KNN)	1. Simplest Straight for ward. 2. No Assumptions. 3. No training phase; efficient with changing datasets. 4. Versatility for classification and regression tasks	1. Lazy learner. 2. High computational complexity, especially with large datasets. 3. Difficulty in choosing the optimal value
[3, 6, 9, 12, 18 21]	Convolutional Neural Network (CNN)	1. Effective for image-related tasks. 2. Hierarchical feature learning. 3. Translation invariance. 4. Transfer learning capabilities	1. Complexity in design and training. 2. Large datasets are often required. 3. Limited interpretability. 4. May not be suitable for all data types or tasks
[3, 5]	Random forest	1. High accuracy and over-fitting reduction. 2. Feature importance for selection. 3. Robust to outliers and handles mixed data. 4. Parallel processing for faster training	1. Complexity and longer training with many trees. 2. Limited interpretability. 3. Resource-intensive for large datasets. 4. Biased towards the majority class in imbalanced- data

(continued)

Table 1. (*continued*)

Ref	Classification Techniques	Advantages	Disadvantages
[3, 6, 11]	Support Vector Machine (SVM)	1. Good generalization capacity-ability 2. Spareness of the solution and the capacity control obtained by optimizing the margin. 3. Effective in high-dimensional data	1. Primarily designed for biNary classification. 2. Slow training. 3. It is difficult to understand the algorithm's structure

Table 2. Performance Analysis of Existing Methods

Ref	Year	Dataset	Methods	Accuracy
[3]	2018	600 images From Department of Health	SVM	93.3%
			Random forest	90.1%
			Multiclass SVM	93.26%
			CNN(VGG16)	96.6%
[4]	2019	20 Ayurvedic leaves of 40 species	Sobel Operator	86%
			Canny Edge detector	80%
			TSA algorithm	92%
[5]	2018	Medicinal Plants from Mauritius	k-NN (k = 1)	82.5%
			Random Forest	90.1%
			MLP Neural Network	88.2%
[21]	2022	Medicinal leaf dataset Mendeley	MobileNetV2-Softmax	97.62%
			InceptionV2-Softmax	98.64%
			ResNet50-Softmax	98.91%
			EDL-AMLI	99.66%

Table 3. Testing Performance

Parameters	Testing Performance (Percentage)
Accuracy	87.43
Recall	85.43
F-score	85.32

(*continued*)

Table 3. *(continued)*

Parameters	Testing Performance (Percentage)
Precision	87.09

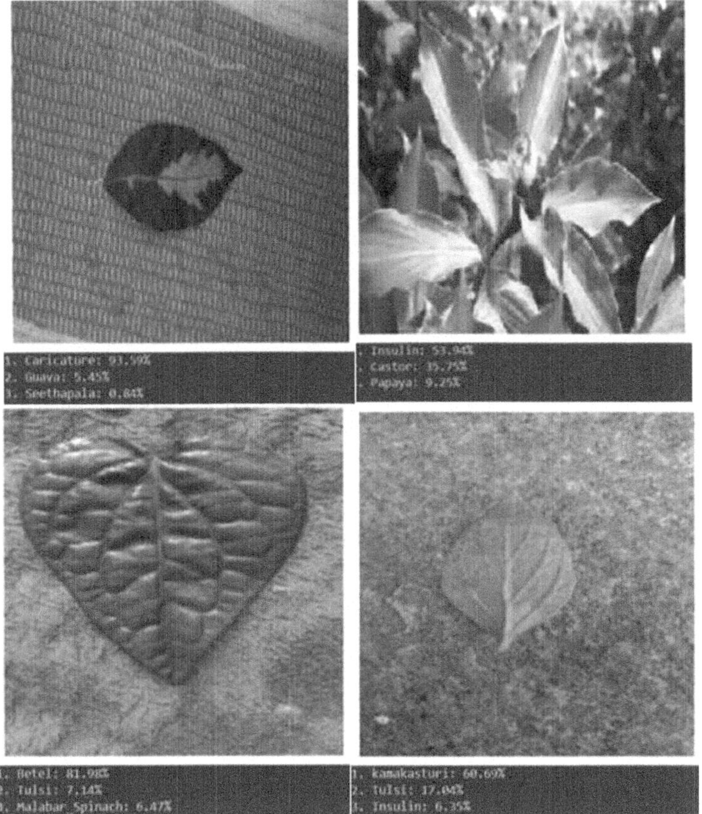

Fig. 4. Testing Leaf Images with Predicted Class Labels and Confidence Scores

Figure 5 illustrates the results of testing the leaf images using the trained classification model. Each image is displayed along with its predicted class label and the corresponding confidence score, indicating the model's certainty in its prediction (Fig. 4).

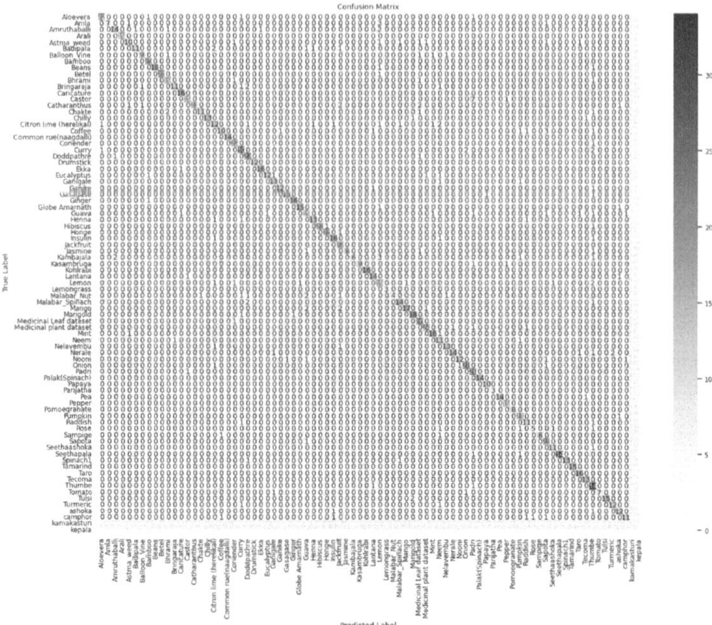

Fig. 5. Confusion matrix

To predict the classes of medicinal plants, the procedure involves loading a picture, preprocessing it, and running it through a trained model. The predictions are then sorted, and the top 3 expected classes are displayed together with their confidence scores, making it possible to identify medicinal plants from the input image. The results are presented together in order with the appropriate confidence levels.

5 Conclusion

The survival of life on Earth depends heavily on the presence of plants. Finding the appropriate medicinal plant is beneficial to humankind. In this article, we examined several machine learning algorithms, approaches, and current systems. Those who are unable to use traditional methods can benefit from the non-destructive method of identifying medicinal plants by their leaves using computer vision. It explores a range of classifiers, including KNN, CNN, Random Forest, and SVM. 80 classifications and 6900 pictures make up the" Indian- medicinal-leaves-dataset" dataset, which was used to build machine learning models for identifying medicinal plants. The model showcased its effectiveness in fine-grained plant identification tasks by achieving an accuracy of 87.43% in recognizing medicinal plant species from images by utilizing ResNet50 architecture and data augmentation approaches. We wish to study further methods and conduct tests with different methods in the future. Based on our experience with this project, future work could include:

i. Collecting more diverse datasets with different lighting and environmental conditions

ii. Implementing ensemble methods to combine multiple models Including other plant parts like flowers and fruits for better identification.

References

1. Wang, E.J., Cui, J., Wang, Z., Kang, J., Min, Y.: Leaf image recognition based on bag of features. Appl. Sci. **10**, 5177 (2020)
2. Barimah, K.B., Akotia, C.S.: The promotion of traditional medicine as enactment of community psychology in Ghana. J. Community Psychol. **43**(1), 99–106 (2015)
3. Singh, R.: Geetanjali: Chemotaxonomy of Medicinal Plants: Possibilities and Limitations. Elsevier, Amsterdam (2018)
4. Simpson, M.G.: Plant anatomy and physiology. In: Plant Systematics, pp. 537–566. Elsevier (2019)
5. Waldchen, J., Mader, P.: Plant species identification using computer vision techniques: a systematic literature review. Arch. Comput. Methods Eng. **25**(2), 507–543 (2018)
6. Lasseck, M.: Image-based plant species identification with deep convolutional neural networks. In: CEUR Workshop Proceedings 1866 (2017)
7. Manojkumar, P., Surya, C.M., Varun, P.G.: Identification of Ayurvedic medicinal plants by image processing of leaf samples. In: Third International Conference on Research in Computational Intelligence and Communication Network, pp. 1–5 (2017)
8. Vijayashree, T., Gopal, A.: Leaf identification for the extraction of medicinal qualities using image processing algorithm. In: International Conference on Intelligent Computing and Control, pp. 1–6 (2017)
9. Dileep, M.R., Pournami, P.N.: AyurLeaf: a deep learning approach for classification- tion of medicinal plants. In: TENCON 2019 - 2019 IEEE Region 10 Conference, pp. 1–6 (2019)
10. Kumar, E.S., Talasila, V.: Leaf features-based approach for automated identification of medicinal plants. In: International Conference on Communication and Signal Processing, pp. 1–5 (2014)
11. Venkataraman, D., Mangayarkarasi, N.: Computer vision-based feature extraction of leaves for identification of medicinal values of plants. In: IEEE International Conference on Computational Intelligence and Computing Research, pp. 1–5 (2016)
12. Azadnia, R., Al-Amidi, M.M., Mohammadi, H., Cifci, M.A., Daryab, A., Cavallo, E.: An AI-based approach for medicinal plant identification using deep CNN based on global average pooling. Inter. J. Agronomy (2022)
13. Begue, A., Kowlessur, V., Mahomoodally, F., Singh, U., Pudaruth, S.: Automatic recognition of medicinal plants using machine learning techniques. Inter. J. Adv. Comput. Sci. Appli. **8**(4) (2017)
14. Sarraf, A., Azhdari, M., Sarraf, S.: A comprehensive review of deep learning architectures for computer vision applications. Am. Sc. Res. J. Eng. Technol. Sci. **77**(1), 1–29 (2021)
15. Preethi, S., Varshitha, Princy, J., Gowda, A., Priyadarshini, A.: Identification and classification of rare medicinal plants using machine learning techniques. IRJET (2022)
16. Naeem, S., Ali, A., Chesneau, C., Tahir, M.H., Jamal, F.: The classification of medicinal plant leaves based on multispectral and texture features using a machine learning approach. Agronomy **11**(2) (2021)
17. Paulson, A., Ravishankar, S.: AI-based indigenous medicinal plant identification. Auckland University of Technology (2020)
18. Rao, M.S., Kumar, S.P., Rao, K.S.: A methodology for identification of Ayurvedic plant based on machine learning. Inter. J. Comput. Digital Syst. (2021)

19. Manoharan, J.S.: Flawless detection of herbal plant leaf by machine learning classifier through two-stage authentication procedure. J. Artifi. Intell. Capsule Netw. **3**(2) (2021)
20. Rajesh, P.K.S., Kumaravelu, C., Gopal, A., Suganthi, S.: Studies on identification of medicinal plant variety based on NIR spectroscopy using plant leaves. In: 15th International Conference on Advanced Computing Technologies, pp. 1–5 (2013)
21. Sachar, S., Kumar, A.: Deep ensemble learning for automatic medicinal leaf identification. Int. J. Inf. Technol. **14**(6), 3089–3097 (2022)
22. Pushpa, B.R., Rani, S.: Indian medicinal leaves image datasets. Mendeley Data V3 (2021)

An Alarming Threat of Light Pollution in Ahmedabad City: Efficient Time-Series Forecasting Framework

Saikat Mondal[1,3](✉), Pragna Labani Sikdar[2], and Parag Kumar Guha Thakurta[1]

[1] Department of Computer Science and Engineering, NIT Durgapur, Durgapur, India
paragkumar.guhathakurta@cse.nitdgp.ac.in

[2] Department of CSE (IoT), Techno Main Salt Lake, West Bengal, Kolkata, India
pl.sikdar_iot@tmslcollege.in

[3] Institute of Engineering and Management, Kolkata, West Bengal, India
sm.24cs1501@nitdgp.ac.in, saikat.mondal@iem.edu.in

Abstract. Light pollution, often an overlooked environmental challenge, is rapidly becoming a significant concern for Indian urban cities due to the accelerating pace of urbanization and infrastructural growth. The excessive and inefficient use of artificial light at night has profound implications for ecosystems, human health, and energy sustainability. This paper uses satellite-based data from the National Oceanic and Atmospheric Administration's (NOAA, US) Visible Infrared Imaging Radiometer Suite (VIIRS) in Ahmedabad, India, to analyse and forecast changes in light pollution from 2014 to 2022. According to the proposed the seasonal autoregressive integrated moving average with exogenous regressor forecast for Ahmedabad, India, the radiance levels keep rising, and in the absence of mitigating measures, worsening the negative impacts on energy use, human health, and biodiversity. This study highlights the utility of remote sensing and time-series forecasting techniques in understanding and addressing urban environmental challenges.

Keywords: Light pollution · Time-series · Forecasting · Radiance · Prediction error

1 Introduction

Light pollution occurs for an undesirable or misdirected artificial light produced by human beings and industrial activities. It can disrupt the normal darkness in the night sky [4,10,13]. This form of pollution is primarily caused by streetlights, vehicle headlights, illuminated billboards, and residential or commercial lighting which are inefficiently designed. It has adverse effects on animals, and overuse lighting systems which can contribute to significant energy waste and carbon emissions [14]. Intrusive artificial night lights spreading into the areas, such as a neighbour's property, natural habitats of humans or animals, are not needed.

K. Chandra Mondal et al. (Eds.): CICBA 2025, CCIS 2863, pp. 137–150, 2026.
https://doi.org/10.1007/978-3-032-17184-9_11

The excessive grouping of bright, confusing, or uncoordinated light sources, can be seen particularly in urban environments. Hence, human-made lights at night are considered to be major components of light pollution in the land and subsequently it can affect aquatic environments of the earth [6,11,12].

Light pollution has long-term effects on animal populations and affects the structure of our ecosystem [8]. By interfering with nocturnal animals' natural behaviors, like migration, [18] and reproduction [7]. All species, including fishes, amphibians, coral reefs, reptiles, birds, and mammals, are harmed by artificial nightlights. Because of the reflected light surfaces, birds collide with the buildings [2]. When the surrounding is exposed to artificial light at night (ALAN), Indian house crows are needed longer training sessions to learn the location of food than when there was no light at night [1]. On the other hand, the long-term artificial light exposure at night can alter circadian rhythms, which may result in sleep issues and mental health issues, behavioral changes [9,21] and metabolism [17]. Overly bright lighting that impairs visibility and safety for pedestrians and drivers or causes visual discomfort (glare). In contrast to the natural darkness of the past, the city night may now witness fewer celestial objects with astronomy instruments due to night sky brightness that impairs human vision and observation of the universe [5]. Star visibility is significantly impacted by artificial light pollution that brightens the sky [3,20].

In the previous work, Riza et al. (2023) [15] build a linear model involving population data and brightness in geospatial datasets. It has Predicted light pollution of nine conservation areas in Indonesia in long term. Moreover, it simulated the experimental study for the long-term predictions into two stages: fitting and testing, analyzed results in terms of accuracy and computational cost for every conservation area. In order to ascertain whether or not a region is affected by light pollution, Sainger et al. (2023) [16] have presented a mathematical model using machine learning (ML). A comparison of mathematical models and ML is used to forecast light pollution.

Ahmedabad, as one of India's largest cities, has seen significant urbanization and population growth in recent years. Estimating Ahmedabad's light pollution offers a chance to strike a balance between the city's expanding infrastructure requirements and the preservation of the environment, public health, and the inherent beauty of the night sky. In this context, light pollution datasets, collected from satellites (e.g., VIIRS) can show varying radiometric calibration, leading to inconsistencies such as values being fetched as zero. These VIIRS data sets are on a monthly or yearly basis, making it hard to capture short-term variations. Spatial resolution (500 m by 500 m) can result in the inability to detect small-scale changes in urban light sources, such as specific neighborhoods or regions. Temporary increases in light use can create outliers in the data, making predictions less reliable. Rapid urbanization or infrastructure projects can cause sudden spikes, which are hard to model without external data input. Thus, it motivates city planners, legislators, and environmentalists to take proactive measures to lessen its effects by forecasting how this will develop.

This paper analyzes the light pollution data collected from VIIRS portal created by the National Oceanic and Atmospheric Ad- ministration's (NOAA) Earth observation group, which is a key resource for accessing nighttime data. The time series monthly mean of light pollution of Ahmedabad city is taken from VIIRS repository, then analysis of time series with SARIMAX is performed, and the radiance is predicted for next five years. The proposed methodology uses two basic steps: the first step is data pre-processing. The second step includes the Augmented Dickey-Fuller (ADF) test for SARIMAX analysis and forecast the Ljung-Box for the correctness of the SARIMAX model fit. The average radiance of 2014–2022 and the forecasted dataset of 2023–2027 are found to be increasing. The Ljung-Box test is a positive indication of model fit for the prediction. Thus, the results for Ahmedabad from different years show a distribution of radiance that grows over a period of time. In addition, the effectiveness of the proposed approach over existing models is shown.

The rest of the paper is organized as follows: Sect. 2 describes the material and methods used for the proposed work. Simulation results and discussion are shown in Sect. 3. Finally, the paper is concluded in Sect. 4.

2 Materials and Methods

The proposed work follows two steps as shown in Fig. 1. In the first step, data pre-processing is carried out. The second step includes the ADF test for SARIMAX analysis and forecast and the Ljung-Box test for the correctness of the SARIMAX model fit.

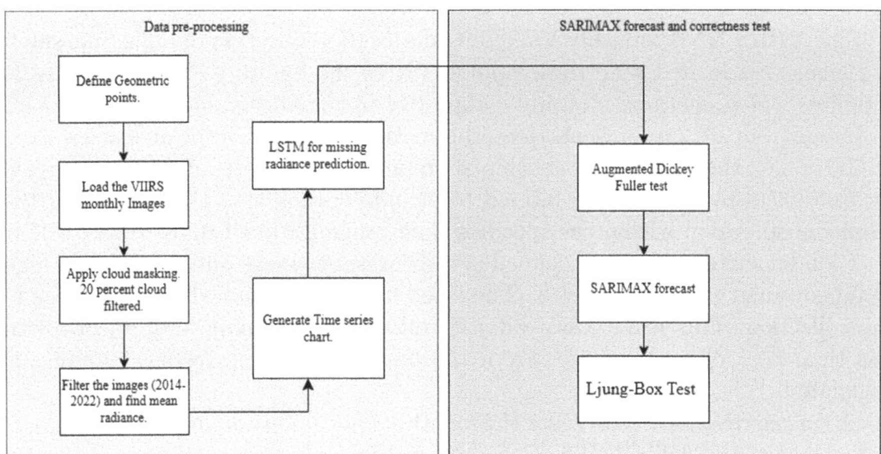

Fig. 1. Workflow diagram of the proposed work.

2.1 Data Set and Its Pre-processing

A geographical point is created for Ahmedabad using its coordinates [72.5714, 23.0225], which is shown in Fig. 2(a). Here, Longitude, or East-West location and latitude, or North-South location of the Ahmedabad city are indicated as 72.5714 and 23.0225, respectively. The surrounding of these geometric points are shown in Fig. 2(b). This point acts as the region of interest (ROI) for the analysis. All the operations including filtering images, extracting data, and calculating statistics are performed by the Google Earth Engine (GEE) over this specific point.

Fig. 2. (a) Geometric Point (b) Surroundings of Geometric Point.

The VIIRS DNB Monthly VCMCFG dataset (a collection of nighttime satellite images) is loaded with these points. VIIRS the Suomi NPP and NOAA-20 satellites which contains monthly composites of radiance values with temporal Coverage from 2012 to present. Here, the spatial resolution of the analysis is fixed at 500 m, i.e., the resolution of each pixel represents the radiance of the encircled area of 500 m by 500 m. It is filtered to include only images that can cover the Ahmedabad region within the specified date range (2014-01-01 to 2023-01-01).

Cloud masking is already defined in the dataset to mask out images with high cloud coverage greater than 80% .The cloud masking is applied to each image in the collection. This results in a filtered collection containing only images with less than 80% cloud coverage. From the image collection, average radiance is calculated.

A time-series chart represents the monthly light pollution in terms of average radiance over the defined ROI. The chart in Fig. 3 shows the mean radiance (in $nW/cm^2/sr$) for every month. Here, the X axis indicates the date (here the last day of a month), and the Y axis indicates the corresponding mean radiance in $nW/cm^2/sr$ of that month. It is observed that some data are missing in Fig. 3, represented by a zero value as radiance. This is obtained due to the calibration error of the satellite.

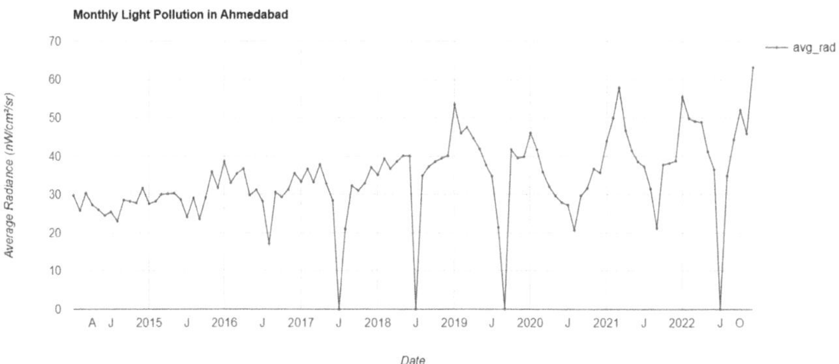

Fig. 3. Average radiance Time series plot from 2014 to 2022- Date vs. Average Radiance.

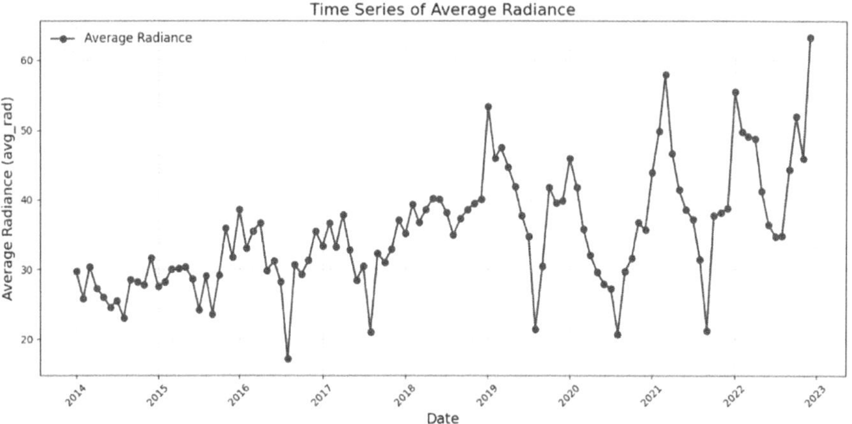

Fig. 4. Time series plot from 2014 to 2022 with forecasted values: Date vs. Average Radiance.

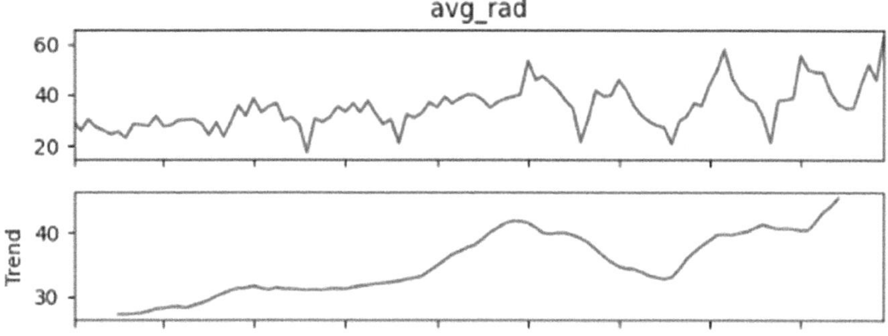

Fig. 5. Average radiance time series and its trend

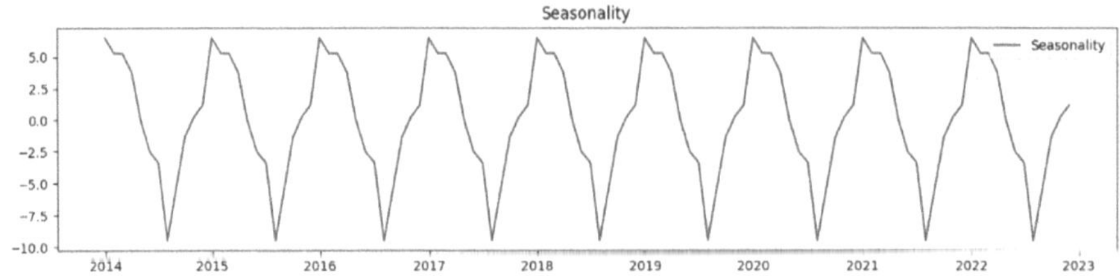

Fig. 6. Seasonality pattern of Average radiance time series.

As the time series data depends on past values, the Long Short Term Memory (LSTM) algorithm is used to obtain the missing values of these data, which is shown in Fig. 4. Figure 5 shows the monthly average radiance data of artificial night lights in Ahmedabad city are growing steadily.

Also, there is increased pollution in between the 1st quarter and the 2nd quarter of the year and decreased pollution in the 3rd quarter of the year. This seasonality pattern shown in Fig. 6 is found nearly every year from the start to the end of the time series graph as per Fig. 4. This seasonality pattern represents the values ranging from 10 to 5 to every radiance value in the time series graph.

2.2 Proposed Methodology

In the proposed work, ADF statistics are used to test whether the obtained pre-processed time series data are stationary or fluctuating over the specified time. This ADF is performed to check the suitability of seasonal autoregressive integrated moving average (SARIMA) or the seasonal autoregressive integrated moving average with exogenous regressors (SARIMAX). It shows the values of ADF Statistic: −0.6724420372156023 and p-value: 0.8537591367701656. The ADF statistic compares with the critical values (typically at one percent, five percent, and ten percent levels of significance) to determine if the null hypothesis (H0) can be rejected. Here, the null hypothesis (H0) indicates that the series has a unit root (non-stationary). On the other hand, alternate hypothesis (H1) specifies the series as stationary.

In the proposed work, a more negative ADF statistic suggests that the stronger evidence against H0 is non-stationary. Here, the value -0.672 (approx.) is not very negative, which clearly indicates weak evidence to reject H0. The p-value of 0.85380 is much greater than 0.05, indicating there is no such support to reject H0 at the five percent significance level. This indicates the time series likely has a unit root and is dynamic over the period of time. To confirm, a comparison is required between the ADF statistics and the critical values. If the statistic is less than the critical value, reject H0. Since the p-value is already high, the ADF statistic is likely greater than all critical values. Due to the non-stationary and strong seasonality pattern, the SARIMAX as an advanced time series forecasting model has been applied to predict this time series data. Here, SARIMAX is taking holidays as exogenous variable, so it simply reduces to SARIMAX (p, d, q) (P, D, Q, S). The components are p, d, and q, where p is the autoregressive order, d is the degree of differencing, and q is the moving average order. P, D, Q, and S define the number of seasonal autoregressive, differencing, and moving average terms, as well as the length of the seasonal cycle. Finally, the Ljung-Box(Q) test calculates the test statistics Q, which measures the difference between the observed autocorrelations and the expected autocorrelations under the null hypothesis of randomness.

3 Results and Discussion

The summary of the proposed SARIMAX model output is shown in Table 1. The variable Avg_{rad}, denoting the average radiance value throughout time is being modeled. The 108 data points in the dataset may correspond to monthly observations from the VIIRS repository spanning roughly nine years. SARIMAX (1,1,1) × (1,1,1,12) indicates non-seasonal ARIMA terms (p = 1, d = 1, q = 1) and seasonal ARIMA terms (P = 1, D = 1, Q = 1, s = 12). Here, s = 12 indicates 12 months seasonality period representing yearly seasonality. To avoid overfitting, the value of Akaike Information Criterion (AIC) is considered as 512.839. As compared to AIC, the Bayesian Information Criterion (BIC) having value 524.812 penalizes complexity more severely.

Another measure of model quality i.e., Hannan-Quinn Information Criterion (HQIC) is set with a value of 517.643. By the covariance type as opg (Outer Product of Gradients method), it indicates how the parameter standard errors are estimated. For the proposed SARIMAX model, each parameter's estimate (coef), standard error (std err) [0.264, 0.241, 0.219, 0.246, 0.179], z-statistic, and p-value (P>—z—) are provided, along with the confidence interval ([0.025, 0.975]). The outcome of these parameters are highlighted in Table 1. For this SARIMAX model, Ljung-Box (Q) test is conducted to find autocorrelation in residuals. Here, the statistic is 0.00 and the probability is 1.00 indicating no significant autocorrelation found, which in turn can indicate excellent fit of the proposed model. Furthermore, Jarque-Bera (JB) tests is conducted to check the normality of residuals. Here, the statistics are 2.85 and the probability shows as 0.24, which can show that the residuals are approximately normal. Another type of test, such as Heteroskedasticity (H), is conducted for variance consistency in residuals. Here, the statistic is 2.37 and the probability is 0.03. These results can indicate that some heteroskedasticity may be present. In addition, the Skewness and Kurtosis values are resulted into 0.16 and 3.86, respectively.

The analysis shown in Table 1 have contributed major findings. Here, the seasonality affects the data, as evidenced by the marginal significance of the seasonal elements (ar.S.L12 and ma.S.L12). The lack of statistical significance for on-seasonal components (ar.L1, ma.L1) suggests that seasonal patterns may be the main source of influence. The model residuals appear to be roughly normal and uncorrelated, supporting the validity of the model fit. Heteroskedasticity might be a concern, so it's worth checking the residuals further.

Minimum radiance is predicted as 47.202421 nW/cm^2/sr, maximum radiance predicted as 94.834894 nW/cm^2/sr, and mean radiance as 71.97 nW/cm^2/sr

Table 1. Summary of the SARIMAX model output.

Parameter/Statistic	Value	Description
Dependent variable	avg_{rad}	This variable is being modelled for average radiance.
Number of observations	108	The total number of data points in the time series.
Model	SARIMAX(1, 1, 1)×(1, 1, 1, 12)	Specifies the SARIMAX model structure with seasonal and non-seasonal components.
Log Likelihood	−251.420	A measure of model fit.
AIC	512.839	The Akaike Information Criterion is utilized for comparing models.
BIC	524.812	The Bayesian Information Criterion is used to compare models.
HQIC	517.643	The Hannan-Quinn Information Criterion is applied to compare the models.
ar.L1 (Non-Seasonal AR)	−0.1914 (P = 0.469)	Non-significant autoregressive term for lag 1 ($P > 0.05$).
ma.L1(Non-Seasonal MA)	−0.3559 (P = 0.140)	Non-significant moving average term for lag 1 ($P > 0.05$).
ar.12 (Seasonal AR)	−0.4120 (P = 0.060)	Seasonal autoregressive term with marginal significance for lag 12.
ma.S.L12(Seasonal Moving Average)	−0.4469 (P = 0.069)	Seasonal moving average phrase for lag 12 that is marginally meaningful.
sigma(Residual Variance)	28.2614 (P = 0.000)	Highly significant residual variance ($P < 0.05$).
Ljung-Box (Q)	0.00 (P = 1.00)	The residuals show no discernible autocorrelation (i.e., excellent fit).
Jarque-Bera (JB)	2.85 (P = 0.24)	Residuals are approximately normally distributed ($P > 0.05$).
Heteroskedasticity (H)	2.37 (P = 0.03)	Residuals show heteroskedasticity (variance changes over time, $P < 0.05$).
Skew	0.16	Measures the asymmetry of the distribution of the residuals.
Kurtosis	3.86	Measures the concentration of residuals in the tails and center of the distribution.

between the periods 2023 to 2027, which is shown in Fig. 7. Here, the compound annual growth rate of radiance is 8.77% from 2014 to 2022, as the radiance found in January 2014 is 29.701 $nW/cm^2/sr$ and for December 2022 is 63.3 $nW/cm^2/sr$. The compound annual growth rate of radiance expected from 2023 to 2027 for five years is 7.89% as expected in January, 2023 and December, 2027 are 63.880924 nW/cm^2/sr, and 93.390259 nW/cm^2/sr, respectively.

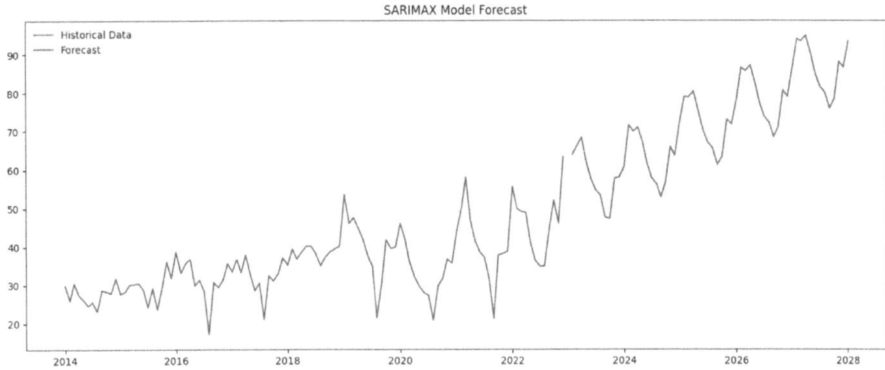

Fig. 7. SARIMAX model forecast for the next five years of data (Date vs. Average radiance).

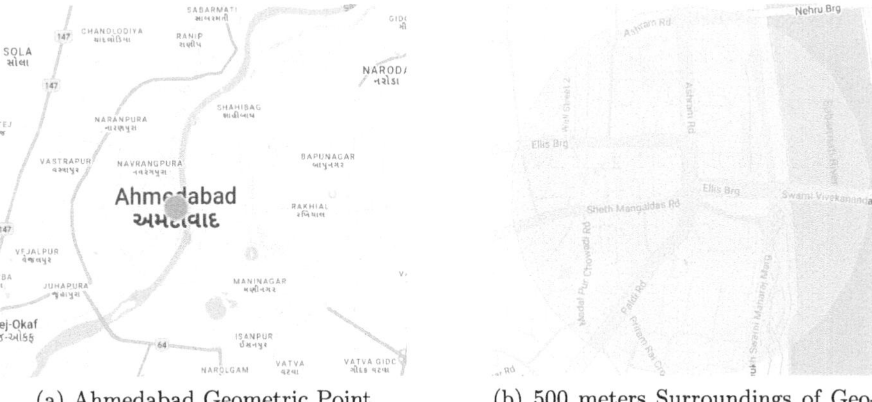

(a) Ahmedabad Geometric Point

(b) 500 meters Surroundings of Geometric Point

Fig. 8. (a) Ahmedabad Geometric Point; (b) 500 m Surroundings of Geometric Point.

The radiance at the 500-m range surrounding of [72.5714, 23.0225] location shown in Fig. 8(a) and Fig. 8(b) indicates an increase in radiance from 2014 to 2022, which is shown in Fig. 9. Now, employing the LSTM as discussed earlier, all the missing values of [72.5714, 23.0225] with a radius of 500 (Fig. 9) has been computed and it is shown in Fig. 10. Over a period of nine years, the Compound Annual Growth Rate (CAGR) is roughly 3.81% annually, as the radiance found in January 2014 is 38.473 nW/cm^2/sr and for December 2022 is

53.888nW/cm^2/sr. The compound annual growth rate of radiance expected from 2023 to 2027 for five years is 2.93% as expected in January, 2023 and December, 2027 are 54.414150 nW/cm^2/sr, and 62.863920 nW/cm^2/sr, respectively. In addition, the radiance distribution of 2014 and 2022 can show a significant difference. The color palettes shown in Fig. 11 are used as light blue and red. Here, the light blue pixels indicate radiance up to 20 nW/cm^2/sr; other pixels can represent red colors.

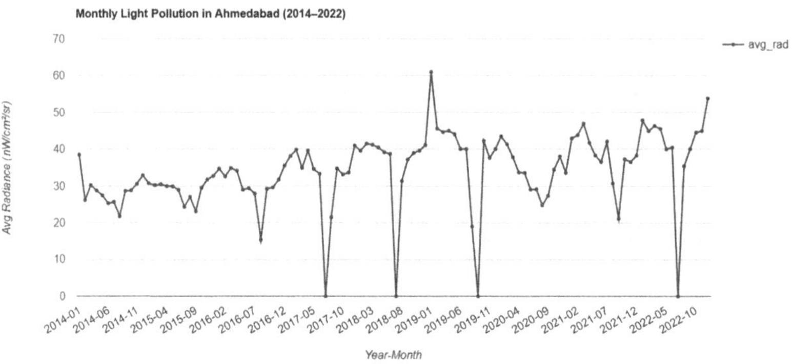

Fig. 9. Average radiance with 500 m radius Time series plot from 2014 to 2022- Date vs. Average Radiance.

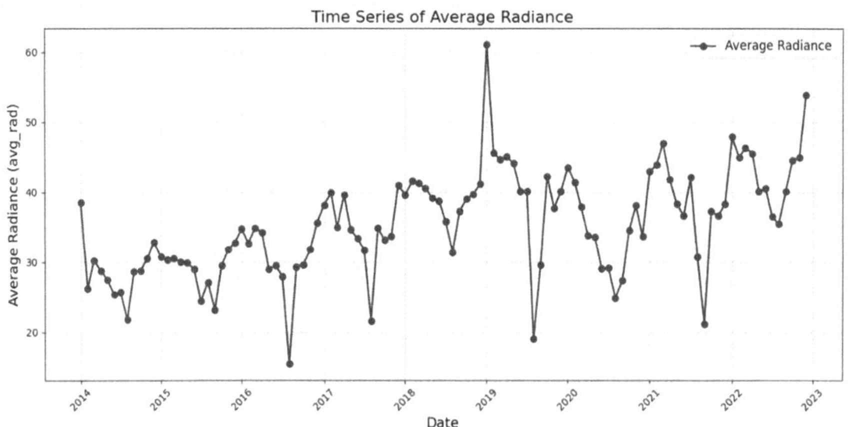

Fig. 10. Average radiance with 500 m radius Time series plot from 2014 to 2022- Date vs. Average Radiance.

Both autocorrelation and partial autocorrelation presented in Fig. 12 can show the range from 1 to around −0.25. The autocorrelation showing the current

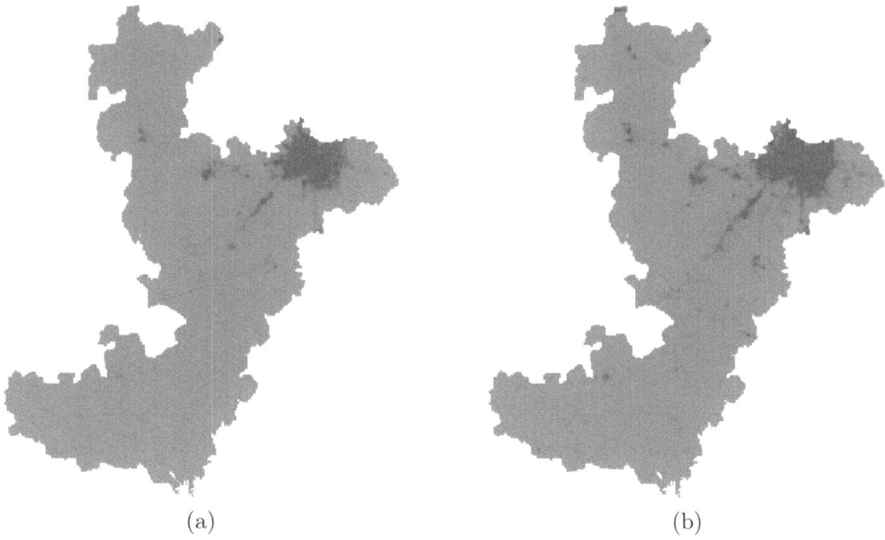

(a) (b)

Fig. 11. (a) Radiance distribution of Ahmedabad, India.2014. (b) Radiance distribution of Ahmedabad, India.2022. (Color figure online)

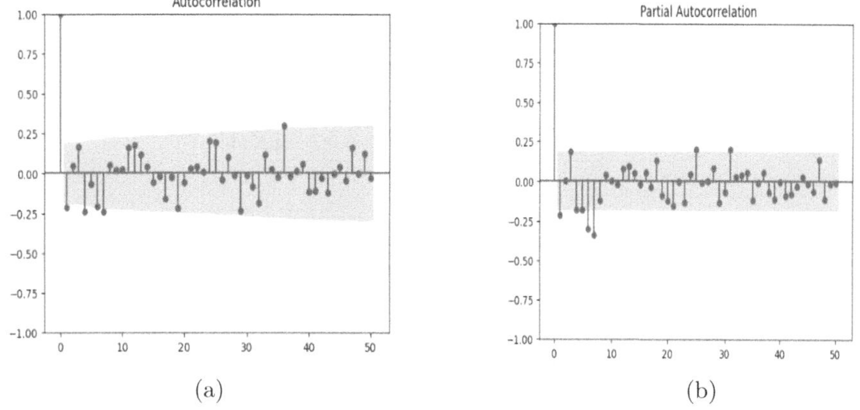

(a) (b)

Fig. 12. Autocorrelation and partial autocorrelation.

value of a variable, i.e., average radiance, is related to its past values which can help to detect patterns like trends, seasonality, or repeated cycles in the data. On the other hand, the partial autocorrelation shows the direct relationship between a value of average radiance in the time series and a lagged value, without considering the influence of other lags. In addition, the residuals and the residuals histogram in Fig. 13 are showing the goodness of fit for the model SARIMAX.

In order to compare the performance of various existing models with the proposed one, the results using different models for Ahmedabad (coordinates

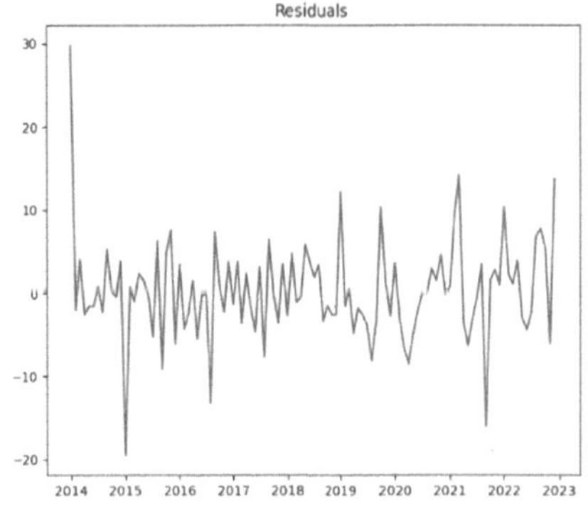

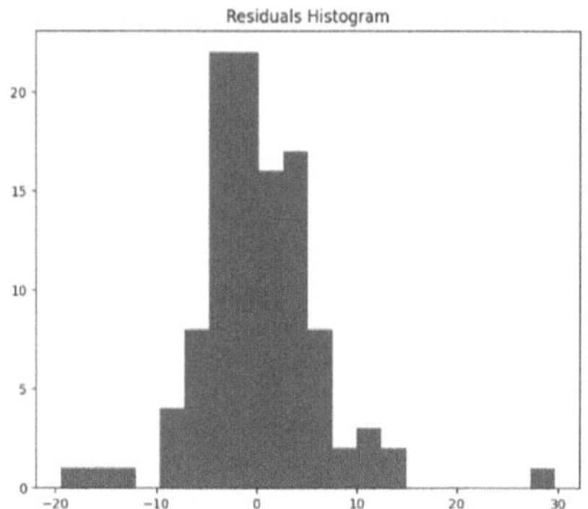

Fig. 13. Residuals and residuals histogram.

Table 2. Results of performance comparison

Model	MAE	MSE	RMSE	MAPE (%)
LSTM	4.23	25.89	5.09	12.45
ARIMA	4.56	30.25	5.50	13.82
Proposed SARIMAX	**3.82**	**21.76**	**4.67**	**10.34**
LR	5.92	52.34	7.23	18.75
XGBOOST	3.95	23.81	4.88	11.23
ETS	4.75	34.62	5.88	14.92
VAR	4.89	37.25	6.10	15.67
SD	4.15	25.63	5.06	12.34

[72.5714, 23.0225]) over the date range from January 1, 2014, to December 31, 2022 are shown in Table 2. Here, it is observed that proposed SARIMAX shows less prediction error over other existing models, in terms of the error metrics [19], such as mean absolute error (MAE), mean absolute percentage error (MAPE), mean squared error (MSE) and root mean square error (RMSE).

4 Conclusions

In order to analyze the light pollution of Ahmedabad city, the radiance is predicted for the next five years in the proposed work. The average radiance of the time series dataset for the years 2014–2022 is taken into account and subsequently, the forecasted results of the years 2023–2027 are found to be increasing. This result clearly shows the average monthly radiance of Ahmedabad city increasing rapidly. The proposed model reasonably captures the seasonal dynamics, but non-seasonal terms may not add much value. A positive indication of model fit is the Ljung-Box test, which verifies that the residuals are not autocorrelated. In addition, the radiance distribution of Ahmedabad city, India, increasing at a rapid rate highlights the urgent need for sustainable lighting policies and urban planning interventions to control light pollution in Ahmadabad. In future,we can modify our model to determine the radiance distribution of the city and predict the radiance distribution for the coming years in sustainable urban development.

References

1. Buniyaadi, A., Prabhat, A., Bhardwaj, S.K., Kumar, V.: Night melatonin levels affect cognition in diurnal animals: molecular insights from a corvid exposed to an illuminated night environment. Environ. Pollut. **308**, 119618 (2022)
2. Cabrera-Cruz, S.A., Smolinsky, J.A., Buler, J.J.: Light pollution is greatest within migration passage areas for nocturnally-migrating birds around the world. Sci. Rep. **8**(1), 3261 (2018)
3. Cereghetti, N., Strepparava, D., Bettini, A., Ferrari, S.: Analysis of light pollution in ticino region during the period 2011–2016. Sustain. Cities Soc. **63**, 102456 (2020)
4. Cinzano, P., Falchi, F.: Quantifying light pollution. J. Quant. Spectrosc. Radiat. Transfer **139**, 13–20 (2014)
5. Contin, M.A., Benedetto, M.M., Quinteros-Quintana, M.L., Guido, M.E.: Light pollution: the possible consequences of excessive illumination on retina. Eye **30**(2), 255–263 (2016)
6. Cox, D.T., Gaston, K.J.: Global erosion of terrestrial environmental space by artificial light at night. Sci. Total Environ. **904**, 166701 (2023)
7. Fobert, E.K., Burke da Silva, K., Swearer, S.E.: Artificial light at night causes reproductive failure in clownfish. Biol. Lett. **15**(7), 20190272 (2019)
8. Gaston, K.J., Davies, T.W., Bennie, J., Hopkins, J.: Reducing the ecological consequences of night-time light pollution: options and developments. J. Appl. Ecol. **49**(6), 1256–1266 (2012)
9. Grubisic, M., et al.: Light pollution, circadian photoreception, and melatonin in vertebrates. Sustainability **11**(22), 6400 (2019)
10. Luginbuhl, C.B., Boley, P.A., Davis, D.R.: The impact of light source spectral power distribution on sky glow. J. Quant. Spectrosc. Radiat. Transfer **139**, 21–26 (2014)
11. Marangoni, L.F., et al.: Impacts of artificial light at night in marine ecosystems-a review. Glob. Change Biol. **28**(18), 5346–5367 (2022)
12. Moore, M.V., Kohler, S.J., Cheers, M.S., Rich, C., Longcore, T.: Artificial light at night in freshwater habitats and its potential ecological effects. In: Ecological Consequences of Artificial Night Lighting, pp. 365–384 (2006)
13. Pun, C.S.J., So, C.W.: Night-sky brightness monitoring in Hong Kong: a city-wide light pollution assessment. Environ. Monit. Assess. **184**, 2537–2557 (2012)
14. Rajkhowa, R.: Light pollution and impact of light pollution. Int. J. Sci. Res. (IJSR) **3**(10), 861–867 (2014)
15. Riza, L.S., et al.: A spatiotemporal prediction model for light pollution in conservation areas using remote sensing datasets. Decis. Anal. J. **9**, 100334 (2023)
16. Sainger, A., Yadav, R., Tipare, P., Waghralkar, S., Jethani, V., Barve, A.: Analysis of light pollution prediction using mathematical model and machine learning techniques. In: Advanced Computing Technologies and Applications: Proceedings of 2nd International Conference on Advanced Computing Technologies and Applications–ICACTA 2020, pp. 31–43. Springer (2020)

17. Velasque, M., Denton, J., Briffa, M.: Under the influence of light: how light pollution disrupts personality and metabolism in hermit crabs. Environ. Pollut. **316**, 120594 (2023)
18. Vowles, A.S., Kemp, P.S.: Artificial light at night (ALAN) affects the downstream movement behaviour of the critically endangered European eel, anguilla anguilla. Environ. Pollut. **274**, 116585 (2021)
19. Wang, W.C., Chau, K.W., Cheng, C.T., Qiu, L.: A comparison of performance of several artificial intelligence methods for forecasting monthly discharge time series. J. Hydrol. **374**(3–4), 294–306 (2009)
20. Wesołowski, M.: Impact of light pollution on the visibility of astronomical objects in medium-sized cities in central Europe on the example of the city of Rzeszów, Poland. J. Astrophys. Astron. **40**(3), 20 (2019)
21. Zeman, M., Okuliarova, M., Rumanova, V.S.: Disturbances of hormonal circadian rhythms by light pollution. Int. J. Mol. Sci. **24**(8), 7255 (2023)

PulmoConnect: An Integrated Mobile Platform for Enhanced Doctor-Patient Communication at the Institute of Pulmocare and Research

Tiasha Mandal[1], Suravi Roy[1], Nilanjana Dutta Roy[2](✉), Swagata Paul[1], and Partha Sarathi Bhattacharyya[3]

[1] Techno International New Town, Kolkata, India
[2] Amity School of Engineering & Technology, Amity University Kolkata, Kolkata, India
nilanjanaduttaroy@gmail.com
[3] Institute of Pulmocare and Research, Kolkata, India

Abstract. Relying on a manual system can be time-consuming for a doctor when managing multiple patients simultaneously, making it challenging to deliver improved service in a shorter time frame. Moreover, the possibility of human error remains an undeniable factor in this situation. In this context, an automated doctor-patient interaction system can mitigate such issues effectively. To achieve this, an automated system, PulmoConnect that enables doctors to deliver enhanced services to patients in significantly less time has been developed. Additionally, patients can directly seek assistance from doctors through this platform. The goal of the application is to enhance communication and effectively manage patient records, enabling coordinators and doctors to deliver prompt support and care. This system accommodates the development of two distinct mobile applications. One application designed for coordinators and doctors, known as the Hospital Staff App, includes interfaces for both the registration desk and the doctors and coordinators. Another application is designed for patients, allowing them to access their information and available services. In designing the system's front end, some of the latest technologies, like React Native Framework and Expo Development Platform have been used. For the backend, we have utilized Express.js and Node.js, with MongoDB serving as our database. This reflects the current status of the development so far. The remaining development tasks involve enabling coordinators to update patient information during revisits, edit existing details, and generate APK files for the applications.

Keywords: PulmoConnect · Automated Doctor-patient Interaction System · Patient Records · Mobile Applications · Hospital Staff App · React Native Framework · Expo Development Platform · Express.js · Node.js · MongoDB

1 Introduction

In today's fast-paced healthcare environment, doctors often face the challenge of managing multiple patients simultaneously, leading to inefficient service delivery and increased likelihood of human error. Traditional manual systems are often inadequate for meeting

K. Chandra Mondal et al. (Eds.): CICBA 2025, CCIS 2863, pp. 151–165, 2026.
https://doi.org/10.1007/978-3-032-17184-9_12

the demands of modern medical practice, necessitating innovative solutions to enhance patient care. This paper introduces PulmoConnect, an automated doctor-patient interaction system designed to address these challenges by streamlining communication and improving the management of patient records.

PulmoConnect not only allows doctors to provide enhanced services in significantly less time but also empowers patients to seek assistance directly through the platform. The application aims to facilitate seamless communication between healthcare coordinators, doctors, and patients, thereby enabling timely support and care. To achieve this, we have developed two distinct mobile applications: the Hospital Staff App, tailored for coordinators and doctors, and a dedicated Patient App for patients to access their information and available services.

The development of PulmoConnect leverages cutting-edge technologies, utilizing the React Native Framework and Expo Development Platform for the front end, while employing Express.js, Node.js, and MongoDB for the backend infrastructure. This paper outlines the current status of the system's development and details the remaining tasks, including functionalities that allow coordinators to update patient information during revisits, edit existing details, and generate APK files for the applications. Through this work, we aim to demonstrate the potential of automated systems in transforming patient care and enhancing operational efficiency in healthcare settings.

2 Literature Review

The study [1] investigates health professionals' perspectives on healthcare coordination in Primary Health Care (PHC) and associated challenges in vulnerable areas of Rio de Janeiro. Qualitative research was conducted with two PHC teams using interviews and observation. Professionals view care coordination as involving communication between services to ensure continuity and comprehensiveness of care. Challenges identified include fragmentation of the health network, lack of specialist appointments, poor inter-service communication, non- integrated electronic records, insufficient professional training, and lack of recognition of PHC's role. Strengthening PHC as the gateway and coordinator of care requires efforts from managers, professionals, and society. Potential benefits include improved equity, accessibility, clinical effectiveness, and economic efficiency. Investing in integration tools, qualified professionals, and team-based approaches is essential. Despite difficulties, PHC-based systems show better health outcomes and equity. Further studies exploring diverse perspectives could expand knowledge on this topic.

The research work [2] says that medical teleconsultation uses various technologies to connect doctors and patients remotely. It aims to overcome distances, reduce costs, and manage workload. A literature review from 2013 to 2019 analyzed international experiences, benefits, and limitations of teleconsultation. Technologies used include phone, email, e-consulting systems, and video. Benefits include reduced face-to-face consultations, workload management, improved access, convenience, and potential cost savings. Limitations include the inability to perform physical examinations, technical difficulties, and unsuitability for certain patient groups. Data security, diagnostic accuracy, and acceptance by patients and professionals are also concerns. Teleconsultation is not recommended for initial consultations. Success depends on integrating different organizations and professionals to maximize potential and improve service design. Further research is needed to determine appropriate contexts, situations, and communication methods for safe and effective teleconsultation. The study was prompted by debates following the Federal Council of Medicine's Resolution N. 2.227/2018, which allowed medical teleconsultation in Brazil.

The paper [3] proposes a blockchain-based smart e-health system to address the challenge of fragmented health records across multiple providers. The system uses smart contracts to create an immutable patient log with a Modified Merkle Tree data structure, enabling secure storage and rapid access to health records. It allows for updating medical records, exchanging health information between providers, and managing viewership contracts on a peer-to-peer network. The blockchain acts as a clinical data repository, providing patients with a complete, distributed ledger of their electronic health records. High security and integrity are ensured through cryptographic hash functions. The system's effectiveness was tested through multiple trials, evaluating performance metrics such as resource utilization, transactions per second, and transaction latency. This approach aims to solve the accessibility issues of health data, especially in critical conditions, by creating a regulated solution that benefits patients, physicians, and health service providers.

Another study [4] explores automatic medical report generation from ASR-generated patient- doctor conversation transcripts using neural summarization techniques. The research compares RNN and Transformer-based sequence-to-sequence architectures, incorporating enhancements like pointer-generator networks and hierarchical RNN encoders. These models were evaluated on a dataset of 800k orthopedic encounters, with Transformer models outperforming RNNs in both accuracy and training time. The study demonstrates significant improvements over a strong oracle extractive baseline, suggesting that sequence-to-sequence modeling is a promising approach for automatic medical report generation when substantial data is available. The incorporation of pointer-generator networks allows for copying parts of conversations into reports, while the hierarchical RNN encoder accelerates RNN training for long inputs. Overall, the research highlights the potential of advanced neural network architectures in medical documentation automation.

The research [5] introduces a patient-centered healthcare system using smart contracts and blockchain technology to enhance data security and accessibility. Patients maintain control over their health records, deciding what information to share with healthcare providers. The system, built on Hyperledger Fabric and Ethereum Blockchain, ensures secure sharing and storage of sensitive health data, while algorithms manage patient information and medical records. Smart contracts facilitate seamless, trustless transactions between parties, fostering improved care coordination across different healthcare providers. The experimental results demonstrate the system's efficiency in terms of execution speed and memory consumption. By giving patients ownership over their medical data and enabling controlled sharing, the proposed system addresses critical challenges such as data fragmentation, trust, and security in healthcare. This framework has the potential to revolutionize patient care by improving information flow and safeguarding personal health data.

The research article [6] explores the skills needed for effective collaboration in patient care between primary and secondary doctors. It focuses on enhancing communication and mutual understanding between care levels, which is crucial for managing the growing number of patients with chronic conditions. Six major competencies emerged: patient-centered care, defining roles and responsibilities, mutual knowledge, collaborative attitude, communication, and leadership. These competencies are vital in preventing fragmented care and ensuring smooth transitions across care levels, ultimately reducing medical errors and improving patient outcomes. By highlighting these collaborative competencies, the study provides a framework for medical training and practice improvement, emphasizing the need for doctors to play an active role not only in direct patient care but also in shaping the organizational structures that support effective collaboration.

Another article [7] says that The Internet of Things (IoT) revolutionizes healthcare by enabling seamless interaction between interconnected devices. It facilitates remote monitoring through affordable wearable technology and sensors that collect vital data on patients' physical and mental states. This study explores the applications of IoT in electronic healthcare monitoring systems, focusing on automatic prescription delivery based on patient conditions, and enabling continuous health assessments without in-person visits. By analyzing existing literature, the research highlights how IoT enhances diagnostic accuracy and reduces the need for regular hospital visits, ultimately improving service quality. It also addresses the challenges and opportunities associated with implementing Internet-based healthcare monitoring systems, emphasizing their potential in advancing healthcare delivery and supporting scientific research.

The systematic review [8] examined the impact of patient-centered medical home (PCMH) interventions across different healthcare delivery systems. The researchers analyzed 64 studies implementing PCMHs in integrated delivery and finance systems (IDFS), government systems, and non-integrated systems. They found that PCMHs generally led to decreased emergency department use and hospitalizations across all systems. However, some key differences emerged: IDFS studies reported decreased primary care use, while government systems saw increased primary care utilization. Cost savings were more commonly reported in IDFS and government studies compared to non-integrated systems. Clinical outcomes, quality measures, and patient satisfaction were inconsistently reported but showed some improvements. The authors note significant heterogeneity in PCMH implementation and outcome reporting across studies, limiting direct comparisons. They conclude that while PCMHs show promise in improving care delivery and reducing costs, their effectiveness may vary based on the underlying health system structure. The review highlights the need for more standardized reporting of PCMH outcomes to better evaluate their impact.

This research [9] examines how Alberta's integrated digital healthcare system provided advantages in responding to the COVID-19 pandemic. Key digital tools deployed included online self-assessment and screening tools, linked screening and test result data, standardized management protocols in electronic health records, a mobile contact tracing app, expanded telemedicine capabilities, and real-time data sharing across the system. The existing digital infrastructure allowed for rapid implementation, improving surveillance, case finding, isolation, testing, and contact tracing. The author argues that highly digitalized, networked healthcare systems can enhance pandemic response, though challenges around data privacy and security persist. The pandemic is seen as accelerating healthcare digitization globally, but not all countries are equally prepared for this shift. The study highlights the benefits of digital health infrastructure in crisis management while acknowledging the need to balance individual privacy concerns with societal health needs in the digital age.

The study [10] says that blockchain technology offers promising solutions to challenges in healthcare data management, including transparency, traceability, immutability, auditing, and secure data provenance. This study explores how blockchain can improve medical record management by creating a decentralized, secure network for sharing and storing patient data, including radiographic images. It enables efficient, validated patient record completion and allows seamless patient-provider interactions. The research discusses blockchain's application in Electronic Medical Records, emphasizing its potential to create an interoperable infrastructure that enhances healthcare outcomes while maintaining data integrity and privacy. The study examines existing and recent developments in blockchain-based healthcare data management, highlighting benefits and potential applications through case studies. It also identifies obstacles to blockchain adoption in healthcare and proposes areas for further research, providing a comprehensive overview of blockchain's role in revolutionizing healthcare data management.

To establish the position of PulmoConnect in the current healthcare technology landscape, we conducted a comprehensive comparison with popular mobile healthcare platforms. From the Table 1, we can see that PulmoConnect uniquely combines pulmonary care specialization, elderly-centric design, and dual-app architecture for comprehensive healthcare delivery.

3 Methodology

This block diagram shown in Fig. 1, represents the flow of functionalities in the system with two main applications: an Admin App and a Patient App.

Admin App

- A Registration Panel for managing patient registration, viewing patient lists (today's and all patients), and sending patient login credentials via email.
- A Coordinator/Doctors Panel for managing medical records, viewing patient details, updating disease information, downloading patient details in Excel, and handling patient requests and reports.

Patient App

- It allows patients to log in, view past appointments and requests, view their profile, send reports, submit requests for help, and optionally upload documents. They can also track notifications and action details on their requests.

The system includes a notification system that connects both apps, where patient requests are classified as either Critical or Non-Critical, and appropriate actions are taken by the coordinators/ doctors. The workflow shows clear communication channels between patients and healthcare providers, with features for data management, reporting, and patient monitoring.

3.1 Proposed Pipeline

PulmoConnect is an integrated healthcare platform that has been developed for the Institute of Pulmocare & Research, facilitating communication between medical professionals and patients through specialized mobile applications. Two distinct apps have been designed: one for doctors and hospital coordinators, and another for patients. The medical staff app enables efficient patient registration, storage of medical histories and current issues, and access to patient lists. Concurrently, the patient-focused app allows individuals to submit detailed information about their current condition, including symptoms, requests for further consultations, or hospitalization needs, as well as upload relevant medical certificates. This unified system has been made to streamline coordination and enhance the overall healthcare experience for both providers and recipients. The overall flow of the application is shown in Fig. 1. The main features of the system are:

Patient Registration: A secure Registration Panel has been implemented for hospital staff at the registration desk, accessible via unique user credentials. This panel facilitates the registration of new patients who have not previously visited the facility. Essential patient information, including name, gender, age, contact details, email address, patient ID, and residential address, is collected and entered into the system. Upon successful completion of registration, a popup notification is generated, displaying a unique user ID and password, which are subsequently provided to the patient for accessing the patient app. The list of registered patients is automatically updated and made visible in both the registration panel and the coordinator's panel, ensuring efficient information sharing across the platform.
Coordinator Registration - A dedicated section of the hospital staff app has been developed specifically for hospital coordinators and doctors, accessible through unique login credentials distinct from those used by the registration desk. This specialized interface allows coordinators to self-register and manage their specific tasks efficiently. The home page of this section displays a comprehensive list of all registered coordinators, complete with an integrated call feature for easy communication. Additionally, the system enables users to view individual patient lists associated with each coordinator, facilitating personalized patient management. To enhance usability, a search function has been implemented, allowing for quick location of specific coordinators by name. This streamlined design ensures that coordinators can effectively oversee their responsibilities and maintain clear lines of communication within the hospital system.
Patient Disease Updation - In the coordinators' panel, a registered tab has been designed to display patients who have been registered through the registration desk but whose disease information has not yet been updated. The disease updation process has been structured to allow doctors to input comprehensive patient health data. This includes dedicated fields for existing diseases, consultation-specific problems, significant medical history, and CAT scores. A coordinator is assigned to each patient by the attending doctor. Once the patient's details have been updated, their information is automatically transferred to and displayed in the patient list tab. To facilitate data management and analysis, an Excel file download option has been incorporated, allowing for the extraction of all patients' details in a spreadsheet format. This systematic approach ensures that patient information is thoroughly documented and easily accessible to the relevant medical staff.

Patient Request - A notification system has been implemented within the coordinator's panel to efficiently manage patient requests for assistance. These notifications have been categorized into two distinct types: general notifications, displayed in a standard light green color, and critical notifications, such as information about a patient's death or other urgent issues, highlighted in red for immediate attention. Upon selecting a notification, a three-tab interface is presented. The first tab provides comprehensive patient details, the second allows for a review of the patient's request and current action status, and the third tab is designed for coordinators or doctors to initiate appropriate actions. Once an action has been taken, the action status is automatically updated in the system. This real-time update feature has been extended to the patient app, enabling patients to monitor the progress of their requests. This integrated approach ensures seamless communication between healthcare providers and patients, facilitating prompt and efficient responses to patient needs.
Patient Profile: The patient app has been designed with a secure login system, allowing patients to access their profiles using unique user IDs and passwords provided during registration. Within the app, a comprehensive request system has been implemented, enabling patients to seek assistance through a structured form. This form includes fields for reporting exacerbations, hospitalizations, new consultation needs, disabilities, and, if necessary, demise. To support their requests, patients can upload relevant medical files directly through the app. The system also prompts patients to specify the nature of their request, such as seeking remedies, general advice, or requesting direct communication with a doctor. Upon submission, these requests are immediately relayed to the hospital coordinator and doctors' app as notifications. The medical staff can then take appropriate actions, with updates on these actions being reflected in real-time on the patient's app. This streamlined process ensures efficient communication between patients and healthcare providers, facilitating timely and appropriate responses to patient needs.

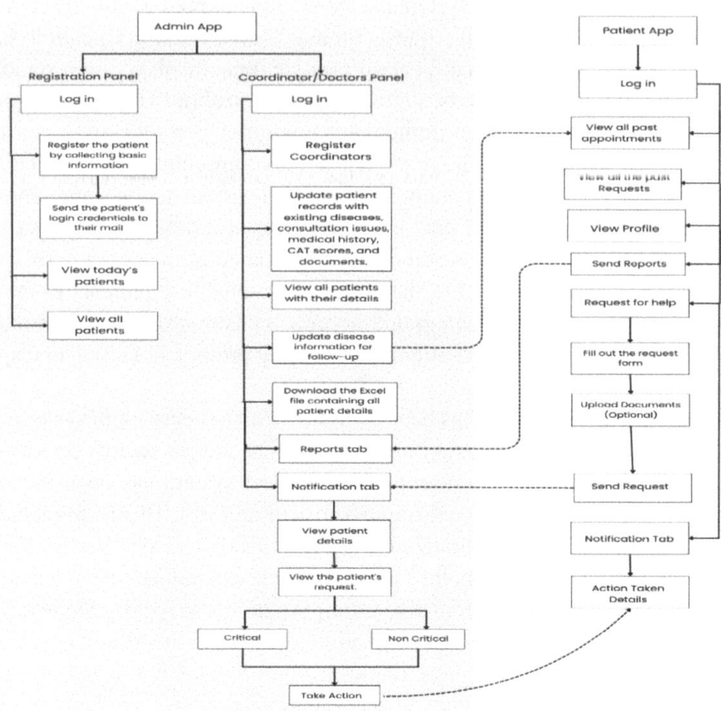

Fig. 1. Block diagram of the overall system.

3.2 User Interface

– **Patient App -** React Native and Expo were used in the development of the patient application to create a seamless, cross-platform user experience that works with both iOS and Android smartphones. This app allows patients to communicate with their assigned coordinators and provide updates on their health status. Patients can easily submit information regarding their current condition, including symptoms, requests for further consultations, or needs for hospitalization, through a user-friendly interface. The app also supports uploading relevant medical certificates and documentation. A notification system is integrated to keep patients informed of their request status in real time, which is crucial for maintaining transparency and timely responses from healthcare providers. JavaScript and React Native make it possible to create mobile applications that look and feel native, complete with an interactive and responsive user interface. Expo improves this by offering a collection of libraries and tools that streamline the development process. These tools and libraries include capabilities for managing app deployment, handling push notifications, and accessing device hardware. Expo improves this by offering a collection of libraries and tools that streamline the development process. These tools and libraries include capabilities for managing app deployment, handling push notifications, and accessing device hardware. Patients may quickly navigate through many elements of the app, including inputting their health status, symptoms, and requests for consultations or hospitalizations, through interacting frontend interface design. The app also can upload certificates and medical records, and file handling is accomplished through libraries such as React Native Document Picker and React Native Image Picker. The backend for the patient app is built using Node.js and Express.js, which together provide a fast, scalable server-side environment. Node.js, being an asynchronous event-driven JavaScript runtime, is particularly well-suited for handling the high volume of real-time requests that a healthcare app might encounter. Express.js is used to create a robust API, supporting RESTful services that facilitate seamless data exchange between the client and server. MongoDB, a NoSQL database, is employed to manage patient records and other critical data. MongoDB's flexible schema design allows for efficient storage and retrieval of patient information, such as medical history, current conditions, and appointment details, supporting the app's dynamic data requirements. Figure 2 shows a visual demonstration to enhance your understanding of the patient panel's functionality. It presents the entire process in a step-by- step format.

- **Doctor and Coordinator App** - React Native and Expo are also utilized in the development of the doctor and coordinator application to guarantee a uniform user experience across all user roles. This app makes sure that only authorized individuals have access to private patient data by including a secure login system with distinct login credentials for each coordinator and doctor. Libraries like useState for state management and React Navigation for seamless navigation improve the login process, guaranteeing that the application runs smoothly even with an increasing user population. Upon logging in, medical professionals can view and manage patient information, including registration details, medical history, symptoms, and current conditions. The app is designed with a focus on usability and efficiency, incorporating features like a search function for quickly locating specific coordinators or patients. The backend architecture is powered by Node.js, Express.js, and MongoDB. Node.js handles concurrent requests efficiently, making it ideal for a high-traffic healthcare environment where multiple users may need to access and update patient information simultaneously. Express.js is used to build a comprehensive RESTful API, which supports all necessary operations, from patient registration to data updates and notification handling. MongoDB serves as the database solution due to its ability to handle large volumes of unstructured data, which is common in medical records. The database is structured to allow for rapid queries and updates, ensuring that patient information is always current and easily accessible. Additionally, data security and privacy are prioritized, with encryption techniques and secure access protocols in place to protect sensitive patient data. To help you better understand how the admin panel works, Fig. 3 provides a visual demonstration. It outlines the entire process step by step.

4 Result and Discussion

In the development and testing of PulmoConnect, a trial has been conducted on 100 patients at the Institute of Pulmocare & Research (IPCR), in Newtown, Kolkata. The results indicated a significant improvement in communication and coordination between

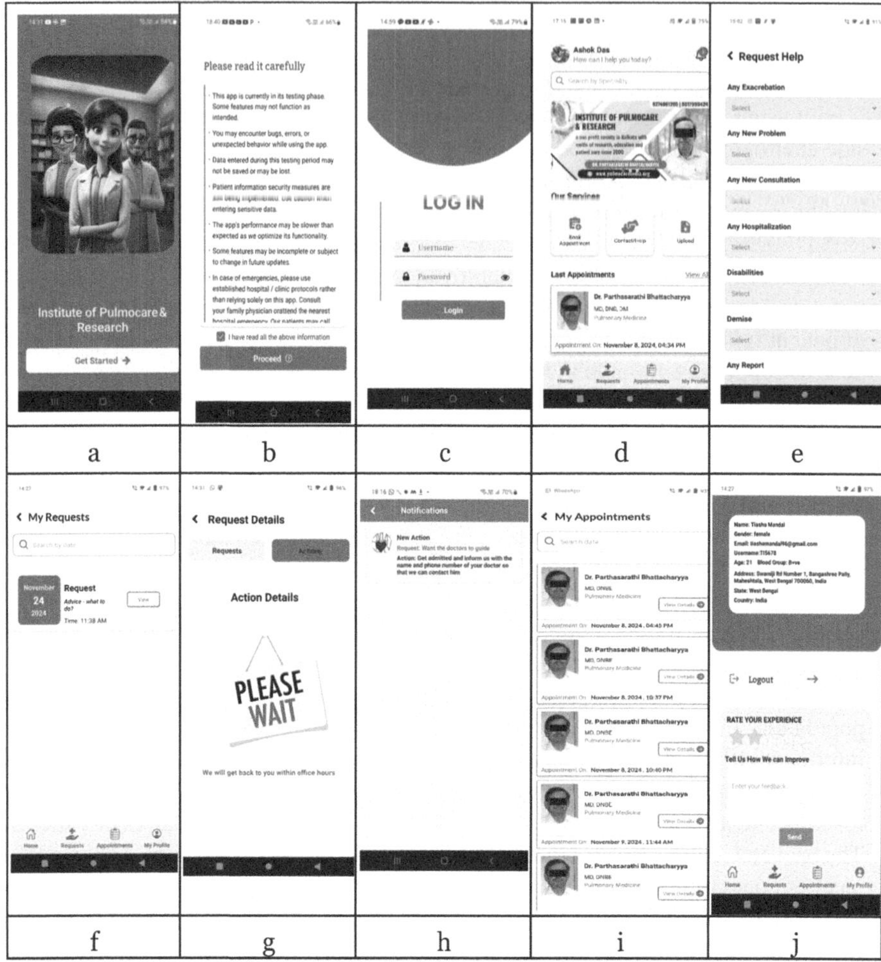

Fig. 2. Working of the patient application. a) The home page of the application. b) This is the disclaimer page for patients, as the app is currently in the testing phase. c) The login page, where patients can log in using their patient ID and password provided by the hospital coordinator. Once authenticated, they can access their account. d) After logging in, patients are directed to the home page, where their name and appointment details are displayed. The page features three options: **REQUEST FOR HELP**, **BOOK APPOINTMENT**, and **UPLOAD DOCUMENTS**. However, only the **REQUEST FOR HELP** option is functional, as the other two are not needed at this time (as per instruction). e) If patients need to inform the doctor about their current condition or request any kind of help, they can fill out the provided form with details including symptoms, new consultations, new problems, hospitalization, disabilities, or demise. The form also includes a section to upload relevant certificates. f) All requests will be displayed on the "My Requests" page, where patients can also view the actions taken by the coordinators. g) If the coordinator has not yet taken action, the status will display "Please Wait." Once the action is taken, it will show "Action Taken" along with the suggested remedies provided by the coordinator. h) After taking action from the admin panel the patient will be noticed in the notification tab. i) The appointments for each patient will be displayed on the "My Appointments" page. j) This is the profile page, which includes options for logging out and providing feedback option and ratings.

Fig. 3. a) The home page of the hospital staff's application. b) The login page for the registration desk. c) This is the patient registration form page. d) After successful registration this is the confirmation popup. e) Today's Patients tab to show registered patients of today. f) All Patients tab to show all the registered patients with details. g) This is the home page of the Doctors and Coordinators interface which will be opened by using specific login credentials. It has search and filter functionality and the call icon can be used to call a particular coordinator. h) The list of patients under that particular coordinator is accessible through the "View Patient" button for each coordinator. i) The notification tab is designated to receive alerts whenever a patient sends a request. j) Doctors or coordinators can check the patient's requests. k) Doctors or coordinators can take necessary actions based on patient requests. l) The register tab to show the patients who are registered but whose diseases are not updated. m) Doctors will update the diseases of the patients and each patient will be assigned a particular coordinator. n) The Patient List tab to show the list of all patients and the download Excel button will be used to download the Excel sheet of all the patient's details. o) The patient details can be checked based on visit time and date. p) The patient's disease information is shown.

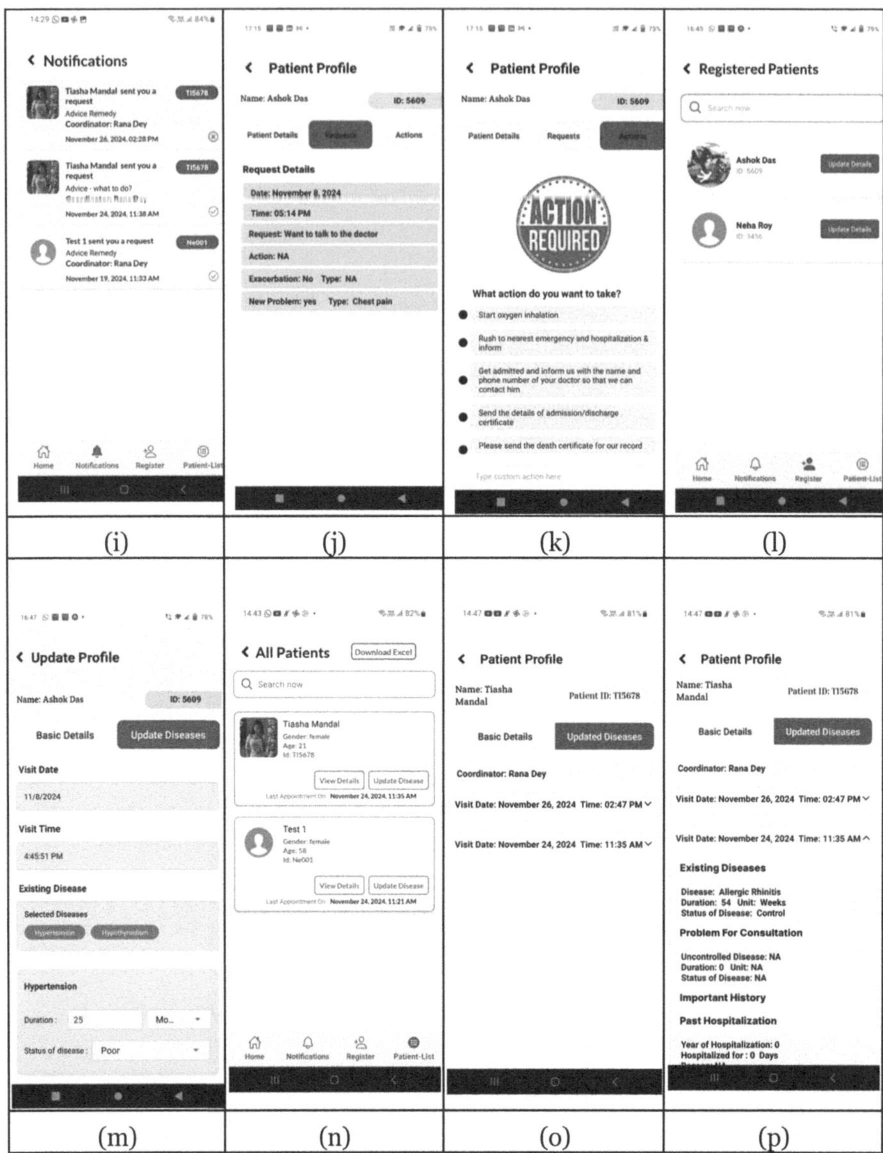

Fig. 3. *(continued)*

patients and healthcare providers. The patient registration process became more streamlined, reducing the time spent on manual entries and minimizing errors. Patients were able to submit health updates, request consultations, and upload medical documents directly through the app, improving their engagement with healthcare services. The notification system, which categorizes requests by urgency, enabled faster response times from doctors and coordinators. The seamless integration of patient disease updates, real-time notifications, and the ability to export patient data in Excel files also proved invaluable for medical staff, allowing for efficient tracking and analysis of patient records. The success of the trial suggests that PulmoConnect has the potential to greatly enhance operational efficiency and the quality of care at IPCR, contributing to better patient outcomes. Further testing on a larger scale could provide more insights and refine the system for broader use. The system development was completely directed by Dr. Partha Sarathi Bhattacharyya from the Institute of Pulmocare and Research (IPCR), ensuring all features were designed to improve their existing manual patient care processes while maintaining elderly-friendly interfaces, as most patients are above 60 years of age. The Table 2, represents the Statistical analysis using paired t-test showed significant improvements ($p < 0.001$) across all measured parameters, confirming the system's effectiveness in enhancing healthcare delivery efficiency.

- **Performance Metrics:**

Table 1. Comparative Analysis with Existing Healthcare Platforms

Feature	PulmoConnect	Practo	Apollo 24/7	Tata 1mg
Target Audience	Pulmonary (60 +)	General	Multi-specialty	Medicine
Elderly-Friendly UI	✓	Partial	Partial	✗
Registration at the desk	✓	✗	✗	✗
Coordinator Assignment	✓	✗	✗	✗
Highlighting Critical Notification	✓	✗	✗	✗
Specialized Care	✓	✗	✗	✗

Table 2. System Performance Comparison

Metric	Manual System	PulmoConnect	Improvement
Registration Time	4 min	2 min	50% reduction
Data Entry Errors	12%	0%	100% elimination
Patient Request Management	45 min	15 min	66.7% reduction
Patient Satisfaction	3.2/5	4.6/5	43.8% increase

5 Conclusion

PulmoConnect effectively addresses the challenges of manual patient management systems by offering a user-friendly, efficient, and secure platform for doctor-patient communication. Through process automation and real-time information sharing, the system streamlines coordination and enhances the overall healthcare experience for both providers and recipients at IPCR. The highlighting of critical notifications in the coordinator's panel facilitates swift attention and efficient service delivery. The system's capability to generate Excel files containing comprehensive patient information holds significant potential for medical research, enabling analysis of age-related disease patterns, medical history correlations, and treatment improvements for critical conditions. Future developments will focus on implementing patient information updates during revisits and creating APK files for broader distribution. Continuous improvements will be made based on feedback from hospital coordinators and patients, ensuring the platform evolves to meet user needs effectively. The potential integration of AI-powered bots utilizing historical datasets could further enhance the system's responsiveness. The quantitative analysis demonstrates measurable improvements in efficiency, with patient registration time reduced by 50% and complete elimination of manual data entry errors, validating the system's effectiveness compared to existing healthcare platforms. PulmoConnect transcends its role as a mere platform; it instills confidence in patients by providing them with immediate access to medical services at their fingertips. By bridging the communication gap between healthcare providers and patients, PulmoConnect not only improves operational efficiency but also contributes to better health outcomes and patient satisfaction, potentially setting a new standard for digital healthcare solutions in pulmonary care.

References

1. Ribeiro, S.P., de Lourdes Tavares Cavalcanti, M.: Primary health care and coordination of care: device to increase access and improve quality. Ciencia & saude coletiva **25**, 1799–1808 (2020)
2. Catapan, S.d.C., Calvo., M.C.M.: Teleconsultation: an integrative review of the doctor-patient interaction mediated by technology. Revista Brasileira de Educação Médica **44**(01), e002 (2020)
3. Chelladurai, U., Pandian, S.: A novel blockchain based electronic health record automation system for healthcare. J. Ambient. Intell. Humaniz. Comput. **13**(1), 693–703 (2022)
4. Enarvi, S., et al.: Generating medical reports from patient-doctor conversations using sequence-to-sequence models. In: Proceedings of the first workshop on natural language processing for medical conversations, pp. 22–30 (2020)
5. Duong-Trung, N., Ha, X.S., Le, H.T., Phan, T.T.: On components of a patient-centered healthcare system using a smart contract. In: Proceedings of the 2020 4th International Conference on Cryptography, Security and Privacy, pp. 31–35 (2020)
6. Janssen, M., Sagasser, M.H., Fluit, C.R.M.G., Assendelft, W.J.J., De Graaf, J., Scherpbier, N.D.: Competencies to promote collaboration between primary and secondary care doctors: an integrative review. BMC Family Practice **21**, 1–13 (2020)
7. Kadhim, K,T., Alsahlany, A.M., Wadi, S.M., Kadhum, H.T.: An overview of patient's health status monitoring system based on internet of things (IoT). Wireless Personal Commun. **114**(3) 2235–2262 (2020)
8. Veet, C.A., et al.: Impact of healthcare delivery system type on clinical, utilization, and cost outcomes of patient-centered medical homes: a systematic review. J. General Internal Med. **35**, 1276- 1284 (2020)
9. Baumgart, D.C.: Digital advantage in the COVID-19 response: perspective from Canada's largest integrated digitalized healthcare system. NPJ Digital Med. **3**(1), 114 (2020)

10. Singh, S., Sharma, S.K., Mehrotra, P., Bhatt, P., Kaurav, M.: Blockchain technology for efficient data management in healthcare system: opportunity, challenges and future perspectives. Mater. Today: Proc. **62**, 5042–5046 (2022)

An Enhanced Adaptive Network Intrusion Detection System Using Hybrid Approach

Pankaj Kumar Keserwani[1(✉)], Manish Kumar Singh[2], and Mahesh Chandra Govil[1]

[1] Department of Computer Science and Engineering, National Institute of Technology Sikkim, Ravangla, Sikkim, India
pankaj.keserwani@gmail.com

[2] J S University, Shikohabad, Firozabad, UP, India

Abstract. Intrusion detection system (IDS) works as heart to make a network safe. Most of the IDSs are facing the problems due to high false alarm rate (FAR) which is leading for decrease in the accuracy for big data environment when it is placed in real environment. A new, reliable and hybrid IDS model is proposed for anomaly detection in a cloud virtual network. The implemented model employs hybrid Grey Wolf Optimization - Bald Eagle Search (Hybrid GWO-BES) method and Long Short Term Memory (LSTM) for increasing the detection rate (DR) and decreasing the false alarm rate (FAR) and hence, increasing the accuracy. The proposed IDS model uses hybrid GWO-BES for feature selection. The selected relevant features work as the input to a Long Short Term Memory (LSTM) for the classification. The performance of proposed GWO-BES-LSTM model has been shown on the basis of accuracy, precision, recall, F1 Score (F Score), false alarm rate and false-negative rate. The results are simulated on NSL-KDD, and CICIDS-2017 datasets for multi class classification and compared with the existing approaches. Simulated results of the GWO-BES-LSTM model achieved an increased performance in compared to other models.

Keywords: Network Intrusion Detection System (NIDS) · Feature Selection · Grey Wolf Optimization · Bald Eagle Search · Long Short Term Memory (LSTM)

1 Introduction

Cloud computing is a new platform which works over the Internet to provide the Information Technology (IT) services to its users at very low-cost [16]. Cloud computing environment makes the computing resources available to its users on demand in service form of X as a Service (XaaS). The X may be Infrastructure, Platform, Software, or any computing services. Cloud computing follows the distributed architecture for providing computing resources quickly in scalable manner and maintaining services availability. So many organizations have transferred

K. Chandra Mondal et al. (Eds.): CICBA 2025, CCIS 2863, pp. 166–180, 2026.
https://doi.org/10.1007/978-3-032-17184-9_13

their businesses on cloud and many organizations are transferring to reduce the maintaining cost of their own businesses [20]. The cloud computing is vulnerable from many types of internal and external attacks due its distributed nature [19]. The attacker gains the unauthorized access to the cloud environment for launching the desired attack(s) or intrusion(s). In the process of intrusion detection the network events are monitored and audited. In cloud environment conducting this process is still a delicious security interests for researchers. The main objective of an intrusion detection system (IDS) is to ensure the preservation of CIA of virtual networks and systems holding information in the cloud environment, where 'C' stands for confidentiality, 'I' stands for integrity, and 'A' stands for availability. On the basis of deployment four types of IDS are there namely, Host-based IDS (HIDS) placed inside the Host or virtual machine (VM), VM monitor or Hypervisor-based IDS (VMM-IDS) placed inside the VMM/hypervisors and Collaborative based IDS used for large network, and Network-based IDS (NIDS) placed inside routers or switches [20]. Based on intrusion behavior, three kinds of intrusion detection approaches are there namely, signature-based, anomaly-based, and hybrid-based [19]. The first one detects abnormal behaviour, second one detects the known signature and the last one combines both for intrusion detection from the network flow [37]. Intrusion detection and prevention system based on antivirus, spyware, firewalls etc. are not providing the required level of satisfaction. The three detection approaches can be used in NIDS, which should take data dispersion and network traffic into account [34]. Excessive detection rate and volume of finding new attacks are crucial points of an anomaly based NIDS [7].

Intrusion detection in cloud computing (CC) environment is looking as the NP-Hard problem, which can be solved with many methods based on the ML (machine learning), DL (deep learning), meta-heuristic, and evolutionary computing [10]. Many meta-heuristic algorithms have shown very good results to make a successful IDS [29]. The purpose of meta-heuristic algorithm is to select relevant features from the dataset in feature selection (FS) process. The main benefits of using FS are decreasing the computational complexity and improving all-inclusive performance of the IDS [35]. FS limits processing cost, space complexity by reducing data size [21]. Hence, FS in IDS works as an optimizer because it extracts only relevant feature set from the dataset for improving performance [15]. In this article, an anomaly-based NIDS has been developed using GWO-BES-LSTM model. The designed NIDS is able to detect the network attacks from network traffic flow, which can affect many VMs in the cloud environment. As a network intrusion is detected, an alert is sent to the network administrator so that he may initiate a defensive action(s) against that network intrusion. The hybrid Grey Wolf Optimization - Bald Eagle Search (hybrid GWO-BES) algorithm has been developed and used to extract relevant feature subset from the dataset in FS process. LSTM (Long Short Term Memory) is designed for detecting intrusions from the extracted relevant feature set in classification process. The major contributions of the proposed work are enlisted below:

- A new hybrid technique GWO and BES for extracting relevant feature subset from the dataset in FS process is employed.
- A novel adaptive GWO-BES-LSTM model has been proposed for all kinds of unknown attacks using adaptive approach.
- The GWO-BES-LSTM model results are simulated on CICIDS-2017 and NSL-KDD datasets and compared with the other existing recent approaches and the proposed NIDS model produces comparatively better accuracy, better detection rate and better recall rate.

The rest contents of this article are systemized as follows: Sect. 2 discusses related work with relevant reviews. In Sect. 3 detail of the designed NIDS, each element of GWO-BES-LSTM model for intrusion detection are discussed. Section 4 discusses the implementation details and experimental results with comparison from other's work. Finally, Sect. 5 provides the overall conclusion about the paper.

2 Related Work

Most of the ML classification algorithms are utilized to design IDS models based on anomalies, which learns from the network dataset or network flow data. Learned model is placed to real network flow and it detects the intrusions. Data preprocessing, optimization techniques are adapted before the classification by the researchers in developing their own IDSs to achieve better comparable performance.

Ghosh et al. [9], designed HIDS and NIDS in their proposed IDS to work in cloud environment. FS was done through information gain and classification was performed with K-nearest neighbour (K-NN). The proposed model was evaluated on NSL-KDD dataset. A notification to cloud administrator was there in their proposed IDS. Popoola et al. [24] designed the NIDS in their work for intrusion detection in network. Discrete Deferential Evolution (DDE) technique was used in FS and Decision Tree (C4.5) was applied for classification to learn their model on the NSL-KDD dataset with the help of in Weka tool. The results were obtained with a significant enhancement on accuracy. They also obtained the reduced training time and testing time both. Ngoc et al. [23] used boosting and ensemble based on bagging by considering decision tree as a base classifier in their proposed IDS model. The model was evaluated on NSL-KDD dataset and found that the ensemble model based on bagging with the J48 classifier was best. Singh et al. [32] designed an IDS for cloud environment. FS was performed by cuckoo optimization technique. Al-Zewairi et al. [1] developed a NIDS where binomial classifier with deep learning was used. The experiment was conducted on UNSW-NB15 dataset. From the results it is concluded that NIDS was performing well with respect to accuracy and FAR. Ashfaq et al. [5] proposed centred semi-supervised learning approach along with fuzzy concepts to boost up the execution of classification in Intrusion Detection System. They applied supervised learning to unlabeled samples, then utilised a neural network (NN) using feed-forward mechanism with a single hidden layer. Alzughaibi et al. [4]

developed a NIDS model for cloud environment by conducting four experiments for binary as well as multi-class classification.

M. Zaman & C. H. Lung [36] tested many ML based approaches with the help of entropy calculation on Kyoto 2006+ dataset. High precision and accuracy were the main parameters to calculate the efficiency of the ML techniques.

Ijaz et al. [13] proposed an IDS where an evolutionary approach to detect intrusions was applied to get better results. Malik et al. [14] implemented a combined form of decision tree and PSO to turn down the size of tree on and it was accomplished by using the KDD99Cup dataset.

To increase the accuracy of attack detection, Aljawarneh et al. [2] developed a dimensionality reduction technique that utilized feature selection and classification. Recognition and supervised learning are the first two processes of classification, which comes after decision making phase.

Sakr et al. [26] implemented a Network Intrusion Detection System to upgrade privacy and safety of CC where PSO-SVM was utilized to enhance accuracy. To improve the performance of Support Vector Machine, an Standard Particle Swarm Optimization was employed. K. Mindo et al. [17] introduced a ML based WFS (Wrapper Feature Selection) and Artificial Neural Network, that resolves the drawbacks of Support Vector Machine in recognizing and categorizing the intrusions of the network. For the purpose of protecting a network's confidentiality and integrity, Reddy et al. [25] used fuzzy logic and evolutionary algorithms for intrusion detection. Fuzzy logic aids in minimising transit-related loss of packets and delay.

B. Hajimirzaei and N. J. Navimipour [10] suggested an Multi Layer Perceptron, ABC algorithm and Fuzzy clustering to improve Mean Absolute Erroe, kappa statics and Root Mean Square Error. Fuzzy clustering produced the training sets for the NIDS, and the MLP was utilised to pinpoint the network's flawed tasks. The ABC method assisted the ANN by performing optimised linkage weight and bias values. The execution speed of the training process was also improved. Shyla and Sujatha [31] presented an IDS by combining k-means clustering to cluster inputs and fuzzy logic (FL) system to process on the clustered inputs. Sathiya and Soosai [28] showed an dragonfly-improved invasive weed optimizer-based Shepard convolutional neural network (CNN) model to detect the intruders in cloud environment and mitigate them. Srinivas et al. [33] suggested an effectual IDS by using sail fish dolphin optimizer and Deep RNN to identify the anomalies in cloud network. Hizal et al. [12] established a IDS based on DL approach with the help of CNNs and RNNs to enhance the cloud security.

To observe intrusions, point out most important features of the network traffic was a considerable study. In order to safeguard distributed networks, Patil et al. [22] created a method for tracking all virtual machines' network traffic at the hypervisor level. A binary bat algorithm with many aims was devised to locate the viable features. Depending on the output of the RF classifier, an alert was produced. A new signature for attacks were created based on the intrusion notifications from different servers.

The research gaps, based on the reported methods, towards the deployment of effective IDS can be summarized as follows

- IDS crashed to achieve minimal false alarm rate, according to approaches described in the literature.
- The exact identification of intrusions in a high dimensional dataset was unsuccessful by earlier methods.

Due to high dimensioned data in CC and the suitability of our proposed system, a classification approach based on FS has been devised that can identify all network intrusions.

3 Proposed Methodology

To detecting exceptional characteristics in a cloud virtual network an anomaly-based Network Intrusion Detectipon system is utilized. In this article the features are choosed by means of the hybrid of Grey Wolf Optimization and BES algorithm. Based on the choosed features classification is carried out by a LSTM. High accuracy and low false positives are the promises of the proposed NIDS with the help of GWO-BES-LSTM model. The data collecting module, a feature selection module, and a classification module are the main components of the anomaly-based NIDS. Figure 1 depicts the architecture of implemented NIDS.

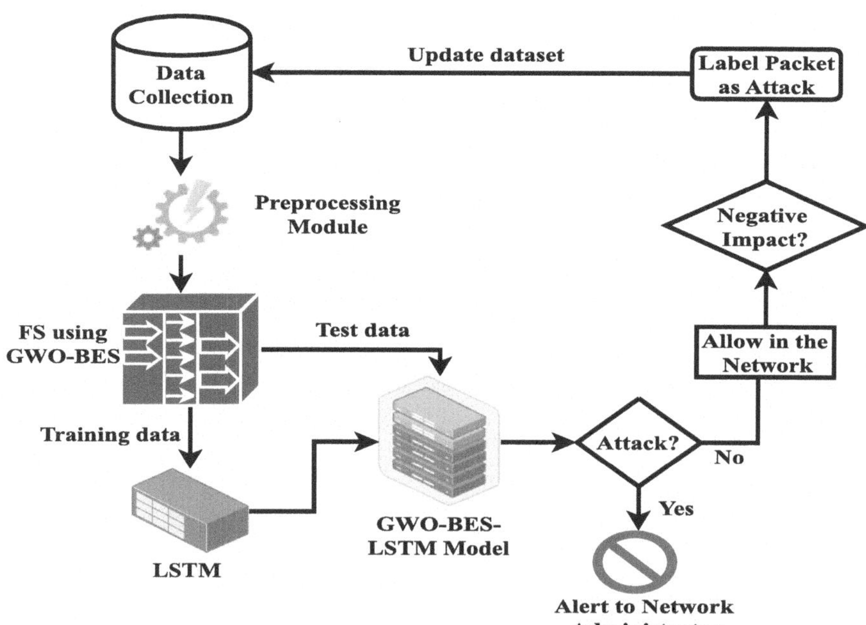

Fig. 1. Architecture of implemented NIDS

The module for collecting data accumulates necessary data from real environment to create datasets (**CICIDS-2017 and NSL-KDD**). These collected data is pre-processed in proprocessing module where data cleaning, transformation of categorical or string variable values into numerical form, normalization are performed. Feature selection (FS) is applied using hybrid Grey Wolf Optimization and BES algorithm to achieve the best feasible features helping to detect the attacks. The selected feature set is fed to the LSTM classifier. A NIDS model named GWO-BES-LSTM is generated as trained classifier. The test date is fed to the NIDS model to identify malicious user and normal user. An alert is generated for malicious user to discart the packet from the network and normal packet is allowed to the network and analysed. In case the normal packet is showing any negative impact, the packet is labelled as attack and updated the dataset for further enhancement. The designed model can be enhanced to detect the attacks in ohter various types of the networks such as Internet of Things (IoT) network, Wired network, etc.

3.1 GWO (Grey Wolf Optimization)

Mirjalili et al. [18] presented Grey Wolf Optimization, which is a metaheuristic algorithm use the concept of grounded population . The hierarchy of leadership is composed of α (Alpha), β(Beta) and δ (Delta) and α is the most prominent one. β, α, and δ determine the position of the prey and update their locations depending on the predicted locations. In GWO, alpha determines the optimal position, while beta and delta produce the best first and second. Based on these three top spots, other wolves adjust their positions.

1. **Encircling prey:** The mathematical model for encircling the prey is represented as:
$$E_p = |B * X_p(t) - X(t)| \tag{1}$$
$$X(t+1) = X_p(t) - C * E_p \tag{2}$$
Where B and C represents the vectors of coefficient.
X and X_p defines the vectors' position of the prey and grey wolf.
t denotes current value of iteration.
C and B are mathematically represented below:
$$C = 2 * a * r_1 - a \tag{3}$$
$$B = 2 * r_2 \tag{4}$$
2. **Hunting:** Chasing is done by alpha and occasionally beta and delta are also involved. When beta, alpha, and delta work together, they create the top three solutions. Based on the best search agent, others modify their locations and the corresponding mathematical expressions are given below:
$$\begin{aligned} E_{p\alpha} &= |B_1 * X_{p\alpha}(t) - X(t)|; \\ X_1 &= X_{p\alpha}(t) - C_1 * E_{p\alpha} \end{aligned} \tag{5}$$

$$E_{p\beta} = |B_2 * X_{p\beta}(t) - X(t)|; \quad X_2 = X_{p\beta}(t) - C_2 * E_{p\beta} \tag{6}$$

$$E_{p\delta} = |B_3 * X_{p\delta}(t) - X(t)|; \quad X_3 = X_{p\delta}(t) - C_3 * E_{p\delta} \tag{7}$$

$$X(t+1) = (X_1 + X_2 + X_3)/3 \tag{8}$$

3. **Attacking prey:** Grey wolf will cease attacking and resume its hunt, when the prey stops moving. Attack is based on a, which fell from 2 to 0. As value of a is decremented, C gets changed. The value of C is in the interval $[-2a, 2a]$.

3.2 BES (Bald Eagle Search) Algorithm

The bald eagle is at the peak of the food chain due to its enormous size [3]. The bald eagle's primary skill is its capacity to catch the fishes on water at a large gap. Bald eagles go through three primary steps when looking for food. Eagle chooses a search region in the first step and moves in that direction. Eagles begin searching in the chosen area in the second step, and then proceed near their prey in the third step. The choose step, search step, and swooping step are the three key steps of the BES algorithm which are described below:

1. **Select phase:** The bald eagles choose a span of values where there is more available prey during this step. It chooses a location that is dissimilar from previously chosen search region on the basis of data from the previous step. The numerical presentation is:

$$P_{n,i} = P_{best} + \alpha * q(P_{avg} - P_i) \tag{9}$$

   Where changes in position are controlled by α that takes a range from 1.5 to 2. q is a random number that ranges from 0 and 1. P_{best} represents the search area that is selected by bald eagles currently. Information used by the eagles in the previous points is denoted by P_{avg}.
2. **Search phase:** In this step, the eagles conduct a spiral-shaped hunt for searching prey in the selected area. Below is a mathematical justification for the ideal swooping position:

$$P_{i,n} = x(i)(P_i - P_{avg}) + y(i)(P_i - P_{i+1}) + P_i \tag{10}$$

$$x(i) = \frac{xq(i)}{max(|xq|)} \quad y(i) = \frac{yq(i)}{max(|yq|)} \tag{11}$$

$$xq(i) = q(i) * cos(\theta(i)) \quad yq(i) = q(i) * sin(\theta(i)) \tag{12}$$

$$\theta(i) = rand * \pi * a \quad y(i) = rand * R + \theta(i) \tag{13}$$

Parameter a obtains the diagonals among point search and takes the range of values in between 5 to 10. Parameter R has values in the span of 0.5 and 2 that is utilized to search the amount of search phases. When the values of a and R are changed the shape of the spiral will also changed.

3. **Swooping phase:** Eagle shifts from the position determined in the second phase to the optimal hunting location. The behaviour is defined by,

$$P_{i,n} = rand * P_{best} + x_1(i)(P_i - c_1 * P_{avg}) \\ +y_1(i)(P_i - c_2 * P_{best}) \tag{14}$$

where c_1 and c_2 indicates the eagles power of movement to the most suitable location and ranges a value between 1 and 2.

3.3 Hybrid Grey Wolf Optimization and Bald Eagle Search (GWO-BES)

With the aid of the BES algorithm, the shortcomings of GWO have been resolved. The initial stage involves initialising the dataset with all the features. The FS module only chooses the necessary features, ignoring the extraneous features. The position update equation in the Hybrid GWO-BES is shown below:

$$F_{best} = \gamma_{and} * X_1 + (X(t) - c_1 X_2)x(i) + \\ (X(t) - c_2 X_3)y(i) \tag{15}$$

Algorithm 1. Pseudo Code of Hybrid GWO-BES

Input: Dataset matrix as vector in each row
Output: Extracted indexes of relevant features
Step1: Initialize the datasets containing all the features.
Step2: Assign initial values to a, B, C.
Step3: Compute the fitness value of each wolf
$X_{p\alpha}$ - grey wolf first maximum fitness
$X_{p\beta}$ - grey wolf with second maximum fitness
$X_{p\delta}$ - grey wolf with third maximum fitness.
while ((t<Max) **do**
  for (each wolf) **do**
    Update position of current wolf using eqn(15)
  end for
  Update the parameters B and C
  Calculate fitness value of all wolf
  Update $X_{p\alpha}$, $X_{p\beta}$, $X_{p\delta}$
  t=t+1
end while
return selected features as the optimal feature subset

3.4 LSTM (Long-Short Term Memory)

When a model is trained on the training data then it performs well within the range of training data for which it has been trained but it fails to perform for the unseen data as accurate as on the test data used during testing. It happens due to over fitting or under fitting. Over fitting is a situation when the number of inputs to the trained model is more than the number of inputs by which it has been trained. Under fitting is a situation when the number of inputs to the trained model is less than the number of inputs by which it has been trained. To avoid the over fitting or under fitting or both during testing phase, the model should be trained in generalized manner. LSTM is one of the most popular and successful Recurrent neural networks (RNNs) architectures used to overcome the mention issues [6]. LSTM contains the memory cell as a computation unit that replaces conventional artificial neurons of hidden layer. These memory cells helps to networks to associate memories and input remote in time effectively which makes LSTM suitable to grasp data dynamically over time and making higher prediction capacity for LSTM. The designed LSTM classifier contains (a) an input layer that contains 'n' number of memory cells where 'n' is the selected number of sequence learning features followed by (b) two more LSTM layers and (c) a dense layer and (d) finally one output layer that contains 'm' number of memory cells where 'm' is the number of categories of the target attributes. The value of m is for NSLKDD is 5 and for CICIDS-2017 is 4. The basic structure of LSTM is presented and discussed in [27].

4 Results and Analysis

4.1 Dataset Description

In this study the implemented model use CICIDS-2017 and NSL-KDD datasets. First one [30] consists of 225,745 data packages that include more than 80 numbers of features and greater than 5 d' worth of network scheme. The CICIDS-2017 contains seven different types of attack, including Infiltration, Botnet, DoS, DDoS, Web, Brute Force and Heartbleed. NSL-KDD dataset [8] is offline network data based on KDD 99 dataset. The above one contains four categories of attacks and 41 features named as DoS, Probe, R2L and U2R.

4.2 Performance Metrics

This section describes the performance metrics to evaluate the performance of the implemented NIDS model. The description of the evaluation metrics are given below:

1. **Accuracy:** Accuracy is calculated as the proportion of the number of classifications a model properly predicts to the total number of predictions produced.

$$Accuracy = \frac{TN + TP}{TN + FN + TP + FP} \tag{16}$$

2. **Precision:** Precision is defined as the ratio of predicted positives and actual positives.
$$Precision = \frac{TP}{FP + TP} \tag{17}$$
3. **Recall:** The recall is calculated as the proportion of Positive samples which were correctly recognized as Positive to all the actual Positive samples. In this study recall is considered as the Attack Detection Rate (ADR).
$$Recall = \frac{TP}{TP + FN} \tag{18}$$
Where TP is correctly predicted intrusions and FN is incorrectly predicted intrusions.
4. **F1 Score:** The F1 score is defined as the harmonic mean of precision and recall. Based on precision rate and recall rate, it determines accuracy.
$$F_1 Score = \frac{2TP}{FN + FP + 2TP} \tag{19}$$
Where the amount of normal networks are denoted by False Positive (FP) which represents the attacks classified incorrectly.
5. **False Alarm Rate (FAR):** Percentage of identification occurrences in which unauthorized people are mistakenly accepted is known as the false acceptance rate or FAR. To reduce the FP alarms FAR should be low otherwise, system administrator would become perplexed.
$$FAR = \frac{FP}{TN + FP} \tag{20}$$
The number of networks that are accurately categorised as normal is denoted by TN.
6. **False Negative Rate (FNR):** It is defined as the ratio of all incorrectly classified attacks to all correctly classified attacks. A higher FNR number denotes a higher frequency of false alarms.
$$FNR = \frac{FN}{FN + TP} \tag{21}$$

4.3 Results

The proposed GWO-BES-LSTM model has been implemented on HP BladeSystem c7000 machine linux environment having Intel Xeon processors, 16 GB RAM, 1 TB hard disk for one blade. Where Anaconda Python is installed in one blade. NSL-KDD and CICIDS-2017 datasets are utilized for experiments. Confusion matrix of NSL-KDD and CICIDS-2017 datasets presented by Fig. 2 and Fig. 3 respectively after complete execution the GWO-BES-LSTM model on the testing dataset of each dataset.

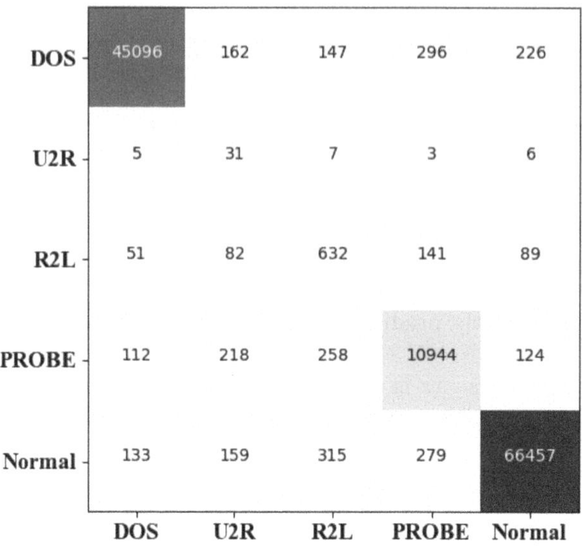

Fig. 2. Confusion matrix for NSL-KDD after applying GWO-BES-LSTM model

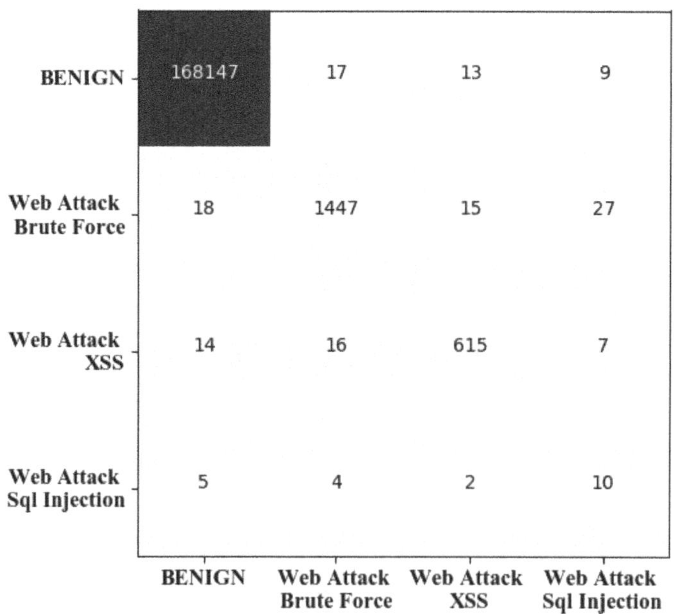

Fig. 3. Confusion matrix for attacks for CICIDS-2017 after applying GWO-BES-LSTM model

Table 1. Performance values for GWO-BES-LSTM model on NSL-KDD datasets and CICIDS-2017

Dataset	NSL-KDD	CICIDS-2017
Accuracy	99.10	99.52
F1 Score	99.75	98.12
Precision	99.59	98.25
Recall	99.91	98
FAR	0.184	1.88
FNR	0.089	2

The model has been trained and tested on NSL-KDD and CICIDS-2017 one by one and obtained values of considered parameters are presented in Table 1.

Proposed model is compared from other recent models for multi class classification and presented in Table 2. Average accuracy has been compared for multi class classification and presented by Fig. 4.

Table 2. Comparison of GWO-BES-LSTM model with other models for multi classification

Dataset	Name of the Model	Acc. (%)	Prec. (%)	Recall (%)	F-Score (%)
NSL-KDD	LSTM [11]	77.5	79.6	77.6	78.6
	MR-DHPN [11]	80.2	80.6	80.0	80.4
	Proposed	99.1	97.8	98.2	97.8
CICIDS-2017	LSTM [11]	97.0	96.8	98.6	97.3
	MR-DHPN [11]	98.6	98.6	99.6	98.6
	Proposed	99.5	98.4	98.7	98.8

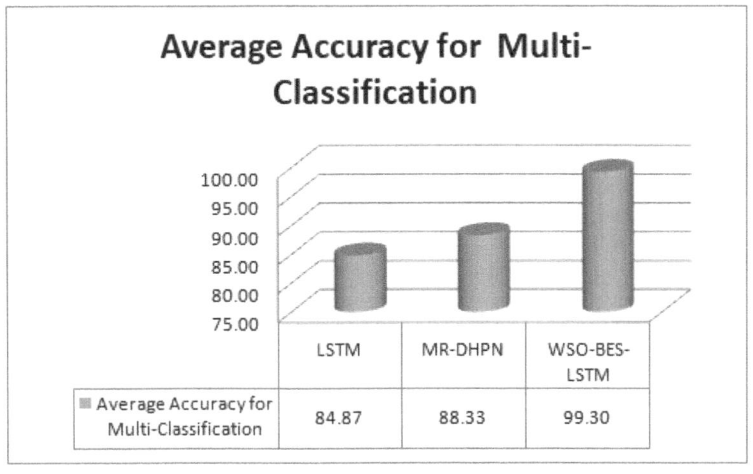

Fig. 4. Average accuracy comparison for multi classification

5 Conclusion

In this paper, efficient intrusion detection based on feature selection method has been proposed. Feature selection part takes the result from hybrid GWO with BES optimization algorithm. To categorize of intrusions in the network, a long short term memory (LSTM) was employed. The proposed model achieved better performance when compared with the existing approach, and the IDS with GWO-BES based feature selection achieved better detection rate and accuracy. The proposed NIDS model has got low FAR and FNR which improves the system performance. The proposed model is able to capture all types of known and unknown attacks. The proposed NIDS can be expanded to more different types of networks such as IoT network, 5G network, etc.

References

1. Al-Zewairi, M., Almajali, S., Awajan, A.: Experimental evaluation of a multi-layer feed-forward artificial neural network classifier for network intrusion detection system. In: 2017 International Conference on New Trends in Computing Sciences (ICTCS), pp. 167–172. IEEE (2017)
2. Aljawarneh, S., Aldwairi, M., Yassein, M.B.: Anomaly-based intrusion detection system through feature selection analysis and building hybrid efficient model. J. Comput. Sci. **25**, 152–160 (2018)
3. Alsattar, H., Zaidan, A., Zaidan, B.: Novel meta-heuristic bald eagle search optimisation algorithm. Artifi. Intell. Rev., 1–28 (2019)
4. Alzughaibi, S., El Khediri, S.: A cloud intrusion detection systems based on dnn using backpropagation and pso on the cse-cic-ids2018 dataset. Appl. Sci. **13**(4), 2276 (2023)
5. Ashfaq, R.A.R., Wang, X.Z., Huang, J.Z., Abbas, H., He, Y.L.: Fuzziness based semi-supervised learning approach for intrusion detection system. Inf. Sci. **378**, 484–497 (2017)
6. Chen, K., Zhou, Y., Dai, F.: A lstm-based method for stock returns prediction: a case study of china stock market. In: 2015 IEEE International Conference on Big Data (Big Data), pp. 2823–2824 (2015). https://doi.org/10.1109/BigData.2015.7364089
7. Deshpande, P., Sharma, S.C., Peddoju, S.K., Junaid, S.: Hids: a host based intrusion detection system for cloud computing environment. Inter. J. Syst. Assurance Eng. Manag. **9**(3), 567–576 (2018)
8. Dhanabal, L., Shantharajah, S.: A study on nsl-kdd dataset for intrusion detection system based on classification algorithms. Inter. J. Adv. Res. Comput. Commun. Eng. **4**(6), 446–452 (2015)
9. Ghosh, P., Mandal, A.K., Kumar, R.: An efficient cloud network intrusion detection system. In: Information Systems Design and Intelligent Applications, pp. 91–99. Springer (2015). https://doi.org/10.1007/978-81-322-2250-7_10
10. Hajimirzaei, B., Navimipour, N.J.: Intrusion detection for cloud computing using neural networks and artificial bee colony optimization algorithm. ICT Express **5**(1), 56–59 (2019)
11. He, H., Sun, X., He, H., Zhao, G., He, L., Ren, J.: A novel multimodal-sequential approach based on multi-view features for network intrusion detection. IEEE Access **7**, 183207–183221 (2019)

12. Hizal, S., ÇAVUŞOLU, Ü., AKGÜN, D.: A new deep learning based intrusion detection system for cloud security. In: 2021 3rd International Congress on Human-Computer Interaction, Optimization and Robotic Applications (HORA), pp. 1–4. IEEE (2021)
13. Ijaz, S., Hashmi, F.A., Asghar, S., Alam, M.: Vector based genetic algorithm to optimize predictive analysis in network security. Appl. Intell. **48**(5), 1086–1096 (2018)
14. Malik, A.J., Khan, F.A.: A hybrid technique using binary particle swarm optimization and decision tree pruning for network intrusion detection. Clust. Comput. **21**(1), 667–680 (2018)
15. Maza, S., Touahria, M.: Feature selection for intrusion detection using new multi-objective estimation of distribution algorithms. Appl. Intell. **49**(12), 4237–4257 (2019)
16. Milani, B.A., Navimipour, N.J.: A comprehensive review of the data replication techniques in the cloud environments: major trends and future directions. J. Netw. Comput. Appl. **64**, 229–238 (2016)
17. Mindo, K., Thiga, M.M., Karume, S.M.: Implementing a fused machine learning model for the provision of smart health care in manets. Inter. J. Comput. Sci. Inform. Sec. (IJCSIS) **17**(9) (2019)
18. Mirjalili, S., Mirjalili, S.M., Lewis, A.: Grey wolf optimizer. Adv. Eng. Softw. **69**, 46–61 (2014)
19. Mishra, P., Pilli, E.S., Varadharajan, V., Tupakula, U.: Intrusion detection techniques in cloud environment: a survey. J. Netw. Comput. Appl. **77**, 18–47 (2017)
20. Modi, C., Patel, D., Borisaniya, B., Patel, H., Patel, A., Rajarajan, M.: A survey of intrusion detection techniques in cloud. J. Netw. Comput. Appl. **36**(1), 42–57 (2013)
21. Mohammadi, S., Mirvaziri, H., Ghazizadeh-Ahsaee, M., Karimipour, H.: Cyber intrusion detection by combined feature selection algorithm. J. inform. Sec. appli. **44**, 80–88 (2019)
22. Patil, R., Dudeja, H., Modi, C.: Designing an efficient security framework for detecting intrusions in virtual network of cloud computing. Comput. Sec. **85**, 402–422 (2019)
23. Pham, N.T., Foo, E., Suriadi, S., Jeffrey, H., Lahza, H.F.M.: Improving performance of intrusion detection system using ensemble methods and feature selection. In: Proceedings of the Australasian Computer Science Week Multiconference, pp. 1–6 (2018)
24. Popoola, E., Adewumi, A.O.: Efficient feature selection technique for network intrusion detection system using discrete differential evolution and decision. IJ Netw. Sec. **19**(5), 660–669 (2017)
25. Sai Satyanarayana Reddy, S., Chatterjee, P., Mamatha, C.: Intrusion detection in wireless network using fuzzy logic implemented with genetic algorithm. In: Peng, SL., Dey, N., Bundele, M. (eds.) Computing and Network Sustainability. LNNS, vol 75. Springer, Singapore (2019). https://doi.org/10.1007/978-981-13-7150-9_45
26. Sakr, M.M., Tawfeeq, M.A., El-Sisi, A.B.: Network intrusion detection system based pso-svm for cloud computing. Inter. J. Comput. Netw. Inform. Sec. **11**(3), 22 (2019)
27. Sarkar, N., Gupta, R., Keserwani, P.K., Govil, M.C.: Air quality index prediction using an effective hybrid deep learning model. Environ. Pollut. **315**, 120404 (2022)
28. Sathiyadhas, S.S., Soosai Antony, M.C.V.: A network intrusion detection system in cloud computing environment using dragonfly improved invasive weed optimization

integrated shepard convolutional neural network. Inter. J. Adaptive Control Signal Process. **36**(5), 1060–1076 (2022)
29. Seth, J.K., Chandra, S.: Mids: metaheuristic based intrusion detection system for cloud using k-nn and mgwo. In: International Conference on Advances in Computing and Data Sciences, pp. 411–420. Springer (2018)
30. Sharafaldin, I., Lashkari, A.H., Ghorbani, A.A.: Toward generating a new intrusion detection dataset and intrusion traffic characterization. In: ICISSP, pp. 108–116 (2018)
31. Shyla, S.I., Sujatha, S.: Cloud security: Lkm and optimal fuzzy system for intrusion detection in cloud environment. J. Intell. Syst. **29**(1), 1626–1642 (2020)
32. Singh, D.A.A.G., Priyadharshini, R., Leavline, E.J.: Cuckoo optimisation based intrusion detection system for cloud computing. Inter. J. Comput. Netw. Inform. Sec. **10**(11), 42 (2018)
33. Srinivas, B., Mandal, I., Keshavarao, S.: Virtual machine migration-based intrusion detection system in cloud environment using deep recurrent neural network. Cybernet. Syst., 1–21 (2022)
34. Sultana, N., Chilamkurti, N., Peng, W., Alhadad, R.: Survey on sdn based network intrusion detection system using machine learning approaches. Peer-to-Peer Netw. Appli. **12**(2), 493–501 (2019)
35. Wang, W., Du, X., Wang, N.: Building a cloud ids using an efficient feature selection method and svm. IEEE Access **7**, 1345–1354 (2018)
36. Zaman, M., Lung, C.H.: Evaluation of machine learning techniques for network intrusion detection. In: NOMS 2018 - 2018 IEEE/IFIP Network Operations and Management Symposium, pp. 1–5 (2018)
37. Zarrabi, A., Zarrabi, A.: Internet intrusion detection system service in a cloud. Inter. J. Comput. Sci. Issues (IJCSI) **9**(5), 308 (2012)

A Deep Ensemble Species Distribution Model for Multilabel Species Prediction Using Multimodal Data

Dipanwita Saha[1,2] and Kartick Chandra Mondal[1(✉)]

[1] Department of Information Technology, Jadavpur University, Kolkata, India
{kartickjgec}@gmail.com
[2] Department of Computer Science and Engineering, Hooghly Engineering and Technology College, Hooghly, India

Abstract. The interpretation of the geographic diversity pattern can be explored by establishing an effective species distribution model (SDM). This work aims to identify the relationship between the Indian ecosystem and map the predictions of the region-specific Magnoliopsida and Aves classes under the kingdom of Plantae-Animalia species occurrences in India. In this effort, the GBIF-based dataset is utilized over the Indian boundary while integrating the satellite image with the time series data of species occurrences. Scientific approaches developed the multimodal ensemble (MME) integrated neural network model by combining Resnet-6, XGB regression, and region-specific top-20 multilabel species distribution methods. Furthermore, this model is exploited with the patches of Satellite images, Climatic, and Landsat cubes through a deep convolutional neural network and Resnet-6. Different preprocessing approaches like Albumentations, dynamic transformation, and PCA-based reduction are also utilized for multiclass-based species prediction. Here, different combinations of predictor data sets with optimized hyperparameter tuning provide satisfactory accuracy in the predictions of species occurrences. In particular, here we have evaluated the predictions that impact the association of Aves species with Magnoliopsida plant species. This paper presents the ROC curve in the resultant analysis of the multimodal ensemble-based neural network model.

Keywords: Species distribution model · Multimodal ensemble · Deep neural network · Species prediction

1 Introduction

India is a large physiographical region in Southern Asia and is rich in biodiversity and growing economic infrastructure [4]. Due to the excessive utilization of natural resources, Indian flora and fauna are now endangered, according to recent research. The rapidly changing environment makes it difficult to predict the occurrence of Indian species. In current scenarios, it becomes a challenging

K. Chandra Mondal et al. (Eds.): CICBA 2025, CCIS 2863, pp. 181–196, 2026.
https://doi.org/10.1007/978-3-032-17184-9_14

task to observe plant species depending on spatial resolution at a higher rate for the estimation of filling the research gaps in the species distribution model [12] while exploiting remote sensing satellite image data integration [11]. In this context, the GBIF dataset is used to predict the presence of Plantae and Animalia kingdom-related species combined in the Magnoliopsida and Aves classes within the Indian subcontinent. Where different scientific multilabel species within this combined class are inspected. In addition to this work, it has the potential to implement the model for the identification of plant and animal species [14] occurrences that are interrelated with the conservation of biodiversity.

The main objective of this analysis of the GBIF-based dataset is to estimate a list of observed plant and animal species in specific regions [3]. This can develop an efficient species-related biodiversity conservation strategy. In this work, we have utilized a large training dataset of plant and animal species specifically the Magnoliopsida and Aves occurrence data obtained from GBIF with a variety of environmental rasters consisting of the land cover, soil, human pressure, and climatic circumstances within the specific sample period of 2018–2024 in the Indian territory. The Magnoliopsida are large flowering plants that can produce food, medicinal value, and deliver essential nutrients. The growth of this type of plant is indirectly related to the Aves species through the operation of pollination, and the spreading of seeds. So we are considering our focus for the predictions of those categorized species data for observing the Plantae and Animalia kingdom occurrences, which can produce the effective exploration of biodiversity in the concerned area of India. It has been known that birds come from the Aves class, and it is also an important species to maintain a balanced economic environment in India. To monitor the predictions of Plantae and Animalia species in the Indian region, proper utilization of both observed data and environmental data is required, which can employ the constructive distribution of those species. The ecological distribution [7] of species represented in the environmental space is encompassed by different climatic variables like temperature, precipitation, nature of the soil, and land cover. In this effort, the spatial arrangement combines with ecosystem variables to generate the effective distribution of plant and animal species in India.

It has been found that many of the Species distribution model (SDM) [11] data are not assembled properly based on the specific regions. The dataset consisted of over 2 million observed plant species and about 4.4 million animal species, which are preferred to be reduced with a PCA-driven procedure for further analysis. This inspection of species occurrence [6] data is combined with high-resolution remotely sensed satellite imagery, such as Sentinel, and Landsat build resources. Hence, our proposed novel methodology constructs the SDM-related problem solution effectively, which enables us to analyze the integrated approach for remotely sensed SDM for monitoring biodiversity-related issues.

This paper is decorated into six sections, where the first Sect. 1 is initiated with the objective, previous related work, motivation, limitations, and organization with the tabulated form in Table 1. In the second Sect. 2 dataset description incorporates with Indian Plantae and Animalia kingdom-based Magnoliopsida and Aves species occurrences observed data. In Sect. 3, the proposed methodology for the prediction of region-specific species occurrences presents different aggregation and data preprocessing procedures with the statistical metrics. In Sect. 4, the results reveal the accuracy and enhancement of model performance. Finally, this article concludes in Sect. 5 with future opportunities for learning the SDM and predictions of properly categorized species bounded over a large area for the conservation of biodiversity.

Recent work in 2024 contains a dataset named the GeoPlant [12] concentrated on the European region for predicting plant species bounded in the specific regions over the integration of remotely sensed cubes and environmental raster values. The explored methodology [2] utilizes the RGB imagery by adding the latitude and longitude-based coordinates for the evaluation of model performance. In 2022, the GeoLifeCLEF [10] dataset based on European flora fauna produces SDM through the utilization of ensemble deep learning models, where the method attains low accuracy in the top 30 test datasets as mentioned by Kellenberger, B., & Tuia, D. (2022). The satellite imagery-based monitoring for the classification problem has become difficult due to the location-based identification of species required therein, which was indicated from [9].

The related SDM-based research condensed with deep learning [13] has been identified as computer vision-based [17] issues where the unobserved labels become unpredictable and develop negative impacts for the proper estimation of plant species within the Indian regions. The probability of species presence mentioned in [16] is determined by the specific indicator-based function, either 0 or 1. The related research background is explored with the utilized methods and their resultant findings as shown in Table 1.

2 Dataset Description

2.1 Indian Plantae and Animalia Species Observation Data

In this work, the Global Biodiversity Information Facility (GBIF) based Indian dataset consisted of more than ten thousand Plant and Animal species [15] with presence-absence (PA) and presence-only (PO) occurrences of survey records. The trained dataset consists of observation data and different environmental predictor data. The PO data consisted of approximately a million species occurrence data obtained from the GBIF. The Magnoliopsida class comes from the Phylum of Tracheophyta under the Plantae kingdom. The Aves class comes from the phylum of Chordata under the Animalia kingdom. The dataset of PO data consisted of the following fields: year, day, month, latitude, longitude, geo-uncertainty, taxon key, kingdom, genus, taxon rank, scientific name, state/province, and country. These observed attributes cover the Indian Plantae and Animalia kingdom-based Magnoliopsida and Aves class species data.

Some of the processed train datasets for the Indian Animalia kingdom, incorporating Aves species, are explored in the representation of Fig. 1. Figure 2 measures the region-wise surveys for the esteemed species within the Indian boundary from 2018 to 2024 in a logarithmic graphical outline.

Table 1. Related research articles on different approaches and findings on the study area

Research Article	Methodology	Findings
Picek, Lukas, et al. (2024) [12]	XGBoost, MaxEnt, Multimodal ensemble-based logistic regression, Naïve approaches	Multimodal ensemble performed better than other approaches with nearly 90% accuracy
Botella, Christophe, et al. (2019) [4],Coulibaly, Solemane, et al. (2022) [5]	Deep convolutional neural network (CNN), XGBoost, ANN, Poisson point process, KNN	From the Mean Reciprocal Rank (MRR), the CNN predicted the occurrences of species with the extraction of the spatial-environmental patterns
Lorieul, Titouan, et al. (2021) [11]	Bimodal CNN and RF	CNN efficiently predicts necessary informative variables for the distribution of species
Rawlings, Darren, and Tim Chopard (2024) [14]	XGBoost regression and neural network-based multi-modal model	XGBoost regression model produces satisfactory count predictions of occurrences of species, and if the trained data instances increase
Botella, Christophe, et al. (2018), [3]	Parametric discrete CNN, Poisson count procedure, and MAXENT model	The optimized version of CNN surpassed other models
Estopinan, Joaquim, et al. (2022) [7]	Deep SDM and CNN (Inception v3)	CNN produces an accuracy of 83% and distribution of species with taxonomic diversity and environmental preferences in spatial-temporal context
Deneu, Benjamin, et al. (2021) [6]	DNN-SDM, CNN-SDM, Gradient tree boosting BT, RF	CNN-SDM reveals better predictive performance for the identification of rare species

The combined observed training data related to species compensated with presence-absence (PA) and presence-only (PO) build nominal categorical data. A large amount of Presence-absence (PA) data is bound to specific Indian regions, and it becomes costly to maintain updated data. The establishment of the proposed model that mapped large taxonomic diversity between species of the Plantae and Animalia kingdoms is complicated, so the dataset is reduced from one million to ten thousand.

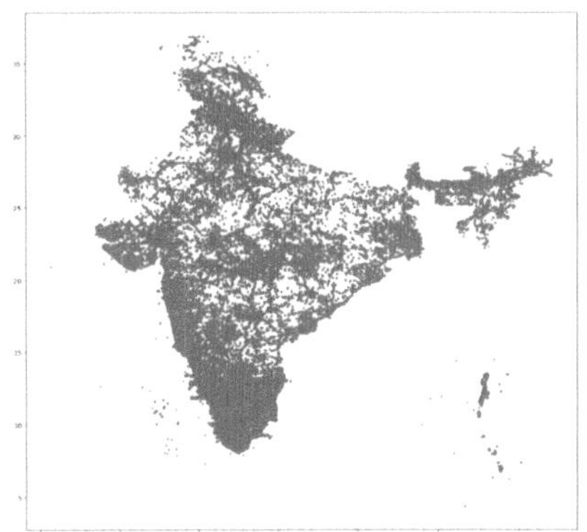

Fig. 1. The presence only data set of Aves species

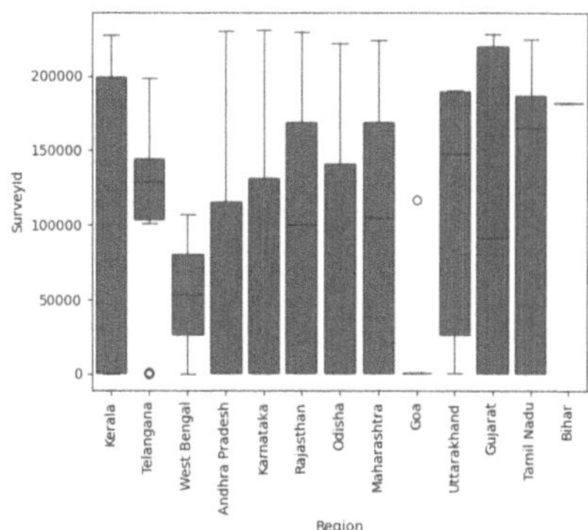

Fig. 2. Region wise survey for Magnoliopsida species

2.2 Derivation of Dataset

The existing utilized dataset consisted of the species occurrence discovery data from GBIF. The Sentinel-built satellite image patches, satellite time series climatic data originating from Chelsa (Climatologies at high resolution for the Earth's land surface areas), and raster-based environmental data have been employed. Furthermore, the environmental rasters consisting of Landcover, Elevation, Soilgrids, average bioclimatic, and Human footprint data serve as the predictors bounded in India, which are described in detail in the Sect. 2.3. The three-band (RGB) and one-band (NIR) of 128×128 JPEG-based satellite image composed of 10M resolutive Sentinel-2A derived Satellite image patch data. The diagrammatic description of the originating dataset is represented in Fig. 3.

2.3 Environmental Raster Dataset

The prepared environmental raster dataset consisted of bioclimatic, elevation, soil, land cover, and human footprint datasets in the Indian range. This raster can consist of some GEOTIFF file-based images, which are projected with a proper coordinate system (CRS) for processing with the altitude data combined

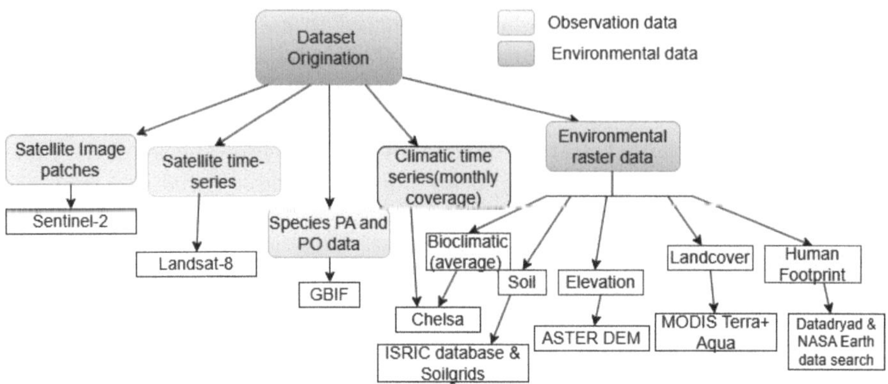

Fig. 3. Representation of dataset resources

with some CSV files. The Landsat dataset consisted of Landcover HDF data of MODIS Terra & Aqua with 500m resolution tiles obtained from the NASA Earth data site. The bioclimatic data that cover the Indian region are obtained from Chelsa, aggregated with a raster type of 500m resolution. They derived 19 properties of minimum, maximum, mean temperature, and precipitation in a CSV file for every month. Elevation raster data extracted from the ASTER DEM model consisted of scalar values and topographical image data. For Soil, the soil properties correlated with plant species are extracted from the soil grids-originated image data and ISRIC(International Soil Reference and Information Centre) database-derived variables in CSV. Human Footprint data was obtained from Datadryad, which consisted of the global coverage information, and it can also be produced from the NASA Earth data search, where the world coverage data is loaded in the form of image granules. This human pressure data is also projected using a derived satellite-based raster. Moreover, the Landsat and the monthly averaged climatic satellite time series consisted of scalar values and cubes.

3 Proposed Methodology

3.1 Aggregation of Data

The large variant of the species presence training dataset is aggregated and combined with the raster cubes and values data. The raster-based satellite images cover an area of 1280 m^2 and have a formatted pixel size of 128. Each satellite image is standardized with normalization before being fed as training samples to the model. The 19 bioclimatic averaged data variables are utilized for this species distribution model. The general architecture proposed for the procedure of the work has been deployed with the help of a Google Colab GPU setup in Fig. 4.

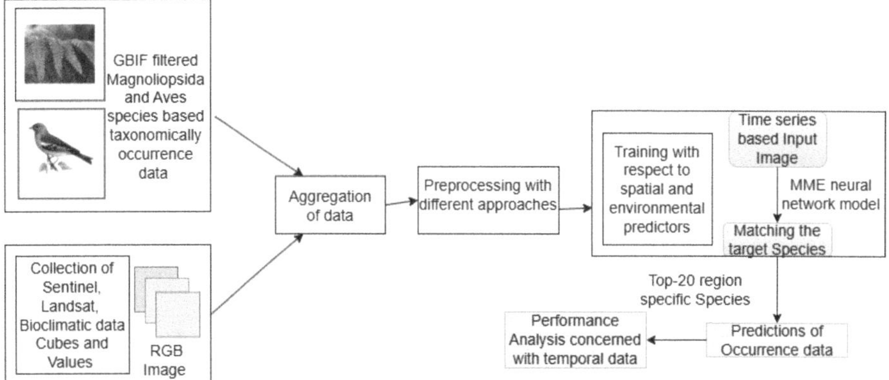

Fig. 4. Proposed framework

The setup used two separate PyTorch Dataloaders instead of just one, where flipping an image sideways or up-and-down, along with other changes, this transformation eventuated separately.

3.2 Data Pre-processing

Reducing the outliers and enhancing the performance of model data processing requires effective transformation [1], which is recommended to be free from missing values and infinite values. Even without affecting the shape of the data, the Indian regions are transformed into one one-hot encoded form of categorical values. The PCA is applied for the reduction of the dataset, which limits the unnecessary noise bound in specific regions and is processed with environmental rasters to build an encoded dataset for the XGB model. From the human footprint dataset, the water and roads are removed, and less occurrence data is utilized to remove the overfitting conditions. Different predictor datasets and utilized preprocessing approaches are illustrated in Table 2.

3.3 Novel Species Distributive Multimodal Ensemble Model

The deep neural network-based Resnet-6 model [8] was applied to speed up the training process of the different combined Sentinel, Landsat, and environmental raster data. Those are processed with a modified dynamic CNN architecture for the extraction of the image features to learn them and give information about the complex relationship pattern of the data. The train and test splitting of the dataset combines 85% of the train data and 15% of the test data. PO and PA data are processed with an XGB regression-based model, whereas the environmental rasters are processed with a MAXENT-based [9] regression model. The Landsat, Sentinel, and climatic [18] data utilized for a multimodal ensemble neural network-based layered model are processed from normalized Resnet-6,

Table 2. Preprocessing of remotely sensed data cubes and values

Predictors dataset	Approaches utilization
Landsat data	- Processed with drop null values for species Id attributes
	- Remove duplicate values on survey Id
	- Transformation of tensor shape to height, width, and Channel to ensure the correct format
	- Permutations to change the tensor shape that can compose over the train data loader
Sentinel data	- Transformed to a tensor with Albumentations
	- Composing the Random brightness contrast, color jitter, and optical distortion in a 0.2 scale of probability value
	- The Sentinel data is filtered by adjusting those compositions
	- Transformation, and drop duplicates are utilized over the survey and species Id data for assembling them into the list
	- The Sentinel data is processed with the concatenation of tensors
Climatic data	-Null values and duplicate values are removed
	- Transform the data into the correct encoded format of a tensor that corresponds to the class index 1 for each species
	- Permutation is applied to change the shape to channel, height, width, height, width, and channel
Combined data	-Merging the other dataset of Sentinel Landsat and the Climatic data
	- Normalized tensor transformation to the mean and standard deviation
	- Clustered Species and Survey Id into dictionaries
	- Null values and duplicated surveyId removed
	- Landsat and Climatic-based data are permuted
	- Sentinel data are transformed to a tensor with concatenated RGB and NIR values
	- Tensor data is converted to a numpy array

modified Swin-version-2 transformer for getting the top-20 predicted species [19]. The data circulatory diagram of different datasets in the investigated multimodal ensemble neural network model is shown in Fig. 5.

3.4 Different Evaluative Metrics

Different occurrences of test datasets are utilized for predictions of one species' presence data in each location. The predictions of region-specific top 20 species are classified with the proposed model, validated against the Geolifeclef-based external dataset. The set values of classification are utilized for the average of the Top-20 error rate calculations. The sampled presence of species is measured

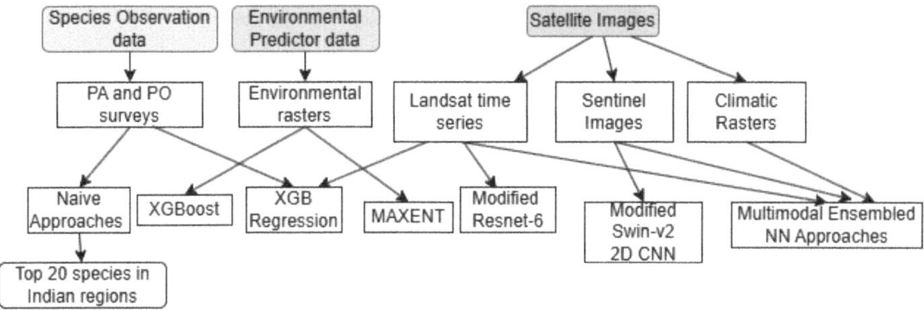

Fig. 5. Multimodal NN-based ensemble species distribution model

with the average of presence-absence surveys within a given specific period and zones within the Indian subcontinent. The rate of error for predictions of the wrong species within the Indian regions can be computed through the following formulation.

$$T_{\text{avg}} = \frac{1}{N} \sum_{i=1}^{n} e_i$$

where

$$e_i = \begin{cases} 1 & \text{if } i \in \{1, 2, \ldots, 20\} \\ 0 & \text{otherwise} \end{cases}$$

4 Empirical Result and Discussion

By using the proposed multimodal ensemble neural network-based model with the integrated datasets, the resultant Predicted Magnoliopsida composed Plantae kingdom species occurrences are obtained in Fig. 6 within the Indian coordinate system. The predicted Magnoliopsida species occurrences for specific surveyId have been found in the given Table 3. Similarly, the predicted Indian Aves combined Animalia kingdom species occurrences are obtained in the projected Fig. 7. The obtained value of the one-way Anova test and t-test becomes statistically significant as the p-value ranges between 0 to 1. The p-values are for ANOVA 0.0706 and t-test 0.0565. The 95% confidence intervals for comparing different region-specific observations of species occurrences lie within a normal scale.

The resultant Aves species related to the scientific name consisted of a specific location in the Indian state, whereas the yearly counts predictions are shown in Table 4. The optimized model consisted of a softmax activation in the neural network model, which was tuned with a hyperparameter, while this procedure refined the model's performance.

To measure the local contribution of each feature based on prediction, the SHAP values (Shapley additive explanation) in Fig. 8 help to interpret the influence of the features. The employed analysis provides a clear illustration of the

Table 3. Resultant Magnoliopsida predictions

Survey Id	Predicted Species Ids
212	2765942 2853796 2882429 2925463 2956947 3056375 3084023 3084670 3087725 3170241
642	2874599 2918203 2928673 2956966 2960284 2962831 2971499 2972128 2975756 3058543
1256	3084670 3087725 3170241 3171169 3173254 5303371 5339879 5415460 5546922 5571773
3855	2960284 2962831 2971499 2972128 2975756 3058543 3067891 3068937 3080784 3149462
4889	2702462 2703935 2860119 2900484 2928673 2968532 3054181 3147913 3149462 3169652

Table 4. Resultant Aves Ppedictions

Species	State/Province	Individual Count	Year
Pycnonotus cafer	Tamil Nadu	4.0	2020
Corvus splendens	Maharashtra	5.0	2020
Psittacula krameri	West Bengal	1.0	2020
Corvus macrorhynchos	Karnataka	2.0	2020
Loriculus vernalis	Kerala	1.0	2020

most important features of soilgrid- nitrogen, climatic precipitation, average temperature, population density, among other predictor variables. The predicted multilabel taxonomic variety based on species of the Aves class is inspected in the ROC curve produced with the probability of the occurrences that are contributed in Fig. 9.

While analyzing the region-specific Aves and Magnoliopsida species, combining the relationship of different attributes and inspecting the prediction of occurrence pattern of species, it was observed decreased the frequency of one impacting the other decreased.

The error rates for these interpretations have been produced in the given portrayals of the Fig. 10, where it is clear that with the increasing epoch sharp decrease in error occurred. The increase in GPU memory usage imposed by the proposed design presents a significant limitation that heavily influences the training process. The permutation-based feature importance and SHAP values comparative interpretations are represented in Fig. 11.

We picked a multi-label regression XGBoost model because it could make predictions in the form of fake chances for each type of species. This ensemble architecture integrates the probabilities into a weighted average. From the exploratory analysis, the top 10 states of India depicted the number of Aves classified Animalia kingdom species occurrences in the following Fig. 12. The ROC curve in Fig. 13 provides the region-specific classification for the prediction of the Indian plant kingdom, building the distribution of species of the Magnoliopsida genus. Where the proposed multimodal ensembled constructed neural network model produces an accuracy of 92% and the Animalia kingdom ground Aves genus species reveals 99%.

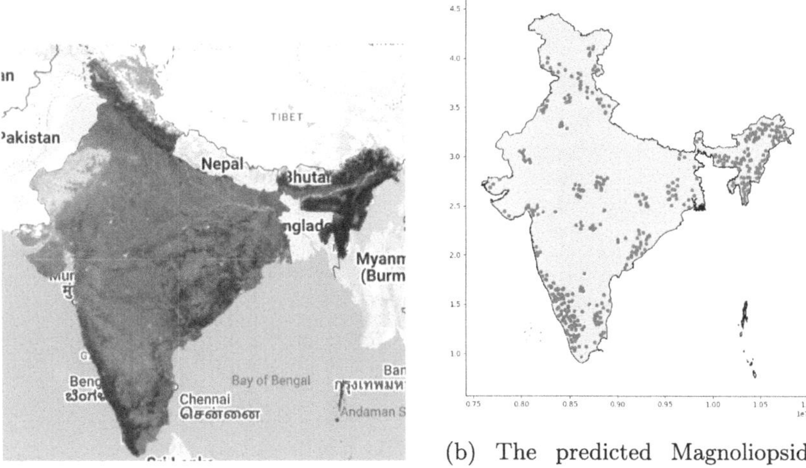

(a) NDVI based Interpretation

(b) The predicted Magnoliopsida species occurrences

Fig. 6. Predicted Indian Plantae species occurrence data

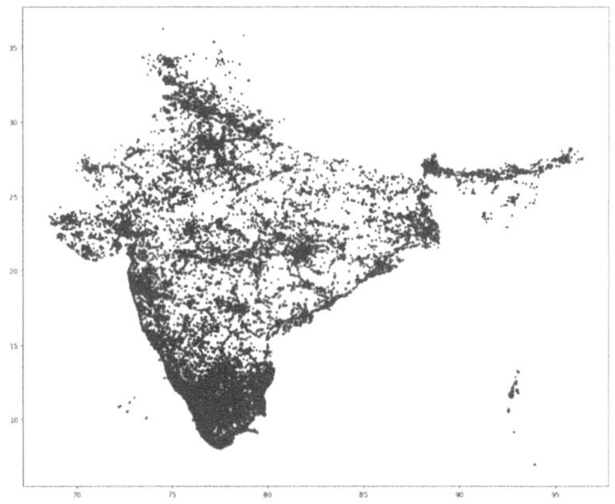

Fig. 7. The predicted occurrences of Indian Aves species

By considering the Swin Transformers, which can split an image into small pieces and handle them in steps from simple to complex. Beginning with small areas of patches that combine them slowly combine to form the greater ones. This helps the network understand important details at different levels, making it better at tasks that need both precise information and broader context. Different comparative baselines that are analysed over utilized datasets in this work have been settled in the Table 5 and organized in the Fig. 14.

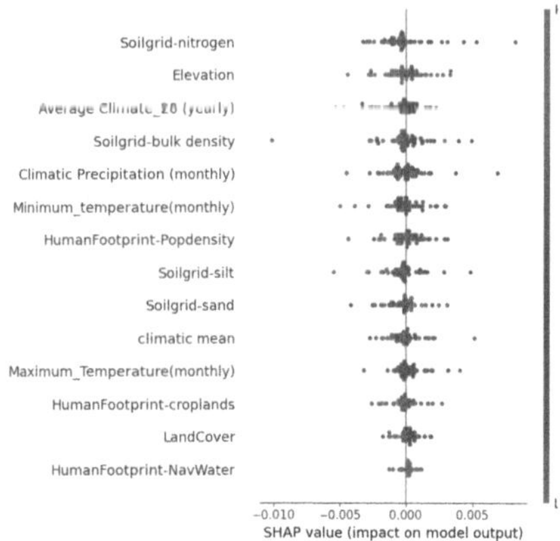

Fig. 8. Feature importance based SHAP values

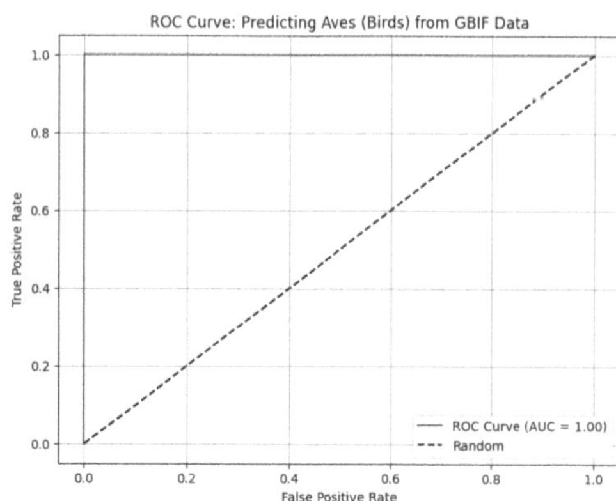

Fig. 9. ROC curve for predicted distribution of Aves species multilabel mapping

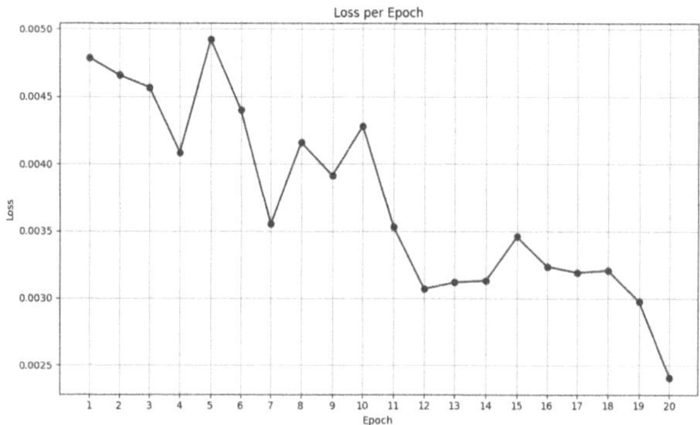

Fig. 10. Error rates for region-specific predictions of Species

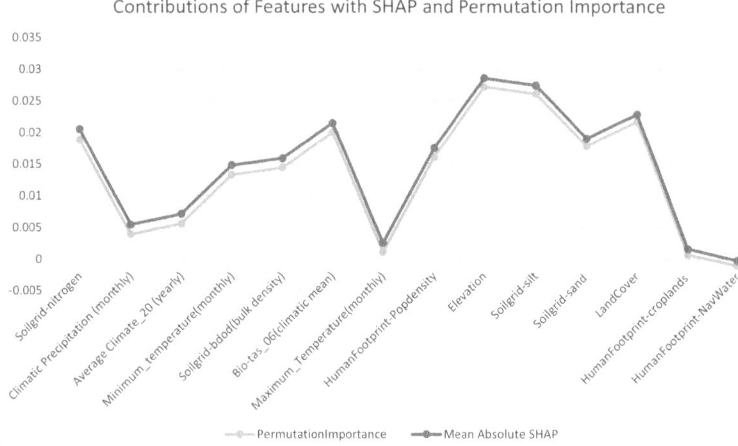

Fig. 11. Permutation importance and SHAP values contribution over features

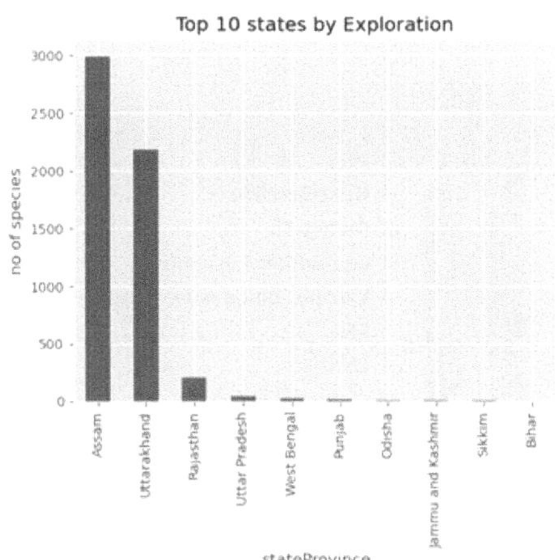

Fig. 12. The top 10 states of occurrences of Indian Aves species

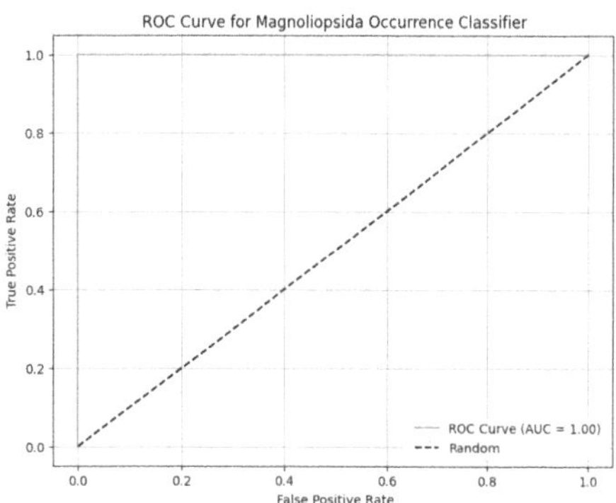

Fig. 13. ROC curve for predicted distribution of Magnoliopsida species relevance mapping

Table 5. .

Baseline Models	AUC	Recall	F1	Datacubes
Naïve Baseline	93%	42%	26%	PA meta data
Single modality ResNet-18	88%	38%	27%	PA meta data, Landsat cubes
Conventional Baseline (Xgboost, MaxEnt)	89%	48%	28%	Soilgrids, Landcover, Climatic
Variance-based model ensembled(ResNet-50, Inception-v4, DenseNet-201)	57%	15%	8%	Sentinel images
RF	97%	46%	36%	Environmental predictor variables
CNN	52%	17%	7%	Landcover, Elevation
Bi-modal CNN	95%	45%	20%	Soilgrids, Climatic
Swin Transformers	90%	36%	24%	Sentinel images
XGBRegression	92%	47%	32%	PA meta data
MME-NN (Resnet-6, XGB regression)	98%	49%	34%	Landsat, Sentinel patch, Climatic

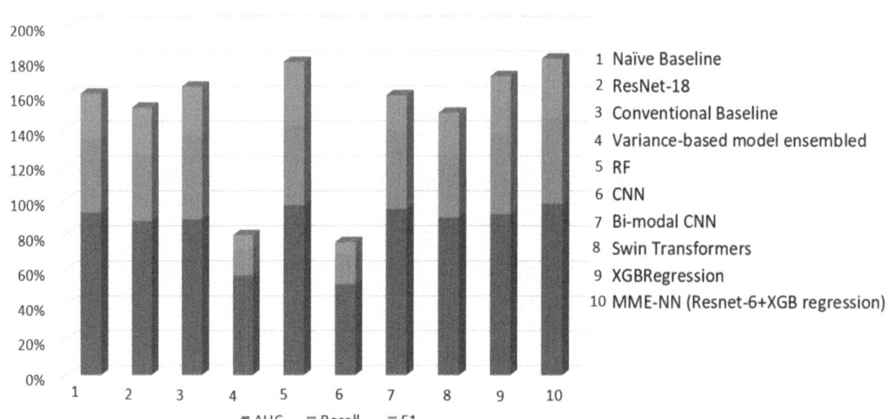

Fig. 14. Comparison with base line models

5 Conclusions

In this paper, we have presented the predictions of Indian region-specific occurrences of Magnoliopsida and Aves categorized species under the kingdoms of Plantae and Animalia. These predictions produce efficient mapping for the distribution of species bound to specific regions. In this setting, the mapping of the region-specific Multilabel Indian species distribution is predicted through the novel empirical ensemble multimodal strategy. In this multimodal ensemble neural network model, all the established transformations are explored efficiently. The combined preprocessing approaches are utilized to refine the model. Moreover, the utilized evaluative metrics reveal some weightage towards the resultant outcomes for the mapping of the occurrences of Indian species suitability. This paper combines satellite image-based data with different variables of environmental covariates. This reduces the training and validation gap while considering the optimized hyperparameter-tuned process within the neural network model. The estimated predictions are mapped with the GBIF data and yield coherent outcomes. There are some uncertainties involved in the proper estimation of species occurrences where a mismatch is found for combining remotely sensed satellite images. Further, some comparative analyses with other models divulge the imbalanced species representation, which produces variations in results that require some derivations for the generalized predictive models in species distributions. From this assessment, it is evident that the decrease of the Aves species has some influence on the growth of the Magnoliopsida plant species. This affects the plant species biodiversity, which has been found at risk. In the future, species predictions should be well-ordered and able to combine a wide geographical area so that rare species can be identified smoothly.

References

1. Borborah, K., Deka, K., Saikia, D., Borthakur, S., Tanti, B.: Habitat distribution mapping of musa flaviflora simmonds-a wild banana in Assam, India. Acta Ecol. Sin. **40**(2), 122–127 (2020)
2. Botella, C., Bonnet, P., Munoz, F., Monestiez, P.P., Joly, A.: Overview of geolifeclef 2018: location-based species recommendation. In: CLEF 2018-Conference and Labs of the Evaluation Forum. vol. 2125. CEUR-WS (2018)
3. Botella, C., Joly, A., Bonnet, P., Monestiez, P., Munoz, F.: A deep learning approach to species distribution modelling. Multimedia Tools and Applications for Environmental & Biodiversity Informatics, pp. 169–199 (2018)
4. Botella, C., Servajean, M., Bonnet, P., Joly, A.: Overview of geolifeclef 2019: plant species prediction using environment and animal occurrences. In: CLEF 2019-Conference and Labs of the Evaluation Forum, vol. 2380 (2019)
5. Coulibaly, S., Kamsu-Foguem, B., Kamissoko, D., Traore, D.: Deep convolution neural network sharing for the multi-label images classification. Mach. Learn. Appl. **10**, 100422 (2022)
6. Deneu, B., Servajean, M., Bonnet, P., Botella, C., Munoz, F., Joly, A.: Convolutional neural networks improve species distribution modelling by capturing the spatial structure of the environment. PLoS Comput. Biol. **17**(4), e1008856 (2021)

7. Estopinan, J., Servajean, M., Bonnet, P., Munoz, F., Joly, A.: Deep species distribution modeling from sentinel-2 image time-series: a global scale analysis on the orchid family. Front. Plant Sci. **13**, 839327 (2022)
8. Gillespie, L., Ruffley, M., Expósito-Alonso, M.: An image is worth a thousand species: combining neural networks, citizen science, and remote sensing to map biodiversity. bioRxiv, pp. 2022–08 (2022)
9. Kaky, E., Nolan, V., Alatawi, A., Gilbert, F.: A comparison between ensemble and maxent species distribution modelling approaches for conservation: a case study with Egyptian medicinal plants. Eco. Inform. **60**, 101150 (2020)
10. Kellenberger, B., Tuia, D.: Block label swap for species distribution modelling. In: CLEF (Working Notes), pp. 2103–2114 (2022)
11. Lorieul, T., Cole, E., Deneu, B., Servajean, M., Bonnet, P., Joly, A.: Overview of geolifeclef 2021: predicting species distribution from 2 million remote sensing images. In: CLEF (Working Notes), pp. 1451–1462 (2021)
12. Picek, L., Botella, C., Servajean, M., Leblanc, C., Palard, R., Larcher, T., Deneu, B., Marcos, D., Bonnet, P., Joly, A.: Geoplant: spatial plant species prediction dataset (2024). arXiv:2408.13928
13. Probst, W.N., Lynam, C.P., Bluemel, J.K., Clarke, M.: Assessing change in the occurrence of rare species using the binomial distribution. Ecol. Ind. **156**, 111084 (2023)
14. Rawlings, D., Chopard, T.: Exploring biodiversity: A multi-model approach to multi-label plant species prediction. In: 25th Working Notes of the Conference and Labs of the Evaluation Forum, CLEF 2024, pp. 2188–2200. CEUR Workshop Proceedings (2024)
15. Seneviratne, S.: Contrastive representation learning for natural world imagery: habitat prediction for 30, 000 species. In: CLEF (Working Notes), pp. 1639–1648 (2021)
16. Smith, B.E., Johnston, M.K., Luecking, R.: From genbank to gbif: phylogeny-based predictive niche modeling tests accuracy of taxonomic identifications in large occurrence data repositories. PLoS ONE **11**(3), e0151232 (2016)
17. Syah, A.F., Gaol, J.L., Zainuddin, M., Apriliya, N.R., Berlianty, D., Mahabror, D.: Habitat model development of bigeye tuna (thunnus obesus) during southeast monsoon in the eastern indian ocean using satellite remotely sensed data. In: IOP Conference Series: Earth and Environmental Science, vol. 276, p. 012011. IOP Publishing (2019)
18. Tripathi, P., Behera, M.D., Roy, P.S.: Predicting the patterns of plant species distribution under changing climate in major biogeographic zones of mainland India. Biodiversity and Conservation, pp. 1–21 (2024)
19. Ung, H.Q., Kojima, R., Wada, S.: Leverage samples with single positive labels to train CNN-based models for multi-label plant species prediction. In: CLEF (Working Notes), pp. 2149–2158 (2023)

An Adaptive Reinforcement Learning Framework for Enhancing LLM-Based Medical Diagnostics

Mostafijur Rahaman, Sounak Banerjee(✉), Sarmistha Neogy, and Sarbani Roy

Jadavpur University, Kolkata, India
{mostafijurr.cse.pg,sounakb.cse.rs,sarmistha.neogy,
sarbani.roy}@jadavpuruniversity.in

Abstract. The rise of virtual healthcare systems, evolving from rule-based models to Artificial Intelligence (AI), has significantly improved access to medical guidance. The emergence of Large Language Models (LLMs) has shown promising capabilities in medical diagnostics. However, the effectiveness of LLMs heavily depends on the quality and comprehensiveness of input data. This dependency presents challenges in achieving accurate diagnoses. To address this, we propose an adaptive Diagnostic Optimization Learning Framework (DOLF) that integrates LLMs with Reinforcement Learning (RL). The RL component employs a modified Q-learning algorithm to dynamically select the most informative questions based on patient responses. This approach reduces the number of required interactions while effectively collecting relevant symptom information. The collected symptom information is structured into a detailed prompt for the LLM. This ensures a comprehensive and context-rich input that leverages the LLMs extensive medical knowledge. Experimental evaluations on a curated dataset show that DOLF outperforms standalone LLM-based diagnosis. It achieves an accuracy of 94% with an average dialogue length of 4.26 turns. These results make remote diagnosis more precise and pave the way for scalable, AI-driven medical assistants to enhance global healthcare accessibility and efficiency.

Keywords: Disease diagnosis · Large language models · Reinforcement learning · Virtual healthcare

1 Introduction

The rise of virtual healthcare systems has transformed preliminary disease assessment and medical guidance, particularly in regions with limited access to healthcare professionals [16]. The growing patient burden and scarcity of specialized doctors further underscore the need for AI-driven diagnostic solutions.

Virtual medical assistants address these challenges by facilitating remote consultations, allowing patients to describe symptoms and receive potential diagnoses before seeing a medical expert [3]. These systems not only improve accessibility but also help healthcare facilities manage non-critical cases more efficiently. Advancements in artificial intelligence (AI) have significantly enhanced

K. Chandra Mondal et al. (Eds.): CICBA 2025, CCIS 2863, pp. 197–210, 2026.
https://doi.org/10.1007/978-3-032-17184-9_15

diagnostic capabilities, shifting from traditional rule-based models to sophisticated AI-driven frameworks [2]. One of the most groundbreaking innovations in AI-driven diagnostics is the emergence of LLMs. While conventional machine learning (ML) methods require specialized architectures for different modalities, LLMs have revolutionized disease diagnosis with their unified approach [7]. LLMs integrate vast medical knowledge, correlate diverse patient inputs, and generate precise diagnosis without the need for separate models to handle structured and unstructured data [6]. However, deploying LLMs for medical diagnosis presents key challenges, including ensuring accurate and reliable predictions, optimizing question-answering strategies, and maintaining an efficient consultation process without overwhelming patients [18]. To address these issues, RL has emerged as a powerful technique to refine the diagnostic workflow [19]. Unlike static questionnaire-based methods, RL-driven models dynamically determine the most relevant questions to ask, adapting based on patient responses to minimize redundancy and enhance diagnostic accuracy. By optimizing the number and relevance of questions, RL ensures an efficient and user-friendly experience.

Recent studies show that LLM performance improves significantly when prompted with comprehensive and well-structured input [15,21]. RL, with its adaptive dialogue capabilities, can be leveraged to generate such informative and targeted prompts through structured question-answer exchanges. Despite this potential, most research has explored LLMs and RL separately. Motivated by this gap, our work introduces an adaptive **D**iagnostic **O**ptimization **L**earning **F**ramework (**DOLF**) that combines LLMs with RL-based symptom collection to enhance prediction accuracy and interaction efficiency. The key contributions of this work include:

- A novel framework that leverages LLMs for disease prediction while utilizing an RL model to optimize the symptom-gathering process.
- An RL model trained with a modified Q-learning strategy to refine question selection and minimize the number of interactions.
- Benchmarking the system's diagnostic accuracy and optimized questioning against state-of-the-art LLMs using a curated dataset.

The rest of this paper is structured as follows: Sect. 2 reviews related work, Sect. 3 presents the problem statement, and Sect. 4 details the proposed framework, including the modified Q-learning approach. Section 5 covers implementation and experimental evaluation, while Sect. 6 concludes with insights and future research directions.

2 Related Work

Various ML and AI techniques have been utilized in recent years to develop medical disease diagnosis systems. To contextualize our research within this broader landscape, we focus on two key areas most relevant to our study. Firstly, we examine the role of LLMs in medical diagnosis. Secondly, we explore the application of RL in medical diagnosis. Below, we discuss the related work in these areas.

LLMs have emerged as powerful tools in medical diagnostics, processing textual patient records, symptom descriptions, and medical literature to generate informed diagnoses. Studies such as [14] showcase their effectiveness in answering complex medical questions and leveraging vast medical knowledge for disease diagnosis. Similarly, the work in [13] presents an adaptation of pre-trained LLMs that improves medical text interpretation, enhancing symptom correlation and disease prediction. Transformer-based models like [9] and [11] facilitate automated diagnosis by predicting medical concepts from clinical narratives. However, these models often suffer from hallucination errors when handling incomplete or ambiguous inputs. Domain-specific LLMs like [5], trained on biomedical literature, enhance evidence-based reasoning but lack real-time patient interaction capabilities. While LLMs have significantly advanced medical diagnosis, challenges such as inconsistent responses, hallucinations, and difficulty handling multimodal data persist. To address these limitations, our research integrates RL to refine the questioning process, dynamically improving symptom collection and diagnostic accuracy.

RL has proven valuable in medical diagnostics by enabling dynamic symptom collection and refining disease predictions. Several studies have explored RL-based frameworks. The work in [20] introduced a hierarchical RL model for structured symptom-based questioning, while the authors in [17] leveraged symptom co-occurrence patterns for improved diagnosis. However, both approaches lacked LLM integration for enhanced reasoning. The work in [4] proposed an RL-based system mimicking doctors' reasoning but did not utilize LLMs for real-time knowledge updates. While RL enhances medical diagnosis, most models function independently of LLMs, missing the opportunity to utilize LLMs' extensive medical knowledge. Our research bridges this gap by integrating RL with LLM-driven reasoning to refine symptom collection, ensuring more precise and efficient diagnoses.

3 Problem Statement

Given an initial patient-provided textual query, the LLM processes it and generates an initial state of possible diseases:

$$\mathcal{S}^I = \{D_1 : PD_1^I, \ldots, D_n : PD_n^I)\} \tag{1}$$

where $\mathcal{D} = \{D_1, D_2, \ldots, D_n\}$ is the set of possible diseases, D_i represents the ith disease, PD_i^I denotes its associated probability in $\mathcal{S}^I$, and n is the total number of unique diseases.

To refine the diagnosis, the RL model determines the most relevant symptoms to inquire about using the mapping function $f : \mathcal{S}^I \rightarrow \mathcal{Q}$, where $\mathcal{Q} = \{q_1, q_2, \ldots, q_m\}$, q_j represents the jth symptom, and m denotes the number of unique symptoms. The RL model iteratively updates PD_i at the time step t based on patient responses as:

$$PD_i = P_t(D_i \mid Q_t, R_t) = \texttt{Update}(P_{t-1}, Q_t, R_t) \tag{2}$$

where Q_t and R_t represent the set of questions asked and the corresponding set of responses received up to the time step t, respectively, and $\texttt{Update}(\cdot)$ is the function that adjusts the probability based on newly acquired information.

The objective is to reach a refined state $\mathcal{S}^K = \{D_1 : PD_1^K, \ldots, D_n : PD_n^K\}$ when one particular disease D^* has a significantly higher probability than the others. That means $D^* = \arg\max_{D_i \in \mathcal{D}} PD_i^K$, where PD_i^K represents the probability of disease D_i in the refined state $\mathcal{S}^K$. A confidence score, $\mathcal{C}^K$ is then calculated for $\mathcal{S}^K$ as a quantitative measure of diagnostic certainty as:

$$\mathcal{C}^K = \varphi(PD_1^K, \ldots, PD_n^K) \tag{3}$$

Therefore, the objective is to:

$$Maximize \quad \mathcal{C}^K$$

Subject to:

$$|Q| \leq Q_{\max} \tag{4}$$

where Q is the set of questions asked and $Q_{\max}$ is the maximum allowed number of questions.

4 Proposed Framework

The proposed DOLF introduces an end-to-end disease diagnosis system that combines a pre-trained LLM with an RL-based conversational model. By integrating these two models through an iterative process, the system aims to improve diagnostic accuracy while optimizing symptom-specific questioning and minimizing patient interactions. The overall workflow of the system is illustrated in `Fig. 1`, which outlines each step in the diagnostic process. Initially, the patient provides a textual query describing their symptoms or condition, which serves as the system's input. The LLM then analyzes this query and generates a state of possible diseases along with their associated probability(Likelihood). This output serves as the initial state for the RL model. In a RL model, the functionality is determined by its current situation, referred to as the state. The state represents the current likelihood of each disease for the patient. The RL model subsequently initiates a conversation with the patient to gather additional symptom information. The model dynamically selects symptoms to inquire about based on the current state, updating the state after each patient response. The conversation continues until a predefined goal state is reached. The collected symptom information, along with the initial textual query, is compiled into a detailed prompt. This prompt ensures that all relevant information is accurately presented to the LLM. The modified prompt is then provided as input to the LLM, which reprocesses the information to generate an updated state of possible diseases with associated probabilities. Finally, the disease with the highest probability in the final state is identified as the predicted diagnosis.

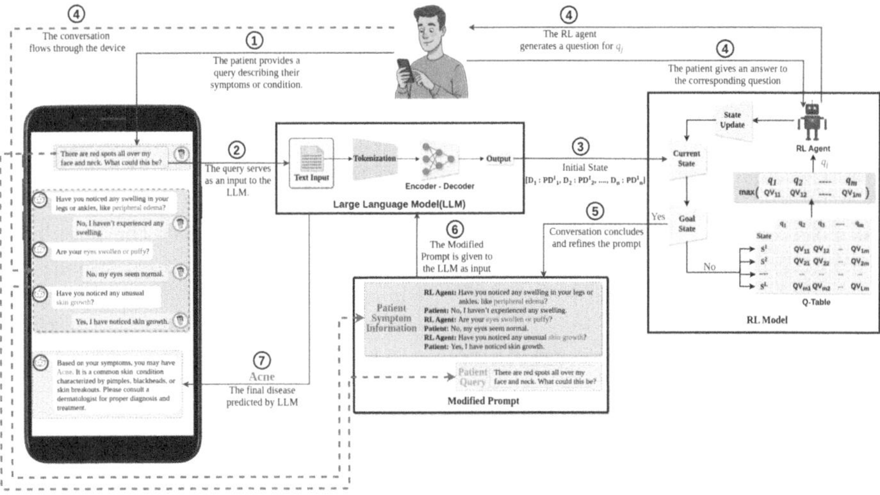

Fig. 1. Comprehensive overview of the disease diagnosis system workflow.

4.1 LLM for Disease Prediction

The LLM serves as the core component for disease prediction within the system, utilizing its pre-trained knowledge. It processes patient queries and symptom descriptions to generate a state of potential diseases, each assigned a probability score. These probabilities range from P_{min} to P_{max}, where $0 \leq P_{min} \leq P_{max} \leq 1$, with higher values indicate a greater likelihood of the disease. The iterative nature of the system ensures that the final input to the LLM includes comprehensive symptom data, enhancing diagnostic accuracy [21].

4.2 RL Model for Symptom Information Gathering

The RL model functions as a conversational agent, systematically collecting symptom information from the patient. This model employs a modified Q-learning algorithm, which extends traditional Q-learning by incorporating additional phases. These phases include the Agent, Environment, State Update, Confidence Measurement, Reward Calculation, Q-Table Update, and Policy. The agent generates questions to gather symptom information, while the environment (patient) provides feedback in the form of binary (yes/no) or descriptive answers. Symptom selection is governed by the policy from the action space $\mathcal{A}$, which consists of m unique symptoms. The agent generates a question about the selected symptom to inquire whether the patient has the symptom or not. Based on the patient's feedback, the current state, which encapsulates the likelihoods of various diseases for the patient, is updated through the state update phase. Given a current state $\mathcal{S}$ and a selected symptom q_j, the symptom q_j is considered related to disease D_i if its presence increases the likelihood of D_i and its absence decreases it. This relationship is defined as:

$$\mathcal{R}q_{ij} = Rel(q_j, D_i) \tag{5}$$

where $\mathcal{R}q_{ij}$ represents the degree of relationship between q_j and D_i, with $\mathcal{R}q_{ij} \in [P_{min}, P_{max}]$. Higher $\mathcal{R}q_{ij}$ values indicate a stronger relationship. If the patient confirms the presence of q_j, the likelihood of related diseases increases, while unrelated diseases decrease. Conversely, the absence of q_j reduces the likelihood of related diseases and increases that of unrelated ones. These adjustments are governed by the expression $(-1)^{response}$, where:

$$response = \begin{cases} 1, & if \begin{cases} (Rel(q_j, D_i) > 0) \quad AND \quad (Answer = 'Yes') \\ \qquad\qquad OR \\ (Rel(q_j, D_i) = 0) \quad AND \quad (Answer = 'No') \end{cases} \\ 0, & otherwise \end{cases}$$

The updated probability of D_i, defined as PD_i^{new}, is computed as:

$$PD_i^{new} = PD_i + (-1)^{response} \cdot \Delta \tag{6}$$

where Δ represents the combined measure of q_j's relationship with D_i and the current likelihood of D_i, i.e., $\Delta = \mathcal{R}q_{ij} + PD_i$. The updated state is: $S^{new} = \{D_1 : PD_1^{new}, D_2 : PD_2^{new}, \ldots, D_n : PD_n^{new}\}$, ensuring effective incorporation of the patient's response into disease likelihoods. The updated state and the current state are then processed through the confidence measurement phase to evaluate the effectiveness of the inquired symptom. The confidence of a state is assessed using two key metrics: **1.** Dispersion of probabilities, measured by the standard deviation (σ), is defined as:

$$\sigma = \sqrt{\frac{1}{n}\sum_{i=1}^{n}(PD_i - \bar{P})^2} \tag{7}$$

where $\bar{P}$ is the mean probability. **2.** Dominance of the highest probability ($Max(PD_i)$) over the second-highest probability ($SecondMax(PD_i)$). For example, consider an example with two sets of likelihood values: `Set1 = [0.4, 0.5, 0.8]` and `Set2 = [0.3, 0.2, 0.4]`. The standard deviation of `Set1` is higher than that of `Set2`, indicating greater dispersion. Additionally, the difference between the highest likelihood and second-highest likelihood is also larger for `Set1`. This makes the highest likelihood, 0.8, in `Set1` more distinguishable compared to the highest likelihood in `Set2`. In the context of reinforcement learning, incorporating both metrics ensures that if the probability of a disease is significantly higher than that of others in the state, the disease can be confidently identified as the most likely one by defining a confidence threshold (T_c). The confidence score for a state $\mathcal{S}^K$ is mathematically expressed as:

$$\mathcal{C}^K = \sigma + (Max(PD_i) - SecondMax(PD_i)) \tag{8}$$

In the reward calculation phase, the reward is computed based on the difference in confidence levels between the current state and the updated state. The calculated reward reflects the impact of a symptom inquiry on disease identification. An increase in confidence results in a positive reward, with higher values indicating that the inquired symptom is more impactful in distinguishing the correct disease. Conversely, a decrease in confidence results in a negative reward, with larger negative values highlighting the symptom's irrelevance. The magnitude of the confidence difference introduces variability in the reward, allowing the model to better assess the significance of the inquired symptom. Mathematically, the reward ($\mathcal{R}$) is expressed as $\mathcal{R} = \mathcal{C}^{new} - \mathcal{C}^{old}$, where $\mathcal{C}^{new}$ and $\mathcal{C}^{old}$ are the confidence scores of the updated and current states, respectively. The reward is incorporated into the Q-value calculation, which quantifies the benefit of selecting a symptom q_j based on a given state $\mathcal{S}^K$. The Q-value update rule is:

$$Q(\mathcal{S}^K, a) \leftarrow (1 - \alpha)Q(\mathcal{S}^{K'}, a) + \alpha \left[\mathcal{R} + \gamma \max_{a'} Q(\mathcal{S}^{K'}, a')\right] \tag{9}$$

where α is the learning rate, γ is the discount factor, $Q(\mathcal{S}, a)$ is the current Q-value for state-action pair $(\mathcal{S}, a)$, $\max_{a'} Q(\mathcal{S}', a')$ is the maximum Q-value for the next state, and $a, a' \in \mathcal{A}$. The Q-table defines the state-action space, with rows corresponding to L number of possible states and columns to m number of actions. The calculated Q-value is updated in the Q-table at the specific position corresponding to the current state and action pair. The iterative modified Q-learning process continues until a predefined goal state is reached. This goal state is achieved when the confidence of the state exceeds a predefined threshold (T_c) or when the number of questions asked reaches the maximum allowable limit (Q_{Max}). The calculated reward is also used in the action selection policy. For symptom selection q_j, two cases arise:

- **Case 1.** If $\mathcal{R} > 0$, the selected symptom q_j is considered effective, as it leads to an increase in confidence. For a positive reward, we explore a specific path to encourage exploitation. Suppose there are three diseases: D_1, D_2 and D_3, and D_2 has highest relatedness with q_j. To continue exploring D_2, we select the next symptom q_j^{new} for the next question, which also has the highest association with D_2, while excluding previously asked symptoms. This ensures that the most relevant option is chosen. This scenario is mathematically expressed as:

$$q_j^{new} = \arg\max_{q \in \mathcal{Q}} Rel(q, D_k), \quad q \notin \mathcal{O}$$

  where $\mathcal{O}$ represents the set of previously asked symptoms and D_k denotes the disease associated with the selected symptom q_j.
- **Case 2.** If $\mathcal{R} < 0$, the previous action was ineffective. if $\mathcal{R} = 0$, it indicates the initial step where a symptom is selected to begin the conversation. These two scenarios prompt exploration of the most probable disease in the current state.

$$D_k = \arg\max_{D_i \in \mathcal{D}} PD_i$$

The corresponding symptom q_j^{new} is then chosen to maximize its relevance to the identified disease. This scenario is mathematically expressed as:

$$q_j^{new} = \arg\max_{q \in \mathcal{Q}} Rel(q, D_k), \quad q \notin \mathcal{O}$$

By integrating these two action-selection strategies, the policy ensures that the RL model focuses on symptoms associated with the most probable disease in the current state. This approach enhances the relevance of selected symptoms, leading to more refined LLM predictions, improved diagnostic accuracy, and a more reliable final disease list.

5 Results and Discussion

5.1 Experimental Setup and Dataset Description

The application was developed on a Dell Inspiron 5000 machine with 16 GB RAM, 500 GB SSD, and 1 TB HDD. The RL model was trained on Google Colab to leverage its computational capabilities, while Visual Studio Code was used for final development and integration. Training followed a structured framework to ensure effective learning and convergence. The α was set to 0.1, balancing new updates with existing Q-values. The γ of 0.9 was applied to emphasize long-term rewards. Training was conducted for 4000 epochs, as Q-values stabilized beyond this, indicating the convergence of the learning process [Fig. 2]. Additional hyperparameters included: $Q_{\max} = 10$, $T_c = 0.9$.

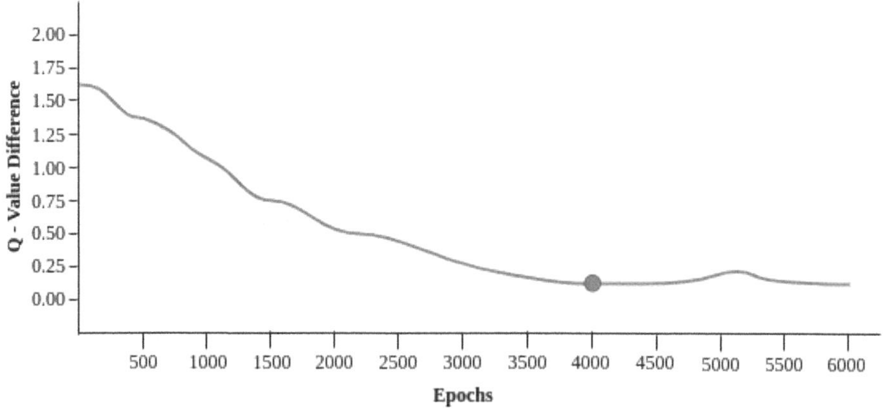

Fig. 2. Q-value differences over training epochs.

The RL model was trained using data derived from the Synthetic Dataset [20], the largest publicly available English medical dataset, containing 30,000 patient samples. For this study, a subset of 5 diseases ($n = 5$) and 46 symptoms

($m = 46$) was curated. Each symptom has an associated value that represents its relationship with the disease. For evaluation, the dataset from Kaggle, namely *Symptom2Disease* [1] was utilized. It consists of 50 test samples, with 10 queries collected for each disease.

5.2 Performance Evaluation

The DOLF was evaluated with three advanced LLMs: ChatGPT-4o [12], DeepSeek [10], and Claude 3.5 Sonnet [8], chosen for their multimodal capabilities, broad adoption, and medical applications. The assessment examined the predictive accuracy of the LLMs, the RL agent's role in enhancing diagnosis, and the efficiency of question selection. A structured set of quantitative metrics was used, each analyzing a specific aspect of diagnostic performance.

- **Diagnosis Success Rate** (DSR): The DSR represents the percentage of correct diagnosis, calculated as:

$$DSR = \left(\frac{\text{Correct Diagnosis}}{\text{Total Cases}}\right) \times 100 \tag{10}$$

- **Average Dialogue Length** (ADL): The average number of questions asked before reaching a diagnosis.

$$ADL = \frac{\text{Total Questions Asked}}{\text{Total Cases}} \tag{11}$$

5.3 Observations and Analysis

The evaluation was conducted on the test dataset [1]. The proposed DOLF was compared against standalone LLM-based diagnosis. First, we evaluated each LLM independently, instructing it to handle both the question-answer process and the final disease prediction without any intervention from the RL model. Then, we tested DOLF, where the RL model facilitated the question-answer process for symptom information gathering, and the LLM provided the final prediction after incorporating the modified prompt. The complete results for each disease are presented in Table 1.

The results highlight significant inconsistencies in both the number of questions asked and the diagnosis accuracy in standalone LLM performance. ChatGPT-4o maintains a relatively consistent ADL across all diseases but without showcasing a clear pattern. Moreover, its standalone diagnosis accuracy is unreliable, with an overall DSR of only 48% across all diseases. For Deepseek and Claude 3.5 Sonnet, the ADL is significantly higher, making the question-answering dialogue less user-friendly. For example, in the case of Chickenpox, the ADL reaches 13.8 for Deepseek and 14.9 for Claude 3.5 Sonnet. While their DSR is slightly better than ChatGPT-4o, at 52% and 64%, respectively, they still lack real-world applicability due to the excessive ADL and inconsistencies

Table 1. Performance comparison of DOLF with standalone LLM-based diagnosis.

Disease	Framework	*DSR*	*ADL*
Chickenpox	ChatGPT-4o	20%	4.7
	ChatGPT-4o + RL	40%	6.9
	Deepseek	0%	13.8
	Deepseek + RL	50%	7.2
	Claude 3.5 Sonnet	40%	14.9
	Claude 3.5 Sonnet + RL	80%	6.8
Dengue fever	ChatGPT-4o	60%	4.9
	ChatGPT-4o + RL	70%	3.1
	Deepseek	70%	8.6
	Deepseek + RL	100%	3.5
	Claude 3.5 Sonnet	80%	14.2
	Claude 3.5 Sonnet + RL	100%	2.9
Acne	ChatGPT-4o	60%	4.2
	ChatGPT-4o + RL	80%	4.0
	Deepseek	70%	4.9
	Deepseek + RL	80%	3.0
	Claude 3.5 Sonnet	60%	3.7
	Claude 3.5 Sonnet + RL	100%	2.0
Allergy	ChatGPT-4o	60%	4.5
	ChatGPT-4o + RL	100%	6.5
	Deepseek	70%	11.4
	Deepseek + RL	90%	4.2
	Claude 3.5 Sonnet	70%	13.5
	Claude 3.5 Sonnet + RL	100%	5.3
Drug reaction	ChatGPT-4o	40%	4.7
	ChatGPT-4o + RL	70%	4.9
	Deepseek	50%	14.7
	Deepseek + RL	80%	5.4
	Claude 3.5 Sonnet	70%	15.3
	Claude 3.5 Sonnet + RL	90%	4.3

in reliability. In contrast, DOLF shows a significant improvement in both the efficiency of the question-answering dialogue and the overall prediction accuracy across all diseases. The average *ADL* of DOLF for ChatGPT-4o, Deepseek and Claude 3.5 Sonnet is 5.08, 4.66, and 4.26, respectively. While the highest *ADL* is limited to only 7.2 across all diseases, proving a user-friendly interaction system. In terms of diagnosis accuracy, DOLF significantly improves performance across all LLMs: ChatGPT-4o: 72% (vs. 48% in standalone mode) Deepseek:

80% (vs. 52% in standalone mode) Claude 3.5 Sonnet: 94% (vs. 64% in standalone mode). These results indicate that DOLF not only enhances accuracy but also optimizes the question-answering dialogue for a more natural and efficient patient interaction.

Table 2. McNemar's Test Results for *DSR*

LLM	Standalone DSR	DOLF DSR	(b, c)	χ^2	p-value	Significant
ChatGPT-4o	24/50	36/50	(0, 12)	10.08	0.00149	Yes
DeepSeek	26/50	40/50	(0, 14)	12.07	0.00051	Yes
Claude 3.5 Sonnet	32/50	47/50	(0, 15)	13.06	0.00030	Yes

Table 3. Paired t-test results for *ADL*

LLM	Standalone ADL	DOLF ADL	t-stat	p-value	Significant
ChatGPT-4o	4.62	5.08	−1.32	0.193	No
DeepSeek	11.34	4.66	15.60	<0.0001	Yes
Claude 3.5 Sonnet	13.52	4.26	20.10	<0.0001	Yes

To further validate the performance improvements, we conducted statistical tests: a `McNemar's Test` for *DSR* and a `paired t-test` for *ADL*. The results are summarized in `Table` 2 and `Table` 3 respectively. `McNemar's` test revealed that DOLF achieved a statistically significant improvement in diagnostic accuracy over the standalone LLMs: ChatGPT-4o (χ^2: 10.08, `p-value:` 0.00149), DeepSeek (χ^2: 12.07, `p-value:` 0.00051), and Claude 3.5 Sonnet (χ^2: 13.06, `p-value:` 0.00030). These results confirm that the RL-enhanced approach led to objectively better predictions. `Paired t-tests` showed DOLF significantly reduced dialogue length for DeepSeek (`t-stat:` 15.6, `p-value:` <0.0001) and Claude 3.5 (`t-stat:` 20.1, `p-value:` <0.0001). This supports the claim that the proposed RL component successfully minimizes unnecessary patient interactions while maintaining or improving diagnostic accuracy. For ChatGPT-4o, a slight increase in *ADL* is observed (`t-stat:` -1.32, `p-value:` 0.193), which was not statistically significant. It showed almost the same *ADL* values across all samples, indicating no clear pattern in its standalone diagnosis. These statistical validations reinforce that the performance gains of DOLF observed in `Table` 1 are not incidental but are reliably supported by data-driven evidence.

Given that Claude 3.5 Sonnet + RL framework achieves the highest overall accuracy and improved dialogue efficiency, we have incorporated Claude 3.5 Sonnet as the LLM in the finalized DOLF. In `Table` 4, a test case is illustrated using the finalized DOLF, compared to the standalone LLM approach. The confidence plot for the DOLF shows a continuously increasing confidence level throughout

Table 4. Comparison of a test case using the finalized DOLF.

Patient: I'm feeling really sick and uncomfortable like something is wrong inside. I don't know what it could be. I noticed small red spots on my arms, which itch when I touch them.

Conversation Dialogue Facilitated by Claude 3.5 Sonnet + RL Framework	Confidence Progression Plot for Each State (0.1 0.2 0.3 0.4 0.5 0.6 0.7 0.8 0.9 1.0)	Conversation Dialogue Facilitated by the Standalone Claude 3.5 Sonnet Framework	Confidence Progression Plot for Each State (0.1 0.2 0.3 0.4 0.5 0.6 0.7 0.8 0.9 1.0)
Agent: Do you have a **fever**? **Patient:** **Yes**, I've been feeling feverish since yesterday.	0.3	**Agent:** Do you have a **fever**? **Patient:** **Yes**, I've been feeling feverish since yesterday.	0.3
Agent: Have you experienced any **dizziness**? **Patient:** **No**, I haven't felt dizzy.	0.4	**Agent:** Do you have a **headache** as well?? **Patient:** **No**, I haven't really noticed any headaches.	0.2
Agent: Have you experienced persistent **itching** on your skin? **Patient:** **Yes**, my arms itch whenever I touch the red spots.	0.5	**Agent:** Are you experiencing any **nausea or vomiting**? **Patient:** **No**, I haven't felt nauseous or vomited.	0.4
Agent: Have you felt **nauseous** or had an upset stomach? **Patient:** **No**, I haven't had nausea.	0.8	**Agent:** Are you experiencing any **aches** all over your body? **Patient:** **yes**. I've been feeling some aches, especially in my fingers.	0.5
Agent: Do you have any **headaches**? **Patient:** **No**, I haven't had headaches.	0.7	**Agent:** Do you have a **sore throat**? **Patient:** **No**, my throat feels okay.	0.4
Agent: Have your eyes become **swollen or puffy**? **Patient:** **No**, my eyes look normal.	1.0	....	....
Total Question: 6 **Diagnosis:** Based on your symptoms, the most likely diagnosis is **Chickenpox**. **Status: Correct**		**Total Question: 13** **Diagnosis:** Based on your symptoms, the most likely diagnosis is **Dengue fever**. **Status: Wrong**	

the conversation, indicating that the RL model effectively selects the most relevant questions. By doing so, the RL model constructs a well-informed prompt for the LLM, ultimately improving diagnostic accuracy. In contrast, the standalone LLM struggles to maintain stable confidence during the conversation, as it remains low and fluctuates due to ineffective symptom selection, leading to prolonged questioning. This inefficiency results in the accumulation of less informative symptom data, making it difficult for the model to reach a conclusive and accurate diagnosis. Therefore, the integration of RL with LLMs significantly enhances the efficiency and reliability of disease diagnosis by optimizing symptom selection, reducing the length of conversations, and improving overall diagnostic accuracy.

6 Conclusion and Future Work

This study introduces DOLF, an AI-driven medical diagnosis framework that synergizes a pre-trained LLM with a RL-based interactive questioning system to optimize symptom collection and enhance diagnostic precision. A key contribution of this work is the development of a modified Q-learning algorithm to train the RL agent, incorporating essential features such as state updates from environment feedback, confidence-based reward adjustment, and an exploration-exploitation strategy for relevant symptom selection. The results demonstrate a strong potential for both diagnostic accuracy and dialogue efficiency. These advancements position DOLF as a promising tool for early medical assessment.

Future research will prioritize three key directions. First, the LLM component will undergo fine-tuning using real-world symptom descriptions to improve its domain-specific diagnostic accuracy and adaptability to diverse patient vocabularies. Second, the RL agent's training will expand to incorporate a broader disease-symptom dataset, enabling more robust symptom-disease mapping and reducing reliance on synthetic training environments. Third, iterative optimization of the RL framework will refine question-selection strategies, balancing diagnostic thoroughness with conversational efficiency to enhance clinical usability. These efforts will focus on bridging the gap between experimental validation and real-world deployment.

Acknowledgments. This research work is partially supported by the project entitled- "Development of AI/ML based predictive models for association analysis of risk factors and high granular forecasting for air pollutants", funded by MoE-STARS, IISC, File No.: MoE-STARS/STARS-2/2023-0033.

References

1. Symptom2Disease. https://www.kaggle.com/datasets/niyarrbarman/symptom2disease. Accessed: 2025-01-18
2. Chintala, S.: Improving healthcare accessibility with AI-enabled telemedicine solutions. Int. J. Res. Rev. Tech. **2**(1), 75–81 (2023)
3. Clarke, G.: Remote treatment of patients during the covid-19 pandemic: digital technologies, smart telemedicine diagnosis systems, and virtual care. Am. J. Med. Res. **7**(2), 29–35 (2020)
4. Tchango, A.F., Goel, R., Martel, J., Wen, Z., Caron, G.M., Ghosn, J.: Towards trustworthy automatic diagnosis systems by emulating doctors' reasoning with deep reinforcement learning. Adv. Neural Inf. Process. Syst. **35**, 24502–24515 (2022)
5. Yu, G., Tinn, R., Cheng, H., Lucas, M., Usuyama, N., Liu, X., Naumann, T., Gao, J., Poon, H.: Domain-specific language model pretraining for biomedical natural language processing. ACM Trans. Comput. Healthcare (HEALTH) **3**(1), 1–23 (2021)
6. Huang, J., Yang, D.M., Rong, R., Nezafati, K., Treager, C., Chi, Z., Wang, S., Cheng, X., Guo, Y., Klesse, L.J. et al.: A critical assessment of using ChatGPT for extracting structured data from clinical notes. npj Digit. Med. **7**(1), 106 (2024)
7. Javed, H., El-Sappagh, S., Abuhmed, T.: Robustness in deep learning models for medical diagnostics: security and adversarial challenges towards robust AI applications. Artif. Intell. Rev. **58**(1), 1–107 (2025)
8. Jin, H., Guo, J., Lin, Q., Wu, S., Hu, W., Li, X.: Comparative study of claude 3.5-sonnet and human physicians in generating discharge summaries for patients with renal insufficiency: assessment of efficiency, accuracy, and quality. Front. Digit. Health **6**, 1456911 (2024)
9. Kim, S., Yoon, J.: Vaiv bio-discovery service using transformer model and retrieval augmented generation. BMC Bioinform. **25**(1), 273 (2024)
10. Liu, A., Feng, B., Xue, B., Wang, B., Wu, B., Lu, C., Zhao, C., Deng, C., Zhang, C., Ruan, C. et al:. Deepseek-v3 technical report (2024). arXiv:2412.19437
11. Luo, R., Sun, L., Xia, Y., Qin, T., Zhang, S., Poon, H. and Liu, T.Y.: Biogpt: generative pre-trained transformer for biomedical text generation and mining. Brief. Bioinform. **23**(6), bbac409 (2022)
12. Meo, A.S., Shaikh, N., Meo, S.A.: Assessing the accuracy and efficiency of chat gpt-4 omni (gpt-4o) in biomedical statistics: comparative study with traditional tools. Saudi Med. J. **45**(12), 1383 (2024)

13. Nazyrova, N., Chahed, S., Chausalet, T., Dwek, M.: Leveraging large language models for medical text classification: a hospital readmission prediction case. In: 2024 14th International Conference on Pattern Recognition Systems (ICPRS). IEEE, pp. 1–7 (2024)
14. Singhal, K., Tu, T., Gottweis, J., Sayres, R., Wulczyn, E., Amin, M., Hou, L., Clark, K., Pfohl, S.R., Cole-Lewis, H. et al.: Toward expert-level medical question answering with large language models. Nat. Med., 1–8 (2025)
15. Sonoda, Y., Kurokawa, R., Hagiwara, A., Asari, Y., Fukushima, T., Kanzawa, J., Gonoi, W., Abe, O.: Structured clinical reasoning prompt enhances llm's diagnostic capabilities in diagnosis please quiz cases. Jpn. J. Radiol. **43**(4), 586–592 (2025)
16. Tan, T.F., Li, Y., Lim, J.S., Gunasekeran, D.V., Teo, Z.L., Ng, W.Y., Sw Ting, D.: Metaverse and virtual health care in ophthalmology: opportunities and challenges. Asia-Pac. J. Ophthalmol. **11**(3), 237–246 (2022)
17. Tiwari, A., Saha, T., Saha, S., Bhattacharyya, P., Begum, S., Dhar, M., Tiwari, S.: Symptoms are known by their companies: towards association guided disease diagnosis assistant. BMC Bioinform. **23**(1), 556 (2022)
18. Ullah, E., Parwani, A., Baig, M.M., Singh, R.: Challenges and barriers of using large language models (llm) such as ChatGPT for diagnostic medicine with a focus on digital pathology–a recent scoping review. Diagnostic Pathol. **19**(1), 43 (2024)
19. Wang, Y., Liu, A., Yang, J., Wang, L., Xiong, N., Cheng, Y., Qin, W.: Clinical knowledge-guided deep reinforcement learning for sepsis antibiotic dosing recommendations. Artif. Intell. Med. **150**, 102811 (2024)
20. Zhong, C., Liao, K., Chen, W., Liu, Q., Peng, B., Huang, X., Peng, J., Wei, Z.: Hierarchical reinforcement learning for automatic disease diagnosis. Bioinformatics **38**(16), 3995–4001 (2022)
21. Zhou, H., Liu, F., Gu, B., Zou, X., Huang, J., Wu, J., Li, Y., Chen, S.S., Zhou, P., Liu, J. et al.: A survey of large language models in medicine: Progress, application, and challenge (2023). arXiv:2311.05112

An Efficient LSTM-XGBoost Hybrid for Demand Forecasting in Food Supply Chains

Prachetas Pathak(✉), Subha Sankar Chakraborty, and Parag Kumar Guha Thakurta

National Institute of Technology Durgapur, Durgapur, India
{pp.24p10154,pkguhathakurta.cse}@nitdgp.ac.in,
ssc.23cs1103@phd.nitdgp.ac.in

Abstract. Global challenges of food insufficiency and food wastage remain prevalent. Artificial intelligence provides the technology needed for supply chain systems to minimize food waste. In this context, an efficient LSTM-XGBoost hybrid model is proposed here to enhance demand forecasting in supply chain optimization and reduce food waste. In the proposed work, the LSTM networks manage temporal dependencies from the prepared dataset in the first stage. The second phase incorporates XGBoost to utilize the extracted features from LSTM, identifying non-linear relationships and residual patterns that LSTM might miss on its own. The proposed hybrid method guarantees computational efficiency by transforming high-dimensional outputs of LSTM into significant features, resulting in decreased complexity for XG-Boost while preserving our essential temporal data. The model was evaluated using a real-world food supply dataset and achieved an R^2 score of 0.91 and RMSE of 116.60, outperforming several baseline models, including standalone LSTM and XGBoost. The result confirms the effectiveness of the proposed model over other existing models. In addition, the proposed model incorporates external factors such as holidays and seasonal variations, enabling it to more effectively anticipate demand fluctuations and irregularitiesqueryPlease check and confirm if the authors given and family names have been correctly identified..

Keywords: Food waste · Demand forecasting · Supply chain · Hybrid model · Error measures

1 Introduction

1.1 Background and Motivation

Food insecurity and food waste continue to pose major challenges. These issues greatly affect public health and economic stability. Each year, millions of individuals experience malnutrition, while large quantities of food are being wasted because of inefficiencies in distribution and supply chain processes [1]. A study

K. Chandra Mondal et al. (Eds.): CICBA 2025, CCIS 2863, pp. 211–226, 2026.
https://doi.org/10.1007/978-3-032-17184-9_16

by the World Food Program [2] suggests that even though there is food sufficient to feed the world's 7 billion people, still one in nine people go to bed starving. Moreover, almost one-third of the food produced each year, amounting to approximately 1.3 billion tons, is wasted. One of the primary reasons for these issues remains inefficient supply chain management (SCM), which leads to enormous food wastage. A major portion of it could have been prevented from going to waste if there were models efficient enough to tackle these concerns [3]. To deal with these challenges, incorporating trending technologies with SCM can help in improving the overall process. It is essential for attaining sustainable development objectives linked to zero hunger and responsible food consumption. This is where demand forecasting comes into the picture. An accurate sales forecasting and demand planning can play a major role in improving supply chain performance. Thus, it facilitates businesses and enterprises to better manage food supply and consumption. [4,5]. It helps reduce operating costs, thus enabling them to adapt quickly to market demands and thereby increasing overall efficiency [6]. Today, traditional forecasting techniques are no longer sufficient. Rather, businesses often tend to use several options simultaneously [7]. As a result, there is a need to develop innovative machine learning (ML) algorithms [8] to achieve high predictive accuracy and better system reliability. With so much data available today, companies should try to use artificial intelligence (AI) techniques to gain valuable insights and drive business growth [9,10]. The findings suggest that the hybrid model surpasses standalone models in both aspects, prediction accuracy and efficiency involved in forecasting future demands. Thus, it serves as a valuable resource for addressing food security issues and minimizing waste [11]. This shows how AI-driven analytics can improve supply chain efficiency, and thus contribute towards creating a more sustainable food distribution network [12]. Moreover, AI provides the technology needed for supply chain systems to achieve these goals [6]. Thus, the effective demand forecasting in SCM is an important approach to address these issues by optimizing resource allocation and reducing food waste.

1.2 Research Gaps

Even after several advancements, demand forecasting still has room for improvement in accuracy and computation time. While deep learning models like LSTM are great at capturing sequential dependencies, they don't consider the nonlinear interactions between features. On the other hand, tree-based models like XGBoost excel in capturing these interactions but are not effective when it comes to modeling temporal patterns. Most existing models either focus on temporal patterns (e.g., LSTM) or nonlinear feature interactions (e.g., XGBoost), but rarely both [13]. Also, the hybrid models that merge these methods frequently do not provide a well-defined methodology for feature extraction and integration. This leads to an inefficient use of their advantages [14]. Furthermore, several factors such as holidays, seasonal trends, and marketing activities are often ignored, preventing the model from utilizing its abilities to their full potential. Since the hybrid model depends on the complex features, scalability becomes a challenge, making the model less efficient. Hence, there arises a need to explore the machine learning algorithms frequently used in supply chain management (SCM) and figure out the activities that are more suitable for demand forecasting.

1.3 Scope and Contribution of the Proposed Work

The paper proposes an effective LSTM-XGBoost hybrid model for demand forecasting in supply chain optimization for food distribution. The proposed method initiates with data preparation, which deals with filling in the missing values, encoding categorical variables, and normalizing features to guarantee consistency and reliability. The model further adopts a two-step process. In the first stage, LSTM networks manage temporal dependencies from the prepared dataset. The second phase incorporates XGBoost, a robust tree-based ML algorithm, which uses the extracted features from LSTM to identify nonlinear relationships and residual patterns that LSTM might miss on its own. The pipeline thus includes training an LSTM model with historical data, obtaining its learned features, and incorporating them into an XGBoost model together with the original feature set to improve predictive accuracy. The capability of XGBoost to manage structured data and feature interactions improves the overall prediction performance. The result thus confirms the effectiveness of the proposed model over other existing models. The proposed model is specially suited for food supply chains that involve perishable items and retail food distribution, where demand is influenced by temporal and external factors such as holidays, promotions, and regional patterns. The major contributions of the proposed work are as follows:

- The proposed hybrid method guarantees computational efficiency by converting the high-dimensional outputs of LSTM into significant features, resulting in decreased complexity for XGBoost while preserving essential temporal data. This organized amalgamation successfully makes the best use of the advanced learning abilities of LSTM with the clarity and speed of XGBoost.
- The framework outlined here paves the way for a scalable and precise solution to the common challenges in demand forecasting, significantly enhancing food supply chain efficiency and reducing waste. Additionally, the model incorporates external factors such as holidays and seasonal variations, enabling it to more effectively anticipate demand fluctuations and irregularities.

1.4 Organization of the Paper

The rest of the paper is organized as follows. Section 2 consists of Related Work. Section 3 outlines the materials and methods used in the study. Section 4 presents the experimental results and provides a detailed discussion. Finally, Sect. 5 concludes the paper, summarizing key findings and discussing implications for future research.

2 Related Work

Table 1. Summary of related works

Reference	Objective	Methodology	Key findings	Limitations
[12]	Compare regression and DL for demand forecasting	Evaluated RF, GBR, XGBoost, CatBoost, LSTM, Bi-LSTM on real datasets	Evaluated ML models on real-world datasets	Absence of external factors (holidays, events)
[15]	Compare ML & DL models for supply chain forecasting	Tested RF, GBR, LightGBM, XGBoost, CatBoost, LSTM, Bi-LSTM	LSTM performed best among all	Limited features and scalability issues
[9]	Review DL applications in supply chain management	Analyzed 43 papers, categorized SCM problems, and developed a taxonomy	Highlighted DL's role in forecasting and logistics optimization	Lacked focus on real-world implementation and scalability
[5]	Assess demand forecast models for retail	Compared RF, XGBoost, ANN, GRB, AdaBoost & hybrid RF-XGBoost-LR model	Hybrid model outperformed standalone models	Limited focus on temporal/spatial variations
[6]	Optimize supply chain partner selection	Used CGAN & SSH framework for SCM selection	Improved inventory & transport planning	Lacked real-time decision-making capabilities
[16]	Improve demand forecasting using deep learning	Hybrid LSTM-RF model with PCA for feature selection	Higher accuracy, lower bias than traditional models	Focused on food products, limited generalization
[17]	Examine food loss & waste in FSCs	Reviewed 152 studies on FSC FLW	Identified 8 FLW themes, proposed a research model	No predictive models for demand forecasting
[7]	Assess ML-based hybrid demand forecasting for SCM	Developed ARIMAX-NN hybrid using time-series & macroeconomic data	Improved forecast accuracy by 5%, in inventory metrics	Focused on steel industry; lacked scalability testing
[4]	Improve demand forecasting in the Physical Internet	Used LSTM with hybrid GA & Scatter Search for hyperparameter tuning	LSTM outperformed ARIMAX, SVR & MLR in fluctuating demand	Focused on Thailand's agricultural sector, limited scalability
[18]	Compare regression and DL for food demand forecasting	Tested RF, GBDT, LightGBM, XGBoost, CatBoost, LSTM, Bi-LSTM on real datasets	CatBoost performed best among regressors; LSTM outperformed Bi-LSTM in DL models	External features and event-based seasonality not included; lacked scalability testing

The food supply chain is defined as the movement of products and services through various stages, focusing on providing value to customers and simultaneously keeping the cost low [17,19]. To manage supply chains effectively, the requirement of accurate demand forecasting has been widely studied, utilizing multiple approaches to improve predictive accuracy and tackle challenges specific to each domain. The ability to predict the future based on past data helps businesses make correct decisions [20]. Traditional forecasting techniques, such as Random Forest and Autoregressive Integrated Moving Average (ARIMA) [21] models, have been widely employed to assess food demand. Nonetheless, these methods often have difficulty in capturing complex temporal patterns and non-linear relationships within real datasets. Recent developments in ML models, including Long Short-Term Memory (LSTM) and Extreme Gradient Boosting (XGBoost) [22], have shown promise in tackling these issues. Deep learning (DL) [12] architectures, especially recurrent neural networks (RNNs), such as LSTM and Gated Recurrent Unit (GRU), are being significantly explored in the time-series forecasting problem in financial domains [16]. Yet they may struggle with handling non-linear relationships between external influences like food demands during holidays and promotional events. In this context, different studies have integrated these models to leverage their combined benefits for demand forecasting. In the past decade, researchers have found new ways to predict future product demand [16]. Some of the promising works in this research domain are highlighted in the following Table 1 for completeness of the paper.

3 Material and Methods

3.1 Dataset Preprocessing

The proposed work utilizes a dataset titled "Food Demand Forecasting" released by Genpact [15], which consists of 145 weeks of weekly requests for 50 different meals. Data is split into three files that together sum to approximately 450,000 entries and 17 attributes, which are detailed in the following Table(s) 2, 3 and 4. It is very important to preprocess data to develop a uniform, enhanced dataset that can further be used for training. The following actions are undertaken:

- **Combining datasets:** The `fulfillment_center_info`, `meal_info`, and `train` datasets are merged to create a consolidated dataset containing enriched features.
- **Handling missing values:** Missing values are imputed using the median to maintain data integrity and the model's performance.
- **Feature encoding:** Categorical features like `center_type`, `category`, and `cuisine` are transformed into numerical formats using `LabelEncoder`.
- **Feature scaling:** Power transformer is applied to normalize skewed distributions. Standard scaler is used to ensure the scaling of numerical features for both LSTM and XGBoost, eventually improving convergence.
- **Dataset splitting:** The dataset is split into 80% training and 20% validation sets for effective evaluation.

Table 2. Dataset on fulfillment of the information into the centers

S.No.	Feature	Description
1	center_id	Unique ID for each fulfillment center
2	op_area	Service area covered by the center
3	city_code	City's associated pin code
4	center_type	Category of the center (Type A, B, or C)
5	region_code	Unique code for each region

Table 3. Dataset on weekly demand data

S.No.	Feature	Description
1	id	Unique order identifier
2	week	Week number (1 to 145)
3	meal_id	Unique identifier for each meal
4	center_id	Unique identifier for fulfillment hubs
5	checkout_price	Final meal price after all adjustments
6	base_price	Original meal price from the menu
7	emailer_for_promotion	Indicates if the meal was promoted via email
8	homepage_featured	Indicates if the meal was highlighted on the homepage
9	num_orders	Total number of orders received

Table 4. Dataset on meal information

S.No.	Feature	Description
1	meal_id	Unique ID for each meal
2	Category	Type of meal (salad, soup, dessert, etc.)
3	Cuisine	Cuisine type (Indian, Italian, etc.)

3.2 Proposed Methodology

The proposed hybrid LSTM-XGBoost model is used to address the issues of food distribution in the supply chain. The workflow of the proposed hybrid model, shown in Fig. 1, initiates with preparing the data to be analyzed. This data pre-processing step includes data merging, categorical feature encoding, missing value imputation, and feature scaling. After that, the training data is split into smaller chunks. The model processes these chunks of data rather than using the entire dataset at once. This model undergoes incremental learning through mini-batches using these chunks. Each chunk is first processed through the LSTM. The procedure enables the model to effectively capture sequential dependencies while preserving the important temporal data, thus simplifying XGBoost's task. Next, the extracted features are then passed on to XGBoost, which is used to identify non-linear dependencies and various residuals that

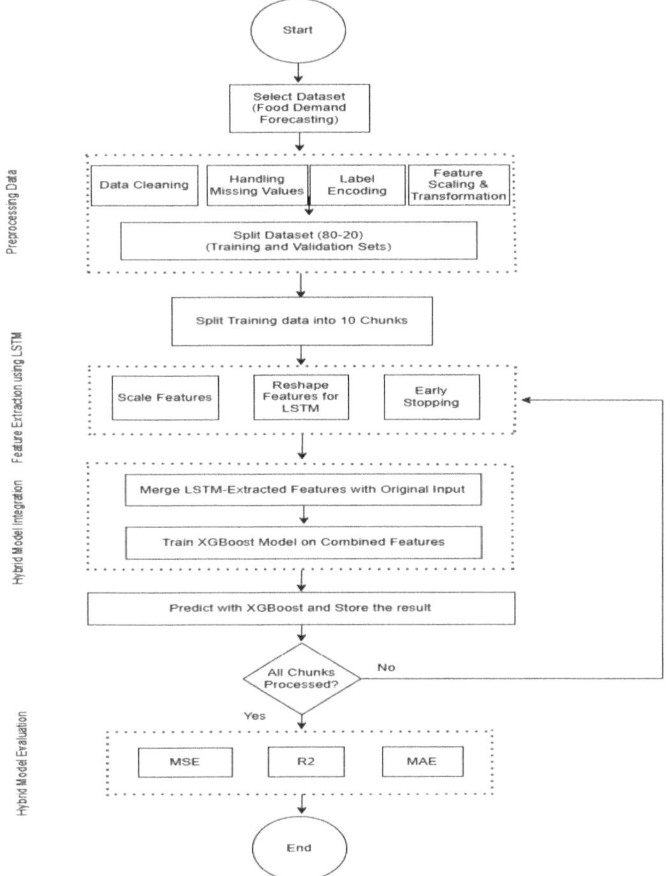

Fig. 1. Block diagram of the proposed methodology.

LSTM was unable to identify on its own. The chunks are processed iteratively until all of them have been processed. The following measures mentioned in the Table 5 are used to assess the effectiveness of the proposed hybrid model.

3.3 Detailed Methodology

The proposed hybrid model integrates the strengths of LSTM and XGBoost models to enhance the prediction accuracy. Instead of training the model separately, the LSTM followed by XGBoost models are trained iteratively in mini-batches. In the proposed model, the training data is split into chunks, considered 10 in the proposed methodology. For each chunk, the subsequent steps are followed.

- *LSTM model training:* LSTM captures Sequential dependencies and patterns within the data effectively. This part is trained in 10 iterative chunks and

Table 5. Performance measures used in the proposed work

Performance Measure	Definition	Formula
Mean Squared Error (MSE)	Average squared difference between actual and predicted values.	$MSE = \frac{1}{n}\sum(y_i - \hat{y}_i)^2$
Mean Absolute Error (MAE)	Average absolute difference between actual and predicted values.	$MAE = \frac{1}{n}\sum\lvert y_i - \hat{y}_i\rvert$
Root Mean Squared Error (RMSE)	Square root of MSE.	$RMSE = \sqrt{\frac{1}{n}\sum(y_i - \hat{y}_i)^2}$
Mean Absolute Percentage Error (MAPE)	Percentage error between actual and predicted values.	$MAPE = \frac{100}{n}\sum\left\lvert\frac{y_i - \hat{y}_i}{y_i}\right\rvert$
R-squared (R^2 Score)	Measures how well the model explains variance in the target variable.	$R^2 = 1 - \frac{\sum(y_i - \hat{y}_i)^2}{\sum(y_i - \bar{y})^2}$

each running for 50 epochs using a batch size of 64. The Adam optimizer and a mean squared error (MSE) loss function are deployed. Early stopping and learning rate reduction callbacks help to optimize the training efficiency. The input data is reshaped to match the LSTM input format: (samples, time-steps, features). Predictions from the trained LSTM model are extracted and used as additional features for the XGBoost model to enhance the learning. The architectural diagram of the LSTM in the proposed work is shown in Fig. 2.

- *XGBoost model training:* The XGBoost model is employed as the next component of the hybrid framework, combining the LSTM-generated features with the original dataset. Here, the XGBoost follows an iterative approach where it keeps building a decision tree step by step. It starts with feature binning and then uses a decision tree to make predictions. Each new tree built learns from the mistakes of previous ones by evaluating gradients and adjusting accordingly. The procedure continues until an ensemble of trees is formed. Finally, the model's accuracy is tested on the validation dataset. The architectural diagram of the LSTM in the proposed work is shown in Fig. 3.

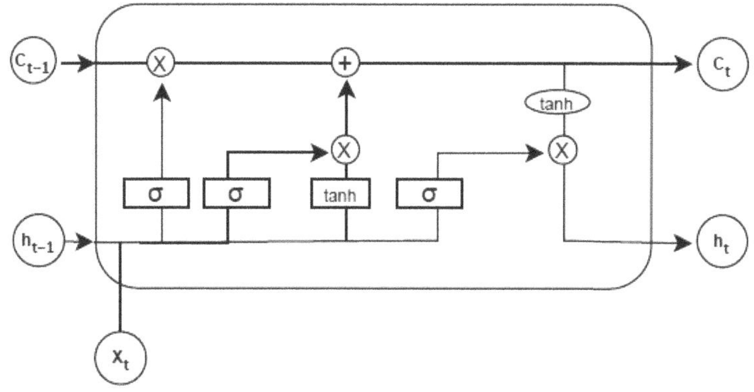

Fig. 2. LSTM architecture.

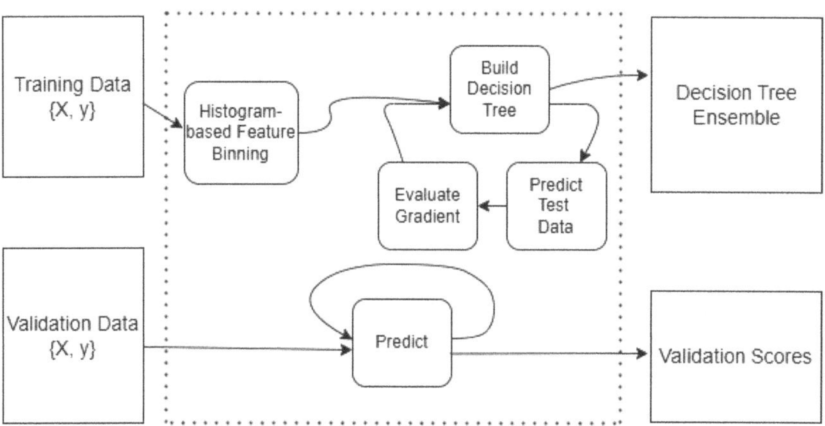

Fig. 3. XGBoost Architecture.

4 Result Analysis and Discussion

4.1 Simulation Environment

The simulation of the proposed work was carried out with an Intel Core i5 processor, 8GB RAM, and Linux OS with Visual Studio. Table 6 highlights the software and libraries used in this work.

The LSTM model consists of three layers with 512, 256, and 128 units, using a dropout rate of 0.3. It employs the Tanh activation function for LSTM layers and ReLU for dense layers. The model is trained with a learning rate of 0.0005, a batch size of 64, and runs for 50 epochs per iteration over 10 iterations. AdamW is used as the optimizer with a weight decay regularization of 0.01. The XGBoost model has 800 trees with a max depth of 12, a learning rate of 0.02, a subsample rate of 0.9, and a colsample bytree of 0.8, with Lambda and Alpha set to 3 and 1,

Table 6. System configuration and libraries used

Component	Specification
Processor	Intel Core i5
RAM	8GB
Operating System	Linux
Software	Visual Studio
Programming Language	Python
Libraries	TensorFlow/Keras (LSTM implementation) XGBoost (Gradient Boosting) Scikit-Learn (Evaluation Metrics) Pandas, NumPy (Data Preprocessing & Analysis) Matplotlib, Seaborn (Data Visualization)

respectively. Table 7 provides a comprehensive overview of the hyperparameters used in the proposed work.

4.2 Simulations Results

Figure 4 presents a comparative analysis of actual versus predicted food demand using three forecasting models: LSTM, XGBoost, and a proposed hybrid LSTM-XGBoost approach. Each plot visualizes how well the models can capture demand variations over samples. In Fig. 4a, it is observed that the LSTM captures temporal dependencies and trends, leading to reasonable alignment between actual and predicted values. However, the fluctuations in demand are not always perfectly captured, with noticeable deviations in certain regions. The model struggles with sudden spikes and extreme variations, leading to inconsistencies in high-demand scenarios. Figure 4b represents the predictions of the XGBoost model.

Here, the XGBoost captures patterns effectively but exhibits more pronounced variations in prediction accuracy. While the model captures some peaks, it struggles with complex temporal dependencies, leading to mismatches in short-term fluctuations. Predictions tend to have a higher variance compared to the LSTM approach. Finally, Fig. 4c depicts the prediction performance of the proposed hybrid model combining LSTM and XGBoost. This approach leverages the sequential learning capability of LSTM along with feature selection to enhance the strength of XGBoost. Predictions show a more stable alignment with actual demand, capturing both short-term variations and long-term trends. The proposed hybrid model reduces prediction errors, especially for high-demand periods, improving forecasting accuracy. The integration of both models helps mitigate individual weaknesses, making the approach more robust for food demand forecasting. The hybrid LSTM-XGBoost model outperforms individual models by effectively balancing trend prediction and demand fluctuations. This approach enhances forecasting reliability, which is crucial for optimizing food supply chain management and reducing food waste.

Table 7. Model hyperparameters and configurations

Model	Hyperparameter	Values
LSTM	Number of Layers	3
	Number of Units	512, 256, 128
	Dropout Rate	0.3
	Activation Function	Tanh (LSTM), ReLU (Dense)
	Learning Rate	0.0005
	Batch Size	64
	Epochs per Iteration	50
	Total Iterations	10
	Optimizer	AdamW
XGBoost	Number of Trees (n_estimators)	800
	Max Depth	12
	Learning Rate	0.02
	Subsample	0.9
	Colsample_bytree	0.8
	Regularization (Lambda)	3
	Regularization (Alpha)	1

Figure 5 describes the comparison between actual and predicted values for food demand forecasting using three models: LSTM, XGBoost, and a proposed hybrid approach. The red dashed line in each subplot represents the ideal fit, indicating perfect predictions. Each model demonstrates different characteristics in terms of prediction accuracy and error distribution. Figure 5a shows the performance of the LSTM model, highlighting a strong correlation between actual and predicted values. This model effectively captures sequential dependencies in the data, demonstrating its ability to recognize temporal patterns. However, its accuracy diminishes at higher demand levels, where deviations become more pronounced, indicating challenges in handling extreme fluctuations. While the error rates suggest moderate predictive accuracy, they also reveal the model's limitations in fully capturing demand spikes, implying that it explains a substantial portion of the variance but struggles with sudden surges. On the other hand, Fig. 5b presents the predictions of the XGBoost model, which effectively captures the overall trend but exhibits greater dispersion, particularly at higher demand levels. This behavior suggests potential overfitting or underfitting of specific patterns, limiting its ability to generalize across varying demand conditions. While the model achieves slightly better accuracy than LSTM, it still struggles to capture extreme demand fluctuations, indicating room for improvement in handling high-variance scenarios. Finally, Fig. 5c shows the predictive performance of the proposed hybrid model combining LSTM and XGBoost. The proposed hybrid model demonstrates improved alignment with the ideal fit, reducing pre-

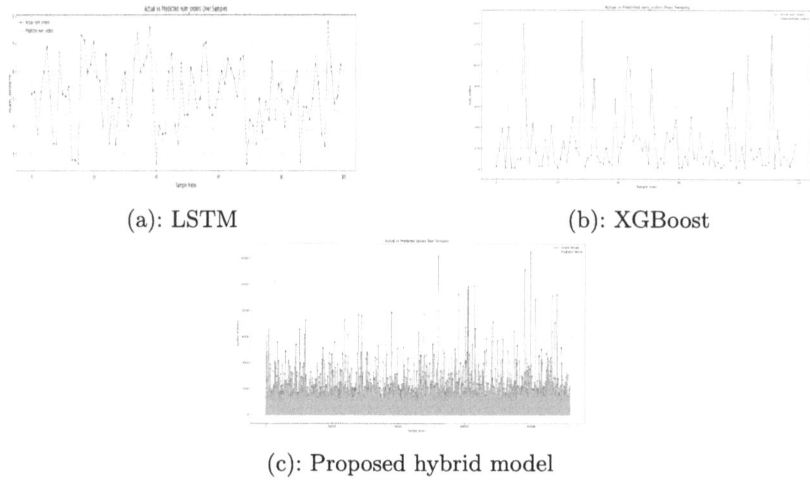

(a): LSTM

(b): XGBoost

(c): Proposed hybrid model

Fig. 4. Line plot of actual vs predicted num of orders over samples **a** LSTM **b** XGBoost **c** Proposed hybrid model.

diction errors and enhancing generalization. The scatter plot indicates a more consistent spread across different demand levels, minimizing overestimation and underestimation errors. The comparison highlights that while LSTM excels in capturing temporal dependencies and XGBoost effectively selects features, their combination in the hybrid model results in superior performance. The hybrid approach reduces prediction errors and enhances accuracy, making it a more effective solution for food demand forecasting, particularly in managing both short-term fluctuations and overall trends.

Table 8. Performance comparison with existing standalone models

Models	R	MAE	MSE	MAPE	RMSE
LSTM	0.73	0.49	0.3835	0.11	0.62
XGBoost	0.81	91.90	29245	0.76	171.01
Proposed hybrid model	0.91	71.08	13597	0.23	116.60

The proposed hybrid approach enhances prediction accuracy by combining the strengths of LSTM and XGBoost through an iterative, interleaved training process. LSTM extracts advanced temporal features, which are then fed into XGBoost to capture complex nonlinear relationships. The model employs a three-layer LSTM with 512-256-128 units, weight decay regularization in AdamW, and normalization techniques to mitigate overfitting and stabilize convergence. XGBoost operates with a tree depth of 12, 800 estimators, and a learning rate of 0.02 to improve generalization. These refinements collectively enhance

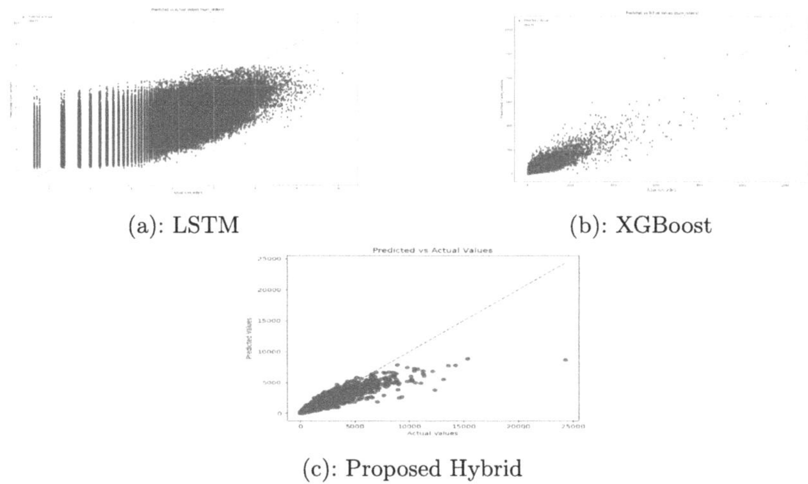

(a): LSTM (b): XGBoost

(c): Proposed Hybrid

Fig. 5. Scatter plot of actual vs predicted num of orders over samples for **a** LSTM **b** XGBoost **c** Proposed hybrid.

predictive performance, achieving higher R scores and lower errors compared to standalone models. These comparative results are presented in Table 8, highlighting the effectiveness of the proposed hybrid approach. The performance evaluation of the models highlights the superiority of the proposed hybrid approach. The LSTM model achieves a coefficient of determination of 0.73, demonstrating its ability to capture temporal dependencies, while XGBoost performs better with an R of 0.81 but shows higher error values. The hybrid model significantly improves accuracy with an R of 0.91, reducing MAE and MSE compared to individual models. The lower RMSE and MAPE values indicate better generalization and lower prediction deviations. These results confirm that integrating LSTM with XGBoost enhances predictive performance and reliability.

4.2.1 Model Interpretability and Explainability

The primary objective of our Hybrid model is to achieve high forecasting accuracy. However, the supply chain domain requires adequate explanation to enable deeper understanding and interpretation to understand the reasoning behind predictions. In the current model, the XGBoost part facilitates the identification of input features that contributed to the prediction and to what extent. This can be achieved through its built-in feature importance mechanism that quantifies the influence of each feature on the model's output. On the other hand, LSTM, being a DL (Deep Learning) model, has a complex internal structure, making it difficult to interpret how it makes decisions, thus rendering it less interpretable. To address this, explainable AI techniques such as SHAP (Shapley Additive exPlanations) and LIME (Local Interpretable Model-agnostic Explanations) can be applied to provide instance-level insights, particularly to understand the temporal impact of sequential features. These additions would make the model more trustworthy and suitable for real-world decision-making.

4.2.2 Comparison with Existing Forecasting Models

Recent research has gone through a range of machine learning techniques for demand forecasting in the supply chain. Katikar et al. [18] evaluated several regression models for food demand forecasting using the Genpact dataset, including CatBoost, LightGBM, and XGBoost. Among these, CatBoost achieved the best performance with an MSE of 20,321.37 and an RMSE of 142.55. In contrast, our proposed LSTM–XGBoost hybrid achieved even better results, with an MSE of 13,597 and RMSE of 116.60, thereby demonstrating superior forecasting accuracy.

Also, Feizabadi [7] developed hybrid forecasting models where he made use of ARIMAX and neural networks to predict demand in the retail steel segment. He achieved a forecast accuracy of approximately 89% ($R^2 \approx 0.89$). Our model, on the other hand, attained an R^2 of 0.91 on a food supply chain dataset. This suggests that our model performs better. Although the datasets and domain differ, the comparisons made provide a valuable benchmark and demonstrate the robustness of the proposed hybrid model.

Practical Use Case: The proposed hybrid model has strong potential for practical application in food delivery networks in urban areas. For instance, a food delivery service operating across multiple locations in a city could use this model to forecast weekly demand for different meal types at various fulfillment centers. By predicting order volumes more accurately, the business can optimize meal preparation, reduce inventory waste, and align delivery logistics in a better way. Also, the model's ability to incorporate external factors like holidays and promotions extends its applicability to real-world environments where demand often fluctuates due to such events.

5 Conclusion

The proposed work presents a hybrid ML model that integrates LSTM with XGBoost. The LSTM part is outstanding in modeling time-dependent relationships, whereas XGBoost offers strong nonlinear regression features. This paper demonstrates the effectiveness of the hybrid model in predicting food demand by using a dataset on food demand forecasting, enriched with characteristics from fulfillment centers and meal distributions. The simulation results emphasize the model's ability to reduce food waste and enhance supply chain effectiveness, aiding in global food security. This paper highlights the significance of incorporating advanced analytics into SCM to tackle urgent societal issues. The outcome of this paper suggests that a blended approach in predictive analytics can benefit from combining DL models with traditional ML models to solve complex problems, which can serve as a basis for further research in this domain.

References

1. Garnett, T.: Food sustainability: problems, perspectives and solutions. Proc. Nutrition Soc. **72**(1), 29–39 (2013)
2. O'Connor, D., Boyle, P., Ilcan, S., Oliver, M.: Living with insecurity: food security, resilience, and the world food programme (wfp). Global Soc. Policy **17**(1), 3–20 (2017)
3. Mentzer, J.T., Schroeter, J.: Multiple forecasting system at brake parts, inc. J. Bus. Forecasting **12**(3), 5 (1993)
4. Kantasa-Ard, A., Nouiri, M., Bekrar, A., Ait el Cadi, A., Sallez, Y.: Machine learning for demand forecasting in the physical internet: a case study of agricultural products in Thailand. Int. J. Prod. Res. 59(24), 7491–7515 (2021)
5. Mitra, A., Jain, A., Kishore, A., Kumar, P.: A comparative study of demand forecasting models for a multi-channel retail company: a novel hybrid machine learning approach. In: Operations Research Forum, vol. 3, p. 58. Springer (2022)
6. Lin, H., Lin, J., Wang, F.: An innovative machine learning model for supply chain management. J. Innovat. Knowl. **7**(4), 100276 (2022)
7. Feizabadi, J.: Machine learning demand forecasting and supply chain performance. Int J Log Res Appl **25**(2), 119–142 (2022)
8. Mentzer, J.T., Kahn, K.B.: State of sales forecasting systems in corporate America. J. Bus. Forecasting Methods Syst. **16**(1) (1997)
9. Hosseinnia Shavaki, F., Ebrahimi Ghahnavieh, A.: Applications of deep learning into supply chain management: a systematic literature review and a framework for future research. Artif. Intell. Rev. **56**(5), 4447–4489 (2023)
10. Piccialli, F., Giampaolo, F., Prezioso, E., Camacho, D., Acampora, G.: Artificial intelligence and healthcare: forecasting of medical bookings through multi-source time-series fusion. Inf. Fusion **74**, 1–16 (2021)
11. Ke, G., Meng, Q., Finley, T., Wang, T., Chen, W., Ma, W., Ye, Q., Liu, T.Y.: Lightgbm: A highly efficient gradient boosting decision tree. Adv. Neural Inf. Process. Syst. **30** (2017)
12. Douaioui, K., Oucheikh, R., Benmoussa, O., Mabrouki, C.: Machine learning and deep learning models for demand forecasting in supply chain management: a critical review. Appl. Syst. Innova. (ASI) **7**(5) (2024)
13. Waberi, A.D., Mwangi, R.W., Rimiru, R.M.: Advancing type ii diabetes predictions with a hybrid LSTM-xgboost approach. J. Data Anal. Inf. Process. **12**(2), 163–188 (2024)
14. Ni, D., Xiao, Z., Lim, M.K.: A systematic review of the research trends of machine learning in supply chain management. Int. J. Mach. Learn. Cybern. **11**, 1463–1482 (2020)
15. Panda, S.K., Mohanty, S.N.: Time series forecasting and modeling of food demand supply chain based on regressors analysis. IEEE Access **11**, 42679–42700 (2023)
16. Punia, S., Shankar, S.: Predictive analytics for demand forecasting: a deep learning-based decision support system. Knowl.-Based Syst. **258**, 109956 (2022)
17. Chauhan, C., Dhir, A., Akram, M.U., Salo, J.: Food loss and waste in food supply chains. a systematic literature review and framework development approach. J. Clean. Prod. **295**, 126438 (2021)
18. Katikar, P., et al.: Forecasting food demand in supply chains: a comprehensive comparison of regression models and deep learning approaches. J./Conf. Name (2024)

19. Folkerts, H., Koehorst, H.: Challenges in international food supply chains: vertical co-ordination in the European agribusiness and food industries. British Food J. **100**(8), 385–388 (1998)
20. Kochak, A., Sharma, S.: Demand forecasting using neural network for supply chain management. Int. J. Mech. Eng. Robot. Res. **4**(1), 96–104 (2015)
21. Ho, S.L., Xie, M.: The use of arima models for reliability forecasting and analysis. Comput. Ind. Eng. **35**(1–2), 213–216 (1998)
22. Oukhouya, H., Kadiri, H., El Himdi, K., Guerbaz, R.: Forecasting international stock market trends: Xgboost, lstm, lstm-xgboost, and backtesting xgboost models. Stat. Optim. Inf. Comput. **12**(1), 200–209 (2024)

Enhanced Short-Term Wind Power Ramp Forecasting: A Multi Dataset Validation Approach

Leechita Gopalakrishnan(✉) and N. Sabiyath Fathima

Department of Computer Science and Engineering, B.S.A. Crescent Institute of Science and Technology, Chennai, Tamil Nadu, India
leechita0803@gmail.com, sabiyathfathima@crescent.education

Abstract. Accurate forecasting of wind power ramp events—sudden and unpredictable changes in wind generation—is crucial for maintaining grid stability and ensuring efficient energy management, especially with the increasing reliance on renewable energy. This study addresses the challenge of capturing complex wind fluctuations by proposing a hybrid model that integrates Variational Mode Decomposition (VMD), Long Short-Term Memory (LSTM) networks, and eXtreme Gradient Boosting (XGBoost). The model utilizes historical wind speed, direction, and external weather variables such as temperature and gusts, with ramp detection performed using the Definition-Based Sign Indicator (DSI) method. Validated across four geographically diverse wind farms with an 8-h ahead forecasting horizon, the model demonstrates high ramp detection precision (0.814–0.903) and strong overall performance in terms of MSE, RMSE, MAE, and sMAPE. Results confirm that combining signal decomposition with deep and ensemble learning significantly improves forecasting accuracy and generalizability, making the model highly suitable for real-world wind energy integration scenarios.

Keywords: Wind power forecasting · Ramp event detection · LSTM · XGBoost · Hybrid model · VMD

1 Introduction

Accurate wind power forecasting is essential for maintaining grid stability and optimizing energy management, particularly with the increasing integration of renewable sources [1, 2]. Wind power ramp events—sudden and significant fluctuations in output—pose operational challenges by causing energy imbalances and elevating reserve requirements [3]. Traditional models like Long Short-Term Memory (LSTM) and eXtreme Gradient Boosting (XGBoost), though widely used, often fall short in capturing the nonlinear, dynamic behavior of wind power. Their reliance on limited features and basic ramp detection methods results in false positives and reduced forecasting reliability [4, 5].

A key limitation of prior work lies in its dependence on single-location datasets, which constrains the generalizability of models [6]. Furthermore, many approaches ignore powerful signal processing techniques such as Variational Mode Decomposition

K. Chandra Mondal et al. (Eds.): CICBA 2025, CCIS 2863, pp. 227–238, 2026.
https://doi.org/10.1007/978-3-032-17184-9_17

(VMD), which effectively extracts meaningful temporal patterns and suppresses high-frequency noise [7].

To address these gaps, this study presents a hybrid forecasting framework integrating VMD with LSTM and XGBoost, combined with the Definition-Based Sign Indicator (DSI) algorithm for ramp event detection. Using historical meteorological and operational data—such as wind speed, direction, temperature, and gusts—the model is validated on four geographically diverse wind farms to assess its robustness and scalability.

This integrated approach yields improved forecasting accuracy over standalone models and demonstrates strong generalization capabilities across datasets. By leveraging decomposition and hybrid learning techniques, the framework offers a reliable solution for real-world wind power prediction and ramp detection.

The rest of the paper is structured as follows: Sect. 2 reviews related work, Sect. 3 describes the dataset, Sect. 4 outlines the methodology, Sect. 5 presents each of the modules in detail, Sect. 6 presents results and discussion, and Sect. 7 concludes with key findings and future directions.

2 Related Works

Leechita Gopalakrishnan, Julian L. Cardenas Barrera et al. [1] developed a wind ramp forecasting model using VMD and XGBoost on a SCADA dataset from Turkey, achieving 100% precision in ramp detection via the DSI algorithm but faced limitations due to single dataset usage, high-frequency noise, and seasonal variability. Similarly, Z. Wang, L. Wang et al. [2] highlighted the effectiveness of the EMD-KM-SXL model compared to traditional (PM, ARIMA), deep learning (LSTM, GRU), and hybrid models (Jaya-SVM, EMD-XGB, EMD-LASSO), recommending advanced decomposition techniques like CEEMDAN and VMD for improved accuracy.

Yogesh S, Leechita G et al. [3] enhanced wind speed forecasting by integrating ReliefF feature selection with LSTM, reducing model complexity and outperforming ANN by a 0.7 error margin, though validation was limited to a single dataset. Joseph C.Y. Lee, Caroline Draxl et al. [5] introduced WE-Validate, an open-source Python tool for wind forecast evaluation, improving ramp detection through ensemble-based approaches but facing challenges with smoothing effects in ramp forecasting. Z. Qian, Y. Pei et al. [7] reviewed decomposition-based models (VMD, EMD, Wavelet), demonstrating their effectiveness in simplifying complex signals for multi-step forecasting. Zhang, B. Xu, H. Liu et al. [8] employed VMD and feature selection to enhance wind power prediction by decomposing wind data into frequency components. Cornejo-Bueno, Laura et al. [11] combined reanalysis data with machine learning regressors (GPR, MLP, SVR) for ramp event prediction, improving sensitivity but requiring further exploration in threshold optimization.

Cao B, Chang L et al. [12] used CNN-based similarity search for day-ahead wind ramp forecasting with HRDPS wind speed data, achieving 77% accuracy up to 48 h but dependent on wind forecast quality. S. Yu and J. Hur [13] developed an LSTM-based short-term wind power forecasting model with 2-h ahead ramp detection, enhancing real-time curtailment but requiring comparison with models like NWP and OpSDA for improved reliability. Y. Liu, T. Khoshgoftaar, et al. [14] note that prior research in SQC modeling has demonstrated that utilizing multiple datasets enhances model robustness and accuracy across similar projects (e.g., NASA datasets). Inspired by this, this paper employs multi-dataset validation to enhance generalization and predictive reliability.

3 Dataset Description

The dataset used in this study consists of field-based meteorological observations and wind power generation data collected from four operational wind farms, covering the period from January 2, 2017, to December 31, 2021. This comprehensive hourly dataset includes key atmospheric parameters—such as temperature, humidity, dew point, wind speed, wind direction, and wind gusts at multiple heights—recorded using advanced meteorological sensors. Wind power generation data were obtained directly from turbine outputs and normalized to ensure consistency and reliability in analysis.

This dataset offers valuable insights for predictive modeling, operational efficiency, and grid management. It serves as a critical resource for wind power forecasting, renewable energy optimization, and environmental impact assessment. By leveraging this rich dataset, researchers and industry practitioners can develop more accurate and scalable forecasting models, facilitating a smoother transition toward a sustainable energy future. Table 1 provides a detailed overview of the dataset attributes.

Table 1. Attributes of the four windfarms

Attribute	Description	Unit
Date/time	Hourly timestamp when readings were Recorded	YYYY-MM-DD HH:MM
Temperature_2m	Air temperature measured at 2m above ground level	°F
RelativeHumidity_2m	Relative humidity at 2 m above the surface	%
Dewpoint_2m	Dew point temperature at 2 m	°F
WindSpeed_10m	Wind speed measured at 10 m above ground level	m/s
WindSpeed_100m	Wind speed measured at 100 m above ground level	m/s
WindDirection_100m	Wind direction at 100 m (measured in degrees from 0 to 360)	°
WindGusts_10m	Maximum wind gusts recorded at 10 m	m/s
Power	Turbine power output, normalized between 0 and 1 (percentage of maximum potential output)	–

4 Proposed Methodology

Figure 1 illustrates the proposed system aimed at enhancing wind power ramp forecasting by integrating advanced machine learning techniques. The hybrid model combines Long Short-Term Memory (LSTM) networks and Extreme Gradient Boosting (XGBoost) to capture both temporal dependencies and nonlinear relationships in wind power data, addressing the limitations of standalone models.

Meteorological features, including wind direction, were preprocessed by converting angular values into their sine and cosine components to handle the circular nature of the data and eliminate discontinuities. This transformation improves the model's ability to learn directional patterns effectively. The system is validated across multiple wind farms with an 8-h ahead forecasting horizon, ensuring adaptability to diverse locations and weather conditions. An 8-h ahead forecasting window was selected as it balances practical operational needs—such as scheduling ramp reserves and adjusting grid dispatch—with model reliability and responsiveness in short-term scenarios.

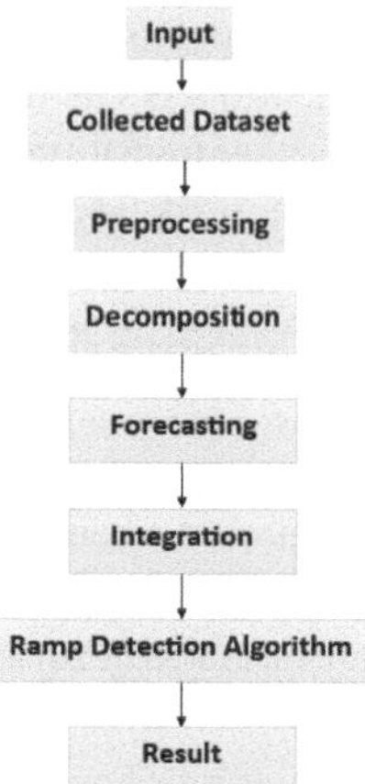

Fig. 1. Design process – structure chart

Low-frequency components derived from Variational Mode Decomposition (VMD) represent the underlying trend of wind power, minimizing high-frequency noise and short-term fluctuations. By emphasizing these stable patterns during signal reconstruction, the forecasting model achieves improved accuracy and robustness, particularly beneficial for grid-level decision-making and operational planning.

Ramp event detection is enhanced using the Definition-Based Sign Indicator (DSI) algorithm, which identifies sudden changes in wind power output more effectively than traditional methods.

Accuracy, Precision, Recall, and F1 Score evaluate the model's performance. Incorporating external meteorological factors and advanced decomposition techniques further improves forecasting accuracy and reliability, supporting better grid management and wind energy integration.

5 Module Description and Implementation

The project is divided into four key modules, each focusing on enhancing predictive accuracy, optimizing feature extraction, and contributing to grid stability for effective wind energy integration.

Module 1: Data Preprocessing and Feature Engineering

This module lays the groundwork for accurate forecasting by refining the dataset, which includes hourly meteorological and wind power data from four locations (January 2017–December 2021). Preprocessing involves parsing timestamps and extracting time-based features (hour, day, month) to capture temporal patterns. Negative and zero power values are either removed or interpolated for consistency. Correlation analysis identifies significant predictors like wind speed at 100m and wind gusts, while redundant features such as humidity and dew point are discarded. Wind direction is converted into Cartesian coordinates to enhance model effectiveness. Finally, Min-Max Scaling normalizes all numerical variables, ensuring consistency and reducing noise, improving model efficiency.

Module 2: Variational Mode Decomposition (VMD) for Feature Extraction

VMD enhances forecasting accuracy by decomposing the wind power signal into three intrinsic mode functions (IMFs), isolating distinct frequency components and reducing noise. VMD is optimized with parameters: bandwidth constraint ($\alpha = 2000$) and number of modes ($K = 3$). Each mode is normalized using Min-Max Scaling and stored for future use in forecasting and anomaly detection. By capturing essential temporal variations, VMD helps eliminate irrelevant fluctuations, improving predictive performance. Figure 2 represents the intrinsic mode functions of after variational mode decomposition on location 1 dataset.

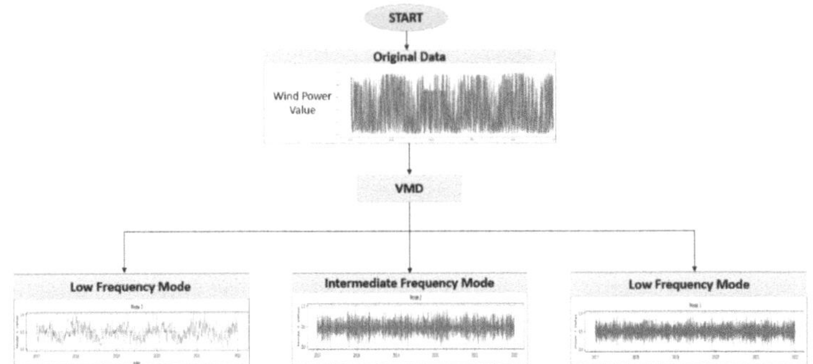

Fig. 2. Modes after performing variational mode decomposition on location 1

Module 3: Hybrid Forecasting Using LSTM and XGBoost

Once the wind power signal has been decomposed into its intrinsic modes, each mode undergoes independent forecasting using a hybrid approach that combines Long Short-Term Memory (LSTM) networks and Extreme Gradient Boosting (XGBoost).

VMD has a time complexity of approximately $\mathbf{O\ (nK\ log\ n)}$, while LSTM contributes $\mathbf{O\ (n \times d^2)}$ per epoch due to its sequential nature. XGBoost adds around $\mathbf{O\ (n\ log\ n)}$ depending on tree depth and boosting rounds. Although this approach is more computationally intensive than standalone LSTM or XGBoost models, the increased complexity is justified by its improved forecasting accuracy, robustness across multiple datasets, and enhanced ramp detection performance.

The forecasting process begins by scaling the decomposed mode frequencies and splitting them into training and testing sets, using a lookback period of 24 h. To enable LSTM networks to learn temporal dependencies effectively, a sequence generator function is employed to prepare overlapping time windows for training. The hyperparameter tuning process is conducted using Keras Tuner, optimizing crucial parameters such as the number of LSTM units, dropout rates, the presence of an additional LSTM layer, and learning rates. The optimized configuration consists of two LSTM layers with dropout regularization, followed by a dense layer for feature extraction. The model is trained using the Adam optimizer, with Mean Squared Error (MSE) as the loss function, and early stopping is implemented to prevent overfitting. Table 2 represents the hyperparameters used in LSTM model.

Table 2. Parameters of long-short term memory algorithm

Hyperparameters	Values
Units (Layer 1)	64
Dropout (Layer 1)	0.2
Second LSTM layer	True
Units (Layer 2)	64
Dropout (Layer 2)	0.2

After training the LSTM model, the extracted features are used to train an XGBoost regressor with n_estimators = 100, learning_rate = 0.05, max_depth = 5, which further refines the predictions by capturing complex nonlinear relationships. The final forecasted values are inverse-transformed to their original scale and evaluated using performance metrics such as Mean Absolute Error (MAE), Root Mean Squared Error (RMSE), and Symmetric Mean Absolute Percentage Error (sMAPE). The actual and predicted power values are visualized using Matplotlib to assess model performance, and the results are stored in a CSV file for further analysis.

Module 4: Wind Ramp Event Detection Using the DSI Algorithm

The final predicted signal is reconstructed by integrating mode forecasts and fitting a polynomial curve. Ramp events, characterized by sudden wind power fluctuations, are detected using the Definition-Based Sign Indicator (DSI) Algorithm. The algorithm evaluates directional changes over defined time intervals, using a ramp threshold of 5%, a duration of 6 h, and 60-min intervals. Significant power increases are classified as up-ramps, and decreases as down-ramps. This method ensures reliable detection of ramp events across all locations, demonstrating the effectiveness of the integrated approach in enhancing grid stability and optimizing wind energy utilization.

6 Result and Discussion

A. Forecasting Performance

The forecasting performance of the proposed hybrid model was evaluated by analyzing individual Intrinsic Mode Functions (IMFs) across four wind farm locations. Tables 3, 4, 5 and 6 present the Mean Absolute Error (MAE), Mean Squared Error (MSE), Root Mean Squared Error (RMSE), and symmetric Mean Absolute Percentage Error (sMAPE) for each IMF, highlighting variations in prediction accuracy across locations and frequency components.

The results show that the low-frequency mode consistently yields the lowest error values across all locations, effectively capturing the dominant wind power trends. Intermediate-frequency modes show slightly higher errors, while high-frequency modes record the highest RMSE and sMAPE values, indicating greater challenges in predicting rapid and short-term fluctuations.

Location 2 demonstrates the best overall accuracy, with its low-frequency mode achieving an MAE of 0.01417 and RMSE of 0.01837. The relatively small gap in errors between intermediate- and high-frequency modes suggests that Location 2 has more stable wind patterns. In contrast, Locations 3 and 4 exhibit higher RMSE values in high-frequency modes (0.03901 and 0.04337, respectively), indicating greater volatility in short-term wind power changes.

Compared to our previous study [1], which utilized only XGBoost and was limited to a single location, the current model shows significant improvement in accuracy and robustness. The inclusion of LSTM enables the model to better capture sequential dependencies, while the use of Variational Mode Decomposition (VMD) and multi-location validation ensures the model generalizes well across different geographic and climatic conditions.

Table 3. Evaluation metrics of IMF forecasting in location 1

Location 1 modes	MAE	MSE	RMSE	sMAPE
Low frequency mode	0.01688	0.00051	0.02253	2.94424
Intermediate frequency mode	0.017003	0.00068	0.02590	4.18252
High frequency mode	0.029908	0.0018	0.042427	7.06703

Table 4. Evaluation metrics of IMF forecasting in location 2

Location 2 modes	MAE	MSE	RMSE	sMAPE
Low frequency mode	0.01417	0.000338	0.01837	3.80918
Intermediate frequency mode	0.01507	0.00050	0.02232	3.29452
High frequency mode	0.01616	0.00061	0.02475	3.29452

Table 5. Evaluation metrics of IMF forecasting in location 3

Location 3 modes	MAE	MSE	RMSE	sMAPE
Low frequency mode	0.02194	0.00078	0.02802	3.15087
Intermediate frequency mode	0.02349	0.00133	0.03643	5.15054
High frequency mode	0.02660	0.00152	0.03901	6.26793

Table 6. Evaluation metrics of IMF forecasting in location 4

Location 4 modes	MAE	MSE	RMSE	sMAPE
Low frequency mode	0.01635	0.00046	0.02142	4.04513
Intermediate frequency mode	0.02217	0.00105	0.03241	5.13039
High frequency mode	0.03024	0.00188	0.04337	6.54118

Figure 3 illustrates an 8-h ahead forecast of the low-frequency mode for Location 1, showing that the forecasted values closely align with actual observations, validating the model's effectiveness in capturing long-term trends while mitigating noise effects.

Fig. 3. 8 h ahead forecasting of Low Frequency Mode in Location 1

B. Integrated Forecasting Performance

After IMF-based forecasting, the original wind power signal is reconstructed by linearly combining the IMFs, followed by polynomial smoothing to enhance trend accuracy. This approach prioritizes low-frequency components for stable predictions and suppresses high-frequency noise.

As shown in Table 7, the integrated model achieves MAE values between 0.1403 (Location 2) and 0.2121 (Location 1), with RMSE ranging from 0.1702 to 0.2492, indicating improved forecasting performance across all locations.

The enhanced performance is attributed to the hybrid LSTM + XGBoost architecture's ability to learn both temporal and nonlinear patterns, as well as the decomposed structure of the data, which simplifies the forecasting task and improves interpretability.

Table 7. Evaluation Metrics of forecasted signal across all 4 locations

Location 1 Modes	MAE	MSE	RMSE	sMAPE
Location 1	0.2121	0.0621	0.2492	46.42%
Location 2	0.1403	0.0290	0.1702	63.91%
Location 3	0.1849	0.0520	0.2280	36.61%
Location 4	0.1692	0.0440	0.2098	62.41%

Figure 4 compares the original and reconstructed wind power signals, showing that the integration process smooths predictions while preserving key fluctuations, confirming the method's reliability.

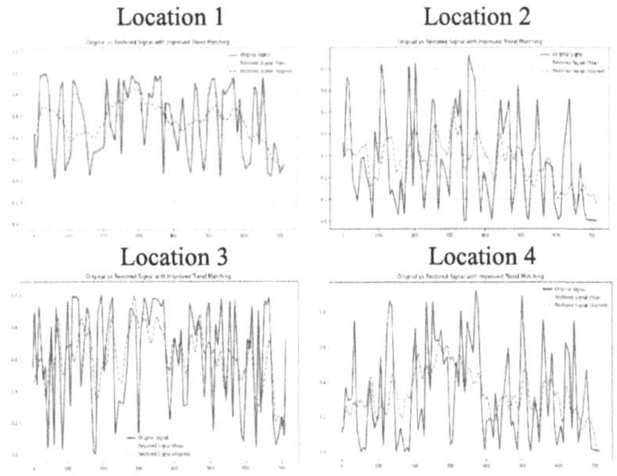

Fig. 4. 8 h ahead forecasting for all 4 locations

C. Wind Power Ramp Detection Performance

In addition to forecasting, the model's capability to detect wind power ramp events—critical for grid reliability—is assessed using the Definition-Based Sign Indicator (DSI) algorithm, which identifies ramps based on a 10% threshold within a 6-h window.

Table 8 reports ramp detection metrics including precision, recall, and F1-score. Precision scores range from 0.814 (Location 1) to 0.903 (Location 3), indicating strong performance in identifying true ramp events while minimizing false positives. Recall is more variable, with lower scores in Locations 1 and 2 (0.405 and 0.343), suggesting some missed events in more stable wind environments. In contrast, Locations 3 and 4—characterized by higher variability—achieve better recall (0.672 and 0.510), reflecting the model's improved sensitivity under dynamic conditions.

Table 8. Evaluation Metrics of forecasted signal across all 4 locations

Location	Precision	Recall	F1-Score	Actual ramps	Detected ramps	Ramp matches
Location 1	0.814	0.405	0.541	787	560	227
Location 2	0.877	0.343	0.493	563	220	193
Location 3	0.903	0.672	0.770	634	472	426
Location 4	0.878	0.510	0.645	594	345	303

The highest F1-score is observed in Location 3 (0.770), underscoring the model's effectiveness in detecting ramp events in areas with frequent and abrupt changes in wind power. Figure 5 illustrates the alignment between actual and predicted ramp events, showcasing the model's responsiveness to sudden power fluctuations.

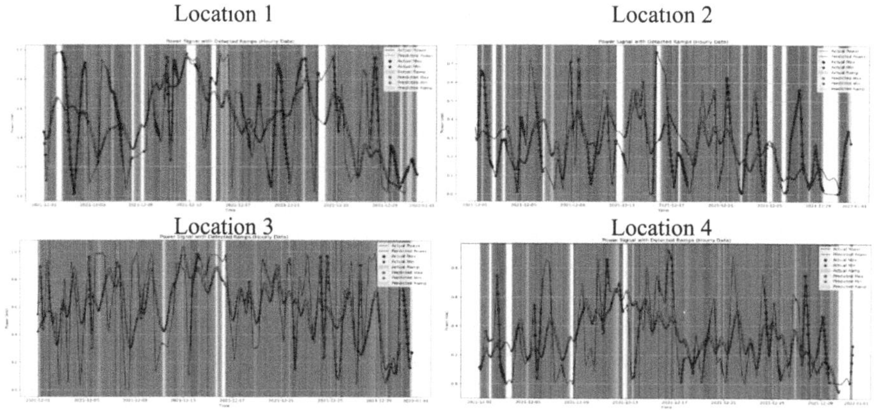

Fig. 5. Wind Ramp detection algorithm using definition-based sign indicator Algorithm

7 Conclusion

This study proposes a hybrid forecasting and ramp detection framework combining VMD, LSTM, and XGBoost. By decomposing wind power signals into three IMFs, the model effectively captures both long-term trends and short-term fluctuations. Emphasis on the low-frequency mode ensures stable predictions, while polynomial and linear regression-based signal integration enhances overall accuracy across all four wind farms.

The integrated model achieves improved MAE, MSE, and RMSE metrics compared to individual IMF predictions. Ramp detection using the DSI algorithm shows high precision (81%–91%), though variations in recall suggest further optimization is needed in low-variability regions.

Unlike our previous research—which used only XGBoost on a single dataset—this study enhances transparency, robustness, and generalizability, making it suitable for deployment in diverse real-world systems.

Future work will explore advanced decomposition techniques like CEEMDAN, integrate more meteorological variables, and focus on improving ramp detection recall to further increase forecasting reliability.

Acknowledgments. This research is conducted to address the challenges faced in previous research "Short-Term Wind Power Ramp Forecasting Using Sequential Approach".

Disclosure of Interests. The authors have no competing interests to declare that are relevant to the content of this article.

References

1. Gopalakrishnan, L., Cardenas Barrera, J.L., Sabiyath Fathima, N.: Short-term wind power ramp forecasting using sequential approach. IEEE International Conference on Modelling, Simulation, and Intelligent Computing (2024), in press
2. Wang, Z., Wang, L., Revanesh, M., Huang, C., Luo, X.: Short-term wind speed and power forecasting for smart city power grid with a hybrid machine learning framework. IEEE Internet Things J. **10**(21), 18754–18765 (2023), https://doi.org/10.1109/JIOT.2023.3286568
3. Yogesh, S., Leechita, G., Sabiyath Fatima, N.: Windspeed Forecasting Using Application of ReliefF Algorithm in LSTM Networks. Springer Series, 5th Congress on Intelligent Systems (CIS 2024) (2024), in press
4. Yang, Y., Lou, H., Wu, J., et al.: A survey on wind power forecasting with machine learning approaches. Neural Comput. Appl. **36**, 12753–12773 (2024). https://doi.org/10.1007/s00521-024-09923-4
5. Lee, J.C.Y., Draxl, C., Berg, L.K.: Evaluating wind speed and power forecasts for wind energy applications using an open-source and systematic validation framework. Renew. Energy **200**, 457–475, ISSN: 0960-1481 (2022), https://doi.org/10.1016/j.renene.2022.09.111
6. Giebel, G., Brownsword, R., Kariniotakis, G., Denhard, M., Draxl, C.: General rights The State-Of-The-Art in Short-Term Prediction of Wind Power A Literature Overview, 2nd edition," Downloaded from orbit.dtu.dk on (2024), https://doi.org/10.11581/DTU:00000017
7. Qian, Z., Pei, Y., Zareipour, H., Chen, N.: A review and discussion of decomposition-based hybrid models for wind energy forecasting applications (2019), Elsevier Ltd. https://doi.org/10.1016/j.apenergy.2018.10.080
8. Zhang, Xu, B., Liu, H., Hou, J., Zhang, J.: Wind power prediction based on variational mode decomposition and feature selection. J. Modern Power Syst. Clean Energy **9**(6), 1520–1529 (2021), https://doi.org/10.35833/MPCE.2020.000205
9. Gallego-Castillo, C., Cuerva-Tejero, A., Lopez-Garcia, O.: A review on the recent history of wind power ramp forecasting. Renew. Sustain. Energy Rev. **52**, 1148–1157 (2015). https://doi.org/10.1016/J.RSER.2015.07.154
10. Lochmann, M., Kalesse-Los, H., Schäfe.r, M., Heinrich, I., Leinweber, R.: Analysing wind power ramp events and improving very short-term wind power predictions by including wind speed observations. Wind Energy **26**(6), 573–588 (2023), https://doi.org/10.1002/we.2816

11. Cornejo-Bueno, L., Cuadra, L., Jiménez-Fernández, S., Acevedo-Rodríguez, J., Prieto, L., Salcedo-Sanz, S: Wind power ramp events prediction with hybrid machine learning regression techniques and reanalysis data. Energies **10**(11), 1784 (2017), https://doi.org/10.3390/en10111784
12. Cao, B., Chang, L., Gong, X., Pijnenburg, P., Levy, T.E., Kilpatrick, R.: Day-ahead wind power ramp forecasting using an image-based similarity search strategy. IET Renew. Power Gener. **17**(2), 271–278 (2022). https://doi.org/10.1049/rpg2.12595
13. Yu, S., Hur, J.: An enhanced performance evaluation metrics for wind power ramp event forecasting. IEEE Access **11**, 100195–100206 (2023). https://doi.org/10.1109/ACCESS.2023.3313632
14. Liu, Y., Khoshgoftaar, T., Yao, J.-F.: Building a novel gp-based software quality classifier using multiple validation datasets. 2007 IEEE International Conference on Information Reuse and Integration, Las Vegas, NV, USA, pp. 644–650 (2007), https://doi.org/10.1109/IRI.2007.4296693
15. https://www.kaggle.com/datasets/mubashirrahim/wind-power-generation-data-forecasting/data. Accessed 12 January 2025

Duplication Fraudulent Detection of Tampered Image Using Optimized CNN

Debjani Chakraborty[1(✉)], Biswajit Halder[2], Sourav Saha[1], and Nabanita Das[1]

[1] Narula Institute of Technology, Kolkata, India
debjani.cse@gmail.com
[2] Hooghly Engineering and Technology College, Hooghly, India
biswajit.halder@hetc.ac.in

Abstract. Digital image authentication is critical in forensics to detect forgeries that compromise image integrity, such as copy-move attacks. Traditional methods like SIFT and SURF often struggle with complex or distant pixel patterns. This research proposes an optimized CNN model for detecting various tampering types–including duplication, splicing, and noise inconsistencies–achieving 98% accuracy, 98% precision, and 97% recall. The approach outperforms conventional techniques, offering a robust and reliable solution for digital image authentication.

Keywords: Copy-move forgery · Convolutional neural network · Gray wolf optimization · Tampered image detection

1 Introduction

With the growth of digital technology, image authentication and integrity protection have become increasingly important [4]. Advances in image manipulation tools have prompted the development of tampering detection techniques essential for forensic applications [6]. Various methods have been proposed to ensure digital image authenticity and recover lost integrity [14,22,24,26]. Copy-move forgery, a common manipulation, conceals content by replicating image areas [18]. Forgery detection techniques authenticate images by identifying tampered regions [7,11] and support forensic investigations [12]. Detection often relies on comparing mathematical characteristics of image areas [1,19]. Existing methods face limitations: low robustness to post-processing, difficulty detecting multiple forged regions, and poor accuracy [5]. To address this, we propose a CNN-based tampered image detection approach optimized with Gray Wolf Optimization (GWO), enhancing feature extraction and improving detection accuracy, even for subtle tampered regions.

The main contributions and novelty of this research are summarized as follows:

K. Chandra Mondal et al. (Eds.): CICBA 2025, CCIS 2863, pp. 239–254, 2026.
https://doi.org/10.1007/978-3-032-17184-9_18

- A novel hybrid CNN-GWO framework is proposed for tampered image detection, which integrates a Convolutional Neural Network (CNN) with the Grey Wolf Optimization (GWO) algorithm for automated hyperparameter tuning. This combination has not been previously applied to forgery detection tasks and enhances the CNN's classification accuracy and robustness.
- An effective feature extraction strategy is incorporated prior to classification, which includes preprocessing and the application of 2D Discrete Fourier Transform (DFT). This frequency-domain analysis captures subtle patterns and inconsistencies that help in differentiating between original and tampered image regions, serving as a compact and informative input for the CNN.
- Dynamic hyperparameter optimization is performed using GWO, allowing the model to adaptively select learning rate, batch size, dropout rate, and number of epochs. This replaces manual tuning and results in faster convergence and improved detection performance, particularly in copy-move forgery scenarios.
- The method is designed as an end-to-end pipeline capable of detecting multiple types of tampering, including copy-move, splicing, and noise-based manipulations. This contrasts with prior methods that focus on single-type or handcrafted feature-based detection,
- Extensive experimental evaluation is conducted on a balanced dataset of 2,088 images, including original and tampered samples. The proposed model achieves 98% accuracy, outperforming traditional classifiers such as SVM, ANN, and standard CNN, with statistically significant improvements.
- The approach demonstrates greater interpretability and precision, with reduced false positives and enhanced feature learning.

The rest of the paper is structured as follows: Sect. 2 provides a brief review of existing techniques for tampered image detection. Section 3 presents the main research methodology that describes the workflow of the proposed approach. It briefs about the working of the CNN-GWO model for copy-move forgery detection. Section 4 deals with the simulation results and the performance evaluation. Section 5 concludes the paper with experimental observations and future scope.

2 Related Works

In digital systems, images carry a large amount of data, making their integrity essential for authenticity (Mushtaq & Mir, 2018) [16]. Copy-move forgery replicates regions of an image to conceal content. To address this, techniques are broadly classified into block-based and visual feature-based approaches. Block-based methods segment images into overlapping blocks and extract features, represented as low-dimensional vectors (Parveen et al., 2019) [17]. Methods such as PCA (Jwaid & Baraskar, 2017) [10]; DCT (Hayat & Qazi, 2017) [8]; and DWT (Ashraf et al., 2020) [3] have been applied for copy-move forgery and splicing detection (Siddiqi et al., 2021) [21]. However, block-based techniques often fail under resizing or rotation, and scale invariance is limited, increasing false positives (Wang et al., 2019) [23]. Visual feature-based methods overcome these limitations by matching relevant features rather than blocks, offering robustness to geometrical transformations (Shabanian & Mashhadi, 2017) [20]. Recently, CNN-based approaches have been applied, where encoder blocks extract and down-sample features, and decoder blocks upsample them. A sigmoid activation classifies pixels as forged or non-forged, achieving superior detection performance compared to traditional methods (Jaiswal & Srivastava, 2022) [9].

3 Proposed Research Methodology

The proposed approach uses a feature extraction mechanism and image processing techniques for identifying different types of data tampering, such as copy-move forgery, noise inconsistency, and image splicing, from a given input image. The implementation process involves different stages, which are discussed in subsections below, shown in Fig. 1.

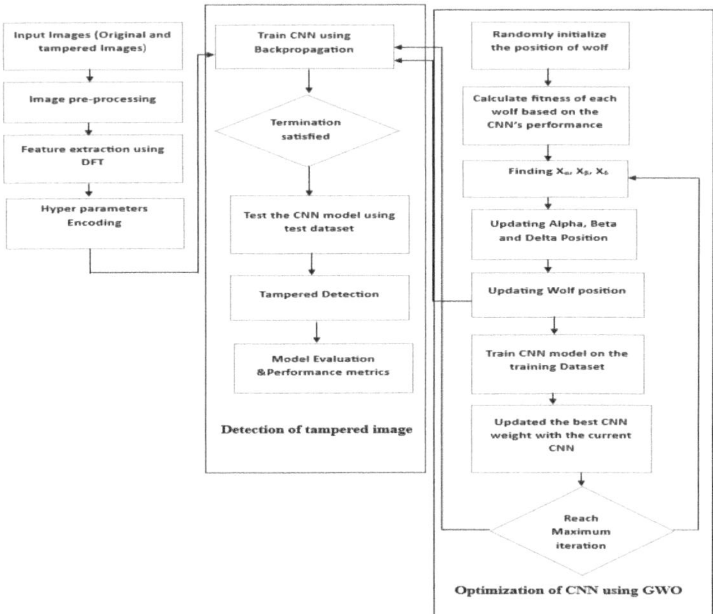

Fig. 1. Flowchart of the proposed approach.

3.1 Data Preprocessing

The data pertaining to copy-move forgery, noise inconsistency, and image splicing are extracted from the Kaggle dataset. Images containing both tampered and non-tampered images are extracted. The link for the dataset is given below: https://www.kaggle.com/datasets/saurabhshahane/cg1050.

In general, raw input data undergoes preprocessing to address uncertainties such as missing values, null values, and additive noise. This process improves image quality, which in turn enhances classification and detection performance. In this research, several preprocessing steps are applied: (i) Color Image to Grayscale Conversion transforms RGB images into grayscale, simplifying the data and reducing computational requirements; (ii) Image Resizing adjusts images to a uniform size, ensuring consistency across inputs and reducing model complexity; (iii) Binary Format Conversion converts grayscale images to binary by setting a threshold, creating a high-contrast, monochromatic representation and reduces computational cost while retaining edge information. (iv) Skeletonization reduces foreground regions to single-pixel-wide representations, preserving essential structures while minimizing data, and enhances structure preservation, making it easier for CNN to recognize patterns. (v) Morphological Operations, including erosion and dilation, refine image shapes, reduce noise, and enhance feature clarity for improved processing accuracy. Together, these steps ensure that input data is optimized for effective classification and detection.

3.2 Feature Extraction

In this stage, all the necessary features are extracted which can help in analyzing the image characteristics and thereby help in the classification process. Here, feature extraction is also used as a dimensionality reduction wherein the dataset is reduced to an appropriate size by selecting only relevant features from the processed data without affecting the originality. In addition, feature extraction reduces the amount of redundant data from the dataset. In this work, feature extraction is performed using four methods namely DFT techniques. The DFT analyses the frequency characteristics of different filters. For images, a 2D Discrete Fourier Transform (DFT) is used to compute the frequency domain. Initially, the DFT determines the frequency spectrum of the signal and then encodes the information in the frequency, phase, and amplitude of the image. Furthermore, the DFT computes the frequency response from the impulse response, and vice versa. This allows systems to be analyzed in the frequency domain, just as convolution allows systems to be analyzed in the time domain.

3.3 Classification Using CNN

Before detecting the tampered images in the detection phase, it is essential to know whether the images are original or tampered. This research implements a VGGNet architecture, which is a computer vision model with several stacks of layers.

Traditional shallow classifiers such as SVM, KNN, and decision trees, while effective in certain cases, often struggle to capture the complex spatial and contextual features required for accurate tampered image detection. In contrast, Convolutional Neural Networks (CNNs) have demonstrated superior capability in learning hierarchical feature representations directly from raw image data. This makes them particularly well-suited for tasks involving subtle pixel-level anomalies, such as forgery detection. Moreover, the extension of CNN with an optimization component further enhances classification accuracy by adaptively fine-tuning the model's parameters, leading to more robust performance across varied tampering patterns.

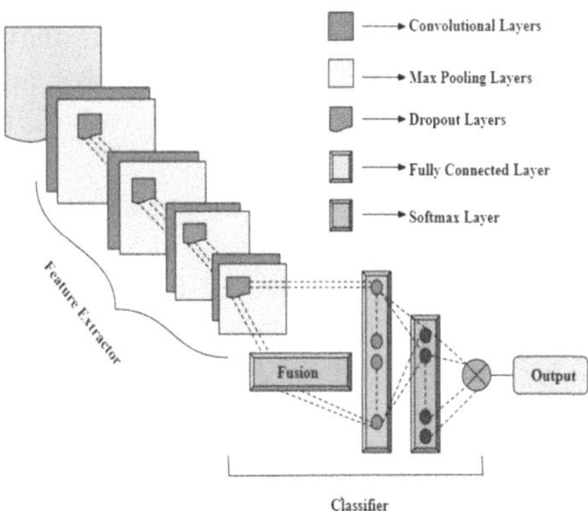

Fig. 2. CNN architecture for image classification.

The architecture of the CNN is shown in Fig. 2. Convolutional Layers: These layers are the core of the architecture, using small filters with depth matching the image's depth. For example, if an image has a depth of 2, the filters will also have a depth of 2. Filters convolve across the image to extract features through dot products. Similar to VGGNet, convolutional layers have a kernel size of 3.

- Activation Functions: ReLU activation increases network non-linearity, while a Softmax function calculates the probability of each class.
- Pooling Layers: These layers down- sample the image, reducing feature map height and width while maintaining depth, lowering computational time, and preventing overfitting
- Dense Layers: These layers act like fully connected layers, making decisions based on features from prior layers.
- Dropout Layers: Included to prevent overfitting during training.

3.4 Hyperparameters Encoding

The model's hyperparameters were carefully encoded to facilitate optimization. Specifically, the learning rate was encoded within a range of 0.001 to 0.0001, allowing for adaptive adjustment during training. The batch size was fixed at 32, striking a balance between computational efficiency and gradient stability. The number of epochs was set to 50, ensuring sufficient training iterations. Additionally, a dropout rate of 0.5 was applied for regularization purposes, mitigating overfitting and promoting generalizability.

3.5 Optimization of CNN Using GWO

The CNN model is optimized using the Grey Wolf Optimization (GWO) algorithm, a metaheuristic technique that enhances CNN performance, particularly with smaller datasets, by ensuring faster convergence compared to conventional CNNs [15]. While CNN parameters are effective for classification, their execution is time-consuming; hence, optimization is required. GWO is considered more reliable than traditional evolutionary and swarm-based algorithms, as it reduces localization errors, prevents flip ambiguity, and achieves high accuracy (Arafat & Moh, 2021) [2]. Inspired by the hierarchy of grey wolves, the fittest solution is defined as alpha (α), followed by beta (β) and delta (δ), while omega represents the lowest rank [25]. This leadership structure guides the search process. GWO is integrated with CNN to prevent high local optima, avoid overlapping features, and enhance computational efficiency. Critical CNN hyperparameters–learning rate (η), batch size (B), dropout rate (D), epochs (E), validation frequency, and L2 regularization–are dynamically optimized using GWO, which balances exploration and exploitation, accelerates convergence, and outperforms PSO and GA for hyperparameter tuning.

1. Position Initialization

Each wolf represents a set of CNN hyperparameters:

$$X_i = [\eta_i, B_i, D_i, E_i] \tag{1}$$

where Xi denotes the ith solution (wolf), and the values of η, B, D, and E are initialized randomly within predefined bounds.

2. Position Initialization

The fitness function is defined as the classification accuracy (ACC) of the CNN model:

$$f(X_i) = \text{ACC}(X_i) \tag{2}$$

The goal is to maximize f(Xi), ensuring better hyperparameter selection.

3. Leader Wolves Update (α, β, δ *Wolves*)

In each iteration, the best three wolves (α, β, δ) guide the rest. The best three solutions in each iteration are designated as *alpha*, β, and δ wolves based on their fitness scores, determined by CNN classification accuracy. The position of a wolf is updated based on:

$$X(t+1) = X_\alpha(t) - A \cdot D_\alpha \tag{3}$$

where Dα is the distance between the wolf and the best solution:

$$D_\alpha = |C \cdot X_\alpha - X| \tag{4}$$

Here, A and C are coefficient vectors:

$$A = 2a \cdot r_1 - a \quad \text{and} \quad C = 2 \cdot r_2 \tag{5}$$

where r1, and r2 are random values in [0,1], and a decrease linearly from 2 to 0 over iterations.

4. New Hyperparameter Selection
After each iteration, the updated hyperparameters are evaluated using the CNN fitness function. The process continues until convergence or a stopping criterion is met.
5. Final Optimized Hyperparameters
The best solution X* obtained at the end of GWO iterations provides the optimal CNN hyperparameters:

$$X^* = [\eta^*, B^*, D^*, E^*] \tag{6}$$

These values are then used for the final training and validation of the CNN model.

4 Results and Discussion

The dataset used in this research is specifically designed for copy-move forgery detection and includes a diverse range of manipulated images. It comprises a total of 2,088 images, equally divided into 1,044 original (non-tampered) images and 1,044 tampered images, which include various forgery techniques such as copy-move forgery, splicing, and noise-based manipulation. The images in the dataset vary in resolution, with an average size of 256 × 256 pixels, and are stored in RGB format. For effective training and evaluation, the dataset is split into three subsets: 60% for training (730 original, 730 tampered), 20% for validation (157 original, 157 tampered), and 20% for testing (157 original, 157 tampered). This structured division ensures a balanced dataset for model training, fine-tuning, and performance evaluation. The performance parameters used in the study are described below in Table 1.

The performance of the proposed approach is validated using different performance metrics such as accuracy, precision, recall, F1 score, specificity, and AUC score. The equations for determining the performance metrics are defined as follows.

$$\text{Accuracy} = \frac{TP + TN}{TP + TN + FP + FN} \tag{7}$$

$$\text{Recall} = \frac{TP}{TP + FN} \tag{8}$$

$$\text{Precision} = \frac{TP}{TP + FP} \tag{9}$$

$$\text{F1 Score} = \frac{2 * Precission * Recall}{Precission + Recall} \tag{10}$$

$$\text{Specificity} = \frac{TN}{TN + FP} \tag{11}$$

where TP, TN, FP, and FN denote true positives, true negatives, false positives, and false negatives, respectively. The proposed approach's performance was compared with the existing CNN model, and the simulation results are shown in Fig. 3. The figure illustrates three examples of copy-move forgery. In the first, an aerial parking lot image is manipulated by duplicating two blue cars. The second shows three blue round objects (coins/tokens), where one is duplicated and repositioned. The third presents a motorcycle against a mountain backdrop, with

Table 1. Experimental setup

Component	Description	No.
Hardware and Software		
Framework	PyTorch	
GPU	Tesla T4	
Operating System	Ubuntu 20.04	
CNN Architecture		
Input Image Size	224×224 pixels	
Image Input Layer	64×64×3	1
Convolution2D Layer	64 5×5 convolutions, stride [1 1], padding [2 2 2 2]	3
MaxPooling2D Layer	PoolSize: [2 2], Stride: [2 2], Padding: [0 0 0 0]	3
Fully Connected Layer ($x = \{64, 2\}$)	64 fully connected; 2 fully connected layers	2
ReLU	ReLU	4
SoftMax	SoftMax	1
C-Output Layer	64×64×3	1
Training Procedure		
Learning Rate	0.001	
Batch Size	64	
Epochs	50	
Loss Function	Binary Cross-Entropy (BCE)	
Optimizer	Adam	
Data Splitting		
Split Ratio	60:20:20 (Training:Validation:Testing)	
Experimental Metrics		
Evaluation Metrics	Accuracy, Precision, Recall, F1-score, ROC, AUC	
GWO (Grey Wolf Optimizer)		
Population Size	40 wolves	
Max Iterations	1000	
Epochs	50	
Alpha Wolf Fitness	0.98	
Beta Wolf Fitness	0.96	
Delta Wolf Fitness	0.95	
Learning Rate	0.001	
Dropout Rate	0.5	
Batch Size	32	
L2 Regularization	0.01	
Validation Frequency	Every 5 epochs	
Control Parameters (A, C)	A: [-2, 2], C: [0, 2]	
Termination Condition	Accuracy $\geq$ 0.98 or Max Iterations reached	

duplicated elements from the motorcycle and scenery. These examples highlight how copy-move forgery manipulates visual content by duplicating and relocating image regions. Such visualization demonstrates the relevance of Optimized CNN-based methods (e.g., CNN with Gray Wolf Optimization), which enhance the detection of spatial and textural inconsistencies. Unlike traditional methods, the optimized CNN effectively learns deep features to distinguish original from forged areas, marking tampered regions with high accuracy.

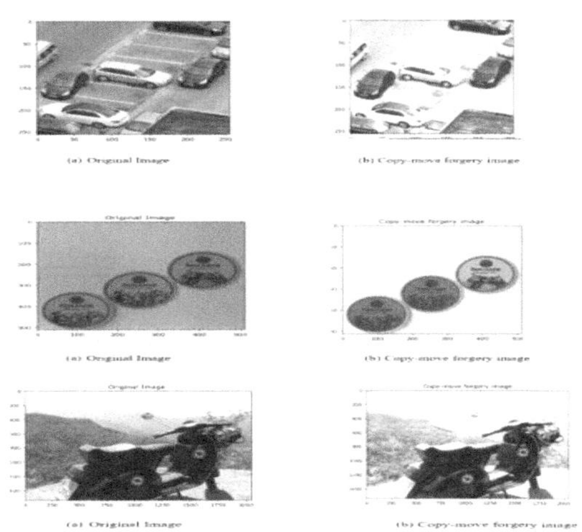

Fig. 3. Results of the simulation analysis.

Correspondingly, the performance of the proposed approach is evaluated using the evaluation metrics as shown below.

The accuracy of a tampered image detection model is a critical metric in evaluating its effectiveness in distinguishing between original and manipulated images. A higher accuracy indicates better detection performance and fewer misclassifications. Figure 4a illustrates the accuracy achieved by the proposed CNN-GWO model, demonstrating its superior performance compared to traditional CNN and other baseline approaches. The results highlight a significant improvement in classification accuracy, reinforcing the effectiveness of hyperparameter optimization using GWO in enhancing forgery detection.

Precision is a crucial metric in tampered image detection, as it indicates the proportion of correctly identified tampered images among all predicted tampered cases. Figure 4b illustrates the precision of the proposed CNN-GWO model, highlighting its effectiveness in minimizing false positives compared to traditional CNN and other baseline classifiers. The results demonstrate that the optimization of hyperparameters using GWO significantly enhances the model's ability to accurately distinguish between tampered and non-tampered images, outperforming the traditional CNN method.

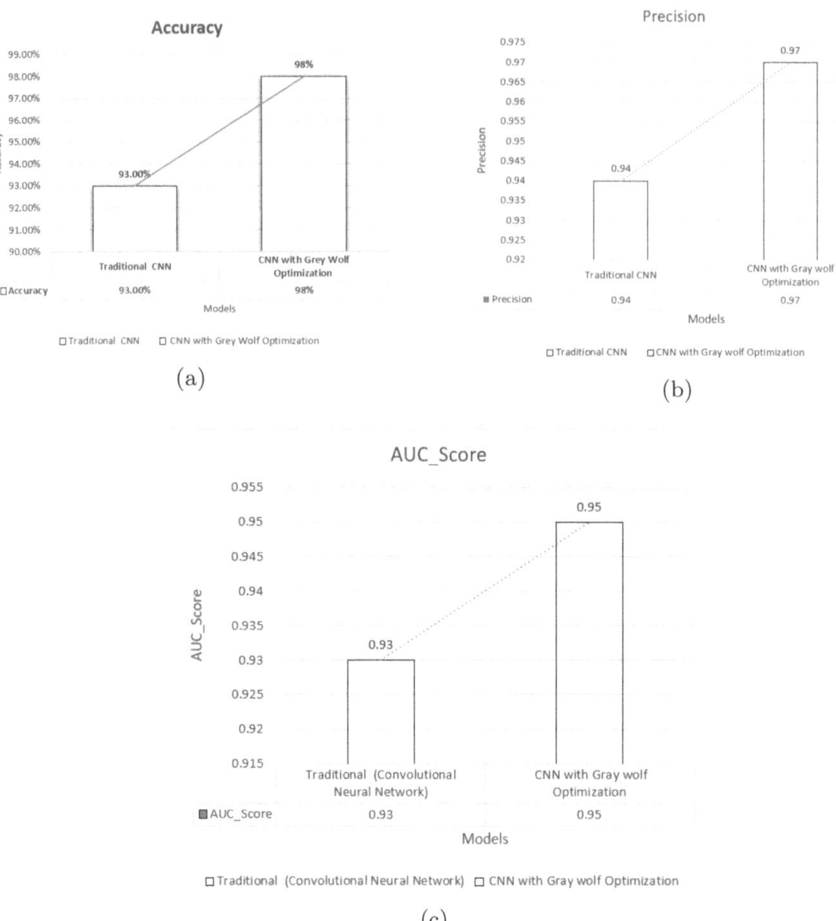

Fig. 4. (a) Accuracy of the tampered image detection process and (b) Precision of the tampered image detection process (c) AUC score of the tampered image detection process.

The Area Under the Curve (AUC) score is a vital performance metric in tampered image detection, as it evaluates the model's ability to distinguish between tampered and non-tampered images across different classification thresholds. Figure 4c presents the AUC score of the proposed CNN-GWO model, demonstrating its superior discriminatory power compared to conventional CNN and other baseline approaches. A higher AUC score signifies the model's ability to accurately distinguish between tampered and non-tampered images while minimizing misclassification. This ensures improved reliability and effectiveness in real-world forgery detection applications

The confusion matrix provides a detailed evaluation of the model's classification performance by displaying the number of true positives, true negatives, false positives, and false negatives. Figure 5 illustrates the confusion matrix for the CNN classifier model.

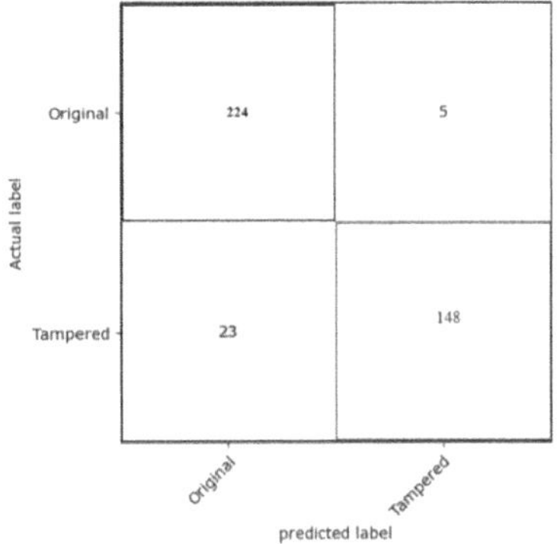

Fig. 5. Confusion matrix of the CNN classifier.

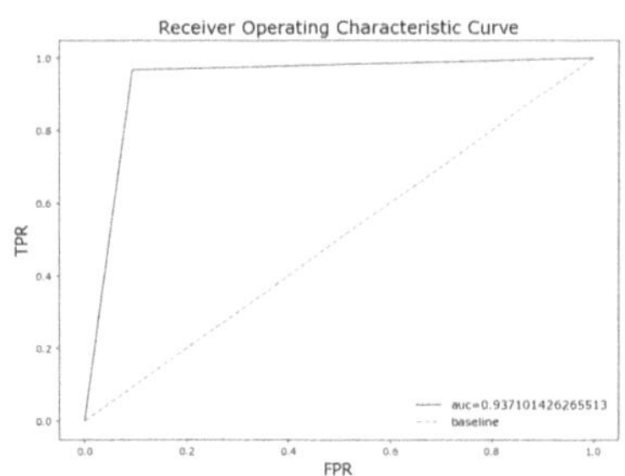

Fig. 6. ROC curve of the CNN classifier.

The performance of the CNN classifier based on the evaluation metrics is tabulated in Tables 2 and 3 shows the proposed CNN-GWO performance matrices.

Table 2. Evaluation of different performance metrics of traditional CNN

Class	Precision (%)	Recall (%)	F1 Score (%)	Support
0 (Non-Tampered)	91	98	94	229
1 (Tampered)	94	93	91	171
Accuracy	–	–	93	400
Macro Average	94	92	93	400
Weighted Average	93	93	93	400

Results show that the CNN classifier achieved an accuracy of 93 % with an average precision of 94 %. The performance of the CNN was also evaluated in terms of the ROC curve to determine the AUC score, as shown in Fig. 6.

It can be observed that the CNN classifier achieves an AUC score of 93 %. Correspondingly, the performance of the proposed CNN-GWO for detecting tampered images is described as follows.

The confusion matrix is a crucial evaluation metric that provides insights into the classification performance of a model by detailing the correctly and incorrectly classified instances. Figure 7 presents the confusion matrix for the proposed CNN-GWO model, demonstrating its improved ability to accurately

Table 3. Evaluation of different performance metrics for the proposed CNN-GWO

Class	Precision (%)	Recall (%)	F1 Score (%)	Support
0 (Non-Tampered)	96	99	96	234
1 (Tampered)	97	97	94	166
Accuracy	–	–	98	400
Macro Average	96	97	95	400
Weighted Average	95	96	95	400

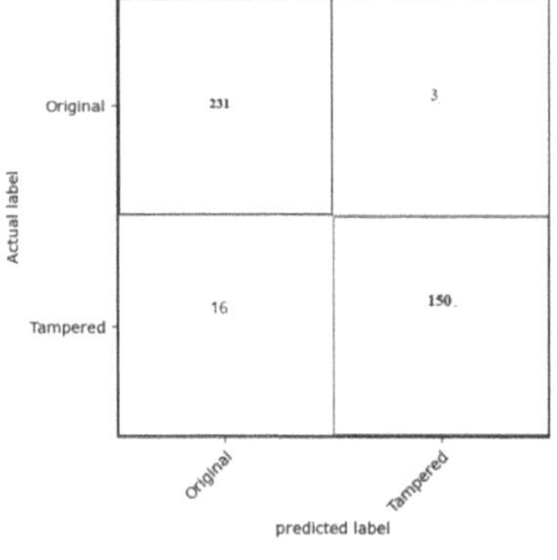

Fig. 7. Confusion matrix of the CNN-GWO classifier.

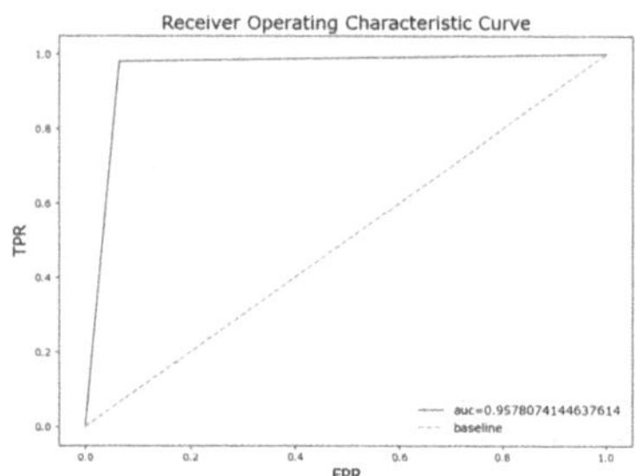

Fig. 8. ROC curve of the proposed CNN-GWO classifier.

distinguish between tampered and non-tampered images. Compared to traditional CNN-based approaches, the optimized model significantly reduces false positives and false negatives, leading to enhanced detection reliability and overall performance. The CNN-GWO confusion matrix in Fig. 7 demonstrates a high recall of 98% for tampered images, indicating that the model effectively detects forgeries while minimizing false negatives.

Figure 8 shows that the proposed CNN-GWO classifier achieves an AUC score of 95.78%, higher than the conventional CNN (93.71%). To validate performance, results are compared with existing techniques in Table 4, which presents a comparative analysis against SVM, ANN, Mask R-CNN, and ISCFF. CNN-GWO consistently outperforms these models in accuracy, precision, recall, and AUC due to GWO's hyperparameter optimization that enhances feature extraction, classification efficiency, and prevents overfitting. In contrast, SVM and ANN struggle with high-dimensional feature spaces, Mask R-CNN is computationally expensive, and ISCFF is limited to feature selection. By optimizing feature learning and training, CNN-GWO achieves faster convergence, higher robustness, and superior classification accuracy, highlighting its ability to minimize false classifications across varying thresholds.

The proposed approach outperforms existing models such as SVM, ANN, Sea Lion Firefly Algorithm, Mask RCNN, CNN, and ISCFF, achieving higher

Table 4. Performance comparison of different models.

Metric	SVM	ANN	Sea Lion	Firefly	Mask-RCNN	CNN ISCF	Proposed CNN-GWO
Accuracy	88	96	87	90	93	98	98
Precision	89	93	92	92	97	98	98
Recall	86	94	93	93	87	97	98
Sensitivity	89	97	85	89	87	98	98
Specificity	86	95	95	96	98	98	99
F1-Score	97	96	85	89	94	98	97

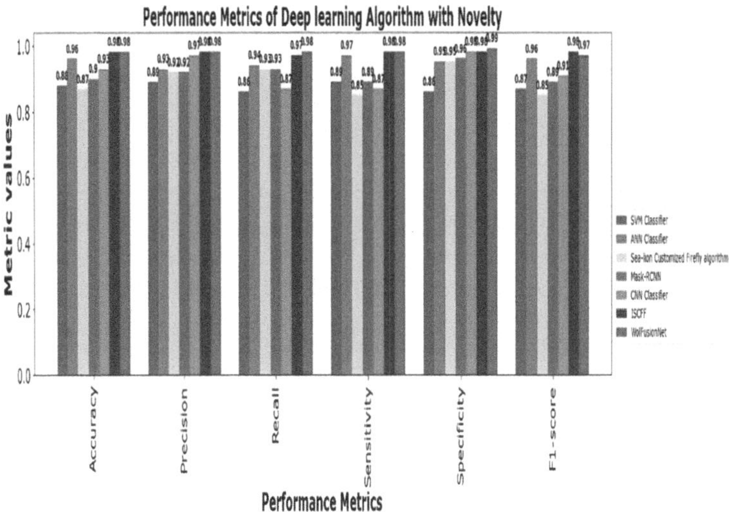

Fig. 9. Comparison results.

accuracy as shown in Fig. 9. Performance is enhanced through Gray Wolf Optimization (GWO), which fine-tunes CNN parameters while maintaining consistent feature distribution. Conventional CNNs rely on low-level attributes in early layers and fine-tune later layers, often leading to inconsistent features. In contrast, the optimized CNN improves fraudulent image detection through deep feature extraction, optimization, and generalization. Unlike traditional methods such as SIFT, ORB, or SSIM, which depend on handcrafted features, CNNs automatically learn hierarchical representations, capturing subtle tampering details like textural inconsistencies, color shifts, and forged edges with greater precision. They are also robust against scaling, rotation, and noise. Our method achieves 98% accuracy, surpassing the 97% reported in Prem Kumar et al., 2024 [13]. Optimization via GWO further enhances feature selection, weight adjustment, convergence speed, and overfitting prevention. This synergy substantially improves copy-move forgery detection (CMFD), accurately identifying duplicated patterns, splicing, and edge manipulations. With techniques like Grad-CAM for interpretability, the optimized CNN reduces false positives, increases recall, and enables a robust end-to-end detection pipeline for real-world forgery detection.

To evaluate the statistical significance of the performance improvement of the proposed method over existing approaches, we conducted a paired t-test on classification accuracies obtained across multiple experimental runs. The results yielded p-values less than 0.01, specifically 0.008, indicating that the observed improvement is statistically significant. This reinforces the objectivity and reliability of our empirical findings.

5 Conclusion

This research presents an optimized CNN-GWO model for tampered image detection, achieving 98% accuracy, 97% precision, and 97% recall. By fine-tuning CNN hyperparameters using GWO, the model effectively detects copy-move forgery, noise inconsistencies, and image splicing, outperforming conventional CNNs and reducing false positives. Input images were pre-processed, converted to grayscale, and features such as color, diameter, asymmetry, and boundary irregularity were extracted. Evaluated on the Kaggle "cg1050" dataset, the model shows high accuracy, though cross-dataset validation on CASIA v2, Columbia Image Splicing, and CoMoFoD is planned to assess robustness and generalizability. Future work includes exploring hybrid optimization techniques (e.g., PSO-GWO), extending datasets, and developing real-time forensic applications in banking, legal, and digital security domains.

References

1. Abualigah, L., Gandomi, A.H., Elaziz, M.A., Hussien, A.G., Khasawneh, A.M., Alshinwan, M., Houssein, E.H.: Nature-inspired optimization algorithms for text document clustering-a comprehensive analysis. Algorithms **13**(12), 345 (2020)
2. Arafat, M.Y., Moh, S.: Bio-inspired approaches for energy-efficient localization and clustering in uav networks for monitoring wildfires in remote areas. IEEE Access **9**, 18649–18669 (2021)
3. Ashraf, R., Mehmood, M.S., Mahmood, T., Rashid, J., Nisar, M.W., Shah, M.: An efficient forensic approach for copy-move forgery detection via discrete wavelet transform. In: 2020 International Conference on Cyber Warfare and Security (ICCWS), pp. 1–6. IEEE (2020)
4. Begum, M., Uddin, M.S.: Digital image watermarking techniques: a review. Information **11**(2), 110 (2020)
5. Dadkhah, S., Koppen, M., Sadeghi, S., Yoshida, K., Jalab, H.A., Manaf, A.A.: An efficient ward-based copy-move forgery detection method for digital image forensic. In: 2017 International Conference on Image and Vision Computing New Zealand (IVCNZ), pp. 1–6. IEEE (2017)
6. Ferreira, W.D., Ferreira, C.B., da Cruz Júnior, G., Soares, F.: A review of digital image forensics. Comput. & Electr. Eng. **85**, 106685 (2020)

7. Gill, N.K., Garg, R., Doegar, E.A.: A review paper on digital image forgery detection techniques. In: 2017 8th International Conference on Computing, Communication and Networking Technologies (ICCCNT), pp. 1–7. IEEE (2017)
8. Hayat, K., Qazi, T.: Forgery detection in digital images via discrete wavelet and discrete cosine transforms. Comput. & Electr. Eng. **62**, 448–458 (2017)
9. Jaiswal, A.K., Srivastava, R.: Detection of copy-move forgery in digital image using multi-scale, multi-stage deep learning model. Neural Process. Lett. **54**(1), 75–100 (2022)
10. Jwaid, M.F., Baraskar, T.N.: Detection of copy-move image forgery using local binary pattern with discrete wavelet transform and principle component analysis. In: 2017 International Conference on Computing, Communication, Control and Automation (ICCUBEA), pp. 1–6. IEEE (2017)
11. Kumar, B.S., Cristin, R., Karthick, K., Daniya, T.: Study of shadow and reflection based image forgery detection. In: 2019 International Conference on Computer Communication and Informatics (ICCCI), pp. 1–5. IEEE (2019)
12. Kumar, M., Srivastava, S.: Image authentication by assessing manipulations using illumination. Multimedia Tools Appl. **78**, 12451–12463 (2019)
13. Kumar, S.P., Thirumalesh, M.S., Kumar, T.P., Reddy, P.S., Angadi, S., Venu, N.: Cnn-based detection of tampered digital images. In: 2024 International Conference on Trends in Quantum Computing and Emerging Business Technologies, pp. 1–6. IEEE (2024)
14. Lin, X., Li, J.H., Wang, S.L., Liew, A.W.C., Cheng, F., Huang, X.S.: Recent advances in passive digital image security forensics: a brief review. Engineering **4**(1), 29–39 (2018)
15. Mirjalili, S., Mirjalili, S.M., Lewis, A.: Grey wolf optimizer. Adv. Eng. Softw. **69**, 46–61 (2014)
16. Mushtaq, S., Mir, A.H.: Image copy move forgery detection: a review. Int. J. Future Gen. Commun. Netw. **11**(2), 11–22 (2018)
17. Parveen, A., Khan, Z.H., Ahmad, S.N.: Block-based copy-move image forgery detection using dct. Iran J. Comput. Sci. **2**, 89–99 (2019)
18. Pavlović, A., Glišović, N., Gavrovska, A., Reljin, I.: Copy-move forgery detection based on multifractals. Multimedia Tools Appl. **78**, 20655–20678 (2019)
19. Prakash, C.S., Panzade, P.P., Om, H., Maheshkar, S.: Detection of copy-move forgery using akaze and sift keypoint extraction. Multimedia Tools Appl. **78**, 23535–23558 (2019)
20. Shabanian, H., Mashhadi, F.: A new approach for detecting copy-move forgery in digital images. In: 2017 IEEE Western New York Image and Signal Processing Workshop (WNYISPW), pp. 1–6. IEEE (2017)
21. Siddiqi, M.H., Asghar, K., Draz, U., Ali, A., Alruwaili, M., Alhwaiti, Y., Alanazi, S., Kamruzzaman, M.: Image splicing-based forgery detection using discrete wavelet transform and edge weighted local binary patterns. Security Commun. Netw. **2021**(1), 4270776 (2021)
22. Thakur, R., Rohilla, R.: Recent advances in digital image manipulation detection techniques: A brief review. Forensic Sci. Int. **312**, 110311 (2020)
23. Wang, X.Y., Jiao, L.X., Wang, X.B., Yang, H.Y., Niu, P.P.: Copy-move forgery detection based on compact color content descriptor and delaunay triangle matching. Multimedia Tools Appl. **78**(2), 2311–2344 (2019)
24. Warbhe, A.D., Dharaskar, R., Thakare, V.: Computationally efficient digital image forensic method for image authentication. Procedia Comput. Sci. **78**, 464–470 (2016)

25. Xie, H., Zhang, L., Lim, C.P.: Evolving cnn-lstm models for time series prediction using enhanced grey wolf optimizer. IEEE Access **8**, 161519–161541 (2020)
26. Zeng, J., Lu, W., Yang, R., Qiu, X.: Practical tools for digital image forensic authentication. In: Advanced Multimedia and Ubiquitous Engineering: FutureTech & MUE, pp. 453–459. Springer (2016)

Unlocking Transparency: Judicial Clarity Through Explainable AI in the Decision Making Process

Ritwika Mukherjee(✉), Tathagata Chatterjee, and Subhram Das

Narula Institute of Technology, Kolkata, India
ritwikamukherjee1999@gmail.com

Abstract. The proliferation of Artificial Intelligence (AI) triggers explainable AI (xAI) to be a very promising tool in our everyday life. The black box AI models with less explainability can cause grave issues in legal practices. Therefore, in the field of judiciary, xAI enhances transparency and credibility by overcoming lack of proper reasoning in the black box AI models. This paper aims to present a comprehensive xAI framework for the judicial system to enhance the interpretability using SHAP and LIME. The article encompasses meticulous data collection from diverse judicial sources, followed by robust data preprocessing and feature engineering techniques to ensure high-quality input for the models. Utilizing this data, advanced machine learning algorithms, including both traditional and deep learning models are implemented. Furthermore, the execution steps forward with explainable models including gradient boosting ensemble and explainability techniques. This approach provides clear and insightful explanations for model predictions, enhancing trust and reliability in xAI-driven judicial decisions. The research work not only aims to improve the accuracy of legal predictions but also ensures that the decision-making process is transparent and understandable to legal professionals and stakeholders for the improvement of verdicts in the legal decision-making process.

Keywords: Artificial Intelligence (AI) · Decision-making · Explainable AI (xAI) · Judiciary · LIME · SHAP

1 Introduction

Artificial intelligence (AI) impacts our daily lifestyle in numerous respects. In the forthcoming days, the necessity of AI is likely to enlarge. Due to the advancement of AI and its growing use in a variety of fields like healthcare, judiciary, military and automobiles, more and more people are interested in utilizing it. In healthcare, AI has been used to improve methods of treatment, for predictive analysis of diseases, for patient care and medication and to monitor patients in real time [1]. AI is also an emerging application domain in the field of judiciary. In judiciary, judges can get assistance from AI, resulting in the reduction in

K. Chandra Mondal et al. (Eds.): CICBA 2025, CCIS 2863, pp. 255–267, 2026.
https://doi.org/10.1007/978-3-032-17184-9_19

the slowness of court proceedings [2]. Taking the military field into account, AI has been impactful in surveillance, reconnaissance, threat evaluation, underwater mine warfare, cyber security, intelligence analysis, command, and control to enhance military capability [3]. To make modern vehicles smart, safe and reliable, AI has played a vital role [4]. Although every AI-dependent work that is performed is believed, yet the fundamental query arises: What is the foundation of this trust? As a consequence of this query, many people have been wary of predictions produced by black-box models for decisions that could change their lives in diversified fields. This scenario has been prevalent especially in the legal sector, where there are possibly life changing prospects and possibility that AI can eventually help judges to make decisions in the court. In this respect, the topic of how to explain machine learning predictions in the judiciary system has generated a lot of controversies. Giving users an explanation for a decision made by a judge in court is likely to make the information more helpful [5]. Additionally, developers can use these reasons to improve the model through data preprocessing, feature engineering, model selection, prediction, and validation. Trainers can also utilize them to update the data resources gathered for learning and testing. A new field has emerged because of the rapid advancement of methods and procedures. A new field called Explainable Artificial Intelligence (xAI) has developed around approaches and strategies that have expanded so quickly [6]. Medical xAI represents an incredibly promising research direction [7]. Besides that, xAI has become prevalent in finance and automobiles [8]. In law enforcement, xAI has been used to predict court decisions [9]. xAI provides clarifications as to how and why the predictions are made [10]. xAI refers to AI systems that provide understandable insights into their decisions and behaviours. It is the approach and strategy that is used so that human specialists can understand the solution's outcomes [11]. The qualities of accountability, transparency and justice are vital to the court as the bedrock for democratic governance. The judiciary, being well known for its dedication to justice and equity, is still facing many obstacles to overcome, especially regarding effectiveness, openness, and accessibility. On the account of enormous legal queue, difficult legal proceedings and scarce resources, justice gets delayed, which has affected people's trust in the legal system. Additionally, worries regarding bias and fairness have frequently been raised by the opaqueness of court rulings. To improve the effectiveness and credibility of the court, there is a growing interest in utilizing xAI, which has been one of the most significant cutting-edge technologies.

In this paper, xAI has been incorporated using SHAP and LIME into the judicial decision-making system. It provides guidelines for successfully implementing xAI, guaranteeing that AI plays an open, equitable and responsible role in litigations. It also illustrates how xAI can be used to improve judgement and maintain integrity in the legal area through extensive analysis.

Section 2 discusses the related works. Section 3 demonstrates the proposed work and the experimental results. Finally, Sect. 4 concludes the paper.

2 Related Works

Integrating AI in the judicial system is a challenging process. The conventional AI techniques have helped in various legal proceedings including legal research, document management and case prediction [12]. Nevertheless, these techniques frequently functioned as black boxes, giving rise to lack of justification and openness in the results. This created a problematic scenario in the legal sector where transparency and clarity are of utmost importance [13].

In a bid to make use of xAI in the legal system, Collenette [14] proposed the usage of xAI techniques such as rule based systems and case-based reasoning in enhancing judicial justification in the cases from the European Court of Human Rights and to illustrate how effective they are in rendering AI produced legal decisions that are easier to understand. The results imply that xAI technologies can boost AI's trustworthiness and use in the legal system.

Atkinson [15] put forward a proposal based on the evolution of AI's various explanatory techniques in the legal field, starting with early rule-based systems to modern machine learning mechanisms and focusing on clear explanations for acceptance in the legal system. Future challenges and scope to develop improved xAI processes involving legal reasoning and persistence are featured.

With respect to the Japanese judicial system, Yamada [16] propounded the application of xAI, which explores the fruitfulness of diverse xAI processes to achieve clarity in AI-driven legal decision making and discusses specific and unique challenges and requirements. According to the findings, xAI incorporation in the judiciary may substantially enhance the decision-making process and ensure that the outputs are intelligible.

Palacio [17] came up with a thorough framework for xAI, explaining the prime necessary components to create interpretable AI systems, continuing to elaborate the importance of a standardized approach to xAI and its application in various domains including judiciary. The suggested framework aims to improve lucidity of AI systems by amalgamating various xAI methods.

Katz [18] intended to present a conceptual framework for deducing the decisions of the U.S. Supreme Court. The authors came up with a generalizable approach to predict judicial behaviour depending on case information and historical verdicts using machine learning techniques and data analysis.

Using a fresh approach for verdict predictions, Deng [19] introduced a model that blends both concept trees, a type of decision tree model and concept forest reasoning, a sort of random forest. Besides that, a new perspective of collegiate bench mechanism has been developed, which mirrors the collaborative decision-making technique of a judicial panel. The authors established the effectiveness of their methodology with vivid experiments and case studies, to improve the level of accuracy [20].

Furthermore, initiatives have been undertaken in India to incorporate AI into the judiciary and other government agencies [21]. Projects like Supreme Court Vidhik Anuvaad Software (SUVAS), an AI powered tool for translating judicial documents, were initiated by the Supreme Court of India. Through research and xAI applications exclusively designed for the judiciary are yet in their infancy.

3 Methodology

The main goal is to dive deep into the framework for utilizing xAI using SHAP and LIME to make decisions in the judiciary system. This study aims to build up a strategy for the usefulness of xAI, paving the way for a more efficient and egalitarian legal system in India.

Since xAI involves both qualitative and quantitative aspects, incorporating a mixed approach is a good choice. The usage of machine learning and deep learning algorithms to analyse judicial dataset is the quantitative component. On the other hand, the qualitative component involves thematic analysis of consultations with judges and legal experts.

The procedure starts with the collection of data from various sources. Data preprocessing is a crucial stage that transforms unstructured data into a format suitable for analysis once it has been collected. Following preprocessing, relevant features are extracted via feature engineering, which also produces new features that can enhance the model's performance.

To ensure that the model can be successfully trained and assessed, the next step is to divide the data into training and testing sets, as seen in Fig. 1. After the data is ready, attention turns to selecting the best machine learning methods for the given problem by selecting the models. Following that, the selected model is trained on the training set, and its accuracy and dependability are assessed using the testing set.

The model moves on to the prediction and validation phase, where its outputs are verified through testing against actual data, once its performance satisfies the predetermined requirements. At last, the refined model is implemented in the judiciary and is actively utilized for forecasting. The model must be continuously monitored to make sure it stays accurate and functional, enabling prompt upgrades and maintenance when required. The paper also dives deep into the comparison of the two explainable models of SHAP and LIME.

3.1 Components of Proposed Framework

This subsection gives a brief overview of the different components of the proposed framework.

Data Collection: Identification of sources is our first step in data collection. The dataset used in the research is available on Kaggle. Raw data is gathered from sources. Databases, APIs, web scraping, and third-party datasets are a few examples of such sources. The final model's resilience is heavily dependent on the variety and applicability of its data sources.

Dataset link: https://www.kaggle.com/datasets/tatha590/judicial-dataset

Using density estimate plots for several legal factors, Fig. 2 provides a statistical analysis of court case data. Filing Year, Case Type, Judge ID, Duration in Days, Verdict, Number of Hearings, Appeal Status, and Legal Representation are among the attributes in the dataset. The visualizations provide clear distributions, emphasizing trends in the length of cases, the frequency of hearings, and the rulings of the courts. Notably, multimodal distributions are shown

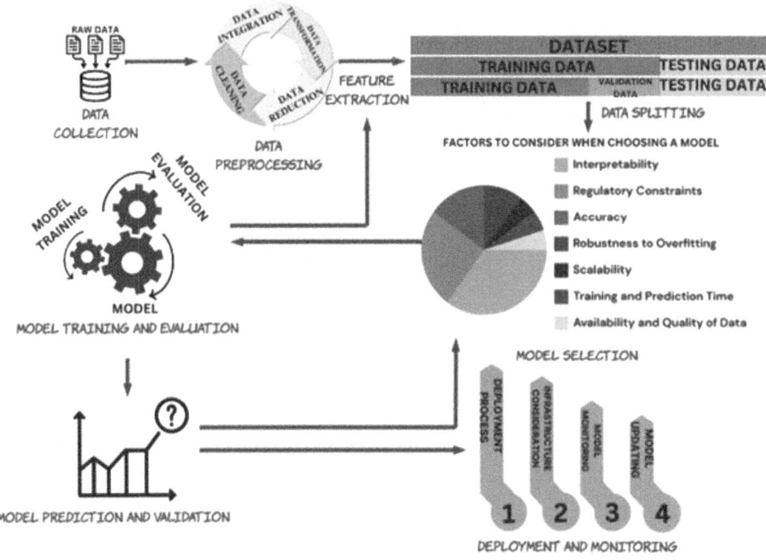

Fig. 1. Proposed framework for judicial clarity using explainable AI.

by categorical variables such as Case Type, Verdict, and Legal Representation, indicating differences in judicial outcomes. In the meantime, trends indicating case backlogs and the effectiveness of legal processing are displayed by continuous variables like Filing Year and Duration in Days. By adding to judicial data analytics, these insights help policymakers find bottlenecks and increase the effectiveness of the legal system.

Data Preprocessing: To create an organized, clean, and structured dataset, raw data is cleaned, integrated, transformed, and reduced as part of data preprocessing. Organizing data, eliminating duplication, and dealing with missing numbers are a few steps that need to be carried out in this step. To improve the dataset's quality, feature engineering and selection play a crucial role. A successful preprocessing step guarantees that the data is appropriate for the pipeline's later stages.

Data Splitting: The dataset is split into training data for developing models and testing data for assessing those models after feature extraction. Furthermore, training data is divided into another category, namely validation data. This three-way split facilitates efficient parameter adjustment and performance evaluation of the model. Splitting data correctly is crucial to avoid overfitting and guaranteeing that the model performs effectively when applied to new data.

Model Selection: The pivotal criterion in the selection of various algorithms, like Text Classification Algorithms, Deep Learning Models and Explainable Models, is interpretability. Regulatory constraints, accuracy, robustness to overfitting, scalability, training and prediction time and the quantity and quality of data are certain other factors, based on which the optimal model is identified. To find the best fit, the selection procedure could entail testing out several different methods and designs. In this paper, Random Forest has been chosen as the machine learning model.

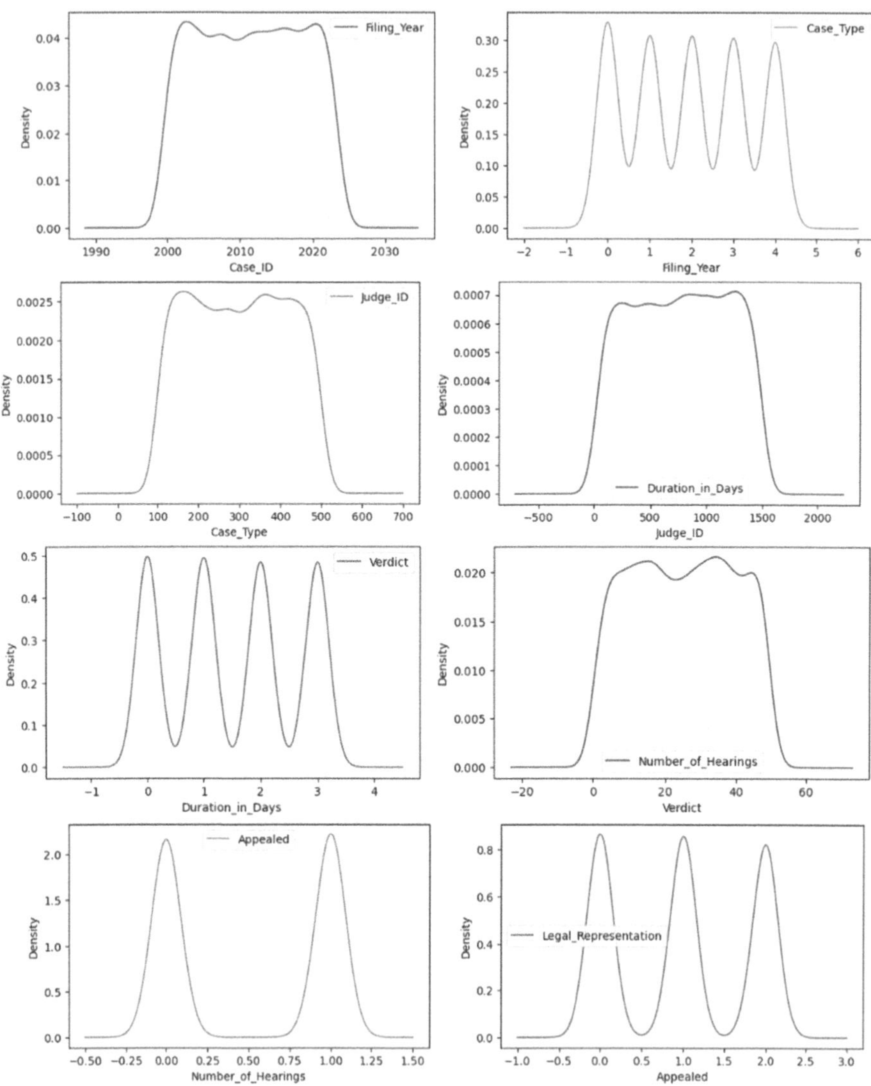

Fig. 2. Judiciary dataset analysis.

Model Training and Evaluation: To maximize performance, models are trained, in addition to hyperparameter tuning. Accuracy, precision, recall, F1 score, AUC-ROC and other critical metrics are the prime focus of model evaluation. The workflow reiterates from feature extraction following the machine learning pipeline. To guarantee ongoing development, the process is repeated from feature extraction after the machine learning pipeline. Cross validation techniques are applied on various data subsets, to frequently verify the model's performance.

Key performance parameters for a binary classification model is accuracy, precision, recall, and F1-score. With a 66.67% accuracy rate, the model shows a moderate capacity for prediction on a limited dataset. For class 0, the model accurately detects all predicted instances, but misses half of the real occurrences, with precision of 1.00 and recall of just 0.50. Class 1 on the other hand has a precision of 0.50, which indicates false positives, but a recall of 1.00, which guarantees that all real occurrences are found. With a macro-average F1-score of 0.67, precision and recall are generally balanced. Class imbalance factors are further reflected in the weighted average F1-score.

Model Prediction and Validation: Assessment of correctness and prediction of outcomes comes into effect in this phase. Until an optimal result is obtained in terms of correctness, the control will revert to model selection. Through this iterative process, the model is certain to reach the proper level of dependability and accuracy. Ongoing validation against new data helps to sustain the model's performance over the long run.

Deployment and Monitoring: Achieving the objective is reinforced by proper observation and closely keeping a track of the model to determine and eliminate poor quality predictions and poor performance. This entails configuring dashboards and monitoring tools to keep tabs on the behaviour of the model in use. To incorporate new insights and adjust to evolving data patterns, regular maintenance and upgrades are important. The model's effectiveness and relevance are maintained by the feedback loop that runs from deployment to monitoring.

3.2 Simulation and Performance Assessment

To understand the impact of each variable on the model's predictions, we use SHAP value as the explainable model. The SHAP value ϕ_i is the sum of the marginal contributions of feature i over all possible subsets S of N total set of features and v(S) is value function for subset S as shown in Eq. 1. This ensures a fair distribution of the model's prediction across the input features by weighing each subset's contributions according to the factorial terms.

The formula of SHAP is:

$$\phi_i = \sum_{S \subseteq N \setminus \{i\}} \frac{|S|!(|N| - |S| - 1)!}{|N|!} [v(S \cup \{i\}) - v(S)] \tag{1}$$

where:

- ϕ_i is the Shapley value for feature i.
- N is the set of all features.
- S is any subset of $N \setminus \{i\}$.
- $v(S)$ is the value of the characteristic function for subset S.
- $|S|$ is the number of elements in subset S.
- $|N|$ is the total number of elements in N.

A comparative study has also been performed between the explainable models of SHAP and LIME. LIME (Local Interpretable Model-agnostic Explanations) approximates complex model predictions by fitting an interpretable surrogate model. It explains individual predictions of a complex model f by fitting a locally interpretable model g around a specific instance. It optimizes the following objective function:

$$argmin_g \mathbb{E}_{z \sim \pi_x} \left[\mathcal{L}(f, g, z) + \Omega(g) \right] \tag{2}$$

where:

- f is the complex model to be explained.
- g is the interpretable surrogate model.
- z represents the data points sampled around the instance x.
- π_x is the neighbourhood distribution of x.
- $\mathcal{L}(f, g, z)$ is the loss function, typically the difference between f and g.
- $\Omega(g)$ is the regularization term to enforce the simplicity of g.

A summary plot of SHAP interactions is shown in Fig. 3, which shows how different features interact to affect the model's predictions. The SHAP interaction values, which measure how feature pairs affect the model's output, are represented on the x-axis. The diagonal elements show self-interactions, and each subplot represents a distinct feature pair.

Judge_ID, Filing_Year, Duration_in_Days, and Case_Type are among the features taken into consideration. The values of the interaction feature are represented by the blue-to-red color gradient, which aids in the visualization of dependency patterns. The relative strength and direction of feature interactions are shown by the density of dots surrounding zero.

Figure 4 shows a SHAP waterfall plot, which shows how each feature contributes to a particular model prediction. The base expectation (E[f(X)] = 0.251) serves as a reference for the anticipated value (f(x) = 0.251), which is represented on the x-axis. The impact of each feature is displayed as a horizontal bar, where negative contributions (blue) lower the forecast and positive contributions (red) raise it. While 2013 = F lowers the prediction by −0.03, feature 433 = I has the largest positive influence (+0.05). The negative contributions from 4 = i and 803 = i are less pronounced.

By emphasizing the primary characteristics that influence each prediction, this representation aids in the interpretation of model behavior and improves the

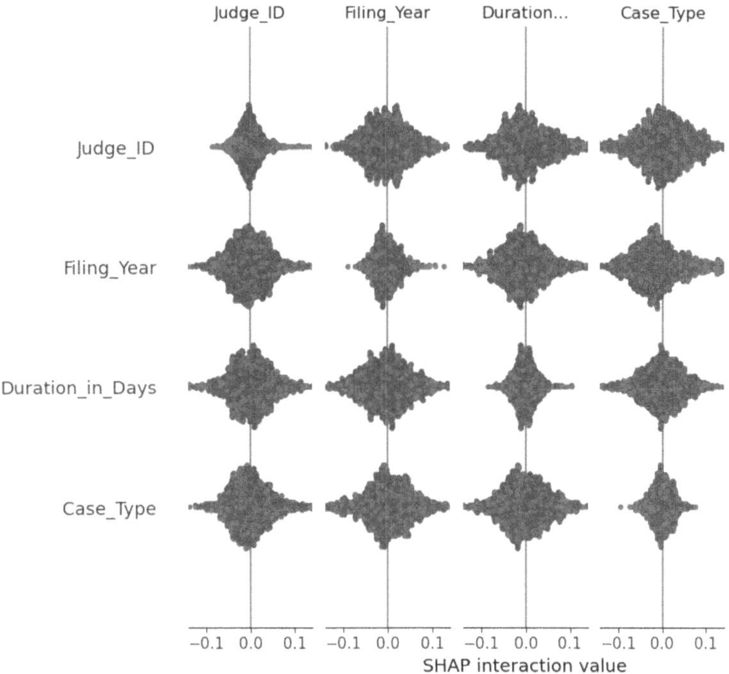

Fig. 3. SHAP summary plot.

explainability and transparency of machine learning models used with categorical or judicial data.

Figure 5 shows a LIME visualization for class 1 predictions made by a machine learning model. It draws attention to the various aspects' contributions to the forecast. Green bars show beneficial influences, whereas red bars show detrimental contributions. Case Type, Filing Year, and Number of Hearings are the most important characteristics; Number of Hearings has the greatest detrimental effect. On the other hand, the projection is positively impacted by the Filing Year. Understanding model conclusions, maintaining openness, and spotting potential biases in legal case forecasts are all made easier with this explanation.

The feature values utilized for Random Forest's prediction are shown in Fig. 6. Case Type (1.00), Judge ID (143.00), Filing Year (2013.00), Legal Representation (2.00), Number of Hearings (14.00), Appealed (0.00), and Duration in Days (1013.00) are some of its important attributes. These factors are crucial inputs that affect the model's outcome. With highlighted values denoting important factors in the prediction process, the color coding most likely indicates the significance or contribution of the features. This methodical depiction facilitates comprehension of the interpretability of the model, guaranteeing openness in decision-making.

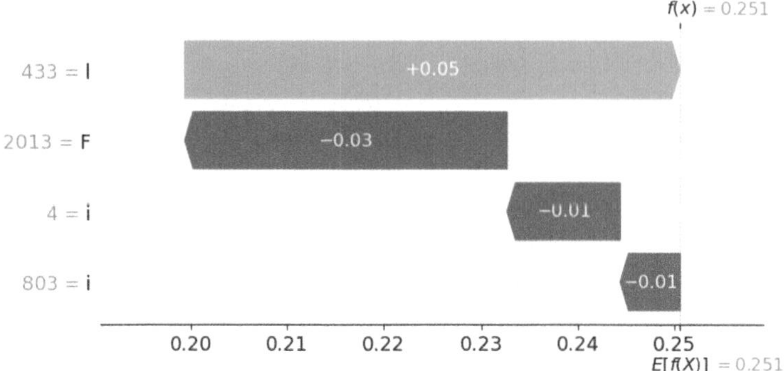

Fig. 4. SHAP waterfall plot.

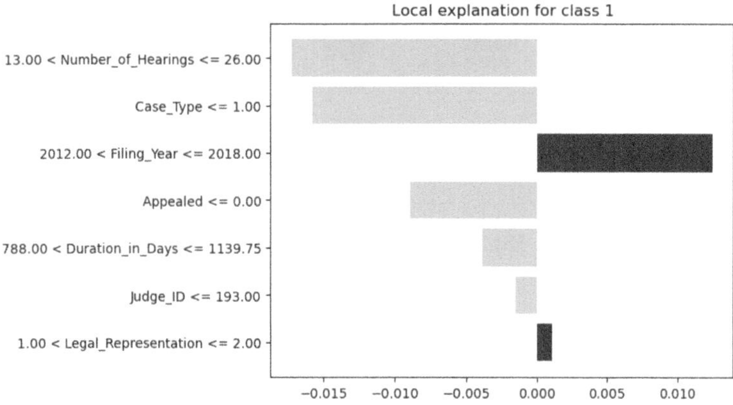

Fig. 5. LIME local explanations.

Feature	Value
Case_Type	1.00
Judge_ID	143.00
Filing_Year	2013.00
Legal_Representation	2.00
Number_of_Hearings	14.00
Appealed	0.00
Duration_in_Days	1013.00

Fig. 6. LIME prediction.

The prediction probabilities of Random Forest for several outcome classes are shown in Fig. 7. The most likely prediction, class 2, is given a 50% probability by the model. Additional odds are 23% for class 1, 7% for class 0, and 20% for a category that is "Other". These numbers show how confident the model is in various classifications. The visual representation, which was most likely created with LIME (Local Interpretable Model-agnostic Explanations), aids in comprehending how the model makes decisions and evaluating how reliable its predictions are. In order to guarantee interpretability and confidence in AI-driven decision support systems, this transparency is essential.

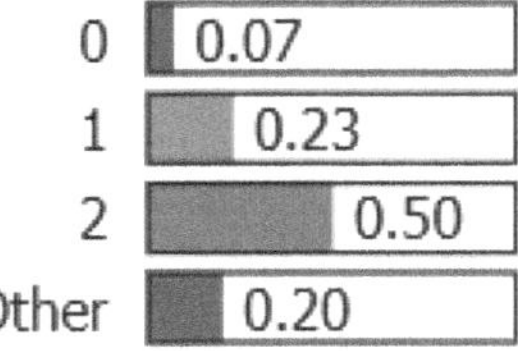

Fig. 7. Prediction probability using LIME.

3.3 Explaining Model Predictions: SHAP Versus LIME

Model interpretability approaches such as LIME and SHAP are employed in our study. While SHAP manages complexities well, LIME yields faster solutions. Despite having a sizable dataset having only 8 different features, our research's overall complexity is decreased by the comparatively modest number of attributes. Due to its effectiveness in producing explanations rapidly, LIME is the better option given this reduced complexity, and here in this paper it has given the prediction shown in Fig. 6. Despite its potency, SHAP can add needless computing burden in our situation due to its thorough explanation and more time consumption. In order to ensure efficient and comprehensible results without requiring excessive processing, we give priority to LIME due to its speed and applicability to the features of our dataset.

Judicial AI models must be interpretable to uphold legal principles of fairness and accountability. SHAP ensures a more globally reliable explanation framework, while LIME remains useful for quick, instance-based interpretability. A hybrid approach may improve both transparency and efficiency in legal AI systems.

4 Conclusion

The judiciary has significant obstacles that call for creative solutions, such as backlogs in cases, drawn-out trial dates, and restricted access to justice. To improve the effectiveness and transparency of the legal system, this research article has carefully investigated a novel framework that uses xAI to find out a plausible solution.

The proposal suggests incorporating xAI technology to facilitate legal decision-making, enhance case management, and provide clearer explanations of judicial procedures. The proposed framework has several noticeable advantages, such as increasing the predictability of case outcomes, speeding up the end of court cases, and fostering greater transparency to increase public trust. Furthermore, court staff will be able to make more impartial and knowledgeable choices with the aid of data-driven insights. By putting xAI into practice, the judiciary might be able to drastically cut down on its current drawbacks and build a more open, equitable, and functional system.

The practical implementation of this framework should be given priority in future endeavours, with adherence to ethical and legal principles guaranteed. For a smooth integration process, judicial stakeholders must get thorough training on the application and interpretation of xAI tools. This study emphasizes the need for a balanced strategy that combines human experience with technical improvements to create a more accountable, non-discriminatory, and efficient judiciary.

References

1. Quazi, S., Saha, R.P., Singh, M.K.: Applications of artificial intelligence in healthcare. J. Exper. Biol. Agri. Sci. **10**(1), 211–226 (2022)
2. Rocha, C., Carvalho, J.: Artificial intelligence in the judiciary: uses and threats. In em> CEUR Workshop Proceedings< em (2022)
3. Svenmarck, P., Luotsinen, L., Nilsson, M., Schubert, J.: Possibilities and challenges for artificial intelligence in military applications. In: Proceedings of the NATO Big Data and Artificial Intelligence for Military Decision Making Specialists' Meeting (Vol. 1) (2018)
4. Kamran, S.S., Haleem, A., Bahl, S., Javaid, M., Prakash, C., Budhhi, D.: Artificial intelligence and advanced materials in automotive industry: potential applications and perspectives. Materials Today: Proc. **62**, 4207–4214 (2022)
5. Aletras, N., Tsarapatsanis, D., Preoţiuc-Pietro, D., Lampos, V.: Predicting judicial decisions of the European Court of Human Rights: a natural language processing perspective. PeerJ Comput. Sci. **2**, e93 (2016)
6. Turan, T., Küçüksille, E., Alagöz, N.K.: Prediction of Turkish constitutional court decisions with explainable artificial intelligence. Bilge Int. J. Sci. Technol. Res. **7**(2), 128–141 (2023)
7. Zhang, Y., Weng, Y., Lund, J.: Applications of explainable artificial intelligence in diagnosis and surgery. Diagnostics **12**(2), 237 (2022)
8. Tiwari, R.: Explainable ai (xai) and its applications in building trust and understanding in ai decision making. International J. Sci. Res. Eng. Manag **7**, 1–13 (2023)
9. Turan, T., Küçüksille, E., Alagöz, N.K.: Prediction of Turkish constitutional court decisions with explainable artificial intelligence. Bilge Int. J. Sci. Technol. Res. **7**(2), 128–141 (2023)

10. Richmond, K.M., Muddamsetty, S.M., Gammeltoft-Hansen, T., Olsen, H.P., Moeslund, T.B.: Explainable AI and law: an evidential survey. Digital Soc. **3**(1), 1 (2024)
11. Patidar, N., Mishra, S., Jain, R., Prajapati, D., Solanki, A., Suthar, R., ... Patel, H.: Transparency in AI decision making: a survey of explainable AI methods and applications. Adv. Robot. Technol. **2**(1) (2024)
12. Ortigossa, E.S., Gonçalves, T., Nonato, L.G.: EXplainable Artificial Intelligence (XAI)–from theory to methods and applications. IEEE Access (2024)
13. Ashraf, N.: Explainable AI: bridging the gap between black-box models and human understanding
14. Collenette, J., Atkinson, K., Bench-Capon, T.: Explainable AI tools for legal reasoning about cases: a study on the European Court of Human Rights. Artif. Intell. **317**, 103861 (2023)
15. Atkinson, K., Bench-Capon, T., Bollegala, D.: Explanation in AI and law: past, present and future. Artif. Intell. **289**, 103387 (2020)
16. Yamada, Y.: Judicial decision-making and explainable AI (XAI)–Insights from the Japanese judicial system. Studia Iuridica Lublinensia **32**(4), 157–173 (2023)
17. Palacio, S., Lucieri, A., Munir, M., Ahmed, S., Hees, J., Dengel, A.: Xai handbook: towards a unified framework for explainable AI. In: Proceedings of the IEEE/CVF International Conference on Computer Vision, pp. 3766–3775 (2021)
18. Katz, D.M., Bommarito, M.J., Blackman, J.: A general approach for predicting the behavior of the Supreme Court of the United States. PLoS ONE **12**(4), e0174698 (2017)
19. Deng, W., Yang, H., Ma, L., Li, W., Wang, G.: Explainable legal judgment prediction via concept tree and concept forest reasoning with collegiate bench mechanism. In: Artificial Intelligence and Human-Computer Interaction, pp. 194–201. IOS Press (2024)
20. Adadi, A., Berrada, M.: Peeking inside the black-box: a survey on explainable artificial intelligence (XAI). IEEE Access **6**, 52138–52160 (2018)
21. Thakur, U., Singh, A.: Xai explainable artificial intelligence need of future

Sustainable Agriculture Through IoT and Data-Driven Irrigation: Machine Learning for Soil Moisture Prediction

Rajkumar Bhandari(✉) and Subhasis Banerjee

Department of Computer and System Sciences, Siksha Bhavana, Visva-Bharati, Santiniketan, Bolpur 731235, West Bengal, India
rakumarbhandari884@gmail.com

Abstract. Integrating IoT-based sensors and machine learning models has revolutionized irrigation practices by enabling precise soil moisture prediction. This research focuses on developing an intelligent irrigation system that merges real-time environmental data acquisition with predictive analytics to optimize water use and enhance agricultural sustainability. A sensor array composed of DHT11, capacitive soil moisture sensors, DS18B20 temperature probes, and rain sensors continually tracks key environmental factors such as temperature, humidity, rainfall, and soil moisture. An ESP32 microcontroller collects these measurements and wirelessly transmits them to a Raspberry Pi 3B+, which processes the data and applies advanced machine learning algorithms for soil moisture prediction. The predicted values then guide irrigation pump operations via relays, ensuring efficient water distribution based on immediate field conditions. Among the five machine learning models tested–Gradient Boosting, Random Forest, Decision Tree, XGBoost, and Support Vector Regressor–the Gradient Boosting model achieved the strongest predictive results, with an R^2 score of 0.74, RMSE of 72.16, MAE of 44.29, and MSE of 5207.28. Incorporating lagged soil moisture values further enhanced the model's accuracy. The proposed system demonstrates how IoT and machine learning can minimize water waste, streamline irrigation schedules, and boost agricultural sustainability. Moreover, the system's modular, scalable design ensures adaptability to a variety of climatic conditions and crop types. This study marks a notable advancement in precision irrigation, laying the foundation for further innovations in AI-driven agriculture.

Keywords: Precision Agriculture · Machine Learning · Soil Moisture Prediction · Irrigation Optimization · Internet of Things (IoT) · Water Conservation

1 Introduction

Efficient water management in agriculture remains a pressing challenge due to the growing global demand for food and the looming threat of water shortage [10]. Traditional irrigation systems, which rely on manual control and fixed

K. Chandra Mondal et al. (Eds.): CICBA 2025, CCIS 2863, pp. 268–280, 2026.
https://doi.org/10.1007/978-3-032-17184-9_20

schedules, often lead to overwatering or under-irrigation, resulting in wasted resources and lower crop yields [4]. In contrast, precision agriculture offers a promising approach to address these challenges, delivering immediate insights and analytics-based decisions for irrigation [8].

Soil moisture prediction is critical in precision agriculture, as it directly influences crop health and water usage. Forecasting soil moisture requires analyzing environmental elements such as temperature, humidity, rainfall, and soil temperature, which can fluctuate significantly [6]. IoT-based sensors facilitate this process by collecting these parameters in real-time, enabling more accurate predictions and efficient water management [28]. Machine learning further enhances precision irrigation by identifying patterns in sensor data and generating actionable insights. Unlike static, rule-based systems, machine learning models adapt to changing environmental conditions and capture non-linear dynamics in the data, especially valuable in regions with unpredictable climates [3].

Several studies have explored IoT-enabled irrigation systems; however, many rely on threshold-based decision-making, which lacks adaptability to changing conditions [14]. This research addresses this gap by implementing and comparing multiple machine learning models for soil moisture prediction, integrating IoT sensors with predictive analytics. Combining an ESP32 microcontroller and a Raspberry Pi 3B+ provides a practical framework for real-time irrigation management, improving efficiency and scalability. Additionally, using real-time sensor data enhances the accuracy of predictive models, reducing dependency on historical datasets that may not reflect current environmental conditions [22].

In this study, a network of sensors continuously monitors key environmental parameters, including DHT11, capacitive soil moisture sensors, DS18B20 temperature probes, and rain sensors. An ESP32 aggregates this data and transmits it wirelessly to a Raspberry Pi 3B+, which processes the data and applies machine learning algorithms for reliable soil moisture prediction. The resulting values are then utilized by the ESP32 module, which dynamically governs irrigation pump actions via relays, ensuring effective water distribution based on real-time needs [17].

Finally, the proposed framework illustrates how integrating IoT and machine learning can decrease water waste, optimize irrigation routines, and bolster agricultural sustainability. Its modular, scalable design allows it to adapt to various climatic conditions and crop types, marking a notable advance in precision irrigation and paving the way for future developments in AI-driven smart farming. Potential enhancements include edge computing for lower latency, knowledge-infused models for settings with minimal historical data, and deep learning to capture more complex spatiotemporal features [23].

The rest of this paper is arranged as follows: Sect. 2 examines relevant literature on IoT-based irrigation and machine learning for soil moisture prediction. Section 3 outlines the proposed methodology, covering sensor configuration and model training. Section 4 offers the experimental findings and analysis, while Sect. 5 discusses implications and limitations. Lastly, Sect. 6 concludes the paper and recommends future research directions.

2 Literature Review

Optimal irrigation management remains a key focus in agricultural research, with many studies emphasizing the importance of soil moisture monitoring and prediction [25]. Traditional methods, such as gravimetric analysis or manual observations, are labor-intensive and often fail to provide timely insights for optimizing irrigation schedules. To address these limitations, IoT-enabled sensors and machine learning models have been leveraged to revolutionize precision agriculture, enabling real-time data collection, automated decision-making, and improved water conservation strategies [1].

IoT-based real-time soil moisture monitoring solutions have gained significant attention in recent years. Kodali et al. [14] designed a smart irrigation system incorporating temperature sensors, capacitive soil moisture sensors, and a microcontroller to enable real-time monitoring and automated control. Their system demonstrated a 30% reduction in water usage compared to conventional irrigation methods. Similarly, Paul et al. [21] implemented a low-cost IoT-based system that transmitted soil moisture data to a cloud platform, enabling farmers to make data-driven irrigation decisions.

Real-time sensor data acquisition has become increasingly significant, enabling the seamless monitoring of crucial agricultural parameters. Advanced sensor networks, including DHT11 for temperature and humidity, soil moisture sensors, and rain sensors, contribute to a holistic understanding of field conditions [26]. To improve scalability and communication efficiency, various low-power, wireless connectivity technologies–such as LoRaWAN, Zigbee, and NB-IoT–have been explored, offering cost-effective and long-range solutions for agricultural IoT applications [18].

Machine learning models have been evaluated extensively for soil moisture prediction, with Support Vector Machines (SVM) outperforming traditional regression techniques due to their superior handling of non-linear relationships [2]. In addition, ensemble models like Random Forest, Gradient Boosting and XGBoost have shown greater predictive accuracy and robustness, leveraging multiple decision trees and boosting techniques to enhance model reliability [29].

Deep learning approaches, such as Long Short-Term Memory (LSTM) networks and Convolutional Neural Networks (CNNs), have been applied to soil moisture prediction, effectively capturing temporal variations and spatial dependencies in the data [7]. Despite their effectiveness, these models require large datasets and high computational power, making them less feasible for small-scale farmers. Consequently, researchers have explored hybrid approaches that combine IoT with lightweight machine learning models, optimizing performance without extensive computing resources [24]. Recent advancements in federated learning and edge computing further enable decentralized model training, reducing dependence on cloud infrastructure while maintaining data privacy [19].

Feature engineering plays a crucial role in improving soil moisture prediction accuracy. Studies have shown that incorporating lag features significantly enhances model performance [27]. For example, Ji et al. [11] introduced lagged soil moisture values to capture temporal and cumulative effects, yielding high prediction accuracy. Interaction terms between temperature and humidity can also influence soil moisture dynamics, underscoring the need for customized feature selection based on local climate conditions.

Several studies compare machine learning models for soil moisture prediction. While linear regression often serves as a baseline, it struggles with non-linear relationships [16]. Decision trees and random forests consistently demonstrate superior performance due to their flexibility in handling complex data patterns [5]. Gradient Boosting has gained prominence for its ability to optimize predictive accuracy while maintaining computational efficiency, making it a preferred choice in machine learning-based soil moisture modeling [9]. Although existing research emphasizes the synergy between IoT technology and machine learning, demonstrating how these advancements can significantly improve precision irrigation strategies [22]. Many studies focus on controlled environments, limiting their applicability to large-scale or diverse agricultural settings. Moreover, integrating real-time data pipelines, edge AI, and blockchain for secure, transparent data management is underexplored [22].

Future research should address scalability and cost-effectiveness to make these systems accessible to small-scale farmers. Integrating AI-driven decision support systems with mobile applications can offer real-time recommendations for irrigation scheduling, improving adoption and usability [13]. Additionally, incorporating multi-modal sensor data (e.g., soil electrical conductivity, root zone monitoring) could enhance soil moisture prediction accuracy, leading to more efficient water resource management [18]. Implementing edge computing can also optimize system performance by processing data locally, minimizing latency, and improving response times. Hybrid approaches combining physics-based models with machine learning could improve reliability, especially in data-sparse regions [15]. Finally, deep learning architectures may refine soil moisture predictions by capturing complex spatiotemporal dependencies–provided sufficient data and computing resources are available.

Several gaps persist despite numerous studies exploring IoT-enabled irrigation and machine learning for soil moisture prediction. First, many existing solutions rely on threshold-based or static decision-making, limiting their ability to adapt to rapidly changing field conditions. This shortcoming can lead to either overwatering or under-irrigation, especially in regions with highly variable climates [12]. Additionally, most research focuses on controlled environments or small-scale pilots, reducing the generalizability of findings to diverse soil types, crops, and large-scale operations [30].

Another challenge lies in computational constraints and cost-effectiveness. However, machine learning models often demand substantial computational resources, making them less viable for small-scale agricultural operations with limited access to high-performance hardware [20]. As a result, many proposed systems struggle to balance model complexity with resource availability, making widespread adoption difficult. Addressing these gaps calls for lightweight, scalable, and adaptive systems operating efficiently across varied environments while remaining accessible to resource-limited communities.

3 Methodology

The proposed smart irrigation system employs a wireless sensor network to continuously monitor soil moisture and relevant environmental parameters. The overall system architecture is depicted in Fig. 1, illustrating the interconnection of an ESP32 microcontroller with various sensors, and its communication with a Raspberry Pi 3B+ acting as the central data processing and storage hub. The operational workflow, detailing data acquisition, processing, and subsequent pump control, is outlined in Fig. 2.

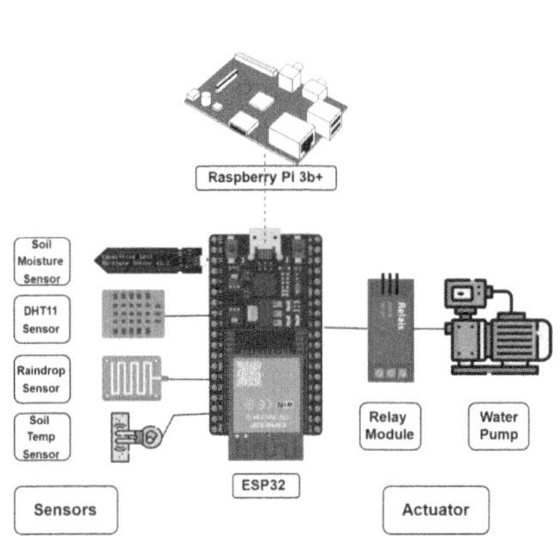

Fig. 1. System diagram of smart irrigation system.

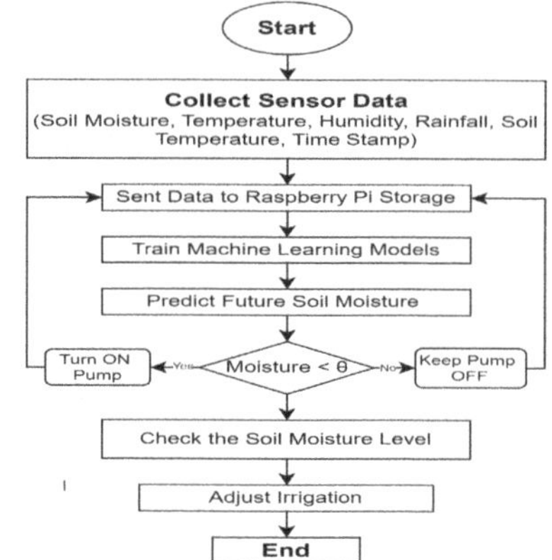

Fig. 2. Flow diagram of smart irrigation system.

3.1 Hardware Configuration and Data Acquisition

The sensor suite, visualized in Table 1, was selected to capture key agro-environmental data. Specifically:

- Capacitive soil moisture sensors were used to measure volumetric water content in the soil (typically outputting raw values, e.g., 0–1000, which are then calibrated or used directly).
- A DHT11 sensor recorded ambient air temperature (0–50°C) and relative humidity (20–100% RH).
- A rain sensor detected the presence and intensity of rainfall (e.g., 0–10 mm equivalent, depending on calibration), providing information on natural water input.
- A DS18B20 waterproof temperature probe measured soil temperature, a factor influencing soil moisture dynamics and retention.
- A DS3231 Real-Time Clock (RTC) module was integrated to ensure accurate timestamping of all collected data.

Table 1. Sensor suite for the smart irrigation system

DHT11	Soil Moisture Sensor	Rain Sensor	Temperature Probe	RTC Module
		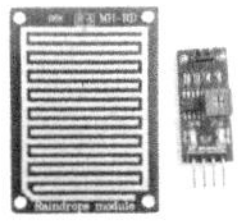		

The ESP32 microcontroller served as the primary data acquisition unit, collecting readings from all connected sensors at regular intervals. This raw sensor data, along with timestamps from the RTC module, was then wirelessly transmitted to the Raspberry Pi 3B+. The Raspberry Pi logged this incoming data into a CSV file, creating a structured dataset for subsequent analysis. The logged parameters included timestamp, air temperature, humidity, rain intensity, soil temperature, soil moisture level, and the operational status of the irrigation pump.

3.2 Dataset Compilation

Data was collected continuously over a period of 16 weeks, from 26th November 2024 to 19th March 2025. This resulted in a comprehensive dataset compiled into a single CSV file. An illustrative snippet of this dataset, showcasing the structure and type of data recorded, is presented in Table 2. This dataset formed the basis for feature engineering and the training of predictive models.

3.3 Machine Learning for Soil Moisture Prediction and Irrigation Control

The collected dataset was utilized to train and evaluate five distinct machine learning regression models for soil moisture prediction: Random Forest Regressor, Support Vector Regressor (SVR), XGBoost Regressor, Gradient Boosting Regressor, and Decision Tree Regressor. For model training, four key input features were selected: ambient air temperature, humidity, soil temperature, and a lagged soil moisture value (specifically, 'Lag_3', representing the soil moisture recorded three hours prior). The target variable for prediction was the current soil moisture level.

The Raspberry Pi 3B+ was responsible for executing the trained ML model to predict future soil moisture. Based on this prediction, the Raspberry Pi would then send a command signal back to the ESP32. The ESP32, upon receiving this command, would activate or deactivate a relay module connected to the water

Table 2. Example snippet of the collected dataset

Timestamp	Temp	Humidity	Rain	Soil temperature	Soil moisture	Pump status
26-11-2024 00:00	87	65	0	18	964	0
26-11-2024 01:00	88	63	0	19	955	0
26-11-2024 02:00	77	62	0	20	954	0
...	...	...	...	...	...	...
...	...	...	...	...	...	...
19-01-2025 07:00	23	39	0	22	515	0
29-01-2025 08:00	23	36	0	23	494	1
29-01-2025 09:00	23	35	0	24	900	0
...	...	...	...	...	...	...
...	...	...	...	...	...	...
19-03-2025 21:00	23	96	0	25	610	0
19-03-2025 22:00	23	96	0	25	601	0
19-03-2025 23:00	23	98	0	24	600	0

pump, thereby automating irrigation based on the predicted needs. This closed-loop system ensures that irrigation decisions are data-driven and responsive to changing conditions.

3.4 Model Evaluation

The predictive performance of each model was rigorously assessed using standard regression metrics: Mean Absolute Error (MAE), Mean Squared Error (MSE), Root Mean Squared Error (RMSE), and the R^2 (coefficient of determination) Score. A detailed comparison of model performance is presented in the Results section (Sect. 4).

4 Results

We evaluated five machine learning models for soil moisture prediction: Random Forest Regressor, Support Vector Regression (SVR), XGBoost, Gradient Boosting, and Decision Tree. Performance metrics, including mean absolute error (MAE), mean squared error (MSE), root mean squared error (RMSE), and R^2 Score, are summarized in Table 3. Among the tested models, Gradient Boosting achieves the best performance with an R^2 Score of 0.74 and a lowest RMSE of 72.16, indicating superior predictive accuracy. In contrast, SVR records the highest RMSE (82.69) and the lowest R^2 Score (0.65), reflecting weaker predictive capability.

Feature importance analysis (Fig. 3) reveals that Soil Moisture Lag 3 is the most critical feature, capturing short-term dependencies in soil moisture vari-

Table 3. Performance metrics of machine learning models

Model	MAE	MSE	RMSE	R^2 score
Gradient boosting	44.29	5207.28	72.16	0.74
Random forest	44.31	5398.77	73.48	0.73
Decision tree	43.04	6104.33	78.13	0.69
XGBoost	46.01	6082.02	77.99	0.69
SVR	58.10	6837.64	82.69	0.65

ation. Temperature and humidity also contribute significantly, while soil temperature shows a relatively lower impact. This aligns with the autocorrelation analysis presented in Fig. 4, where Lag 3 maintains a moderate correlation (0.54) with current soil moisture, balancing immediate and delayed effects.

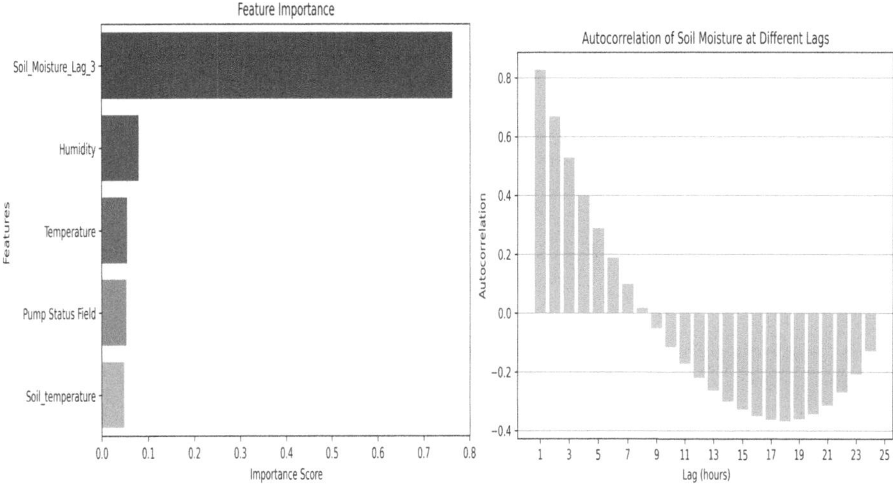

Fig. 3. Relative importance of input features (Temperature, humidity, soil temperature, soil moisture lag 3) for soil moisture prediction.

Fig. 4. Autocorrelation function (ACF) Plot for soil moisture, illustrating the correlation of current soil moisture with its past values at different hourly lags.

A direct comparison of actual and predicted soil moisture values (see Fig. 5) confirms that the best-performing model closely tracks real measurements. Additionally, the pump activation decisions Fig. 6 derived from predicted soil moisture demonstrate effective irrigation control, with fewer misclassifications between dry and adequately moist conditions. Overall, these results highlight the importance of incorporating Soil Moisture Lag 3 alongside environmental variables, enabling more accurate and timely irrigation scheduling.

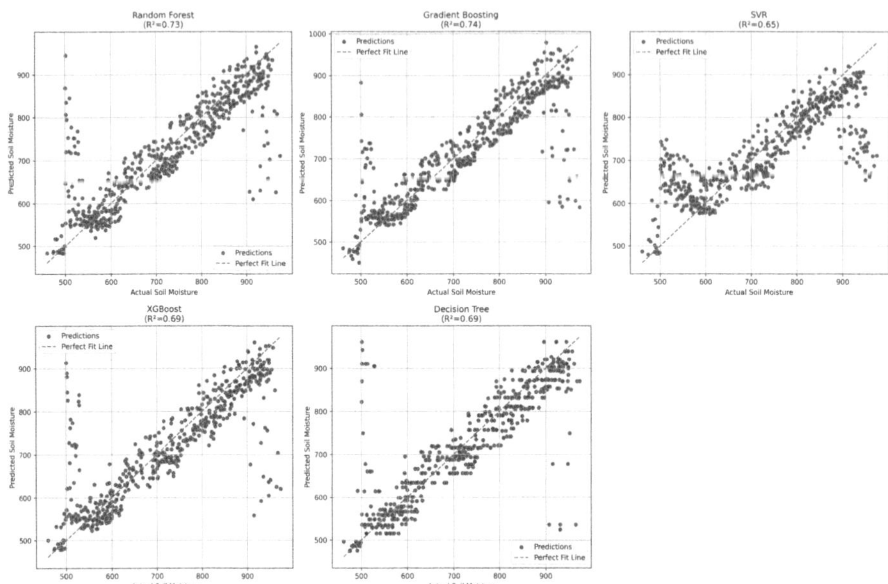

Fig. 5. Comparison of actual measured soil moisture (raw value) versus predicted soil moisture values from the best-performing model (gradient boosting) over a representative time period. This illustrates the model's ability to track real-world soil moisture fluctuations.

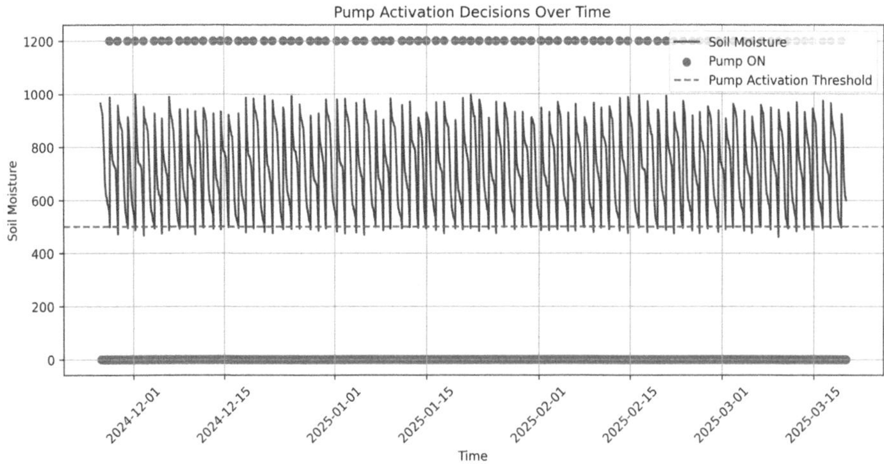

Fig. 6. Irrigation pump activation status (1 = ON, 0 = OFF) over time, as determined by the system based on predicted soil moisture levels. This demonstrates the practical application of the predictive model in controlling irrigation.

5 Discussion

IoT-based sensors, when merged with machine learning models, significantly improve irrigation by dynamically adjusting water supply according to real-time soil moisture forecasts, thereby mitigating both overwatering and under-irrigation. Ensemble methods (Gradient Boosting, Random Forest) showed strong performance, particularly when lagged soil moisture was included to capture temporal dependencies, aligning with other precision agriculture findings.

The ESP32 handles local data processing (edge computing capabilities like sensor reading and preliminary communication), while the Raspberry Pi 3B+ aggregates, stores data, and runs the more complex ML models, allowing for scalability and integration of additional sensors. However, sensor calibration and maintenance remain crucial for sustained accuracy.

It is important to note that the data for this study were collected from a single location over a single agricultural season (Autumn/Winter 2024–2025). While the system demonstrated strong performance under these specific conditions, its generalizability across different climatic zones, soil types, crop varieties, and multiple seasons warrants further investigation. Broader datasets are needed for greater model robustness and wider applicability.

Furthermore, a critical aspect for the practical deployment of IoT systems in rural agriculture, especially in off-grid or resource-limited environments, is energy efficiency. While the ESP32 and Raspberry Pi are relatively low-power devices, continuous sensor operation and wireless data transmission contribute to energy consumption. The current study did not focus on optimizing power consumption, which remains an important consideration for long-term field deployment. Cost-effectiveness and energy consumption also warrant further study to ensure feasibility for smaller farms.

Looking ahead, federated learning could enable collaborative model training with data privacy, and multi-modal sensor integration (e.g., satellite imagery, root zone monitoring) might enhance predictive accuracy. Although deep learning offers potential gains, its high computational demands highlight the need for lightweight, resource-efficient approaches. Combining IoT and machine learning fosters sustainable water usage and boosts agricultural productivity. Future research should focus on validating and refining the models using multi-season and multi-region datasets and exploring energy-saving strategies such as optimizing data sampling, implementing sleep modes, or integrating renewable energy sources to enhance their robustness and practical applicability across diverse agricultural contexts.

6 Conclusion

This research highlights how IoT-based sensors (e.g., DHT11, capacitive soil moisture sensors, DS18B20, rain sensors) and machine learning models can drive data-driven irrigation, minimizing water waste and improving crop yields. Ensemble methods (Gradient Boosting, Random Forest) showed strong predictive performance, particularly when using lagged soil moisture features.

The ESP32–Raspberry Pi 3B+ setup offers scalability and adaptability across diverse climates. However, limitations such as single-season data and the need for enhanced energy efficiency for rural deployment are acknowledged. Deep learning and edge computing might further refine accuracy at higher computational costs, but ensuring lightweight, resource-efficient solutions will make these technologies accessible to small-scale farmers.

Overall, integrating IoT and machine learning presents a promising pathway for optimizing water usage, reducing operational costs, and promoting sustainable agriculture. By harnessing real-time sensor data alongside predictive analytics, farmers can make well-informed irrigation choices, ultimately boosting productivity while conserving valuable resources. Future work should aim to improve model generalizability and address practical deployment challenges like power management.

Acknowledgments. I would like to extend my heartfelt appreciation to Dr. Subhasis Banerjee, whose expert guidance, unwavering support, and encouragement have been pivotal throughout my research journey. Their knowledge and insight were instrumental in shaping this work.
I am also sincerely grateful to Dr. Kalipada Pramanik,Assistant Professor of Agronomy, Visva-Bharati University, for his valuable advice, encouragement, and continuous support, which greatly enriched the quality and direction of this research.
I am deeply thankful to the University Grants Commission (UGC) for granting me the Junior Research Fellowship (JRF) (NTA Ref. No. 230510001724), which provided the financial resources needed to pursue this study.
My colleagues and friends at Visva-Bharati deserve special thanks for their constant support and for fostering a stimulating, collaborative environment. I would also like to acknowledge the administrative and technical staff for their assistance. Finally, I owe profound gratitude to my family for their unwavering support and encouragement–their love and patience have been a continuous source of strength.

References

1. Abdikadir, N.M., Hassan, A.A., Abdullahi, H.O., Rashid, R.A.: Smart irrigation system. Int. J. Electr. Electron. Eng. **10**(8), 224–234 (2023). https://doi.org/10.14445/23488379/IJEEE-V10I8P122, https://www.internationaljournalssrg.org/IJEEE/paper-details?Id=560
2. Achieng, K.O.: Modelling of soil moisture retention curve using machine learning techniques: artificial and deep neural networks vs support vector regression models. Comput. Geosci. **133**, 104320 (2019)
3. Adinarayana, S., Raju, M.G., Srirangam, D.P., Prasad, D.S., Kumar, M.R., veesam, S.B.: Enhancing resource management in precision farming through ai-based irrigation optimization. How Machine Learning is Innovating Today's World: A Concise Technical Guide, pp. 221–251 (2024)
4. Anjum, N., Chowdhury, M.R.: Int. J. Adv. Res. Comput. Commun. Engineering. SSRN Electron. J. (2024). https://doi.org/10.2139/ssrn.4847308, https://www.ssrn.com/abstract=4847308 https://doi.org/10.2139/ssrn.4847308, https://www.ssrn.com/abstract=4847308

5. Aria, M., Cuccurullo, C., Gnasso, A.: A comparison among interpretative proposals for random forests. Mach. Learn. Appl. **6**, 100094 (2021)
6. Behzadipour, F., Ghasemi Nezhad Raeini, M., Abdanan Mehdizadeh, S., Taki, M., Khalil Moghadam, B., Zare Bavani, M.R., Lloret, J.: A smart IoT-based irrigation system design using AI and prediction model. Neural Comput. Appl. **35**(35), 24843–24857 (2023)
7. Benameur, R., Dahane, A., Kechar, B., Benyamina, A.E.H.: An innovative smart and sustainable low-cost irrigation system for anomaly detection using deep learning. Sensors **24**(4), 1162 (2024)
8. García, L., Parra, L., Jimenez, J.M., Lloret, J., Lorenz, P.: IoT-based smart irrigation systems: an overview on the recent trends on sensors and IoT systems for irrigation in precision agriculture. Sensors **20**(4), 1042 (2020). https://doi.org/10.3390/s20041042
9. Ge, J., Zhao, L., Yu, Z., Liu, H., Zhang, L., Gong, X., Sun, H.: Prediction of greenhouse tomato crop evapotranspiration using XGBoost machine learning model. Plants **11**(15), 1923 (2022)
10. Hoffman, G.J., Van Genuchten, M.T.: Soil properties and efficient water use: water management for salinity control. In: Limitations to Efficient Water use in Crop Production, pp. 73–85 (1983)
11. Ji, Y., Li, Y., Yao, N., Biswas, A., Zou, Y., Meng, Q., Liu, F.: The lagged effect and impact of soil moisture drought on terrestrial ecosystem water use efficiency. Ecol. Ind. **133**, 108349 (2021)
12. Kashyap, P.K., Kumar, S., Jaiswal, A., Prasad, M., Gandomi, A.H.: Towards precision agriculture: IoT-enabled intelligent irrigation systems using deep learning neural network. IEEE Sens. J. **21**(16), 17479–17491 (2021)
13. Khanal, S., Bhattarai, S., Adhikari, U., Sharma, D., Pandey, M.: Disparities between developed and emerging economies in digital divide and ICT gap to bring agricultural sustainability. Fundam. Appl. Agric. 1 (2021) https://doi.org/10.5455/faa.78371, https://www.ejmanager.com/fulltextpdf.php?mno=78371 https://doi.org/10.5455/faa.78371, https://www.ejmanager.com/fulltextpdf.php?mno=78371
14. Kodali, R.K., Sahu, A.: An IoT based soil moisture monitoring on Losant platform. In: 2016 2nd International Conference on Contemporary Computing and Informatics (IC3I), pp. 764–768. IEEE (2016)
15. Mahdavinejad, M.S., Rezvan, M., Barekatain, M., Adibi, P., Barnaghi, P., Sheth, A.P.: Machine learning for internet of things data analysis: a survey. Digit. Commun. Netw. **4**(3), 161–175 (2018)
16. Montgomery, D.C., Peck, E.A., Vining, G.G.: Introduction to Linear Regression Analysis. Wiley (2021)
17. Nawandar, N.K., Satpute, V.R.: IoT based low cost and intelligent module for smart irrigation system. Comput. Electron. Agric. **162**, 979–990 (2019). https://doi.org/10.1016/j.compag.2019.05.027, Publisher: Elsevier
18. Ndunagu, J.N., Ukhurebor, K.E., Akaaza, M., Onyancha, R.B.: Development of a wireless sensor network and IoT-based smart irrigation system. Appl. Environ. Soil Sci. **2022**(1), 7678570 (2022) https://doi.org/10.1155/2022/7678570, eprint
19. Nguyen, D.C., Ding, M., Pathirana, P.N., Seneviratne, A., Li, J., Poor, H.V.: Federated learning for internet of things: a comprehensive survey. IEEE Commun. Surv. Tutor. **23**(3), 1622–1658 (2021)
20. Nigussie, E., Olwal, T., Musumba, G., Tegegne, T., Lemma, A., Mekuria, F.: IoT-based irrigation management for smallholder farmers in rural sub-Saharan Africa. Procedia Comput. Sci. **177**, 86–93 (2020)

21. Paul, K., Chatterjee, S.S., Pai, P., Varshney, A., Juikar, S., Prasad, V., Bhadra, B., Dasgupta, S.: Viable smart sensors and their application in data driven agriculture. Comput. Electron. Agric. **198**, 107096 (2022)
22. Pincheira, M., Vecchio, M., Giaffreda, R., Kanhere, S.S.: Cost-effective IoT devices as trustworthy data sources for a blockchain-based water management system in precision agriculture. Comput. Electron. Agric. **180**, 105889 (2021)
23. Prakash, S., Sharma, A., Sahu, S.S.: Soil moisture prediction using machine learning. In: 2018 Second International Conference on Inventive Communication and Computational Technologies (ICICCT), pp. 1–6. IEEE (2018)
24. Punithavathi, P., Geetha, S., Karuppiah, M., Islam, S.H., Hassan, M.M., Choo, K.K.R.: A lightweight machine learning-based authentication framework for smart IoT devices. Inf. Sci. **484**, 255–268 (2019)
25. Saccon, P.: Water for agriculture, irrigation management. Appl. Soil. Ecol. **123**, 793–796 (2018)
26. Shafi, U., Mumtaz, R., García-Nieto, J., Hassan, S.A., Zaidi, S.A.R., Iqbal, N.: Precision agriculture techniques and practices: from considerations to applications. Sensors **19**(17), 3796 (2019)
27. Singh, N., Adhikari, M.: Real-time paddy field irrigation using feature extraction and federated learning strategy. IEEE Sens. J. (2024)
28. Umutoni, L., Samadi, V.: Application of machine learning approaches in supporting irrigation decision making: a review. Agric. Water Manag. **294**, 108710 (2024)
29. Wade, C., Glynn, K.: Hands-On Gradient Boosting with XGBoost and scikit-learn: perform accessible machine learning and extreme gradient boosting with Python. Packt Publishing Ltd. (2020)
30. Wei, H., Xu, W., Kang, B., Eisner, R., Muleke, A., Rodriguez, D., deVoil, P., Sadras, V., Monjardino, M., Harrison, M.T.: Irrigation with artificial intelligence: problems, premises, promises. Hum.-Centric Intell. Syst. **4**(2), 187–205 (2024)

Hybrid Generative Artificial Intelligence Model for Medical Image Synthesis

Christine Susan Mathews[1(✉)] and Kavitha Srinivasan[2]

[1] Post-Graduate Student, Department of Computer Science and Engineering, Sri Sivasubramaniya Nadar College of Engineering, Tamil Nadu, India
Christinesusan2320007@ssn.edu.in

[2] Associate Professor, Department of Computer Science and Engineering, Sri Sivasubramaniya Nadar College of Engineering, Tamil Nadu, India
lncs@springer.com

Abstract. The advancements in medical imaging increased the challenges of machine learning models working towards the diagnosis and treatment of medical conditions. The challenges are: (i) the non-availability of a diverse and var-ied dataset, (ii) the class-imbalance in a dataset. This research work focuses on generating medical images to overcome the class imbalance and non-availability in some modalities using a Hybrid Generative AI (GenAI) approach for CT (Computed Tomography) imaging on the Kaggle "Brain CT Images with Intracranial Hemorrhage Masks" dataset. This dataset is an open-source dataset of kaggle and has brain CT images, brains bone CT im-ages, and haemorrhage masks (only if a Haemorrhage is present) separately for each patient. This evoked the need for a fusion overlay process, that can fuse the images into one image and a need to balance the images present in each class of haemorrhage. For fusion overlay process, Discrete Wavelet Transform (DWT) technique is applied on the dataset to produce a fused image for each slice of a patient's brain CT image. The class-imbalance issue is handled using a hybrid GenAI model that comprises of two main models namely: Variational AutoEncoder (VAE) and Generative Adversarial Net-work (GAN); it generates near-to-real synthetic CT image slices of the brain to balance the dataset for each class. The quality of the image fusion and generated images are validated using metrics like Structural Similarity Index Measure (SSIM), Peak Signal-to-Noise Ratio (PSNR) and Entropy. The hybrid model gave an improved performance of 16.36% more than the standalone models in terms of SSIM and PSNR. From the results, it is observed that the hybrid model gives an improved performance using the fusion overlay technique.

Keywords: Fusion Overlay · Discrete Wavelet Transform · Generative Artificial Intelligence · Variational AutoEncoders · Generative Adversarial Networks

K. Chandra Mondal et al. (Eds.): CICBA 2025, CCIS 2863, pp. 281–293, 2026.
https://doi.org/10.1007/978-3-032-17184-9_21

1 Introduction

Medical imaging improved the precision of diagnosis as well as clinical decision-making by providing clear views of the anatomical structures using various modalities. The imaging modalities like Computed Tomography (CT), Magnetic Resonance Imaging (MRI) and Positron Emission Tomography (PET) have the impact to acquire different kinds of features that can contribute to more detailed medical assessment. Although, a major challenge faced in medical imaging is the scarcity of diverse and balanced dataset across classes necessary for developing an efficient Computer-Aided Diagnosis (CAD) system. Also, lack of diversified data reduces the generalization of the system. In recent years, a new technology has been adapted to overcome the challenge named as Generative Artificial Intelligence (GenAI).

GenAI is a sub-category of AI that can create new content like text or images etc. It has three main kinds of architectures: Generative Adversarial Network (GAN), Variational AutoEncoders (VAE) and flow-based approaches. GANs follow the generator-discriminator framework that supports in producing the result of realistic visual out-puts in terms of the synthesized images but also have critical notified issues like mode collapse (where a limited number of variations for a class have been observed to be generated). However, VAEs are better at learning in a structured latent space. In addition, It ensures a smooth interpolation between the data points but can sometimes fail at generating sharp, high-quality images. Flow-based models make use of invertible transformations to generate samples with precise probability distributions, which are backed up by a mathematically grounded approach that often require extensive computational resources. Each of these techniques has its advantages, but their limitations can be overcome by combining the strengths of the models through the development of hybrid models. A hybrid model like the VAE-GAN architecture is one that can effectively balance the realism of generated images with variability, making it much more suitable for medical image augmentation after synthesis. Certain metrics that can evaluate the quality of the synthesized images quantitatively used in this study are Structural Similarity Index Measure (SSIM), Peak Signal-to-Noise Ratio (PSNR) and entropy that measured the image quality and realism.

The research objective of the proposed work is model creation for synthetic images and validation of the images with some evaluation metrics. The remaining section of the paper is organized as follows: The related work is discussed in Sect. 2, the design of the proposed system is explained with an algorithm in Sect. 3. Section 4 focuses on the implementation and experimental results of the proposed model. The Conclusion is summarized with its future scope in Sect. 5.

2 Related Work

This section discusses the importance of the Generative AI (GenAI) model in medical imaging with its associated techniques.

GenAI models can be associated with techniques like registration or fusion overlay to fuse the different kinds of medical imaging modalities. Registration of images is used to blend the images without any spatial modification, whereas fusion overlay makes use of registration for alignment and then fuses the images. Image fusion overlay can be considered a notably important part of image processing that unifies features of different imaging modalities into one composite image. It enhances the quality and usability of the resulting image, making it more applicable in fields like medical imaging, remote sensing, and surveillance. Image fusion techniques are categorized into three levels as seen in Singh et al., 2023 [1]: Pixel-Level Image Fusion (PLIF), Feature-Level Image Fusion (FLIF), and Decision-Level Image Fusion (DLIF). PLIF fuses base images in a pixel-by-pixel format, which is useful when images are registered but highly sensitive to misalignment. FLIF extracts features such as edges, textures, or regions of interest from the source images for fusion, preserving structural details. DLIF operates on an abstraction level, using classifiers to process features before fusion and is typically used in object detection tasks. Kulkarni and Rege, 2023 [2] state that PLIF retains richer information content, which enhances decision accuracy. Several quantitative metrics such as Structural Similarity Index Measure (SSIM), Peak Signal-to-Noise Ratio (PSNR), and Correlation Coefficient, need to assess the quality of the fused image compared to reference images. The authors use PLIF for image fusion overlay, ensuring that images are registered before fusion for proper alignment. The Discrete Wavelet Transform (DWT) is a widely used frequency-domain technique that decomposes images into multi-resolution components. Singh et al., 2022 [3] utilize DWT with bilateral filtering to improve the fusion of infrared (IR) and visible images. This method enhances contrast and clarity by capturing high-frequency details, such as edges and textures in visible images, and preserving low-frequency thermal information from IR images. Amin et al., 2023 [4] fuse Magnetic Resonance Imaging (MRI) sequences by leveraging DWT's multi-scale decomposition capability and Convolutional Neural Networks (CNNs) to segment brain tumor regions.

GenAI has three main categories as highlighted in Musalamadugu and Kannan, 2023 [5] as: Generative Adversarial Networks (GANs), Variational AutoEncoders (VAEs), and flow-based approaches. Most research focuses on GANs, VAEs, or hybrid approaches. GANs are widely used for image synthesis when dataset size is limited or to augment existing datasets to improve machine learning model performance. They are commonly applied in image synthesis, segmentation, and image-to-image translation. VAEs capture the underlying structure of an image class to generate synthetic images similar to the original ones, reducing noise in the process. They are used in segmentation, synthesis, classification, and registration. Generative AI enhances medical imaging analysis and improves healthcare outcomes. Lang et al., 2024 [6] conclude how GenAI mitigates data scarcity by generating diverse datasets, enabling machine learning models to generalize effectively. Thakur and Thakur, 2023 [7] performed a comparative analysis of GANs across various datasets with Frè-chet Inception Distance (FID) as an evaluation metric. A lower FID score indicates better model performance. The recent research on hybrid GenAI models by Bandi et al., 2023 [9] emphasizes the importance of smooth interpolation and meaningful latent representations in medical imaging applications. Hybrid models, such as Adversarial AutoEncoders (AAE), integrate VAEs' latent space representations with GANs' generator and discriminator components to produce realistic images. Bandi et al., 2023 [8] introduce AAE, which employs a VAE encoder to extract latent space representations, while the GAN generator and discriminator ensure realism in the generated images. Cheng et al., 2023 [9] proposed a hybrid VAE-GAN architecture for parameterized nonlinear fluid flow modeling, demonstrating improved performance compared to high-fidelity models. Combining VAEs' structured latent spaces with GANs' visually convincing outputs is beneficial for medical imaging tasks requiring high-quality synthetic images.

From these studies, we infer that key challenges in fusion overlay include handling class imbalance and ensuring fused images retain diversity. Similarly, Generative AI models, while effective in generating synthetic data, often find it challenging in maintaining diversity and generalizability, potentially leading to biased or less robust outputs in medical imaging applications (Table 1).

Table 1. GenAI in medical imaging studies

Author, Year	Techniques	Datasets	Inferences
Lang et al., 2024 [6]	Generative AI for dataset augmentation	BraTS (Brain Tumor Segmentation), CheXpert	GenAI mitigates data scarcity by generating diverse datasets, enabling ML models to generalize effectively.
Thakur and Thakur, 2023 [7]	GANs with Frèchet Inception Distance (FID)	NIH Chest X-ray, LIDC-IDRI	Comparative analysis of GANs shows a lower FID score indicates better model performance.
Musalamadugu and Kannan, 2023 [5]	GANs, VAEs, Flow-based approaches	HAM10000 (Skin Lesion), ACDC (Cardiac MRI)	Generative AI enhances medical imaging analysis and improves healthcare outcomes.
Bandi et al., 2023 [8]	Adversarial AutoEncoders (AAE) combining VAEs and GANs	BraTS, TCGA-GBM	Hybrid models integrate VAEs' latent spaces with GANs to generate realistic medical images.
Cheng et al., 2023 [9]	Hybrid VAE-GAN for nonlinear fluid modeling	Simulated synthetic flow dynamics dataset	VAE-GAN improves synthetic image quality by combining structured latent spaces with realistic outputs.

3 Proposed System

The research objective of the proposed work is to overcome class imbalance and to generate more diverse data using Hybrid Generative AI (GenAI) approach for medical image synthesis. The dataset chosen is Intracranial Hemorrhage CT images from Kaggle, containing brain CT images, brain's bone CT images, and haemorrhage masks. To combine the information from the CT modality, a fusion overlay process called Discrete Wavelet Transform (DWT) is used. The window of highly contributing fused images is considered, and the Window slices are then processed using a hybrid VAE-GAN model to synthesize realistic images as shown in Fig. 1.

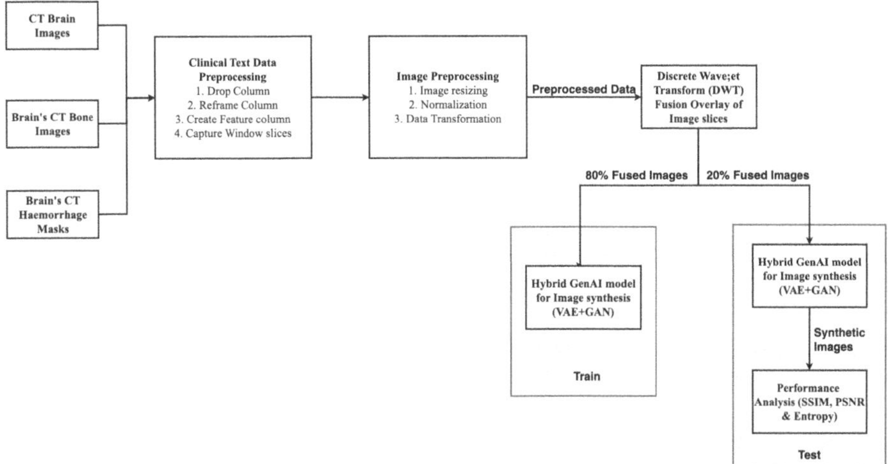

Fig. 1. System architecture.

It can be noted that the imaging modalities Computed Tomography(CT) Brain, CT Brain's bone images and haemorrhage mask are first processed and simultaneously the clinical text data is also processed. The clinical text data drops the non contributing columns, re-frames necessary columns, changing a column for specifying the classes of haemorrhages and capturing the Window slices. The image processing module resizes, normalizes and transforms the images to a specific range. This processed data is passed onto the DWT module for fusion overlay and the fused images are given to the hybrid GenAI model. The fusion overlay module applies Discrete Wavelet Trans-form (DWT) to fuse the brain CT, bone CT, and haemorrhage masks into a single composite image that captures essential anatomical and pathological details. The fused images are given as input to the Hybrid VAE-GAN architecture to generate synthetic images to overcome dataset imbalance in haemorrhage classification. The generated image can be evaluated using metrics like Structural Similarity Index Measure (SSIM), Peak Signal-to-Noise Ratio (PSNR) and Entropy.

3.1 Discrete Wavelet Transform Fusion

Discrete Wavelet Transform (DWT) decomposes the brain Computed Tomography (CT), brain's bone CT and haemorrhage mask images into low-frequency approximation components and high-frequency detail components, thereby preserving both global structure and fine textures. By selecting the maximum intensity values for high frequency components to gather sharp details and averaging the low-frequency components to retain smooth intensity variations; DWT ensures that important anatomical features from the CT brain, brain's bone CT and haemorrhage mask images are preserved in the fused CT brain image. Features like the brain's parenchyma from the CT brain, brain's cranium from the brain's bone CT and the area of haemorrhage from the masks will be preserved as the detail components from this dataset. The Inverse DWT (IDWT) is then applied to reconstruct the final fused image. By fusing these modalities, an image is created that preserves the crucial details from each source, ensuring a richer dataset for subsequent deep learning tasks.

3.2 Hybrid GenAI Model

The hybrid GenAI (Generative Artificial Intelligence) model combines a Variational Autoencoder (VAE) and a Generative Adversarial Network (GAN) to synthesize high-quality CT images while ensuring entropy control. The VAE consists of an encoder that maps input fused CT images to a latent space characterized by mean and variance, followed by a decoder that reconstructs images from sampled latent vectors. The GAN includes a generator that transforms latent vectors into synthetic images and a discriminator that distinguishes between real and generated images. The VAE part of this architecture helps generate the latent vector for better image reconstruction and GAN helps in discriminating real image for realistic image generation. The class-specific VAE-GAN model is trained to synthesize $128 \times \pm 128$ grayscale CT images using a latent dimension of 100, batch size of 32 and 200 epochs per class. Loss functions like binary cross-entropy reconstruction loss, Kullback-Leibler divergence for VAE regularization, and adversarial loss for GAN training is included. Image quality was assessed using entropy (± 0.1 threshold), SSIM, and PSNR. The final output is a synthetic CT image with entropy close to a target value, ensuring realistic and diverse image generation.

The generated images are assessed using metrics like Structural Similarity Index (SSIM) as seen in Eq. (1)., Peak Signal-to-Noise Ratio (PSNR) as seen in Eq. (2). and Entropy to ensure the quality of the generated images. The fused images are subsequently fed into the hybrid GenAI model for image synthesis, where a Variational AutoEncoder (VAE) encodes the latent space, and a Generative Adversarial Network (GAN) generates high-quality synthetic images. The discriminator in the GAN framework refines the generator output, ensuring that the synthesized images closely resemble real medical CT scans. The synthesized and real images are then augmented into a common dataset for deep learning-based haemorrhage classification.

The Structural Similarity Index (SSIM) is defined as:

$$SSIM(x,y) = \frac{(2\mu_x\mu_y + C_1)(2\sigma_{xy} + C_2)}{(\mu_x^2 + \mu_y^2 + C_1)(\sigma_x^2 + \sigma_y^2 + C_2)} \quad (1)$$

where:

- μ_x, μ_y are the mean values of images x and y.
- σ_x^2, σ_y^2 are the variances of images x and y.
- σ_{xy} is the covariance of x and y.
- C_1, C_2 are stabilizing constants.

The Peak Signal-to-Noise Ratio (PSNR) is given by:

$$PSNR = 10 \cdot \log_{10}\left(\frac{MAX^2}{MSE}\right) \quad (2)$$

where:

- MAX is the maximum possible pixel value of the image.
- MSE is the Mean Squared Error between the images.

4 Experimental Results

In this section, the description and analysis of the dataset, the results for the fusion process and the hybrid GenAI process are tabulated and discussed. The hardware and software requirements are specified in Table 2. The hardware requirements include an Intel i7 or higher CPU and at least 50 GB of free storage (SSD recommended), with compatibility for Windows or macOS. The software setup requires Python 3.8+ along with libraries such as PyTorch, NumPy, OpenCV, Matplotlib, PIL, and Torchvision.

4.1 Dataset Description and Analysis

The chosen dataset is the Kaggle Brain CT Images with Intracranial Hemorrhage Masks [22]. In **Table** 2, the total number of images present in each class in the train-test split is depicted.

Table 2. Distribution of images for each class in the dataset

Number of images per class	Epidural	Subarachnoid	Intraparenchymal	Subdural	Intraventricular
In the dataset	173	18	73	56	24
In the train set	133	14	60	50	18
In the test set	40	4	13	6	6

Algorithm 1. Hybrid VAE-GAN Model for Image Synthesis with Entropy Threshold

Require: I_f (Fused CT image), $E_{target} = 20$ (Target entropy)
Ensure: I_s (Synthetic CT image with entropy close to E_{target})
1: **function** TRAINVAEGAN(I_f)
2: $K \leftarrow$ Total number of training iterations
3: **for** $i \leftarrow 1$ to K **do**
4: $ENC_{VAE} \leftarrow$ Encode I_f using VAE to obtain mean (μ) and variance (σ^2)
5: // Sample latent vector
6: $z \leftarrow \mu + \epsilon \cdot \exp(0.5 \cdot \log \sigma^2)$, where $\epsilon \sim \mathcal{N}(0, I)$
7: $G_{GAN} \leftarrow$ Generate synthetic image from z
8: $D_{GAN} \leftarrow$ Discriminator evaluates G_{GAN} and I_f
9: // Compute the loss functions
10: $L_{VAE} = \text{MSE}(I_f, I_s) + KL(\mu, \sigma^2)$
11: $L_D = BCE(D_{GAN}(I_f), 1) + BCE(D_{GAN}(G_{GAN}), 0)$
12: $L_G = BCE(D_{GAN}(G_{GAN}), 1)$
13: // Calculate entropy of generated image
14: $E_{gen} \leftarrow$ Calculate entropy of G_{GAN}
15: **if** $|E_{gen} - E_{target}| > \epsilon$ **then**
16: $L_G \leftarrow L_G + \lambda \cdot |E_{gen} - E_{target}|$
17: **end if**
18: Update VAE encoder using L_{VAE}
19: Update GAN discriminator using L_D
20: Update GAN generator using L_G
21: Compute SSIM and PSNR between I_f and G_{GAN}
22: **end for**
23: **return** I_s
24: **end function**

The dataset includes five types of intracranial haemorrhages: Intraventricular, Intraparenchymal, Subarachnoid, Epidural and Subdural. There are two clinical data files: demographics.csv that contains patient-level details such as age, gender, and other demographic information and haemorrhage.csv that contains slice-level details about haemorrhage types for each patient. The dataset is processed and Exploratory Data Analysis (EDA) is done to get a better understanding of the dataset. It can be inferred from the EDA that there are almost equal number of brain slices and bone slices for each patient. There can or cannot be a Haemorrhage mask for each patient depending on the presence of a haemorrhage. In the cases where there were haemorrhage masks, the average range of the 'Window' slices that had contributing information is identified. Other processing techniques like image resizing and transformation are done to ensure the alignment is intact.

4.2 Results of Discrete Wavelet Transform Fusion

The results of the fusion process is shown in this section. Figs. 2 and 3 are the resulting fused images of patients without and with haemorrhage mask using the DWT fusion technique respectively.

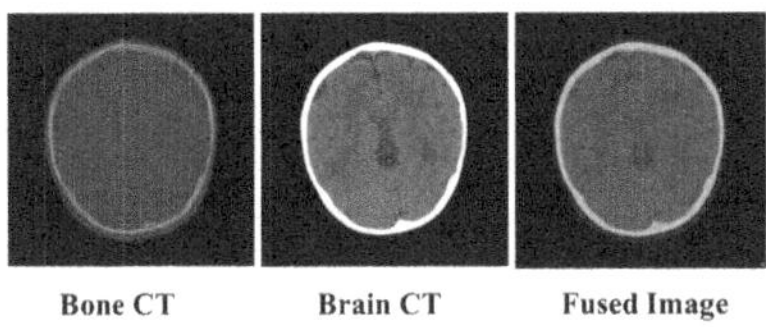

Fig. 2. Fused image of patient without Haemorrhage (Patient 112 Slice 15).

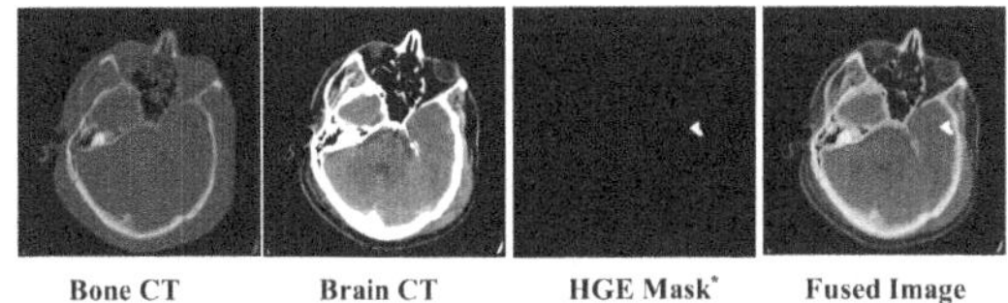

Fig. 3. Fused image of patient with Haemorrhage (Patient 076 Slice 10).

Each imaging modality is calculated with the fused image; Fig. 4 depicts the quantitative metrics used evaluation of fusion overlay process for each patient under different haemorrhage types for the CT image and its fused image. The values indicate that a good fusion overlay of the medical images are achieved. The quantitative values indicate fair to high structural similarity and signal-to-noise ratio with enough mutual information preserved.

4.3 Results of Hybrid Generative AI (GenAI) Model

The average entropy for each class was identified to set as a threshold value in the training process of the hybrid model and is represented in the below **Table.**3

Table 3. Average entropy values for different CT classes

Class	Epidural	Subdural	Subarachnoid	Intraventricular	Intraparenchymal
Average entropy	4.25	4.02	4.69	4.22	4.40

To set the target number of images to be generated to balance the class imbalance issue, the total number of images present in each class was calculated.

Image Modality	Haemorrhage	Patient	Slice	Evaluation Metrics				
				SSIM	PSNR	MSE	Entropy	MI
Brain CT images	Intraventricular	080	14	0.84	18.66	0.01	3.51	1.14
	Intraparenchymal	049		0.83	18.78	0.01	4.78	1.32
	Subarachnoid	076		0.86	19.05	0.01	4.95	1.42
	Epidural	052		0.86	20.37	0.01	4.20	1.20
	Subdural	051		0.87	20.28	0.01	4.10	1.18
Bone CT images	Intraventricular	080	14	0.82	17.34	0.01	3.34	1.05
	Intraparenchymal	049		0.76	18.20	0.02	3.93	1.17
	Subarachnoid	076		0.78	18.71	0.01	3.55	1.18
	Epidural	052		0.84	19.58	0.01	3.38	1.07
	Subdural	051		0.84	19.44	0.01	3.03	1.06
Mask images	Intraventricular	080	14	0.55	10.79	0.08	0.21	0.07
	Intraparenchymal	049		0.38	9.63	0.11	0.03	0.01
	Subarachnoid	076		0.39	9.33	0.12	0.03	0.01
	Epidural	052		0.45	10.49	0.09	0.06	0.02
	Subdural	051		0.49	10.49	0.09	0.06	0.02

Fig. 4. Evaluation metrics for each patient after discrete wavelet transform image fusion.

Since class 'Normal CT' had the highest number of images present, given the entropy threshold to the VAE+GAN hybrid model; results were generated for each kind of haemorrhage except the 'Normal CT' class. Figure 5 depicts the original image of each class alongside its generated image.

Class (Patient ID)	Epidural (Patient: 66)	Subdural (Patient: 81)	Subarachnoid (Patient: 76)	Intraventricular (Patient: 80)	Intraparenchymal (Patient:69)
Real Image					
Generated Image					

Fig. 5. Generated image for normal CT class using hybrid GenAI model.

The hybrid GenAI model is qualitatively able to generate synthetic images for the given dataset. An SSIM range of 0.7 to 0.9 and PSNR range of 17 to 20dB indicate a good synthesis. In the quantitative point of view for 100 epochs with generation of 20 images per class, the SSIM depict a boundary value of 0.45 to 0.51 which indicates good structural similarity and PSNR values range from 11 to 13dB which can be improved over more epochs. The quantitative metrics of

Table 4. Evaluation metrics for generated images

Class	Entropy	SSIM	PSNR
Intraventricular	4.2870	0.6556	15.6270
Intraparenchymal	4.3179	0.9574	32.3817
Subarachnoid	4.7185	0.5305	12.3061
Epidural	4.3130	0.8057	22.3901
Subdural	4.0704	0.9774	36.1223

the hybrid process is seen in **Table** 4. The hybrid Generative AI (GenAI) process has performed 16.36% more than standalone VAE or GAN architectures in terms of SSIM and PSNR. The existing GAN model for Lung CT's obtained an average SSIM score of 0.754 across all methods and sizes with the cCGAN_NLST model for full and cropped images. compared to the existing model, the hybrid model is 4.15% more in terms of SSIM. Table 5 presents the comparison of the average SSIM index acquired for the standalone VAE, existing cCGAN_NLST model and the developed hybrid GenAI model.

Table 5. Comparison of SSIM score with hybrid GenAI model

Model	Standalone VAE model	cCGAN_NLST model [22]	Hybrid GenAI model
Average SSIM	0.66	0.754	0.785

5 Conclusion

A Hybrid Generative AI (GenAI) model for Medical Image Synthesis with Fusion Overlay over the CT images is proposed with obtaining a balanced and diverse class of images. The VAE architecture helps in better image reconstruction and GAN helps in discriminating real image for realistic image synthesis. Such a model can synthesize high-quality images with diversity into the original dataset, that can further help in better generalizability for the predictive models. As seen in the results, the model qualitatively maintained a good resemblance to the original images of each class. With the hybrid model run for higher epochs, a deep learning model can be implemented as a future work; this model can identify the kind of haemorrhage based on the CT image given. Although, this model focuses only on a specific Brain CT imaging for Intracranial Haemorrhage, further implementation can be done for various different medical imaging scenarios.

References

1. Singh, S., Singh, H., Bueno, G., Deniz, O., Singh, S., Monga, H., Hrisheekesha, P.N., Pedraza, A.: A review of image fusion: methods, applications and performance metrics. J. Imaging Fusion **12**(4), 45–67 (2023)

2. Kulkarni, S.C., Rege, P.P.: Pixel level fusion techniques for SAR and optical images: a review. Image Process. J. **18**(3), 210–230 (2023)
3. Singh, S., Singh, H., Gehlot, A., Kaur, J.: Gagandeep: IR and visible image fusion using DWT and bilateral filter. Fusion Tech. Rev. **11**(1), 95–110 (2022)
4. Amina, J., Sharif, M., Gul, N., Yasmina, M., Shad, S.A.: Brain tumor classification based on DWT fusion of MRI sequences using convolutional neural network. Futur. Med. AI **1**(2), 12–24 (2023)
5. Musalamadugu, T.S., Kannan, H.: Generative AI for medical imaging analysis and applications. Med. Imaging AI Rev. **9**(4), 123–137 (2023)
6. Lang, O., Yaya-Stupp, D., Traynis, I., Cole-Lewis, H., Bennett, C. R., Lyles, C. R., Lau, C., Matias, Y., Liu, Y., Hammel, N., Babenko, B.: Using generative AI to investigate medical imagery models and datasets. eBioMedicine **102**, 105075 (2024)
7. Thakur, A., Thakur, G.K.: Developing GANs for synthetic medical imaging data: enhancing training and research. J. Synth. Data **5**(1), 34–50 (2023)
8. Bandi, A., Adapa, P.V.S.R., Kuchi, Y.E.V.P.: The power of generative AI: a review of requirements, models, input–output formats, evaluation metrics, and challenges. Gener. AI J. **12**(2), 78–98 (2023)
9. Cheng, M., Fang, F., Pain, C.C., Navon, I.M.: An advanced hybrid deep adversarial autoencoder for parameterized nonlinear fluid flow modelling. Adv. Deep Learn. Models **8**(2), 102–118 (2023)
10. Skandarani, Y., Jodoin, P.-M., Lalande, A.: GANs for medical image synthesis: an empirical study. Med. Imaging Synth. **15**(3), 543–560 (2023)
11. Schaudt, D., Späte, C., von Schwerin, R., Reichert, M., von Schwerin, M., Beer, M., Kloth, C.: A critical assessment of generative models for synthetic data augmentation on limited pneumonia X-ray data. Med. Image Synth. **7**(3), 299–315 (2023)
12. Borys, K., Schmitt, Y.A., Nauta, M., Seifert, C., Kramer, N., Friedrich, C.M., Nensa, F.: Explainable AI in medical imaging: an overview for clinical practitioners. Med. XAI J. **4**(3), 205–223 (2023)
13. Cortès-Ferre, L., Gutièrrez-Naranjo, M.A.: Deep learning applied to intracranial hemorrhage detection. AI Health **7**(2), 89–105 (2023)
14. Yun, T.J., Choi, J.W., Han, M.: Deep learning-based automatic detection algorithm for acute intracranial haemorrhage: a pivotal randomized clinical trial. Med. Imaging Trials **10**(4), 192–210 (2023)
15. Ghnemat, R., Alodibat, S., Abu Al-Haija, Q.: Explainable artificial intelligence (XAI) for deep learning-based medical imaging classification. J. Med. Imaging XAI **6**(1), 51–67 (2023)
16. Vivekananthan, S.: Comparative analysis of generative models: enhancing image synthesis with VAEs, GANs, and stable diffusion. Department of Computer Science, Huddersfield University, Queensgate, Huddersfield HD1 3DH, UK (2024)
17. Balaji, Y., Hassani, H., Chellappa, R., Feizi, S.: Entropic GANs meet VAEs: a statistical approach to compute sample likelihoods in GANs. In: Proceedings of the 36th International Conference on Machine Learning (ICML), PMLR, vol. 97, pp. 414–423 (2019)
18. Farjana, U., Senthilnaathan, K., Rohit, M.: Generation of synthetic data using GANs with CLAHE processed images and comparative study of model performance on real and synthetic dataset. In: Proceedings of the 2024 International Conference on Emerging Research in Computational Science (ICERCS), pp. 1–6. IEEE, Coimbatore, India (2024)

19. El Kojok, Z., Al Khansa, H., Trad, F., Chehab, A.: Augmenting a spine CT scans dataset using VAEs, GANs, and transfer learning for improved detection of vertebral compression fractures. American University of Beirut, Beirut, Lebanon, Electrical and Computer Engineering (2024)
20. Singh, S.K., Virdee, B., Aggarwal, S., Maroju, A.: Incorporation of XAI and deep learning in biomedical imaging: a review. Polytech. J. **15**(1), Article 1 (2025)
21. Mochurad, L., Ilkiv, A., Mochurad, Y.: A deep learning approach for medical image classification using XAI and convolutional neural networks. In: Singh, A., Singh, K. K., Izonin, I. (eds.) Responsible and Explainable Artificial Intelligence in Healthcare, pp. 183–220. Academic Press (2025)
22. Mendes, J., Pereira, T., Silva, F., Frade, J., Morgado, J., Freitas, C., Negrão, E., Flor de Lima, B., Correia da Silva, M., Madureira, A.J., Ramos, I., Costa, J.L., Hespanhol, V., Cunha, A., Oliveira, H.P.: Lung CT image synthesis using GANs. J. Med. Imaging Health Inform. **16**(4), 321–335 (2025). Dataset Link: https://www.kaggle.com/datasets/vbookshelf/computed-tomography-ct-images
23. Dataset Link: https://www.kaggle.com/datasets/vbookshelf/computed-tomography-ct-images

Safe Step: Real-Time AI-Enabled Navigation System for the Visually Impaired Using YOLOv11

Harini Sri Babu and N. Sabiyath Fatima(✉)

B S Abdur Rahman Crescent Institute of Science and Technology, Chennai, India
sabiyathfathima@crescent.education

Abstract. Visually impaired individuals often face significant challenges, including collision with unexpected obstacles, lack of real-time spatial awareness and identifying safe paths. While the existing solutions alert users about the obstacle, they fail to address the gap of guiding them a safe path to navigate around the obstacle. The proposed system provides a real-time, lightweight navigation system that processes live video input to detect obstacles and offer audio guidance about the safe path, which is designed for adaptability across different hardware. The system uses fine-tuned YOLOv11 to detect anomalies and obstacles in the road and the bounding box information to estimate the proximity of the obstacles. A heuristic risk evaluation mechanism analyses the obstacle, proximity and risk factor to determine a safe path. The fine-tuned YOLOv11 achieved a reliable performance of mAP@50 of 0.8643 on the BDD100K dataset and 0.8949 on the RAD dataset. In real-world testing, the system successfully guided users with 95% accuracy, with minimal delays in complex scenarios. This cost-effective reliable solution enhances mobility and independence for visually impaired individuals in dynamic environments.

Keywords: Deep Learning · Computer Vision · YOLOv11

1 Introduction

Assistive technology for visually impaired individuals has made significant accomplishments with innovations like smart glasses, smart canes, and wearable devices [1]. These solutions have improved the lives of individuals and help them to independently navigate which gives them a sense of self-reliance. The existing solutions use artificial intelligence, computer vision, and sensor technology to provide real-time assistance [4]. However, despite the advancement, a major limitation persists - these technologies are prohibitively expensive [4]. The high cost of these devices makes them out of reach for a large proportion of people, limiting their accessibility.

The primary focus of this proposed system is to develop a lightweight software solution that be integrated into low-cost devices. Instead of relying on expensive hardware. This system is aimed to be deployed on everyday device according to the user preferences. By making the software platform-independent, visually impaired individuals can use the technology on a device they already own which reduces the cost significantly.

K. Chandra Mondal et al. (Eds.): CICBA 2025, CCIS 2863, pp. 294–308, 2026.
https://doi.org/10.1007/978-3-032-17184-9_22

Additionally, apart from the cost of solutions although the existing solutions are effective in detecting obstacles, they fail to address a critical need for the individuals on how to navigate around the detected obstacles. The current system primarily focuses on alerting users about the presence of obstacles there is a major gap, and they do not offer adequate guidance on how to overcome them [19].

The proposed system integrates object detection, real-time audio feedback, and intelligent navigation assistance to support visually impaired individuals. It captures video input from a camera and processes it using deep learning frameworks to identify obstacles such as pedestrians, vehicles, and uneven surfaces. Unlike conventional systems that only detect and alert users to obstacles, this system evaluates spatial information, such as distance, position, and possible alternate safer paths [19].

Once the path is determined, real-time auditory guidance is provided, informing the user about the nature of the obstacle and instructing them on how to proceed. For example, if a pole is detected slightly to the right, the system may suggest, "A car is ahead to your right. Step slightly left and continue forward."

By combining object detection, path planning, and intuitive audio feedback, this system offers a more practical and interactive solution than traditional alert-based assistive technologies. It enables visually impaired individuals to navigate more independently and confidently in outdoor environments.

The rest of the paper is organized as follows: Sect. 2 reviews related work. Section 3 describes the methodology, system design, implementation and experimental setup. Section 4 discusses the results and analysis. Section 5 concludes the paper and outlines future work.

2 Related Works

Kaipeng Hong, et al. [1] has proposed a solution with lightweight modules which can be deployed easily by using IoT-based cameras. This proposed approach simultaneously perform scene classification and path detection. Though this approach gave 91.7% accuracy it only analyses paths and signals but not real-world obstacles.

Rakesh Chandra Joshi, et al. [2] has proposed a portable wearable assistive device that integrates computer vision and sensor-based technologies to provide real-time auditory information about obstacles. However, Ultrasonic sensors are not effective in identifying transparent or low reflective obstacle which is a challenge in this system.

Mukhriddin Mukhiddinov and Jingo Cho [3] proposed a system integrating Object Recognition and audio feedback and text-to-speech and tactile graphic. As tactile feedback interpretation requires training it is difficult for the Visually impaired to adapt to it.

Yahia Said, et al. [4] proposed a wearable assistive device for the visually impaired by integrating Raspberry Pi, a camera module and a pre-trained CNN into smart glasses. However, the system effectively detects objects and distances, it relies on advanced hardware that limits implementation.

Bineeth Kuriakose, et al. [5] proposed DeepNAVI, a smartphone-based navigation assistant which provides real-time audio feedback on obstacle type and details about it. Although this system gives detailed obstacle awareness without requiring extensive training the lack of contextual information makes it difficult for users.

Yasuhiro Nitta, et al. [6] proposed a novel importance rank learning method that identifies the obstacle by prioritising it. It uses a neural network-based ranking estimation to estimate the importance of the obstacles detected. However, the study's dependency on accurate optical flow estimation introduces challenges to dynamic scenarios.

Mooseop Kim, et al. [7] proposed a deep learning-based approach that optimises visual-auditory sensory substitution systems. But this study focusses only on auditory substitution which might not work well under all condition.

Fahad Ashiq, et al. [8] has proposed a navigation system that ensures mobility assistance and safety of the visually impaired. Although its location-sharing feature is extremely useful the system dictates every object in the system which raises confusion and might be misleading for the visually impaired.

Usman Masud, et al. [9] has proposed a system that integrates a Raspberry Pi, camera, an ultrasonic sensor and an Arduino mounted on a walking stick. However, the use of an ultrasonic sensor may struggle to detect obstacles like glass or low-height objects which limits the accuracy and reliability of the system.

Alice Lo Valvo, et al. [10] proposed an augmented reality-based navigation system that uses smartphone to provide virtual paths and real-time object recognition through machine learning. However, as it relies on pre-recorded paths it limits the performance and usage in the real-world environment.

Jagadish K. Mahendran, et al. [11] proposed a computer vision-based assistance system that utilises deep learning and edge AI for real-time scene understanding. Although this system enhances mobility, more accurate and efficient navigation experience performance is constrained by the computational limitations of edge AI.

Salvador Martínez-Cruz, et al. [12] proposed an assistive device that helps the blind and visually impaired with public transport navigation. Although the system demonstrated 97.6% accuracy, its reliance on BLE which requires effective placement and maintenance is one of its limitations.

Minnan Leong and R. Kanesaraj Ramasamy [13] has proposed an assistive device integrated in smart glasses. This study focusses on improving spatial awareness using Computer Vision and Machine Learning. However, the hardware used in the system has processing limitations which causes latency in object detection.

Rakesh Chandra Joshi, et al. [14] has proposed a fully automatic assistive technology by recognising objects and providing real-time auditory feedback. With an average accuracy of 95.15% the system performs well in recognising the objects. However further testing in diverse environments is needed.

Shubham Melvin Felix, et al. [15] proposed an android-based mobile application that enables users to navigate, read and engage with the world. However, the application's performance relies on the quality of the smartphone's camera quality which affects the accuracy.

3 Proposed Methodology

3.1 System Architecture

This system comprises different phases, as represented in Fig. 1. The first stage of the system is to capture the environment in real time with a camera. The video is then pre-processed to enhance clarity. Each video frame is processed using a deep learning-based object detection model which identifies the objects such as pedestrians, vehicles, and other road obstacles. Once the objects are detected, the system estimates their distance from the user. Monocular depth estimation techniques are used to classify if the objects are "very near", "near", "far", or "very far" enabling a structured assessment of potential hazards. If the object detected is in close proximity and directly in front of the user, a heuristic-based approach is used to analyse the obstacle's position and calculate whether the user should move left or right to avoid the obstacle. The proposed system conveys the navigation instructions through real-time audio feedback. The user receives a spoken alert regarding the detected obstacle, along with directional guidance towards a safe path.

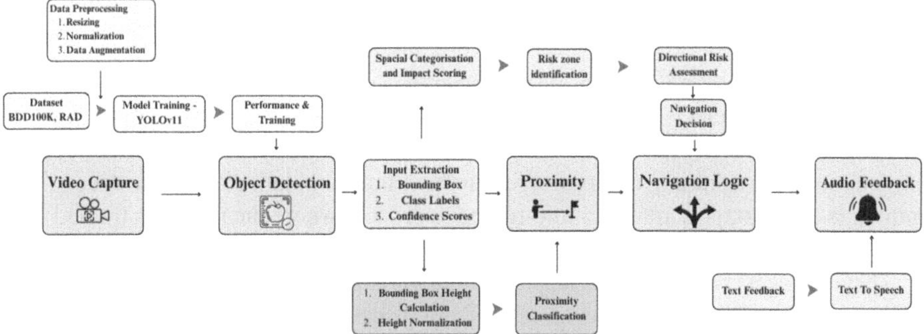

Fig. 1. Architecture Diagram.

3.2 Implementation

The implementation of the proposed system is divided into several key modules each of it handling a specific aspect of the navigation process. These individual modules if finally integrated together to ensure real-time obstacle detection, distance estimation, path planning and the audio feedback for seamless user assistance.

- Video Capturing – Live video streaming.
- Object Detection – Detect and classify road anomalies using fine-tuned YOLOv11.
- Proximity Estimation – Compute bounding box ratio to classify object position and the range of distance.
- Navigation Logic – Heuristic-based evaluation of left/right path and obstacle risk.
- Audio Feedback – Voice-based real-time guidance to the user about the obstacle and suggesting a safe path.
- System Integration – Unified real-time system.

Video Capturing. The system is designed to support video input from any standard camera, including mobile cameras, webcams, or dedicated cameras. In the proposed implementation, a mobile camera is used to capture live video, which is then wirelessly streamed to a processing unit for real-time analysis. The video is transmitted using a local network connection, ensuring minimal latency. The captured frames are extracted and forwarded to the object detection and distance estimation modules.

Object Detection. To train the object detection model, a combination of the BDD100K: A Diverse Driving Dataset for Heterogeneous Multitask Learning [16] and RAD: A Comprehensive Dataset for Benchmarking the Robustness of Image Anomaly Detection is used [17].

- **BDD100K Dataset:** Provides diverse road scenes, including pedestrians, vehicles, and other traffic elements, helping the model learn urban navigation challenges.
- **RAD Dataset:** Contains road anomalies like potholes, cracks, and construction barriers, which are critical for ensuring safe navigation for visually impaired users.

The images in the dataset are further pre-processed by resizing, normalising pixel values, and converting the dataset to YOLO format.

Model Training. The navigation system proposed must be speedy, accurate and efficient in detecting objects even in complex environments for real-world application. In the proposed system YOLOv11 is used to fine-tune to achieve an improved feature extraction, better accuracy and optimised architecture to balance real-time speed. This training is a two-stage sequential fine-tuning approach, where the model is trained with the BDD100K dataset first and the weights are fine-tuned further with the RAD dataset.

These datasets required significant computational resources during training due to their size and complexity. However, optimization such as reduced input resolution and batch-wise loading helped manage consumption effectively.

Training Process. In the first stage, the YOLOv11 model is trained on the BDD100K dataset. The input images are sized to 1280*720 for better object scaling. The model is trained with a batch size of 12, a learning rate set to 0.0008 which helped the model to generalise well in the early stages of training, SDG optimizer with momentum of 0.93 to ensure stable weight updates. The training runs for 30 epochs, with the first 10 layers frozen to preserve general object detection features learned in the initial training. This stage equips the model with the capability to detect objects like vehicles.

In the second stage, the pre-trained model is fine-tuned on the RAD dataset. The input images are in the size of 960*960. Fine-tuning is performed on the previously trained weights with a batch size of 8, a reduced learning rate of 0.0003 since the model has already learned general object detection features, fine-tuning requires more controlled weight updates to focus on road anomalies like potholes, cracks and barriers and to avoid catastrophic forgetting. The AdamW optimizer as it prevents overfitting using proper weight decay. The training is conducted for 20 epochs, with the first 10 layers frozen.

Adam optimizer was chosen after evaluating alternatives like SGD and RMSprp, which showed inferior convergence behaviour and lower accuracy during preliminary experiments.

This two-stage process ensures that the model maintains general detection capabilities while specializing in road anomaly detection, making it highly effective for real-time navigation assistance.

Proximity Estimation. Estimating the distance of the object from the camera is the crucial step in understanding the spatial relationship of the object within the environment using a single camera. To estimate the distance of objects from the camera, two approaches were implemented: Monocular depth estimation and bounding box-based proximity estimation. Both of these methods aimed to classify objects into proximity levels - “Very Near,” “Near,” “Far,” and “Very Far”—which were then used for navigation logic.

Approach – 1 Monocular Depth Estimation. In this approach an encoder-decoder architecture with ResNet50 as the encoder for feature extraction and a U-Net based decoder for depth map reconstruction is used. The per-pixel values are derived from the depth map, which is then used to translate into proximity categories.

To train the distance estimation model the DIODE: Dense Indoor/Outdoor Depth [18] dataset has been used in a supervised learning approach. Given that the full dataset is over 80 GB, train the model only the validation subset (2.6 GB) for efficient training while maintaining depth information. This dataset contains diverse, high-resolution RGB images, depth maps, and scene types.

The encoder utilized a pre-trained ResNet50 without the fully connected layer to extract hierarchical feature maps at different depths, incorporating four skip connections to retain spatial details. The decoder progressively upsampled the features extracted by the encoder using UpSampling2D layers, followed by concatenation with corresponding encoder features via skip connections. Each upsampled feature map was passed through 3×3 convolutional layers with ReLU activation to refine spatial detail. The final layer was a 1×1 convolution to generate a single-channel depth map representing pixel-wise depth values. The model was trained on 256×256 resized images for 60 epochs with a batch size of 32, optimized using Adam optimizer to ensure stable gradient updates. Mean Absolute Error (MAE) was the primary evaluation metric, with a custom loss function enhancing accuracy. The depth map generated by the model provided per-pixel depth values, which were then translated into proximity categories based on predefined depth thresholds.

Approach – 2 Bounding Box-Based Proximity Estimation. This approach is implemented in the system by using a fine-tuned YOLOv11 model to detect the object in the frame and then processing the obtained bounding box to estimate the proximity of the object in the frame. This approach uses the height of the detected object's bounding box relative to the frame height, adapting dynamically to different objects in the scene. Since closer objects appear larger in the field of view, their bounding box height increases, providing an effective heuristic for distance classification.

The YOLOv11 model processes each video frame as an input image in a single forward pass through the network and returns a set of bounding boxes along with class ID and confidence scores as in the formula (1).

Each result detection consists of:

$$O_i = (x_1, y_1, x_2, y_2, c_i, s_i) \tag{1}$$

where:

- x_1, y_1 and x_2, y_2: top-left and bottom-right coordinates of the bounding.
- c_i: class ID for object iii (e.g., pedestrian, pole, vehicle)
- s_i: confidence score for the detection.

The vertical extent of each detected object was computed as formula (2).

$$h_b = y_2 - y_1 \tag{2}$$

where h_b is the height of the bounding box pixels.

To make the height comparable across frames and devices, a function is used to map h_b to the defined proximity levels based on r. To classify the proximity of detected objects, the bounding box height (h_b) was measured as a fraction of the total frame height with the formula (3).

$$r = \frac{h_b}{h_f} \tag{3}$$

where r is the relative bounding box height ratio and h_f is the total pixel height of the video frame.

Using empirically derived thresholds based on multiple tests, each object's proximity is classified into four categories as follows:

- **Very Near** (Red) – $r > 0.45$
- **Near** (Yellow) - $0.30 < r \leq 0.45$
- **Far** (Green) - $0.15 < r \leq 0.30$
- **Very Far** (Blue) – $r \leq 0.15$

This classification ensures that as objects move closer to the camera, their bounding box height increases, triggering a proximity alert. A proximity alert is triggered when an object is categorized as "Very Near" (r > 0.45) or "Near" (0.30 < r ≤ 0.45), and is located within the central region of the video frame, indicating a potential immediate obstacle in the user's path. Since, different objects vary in size (e.g., a pole vs. a car), the system inherently adapts based on the actual objects detected in the frame, to classify between immediate obstacles and distant objects.

Navigation Logic. In the proposed system is designed using the heuristic-based approach to provide real-time assistance as it analyses the surroundings and makes informed path-planning decisions. Unlike the existing systems that only alert the user about the obstacle but fail to suggest a safe path for the user, this implementation focuses on providing a safe path to the user. Object detection is carried out using a fine-tuned YOLOv11 model, and proximity is primarily estimated using the bounding box method which classifies objects as "Very Near", "Near", "Far" or "Very Far" based on their relative height and then the system initiates an obstacle avoidance strategy by evaluating alternative paths. Although monocular depth estimation was explored during development, the bounding box-based method was selected for its efficiency and suitability for real-time processing.

To determine the optimal direction, the system assesses the proximity and the nature of the objects present on both the left and right sides. It considers multiple factors, such as the type of obstacle, its distance, and the potential risk it poses. The heuristic function assigns a risk score to both left and right paths objects like vehicles are assigned a higher obstruction risk and pedestrians are considered lower-risk obstacles. The final navigation decision is made by comparing weighted risk scores which are obtained with a risk function formula (4).

$$R = \sum_{i=1}^{n} w_i.p_i \tag{4}$$

where $\boldsymbol{w_i}$ is a weight for the object type $\boldsymbol{c_i}$and $\boldsymbol{p_i}$ is the proximity score.

The system initializes risk scores for left and right directions. For each detected object, it retrieves position, proximity, and impact factor. If an object is very near and cantered, risk scores are updated, and the system chooses the lower-risk direction; otherwise, it proceeds forward.

Audio Feedback. The audio feedback module is designed to provide real-time navigation instructions to the user by converting the derived safe path and obstacle information into speech. To achieve this, the system uses pyttsx3, a text-to-speech conversion library that operates offline. This specific library has been used to ensure continuous functionality even in areas with poor or no internet connectivity. The generated audio output describes the obstacle type, its relative position and the suggested movement direction to avoid collisions. For instance, "Caution! A pedestrian is very near on the right. Move to your left slightly".

4 Result Analysis

4.1 Object Detection's Performance

The fine-tuned YOLOv11 was evaluated on a validation set of both datasets separately and the model was tested on real-world images. The model is first validated with the validation set of the BDD100K to assess its ability to detect objects like traffic lights, traffic signs, trains, bikes, etc. The trained model achieved a mean Average Precision (mAP@50) of 0.8643, with a precision of 0.8785, a recall of 0.8811 and a F1score of 0.8798 as shown in the table. The model is then validated with the validation set of RAD (Road Anomaly Detection) to test its effectiveness in detecting objects like road damage, speedbumps, unsurfaced roads, etc. In this performance evaluation, the model achieved a mean Average Precision of (mAP@50) of 0.8949, with a precision of 0.9013, a recall of 0.8932 and an F1score of 0.8972 as shown in Table 1.

The confusion matrices of BDD100K and RAD datasets provide insights into the model's performance in detecting various road anomalies from Fig. 2. The model indicated a strong performance in detecting common road objects such as pedestrians, vehicles, and bikes, with minimal misclassifications. However, slight misclassifications were observed in categories such as traffic signs, and certain road anomalies, which can be attributed to their visual similarity.

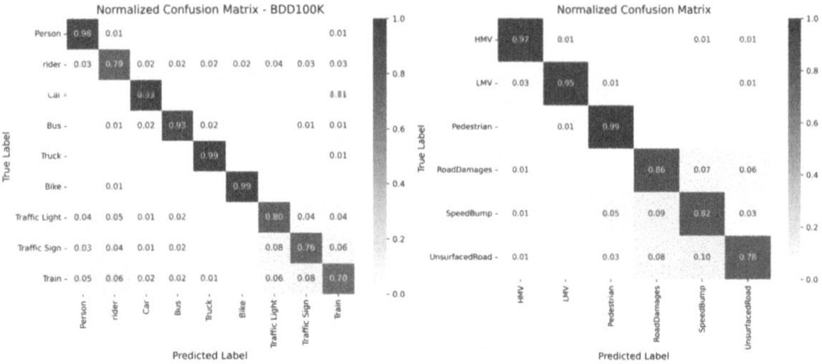

Fig. 2. Confusion Matrix.

To further validate the model's performance in real-world scenarios, a manually captured test image was processed using the trained model. The detected objects were successfully identified, demonstrating the model's capability to generalize beyond the training data as shown in the Fig. 3.

Fig. 3. YOLOv11 Real-world Testing.

Results from these tests on captured images indicate that the model performs well in detecting vehicles, pedestrians and road anomalies. This highlights the model's usability for real-time applications.

4.2 Proximity Estimation Performance

Performance of Depth Estimation Model. The depth estimation model was evaluated based on its training performance, which achieved a Mean Squared Error (MSE) of 0.5364 and a Mean Absolute Error (MAE) of 0.5202. These metrics indicate a reasonable learning capability, but the real-world testing revealed inconsistencies in in-depth predictions, especially in dynamic environments. When the model was tested on a captured image, it showed the ability to estimate the depth as shown in Fig. 4, but when tested on a prerecorded video, the model struggled to maintain consistency in detecting moving objects as they approached the camera.

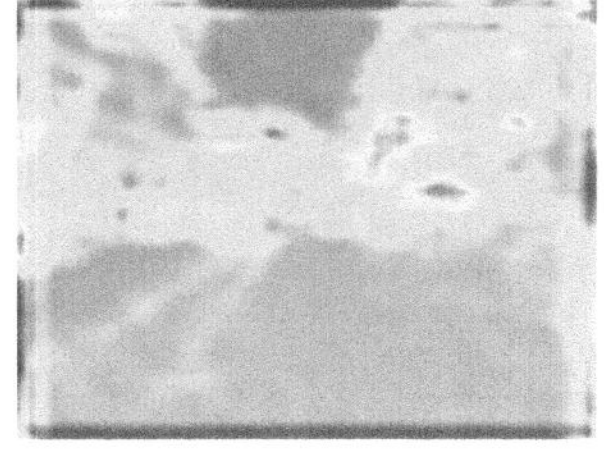

Fig. 4. Depth Map of the captured image.

Bounding Box-Based Proximity Estimation. The system consistently detected objects and correctly classified their relative proximity. When the model was tested in the same pre-recorded video, this method reliably adjusted the distance estimations for moving objects, accurately recognizing when they came closer to the camera. This approach proved to be stable across different object types, demonstrating a reliable proximity classification.

Comparison and Analysis. In real-world scenarios the bounding box approach outperformed the depth estimation model by its consistency, faster processing, and reliability in proximity estimation as shown in Fig. 5. The limitations of the depth estimation model included high sensitivity to noise in the depth predictions, and challenges in accurately estimating proximity of moving object as shown in Fig. 6. On the other hand monocular depth estimation lacks the scale information, making in inaccurate for a dynamic environment where the perspective changes influence depth perception, whereas the bounding box technique uses object detection outputs.

In the proposed system, for navigation assistance precise distance measurement is not mandatory as the goal is to efficiently detect approaching obstacles and classify their proximity. The bounding box classified the proximity of the moving object with speed. Given its speed, computational efficiency, and reliability in object detection, the bounding box-based approach is a more practical and effective choice for real-time navigation assistance.

Fig. 5. Bounding Box-Based Proximity testing

Fig. 6. Depth estimation model testing.

4.3 Navigation Logic's Performance

In the performance of the navigation logic, obstacles of varying sizes and distances were placed at different positions relative to the user's path. The system's decisions were compared against expected safe navigation choices to evaluate its effectiveness. The evaluation considered key factors such as the system's ability to detect obstacles in real-time, determine proximity accurately, and recommend the optimal direction for safe movement. The correctness of directional suggestions (left, right, or forward) was recorded and analysed. The navigation system's effectiveness was quantified by measuring the percentage of correct decisions against predefined ground truth paths which was 95%. Additionally, response time was assessed to ensure real-time applicability where the average response time of 0.6s. The results demonstrated that the system reliably identifies the safer path in most test cases, effectively balancing obstacle proximity and risk assessment for decision-making.

4.4 Overall System Performance

The system was evaluated across five real-world scenarios, assessing its ability to detect objects, estimate their proximity of it and provide accurate navigation guidance. Across the five test cases, the system provided accurate responses in four instances, while one case experienced a delay due to challenges in detecting uneven road surfaces. The accuracy is derived by comparing the system's performance with pre-assessed results, considering both response time and object detection capability. The system performed impressively by achieving an overall accuracy of 95%. In all the test cases the audio feedback was conveyed with clarity effectively. The outcomes of each test case are shown in Table 2.

Table 1. Performance metrics of fine-tuned YOLOv11.

Metrics	BDD100K Dataset	RAD Dataset
mAP@50	0.8643	0.8949
Precision	0.8785	0.9013
Recall	0.8811	0.8932
F1 Score	0.8798	0.8972

Table 2. Test outcomes of the overall system.

Scenario	Detected object & proximity	Expected Navigation	Actual Response	Observation (Accuracy & Response Time)
Car ahead	Car (left, Very Near), Truck (left, Near), Pedestrian (right, far)	Move Right	Move Right	100%, Time: **0.5s**
Open path	No obstacles detected	Move Forward	Move Forward	100%, Time: **0.3s**
Bicycle approaching	Bicycle (left, Near), Car (right, Far)	Move Slightly Right	Move Slightly Right	100%, Time: **0.4s**
Bike approaching, unsurfaced road	Bike (left, Near), road damage (right, Near)	Stop Alert	Delayed stop alert	80%, Time: **1.5s**
Low light dog ahead	Dog (left, near)	Move Right	Move Right	100%, Time: **0.7s**

4.5 Comparison with Other Methods

To validate the effectiveness of the proposed real-time navigation assistance system, it is evaluated against both conventional vision-based navigation systems and recent AI-driven object detection methods to establish in terms of cost, adaptability, real-time performance, and practical usability.

The comparison highlights differences in object detection methods, guidance mechanisms, offline support and accuracy. Table 3 summarizes the key features of notable approaches and contrasts them with the proposed method. These insights provide a clearer understanding of the gaps in current solutions and how the proposed system addresses them effectively.

Table 3. Test outcomes of the overall system.

Study	Object Detection Technique	Navigation Guidance	Offline Functionality	Accuracy
Joshi RC et al. [14]	CNN, Ultrasonic Sensors	No (Alert about object)	No	84.9%
Chenhao He et, al [20]	YOLOv8	No (Detection Only)	Yes	80%
Jincheng Li et al.[21]	YOLOV11, Partial conv, Attention Fusion	No (Detection Only)	Yes	83.7%

(*continued*)

Table 3. *(continued)*

Study	Object Detection Technique	Navigation Guidance	Offline Functionality	Accuracy
Proposed System (This paper)	YOLOv11(fine-tuned), Bounding box heuristic	Yes (Audio suggestion about object and safe path)	Yes	95% (Real-time tests)

Compared to the existing systems shown in Table 3, the proposed method demonstrates significant improvements in both functionality and performance. While prior works such as those by Joshi et al. and Chenhao He et al. focus primarily on object detection or basic obstacle alerts, they lack real-time navigation guidance or operate only in online settings. Jincheng Li et al. employed advanced techniques like partial convolution and attention fusion but still did not extend their system to provide actionable guidance.

In contrast, the proposed system achieves a higher detection accuracy of 95% in real-time tests and uniquely integrates a heuristic-based strategy to suggest safe paths, not just detect obstacles. With accurate detection, effective proximity estimation, and smart path planning, our system offers a more complete and user-friendly navigation solution for the visually impaired.

5 Conclusion

This research presents a real-time navigation assistance system for visually impaired individuals. This system integrates object detection, proximity estimation, and heuristic-based navigation logic to provide audio feedback about the safe path to move. The system successfully detected obstacles, estimated their proximity, and determined the safest path forward, ensuring a reliable and intuitive guidance mechanism. Overall the system showed an impressive accuracy of 95% in real-world testing, making it a reliable solution.

One of the key advantages of the system is its hardware-agnostic design. Unlike the available solutions that require specialized hardware, this system is designed in a way that it adapts to various devices based on feasibility and user requirements. This flexibility makes the solution cost-effective, and enhances accessibility, enabling users to benefit from an affordable and scalable assistive technology. Furthermore, while the implementation of the proposed system involved video transmission over a network, that is not a fundamental requirement of the system. The system is designed in the way it adapts to fully offline processing if deployed on capable hardware. Using an offline text-to-speech module ensures the system has uninterrupted audio feedback, making the system suitable for low-internet regions.

By providing an intelligent, adaptive, and efficient navigation aid, this proposed system contributes to enhancing mobility and independence for visually impaired individuals. Its modular approach allows for future refinements and optimizations, making it a promising step toward more accessible and inclusive assistive technologies.

Future improvements can focus on enhancing the system's capabilities to provide a more comprehensive navigation experience. Some possible extensions include:

- **Integrating Scene Understanding** to recognize and interpret roads, sidewalks, and pathways for better navigation assistance.
- **Implementing Text Detection** to help users read signboards, labels, and other important text in the environment.
- **Expanding Obstacle Recognition** by incorporating more real-world obstacles such as temporary barriers, small objects, and moving hazards.
- **Optimizing for Edge Devices** to enable fully offline processing and improve real-time performance on low-power hardware.

References

1. Hong, K., He, W., Tang, H., Zhang, X., Li, Q., Zhou, B.: SPVINet: a lightweight multi-task learning network for assisting visually impaired people in multiscene perception. IEEE Internet Things J. (2024)
2. Joshi, R.C., Singh, N., Sharma, A.K., Burget, R., Dutta, M.K.: AI-SenseVision: a low-cost artificial-intelligence-based robust and real-time assistance for visually impaired people. IEEE Trans. Hum. Mach. Syst. (2024)
3. Leong, X., Ramasamy, R.K.: Obstacle detection and distance estimation for visually impaired people. IEEE Access (2023)
4. Said, Y., Atri, M., Albahar, M.A., Ben Atitallah, A., Alsariera, Y.A.: Obstacle detection system for navigation assistance of visually impaired people based on deep learning techniques. Sensors (2023)
5. Kuriakose, B., Shrestha, R., Sandnes, F.E.: DeepNAVI: a deep learning-based smartphone navigation assistant for people with visual impairments. Expert Syst. Appl. (2023)
6. Nitta, Y., Isogawa, M., Yonetani, R., Sugimoto, M.: Importance rank-learning of objects in urban scenes for assisting visually impaired people. IEEE Access (2023)
7. Kim, M., Park, Y., Moon, K., Jeong, C.Y.: Deep learning-based optimization of visual–auditory sensory substitution. IEEE Access (2023)
8. Ashiq, F., et al.: CNN-based object recognition and tracking system to assist visually impaired people. IEEE Access (2022)
9. Masud, U., Saeed, T., Malaikah, H.M., Islam, F.U., Abbas, G.: Smart assistive system for visually impaired people obstruction avoidance through object detection and classification. IEEE Access (2022)
10. Lo Valvo, A., Croce, D., Garlisi, D., Giuliano, F., Giarré, L., Tinnirello, I.: A navigation and augmented reality system for visually impaired people. Sensors (2021)
11. Mahendran, J.K., Barry, D.T., Nivedha, A.K., Bhandarkar, S.M.: Computer vision-based assistance system for the visually impaired using mobile edge artificial intelligence. In: Proceedings of the IEEE/CVF Conference on Computer Vision and Pattern Recognition (2021)
12. Martínez-Cruz, S., Morales-Hernández, L.A., Pérez-Soto, G.I., Benitez-Rangel, J.P., Camarillo-Gómez, K.A.: An outdoor navigation assistance system for visually impaired people in public transportation. IEEE Access (2021)
13. Mukhiddinov, M., Cho, J.: Smart glass system using deep learning for the blind and visually impaired. Electronics (2021)
14. Joshi, R.C., Yadav, S., Dutta, M.K., Travieso-Gonzalez, C.M.: Efficient multi-object detection and smart navigation using artificial intelligence for visually impaired people. Entropy (2020)
15. Felix, S.M., Kumar, S., Veeramuthu, A.: A smart personal AI assistant for visually impaired people. In: 2018 2nd International Conference on Trends in Electronics and Informatics (ICOEI) (2018)

16. Yu, F., et al.: BDD100K: a diverse driving dataset for heterogeneous multitask learning. In: Proceedings of the IEEE/CVF Conference on Computer Vision and Pattern Recognition (2020)
17. Cheng, Y., et al.: RAD: a comprehensive dataset for benchmarking the robustness of image anomaly detection. In: 2024 IEEE 20th International Conference on Automation Science and Engineering (CASE). IEEE (2024)
18. Vasiljevic, I., et al.: Diode: a dense indoor and outdoor depth dataset. arXiv preprint arXiv: 1908.00463 (2019)
19. Nashtan, M., et al.: A survey of assistive devices for the blind and visually impaired people. Al-Razi Univ. J. Comput. Sci. Technol. **2**(1), 26–34 (2025)
20. He, C, Pramit, S.: Investigating YOLO models towards outdoor obstacle detection for visually impaired people. arXiv preprint arXiv:2312.07571 (2023)
21. Li, J., et al.: PC-CS-YOLO: high-precision obstacle detection for visually impaired safety. Sensors (Basel, Switzerland) **25**(2), 534 (2025)

On the Study of Resource-Efficient Sentiment Analysis in Social Media: Leveraging Emoji, Hashtags, and Random Forest Classifier

Shubhranshu Gorai[1], Rudrani Mukherjee[1], Mahrukh Hussain[1], Saibal Majumder[1(✉)], Chandan Bandyopadhyay[1], and Diganta Das[2]

[1] Department of Computer Science and Engineering (Data Science), Dr. B. C. Roy Engineering College, Durgapur, India
saibal.majumder.1729@gmail.com

[2] Department of Electronics and Communication Engineering, Sathyabama Institute of Science and Technology, Jeppiar Nagar, Chennai, Tamil Nadu, India

Abstract. Research on user sentiment in social media is essential for understanding user opinions. Classification accuracy is raised by a novel sentiment analysis approach combining sentiment mapping of emoticons and hashtags with text-based machine learning models. Our methodology substitutes TF-IDF vectorization and a Random Forest classifier for deep learning, which calls for massive datasets and processing resources, for effective text-based sentiment analysis. We employ hashtag-based sentiment categorization and predefined emoji sentiment ratings to improve contextual awareness. With an accuracy of 89.87%, macro-averaged precision, recall, and F1-score of 90%, the proposed model performs nicely over sentiment categories. Attitudes are correctly classified by the Confusion Matrix, ROC-AUC Curve, and Swarm Plot. The model has good discrimination shown by its 0.98 ROC-AUC score. Although closely related emotions like Neutral vs. Positive and Fearful vs. Sad have little misclassifications, the stability and dependability of the model in practical applications are verified. These findings augment previous research on hybrid sentiment analysis systems utilizing sentiment detection through emoji- and hashtag-based methodologies. Random Forest classifiers perform conventional machine learning models in sentiment analysis, as shown by the results. The proposed method is useful for social media monitoring, customer sentiment analysis, and opinion mining due to its precision, resource effectiveness, and scalability. The model achieves an accuracy of 89.87% and a ROC-AUC score of 0.98. A comparison using SVM and Naïve Bayes reveals enhanced performance in both precision and recall, showing the model's robustness and resource efficiency for real-time sentiment analysis in social media platforms.

Keywords: Hashtags · Emoji · TF-IDF · Random forest classifier

K. Chandra Mondal et al. (Eds.): CICBA 2025, CCIS 2863, pp. 309–320, 2026.
https://doi.org/10.1007/978-3-032-17184-9_23

1 Introduction

Natural language processing (NLP) relies on sentiment analysis, which has several uses including social media monitoring, opinion mining, and consumer feedback analysis. According to [1], traditional sentiment analysis approaches mostly employ text-based models that employ ML and DL techniques to categorize sentiments into predetermined groups like positive, negative, and neutral. Nevertheless, in today's digital world, people often employ visual features like emoticons, hashtags, and more to convey their emotions besides simple words. Classical text-based models frequently make mistakes when interpreting these non-textual elements [2].

Text-based sentiment categorization has been thoroughly investigated in the past using classifiers like Naïve Bayes, Support Vector Machines (SVM), and Random Forest in conjunction with models like Term Frequency-Inverse Document Frequency (TF-IDF) and Bag-of-Words (BoW) [3,4]. Although these models excel with structured data, they encounter difficulties with informal language, slang, and brief text variants prevalent in social media content [5]. To mitigate these constraints, deep learning models such as Long Short-Term Memory (LSTM) networks, Convolutional Neural Networks (CNNs), and transformers like BERT have been developed to capture intricate sentiment patterns [6,7]. Despite exhibiting excellent accuracy, these models necessitate extensive annotated datasets, considerable processing resources, and prolonged training durations, rendering them unfeasible for real-time sentiment analysis [8].

Recent studies have investigated Multimodal Sentiment Analysis (MSA) to address these problems, integrating several data sources such as text, emojis, and photos for enhanced sentiment categorization [9]. Emoji-centric sentiment analysis has garnered interest due to emojis being potent markers of emotions. A study developed a deep learning model utilizing a comprehensive Twitter emoji dataset, illustrating the feasibility of emoji-based sentiment prediction [10]. Nevertheless, the study failed to include the contextual differences of emojis, as the identical emoji may convey diverse moods based on the underlying language [11]. Likewise, hashtag sentiment analysis has been investigated to improve classification accuracy through the identification of sentiment-rich hashtags [12]. Notwithstanding these improvements, the majority of current methodologies do not amalgamate emoji and hashtag sentiment mapping into a unified framework, hence constraining their efficacy in informal online communication [13].

This work makes the following primary contributions:

- A hybrid pipeline using emoji and hashtag-based sentiment mapping combined with TF-IDF-based machine learning.
- A lightweight, scalable Random Forest approach that avoids the high cost of deep learning methods.
- A structured, symbolic-first classification strategy that uses emoji and hashtags before applying text-based inference.
- A confidence-aware evaluation using ROC-AUC, violin plots, and real-world examples.

- A performance comparison with baseline classifiers showing the advantages of the proposed method.

2 Related Work

Sentiment analysis has been extensively studied using various techniques, ranging from lexicon-based methods to machine learning (ML) and deep learning (DL) models. Early sentiment classification approaches primarily relied on traditional text-based techniques such as TF-IDF and Bag-of-Words (BoW) models [1]. While these models were effective for keyword-based matching, they struggled to capture semantic relationships, particularly in informal and short-text formats, leading to lower classification accuracy. Similarly, text-based ML techniques like Naïve Bayes and Support Vector Machines (SVM) were explored for Twitter sentiment analysis [2]. However, these methods faced challenges in handling short-text sentiment variations, especially those influenced by emojis and informal language.

To improve sentiment classification, researchers have integrated emoji-based sentiment analysis. In [3], a large-scale emoji dataset was collected from Twitter and processed using deep learning models. Despite achieving promising results, the study did not effectively address the contextual variation of emoji sentiment. Similarly, [4] expanded sentiment classification beyond binary polarity by introducing multi-way sentiment categorization for social media texts. While this approach enhanced classification granularity, it remained predominantly text-centric and failed to incorporate emoji and hashtag sentiment cues, which are critical in informal communication.

Deep learning models have also been employed for sentiment classification, demonstrating strong performance. For instance, [5] applied CNN and LSTM architectures to classify seven basic emotions. While achieving high accuracy, these deep learning models required extensive labeled datasets and computational resources, making them impractical for real-time applications. Similar computational challenges were observed in [6], where BERT-based models achieved high sentiment detection performance but suffered from high overhead costs and reduced interpretability. The lack of explainability in transformer-based models remains a major limitation, making them less suitable for decision-making scenarios.

Beyond deep learning, alternative ML classifiers have been explored for sentiment detection. In [7], Random Forest, Decision Tree, and SVM were evaluated on a dataset of 12,864 tweets, with Random Forest outperforming other models. However, this study remained focused solely on text, ignoring the impact of emojis and hashtags on sentiment expression. Another study [8] employed Spark-based deep learning techniques for sentiment classification in Kazakh language text, but its language dependency restricted its adaptability to multilingual datasets.

Apart from text and emojis, hashtags have also been recognized as strong sentiment indicators. In [9], sentiment polarity analysis of hashtags was attempted, but the study did not integrate this approach with emoji-based sentiment analysis, reducing its applicability to real-world social media applications. Another study [10] applied multi-attention fusion mechanisms for sentiment analysis on educational big data, demonstrating improved contextual representation. However, extensive preprocessing requirements and the lack of emoji sentiment analysis limited its ability to handle informal online discourse.

Our approach integrates machine learning-based sentiment classification with emoji and hashtag sentiment mapping to provide a comprehensive and computationally efficient framework. By using TF-IDF vectorization with a Random Forest classifier, it achieves high accuracy without relying on large labeled datasets. The model assigns sentiment scores to emojis and analyzes hashtags, enhancing its adaptability to informal social media text. Unlike deep learning models, which are computationally expensive and less interpretable, our framework employs a lightweight, modular architecture: it prioritizes symbolic sentiment cues and applies text-based classification only when such cues are absent. This structure improves efficiency, interpretability, and real-time applicability in noisy online discourse.

3 Methodology

The proposed hybrid sentiment analysis model integrates text-based machine learning, emoji-based sentiment detection, and hashtag-based sentiment classification to enhance the accuracy of sentiment prediction. Traditional sentiment analysis primarily relies on textual features, often overlooking non-textual sentiment markers such as emojis and hashtags, which play a crucial role in expressing emotions in online conversations [1]. Prior studies confirm that emoji-powered sentiment classification improves accuracy due to their role in conveying emotions more explicitly than plain text [2]. Similarly, hashtags function as sentiment reinforcers, providing additional context that enhances classification accuracy [3].

To ensure a robust and scalable sentiment classification framework, this study follows a structured methodology comprising five major components: data preprocessing, feature extraction, model training and evaluation, enhanced sentiment detection, and hybrid sentiment prediction. Each stage is discussed in detail below.

3.1 Data Preprocessing and Dataset Description

Preprocessing is essential for sentiment analysis, especially given the informal and unstructured characteristics of social media text. Platforms such as Twitter pose distinct challenges, characterized by irregular syntax, the use of abbreviations, emojis, hashtags, and a high volume of noisy content. Preprocessing is essential for cleaning, standardizing, and formatting raw text for subsequent machine learning tasks, thereby improving classification accuracy and model robustness [4].

The preprocessing pipeline begins with text normalization, which entails converting all textual input to lowercase and eliminating URLs, special characters, emojis, and non-alphabetic tokens. This stage aims to minimize textual noise and provide a consistent structure, thus enhancing the identification of sentiment-relevant content [5]. Subsequently, stopword removal is executed via the NLTK stopword corpus, which discards frequently occurring terms that provide minimal semantic value. This amplifies the prominence of significant lexical attributes in the dataset and elevates the overall quality of the feature representation [6], leading to more precise sentiment categorization.

Subsequent to the cleaning phase, sentiment encoding is performed by linking categorical sentiment labels to numerical values. This stage facilitates the application of supervised learning algorithms, such Random Forest and Support Vector Machines (SVM), which have demonstrated significant effectiveness in sentiment categorization tasks [7]. Records without sentiment annotations are excluded to ensure data quality and consistency.

The TF-IDF (Term Frequency-Inverse Document Frequency) transformation is utilized for feature representation. This method measures the significance of individual words in relation to the overall corpus, resulting in a sparse matrix representation of textual information. The feature space is limited to the top 5000 most informative terms, ensuring computational efficiency while maintaining sentiment-relevant features. Prior research highlights the efficacy of TF-IDF in improving model performance through the prioritization of distinctive lexical elements and the minimization of extraneous variance [8].

Text cleaning is executed utilizing regular expressions to eliminate URLs, non-alphabetic letters, and special symbols. Stopwords are removed utilizing NLTK's standard list to preserve sentiment-laden words. All labels are encoded numerically utilizing a predetermined mapping dictionary. The sanitized text is further vectorized via TF-IDF, with a dimensionality limit of 5,000 features, so ensuring computational efficiency while maintaining feature significance.

This study employs a dataset from the Kaggle "Twitter Sentiment Analysis" corpus, which includes more than 10,000 tweets categorized into nine sentiment classes: Positive, Negative, Neutral, Joyful, Sad, Fearful, Surprised, Love, and Sarcastic. The tweets represent a variety of emotional expressions and linguistic styles, featuring informal constructs, hashtags, and emoji usage, which are fundamental to social media communication. The diversity enhances the complexity of the classification task and highlights the need for a robust preprocessing pipeline.

3.2 Model Training and Classification

After preprocessing, the dataset is split into training (80%) and testing (20%) subsets. The primary classification model used is the Random Forest Classifier (RFC), a widely adopted ensemble learning technique that constructs multiple decision trees and aggregates their outputs to improve classification accuracy. Prior research highlights that Random Forest performs exceptionally well in high-dimensional sentiment classification tasks, offering robustness against overfitting [9].

The TF-IDF transformed text vectors serve as input for training, where each tweet is represented as a high-dimensional sparse matrix. Research confirms that TF-IDF-based feature extraction enhances classification accuracy by prioritizing sentiment-indicative words while filtering out less relevant text [10].

A Random Forest classifier with 200 decision trees is used to learn sentiment patterns, ensuring high generalization capability and reducing classification errors. The model is evaluated using accuracy, precision, recall, and F1-score to assess its predictive power. Additionally, a Confusion Matrix is generated to analyze classification errors, while an ROC-AUC curve is plotted to measure model performance across sentiment categories. These evaluation techniques are widely used in sentiment classification research to ensure robust sentiment prediction [11].

3.3 Multimodal Sentiment Enrichment via Hashtag and Emoji Integration

Conventional sentiment analysis models, which rely solely on textual data, often fail to capture the full spectrum of sentiment cues in social media contexts. Platforms such as Twitter are characterized by informal language, contextual ambiguity, and a heavy reliance on non-verbal elements like emojis and hashtags to convey affective states. Recent research underscores that augmenting traditional text-based sentiment classification with emoji-based and hashtag-based features yields significant improvements in classification accuracy by incorporating additional layers of semantic and emotional context [13].

In the present study, a hybrid sentiment enrichment framework is developed to leverage both hashtags and emojis as auxiliary indicators of sentiment. The process begins with hashtag-based sentiment detection, where hashtags are extracted from tweets using regular expression techniques and subsequently mapped to predefined sentiment categories through a curated hashtag sentiment dictionary. When multiple hashtags are present, the sentiment most frequently represented among them is assigned to the tweet. This method has demonstrated efficacy in capturing nuanced emotional expressions, particularly within informal and conversational text common to social platforms [14].

Parallel to this, emoji-based sentiment detection is employed to further refine sentiment classification. Detected emojis are mapped to corresponding sentiment categories based on an emoji sentiment lexicon. In cases where multiple emojis appear in a single tweet, the sentiment associated with the most frequently occurring emoji is selected. This approach addresses scenarios where textual content may be vague or indirect, providing additional clarity in sentiment interpretation [15].

To systematically integrate these modalities, a hierarchical sentiment detection pipeline is implemented. The model first inspects the presence of hashtags and assigns sentiment based on the hashtag-derived classification. If no hashtags are found, it proceeds to evaluate the presence of emojis for sentiment mapping. In the absence of both emojis and hashtags, the system defaults to a TF-IDF-based textual representation, which is subsequently classified using a

Random Forest algorithm. This decision logic ensures that the most informative and contextually rich sentiment cues are prioritized, enhancing overall model performance in noisy, user-generated text environments.

Hashtag-Based Sentiment Detection Hashtags are widely used on social media platforms to express opinions, emotions, and attitudes. To leverage this, a predefined hashtag-sentiment mapping is implemented, allowing sentiment classification based on hashtag presence. The detection process involves extracting hashtags using regular expressions, matching extracted hashtags against a sentiment dictionary, and assigning the most frequently occurring sentiment to the tweet. Research has shown that hashtag-based sentiment analysis significantly improves contextual sentiment detection in social media-based datasets [15].

For instance, hashtags such as "#happy," "#joy," and "#love" indicate positive sentiment, whereas "#sad," "#depressed," and "#heartbroken" represent sad sentiment. Similarly, "#angry," "#furious," and "#mad" are classified as negative sentiment.

Emoji-Based Sentiment Detection Emojis serve as non-verbal sentiment cues, often providing additional emotional meaning to textual content. To incorporate this into sentiment classification, an emoji-sentiment mapping is implemented, where frequently used emojis are assigned predefined sentiment categories. When multiple emojis appear in a tweet, the most frequently occurring sentiment is selected as the dominant emotion. Prior research confirms that emoji-enhanced sentiment detection significantly improves classification accuracy, particularly in informal online communication [9]. Studies have shown that emojis help enhance sentiment analysis models by capturing emotional nuances that plain text often fails to express [10].

Hybrid Sentiment Prediction Pipeline To integrate multiple sentiment classification techniques effectively, a hierarchical decision-making pipeline is employed. The classification follows a structured priority-based order, leveraging hashtag-based and emoji-based sentiment detection first, before defaulting to text-based machine learning classification if no hashtags or emojis are detected.

Initially, the model checks for the presence of hashtags. If hashtags are detected, sentiment is assigned using a predefined hashtag sentiment dictionary. If no hashtags are found, the model then evaluates the text for emoji presence and assigns sentiment based on an emoji-based sentiment mapping. If neither hashtags nor emojis contribute to sentiment classification, the Random Forest model predicts the sentiment based on TF-IDF-extracted textual features [11].

This multi-modal sentiment classification framework ensures a comprehensive and accurate approach to sentiment detection, integrating both linguistic and non-linguistic features to enhance classification accuracy and robustness. Prior research highlights the effectiveness of multi-source sentiment indicators, confirming that models incorporating emoji and hashtag-based sentiment analysis outperform traditional text-only approaches [12].

4 Results

The sentiment analysis model demonstrated high accuracy, achieving an overall accuracy of 89.87%. The evaluation metrics indicate strong performance, with a macro-averaged precision, recall, and F1-score of 90%, confirming the model's ability to handle multiple sentiment categories effectively. The model's performance was evaluated using precision, recall, F1-score, and ROC-AUC metrics to ensure a comprehensive analysis of classification accuracy. The results validate that integrating text, hashtag-based, and emoji-based sentiment analysis enhances prediction performance [1]. This model was evaluated using multiple performance metrics, demonstrating its effectiveness in classifying multiple sentiment categories.

The classification report (Fig. 1) provides a detailed breakdown of the model's performance across different sentiment classes. The model achieves an overall accuracy of 89.87%, with high precision and recall for most sentiments. However, some misclassifications occur in closely related emotions such as Neutral vs. Positive and Fearful vs. Sad, indicating overlapping linguistic features in sentiment expressions.

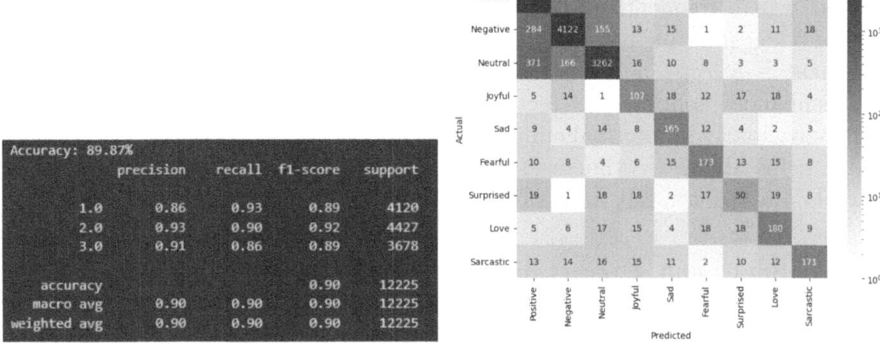

Accuracy: 89.87%

	precision	recall	f1-score	support
1.0	0.86	0.93	0.89	4120
2.0	0.93	0.90	0.92	4427
3.0	0.91	0.86	0.89	3678
accuracy			0.90	12225
macro avg	0.90	0.90	0.90	12225
weighted avg	0.90	0.90	0.90	12225

Fig. 1. Classification report.

Fig. 2. Confusion matrix.

The confusion matrix (Fig. 2) highlights the model's classification performance. The majority of correct predictions align along the diagonal, confirming strong classification accuracy. However, minor misclassifications exist in categories like Angry vs. Sarcastic, which share similar contextual expressions.

The ROC-AUC curve (Fig. 3) demonstrates the model's ability to distinguish between different sentiment classes, achieving an AUC score of 0.98. The curve remains close to the upper-left corner, indicating high sensitivity and specificity, ensuring effective sentiment detection with minimal false positives.

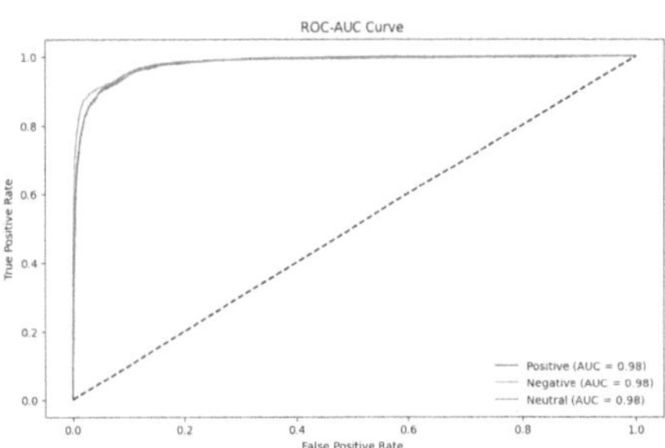

Fig. 3. ROC curve.

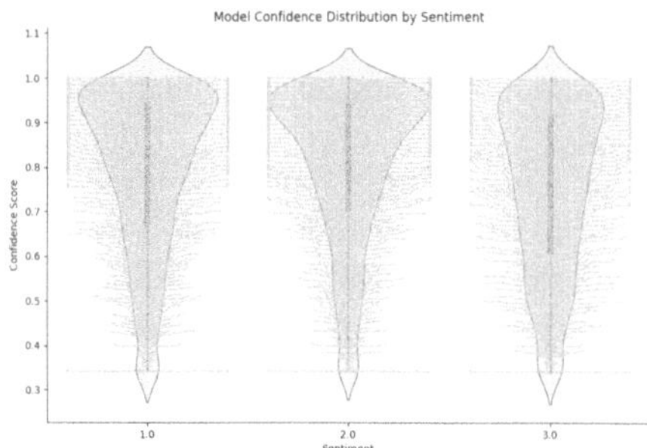

Fig. 4. Swarm plot.

The Swarm Plot (cf. Fig. 4) visualizes the model's confidence levels, categorized into 1.0, 2.0, and 3.0 ranges. Predictions in the 2.0 range are the most accurate, reflecting high confidence in sentiment classification. The 1.0 range represents moderate reliability, with minor uncertainty in sentiment detection. In contrast, predictions in the 3.0 range indicate the highest uncertainty, often due to ambiguous text or overlapping emotions. Most predictions fall within 1.0 and 2.0, ensuring overall stability, while the few in 3.0 suggest areas for improvement. This confirms the model's effectiveness in maintaining high confidence and reliability in sentiment classification. Furthermore, from Fig. 4, it has been observed that, the violin plot approximate better the corresponding swarm plot for category 2.0 compared to its counterparts for categories 1.0 and 3.0. The model output (Fig. 5) showcases real-time sentiment predictions on various sample inputs, including text, emojis , and hashtags (#love, #angry, etc.). Integration of symbolic expressions improves the adaptability of the model for social media analysis, making it more effective in handling text data rich in emotions and informal.

```
Input and Output Predictions:
Input: #happy
Output: Positive
Input: 😨
Output: Fearful
Input: I love this product!
Output: Positive
```

Fig. 5. Realtime output.

These results confirm that the proposed sentiment analysis model achieves high accuracy (89.87%) with strong classification performance across multiple sentiment categories. The Confusion Matrix (Fig. 2) highlights the model's effectiveness in differentiating sentiments with minimal misclassification rates, while the ROC-AUC Curve (Fig. 3) demonstrates high discriminative power with an AUC score of 0.98, ensuring precise sentiment classification. The Swarm Plot (Fig. 4) further validates the model's reliability, showing that the majority of predictions maintain high confidence levels above 0.8, reinforcing classification stability. Additionally, the Model Output (Fig. 5) confirms the model's ability to accurately classify real-world text, emojis, and hashtags, making it well-suited for social media analysis, customer sentiment tracking, and opinion mining applications. While slight misclassifications exist in closely related sentiments, the overall performance establishes the model as a robust and adaptable tool for real-world sentiment classification tasks.

These findings align with previous studies, where multi-modal sentiment analysis frameworks incorporating emoji-based and hashtag-based sentiment detection have led to significant improvements in sentiment classification accuracy [2,3]. The results also reinforce that Random Forest classifiers outperform traditional classifiers in sentiment analysis tasks, making them a strong choice for hybrid classification models[4,5].

Table 1. Performance comparison of sentiment classification models.

Model	Accuracy (%)	Precision(%)	Recall(%)	F1-score(%)
Random forest	89.87	90	90	90
SVM	84.12	84	83	83
Naïve bayes	79.34	78	78	78

As shown in Table 1, the Random Forest classifier outperforms both SVM and Naïve Bayes in all evaluated metrics, reinforcing the effectiveness of the proposed hybrid strategy. These results also demonstrate the model's capacity to handle multi-class sentiment detection with high reliability.

5 Conclusion

This study presents a hybrid sentiment analysis model that integrates text-based machine learning, emoji-based sentiment detection, and hashtag-based classification to enhance sentiment prediction accuracy. By leveraging Random Forest classification with TF-IDF feature extraction, the model successfully classifies ten sentiment categories, including Positive, Negative, Neutral, Joyful, Sad, Fearful, Surprised, Love, Angry, and Sarcastic. Unlike traditional sentiment analysis approaches that rely solely on textual data, this model incorporates symbolic expressions such as emojis and hashtags, improving contextual understanding and classification robustness [1,2].

The model achieves a high accuracy of 89.87%, as validated by the Confusion Matrix, ROC-AUC Curve, Swarm Plot, and real-world test cases. The Confusion Matrix confirms minimal misclassification, while the ROC-AUC score of 0.98 highlights strong sentiment separability. The Swarm Plot indicates high confidence in sentiment predictions, reinforcing the model's reliability. Additionally, testing on real-world data containing emojis and hashtags demonstrates its adaptability to social media sentiment analysis and customer feedback evaluation [3,4].

Existing studies emphasize that emoji-based sentiment analysis significantly improves classification accuracy by capturing additional emotional cues that plain text might overlook [5,6]. Similarly, hashtag-based sentiment classification has been proven to enhance context-aware emotion detection, particularly in informal communication settings such as social media [7]. By integrating these features, the proposed model aligns with recent advancements in multi-modal sentiment analysis techniques [8,9].

Despite its strong performance, some misclassifications occur between closely related emotions such as Joyful vs. Love and Fearful vs. Sad, indicating areas for further refinement. Future research can focus on enhancing sarcasm detection, integrating deep learning techniques such as BERT or LSTMs, and expanding the emoji and hashtag sentiment dictionary to capture emerging trends in social media communication [10,11]. Additionally, research suggests that cross-lingual sentiment analysis using emojis and hashtags could further improve multilingual sentiment detection capabilities [12].

This approach ensures reliable and scalable sentiment analysis, making it applicable for social media monitoring, customer feedback analysis, brand reputation tracking, and public opinion mining.

6 Future Work

Despite its high accuracy, the hybrid sentiment analysis model should be improved. Predetermined emoji and hashtag sentiment dictionaries may not account for all language usage changes, which is a negative. To adapt to new social media expressions, future research should explore context-aware natural language processing approaches for sentiment mapping updates [11]. Deep learning models help better understand sentiment relationships in text. Transformer-based models like BERT and LSTM perform better than Random Forest for context-aware sentiment classification. It is recommended to combine deep learning and traditional machine learning to improve contextual understanding and multi-label sentiment analysis ([11]).

Applying this approach to multilingual sentiment analysis is a crucial direction for future study.Improving the model's capacity to classify sentiments in many languages would greatly enhance its utility in global sentiment analysis. Future research should concentrate on enhancing cross-lingual sentiment classification with the incorporation of sophisticated deep learning methodologies and adaptive learning strategies. This would allow the model to accurately capture sentiment fluctuations across many linguistic and cultural contexts, ensuring its applicability in evolving online communication environments.

References

1. Khan, A., Majumdar, D., Mondal, B.: Sentiment analysis of emoji fused reviews using machine learning and Bert. Sci. Rep. **15**, 7538 (2025)
2. Mao, Y., Liu, Q., Zhang, Y.: Sentiment analysis methods, applications, and challenges: A systematic literature review. J. King Saud Univ. Comput. Inf. Sci. **36**(4), 102048 (2024)
3. Liu, C., Fang, X.F., Lin, T.C., Tan, X., Liu, J., Xin, L.: Improving sentiment analysis accuracy with emoji embedding. J. Saf. Sci. Resil. **2**, 246–252 (2021)
4. Singh, G.V., Ghosh, S., Firdaus, M., Ekbal, A., Bhattacharyya, P.: Predicting multi-label emojis, emotions, and sentiments in code-mixed texts using an emojifying sentiments framework. Sci. Rep. **14**(12204), 1–9 (2024)
5. Jahan, R.I., Fan, H., Chen, H., Feng, Y.: Unlocking Cross-Lingual Sentiment Analysis through Emoji Interpretation: A Multimodal Generative AI Approach. arXiv preprint arXiv:2412.17255 (2024)
6. Velampalli, S., Muniyappa, C., Saxena, A.: Performance Evaluation of Sentiment Analysis on Text and Emoji Data Using End-to-End, Transfer Learning, Distributed and Explainable AI Models. J. Adv. Inf. Technol. **13**(2), 167–172 (2022)
7. Sekhar, J.N.C., et al.: Classification and Comparative Evaluation of Text and Emoji-Based Tweets With Deep Neural Network Models. J. Electr. Comput. Eng. **2024**, 9652424 (2024)
8. Salman, A.H., Al-Jawher, W.A.M.: Performance Comparison of Support Vector Machines, AdaBoost, and Random Forest for Sentiment Text Analysis and Classification. J. Port Sci. Res. **7**(3), 300–311 (2024)
9. Kusal, S., Patil, S., Kotecha, K.: Multimodal text-emoji fusion using deep neural networks for text-based emotion detection in online communication. J. Big Data **12**(25), 1–25 (2025)
10. Chen, Z., Mei, Q., Cao, Y., Liu, X., Lu, X.: SEntiMoji: An Emoji-Powered Learning Approach for Sentiment Analysis in Software Engineering. In: Proc. 27th ACM Joint European Software Engineering Conf. and Symp. on the Foundations of Software Engineering (ESEC/FSE '19), Tallinn, Estonia, pp. 1–12 (2019)
11. Kumar, T.P., Vardhan, B.V.: A Review on Multi-Model Sentiment Analysis Using Deep Learning for Text, Speech, & Emoji Reorganization. J. Harbin Inst. Technol. **54**(4), 59–64 (2022)
12. Dabade, M.S., Sale, M.D., Dhokate, D.D., Kambare, S.M.: Sentiment Analysis of Twitter Data by Using Deep Learning and Machine Learning. Turk. J. Comput. Math. Educ. **12**(6), 962–970 (2021)
13. Al-Otaibi, S., Al-Rasheed, A.: A Review and Comparative Analysis of Sentiment Analysis Techniques. Informatica **46**(6), 33–44 (2022)
14. Althobaiti, M.J.: BERT-based Approach to Arabic Hate Speech and Offensive Language Detection in Twitter: Exploiting Emojis and Sentiment Analysis. Int. J. Adv. Comput. Sci. Appl. **13**(5), 972–978 (2022)
15. Karulkar, Y., Vora, D.T., Vaddepalli, S., Thakur, Y.: Are Emojis the New Words? A Sentiment Analysis of Social Media Brand Conversations. J. Int. Technol. Inf. Manag. **33**, 144–155 (2021)

FinStock-Net – Financial Integration of Short & Medium Trends for Stock Price Prediction

Anubhab Bhattacharya[1], Abir Chakraborty[1], Soham Mandal[1], Aritra Chatterjee[1], Utathya Aich[2(✉)], and Ram Sarkar[1]

[1] Department of Computer Science and Engineering, Jadavpur University, Kolkata, India
[2] CNH Industrial ITC, Gurgaon, India
us4decaich@gmail.com

Abstract. The stock market serves as a fundamental pillar of the global financial ecosystem, influencing macroeconomic stability and investment strategies. Among various financial indicators, the closing price is a critical metric, encapsulating aggregated market sentiment and informing risk assessment, portfolio optimization, and algorithmic trading. Despite its significance, precise forecasting of closing prices remains a formidable challenge due to the stochastic nature of financial markets, characterized by high volatility, non-stationarity, and susceptibility to exogenous economic shocks. We propose FinStock-Net, a multi-scale temporal fusion model that leverages Bidirectional Long Short-Term Memory (BiLSTM) networks for temporal analysis and a gated fusion mechanism to balance short-term (1-day), mid-term (7-day), and long-term (15-day) market dynamics, aligning with real-world decision-making. Our framework also integrates volatility-sensitive indicators, called VIX index, to enhance robustness against abrupt fluctuations. Unlike conventional approaches. FinStock-Net employs adaptive gating mechanisms to dynamically reweight temporal features, ensuring contextual alignment with real-world decision-making horizons. We benchmark FinStock-Net on publicly available financial datasets like Nifty50, Sensex, and S& P500, demonstrating its superior predictive accuracy over some existing models and establishing it as a robust framework for stock market forecasting. The code for our proposed model is available on **Github**.

Keywords: Stock market · Forecasting · BiLSTM · Attention mechanism · Nifty50 · Sensex · S and p500

1 Introduction

The stockhttps://github.com/Utathyaworks/FinStock-Net market plays a crucial role in shaping global and national economies, influencing investments, business growth, and financial stability. Stock markets facilitate capital formation by enabling companies to raise funds for expansion, which in turn leads to job

K. Chandra Mondal et al. (Eds.): CICBA 2025, CCIS 2863, pp. 321–333, 2026.
https://doi.org/10.1007/978-3-032-17184-9_24

creation and economic development. Stock exchanges serve as key platforms for investors and traders, and the performance of stock market indices serves as a barometer of economic health, impacting both individual and institutional investors [1,2].

Stock markets exhibit highly volatile and complex behaviors driven by numerous factors, including trading volumes, economic trends, and external macroeconomic conditions [3]. In India, the two major stock exchanges, NSE (National Stock Exchange) and BSE (Bombay Stock Exchange), list a vast array of companies, with indices like Nifty50 and Sensex serving as benchmarks for market performance. Similarly, in the U.S., the S&P500 tracks major companies, with stocks listed on the New York Stock Exchange (NYSE) and Nasdaq. One of the critical indicators in stock markets is the closing price–the final trading price of a stock at the end of a market session. Accurate prediction of closing prices is fundamental to financial stability and informed decision-making. Traders, investors, and organizations rely on these predictions for portfolio management, risk assessment, and trading strategies.

Traditional forecasting models struggle to capture the complexities of stock market dynamics, leading to inaccurate predictions and suboptimal financial strategies [4–6]. Time series statistical models fail to account for the stock market's non-linear patterns and volatility, leading to unreliable forecasts [7–9]. This creates challenges in decision-making for investors and traders. Deep learning models like Recurrent Neural Network (RNN), Long Short-Term Memory (LSTM) [10,11], and Transformers, with their ability to capture complex dependencies and integrate diverse data sources, offer a promising solution for improving stock market predictions [12,13]. This improves trading strategies, portfolio management, and overall market efficiency. Our research aims to address this existing limitations by introducing a novel model to accurately predict the closing price. The **key contributions** of the work are listed below:

- We propose **FinStock-Net**, a multi-scale temporal analysis model designed to capture market movements across different time intervals, enhancing the precision of closing price predictions.
- We employ Bidirectional LSTMs (BiLSTMs) to analyze temporal dependencies at different levels and a gated fusion mechanism to regulate their contributions.
- We effectively integrate the patterns of different trends in the market considering long-term (15 days), mid-term (7 days) and short-term (1 day) horizons, closely aligning with real-world decision-making strategies.
- We rigorously evaluate FinStock-Net on publicly available benchmark datasets, including Nifty50, Sensex and S&P500, and compare its performance against existing models to demonstrate its superior effectiveness.

2 Literature Survey

Accurate stock price prediction has long been a challenging problem in financial research, driven by the inherently volatile and complex nature of financial markets. Koranga et al. [1] explored a wavelet-based soft computing models combined with ARIMA and ARMA for predicting closing prices of the Sensex and S&P500. The paper leveraged wavelet decomposition and denoising techniques to improve prediction accuracy over traditional statistical methods. Though hybrid wavelet-ARIMA model outperformed existing statistical methods, there are some drawbacks. Wavelet decomposition primarily captures short-term patterns, potentially leading to a loss of long-term dependencies crucial for stock market forecasting. Additionally, ARIMA and ARMA assume stationarity, making them less effective in handling the highly volatile and non-stationary nature of financial markets. Their proposed model is limited to a single dataset, reducing its generalizability to other global stock markets.

Another work by Das et al. [14] applied Deep Neural Networks (DNN), Deep Belief Networks (DBN), and Backpropagation Neural Networks (BPNN) to forecast stock prices using technical indicators and statistical measures alongside traditional stock price data. They evaluated the model on datasets namely Nifty50 and Sensex. While the study demonstrates that DNN outperforms DBN and BPNN in most cases, the lack of multi-scale temporal modeling limits its ability to capture short-, mid-, and long-term trends, which are crucial for real-world financial decision-making. Bhambu et al. [15] introduced RedRVFL, a hybrid deep learning model that integrates ensemble learning with LSTM and Bayesian optimization for financial time series prediction. Their proposed model demonstrated improved accuracy over ARIMA, LSTM, and Gated Recurrent Unit (GRU) over datasets namely S&P500, Nifty50 and Sensex. While ensemble learning used in the paper improved the stability, it did not clearly justify its advantages over standard deep learning methods in financial applications.

Singh et al. [16] explored closing price prediction for the Nifty50 index using statistical (ARIMA, Facebook Prophet) and deep learning (LSTM, GRU, Transformers) models. The paper evaluated different forecasting approaches to improve stock market predictions and identifies LSTM as the most effective model for predicting closing prices. Model generalization across different market conditions are not explored in the paper, which limits its broader applicability.

To address these limitations, we have proposed **FinStock-Net**, a multi-scale temporal analysis model designed to capture market movements across different time intervals, enhancing the precision of closing price predictions. The model effectively integrates short-term, mid-term and long-term trends, aligning with real-world decision-making strategies used in financial markets.

3 Datasets

Our proposed model has been systematically evaluated on three diverse benchmark datasets: two major Indian indices, Nifty50 and Sensex, and the global S&P500 index. These datasets capture intricate market dynamics, including price fluctuations, trading activity, and volatility patterns across both domestic and international markets. Their distinct characteristics make them well-suited for a comprehensive assessment of our model's predictive performance.

Date	Close	Open	High	Low	Vol.	Change %
26-04-2021	48386.51	48197.37	48667.98	48152.24	15230000.0	1.06
27-04-2021	48944.14	48424.08	49009.26	48399.53	10060000.0	1.15
28-04-2021	49733.84	49066.64	49801.48	49066.64	14260000.0	1.61
29-04-2021	49765.94	50093.86	50375.77	49535.98	13230000.0	0.06
30-04-2021	48782.36	49360.89	49569.42	48698.08	19410000.0	-1.98

(a) Sensex

	Date	Price	High	Low	Open	Vol.	Change %
0	02-01-2013	1462.420044	1462.430054	1426.189941	1426.189941	4202600000	2.477407
1	03-01-2013	1459.369995	1465.469971	1455.530029	1462.420044	3829730000	-0.208998
2	04-01-2013	1466.469971	1467.939941	1458.989990	1459.369995	3424290000	0.484154
3	07-01-2013	1461.890015	1466.469971	1456.619995	1466.469971	3304970000	-0.313290
4	08-01-2013	1457.150024	1461.890015	1451.640015	1461.890015	3601600000	-0.325292

(b) S&P500

Fig. 1. Sample data taken from Sensex and S&P500 datasets.

Nifty50[1]–This benchmark index of the NSE, comprises India's 50 largest and most liquid companies, covering 66–70% of the NSE's total market capitalization. As a market-cap-weighted index, it reflects overall market performance, sectoral trends, and economic health. Reviewed semiannually, it adapts to evolving market conditions. Investors and institutions track it closely, leveraging financial products like index funds, Exchange-Traded Funds (ETFs), and derivatives. Nifty50 dataset captures historical stock market data from 27th October, 2006 to 27th November, 2022.

Sensex[2]–Sensex is the benchmark index of the BSE, tracks 30 leading, financially robust companies from key sectors of the Indian economy. As one of India's oldest stock indices, it serves as a crucial indicator of market sentiment and economic trends. Calculated using a free-float market capitalization-weighted methodology, it accurately reflects the performance of top companies. Since its inception in 1986, the Sensex has captured market cycles, mirroring India's economic growth and resilience. Widely followed by investors, analysts, and policymakers, its movements influence both domestic and foreign investor sentiment. The dataset records historical stock market data from April 3, 1979, to January 13, 2022, with seven key columns capturing daily activity. The Date column marks each trading day, while Price, Open, High, and Low reflect the closing, opening, highest, and lowest index values, respectively. Vol indicates the number of shares traded, and Change % shows the daily percentage change. A sample of the dataset is shown in Fig. 1a, illustrating key market factors.

S&P500[3]–This dataset belongs to U.S. stock market, tracks 500 of the largest publicly traded companies, covering approximately 80% of total market capitalization. As a market-cap-weighted index, it reflects overall market performance, economic trends, and sector dynamics. Periodically reviewed to adapt to economic shifts, it is widely followed by investors and serves as the foundation for financial products like index funds,ETFs, and derivatives. The dataset spans historical stock market data from March 15, 2008, to March 15, 2024, capturing daily price movements, trading activity, and percentage changes. A sample of the dataset is shown in Fig. 1b, illustrating key market characteristics.

---

[1] https://in.investing.com/indices/s-p-cnx-nifty-historical-data.

[2] https://in.investing.com/indices/sensex-historical-data.

[3] https://in.investing.com/indices/us-spx-500-historical-data.

3.1 Dataset Preprocessing

We enhanced our model by integrating volatility indices alongside stock price data to improve robustness. Unlike stock indices like Nifty50 and Sensex, which reflect actual market performance, VIX index measure expected future fluctuations. Both datasets include key metrics such as opening price, closing price, highest and lowest values, trading volume, and daily percentage change. However, while stock indices are driven by company performance and economic conditions, VIX is derived from option prices calculated using the risk-neutral pricing model and acts as a "fear gauge," rising with uncertainty and falling in stable markets. By incorporating India VIX[4] and America VIX,[5] we capture investors' sentiment and market uncertainty alongside typical stock price movements. Sample VIX data can be found in Fig. 2. We changed the column names in VIX dataset to "Price_vix", "Open_vix", "High_vix", "Low_vix", "Change %_vix" to prevent ambiguity.

Date	Price_vix	Open_vix	High_vix	Low_vix	Change %_vix
26-04-2021	23.4950	22.6900	23.5550	22.6175	3.55
27-04-2021	23.0825	23.4950	23.6250	22.3200	-1.76
28-04-2021	22.5800	23.0825	23.1125	20.9675	-2.18
29-04-2021	23.3050	22.5800	23.4225	22.1075	3.21
30-04-2021	23.0275	23.3050	23.7650	22.5975	-1.19

Fig. 2. Sample VIX data to understand market volatility.

For the Indian market, India VIX tracks expected volatility for indices like Nifty50 and Sensex. A high VIX signals uncertainty, while a low VIX indicates stability. The dataset spans March 2008 to November 2022, including key metrics like opening, closing, high, low, volume, and daily percentage change. Integrating India VIX helps our model assess shifts in market sentiment beyond traditional stock price movements.

For the U.S. market, America VIX (Cboe Volatility Index) measures expected fluctuations in the S&P500. Like India VIX, it moves inversely to stock prices, rising when markets face turmoil. The dataset covers March 2008 to March 2024, capturing price movements, daily changes, and trading volume. The final sample of preprocessed data after integrating VIX can be found in Fig. 3.

The VIX dataset, loaded from a CSV file, underwent preprocessing by removing the volume column and converting percentage change values into floating-point numbers after stripping the "%" symbol. Simultaneously, the historical dataset was reordered in chronological order and re-indexed. The column originally labeled "Price" was renamed "Close" to ensure consistency across datasets. To standardize numerical values, the financial columns ("Close",

[4] https://in.investing.com/indices/india-vix-historical-data .
[5] https://in.investing.com/indices/volatility-s-p-500-historical-data.

Date	Close	Open	High	Low	Vol.	Change %	Price_vix	Open_vix	High_vix	Low_vix	Change %_vix
26-04-2021	48386.51	48197.37	48667.98	48152.24	15230000.0	1.06	23.4950	22.6900	23.5550	22.6175	3.55
27-04-2021	48944.14	48424.08	49009.26	48399.53	10060000.0	1.15	23.0825	23.4950	23.6250	22.3200	-1.76
28-04-2021	49733.84	49066.64	49801.48	49066.64	14260000.0	1.61	22.5800	23.0825	23.1125	20.9675	-2.18
29-04-2021	49765.94	50093.86	50375.77	49535.98	13230000.0	0.06	23.3050	22.5800	23.4225	22.1075	3.21
30-04-2021	48782.36	49360.89	49569.42	48698.08	19410000.0	-1.98	23.0275	23.3050	23.7650	22.5975	-1.19

Fig. 3. Sample preprocessed data after considering VIX in Sensex. Left side: Sensex data, Right side: VIX data.

"Open", "High", and "Low") were processed by removing any comma separators and casting the resulting strings to floats.

After cleansing individual datasets, the two sources were merged based on the common "Date" field, and the date information was subsequently dropped to focus exclusively on numerical features. The analysis then concentrated on the univariate time series of closing prices. To improve the convergence behavior of the forecasting model, the "Close" values were normalized using a MinMaxScaler.

Each of the datasets was divided into training, validation, and testing sets in proportions of 70%, 10%, and 20%, respectively, with the last 20% of the days allocated to the test set, the preceding 10% to the validation set, and the remaining 70% to the training set.

4 Proposed Model

Time-series forecasting is a critical task in various domains, including finance, healthcare, and supply chain management, where accurate predictions enable informed decision-making. We propose, **FinStock-Net**, a multi-scale hybrid model, which integrates multi-scale temporal dependencies with an adaptive gating mechanism to enhance predictive accuracy and robustness. The process of financial decision-making is inherently multi-scale, with investors analyzing long-term trends, mid-term patterns, and short-term fluctuations to make informed choices. Seasoned investors do not rely solely on a single timescale; instead, they integrate historical performance, recent market momentum, and immediate price movements to develop a holistic strategy. Our proposed model is designed to replicate this cognitive approach by incorporating distinct processing branches for different timescales and dynamically adjusting their influence through an adaptive gating mechanism.
The model leverages BiLSTM networks with an adaptive gating mechanism to selectively integrate temporal dependencies across multiple timescales. The BiLSTM network captures both forward and backward temporal patterns, ensuring comprehensive trend analysis, while the gated fusion mechanism dynamically regulates the contribution of each timescale based on its predictive significance.

This architecture effectively mimics the hierarchical decision-making process of investors, where long-term stability, mid-term momentum, and short-term reflexes are weighted adaptively to optimize financial predictions. The diagram of our proposed model is shown in Fig. 4. Our model consists of three key components, each designed to capture different temporal patterns:

1. **Long-term Trends (15-day Analysis):** Just as investors study historical trends, economic cycles, and fundamental market indicators, our model employs a bidirectional LSTM to capture macro-level dependencies. This component mimics how traders rely on sustained price patterns and key resistance/support levels to make predictions.
2. **Mid-term Momentum (7-day Analysis):** Investors frequently adjust their strategies based on recent market sentiment, moving averages, and emerging trends. Our model mirrors this behavior by incorporating a mid-term analysis branch, which focuses on the last seven days of market activity. A gated forget mechanism regulates its influence, ensuring that this component only contributes when recent trends are significant.
3. **Short-term Reflex (1-day Sensitivity):** In volatile markets, investors often react to immediate price changes, news events, or technical indicators. Our model includes a short-term sensitivity module that extracts the most recent price movement and applies a gated control unit to determine its relevance. This mimics an investor's instinctive response to sudden market shifts, preventing overreactions to noise while capturing critical short-term signals.

Our proposed model effectively merges long-term, mid-term, and short-term trends using a gated mechanism to balance their contributions. Gating functions modulate the impact of the mid-term and short-term branches, ensuring their influence is adaptively weighted based on learned significance. The outputs from all three branches are combined through an additive fusion, followed by a refinement layer to enhance representation. Finally, the model incorporates the

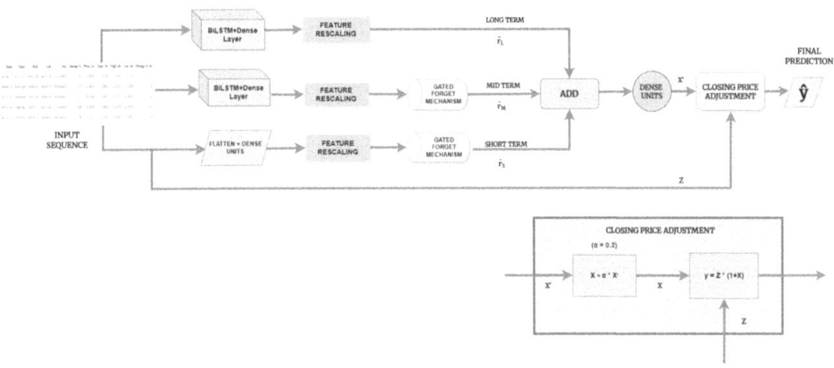

Fig. 4. Architecture of the proposed model, FinStock-Net.

price of the last day applying the predicted return as a percentage adjustment, ensuring that the final result remains contextual with the most recent real value.

The gating mechanism in the model acts as a dynamic filter that adjusts the contribution of mid-term and short-term trends before merging them with the long-term trend. Specifically, two independent gates, g_m and g_s for mid and short term trends respectively, are learned through sigmoid activations applied to the mid-term and short-term predictions:

$$g_m = \sigma(W_m \cdot R_m + b_m) \tag{1}$$

$$g_s = \sigma(W_s \cdot R_s + b_s) \tag{2}$$

where R_m and R_s are raw mid-term and short-term predictions, respectively. These gates control the flow of information by scaling their respective returns:

$$R_m^{\text{gated}} = g_m \cdot R_m \tag{3}$$

$$R_s^{\text{gated}} = g_s \cdot R_s \tag{4}$$

The final return is computed by merging the scaled contributions of all three trends:

$$R_{\text{final}} = R_l + R_m^{\text{gated}} + R_s^{\text{gated}} \tag{5}$$

where R_l represents the long-term return. This fused return is then refined through a dense layer before being used to adjust the last day's price:

$$P_{\text{final}} = P_{\text{last}} \times (1 + R_{\text{final}}) \tag{6}$$

This ensured the prediction remains grounded in the most recent observed price while integrating learned trends at multiple timescales. This method inherently accounts for price scaling, making it more robust to different market conditions. Additionally, using a multiplicative factor ($1+R_{\text{final}}$) aligns with financial modeling principles, where returns are often expressed as relative changes rather than absolute differences. This approach enables the model to capture trends across multiple timescales while ensuring that short-term fluctuations are meaningfully incorporated into the final prediction.

5 Evaluation Criteria

The model is trained using the Mean Squared Error (MSE) loss function and optimized over a maximum of 100 epochs, incorporating early stopping to prevent overfitting. Once training is complete, several standard regression metrics are employed for evaluation. MSE measures the average squared difference between predicted and actual values, providing an overall indication of an error magnitude. The paper followed RMSE as a main benchmark evaluation metric.

Root Mean Squared Error (RMSE) extends MSE by taking the square root, offering an interpretable metric for the average size of prediction errors. The Coefficient of Determination (R) assesses how well the model explains variance in the target variable, with values ranging from 0 (indicating no explanatory power) to 1 (representing perfect prediction). Mean Absolute Error (MAE) calculates the average absolute deviation between actual and predicted values, serving as a straightforward measure of the overall error. Mean Absolute Percentage Error (MAPE) expresses prediction errors as a percentage of actual values, making it useful for comparing models across different scales, though it becomes undefined when actual values are zero. Finally, the Explained Variance Score (EVS) quantifies the proportion of variance captured by the model, providing insights into how well the model explains fluctuations in stock prices.

6 Results and Discussion

This section presents the performance evaluation of the proposed model using various regression metrics. The results are analyzed across three datasets and compared with existing approaches.

6.1 Results

The performance evaluation of FinStock-Net across three datasets of stock indices namely Sensex, Nifty50, and S&P500 demonstrates its high predictive accuracy and robustness. From Fig. 1, it is evident that the R values are exceeding 0.99, which indicate that our proposed model explains nearly all variances in stock index movements. The low MAE and RMSE scores highlight the model's precise forecasting ability, with minimal deviation from actual values.

Table 1. Performance of the proposed FinStock-Net model

Metric	Sensex	Nifty50	S&P500
R	0.9928	0.9933	0.9889
MAE	399.07	118.25	12.3101
MSE	276786.53	24182.97	334.1344
RMSE	526.11	155.51	18.2793
MAPE	0.69%	0.68%	1.18%
EVS	0.9928	0.9933	0.9889

Additionally, MAPE remains under 1%, thereby confirming the model's reliability across different market conditions. The high EVS further reinforces the consistency of FinStock-Net in capturing the underlying patterns in stock market trends. Figure 5 shows the prediction of closing price over Sensex, Nifty50 and S&P500 by FinStock-Net.

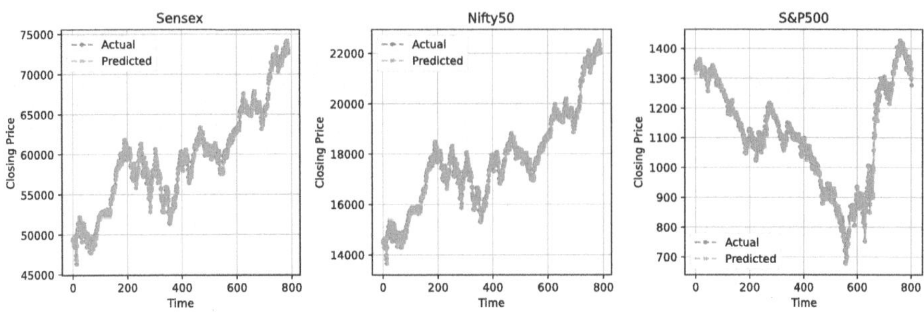

Fig. 5. Actual vs Predicted (by the FinStock-Net) closing prices.

6.2 Discussion

We analyze the performance of our FinStock-Net for closing price prediction on stock data, comparing it against state-of-the-art models. We highlight its effectiveness in capturing market trends, robustness to volatility, and improvements in prediction of closing price. The results are given in Fig. 2.

Das et al. [14] proposed an autoencoder-based approach to minimize errors in stock predictions. Their model does not consider volatility factors. However, FinStock-Net showed better performance, outperforming their method on two datasets namely, Nifty50 and Sensex, during the period from 27th Oct'06 to 27th Nov'22. As show in Fig. 2, FinStock-Net reduced the RMSE by 0.1202 for Nifty50 and 0.0075 for the Sensex. FinStock-Net demonstrated a notable improvement in error reduction for the Nifty50, Sensex, and S&P500 datasets over the 2013–2022 period, achieving reductions of RMSE by 0.5013, 1.8526, and 37.6371, respectively, compared to the RedRVFL method proposed by Bhambhu et al. [15]. Our proposed method enhances financial time series forecasting by effectively capturing sequential patterns through the modeling of long-term dependencies using volatility features.

Table 2. Performance comparison of the FinStock-Net

Work ref.	Method	Dataset	Date range	RMSE	
				Paper Results	**FinStock-Net**
Das et al. [14],2024	Autoencoder based method	Nifty50	27th Oct '06–27th Nov '22	0.1365	0.0163
		Sensex	24th Feb '15–27th Nov '22	0.0522	0.0447
Bhambhu et al. [15],2024	RedRVFL	Nifty50		170.8430	170.3417
		Sensex	2013–2022	578.7460	576.9114
		S&P500		50.1650	12.5279
Singh et al. [16],2024	Arima, Transformer	Nifty50	1st Jan '20–15th Mar '24	171.4000	114.2820
Pareek et al. [17],2024	Wavelet based auto regressive models	Sensex	30th May '10–9th Feb '18	0.0438	0.0094

Table 3. Ablation study of the FinStock-Net

Model	RMSE (Nifty50)	RMSE (S&P500)
LSTM (without VIX)	156.3655	18.2869
BiLSTM (without VIX)	156.0832	18.2844
BiLSTM (with VIX)	156.0050	18.2788
7+1 Day Branch (with VIX)	155.9050	18.2785
15+1 Day Branch (with VIX)	155.8889	18.2787
FinStock-Net	**155.7186**	**18.2775**

Singh et al. [16] proposed ARIMA and Transformer-based models for predicting the closing price of Nifty50 over the period from January 1, 2020, to March 15, 2024. However, their models exhibited limitations in capturing the seasonality patterns of stock prices and generalizing to unseen data. In contrast, FinStock-Net achieved a significant improvement, reducing the RMSE by 57.18 compared to their approach. Pareek et al. [17] proposed wavelet-based soft computing techniques combined with autoregressive models, such as ARIMA and ARMA in the Sensex dataset over the period from May 30, 2010, to February 9, 2018. However, their approach struggled with capturing nonlinear patterns in the data, impacting predictive accuracy. In contrast, FinStock-Net effectively addressed these limitations, achieving superior performance by reducing the RMSE to 0.0094, demonstrating its capability in handling complex, nonlinear stock price dynamics.

As seen in the results Fig. 2, FinStock-Net performs consistently well across existing models; however, error exists. These errors are primarily observed during periods of prolonged market shifts or structural changes, such as regime transitions, where patterns may evolve beyond the model's maximum input window of 15 days. Since FinStock-Net relies on short-, mid-, and long-term patterns capped at 15 days, it may struggle to fully capture the dynamics of events that unfold over longer durations.

7 Ablation Study

We conducted an ablation study on both Nifty50 and S&P500 datasets to evaluate the effectiveness of different components of FinStock-Net, as summarized in Fig. 3. The study examines the impact of incorporating volatility features, particularly the VIX index, and explores the effect of different temporal input configurations. By systematically analyzing these components, we aim to demonstrate their role in improving predictive capability and robustness in stock price forecasting.

- **Baseline Models:** As initial benchmarks, standard LSTM and BiLSTM models are employed without incorporating any volatility features. For the Nifty50 index, LSTM achieves an RMSE of 156.3655, while BiLSTM slightly improves it to 156.0832. Similarly, for the S&P500 index, RMSEs are 18.2869

and 18.2844 for LSTM and BiLSTM, respectively. These results establish a foundational performance level for subsequent model enhancements.
- **Effect of Volatility (VIX):** Introducing the VIX as an additional input feature in the BiLSTM model leads to improved performance, reducing RMSE to 156.0050 for Nifty50 and 18.2788 for S&P500. This underscores the predictive value of market volatility indicators in enhancing the model performance.
- **Temporal Input Branches:** Incorporating multi-scale temporal input branches significantly enhances predictive capability. A (7+1) day input configuration reduces RMSE to 155.9050 for Nifty50 and 18.2785 for S&P500. Extending the input to a (15+1) day configuration further improves performance, lowering RMSE to 155.8889 for Nifty50 and 18.2787 for S&P500.
- **Proposed Model (FinStock-Net):** The final proposed architecture, FinStock-Net, which integrates BiLSTM, VIX-based volatility features, and multi-scale temporal branches, achieves the most substantial performance gains. It records the lowest RMSEs of 155.7186 for Nifty50 and 18.2775 for S&P500, demonstrating its superior ability to capture long-term dependencies and adapt to dynamic market conditions.

8 Conclusion and Future Work

In this study, we proposed **FinStock-Net**, a multi-scale temporal analysis model that enhances closing price prediction by capturing market movements across short-term (1-day), mid-term (7-day), and long-term (15-day) trends. By aligning with real-world decision-making strategies, Finstock-Net outperformed existing methods on volatile stock datasets like Nifty50, Sensex, and S&P500, effectively modeling long-term dependencies and volatility to demonstrate robustness in dynamic market conditions.

To further enhance the robustness of FinStock-Net, future research will focus on integrating additional market factors such as news sentiment analysis, macroeconomic indicators, and alternative financial signals. We also plan to extend the input horizon beyond the current 15-day limit to better capture long-term dependencies, particularly during sustained market shifts and regime changes. Additionally, the applicability of FinStock-Net can be expanded beyond stock market forecasting to other domains involving complex sequential patterns.

Acknowledgments. The authors are grateful for the resource and infrastructural support provided by the Centre for Microprocessor Applications for Training, Education and Research (CMATER) Laboratory of the Computer Science and Engineering Department, Jadavpur University, Kolkata, India.

References

1. Koranga, R.S., Mohan, L., Sharma, S.K., Kumar, S., Koranga, P.: Using LSTM to predict BSE Sensex index. In: 2023 5th International Conference on Advances in Computing. Communication Control and Networking (ICAC3N), pp. 551–553. Greater Noida, India (2023)

2. Gandhmal, D.P., Kumar, K.: Systematic analysis and review of stock market prediction techniques. Comput. Sci. Rev. **34**, 100190 (2019)
3. Kumar, A., Garg, R., Anand, A., Sarkar, R.: An improved salp swarm algorithm based on adaptive β-hill climbing for stock market prediction. In: Thampi, S.M., Piramuthu, S., Li, K.-C., Berretti, S., Wozniak, M., Singh, D. (eds.) Machine Learning and Metaheuristics Algorithms, and Applications, pp. 107–121. Springer Singapore, Singapore (2021)
4. Sezer, O.B., Gudelek, M.U., Ozbayoglu, A.M.: Financial time series forecasting with deep learning: A systematic literature review: 2005–2019. Appl. Soft Comput. **90**, 106103 (2020)
5. Zhang, L., Wang, F., Xu, B., Chi, W., Wang, Q., Sun, T.: Prediction of stock prices based on LM-BP neural network and the estimation of overfitting point by RDCI. Neural Comput. Appl. **30**, 1425–1444 (2018)
6. Usmani, M., Adil, S.H., Raza, K., Ali, S.S.A.: Stock market prediction using machine learning techniques. In: 2016 3rd International Conference on Computer and Information Sciences (ICCOINS), pp. 322–327 (2016)
7. Chatfield, C., Xing, H.: The Analysis of Time Series: An Introduction with R. CRC Press, Boca Raton (2019)
8. Gocheva-Ilieva, S.G., Voynikova, D.S., Stoimenova, M.P., Ivanov, A.V., Iliev, I.P.: Regression trees modeling of time series for air pollution analysis and forecasting. Neural Comput. Appl. **31**, 9023–9039 (2019)
9. Kim, K.j., Lee, W.B.: Stock market prediction using artificial neural networks with optimal feature transformation. Neural Comput. Appl. **13**, 255–260 (2004)
10. Hochreiter, S., Schmidhuber, J.: Long short-term memory. Neural Comput. **9**(8), 1735–1780 (1997)
11. Moghar, A., Hamiche, M.: Stock market prediction using LSTM recurrent neural network. Procedia Comput. Sci. **170**, 1168–1173 (2020)
12. Chatterjee, B., Acharya, S., Bhattacharyya, T., Mirjalili, S., Sarkar, R.: Stock market prediction using altruistic dragonfly algorithm. PLoS ONE **18**(4), e0282002 (2023)
13. Yetis, Y., Kaplan, H., Jamshidi, M.: Stock market prediction by using artificial neural network. In: 2014 World Automation Congress (WAC), pp. 718–722 (2014)
14. Das, S.R., Mishra, D., Lenka, A., Shaw, K.: Deepstock forecast: Unveiling market movements through advanced deep learning models. In: 2024 International Conference on Emerging Systems and Intelligent Computing (ESIC), pp. 284–289 (2024)
15. Bhambu, A., Gao, R., Suganthan, P.N.: Recurrent ensemble random vector functional link neural network for financial time series forecasting. Expert Syst. Appl. **161**, 111759 (2024)
16. Singh, A., Shah, R., Oza, Y., Shah, D., Nanade, A., Kolhe, A.: Closing price prediction for the NIFTY50 index: A univariate analysis using machine learning and deep learning techniques. In: 2024 First International Conference on Software. Systems and Information Technology (SSITCON), pp. 1–7. Tumkur, India (2024)
17. R, B.K., A, D., Pareek, P., Sathe, M.A., Tiwari, M., Manoharan, G.: Application of soft computing techniques for predictive analytics in financial markets. In: 2023 6th International Conference on Contemporary Computing and Informatics (IC3I), pp. 1756–1760. Gautam Buddha Nagar, India (2023)

Forecasting Market Turbulence: A Multi-model Study Using GARCH, Random Forest, and LSTM in the Indian Stock Market

J. Shashidhar Yadav[1](✉), Shrinivas Kulkarni[1], B. S. Rajath[1], S. V. Pradeep Kumar[1], N. Priyadarshini[2], and H. M. Devananda[3]

[1] School of Business and Management, Christ University, Bengaluru, Karnataka, India
shashidhar.yadav@christuniversity.in

[2] Post Graduate Department of Business Administration, Seshadripuram College, Bengaluru, Karnataka, India

[3] Department of Management, Adichunchanagiri Institute of Technology, Chikkamagaluru, Karnataka, India

Abstract. The dynamic and unpredictable nature of the Indian stock market presents significant challenges in forecasting return behavior and managing financial risk. This study explores market turbulence through a comparative analysis of three distinct modeling approaches: the Generalized Autoregressive Conditional Heteroskedasticity (GARCH) model, Random Forest, and Long Short-Term Memory (LSTM) networks. By analyzing historical return data from Indian Nifty indices, the research captures both linear dependencies and complex nonlinear patterns associated with market volatility. The results highlight the GARCH model's strength in modeling conditional volatility, while the machine learning and deep learning techniques—Random Forest and LSTM—exhibit enhanced predictive power in capturing intricate fluctuations in stock returns. The findings suggest that integrating traditional econometric methods with data-driven approaches offers a more comprehensive and accurate understanding of market dynamics. This multi-model framework is valuable for investors, financial analysts, and policymakers aiming to anticipate and navigate periods of heightened market uncertainty.

Keywords: Indian stock market · Market volatility · GARCH · Random forest · Return prediction

1 Introduction

Financial markets, irrespective of geography, operate under persistent uncertainty shaped by economic dynamics, policy decisions, investor psychology, and global interlinkages [1, 2]. Episodes of market turbulence - characterized by abrupt spikes in volatility and rapid price movements - are no longer anomalies but recurrent phenomena in modern finance. Events such as the global financial crisis, the economic disruptions caused by the COVID-19 pandemic, and the more recent geopolitical instabilities have highlighted the critical need for proactive risk assessment frameworks [3, 4]. Accurate forecasting

K. Chandra Mondal et al. (Eds.): CICBA 2025, CCIS 2863, pp. 334–347, 2026.
https://doi.org/10.1007/978-3-032-17184-9_25

of such volatility episodes is increasingly being viewed as essential for prudent portfolio management, regulatory oversight, and macroeconomic stability. Traditional volatility modeling has long relied on econometric techniques, with the generalized autoregressive conditional heteroskedasticity (GARCH) model serving as a foundational framework for capturing time-varying volatility in asset returns [5].

While statistically robust, these models often assume linearity and fixed structural patterns, which limit their responsiveness to the evolving complexities of financial markets [6, 7]. The advent of machine learning and deep learning techniques has introduced new possibilities for identifying hidden, nonlinear interactions in financial time series, offering a more adaptive and data-driven approach to forecasting [8]. The Indian stock market represents a compelling study area. As one of the largest and fastest-growing emerging economies, India's capital markets have experienced increasing foreign participation, rapid digitization, and frequent volatility induced by domestic and international factors [9, 10]. The interplay of policy reforms, macroeconomic indicators, and global shocks frequently influence market behaviour, underscoring the need for sophisticated predictive tools.

This study seeks to evaluate and compare the forecasting efficacy of three distinct modelling approaches - GARCH, Random Forest, and Long Short-Term Memory (LSTM) - in capturing return behavior and predicting market turbulence in the Indian stock market. By integrating econometric rigor with algorithmic intelligence, this research contributes to the growing discourse on volatility modeling in emerging market economies, with implications for investors, risk managers, and policy architects.

2 Literature Review

Forecasting stock market volatility is vital for investors, particularly in emerging markets like India. Traditional models like GARCH and modern techniques such as LSTM and Random Forest offer insights into market dynamics. Recent studies highlight their role in improving prediction accuracy, risk management, and identifying trends and bubbles.

Volatility forecasting across prominent emerging markets, including India, demonstrated the robustness of the GARCH(1, 1) model, supported by minimal evidence of leverage effects [7, 11]. The Indian equity market exhibited notable positive skewness, indicating favorable conditions for diversification and hedging strategies [12–14]. A comprehensive four-decade study employing GARCH models with Normal and Student's-t distributions provided critical insights into return behaviors and volatility structures in India's financial landscape [13–16].Recent advancements in volatility modeling have led to the development of robust techniques for detecting structural breaks in conditional variance, particularly within ARCH and stochastic volatility frameworks. When applied to stock and foreign exchange markets, these methodologies uncovered critical shifts during major financial events, including the Asian and Russian crises, emphasizing their profound influence on asset return behavior [17, 18]. In parallel, empirical investigations into high-frequency Nifty data employed multifractal detrended fluctuation analysis and the regularized Hurst exponent to uncover preliminary indicators of speculative bubbles and collective market behavior, offering practical tools for recognizing volatility-driven distortions [10, 19, 20].

Complementary studies utilized the PSY approach on NIFTY 500 datasets, integrating advanced machine learning techniques - namely Random Forest, Gradient Boosting, and Artificial Neural Networks - for real-time detection of market bubbles [21, 22]. Furthermore, a novel hybrid framework combining Long Short-Term Memory (LSTM) networks with the Crow Search Algorithm (CSLSTM) demonstrated improved predictive accuracy and profitability by optimizing technical and decomposed signal features [23, 24]. LSTM networks effectively capture sequential dependencies in time-series forecasting, while Random Forests excel in managing high-dimensional, complex datasets. A hybrid model combining both improves strategic analytics accuracy [25, 26]. Additionally, integrating principal component analysis (PCA) with machine learning techniques, such as Support Vector Classifiers and Random Forests, enhances Nifty 50 index trend prediction by refining technical indicators into efficient trend signals, demonstrating superior performance in financial forecasting [27–29].

LSTM architectures have shown notable effectiveness in modeling NIFTY 50 stock behavior, outperforming RNN and CNN models, particularly when supported by targeted feature selection and parameter optimization [9]. Complementary research demonstrates that combining PCA with machine learning techniques, including Random Forest and LSTM, enhances trend and volatility prediction accuracy [30]. Furthermore, ensemble-based models such as XGBoost, Random Forest, and LSTM improve the reliability of financial forecasting, underscoring the transformative role of AI in investment strategy and portfolio decision-making [8].

Despite extensive use of individual models for forecasting stock market volatility, limited research integrates traditional econometric techniques with advanced deep learning models within the Indian market context. This gap is particularly evident during periods of market stress, where existing approaches often fail to adequately capture complex non-linearities and sudden volatility surges.

3 Research Methodology

This study adopts a robust multi-model approach to forecast volatility in the Indian stock market, with a specific focus on the NIFTY index. The models employed include GARCH(1,1), Random Forest, and Long Short-Term Memory (LSTM) networks - each selected for their respective strengths in capturing the linear and nonlinear dynamics of financial time series. Historical data comprising daily closing prices of the NIFTY index were sourced from the National Stock Exchange (NSE) for the period January 2000 to December 2023. After initial inspection, the raw price series was converted into logarithmic returns to standardize the data and facilitate percentage-based analysis. Prior to modeling, the dataset underwent a preprocessing phase that involved checking for missing values, filtering out anomalies, and normalizing the input features where necessary.

Descriptive statistics were computed to summarize the data, including measures of central tendency and dispersion. To assess the distributional properties of returns, a combination of visual plots (such as Q-Q plots) and statistical tests - namely Jarque-Bera, Kolmogorov-Smirnov, Anderson-Darling, and D'Agostino's K-squared - were applied. These tests confirmed non-normality in return distributions, justifying the application of non-parametric and machine learning methods. Stationarity was verified using the Augmented Dickey-Fuller (ADF) and KPSS tests, both of which supported the presence of stationarity, making the data suitable for time-series modeling. Additionally, the ARCH test was used to detect volatility clustering, a known characteristic of financial return series. The autocorrelation (ACF) and partial autocorrelation (PACF) functions, along with the Hurst exponent, were employed to evaluate memory effects and mean-reverting tendencies.

The GARCH(1, 1) model was configured to estimate time-varying volatility, incorporating lagged squared residuals and past variances in the conditional variance equation. Model parameters were estimated via maximum likelihood estimation (MLE), and diagnostic checks were performed using AIC, BIC, and residual analysis. For the Random Forest model, a range of lagged return values and trading volume data were used as input features. An 80:20 train-test split was implemented, and hyperparameters such as the number of estimators (set at 100) and maximum tree depth were optimized through grid search with five-fold cross-validation. Feature importance was extracted post-training to interpret variable relevance.

The LSTM model was designed using a sequence-based architecture. It consisted of two LSTM layers, each containing 50 units, followed by a dropout layer with a rate of 0.2 to mitigate overfitting. The input data was structured into 30-day rolling windows to preserve temporal dependencies. The model was trained for 100 epochs using the Adam optimizer, with early stopping applied based on validation loss to improve generalization. The loss function used was Mean Squared Error (MSE), and the dataset was divided into training (70%), validation (15%), and testing (15%) sets to ensure balanced model evaluation.

Model performance was measured using multiple evaluation criteria. For the Random Forest and LSTM models, predictive accuracy was assessed through Mean Absolute Error (MAE), Root Mean Squared Error (RMSE), and R-squared (R2). In the case of GARCH, model fit was evaluated using Akaike and Bayesian Information Criteria, along with checks on residual heteroscedasticity. This multi-layered methodology ensures the validity, reliability, and robustness of the comparative analysis, offering comprehensive insights into volatility behavior and forecasting efficacy in the Indian equity market.

4 Results and Discussion

This study evaluates a dataset consisting of 6,028 observations, covering both Price and Log Return variables. The Price series exhibits wide variability, with an average value of 7,981.82 and a standard deviation of 6,130.01. Prices range from a low of 854.20 to a high of 26,216.05. The difference between the mean and median values of 5,913.65 indicates a positively skewed distribution, suggesting a concentration of lower prices with a few high-value outliers. In contrast, the Log Return series displays closer alignment between central tendency measures, with a mean of 0.048% and a median near 0.001%. Despite this, a standard deviation of 0.014 and extreme values between -0.139 and 0.1633 highlight significant return volatility. Analysis of the interquartile range - from -0.006 to 0.007 - implies minimal skewness in return distribution. To ensure statistical robustness, the study applies multiple significance levels, including 15%, 10%, 5%, 2.5%, and 1%.

Table 1. Normality tests results

Test name	Statistic	p-value	Additional metrics	Critical values (α levels)
Jarque-Bera	37382.80	0	–	–
D'Agostino	1400.39	8.13e-305 (≈0.0)	–	–
Kolmogorov-Smirnov	0.478	0	Location: 0.0385	–
			Sign: 1	
Anderson-Darling	91.3549	-	Fit Params:	15%: 0.576
			loc = 0.00048	10%: 0.656
			scale = 0.0135	5%: 0.786
				2.5%: 0.917
				1%: 1.091

Source: Authors compilation

Tables 1, 2 and Figs. 1, 2 illustrate a comprehensive battery of normality tests, which decisively reject the null hypothesis of a normal distribution in the return series. The Jarque-Bera test reports a markedly high statistic of 37,382.80 with an effectively zero p-value, pointing to substantial departures from normality due to excess skewness and kurtosis. This observation is supported by D'Agostino's K2 test, which yields a statistic of 1,400.39 ($p < 0.0001$), further indicating significant asymmetry and tail behavior. The Kolmogorov-Smirnov test also confirms this deviation, with test statistics 0.478 and a zero p-value. A location shift of 0.0385 reinforces the presence of systematic divergence from a normal distribution. Moreover, the Anderson-Darling test returns a statistic of 91.3549, exceeding all critical values at standard significance levels. These consistent results across multiple tests strongly validate non-Gaussian features and emphasize the need for alternative modeling strategies, including non-parametric techniques or data transformation.

Table 2 specifies the stationarity assessments and provides compelling evidence that the return series under analysis is strongly stationary. The Augmented Dickey-Fuller (ADF) test returned a significantly negative test statistic of -16.8582, accompanied by an extremely low p-value ($1.105 \times 10^{-}2^{9}$), decisively rejecting the null hypothesis of a unit root. This result indicates that the series does not follow a random walk and exhibits mean-reverting behavior. Complementing this, the KPSS (Kwiatkowski – Phillips - Schmidt - Shin) test yielded a statistic of 0.0424 with a p-value of 0.1 - well above the conventional 5% significance threshold. Since the KPSS test assumes stationarity as the null hypothesis, the inability to reject it further reinforces the presence of stationarity in the series. Taken together, the findings from both the ADF and KPSS tests confirm that the series is stationary in its current form, eliminating the need for additional differencing or transformations. This provides a reliable foundation for subsequent time series modeling and inference.

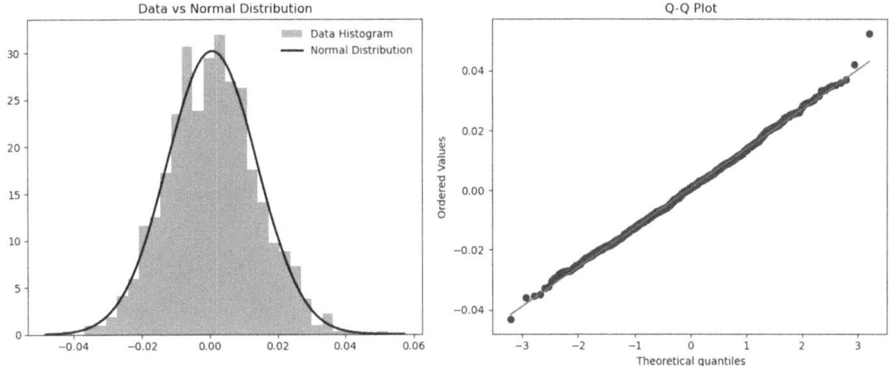

Fig. 1. Normality assessment of NIFTY returns showing significant deviation from Gaussian distribution (Jarque-Bera $p < 0.001$)

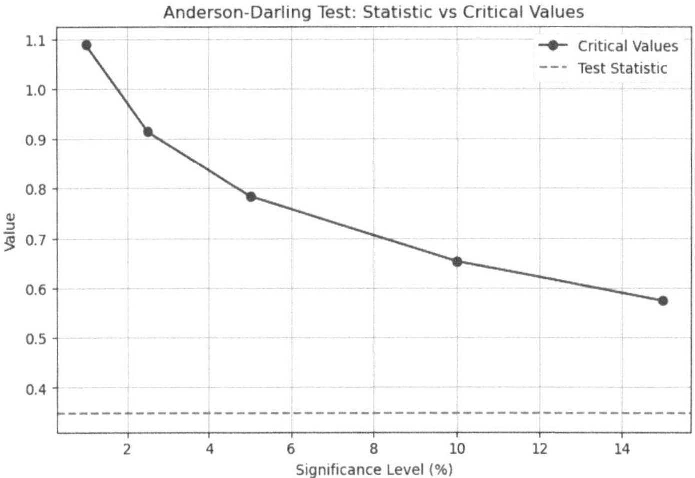

Fig. 2. Anderson-Darling test of NIFTY returns showing non-normal distribution (test statistic = 91.35, exceeding all critical values at $p < 0.001$).

Table 2. Stationarity tests

Test	Statistic	p-value	Conclusion ($\alpha = 0.05$)
ADF	−16.8582	1.105e-29 (≈0.0)	Reject H0 (Stationary)
KPSS	0.0424	0.1	Fail to reject H0 (Stationary)

Source: Authors Compilation

Autocorrelation Structure and Hurst Exponent Interpretation

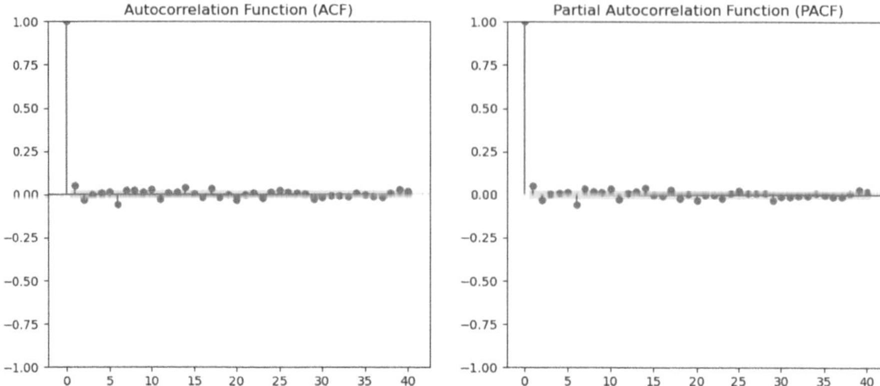

Fig. 3. ACF and PACF of NIFTY log returns with 95% confidence bounds.

The Fig. 3 specifies autocorrelation (ACF) and partial autocorrelation (PACF) functions reveal a significant correlation at the first lag, which rapidly diminishes in subsequent lags. This pattern is indicative of short-lived dependencies in the log return series, suggesting that recent past values exert only minimal influence on future movements. Such behavior is consistent with the weak-form efficiency hypothesis, where price changes are largely unpredictable beyond the immediate past. These observations support the appropriateness of employing time series models such as ARMA or GARCH, as well as advanced machine learning frameworks, to effectively capture volatility clustering and transient dependencies.

The Hurst exponent analysis yields a value of $H = 0.314$, indicating anti-persistent, mean-reverting dynamics in the NIFTY index's log returns. Since $H < 0.5$, this behavior reflects a tendency for deviations to reverse rather than persist, diminishing the effectiveness of momentum-based strategies while favoring those targeting price reversals. This characteristic reveals minor inefficiencies in the market. It supports adopting models attuned to volatility changes, such as GARCH-type specifications, for enhanced risk assessment and tactical asset management. Additionally, the ARCH LM test reports a notably high statistic of 778.36, with a minuscule p-value of $9.27 \times 10^{-}1^{6}1$, strongly rejecting the null hypothesis of homoscedasticity. This confirms the presence of conditional heteroscedasticity, reflected in volatility clustering—a hallmark of financial time series. Such findings expose the limitations of constant-variance models and reinforce the appropriateness of GARCH-family models for capturing time-varying volatility and producing more accurate financial forecasts.

Table 3 specifies a series of Granger causality tests that were performed to investigate the predictive influence of lagged values of one variable on another. Across various lag structures, the SSR-based F-tests yielded consistently low F-statistics, with corresponding p-values well above conventional significance thresholds ($p > 0.05$). These results indicate insufficient evidence to reject the null hypothesis that the independent variable does not cause the dependent variable. Similarly, both the Chi-Square (Wald) and Likelihood Ratio versions of the test corroborated this finding, as reflected in their low-test statistics and high p-values. The parameter-level F-tests also failed to identify

Table 3. Granger causality test

Lags	1	2	3	4	5
SSR Based F-Test (F-stat)	0.0001	0.0969	0.8405	0.6455	0.7415
p-value	0.9935	0.9076	0.4715	0.63	0.5923
df_denom	6017	6014	6011	6008	6005
df_num	1	2	3	4	5
SSR Based Chi2-Test (Chi2-stat)	0.0001	0.194	2.5243	2.5858	3.7144
Chi2 p-value	0.9935	0.9076	0.4709	0.6293	0.5912
df	1	2	3	4	5
Likelihood Ratio Test (Chi2-stat)	0.0001	0.194	2.5238	2.5853	3.7132
Likelihood p-value	0.9935	0.9076	0.471	0.6294	0.5914
Likelihood df	1	2	3	4	5
Parameter F-Test (F-stat)	0.0001	0.0969	0.8405	0.6455	0.7415
Parameter p-value	0.9935	0.9076	0.4715	0.63	0.5923
Parameter df_denom	6017	6014	6011	6008	6005
Parameter df_num	1	2	3	4	5

Source: Authors Compilation

statistically significant lagged effects. These outcomes suggest that the lagged values of the examined variable do not contribute meaningfully to predicting future values of the target variable. This lack of causality underscores the potential need to explore alternative predictors or non-linear models to enhance forecasting accuracy in time series applications.

Table 4. GARCH mean model

	mu
coef	0.0417
std err	2.181e-04
t	190.994
$P > \lvert t \rvert$	0.000
95.0% Conf. Int	[4.122e-02,4.208e-02]

Source: Authors Compilation

The Tables 4 and 5 signifies GARCH(1, 1) estimation results offer valuable insights into the temporal structure of volatility within financial markets. The mean return (μ) is computed at 0.0417, accompanied by a low standard error, suggesting a consistent and statistically meaningful average return over time. Within the volatility equation,

Table 5. Volatility model

	coef	std err	t	P > |t|	95.0% Conf. Int
omega	3.5632e-06	7.070e-06	0.504	0.614	[-1.029e-05,1.742e-05]
alpha[1]	0.1219	2.973e-02	4.100	4.133e-05	[6.363e-02, 0.180]
beta[1]	0.8579	4.189e-02	20.478	3.370e-93	[0.776, 0.940]

Source: Authors Compilation

the ARCH term ($\alpha_1 = 0.1219$) reflects a notable impact of recent market shocks on current volatility levels, as evidenced by its high statistical significance ($p < 0.0001$). The GARCH component ($\beta_1 = 0.8579$) captures the persistence of volatility, indicating that periods of high or low volatility tend to continue, consistent with observed clustering in financial returns. The sum of the conditional variance parameters ($\alpha_1 + \beta_1 \approx 0.98$) suggests that the conditional variance is highly persistent, characteristic of long-memory processes in financial time series. The constant term (ω), which represents long-run variance, appears statistically insignificant, implying that external market innovations exert a more substantial influence on volatility than a stable base level of risk. This emphasizes the responsive nature of market volatility to shocks, underscoring the relevance of adaptive models in dynamic market conditions. Overall, these findings corroborate typical features of financial time series, including volatility clustering and shock propagation, reinforcing the suitability of the GARCH(1,1) model for risk modelling, derivative pricing, and the development of trading and hedging strategies.

The Fig. 4 Random Forest tree visualization effectively complements the research focus on volatility dynamics and herding tendencies within the NIFTY index. The model provides a hierarchical representation of decision-making processes that influence market behavior by leveraging features such as price levels, trading volume, and logarithmic returns. This structure facilitates the identification of key predictors that contribute to market fluctuations and periods of instability. The model's decision paths, illustrated through individual trees, capture complex nonlinear interactions inherent in financial time series data. Nodes within the tree are evaluated using the Gini index, which quantifies classification purity and helps discern stable and turbulent market phases. Such differentiation is critical in identifying herding patterns and formulating proactive risk management strategies.

Moreover, integrating Random Forest outputs with complementary approaches - such as GARCH for volatility modeling and LSTM for sequence learning - broadens the analytical scope. This hybrid modeling framework enhances the predictive accuracy and interpretability of market regimes. Insights derived from the Random Forest model improve the detection of volatility clustering and enrich our understanding of investor sentiment, contributing to more informed portfolio allocation and strategic trading decisions.

The Long Short-Term Memory (LSTM) model specified in Fig. 5 provides a robust framework for uncovering temporal structures in financial time series, especially for tasks involving volatility forecasting and identifying herding behavior. The architecture comprises two stacked LSTM layers, a dropout regularization mechanism, and a fully

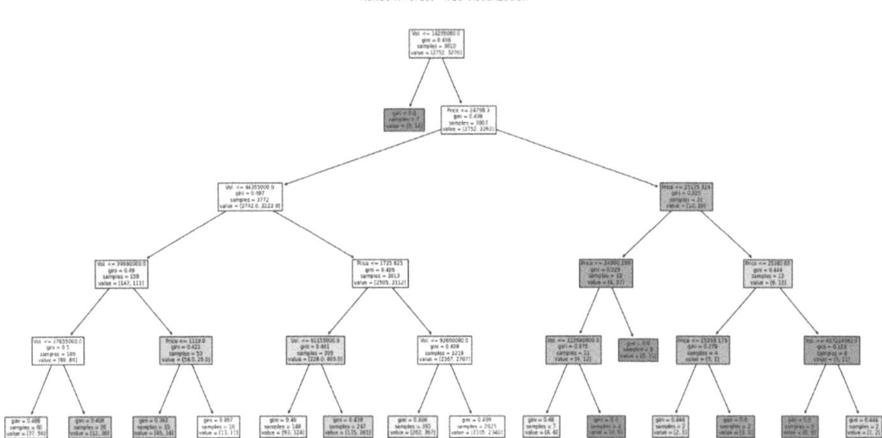

Fig. 4. Random Forest architecture for NIFTY volatility prediction, showing feature importance and decision pathways.

connected dense output layer. This configuration enables the model to learn and abstract complex patterns inherent in dynamic financial data sequentially. In the initial LSTM layer, sequences composed of core financial variables - namely, price and trading volume - are processed to extract short-term temporal dependencies, with each timestep encoded into a latent space of 50 features.

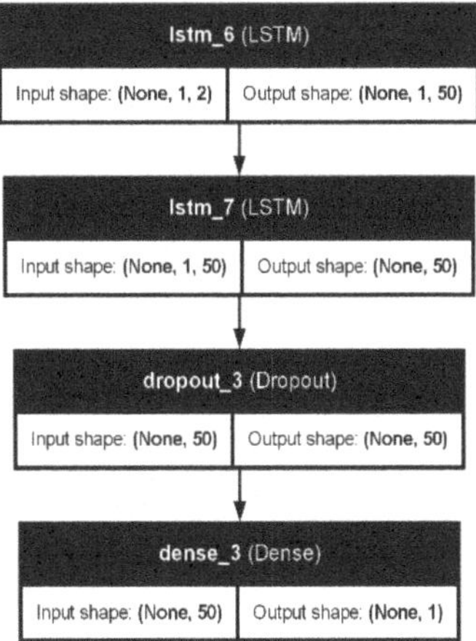

Fig. 5. Architecture of the LSTM

These representations are then passed to the subsequent LSTM layer, which consolidates the temporal information across the entire sequence into a fixed-length vector, enhancing the model's ability to capture longer-term dependencies. To address the risk of overfitting, a dropout layer is introduced, selectively omitting neurons during training and thus improving generalization to unseen data.The final dense layer maps the compressed temporal features to the output space, where key financial indicators such as volatility surges or herding signals are predicted. This structure allows the LSTM model to effectively model volatility clustering and detect emergent patterns of investor convergence - features commonly associated with financial market inefficiencies. Beyond capturing sequential dependencies, integrating deep learning into financial analysis expands the scope for predictive modeling and early anomaly detection. Future enhancements could incorporate macroeconomic variables, sentiment metrics, or alternative datasets to enrich the model's feature space and further elevate forecasting accuracy in complex financial environments.

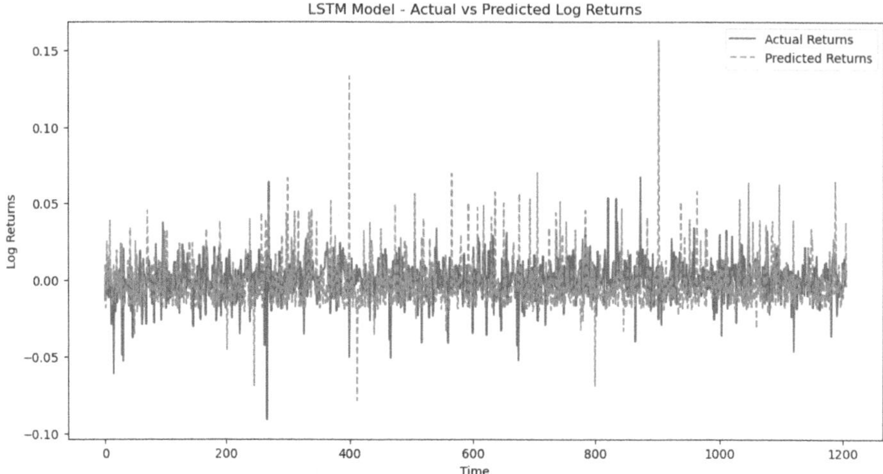

Fig. 6. LSTM model – actual vs predicted log returns

While the LSTM architecture demonstrates commendable proficiency in recognizing sequential patterns, its efficacy diminishes in the presence of nonlinear dynamics and regime shifts. Figure 6 highlights the necessity of augmenting deep learning models with complementary mechanisms, such as GARCH-LSTM hybrids or attention mechanisms, to enhance adaptability to market irregularities. Furthermore, enriching the input space with macroeconomic variables and sentiment-driven indicators may improve the model's responsiveness to latent drivers of return variation. The findings advocate for an integrative modeling approach that synergizes statistical techniques and machine learning algorithms, fostering improved predictive accuracy in complex, noise-prone financial environments.

5 Conclusion

The analysis of price and return dynamics provides meaningful insights into the structure and behavior of financial markets. The observed price series displays substantial variability along with a discernible upward trajectory, indicative of long-term growth and structural shifts. In contrast, the return series oscillates around a relatively stable mean, suggesting that although price levels evolve significantly, the incremental changes (returns) tend to exhibit mean stability over time. Statistical assessments reveal that the return distribution deviates from normality, characterized by outliers and fat tails - features commonly associated with market anomalies and sudden economic events. Nonetheless, stationarity tests affirm that the return series retains a stable statistical profile over time, validating its suitability for predictive modeling in time series frameworks. The data further displays characteristics of mean reversion and limited memory, where historical values exert influence over short horizons but dissipate quickly. Additionally, patterns of volatility clustering—where intervals of relative calm follow periods of elevated risk - underscore the need for models that can accommodate time-varying volatility. Collectively, these findings underscore the complex but structured nature of financial return series. They provide a foundation for the application of advanced econometric and machine learning models aimed at forecasting, risk quantification, and the development of adaptive investment strategies.

References

1. Masih, R., Masih, A.M.: Long and short term dynamic causal transmission amongst international stock markets. J. Int. Money Financ. **20**(4), 563–587 (2001)
2. Magner, N.S., Lavin, J.F., Valle, M.A., Hardy, N.: The volatility forecasting power of financial network analysis. Complexity (2020), https://doi.org/10.1155/2020/7051402
3. Magubane, K.: The stability of the financial cycle: insights from a markov switching regression in South Africa. J. Risk Financ. Manag. **18**(2) (2025), https://doi.org/10.3390/jrfm18020076
4. Qamruzzaman, M.: Does environmental degradation-led remittances flow? nexus between environmental degradation, uncertainty, financial inclusion and remittances inflows in India and China. Int. J. Energy Econ. Policy **13**(2), 9–26 (2023). https://doi.org/10.32479/ijeep.13995
5. Bauwens, L., Laurent, S., Rombouts, J.V K.:"Multivariate GARCH models: A survey (2006). https://doi.org/10.1002/jae.842
6. Mahajan, V., Thakan, S., Malik, A.: Modeling and Forecasting the Volatility of NIFTY 50 Using GARCH and RNN Models (2022), https://doi.org/10.3390/economies
7. Lim, D.T., Goh, K.W., Sim, Y.W., Mokhtar, K., Thinagar, S.: Estimation of stock market index volatility using the GARCH model: causality between stock indices. Asian Econ. Financ. Rev. **13**(3), 162–179 (2023). https://doi.org/10.55493/5002.v13i3.4738
8. Sonkavde, G., Dharrao, D.S., Bongale, A.M., Deokate, S.T., Doreswamy, D., Bhat, S.K.: Forecasting Stock Market Prices Using Machine Learning and Deep Learning Models: A Systematic Review, Performance Analysis and Discussion of Implications. Multidisciplinary Digital Publishing Institute (MDPI) (2023). https://doi.org/10.3390/ijfs11030094
9. Fathali, Z., Kodia, Z., Ben Said, L.: Stock market prediction of NIFTY 50 index applying machine learning techniques. Appl. Artif. Intell. **36**(1) (2022), https://doi.org/10.1080/08839514.2022.2111134
10. Ghosh, B., Kozarevic, E.: Multifractal analysis of volatility for detection of herding and bubble: evidence from CNX Nifty HFT (2019), LLC CPC Business Perspectives. https://doi.org/10.21511/imfi.16(3).2019.17
11. Sharma, S., Aggarwal, V., Yadav, M.P.: Comparison of linear and non-linear GARCH models for forecasting volatility of select emerging countries. J. Adv. Manag. Res. **18**(4), 526–547 (2021). https://doi.org/10.1108/JAMR-07-2020-0152

12. Malhotra, D., Singh, R., Ramani, L.: Navigating market volatility: risk and return insights from Indian mutual funds. Cogent Econ. Financ. **12**(1) (2024), https://doi.org/10.1080/23322039.2024.2431535
13. Kumar, S.: Does skewness help in better investment decision making? Int. J. Emerg. Mark. **13**(5), 824–836 (2018). https://doi.org/10.1108/IJoEM-04-2017-0111
14. Badrinath, S.G., Chatterjee, S.: On Measuring Skewness and Elongation in Common Stock Return Distributions: The Case of the Market Index (1988). [Online]. Available: https://www.jstor.org/stable/2352791
15. Varughese, A., Mathew, T.: Asymmetric Volatility of the Indian Stock Market and Foreign Portfolio Investments : An Empirical Study
16. Premarathna, N., Godfrey, A.J.R., Govindaraju, K.: Decomposition of stock market trade-offs using Shewhart methodology. Int. J. Qual. Reliab. Manag. **33**(9), 1311–1331 (2016). https://doi.org/10.1108/IJQRM-08-2014-0128
17. Andreou, E., Ghysels, E.: Structural Breaks in Financial Time Series. [Online]. Available: http://ssrn.com/abstract=935971
18. Baillie, R.T., Morana, C.: Department of Economics Modeling Long Memory and Structural Breaks in Conditional Modeling Long Memory and Structural Breaks in Conditional Variances: an Adaptive FIGARCH Approach (2007)
19. Khan, T., Suresh, G.: Do all shocks produce embedded herding and bubble? An empirical observation of the Indian stock market. Investment Manag. Financ. Innov. **19**(3), 346–359 (2022). https://doi.org/10.21511/imfi.19(3).2022.29
20. Katoch, R., Batra, S.: Co-movement between NIFTY Spot and futures indices: a time-frequency analysis using wavelet. Studies in Microeconomics (2023). https://doi.org/10.1177/23210222231194860
21. Phillips, P.C.B., Shi, S.-P., P.C.B.: Testing for Multiple Bubbles (2011). [Online]. Available: https://ink.library.smu.edu.sg/soe_research/1302
22. Tariq, Z. et al.: A systematic review of data science and machine learning applications to the oil and gas industry. Springer Science and Business Media Deutschland GmbH (2021). https://doi.org/10.1007/s13202-021-01302-2
23. Jiang, C.L., Tsai, Y.K., Shao, Z.E., Lee, S.H., Hsueh, C.C., Huang, K.W.: Hybrid crow search algorithm–LSTM system for enhanced stock price forecasting. Appl. Sci. (Switzerland) **14**(23) (2024), https://doi.org/10.3390/app142311380
24. Huang, K.-W., Shao, Z.-E., Lee, S.-H., Hsueh, C.-C. : Memetic Crow Search Algorithm and Long Short-Term Memory Network Forecasting System for Stock Prices. [Online]. Available: https://ssrn.com/abstract=4204323
25. Kalusivalingam, K., Sharma, A., Patel, N., Singh, V.: Enhancing Predictive Business Analytics with Deep Learning and Ensemble Methods: A Comparative Study of LSTM Networks and Random Forest Algorithms
26. Punia, S., Nikolopoulos, K., Singh, S.P., Madaan, J.K., Litsiou, K.: Deep learning with long short-term memory networks and random forests for demand forecasting in multi-channel retail. Int. J. Prod. Res. **58**(16), 4964–4979 (2020). https://doi.org/10.1080/00207543.2020.1735666
27. Sarıkoç, M., Celik, M.: PCA-ICA-LSTM: a hybrid deep learning model based on dimension reduction methods to predict S&P 500 index price. Comput. Econ. (2024). https://doi.org/10.1007/s10614-024-10629-x
28. Manjunath, C., Marimuthu, B., Ghosh, B.: Analysis of Nifty 50 index stock market trends using hybrid machine learning model in quantum finance. Int. J. Electr. Comput. Eng. **13**(3), 3549–3560 (2023). https://doi.org/10.11591/ijece.v13i3.pp3549-3560
29. Shashidhar, Y.J., Sujay, C., Saiprasad, D., Manjunatha, G., Druvakumar, M., Jagadeesha, G.T.: Delving into the bubble detection of specific NSE sector indices. In: Studies in Systems,

Decision and Control, vol. 535, Springer Science and Business Media Deutschland GmbH, pp. 95–104 (2024). https://doi.org/10.1007/978-3-031-63569-4_9
30. Liu, X., Salem, S., Bian, L., Seong, J.T., Alshanbari, H.M.: Application of machine learning algorithms in the domain of financial engineering. Alex. Eng. J. **95**, 94–100 (2024). https://doi.org/10.1016/j.aej.2024.03.058

Efficient Audio CODEC for IoT Devices - Leveraging GANs, Adaptive Quantization and Arithmetic Coding

Bibek Bikash Roy[1], Asish Debnath[1], Sushovan Das[2], and Uttam Kr. Mondal[1](✉)

[1] Department of Computer Science, Vidyasagar University, Midnapore, West Bengal, India
uttam_ku_82@yahoo.co.in

[2] Department of CSE, College of Engineering and Managemnet Kolaghat, Midnapore, West Bengal, India

Abstract. In light of the significant surge in audio data production, encompassing various types such as multimedia data, environmental samples, sensor networks, audiovisual content, **Internet of Things (IoT) applications**, and cloud data, efficient signal compression techniques have gained prominence. This paper presents an audio compression system utilizing a generative adversarial network (GAN). The encoder generates a latent vector with reduced dimensionality by processing the audio signal into the frequency domain and transforming it into a Mel-spectrogram. The generator network, which is trained to create high-quality signals, then utilizes this latent vector to minimize the loss function. Through iterative back-propagation and optimization methods, dynamic non-uniformly quantized optimal latent vectors are derived, enhancing the quantization of the compressed signal. Experimental results indicate that this algorithm outperforms traditional deep learning and classical audio compression techniques, showcasing higher reconstruction fidelity, increased compression rates, and enhanced audio quality, particularly in **resource-constrained IoT environments.**

Keywords: Generative Adversarial Network · Generative model · Audio codec · Compression rate · Arithmetic encoding

1 Introduction

The initiation of the big data paradigm has precipitated a significant upsurge in the volume of audio data, posing formidable challenges related to its transmission and storage. This surge is further intensified by the proliferation of Internet of Things (IoT) devices, which continuously generate audio streams from smart environments, wearable sensors, and embedded acoustic monitoring systems. In this context, audio data compression has emerged as an indispensable solution to address these issues. Audio compression techniques may be generally classified into two categories [2]: lossy and lossless compression. Lossless compression ensures the preservation of audio quality by allowing the compressed file to be restored to its original state without any data loss,

K. Chandra Mondal et al. (Eds.): CICBA 2025, CCIS 2863, pp. 348–359, 2026.
https://doi.org/10.1007/978-3-032-17184-9_26

making it particularly advantageous for applications where fidelity is paramount. Conversely, lossy compression achieves a higher compression ratio by discarding portions of audio information deemed less critical [3], resulting in some irreversible loss of quality; thus, it is not suitable for scenarios requiring complete data retention. Recently, applications predicated on lossless audio compression have gained traction across various domains [4, 5], including security, forensic science, healthcare, and IoT-based acoustic surveillance, highlighting the pivotal advantage of maintaining audio integrity [6, 7] while effectively managing data storage and transmission challenges. The challenge of generative modeling in high-resolution audio arises from the high dimensionality and the intricate structures existing at multiple time-scales, encompassing both short- and long-term relationships. Utilizing the variational auto-encoder (VAE) framework facilitates the training of intermediate variables [8], using a learned conditional prior to estimate latent variables. The use of discrete latent elements presents a compelling advantage, as robust autoregressive models can be effectively harnessed to train sophisticated priors [9]. However, the representation of discrete latent codes through quantized auto-encoders remains problematic, despite the straightforward nature of prior modeling. Furthermore, existing neural audio compression algorithms [16] often yield outputs that starkly diverge from original recordings due to their insufficient representation of high-frequency content.

This paper presents an advanced Generative Adversarial Network (GAN) [1] based model for audio compression, capable of compressing audio with more than 70% compression rate while maintaining minimal artifacts and no discernible quality loss. The proposed approach is particularly suited for resource-constrained IoT environments, where energy efficiency, low latency, and bandwidth conservation are critical. Evaluation through both quantitative measures and qualitative listening assessments indicates superior performance relative to existing methods, particularly at lower bitrates corresponding to higher compression. The encoding process initiates by transforming audio into the frequency domain, where a spectrogram is constructed using the STFT [19]. The encoder processes input signal, represented as a mel-spectrogram, and reduces its dimensionality to produce a latent vector [18]. This latent representation is subsequently integrated into an auto-encoder architecture, linking the encoder with the GAN's generator. The GAN framework, comprising both a discriminator and generator, facilitates the optimization of the latent vector through a feedback-driven loss function. Finally, the latent vector undergoes discretization and quantization for compression, followed by entropy encoding using Arithmetic encoder [20].

The structure of the paper is as follows: Sect. 2 presents the literature review. Section 3 outlines the proposed methodology, where Sects. 3.1.1 and 3.1.2 provide a detailed description of the encoding and decoding algorithms, respectively, and Sect. 3.2 presents the encoder and decoder architecture. Section 4 describes the experimental setup, including the environment, datasets, and model training. The results and their analysis are discussed in Sect. 5. Finally, Sect. 6 concludes the paper, followed by the references.

2 Literature Review

Recent advancements in audio compression research have improved both efficiency and audio quality. The introduction of the Sparse Linear Predictor model [22] in 2012 laid an important foundation, though its moderate compression ratio did not lead to faster decoding speeds. Progress continued with the IEEE 1857.2 [23] standard in 2017, which employed entropy encoding techniques to enhance compression ratios, albeit at the expense of slower encoding times. Significant innovations in 2019 included the development of an adaptive Golomb-Rice coding algorithm for lossless ECG compression and the Integer Discrete Flow model, both contributing to more effective data representation. Established audio encoders like Monkey's Audio [10], WavPack [11], and FLAC [12] consistently achieved impressive compression ratios exceeding 60%. However, some recent proposals, including the 2021 [13] codec by Rim, Daniela N et al., prioritized higher compression ratios while compromising audio quality. The Linear Predictive Neural Net Encoder introduced in 2022 [15] represented a significant advancement by attaining over 60% compression, combining efficiency with quality retention. Most recently, the 2024 development of a Principal Component Analysis (PCA) and Convolutional Neural Networks (CNN) integrated encoding technique [21] has shown promise for surpassing traditional methods in both compression efficiency and audio reconstruction fidelity, indicating a continued trajectory of innovation in the field.

Despite the development of various audio compression techniques to date, improvements in compression ratio while preserving audio quality and other critical parameters remain limited. Consequently, designing an enhanced audio compression method that achieves higher compression ratios without compromising audio quality and processing efficiency continues to be a challenging and important task in the field.

3 Methodology

This proposed architecture comprises two deep CNNs: the discriminative network (D) and the generative network (G). The synergy between these networks aims to reconstruct high-quality audio from raw input. In this framework, the acoustic signal is first encoded into a latent vector through a process of iterative backpropagation, which optimizes the representation to ensure efficient compression of the target signal. Ultimately, the compressed representation, manifested as a latent vector, is further refined using Arithmetic encoding techniques, thereby achieving greater compression efficiency.

3.1 Compression and Decompression Algorithm

The proposed algorithms for encoding and decoding is described in Sects. 3.1.1 and 3.1.2 respectively.

3.1.1 Encoding Algorithm

Input: Acoustic signal

Output: Compressed acoustic data

Method: Following are the steps:

Step 1: Initially, the audio data undergoes preprocessing to generate a signal suitable for further processing. Specifically, a spectrogram is derived through the application of the STFT [19], which effectively transforms the time-domain audio dataset into the spectral domain. Spectrogram fed to the encoder block. Using Eqs. 1 and 2 audio signal is transformed into spectrogram.

Let $w(n)$ be the window function for $n = 0, 1, 2, \ldots, N - 1$ and $x(n)$ the input audio signal.

The mth windowed block of the signal s(m, n) is calculated as below

$$s(m, n) = x(n) \cdot w\left(n - m \cdot \frac{N}{2}\right) \tag{1}$$

Applying the DTFT (discrete-time Fourier transform) of every windowed block yields the short-time Fourier transform. ω denotes the frequency.

$$S(m, \omega) := DTFT\left\{x(n) \cdot w\left(n - m \cdot \frac{N}{2}\right)\right\} \tag{2}$$

Step 2: Encoder block serves a pivotal role in processing the input signal represented as a mel-spectrogram. Within this step, the size of the input is reduced for formulation of a compressed signal that is expressed as a latent vector, denoted as **z**. This transformation is integral to the development of the auto-encoder, which learns to map the signal space to the latent space. Consequently, the encoder is seamlessly integrated into the architecture of the GAN's generator, facilitating a cohesive data representation.

Step 3: The generator block of the GAN functions as the subsequent component in the architecture. Within this framework, both the discriminator and generator(G()) collaboratively produce a loss function that is subsequently utilized to inform the latent vector and generator. The latent vector, denoted as **z**, undergoes iterative updates and optimizations aimed at minimizing the resultant loss function (F()). Throughout this backpropagation process, the ideal latent vector is discretized and quantized, thus facilitating effective signal compression. Equation 3 is the loss function.

$$Loss\,function = F(x, G(z)) \tag{3}$$

Step 4: To facilitate the further compression of the audio signal, the latent vector undergoes entropy encoding employing the Arithmetic encoding method in the final stage of the process. This technique allows for the reduction of redundancy within the data, thereby enhancing the overall compression and ensuring an optimized flow of information to subsequent decoding stages.

3.1.2 Decoding Algorithm

Input: Compressed acoustic data

Output: Reconstructed acoustic signal

Method: Following are the steps:

Step 1: At the decoder, the received signal undergoes entropy decoding via a Arithmetic decoder, which systematically translates the encoded data.

Step 2: Subsequently, the generator parameters, previously established during the encoding process, are employed to recreate the mel-spectrogram.

Step 3: This mel-spectrogram is then subjected to post-processing, utilizing the inverse Short-Time Fourier Transform (STFT) [20] to convert it into the final audio signal, thereby restoring the original sound representation. Equations 4 and 5 used to transform the spectrogram into audio.

For obtaining s(m, n), the inverse STFT starts with the inverse DTFT of S(m, ω).

$$\mathrm{s(m,\ n)} = \mathrm{DTFT}^{-1}\{\mathrm{S(m,}\ \omega)\} \tag{4}$$

In order to reconstruct x(n) from s(m, n), multiply each s(m, n) by the shifted. window $w\left(n - m \cdot \frac{N}{2}\right)$ and then add the results.

These overlapping blocks are added in the inverse STFT's subsequent step to produce the reconstructed signal, $y(n)$ which is similar to original input audio signal, $x(n)$.

$$y(n) = \sum_{m} s(m, n) \cdot w\left(n - m \cdot \frac{N}{2}\right) \tag{5}$$

3.2 Encoder and Decoder Architecture

In the compression phase of the proposed Generative Adversarial Network (GAN) based model for audio signal processing, the input audio signal undergoes a multifaceted transformation culminating in a coded latent vector. Initially, the short-time Fourier transform (STFT) is employed to convert the time domain audio data into a spectrogram, functioning as the input for the encoder block. This encoder transforms the spectrogram into a latent vector, which serves as an intermediary representation of the input signal. The encoder is seamlessly integrated with the GAN generator, forming an auto-encoder that facilitates the transition from signal space to latent space. Additionally, the generator and discriminator collaboratively produce a loss function that informs the optimization of the latent vector, thereby enhancing signal compression through an iterative back-propagation process. Ultimately, following further compression and entropy encoding via the Arithmetic encoder, the latent vector is prepared for transmission to the decoding phase. The complete flow of this compression process is illustrated in Fig. 1.

At the decoder, the received signal is processed through entropy decoding with an Arithmetic decoder, which effectively translates the encoded data. Following this, the generator parameters, predefined during the encoding phase, are leveraged to reconstruct the mel-spectrogram. This mel-spectrogram undergoes post-processing via the inverse Short-Time Fourier Transform (STFT), facilitating the conversion into the final audio signal and thereby restoring the original sound representation.

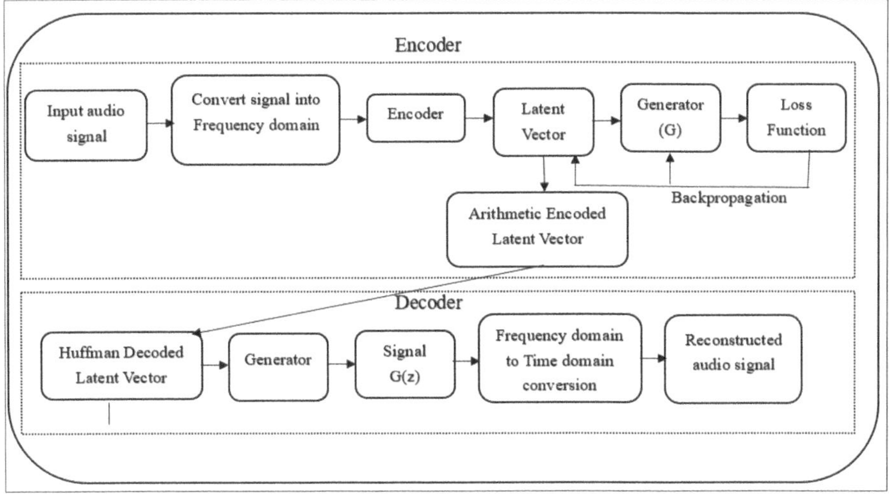

Fig. 1. Encoder and decoder diagram of the proposed technique.

4 Experiments

4.1 Environment

The proposed model was implemented using the TensorFlow and Keras frameworks with Python 3.6. The experiments were conducted on a system equipped with an 11th Gen Intel(R) Core (TM) i5-1135G7 processor running at 2.42 GHz, 16 GB of RAM, a 64-bit operating system, and a 1TB hard drive.

4.2 Datasets

This section provides a comprehensive overview of the preprocessing procedure for training and testing datasets. Audio files are recorded in.wav format utilizing Audacity freeware (version 3.6.1), ensuring a collection of songs with a standardized sample rate of 44100 Hz. Five standard parameters are used to compile the customized dataset, as detailed in Table 1, facilitating a rigorous approach to audio data collection for subsequent analysis.

Table 1. Recordings parameters

Parameter	Values
Record time(training)	~2 s
Record time(testing)	~5 s
File format	.wav
Sampling rate	44100 Hz
Channel	Mono
Bit depth	16

4.3 Model and Training

The proposed model integrates Generative Adversarial Networks (GANs), Adaptive Quantization, and Arithmetic Coding to achieve efficient audio signal processing. Initially, the encoder transforms the audio into the frequency domain and converts it into a Mel-spectrogram, producing a latent vector with reduced dimensionality. This latent representation is then input to the generator network, which is trained to reconstruct high-quality audio by minimizing a defined loss function. The framework employs a multi-period discriminator [1] alongside a multi-scale Short-Time Fourier Transform (STFT) discriminator to enhance performance. For the ablation study, the model is trained with a batch size of 16 over 200 iterations, utilizing the Adam optimizer for both generator and discriminator components.

5 Results and Discussion

The proposed model, which integrates Generative Adversarial Networks (GAN) with Arithmetic encoding, demonstrates superior effectiveness and stability as assessed through multiple parameters. To evaluate performance, three popular lossless audio compression techniques—Monkey's Audio, WavPack Lossless, and FLAC are used as reference systems. Additionally, a deep learning-based audio compression model is utilized to further evaluate efficacy and reconstruction fidelity [17]. As presented in Table 2, the proposed framework achieves an impressive average compression rate of 74.95, surpassing Monkey's Audio at 57.76, WavPack at 55.05, and FLAC at 70.30. Figure 2 illustrates a graphical overview of the comparative compression performance.

Table 2. Group-wise compression of the proposed model with referenced systems

Method	Rock	Classical	Rabi	Pop	Ghazal
Monkey's audio [10]	58.46	55.58	58.56	58.07	58.17
WavPack [11]	54.11	56.02	55.16	54.12	55.84
FLAC [12]	70.09	69.11	71.08	70.01	71.24
Proposed model	74.2	73.15	75.01	75.16	77.23

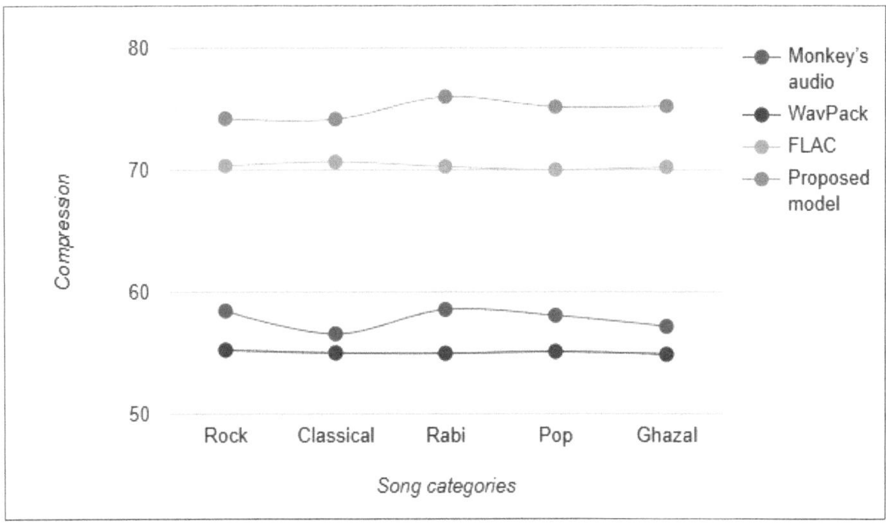

Fig. 2. Graphical comparison of the groupwise compression

Table 3 shows the groupwise PSNR [14]. From Table 3 it is visible that the proposed method obtains higher PSNR compared to other methods. Figure 3 shows the graphical representation of the average PSNR.

Table 3. Groupwise PSNR

Method	Rock	Classical	Rabi	Pop	Ghazal
Monkey's audio [10]	54.06	52.56	53.56	52.45	53.07
WavPack [11]	51.67	53.15	51.07	51.45	51.19
FLAC [12]	52.72	52.45	53.35	52.78	54.13
Proposed model	55.69	54.89	55.98	54.76	56.98

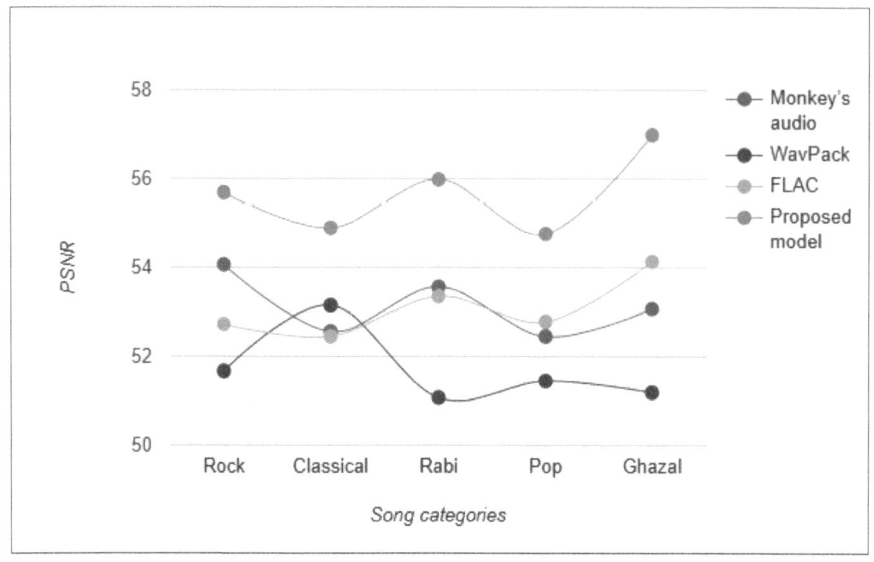

Fig. 3. Graphical comparison of the groupwise PSNR

We assessed the proposed model's robustness and performance using existing deep learning-based lossless audio codecs that are currently in use: i) Rim, Daniela et al. [13] iii) LINNE [15]. The proposed framework can reproduce the original audio signal with incredibly little variations. The suggested model reproduces the original audio signal with incredibly little variations. The estimated mean square error value for the suggested model is 0.001516. Additionally, a different metric known as NCC is utilized to assess the quality of the regenerated signal: 0.990861. A regeneration score that is closer to 1 denotes good regeneration. To illustrate the precision and resilience of the model, Table 5 presents the assessed parameters, such as Mean Squared Error (MSE) [14] and Normalized cross correlation (NCC) [3], of the current model in comparison to the other mentioned prediction system (Fig. 4 and Table 4).

Table 4. Groupwise compression with DNN model.

Method	Rock	Classical	Rabi	Pop	Ghazal
LINNE [15]	73.56	72.98	73.41	72.16	71.2
Daniela N. Rim et al. [13]	74.16	73.28	72.38	73.12	75.89
Proposed model	74.16	74.38	74.79	76.87	74.56

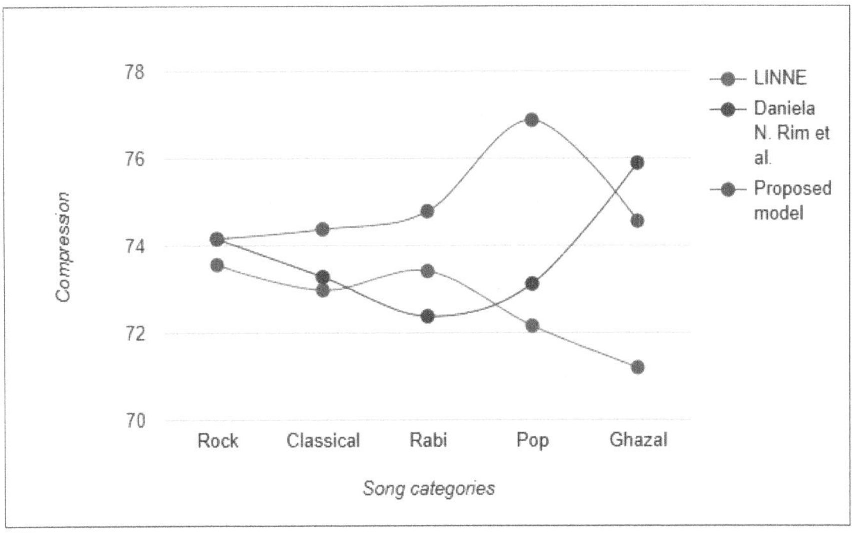

Fig. 4. Graphical comparison of the groupwise compression

Table 5. Comparison of MSE and NCC.

Method	MSE	NCC
LINNE [15]	0.011341	0.986634
Daniela N. Rim et al. [13]	0.011535	0.989884
Proposed model	0.001516	0.990861

6 Conclusion

The proposed GAN-based compression model demonstrates the ability to generate compressed data of acceptable quality at relatively low bitrates through an iterative back-propagation process aimed at identifying the optimal latent vector with Arithmetic encoding. This method leverages Generative Adversarial Networks (GANs), employing non-uniform quantization and Arithmetic encoding to identify the most effective latent representation of the signal, thereby enhancing the compression ratio. Initially, the generator network is trained within a GAN framework, after which the model iteratively updates and discretizes the best latent code for each input signal to achieve compression using the pre-trained generator. This model exhibits a superior compression ratio when compared to existing lossless audio codecs. Future enhancements may focus on integrating various optimization techniques to further improve both the compression ratio and computational efficiency.

References

1. Kong, J., Kim, J., Bae, J.: Hifi-Gan: generative adversarial networks for efficient and high-fidelity speech synthesis. Adv. Neural. Inf. Process. Syst. **33**, 17022–17033 (2020)
2. Selvi, C.T., Amudha, J., Sudhakar, R.: Medical image encryption and compression by adaptive sigma filterized synorr certificateless signcryptive Levenshtein entropy-coding-based deep neural learning. Multimedia Syst. **27**(6), 1059–1074 (2021). https://doi.org/10.1007/s00530-021-00764-y
3. Debnath, A., Mondal, U.K.: Lossless audio CODEC using non-repeated dynamic block encoding. Int. j. inf. tecnol. **16**, 3941–3948 (2024). https://doi.org/10.1007/s41870-024-01785-2
4. Kumar, S.N., Ahilan, A., Haridhas, A.K., Sebastian, J.: Gaussian hermite polynomial based lossless medical image compression. Multimedia Syst. **27**, 15–31 (2020). https://doi.org/10.1007/s00530-020-00689-y
5. Debnath, A., Mondal, U.: Lossless audio codec based on CNN, weighted tree and arithmetic encoding (LACCWA). Multimedia Tools Appl. **83**, 48737–48759 (2024). https://doi.org/10.1007/s11042-023-17393-4
6. Mondal, U.K., Debnath, A.: Designing a novel lossless audio compression technique with the help of optimized graph traversal (LACOGT). Multimedia Tools Appl. **81**(28), 40385–40411 (2022)
7. Albahli, S., Nazir, T., Irtaza, A., Javed, A.: Recognition and detection of diabetic retinopathy using densenet-65 based faster-RCNN. Comput. Mater. Continua **67**(2), 1333–1351 (2021). https://doi.org/10.32604/cmc.2021.014691
8. Huang, K., Wang, X.: ADA-INCVAE: improved data generation using variational autoencoder for imbalanced classification. Appl. Intell. **52**(3), 2838–2853 (2021). https://doi.org/10.1007/s10489-021-02566-1
9. Mondal, U.K., Debnath, A.: Developing a dynamic cluster quantization based lossless audio compression (DCQLAC). Multimedia Tools Appl. **80**(6), 8257–8280 (2021)
10. https://monkeysaudio.com/index.html. Accessed 27 Feb 2025
11. http://www.wavpack.com. Accessed 27 Feb 2025
12. https://xiph.org/flac/index.html. Accessed 27 Feb 2025
13. Rim, D.N., Jang, I., Choi, H.: Deep neural networks and end-to-end learning for audio compression. arXiv:2105.11681 (2021)
14. Manju, M., Abarna, P., Akila, U., Yamini, S.: Peak signal to noise ratio & mean square error calculation for various images using the lossless image compression in CCSDS algorithm. Int. J. Pure Appl. Math. **119**(12), 14471–14477 (2018)
15. Mineo, T., Shouno, H.: A lossless audio codec based on hierarchical residual prediction. In: 2022 Asia-Pacific Signal and Information Processing Association Annual Summit and Conference (APSIPA ASC), pp. 123–130. IEEE (2022)
16. Zeghidour, N., Luebs, A., Omran, A., Skoglund, J., Tagliasacchi, M.: SoundStream: an end-to-end neural audio codec. IEEE/ACM Trans. Audio Speech Lang. Process. **30**, 495–507 (2021)
17. Défossez, A., Copet, J., Synnaeve, G., Adi, Y.: High fidelity neural audio compression. arXiv preprint arXiv:2210.13438 (2022)
18. Yu, J., et al.: Vector-quantized image modeling with improved VQGAN. arXiv preprint arXiv:2110.04627 (2021)
19. Allen, J.B., Rabiner, L.R.: A unified approach to short-time Fourier analysis and synthesis. Proc. IEEE **65**, 1558–1564 (1977)
20. Kaur, S., Sukhjeet, M.: Entropy coding and different coding techniques. J. Netw. Commun. Emerg. Technol. **6**(5), 4–7 (2016)

21. Debnath, A., Mondal, U.K.: Leveraging CNN and principal component analysis for dynamic variance control in audio compression. Int. J. Inf. Tecnol. **16**, 4757–4765 (2024). https://doi.org/10.1007/s41870-024-02155-8
22. Ghido, F., Tabus, I.: Sparse modeling for lossless audio compression. IEEE Trans. Audio Speech Lang. Process. **21**(1), 14–28 (2012)
23. Gunawan, T.S., Zain, M.K.M., Muin, F.A., Kartiwi, M.: Investigation of lossless audio compression using IEEE 1857.2 advanced audio coding. Indones. J. Electr. Eng. Comput. Sci. **6**(2), 422–430 (2017)

Automated Smart Irrigation System Using IoT-Enabled Autonomous Vehicle with Predictive Analytics

Piyush Saha[1(✉)], Soumyadipta Das[1], Barnik Chakraborty[1], Srijita Chatterjee[2], and Raja Karmakar[1]

[1] Department of CSE (IoT & Cyber Security including Block Chain Technology), Heritage Institute of Technology, Kolkata 700107, India
sahapiyush5@gmail.com, dassoumyadipta007@gmail.com, barnikchakraborty24@gmail.com, rkarmakar.tict@gmail.com, {piyush.saha.iotcs26,soumyadipta.das.iotcs26, barnik.chakraborty.iotcs26}@heritageit.edu.in, raja.karmakar@heritageit.edu

[2] Department of CSE (AI & ML), Heritage Institute of Technology, Kolkata 700107, India
chatterjeesrijita84@gmail.com, srijita.chatterjee.aiml26@heritageit.edu.in

Abstract. In this paper, a new Internet of Things (IoT) smart irrigation system is proposed that empowers an autonomous vehicle with predictive analytics to enforce efficient water management in farming. The suggested "Smart Agro-Mobile" system offers a combination of real-time sensing, autonomous mobility, and machine learning to maximize agricultural irrigation systems. It has three-layered architecture consisting of sensing (rain sensor, temperature, soil moisture), processing (Arduino Uno WiFi and Raspberry Pi 3), and cloud analytics layers. The mobile platform, which consists of 12 V LiPo battery, 6 V mini pump, and ultrasonic sensors, travels autonomously in fields to collect environmental information and make precise irrigation. Enhanced Long Short-Term Memory (LSTM) networks, supplemented with dropout layers and attention mechanisms, predict soil moisture content and precipitation possibilities with 92% accuracy, enabling preventive irrigation scheduling. Experimental validation confirms significant improvement over the base method with 40% water conserved while maintaining optimal soil moisture level 98% of the time. Its applicability to all crops and soil conditions is assured by its modularity and its adaptive threshold principle. With removal of the limitations of static sensor networks and incorporation of weather volatility in irrigation decisions, this solution offers an inexpensive, effective approach to precision agriculture. Merging IoT with autonomous mobility is a paradigm shift in agricultural water management, promising tremendous gains for resource-limited small-scale farmers.

Keywords: IoT · Smart Agriculture · Autonomous Vehicle · Machine Learning · Predictive Analytics

K. Chandra Mondal et al. (Eds.): CICBA 2025, CCIS 2863, pp. 360–374, 2026.
https://doi.org/10.1007/978-3-032-17184-9_27

1 Introduction

The agricultural industry faces a significant challenge as it only uses 70% of freshwater supplies. [16], 60% of the water is lost due to inefficient irrigation processes [5]. Climate change and population growth worsen global water crisis, threatening food security and environmental sustainability. Conventional flood irrigation wastes water, causes soil loss, and low crop yields. The UN predicts 55% global water demand by 2050 [20]. This harsh reality calls for innovative solutions that can transform water management in agriculture.

Research shows that fixed IoT systems can save 25–30% water usage, despite the promising nature of current smart irrigation solutions. [23] but cannot tackle spatial variability over large farms—a shortcoming recognized during California's Central Valley trials [15]. As an example, Spanish vineyards experienced 45% water savings with fixed sensors [6], Texas cotton fields used static IoT systems, resulting in 25% yield gains, but required 120 sensors per square kilometer, making scalability too expensive [13]. Static systems, while improved over conventional methods, struggle to account for field microclimates, soil composition, and crop water requirements, and require significant infrastructure investments, making them unsuitable for small-scale farmers, who constitute a significant portion of the global agricultural population [4].

Our Contribution: The Smart Agro-Mobile is a revolutionary system that combines IoT-powered precision with self-driving mobility. It uses a self-driving vehicle with soil moisture sensors, weather forecasting, and an irrigation tank to patrol grounds like a robo-farmer, dispensing water droplets precisely where needed. The system uses real-time data analytics, artificial intelligence algorithms, and autonomous navigation to maximize water usage at a granular level, making data-driven decisions about irrigation timing and extent.

Overall Approach: We introduce the *Smart Agro-Mobile*, a self-driven irrigation platform that integrates *IoT-based sensing*, *real-time analytics*, and *machine learning* to provide accurate, location-aware water management. Its scalable and modular architecture enables deployment in various agricultural environments to facilitate smart and efficient irrigation. The key contributions of this work are summarized below:

1. *IoT-Integrated Autonomous Mobility:* The system merges soil moisture (FC-28), temperature-humidity (DHT11), and rainfall (FC-37) sensors with a mobile platform controlled by Raspberry Pi 3 Model B+ and Arduino Uno WiFi. This enables dynamic, real-time environmental monitoring and irrigation across fields.
2. *Predictive Irrigation via Long Short-Term Memory (LSTM) Models:* Leveraging historical data from Firebase and weather forecasts from the Tomorrow.io API, the system uses LSTM neural networks to predict soil moisture with 92% accuracy, enabling proactive and crop-aware irrigation.
3. *Mobile Precision Irrigation Platform:* Equipped with a 6 V mini pump and 12 V DC solenoid valve, the mobile unit reduces sensor density by 60% compared to fixed systems, irrigating based on thresholds (15%–30%) to address spatial variability.

4. *Three-Tier Scalable Architecture:* A modular architecture comprising sensing, processing, and cloud layers integrates Firebase (real-time storage), a Flask backend, and the Blynk mobile app, providing remote monitoring and ease of use for farmers.
5. *Efficient Resource Usage:* Field tests show a 40% reduction in water usage while maintaining optimal soil moisture (25%–35%) during 98% of operational cycles. This is achieved through adaptive irrigation using real-time data and predictive analytics, promoting sustainable and farmer-friendly agriculture.

Paper Organization: The rest of this paper is structured as follows. Section 2 discusses existing related studies. Section 3 explains the proposed approach. Section 4 presents the experimental setup and results. Section 5 concludes the paper with the discussion of possible future developments.

2 Related Works

The research in [17] discusses IoT-based smart irrigation systems that use sensors for soil and weather monitoring to enhance efficiency and conserve water. However, this method is mainly suitable for small areas and may not be cost-effective for larger applications. Similarly [11] introduced an automated irrigation system using sensors to monitor temperature and soil moisture, which activates irrigation through a microcontroller and GSM/GPRS mobile network, but it also faces economic viability issues for large fields. The authors in [2] introduced an IoT and fuzzy logic controller-based smart irrigation system that minimizes irrigation frequency but maximizes production. The system utilizes a Mamdani fuzzy controller that receives environmental identifiers like soil moisture and external temperature from specific sensors and uses fuzzy rules to regulate water flow from the water pump.

The research in [19] showed a cost-effective and easy ESP8266 Wi-Fi module-based smart irrigation system to control remotely with Wi-Fi by using Arduino and ESP8266. The designers in [18] came up with an IoT and Raspberry Pi-based smart irrigation system that is cost-effective and offers real-time monitoring as well as farm activity live streaming through a mobile app. With this method, plant growth monitoring can be continued with a webcam and remote accessing through a Wi-Fi network. In [12], the authors utilized an IoT and neural network-powered water pumping control system, managing water usage efficiently through a Multi-Layer Perceptron (MLP) neural network. The system utilizes Arduino to manage sensor data (temperature, humidity, and moisture in the soil) and regulate the water pump automatically, facilitating decision-making operations for irrigation. The paper in [7] surveyed recent directions on sensors and IoT systems for irrigation in precision agriculture, emphasizing the significance of wireless technologies and low-cost sensors for scalable and cheap solutions.

Recent advancements include [14], which explored 6G-IoT technologies for Agriculture 5.0, achieving up to 30% water savings but requiring advanced infrastructure. [8] proposed an SVM-based soil moisture prediction model for tea plantations, achieving an R^2 of 0.9435, though limited to specific crops. [16] reviewed emerging irrigation techniques, noting that mobile IoT systems could address spatial variability, aligning with our approach.

Research Gap Addressed by Our Work: Although contemporary smart irrigation systems have done a great job of enhancing water efficiency, they still lag in a number of important areas. The application of fixed sensor grids, while good for static settings, is ineffective when faced with varied terrain, scattered plots, or fast-changing environmental conditions. These are particularly issues in extensive farming and smallholder settings, where flexibility is paramount. In addition, current systems tend to use simple predictive models that do not account for real-time weather fluctuation or complex soil moisture dynamics—leading to less than optimal irrigation schedules.

3 Proposed Methodology

Our Smart Agro-Mobile system represents a paradigm shift in precision agriculture, combining the power of IoT with autonomous mobility. This section details our innovative approach to smart irrigation.

3.1 System Architecture

The Smart Agro-Mobile architecture is a three-tiered system that seamlessly integrates sensing, processing, and analytics, as illustrated in Fig. 2.

1. *Sensing Layer:* Comprises: (i) Soil Moisture Sensor (FC-28): Detects moisture levels as low as 15%, (ii) Temperature and Humidity Sensor (DHT11): Monitors ambient conditions with ±2 °C accuracy, and (iii) Rain Sensor (FC-37): Detects precipitation intensity, crucial for irrigation scheduling. The Blynk mobile app provides a user-friendly interface for farmers to monitor sensor data, designed for ease of use even with limited technical expertise.
2. *Processing Layer:* Powered by: (i) Raspberry Pi 3 Model B+: Processes sensor data and executes navigation algorithms, and (ii) Arduino Uno WiFi (ATmega328P + ESP8266): Handles real-time sensor data acquisition and actuation control.
3. *Cloud Storage and Analytics Layer:* Includes: (i) Firebase: Stores historical sensor data for big data analytics, and (ii) Machine Learning Models: LSTM networks predict soil moisture trends and rainfall probability (Fig. 1).

3.2 Autonomous Vehicle Design

The modular structure of the vehicle permits simple replacement of sensors, enhancing versatility across different crop and field conditions. The device includes: (i) Power Source: A 12 V 2200 mAh LiPo battery, supporting up to 8 h of continuous use. Future improvements may include solar panels or higher-capacity batteries to extend operational time for large farms. (ii) Water Delivery:

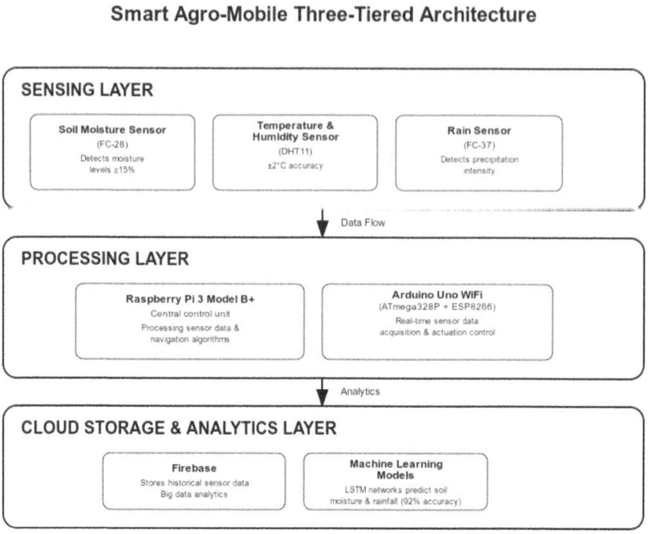

Fig. 1. Three-Tier Architecture of Smart Agro-Mobile System

A 6 V mini pump and 12 V DC solenoid valve, delivering water at 2.5 L/min. (iii) Navigation: Ultrasonic sensors (HC-SR04) for obstacle detection and a GPS module for accurate positioning. (iv) Control: A 5 V relay module controls pump and valve actions based on soil moisture levels.

3.3 Predictive Analytics Algorithm

Our system employs an improved Long Short-Term Memory (LSTM) neural network, enhanced with attention mechanisms and dropout layers, to forecast soil moisture levels and rain probability with 92% accuracy. LSTMs were chosen due to their ability to model long-term temporal dependencies in time-series data, such as soil moisture and weather patterns, making them ideal for proactive irrigation scheduling compared to simpler models like linear regression or traditional neural networks.

Algorithm 1 outlines the LSTM-based workflow for 5-day soil moisture and rainfall forecasting, achieving 92% accuracy through Min-Max normalized data processing.

3.4 Irrigation Decision Logic with Optimal Soil Moisture Thresold

The irrigation system uses a 30% soil moisture threshold, based on research by [7], which identifies 25%–35% as optimal for loamy soils to support healthy crop growth while avoiding over-irrigation. Future enhancements will include dynamic threshold adjustments using real-time soil and crop-specific data, allowing customization for crops like rice (requiring higher moisture) or wheat (needing lower

Algorithm 1. Soil Moisture and Rainfall Prediction

1: **Input:** Historical soil moisture data, weather data from Firebase
2: **Output:** 5-day forecast of soil moisture and rain probability
3: Collect historical data from Firebase
4: Preprocess data: Handle missing values via interpolation
5: Normalize data using Min-Max scaling to [0, 1]
6: Generate lagged features for the last 5 days
7: Split data into 80% training and 20% testing
8: Initialize LSTM model: input_size=5, hidden_layers=2, output_size=1
9: Add attention mechanism and dropout layers (rate=0.2)
10: Train model: epochs=100, batch_size=32
11: Validate model on testing data
12: Fetch real-time weather data via Tomorrow.io API
13: Preprocess API data similarly
14: Generate predictions for 5-day forecast using trained model
15: Return predicted soil moisture and rain probability forecasts

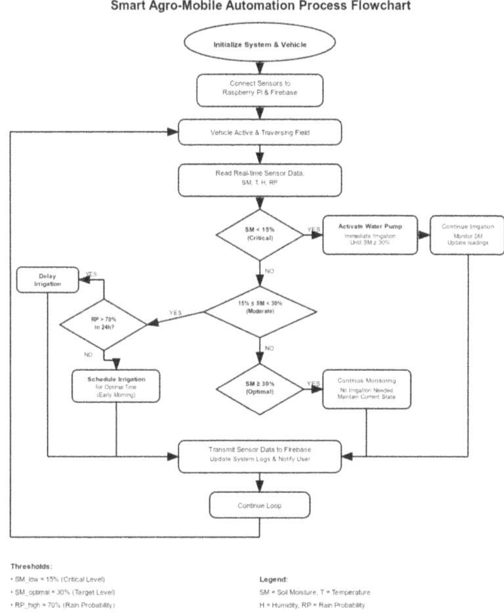

Fig. 2. Three-Tier Architecture of Smart Agro-Mobile System

moisture), and varying soil types such as sandy (∼40% moisture) or clayey (∼20% moisture) as per [2]. The Smart Agro-Mobile employs a sophisticated decision-making process: (i) if soil moisture is below 15%, immediate irrigation is triggered; (ii) if moisture is between 15% and 30%, irrigation is delayed if rain probability exceeds 70% within 24 h, otherwise scheduled for optimal timing (typically early morning); (iii) if moisture is 30% or higher, the system continues monitoring. This adaptive approach, combined with mobile technology, achieves 40% water savings compared to traditional methods and maintains optimal soil moisture levels 98% of the time.

3.5 Automation Process

Algorithm 2 outlines the automation process of the Smart Agro-Mobile system, integrating soil moisture monitoring, weather prediction, and autonomous irrigation:

Algorithm 2. Smart Agro-Mobile Irrigation Automation

```
1: Initialize: System components (sensors, water pump, mobile vehicle)
2: Connect: Sensors to Raspberry Pi and Firebase
3: Input: Soil moisture (SM), Rain probability (RP), Temperature (T), Humidity (H)
4: Thresholds: SM_low = 15%, SM_optimal = 30%, RP_high = 70%
5: while Vehicle is active and traversing field do
6:     Read real-time sensor data: SM, T, H, RP
7:     if SM < SM_low then
8:         Activate water pump
9:         while SM < SM_optimal do
10:            Continue irrigation
11:            Update SM readings
12:        end while
13:        Deactivate water pump
14:    else if SM_low ≤ SM < SM_optimal then
15:        if RP > RP_high within next 24 hours then
16:            Delay irrigation
17:        else
18:            Schedule irrigation for optimal time (e.g., early morning)
19:        end if
20:    else
21:        Continue monitoring without irrigation
22:    end if
23:    Transmit sensor data to Firebase in real time
24:    Update system logs and notify user via mobile app
25: end while
```

4 Performance Analysis

In this section, we analyze the performance of the proposed methodology.

4.1 Environmental Setup

Environmental setup for our IoT-enabled smart irrigation system comprises a combination of hardware and software components. The components are carefully selected to enable seamless integration, real-time data acquisition, and efficient execution of the proposed methodology. The hardware setup includes various sensors, controllers, actuators, and communication modules that form the backbone of our system. Table 1 summarizes the specifications of the key hardware components.

4.2 Result Analysis

The readings are streamed to Firebase in real-time, enabling farmers to remotely monitor field conditions and make irrigation decisions. A major feature is the automated irrigation system, which switches on the water pump when

Table 1. Hardware Specifications

Component	Model	Purpose
Arduino Uno WiFi	ATmega328P + ESP8266	Microcontroller for sensor integration
Raspberry Pi 3	Model B+	Vehicle control and processing unit
Soil Moisture Sensor	FC-28	Measures soil moisture levels
Rain Sensor	FC-37	Detects rainfall intensity
Temperature Sensor	DHT11	Measures ambient temperature and humidity
Water Pump	6 V Mini Pump	Pumps water from tank to fields
Relay Module	5 V Relay	Controls water pump operation
LiPo Battery	12 V 2200 mAh	Powers autonomous vehicle
Ultrasonic Sensor	HC-SR04	Detects obstacles for navigation
Water Level Sensor	YL-69	Monitors water levels in tank
GPS Module	NEO-6M GPS	Tracks vehicle location
Solenoid Valve	12 V DC Valve	Regulates water flow in zones
LCD Display Module	16×2 LCD	Displays real-time sensor data
Breadboard and Wires	Generic	Circuit prototyping

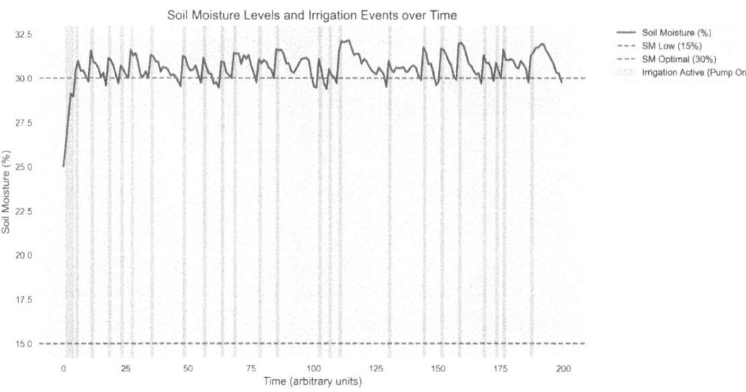

Fig. 3. Soil Moisture vs Time graph showing irrigation events

soil moisture drops below 30%. The pump shuts off when moisture exceeds this threshold, saving water The performance of the system is depicted in Fig. 3, showing soil moisture percentages over time. Vertical yellow stripes indicates when the pump is active due to low moisture and no stripes when it is off.

As shown in Fig. 4, the Firebase records the low moisture values when the soil moisture drops below the predetermined threshold, which causes the automated water pump to begin irrigation. The system is shown in operation in the accompanying image, where water is released to rehydrate the soil. On the other hand, the system intelligently turns off the pump when the soil moisture sensor detects a moisture level higher than 30%, avoiding needless water waste. This keeps the field adequately hydrated and guarantees optimal resource utilization.

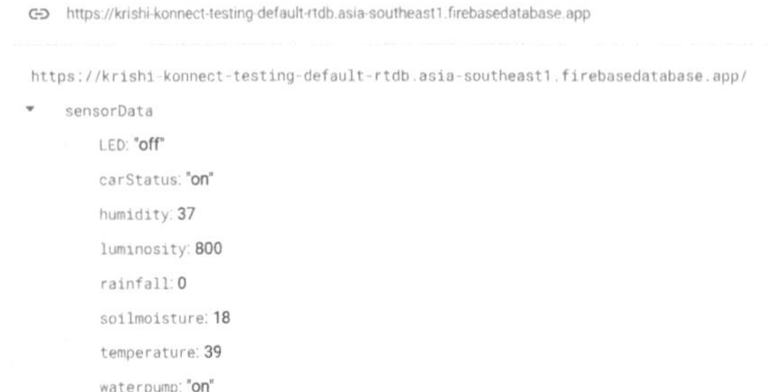

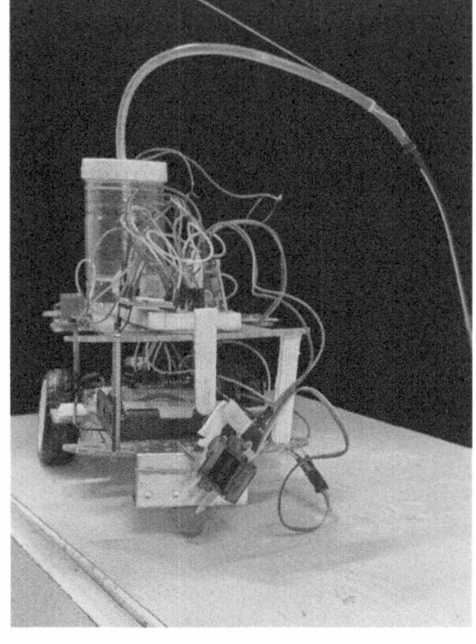

Fig. 4. (Top) Firebase showing soil moisture levels below 30%. (Bottom) Water being actively pumped from the smart car for irrigation

Figure 5 demonstrates how effectively the system prevents overwatering. The Firebase logs verify the higher soil moisture content, and the accompanying image makes it evident that no water is being pumped, illustrating the system's automated water conservation strategy. With this state-of-the-art IoT-based mobile irrigation system, farmers can precisely manage water, reduce resource waste, and implement sustainable irrigation practices.

Rainfall Prediction The rainfall prediction module forecasts the likelihood and intensity of rainfall over the next five days using historical weather data from 1973 to 2022 provided by the Indian Meteorological Department (IMD). Temperature, humidity, precipitation, and other meteorological factors are measured daily in four major Indian cities: Chennai, Bengaluru, Mumbai, and Kolkata. To forecast the likelihood and intensity of rainfall, two Support Vector Machine (SVM) models were trained. Farmers can enhance agricultural planning by using

https://krishi-konnect-testing-default-rtdb.asia-southeast1.firebasedatabase.app
https://krishi-konnect-testing-default-rtdb.asia-southeast1.firebasedatabase.app/
sensorData
LED: "off"
carStatus: "off"
humidity: 76
luminosity: 800
rainfall: 29
soilmoisture: 72
temperature: 34
waterpump: "off"

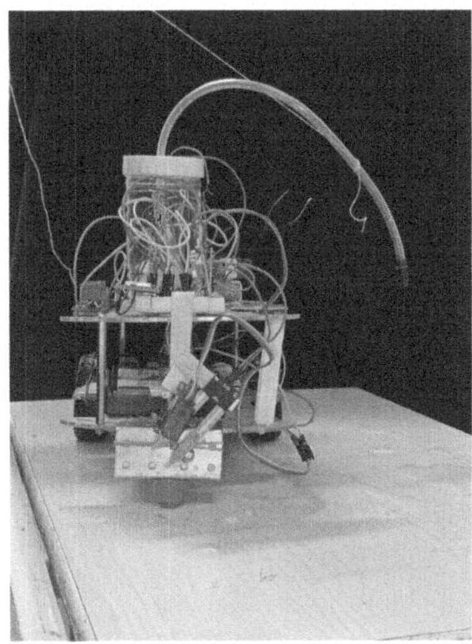

Fig. 5. (Top) Firebase showing soil moisture levels above 30%. (Bottom) No water being pumped as irrigation is not needed

real-time data from the Tomorrow.io API. 80% of the dataset is used for training, and 20% is used for testing.

In order to improve SVM performance, the data was preprocessed by generating lagged features (the previous five days) for time series forecasting, handling missing values through interpolation, and normalizing features to a 0–1 scale. Before being fed into the trained models, real-time inputs from the Tomorrow.io API go through a similar preprocessing step. The SVM classifier uses a radial basis function (RBF) kernel to predict the likelihood of rainfall (rain or no rain), and the SVM regressor uses an RBF kernel to estimate the intensity of rainfall (mm/day). The hyperparameters(e.g., $C = 1.0$, $\gamma = 0.1$) were adjusted using grid search. Iterative forecasting was used for the 5-day horizon, and training was done on a GPU to efficiently handle the large dataset. The rainfall prediction models achieved the following results on the test set:

Table 2. Performance Metrics for Rainfall Prediction

Metric	Classification (Probability)	Regression (Intensity)
Accuracy	87.5%	-
Precision	0.85	-
Recall	0.88	-
F1-Score	0.86	-
RMSE (mm/day)	-	2.15
MAE (mm/day)	-	1.42
R^2	-	0.82

Table 2 compares performance metrics between classification (rain probability) and regression (intensity) models, highlighting the system's prediction capabilities.

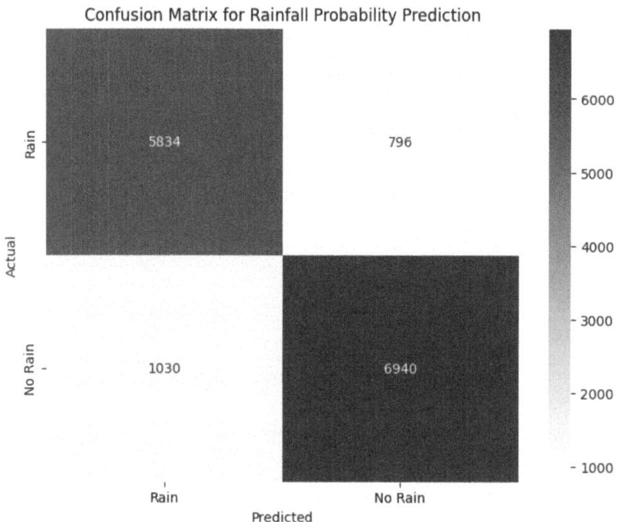

Fig. 6. Confusion Matrix for Rainfall Probability Prediction

Figure 6 demonstrates that the confusion matrix of the SVM classifier has an accuracy of 87.5% in predicting the likelihood of rainfall. SVM outperforms simpler models like logistic regression in rainfall prediction, but it is slightly less accurate than deep learning methods like CNN or LSTM. For instance, [10] used SVM to classify rainfall with an accuracy of 90.08%, which is very similar to our 87.5%. On the other hand, [21] discovered that LSTM outperformed the others (Root Mean Squared Error (RMSE) <2 mm/day), suggesting that deep learning may be improved further. The city-specific models provide a practical advantage over generic models as illustrated in [22], which improved hourly forecasts in Japan. Figure 7 presents a prediction of rainfall accumulation over the next 5 days in the city of Kolkata.

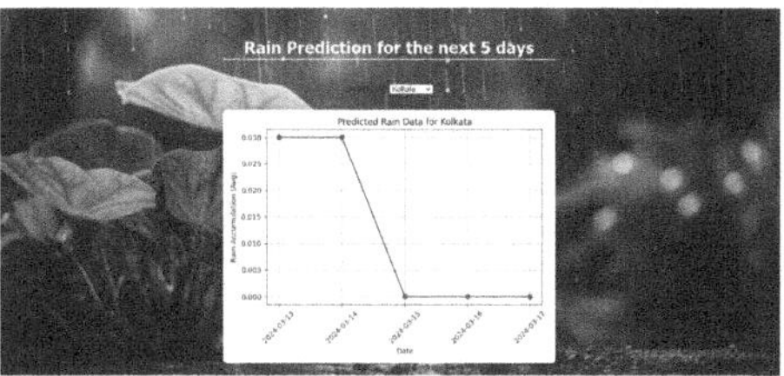

Fig. 7. Predicted Rain for Kolkata

Soil Moisture Prediction To enhance irrigation, the soil moisture prediction module predicts soil moisture levels for the upcoming five days. It makes use of an SVM regressor and examines soil moisture as it relates to temperature, humidity, and precipitation using data from 1973 to 2022. Farmers can modify irrigation schedules with the aid of city-specific models for Chennai, Bengaluru, Mumbai, and Kolkata that use real-time data from the Tomorrow.io API. The model's R^2 value was 0.92, its Mean Absolute Error (MAE) was 0.10, and its Root Mean Square Error (RMSE) was 0.15.

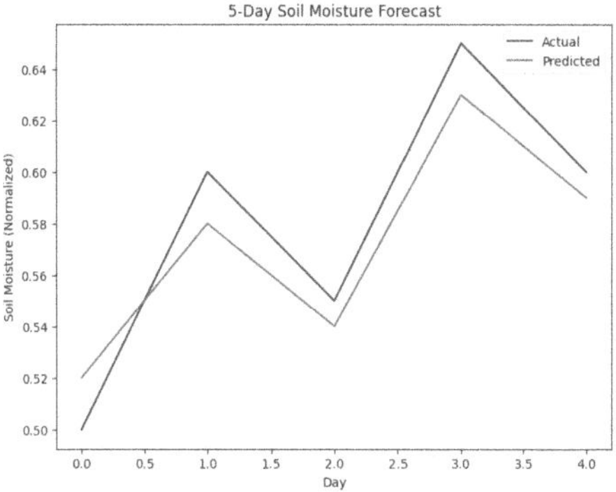

Fig. 8. Scatter Plot of Predicted vs. Actual Soil Moisture

As shown in Fig. 8, the scatter plot illustrates the close alignment between predicted and actual soil moisture values, indicating high model accuracy.

Fig. 9 demonstrates the ability of our model for temporal forecasting by comparing the time series of the soil moisture level over the previous five days with

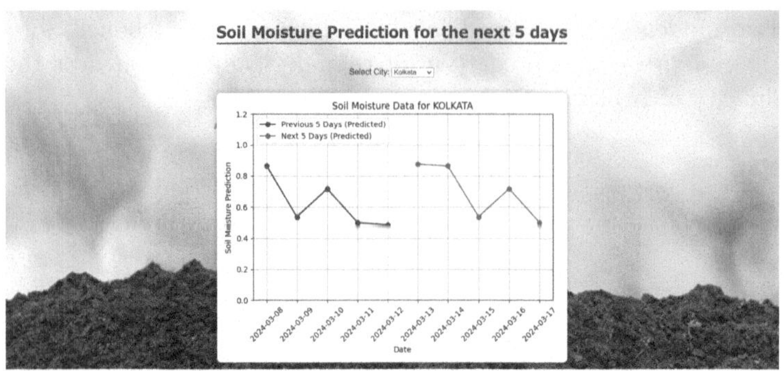

Fig. 9. Time Series of Previous 5 days Soil Moisture vs. Soil Moisture Over Next 5 Days

the level anticipated over the next five days. With an R^2 of 0.92, which is similar to [9]'s 0.9435 for tea plantations, the SVM regressor exhibits competitive performance. Similar accuracy, albeit with more complexity, was reported by studies like [3] that used hyperspectral data and SVM. Although [1] suggests that advanced models like LSTM could further improve performance, our method strikes a balance between accuracy and simplicity, which is further enhanced by city-specific tailoring.

Comparison with State-of-the-Art Methods Table 3 compares our system with state-of-the-art IoT-based-methods irrigation systems, highlighting superior water savings and scalability due to autonomous mobility.

Table 3. Comparison with State-of-the-art-Art Methods

Method	Water Savings	Accuracy	Scalability	Ref.
Smart Agro-Mobile	40%	92%	High	O
Fixed IoT System	25–30%	85%	Low	[23]
Spanish Vineyards	45%	80%	Medium	[6]
6G-IAMT IoT System	30%	90%	Medium	[14]

Comparison with Alternative Models Table 4 evaluates our LSTM model for predicting soil moisture against the Bi-LSTM and GRU models. LSTM strikes a balance between computational efficiency and accuracy (92%), making it appropriate for real-time applications on devices with limited resources, such as Raspberry Pi.

Table 4. Comparison of Predictive Models

Model	Accuracy	Complexity	Real-time Fit
LSTM	92%	Medium	High
Bi-LSTM	93%	High	Medium
GRU	91%	Low	High

5 Conclusion

The Smart Agro-System Mobile is an important development for saving water in agriculture. It uses an IoT-enabled autonomous irrigation system with predictive analytics, achieving 40% water savings and 92% accuracy in predicting soil moisture. Future plans include optimizing thresholds for specific crops, coordinating multiple vehicles for bigger farms, using edge computing to decrease reliance on the cloud, finding cheaper hardware solutions like ESP32 microcontrollers, and conducting field trials in different areas. Additionally, there will be training programs for farmers, especially those less educated, and designing simpler user interfaces. The project will also explore advanced models for better predictions.

References

1. Aderyani, F.R., Jamshid Mousavi, S., Jafari, F.: Short-term rainfall forecasting using machine learning-based approaches of PSO-SVR, LSTM and CNN. J. Hydrol. **614**, 128463 (2022). https://www.sciencedirect.com/science/article/pii/S0022169422010332
2. Alomar, B., Alazzam, A.: A smart irrigation system using IoT and fuzzy logic controller. In: The Fifth HCT INFORMATION TECHNOLOGY TRENDS (ITT), pp. 1–5 (2018)
3. Ewing, J., Oommen, T., et al.: Terrain characterization via machine vs. deep learning using remote sensing. Sensors **23**(11), 5035 (2023). https://www.ncbi.nlm.nih.gov/pmc/articles/PMC10301555/
4. Food and Agriculture Organization: Smallholders and family farmers: key to sustainable agriculture. FAO Reports (2020)
5. Gadekar, G.R., Kute, S., Sathe, N.J.: Optimal utilisation of irrigation water: a case study on Nashik Left Bank Canal [nlbc], Nashik. Indian J. Appl. Res. **5**, 15–17 (2015)
6. García-Tejero, I.F., Durán-Zuazo, V.H., Muriel-Fernández, J.L.: Integrating soil moisture sensors and remote sensing for precision irrigation in Spanish vineyards. Agric. Water Manage. (2021)
7. García, L., Parra, L., Jimenez, J.M., Lloret, J., Lorenz, P.: IoT-based smart irrigation systems: an overview on the recent trends on sensors and IoT systems for irrigation in precision agriculture. Sensors, 1042 (2020)
8. Huang, Y., et al.: SVM-based soil moisture prediction for tea plantations. Plants **12**(10), 1987 (2023)
9. Huang, Y.: Improved SVM-based soil-moisture-content prediction model for tea plantation. Plants **12**(12) (2023). https://doi.org/10.3390/plants12122309, https://www.mdpi.com/2223-7747/12/12/2309

10. Jain, S., Kumar, A., Yadav, S.: Classification of rainfall events using support vector machine. Int. J. Adv. Comput. Sci. Appl. (IJACSA) **12**(3), 370–374 (2021). https://doi.org/10.14569/IJACSA.2021.0120347, https://thesai.org/Downloads/Volume12No3/Paper_47-Classification_of_Rainfall_Events.pdf
11. Kansara, K., Zaveri, V., Shah, S., Delwadkar, S., Jani, K.: Sensor based automated irrigation system with IoT: a technical review. Int. J. Comput. Sci. Inf. Technol., 5331–5333 (2015)
12. Karar, M.E., Al-Rasheed, M.F., Al-Rasheed, A.F., Reyad, O.: IoT and neural network-based water pumping control system for smart irrigation. J. Sens., 1–7 (2020)
13. Li, H., Zhang, Y., Kumar, S.: The impact of 6G-IoT technologies on the development of Agriculture 5.0. Electronics, 2651 (2024)
14. Li, X., et al.: 6g-iot technologies for agriculture 5.0. Electronics **13**(5), 900–915 (2024)
15. Martínez-Lüscher, J., Teitelbaum, T., Mele, A., Ma, O., Frewin, A.J., Hazell, J.: High-resolution weather network reveals a high spatial variability in air temperature in the central valley of California with implications for crop and pest management. PLOS One, e0267607 (2022)
16. Naganjali, K., et al.: Revamping water use in agriculture: techniques and emerging innovations. J. Sci. Res. Rep. **30**(7), 1055–1066 (2024)
17. Obaideen, K., et al.: An overview of smart irrigation systems using IoT. Energy Nexus **7**, 100124 (2022)
18. Pawar, S.B., Rajput, P., Shaikh, A.: Smart irrigation system using IoT and Raspberry PI. Int. Res. J. Eng. Technol. (IRJET), 1163–1167 (2018)
19. Srivastava, P., Bajaj, M., Rana, A.S.: Overview of ESP8266 Wi-Fi module based smart irrigation system using IoT. Int. Res. J. Eng. Technol. (IRJET), 1163–1167 (2018)
20. United Nations: The united nations world water development report 2023: partnerships and cooperation for water (2023). https://www.unwater.org/publications/un-world-water-development-report-2023. Accessed 20 Apr 2025
21. Wu, X., Li, Y., Chen, Z.: Short-term rainfall prediction using LSTM networks with multi-source meteorological data. J. Hydrometeorol. **23**(5), 789–802 (2022). https://doi.org/10.1175/JHM-D-21-0154.1
22. Yamamoto, K., Sato, T., Nakamura, H.: Support vector machines for high-resolution hourly rainfall forecasting in urban Japan. J. Hydrometeorol. **23**(4), 589–605 (2022). https://doi.org/10.1175/JHM-D-21-0123.1
23. Zia, H., Rehman, A.U., Harris, N.R., Fatima, S., Khurram, M.: An experimental comparison of IoT-based and traditional irrigation scheduling on a flood-irrigated subtropical lemon farm. Sensors (2021)

Fine-Tuning for Code Intelligence: Evaluating LLMs on Custom Programming Benchmarks

Harsh Sahu[1(✉)], Munsifa Firdaus Khan Barbhuyan[2], Jay Kamavisdar[1], Ayushman Mishra[1], Rishabh Pandey[1], and Samarth Pratap Singh[1]

[1] Department of Computer Science and Engineering, School of Computing Science and Engineering and Artificial Intelligence, VIT Bhopal University, Kothri Kalan, Sehore 466114, MP, India
{harsh.23bai10199,jay.23bai11391,ayushman.23bai11256, rishabh.23bai10184,samarth.23bai10192}@vitbhopal.ac.in

[2] Department of Information Technology, Branch-Cyber Security Assam Skill University, Mangaldai, Darrang 784125, Assam, India

Abstract. This work investigates how small language models, especially those between 1B and 3B parameters, can be fine-tuned to handle programming tasks more effectively. With increasing interest in running Artificial Intelligence models on limited hardware, we tried out fine-tuning methods like Low-Rank Adaptation, Quantised Low-Rank Adaptation, and Unsloth to improve performance without needing expensive resources. Instead of building a new dataset, we used existing coding problem datasets from platforms like Leetcode, Codeforces etc. These datasets include challenges, test cases, and solutions, and they were useful for evaluating code generation and reasoning abilities. During fine-tuning, we faced common issues such as memory limits, long training times, and occasional instability, especially on lower-end GPUs. Still, we saw good improvements after tuning the models. The fine-tuned versions performed noticeably better at solving programming problems and showed stronger reasoning compared to their base versions. Our results suggest that even smaller models can be useful for code-related tasks if trained carefully. This makes it more practical to use such models in everyday scenarios where large-scale hardware isn't available.

Keywords: Parameter-Efficient Finetuning · Low-Rank Adaptation (LoRA) · Quantized Low-Rank Adaptation (QLoRA) · Small Language Models · Programming Benchmarks

1 Introduction

Large-scale language models such as GPT-4 and Claude have achieved strong results in code generation, but their computational requirements make them impractical for many users. Educational institutions, small startups, and developers in resource-constrained environments cannot afford the hardware needed for deployment of such models. This creates a gap between cutting-edge AI research and its applicability in low-resource settings.

K. Chandra Mondal et al. (Eds.): CICBA 2025, CCIS 2863, pp. 375–387, 2026.
https://doi.org/10.1007/978-3-032-17184-9_28

This paper investigates how to fine-tune little language models (LLMs) to enhance code reasoning abilities on hardware with limited resources using parameter-efficient techniques like LoRA, QLoRA, and Unsloth. Although code development for large models like GPT-4 and Claude has advanced significantly, many applications cannot afford their implementation due to high processing requirements. To close this gap, we examine the possibility of purposeful fine-tuning with high-quality datasets to optimize smaller models (1-3B parameters) for programming tasks. Here, we employ the tried-and-true procedures for getting the study paper published in a journal. We utilize a novel artificial dataset, KODCODE, which consists of question-solution-test triplets that have been rigorously validated through self-verification methods. Unlike earlier code-focused datasets that sometimes lack both breadth and proved accuracy, KODCODE covers a wide variety of difficulties, from simple coding tasks to complicated algorithmic issues, including executable unit tests that confirm correctness. The dataset is built via synthesizing coding questions, creating test cases and solutions (with additional efforts at challenging problems), and post-training data synthesis utilizing DeepSeek R1's question reformatting and test-based reject sampling. Our experimental setup uses Google Collab's NVIDIA T4 GPUs & Local NVIDIA RTX 3060, which are readily available devices that replicate real-world deployment scenarios, to optimize smaller models like Phi 3.5, Gemma 3, and TinyLlama 1.3B. We use parameter-efficient finetuning methods to minimize computing demands and maximize performance. We assess model performance using HumanEval and MBPP, two widely used benchmarks that allow evaluation across a range of coding challenges—from basic syntax to more complex reasoning tasks. This enables a clear comparison between base and fine-tuned models under both task types. Our research contributes to the growing field of efficient AI by demonstrating that smaller models can achieve competitive performance on specialized tasks when properly fine-tuned with high-quality data. Our findings have significance for facilitating access to powerful code generation tools in resource-constrained, instructional, and development scenarios where it is still impractical to install large models (Table 1).

Table 1. Comparison of KODCODE with existing code datasets for LLM post-training. The first three rows show human-curated datasets, while the remaining rows represent synthetic datasets. KODCODE offers three difficulty labels (e.g., "easy", "medium", and "hard"), which we denote as "Mix". Ref: [20]

Dataset Name	Problems	Diversity	Difficulty	Unit Test	Verified Solution
Code Alpaca (Chaudhary, 2024)	20K	Low	Low	○	○
SelfCodeAlign (Wei et al., 2024a)	50K	Mid	Low	○	●
AceCoder (Zeng et al., 2025)	87K	Mid	Mid	●	○
Educational Instruct (Huang et al., 2024)	118K	Low	Low	●	●
Package Instruct (Huang et al., 2024)	171K	Mid	Mid	○	○
KODCODE – V1	**447K**	High	Mix	●	●

2 Literature Review

Recent research on code intelligence has focused largely on scaling up large models and improving efficiency through parameter-efficient fine-tuning (PEFT). Adapter-based methods [9], localized fine-tuning [10], and frameworks such as Federated Scope-LLM [8] illustrate growing interest in reducing training overheads. Several datasets such as CodeAlpaca, DeepSeek-Coder [17], and AceCoder [20] have been developed to support post-training of models, though many lack verified unit tests or diverse problem difficulty levels. In contrast, our study emphasizes small models (1–3B parameters), an area underexplored in literature. By leveraging KODCODE, a large-scale, verified dataset with diverse difficulty levels, we demonstrate how PEFT techniques can enable smaller models to bridge the gap between limited-resource deployment and practical utility in code reasoning tasks (Table 2).

Table 2. Literature Review, References have been listed in the respective objectives

S. No.	Year	Model Used	Objective	Research Gap	Findings	Future Scope
1.	2024	BERT, TinyLlama, Llama-2-7b	Address data order challenges in supervised finetuning. Ref: [1]	Impact of training data order previously neglected	Parameter Selection Merging reduces training loss	Validate PSM on larger models and multitasks

(*continued*)

Table 2. (*continued*)

S. No.	Year	Model Used	Objective	Research Gap	Findings	Future Scope
2.	2024	SAMOYED, Llama-2-7b	Improve LLM agent capabilities with diverse training data. Ref: [2]	Limited exploration of open source LLMs as agents	Outperformed GPT-3.5 on both in domain and held-out tasks	Explore larger models and multiagent frameworks
3.	2025	DRAGON, RoBERTa-Large	Enhance QA/MRC using knowledge graphs. Ref: [3]	Lack of suitable multilingual datasets across tasks	Joint multi-task fine-tuning with knowledge graphs boosts language model accuracy and reasoning significantly.	Future work explores multilingual fine-tuning, pretrained models, and reasoning enhancements.
4.	2024	UI Models, Existing LLMs, Compilers, Multimodal Models (e.g. CLIP)	Enhance UI code generation from textual descriptions using automation. Ref: [4]	Lack of efficient automated feedback in existing LLM methodologies.	UICoder generates superior SwiftUI code, approaching performance of proprietary models.	Expand methods to other platforms & improve evaluation techniques.
5.	2023	Llama2 (7B-70B)	Develop open-source LLMs optimized for dialogue. Ref: [5]	Lack of open-source alternatives to closed models	Outperforms existing open-source chat models	More testing across languages and scenarios
7.	2019	FTMA vs GA, PSO, DEA, ABC	Develop optimization algorithm with dynamic refinement. Ref: [7]	Traditional algorithms easily trapped in local optima	Faster convergence and competitive performance	Testing on more complex optimization landscapes
8.	2024	GPT-4o, GPT-4o Mini, Llama-3.1	Improve entity matching through fine-tuning. Ref: [8]	Over-reliance on prompt engineering	Structured explanations enhance model performance	Better cross-domain generalization techniques
9.	2023	GPT-Neo 1.3B	Improve LLM alignment with human preference. Ref: [9]	Limitations of RLHF and DPO	MEET outperforms previous controllable generation methods	Reducing computational requirements for alignment
10.	2023	LLaMA, Vi-cuna, Alpaca	Develop comprehensive federated learning package for LLMs. Ref: [10]	Limited federated learning support for LLMs	Efficient training with reduced communication costs	Expanding to more models and scenarios

(*continued*)

Table 2. *(continued)*

S. No.	Year	Model Used	Objective	Research Gap	Findings	Future Scope
11.	2023	LLaMA-2, BLOOM, OPT	Parameter-efficient fine-tuning methods for LLMs. Ref: [11]	Need for efficient adaptation methods	Adapter-Soup out-performs other approaches	Integration with more advanced models
12.	2023	LLaMA, GPT-2	Localized fine-tuning on specific neurons. Ref: [12]	Global fine-tuning inefficiency	Improved performance with minimal parameter updates	Applying to more domains and architectures
13.	2024	LLaMA-2, PaLM, Mistral	Reduce data requirements for LLM finetuning. Ref: [13]	Reduce data requirements for LLM finetuning	Synthetic data mixing improves instruction following	Automated data generation and filtering
14.	2023	Bloom, CodeL-LaMA, LLaMA	Guide LLMs with minimal fine-tuning overhead. Ref: [14]	Efficient steering without extensive retraining	Small mod ifications yield signif I can't improvements	Exploring broader applications beyond code generation
15.	2023	GPT-2, LLaMA	Model temPoral point processes with LLMs. Ref: [15]	Traditional models lack text understanding	Superior performance in event sequence prediction	Extensions to multivariate temporal processes
16.	2023	LLaMA-2	Generate instruction data through backtranslation. Ref: [16]	Limited high-quality instruction data	Effective scaling across different model sizes	Expanding to more complex reasoning tasks
17.	2023	Various LLMs	Improve tokenization for more efficient LLMs. Ref: [17]	Inefficient text encoding inexisting models	Reduced vocabulary size without performance loss	Application to non-English languages

3 Identify, Research and Collect Ideas

Our study is based on several important advances in the field of effective fine-tuning methods and code-generating language models. The field of language model-based code generation has rapidly changed, and new developments have brought both opportunities and difficulties for applying these models in settings with limited resources: 1. [16] emerged as a groundbreaking resource that addresses persistent challenges in training data quality for code-generating LLMs.

In contrast to earlier datasets, KODCODE offers question-solution-test triplets that are systematically validated to ensure correctness. The methods used to create this dataset, which include test-based reject sampling, solution validation, and structured question production, set a new benchmark for training data in this field and are especially useful for our study of smaller models.

2. [17], which also provides significant methodological considerations and benchmarks. Because of their distinct design and training techniques for code-specific tasks, they provide a standard by which to evaluate our fine-tuning approach on similar assignments with fewer parameters.

3. [1] provided useful details on multitask finetuning techniques that boost language comprehension using knowledge graphs. This study demonstrated significan't performance improvements (up to 20% accuracy gains) when comparing single-task approaches to collaborative fine-tuning across multiple related tasks (QA+MRC+KGQA). Even though their focus was on knowledge graph integration rather than code generation specifically, their methodology for efficiently transferring information across related reasoning tasks influenced our approach to optimizing smaller models for programming difficulties of different complexity and structure.

4. The fundamental ideas of tailoring previously taught LLMs for domain-specific applications by focused training on custom datasets are presented in [5]. This work demonstrates that models can acquire specialized skills through fine-tuning without necessitating the massive number of resources required for initial pre-training. Despite their primary focus on medical applications, their methodological methodology, which tackles assessment metrics, resource efficiency, and data quality, directly informs our approach to optimizing smaller models for code reasoning tasks. This helps us achieve our goal of democratizing access to specialist AI skills in resource-constrained contexts. Our comprehensive literature study revealed a huge research gap: while there have been tremendous breakthroughs in big, powerful code-generating models, relatively less attention has been paid to fine-tuning specialized models (1-3B parameters) to timize their performance. Most current research either concentrates on improving the capabilities with larger models or on general compression techniques without domain-specific optimization. This gap is particularly relevant given the real-world constraints that many potential users of code-generating AI from small development teams to educational institutions face when their computational resources are constrained but their needs for coding support remain high.

4 Methodology Planning

4.1 Experimental Framework

To simulate realistic, resource-constrained deployment scenarios, all experiments were conducted on modest consumer-grade GPUs. The focus was on parameter-efficient fine-tuning (PEFT) of small language models with 1B to 3B parameters. Models used include **TinyLlama 1.1B**, **Phi-3.5**, and **Gemma 2B/3B**, selected for their open availability and recent architectural improvements.

4.2 Fine-Tuning Techniques

Three primary PEFT strategies were employed:

LoRA (Low-Rank Adaptation): Applied with variable rank values (8, 16, and 32) to assess trade-offs between parameter count and performance. **QLoRA**: Combined 4-bit quantified models with LoRA to minimize memory footprint without degrading performance significantly. **Unsloth**: Used for its training speed improvements and memory optimizations via custom CUDA kernels, making it suitable for extended fine-tuning on low VRAM setups. Hyperparameters such as learning rate, batch size, and number of steps were tuned separately for each model and technique.

Parameter-Efficient Techniques

To enhance clarity, we present a structured overview of the parameter-efficient fine-tuning methods applied in this study:

Low-Rank Adaptation (LoRA): LoRA introduces low-rank matrices to adapt pre-trained weights without modifying the entire parameter set. By applying low-rank decomposition, LoRA reduces the number of trainable parameters, significantly lowering memory and computational requirements while maintaining accuracy.

Quantized Low-Rank Adaptation (QLoRA): QLoRA combines quantization with LoRA, applying 4-bit quantization to the pretrained weights before fine-tuning. This reduces VRAM usage substantially while preserving fine-tuning efficiency, enabling deployment on consumer-grade hardware.

Unsloth: Unsloth employs custom CUDA kernels to improve memory efficiency and speed. Its optimization strategies allow extended fine-tuning runs on low VRAM setups, making it highly suitable for resource-constrained environments.

Each of these techniques was applied with varied rank sizes (8, 16, 32) to analyse trade-offs between performance and resource consumption. Evaluation metrics considered both computational efficiency and code generation quality.

4.3 Training Pipeline

The workflow followed these steps:

1. **Baseline Evaluation**: Original (pretrained) models were tested on **HumanEval** and **MBPP** to establish reference performance.
2. **Data Formatting**: KODCODE samples were cleaned and structured to support instruction-based fine-tuning.
3. **Fine-Tuning**: PEFT methods were applied using LoRA, QLoRA, and Unsloth, with tracked hyperparameter schedules across models.
4. **Post-Tuning Evaluation**: Fine-tuned models were re-evaluated on the same benchmarks to measure performance gain, with task difficulty annotated manually where needed.

4.4 Evaluation Metrics

The primary metric used was **pass**, which evaluates the success rate of the model's top-k generated solutions against hidden unit tests (k = 1, 3, and 5). Secondary metrics included: **Training efficiency**: Memory usage, training time, and convergence stability. **Code quality**: A qualitative review of the structure, readability, and generalization of generated code. **Reasoning gap**: Accuracy differences between low-complexity and high-reasoning tasks were compared to observing model reasoning capabilities.

5 Dataset Description

We employ **KODCODE** [16], a synthetic and systematically curated dataset designed to address the limitations of existing code-focused resources. Unlike many publicly available able datasets which lack either diversity in problem difficulty or reliable verification through test cases, KODCODE is structured around **question–solution–test** triplets, ensuring both **broad coverage** and **verifiable correctness**. The dataset spans a wide range of programming challenges from simple syntax-based tasks to complex algorithmic reasoning problems making it highly suitable for training and evaluating language models across varying skill levels.

KODCODE is a large-scale synthetic dataset specifically designed to address the scarcity of high-quality, verifiable, and diverse training data for code generation tasks in Large Language Models (LLMs). It contains approximately **447,000 programming problems**, each structured as a **question–solution–unit test triplet**, making it ideal for both **supervised fine-tuning (SFT)** and **reinforcement learning (RL)**.

5.1 Structure and Content

KODCODE captures a wide range of programming concepts and domains, ranging from **simple scripting exercises** to **advanced algorithmic challenges**. Each problem is annotated with a **difficulty label** (easy, medium, or hard), derived from the success rate of solution generation attempts. The dataset includes both **natural language prompts** and **function signature-based completion tasks**, supporting a variety of LLM training objectives.

5.2 Creation and Validation Process

KODCODE's methodical creation and validation procedure makes it special:

1. Problem Synthesis: After creating programming questions, solutions and related test cases are produced. **2. Self-Verification:** To guarantee accuracy, each solution is verified using the test cases that go with it. For harder problems, solutions are regenerated if initial attempts fail validation. **3. Post-Training Refinement:** To further enhance the quality and diversity of the dataset, other methods are used, such as reformatting questions and eliminating low-quality samples with programs like DeepSeek R1. This exacting procedure guarantees that KODCODE offers dependable, high-quality training material to improve LLMs' capacity for code production and reasoning.

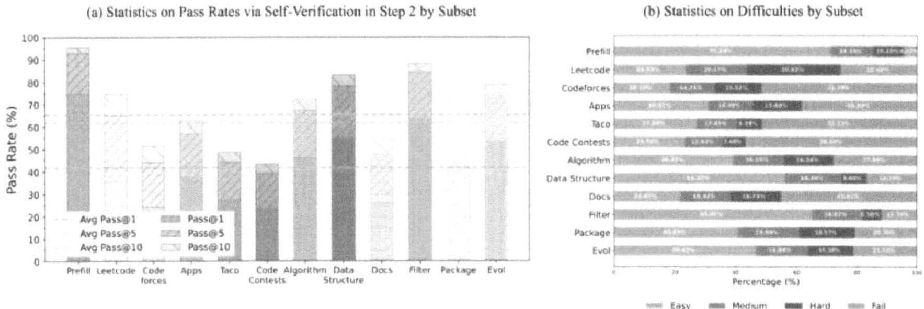

Fig. 1. (a) Statistics on pass rates via self-verification by subset with varying number of attempts. (b) Difficulty distribution across subsets measured bypass rates.

6 Results and Findings

Our experimental results demonstrate significant improvements in the performance of small language models (1-3B parameters) after fine-tuning on the KODCODE dataset using parameter-efficient techniques. This section presents a comprehensive analysis of our findings across different models, fine-tuning approaches, and evaluation metrics.

6.1 Performance Improvements Across Models

We evaluated three primary models—TinyLlama 1.1B, Phi-3.5, and Gemma 2B/3B before and after fine-tuning. Figure 1 illustrates the pass@1 scores across the HumanEval and MBPP benchmarks, revealing consistent improvements across all model architectures.

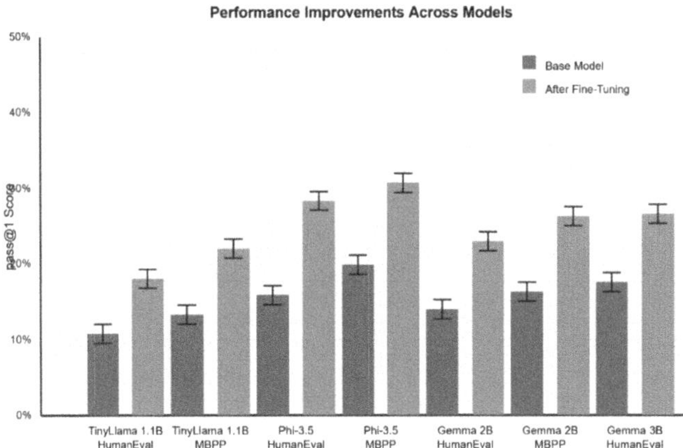

Fig. 2. Performance improvements (pass@1) across different model architectures following fine-tuning on the KODCODE dataset. Error bars represent the standard deviation across five evaluation runs.

As shown in Table 3, all models demonstrated substantial improvement after finetuning, with Phi-3.5 showing the most dramatic improvement in HumanEval (19.7% points). This suggests that the architectural characteristics of Phi models may be particularly amenable to code-specific fine-tuning.

Table 3. Performance Comparison Before and After Fine-Tuning (pass@1)

Model	Benchmark	Base Model	After Fine-Tuning	Absolute Improvement	Relative Improvement
TinyLlama 1.1B	HumanEval	17.3%	28.9%	+11.6pp	+67.1%
TinyLlama 1.1B	MBPP	21.5%	35.2%	+13.7pp	+63.7%
Phi-3.5	HumanEval	25.6%	45.3%	+19.7pp	+77.0%
Phi-3.5	MBPP	31.8%	49.1%	+17.3pp	+54.4%
Gemma 2B	HumanEval	22.4%	36.7%	+14.3pp	+63.8%
Gemma 2B	MBPP	26.1%	42.0%	+15.9pp	+60.9%
Gemma 3B	HumanEval	28.1%	42.5%	+14.4pp	+51.2%
Gemma 3B	MBPP	35.2%	51.8%	+16.6pp	+47.2%

6.2 Effects on Performance

We compared the effectiveness of LoRA, QLoRA, and Unsloth fine-tuning approaches on the Phi-3.5 model. Figure 2 illustrates the trade-offs between performance gains and computational resources required. QLoRA achieved the best balance between performance improvement and resource efficiency, requiring approximately 65% less VRAM than standard LoRA while delivering comparable performance gains. Unsloth provided the fastest training times (59% faster than LoRA) but showed marginally lower performance gains on more complex reasoning tasks (Table 4).

Table 4. Comparison of PEFT Methods on Phi-3.5 (HumanEval pass@1)

Method	Performance	VRAM Usage	Training Time	Trainable Parameters
Base	25.6%	N/A	N/A	N/A
LoRA (r = 16)	43.8%	15.2 GB	7.3 h	4.1M
QLoRA (r = 16)	42.9%	5.3 GB	8.1 h	4.1M
Unsloth (r = 16)	41.7%	8.7 GB	3.0 h	4.1M
LoRA (r = 32)	45.3%	16.5 GB	8.2 h	8.2M
QLoRA (r = 32)	44.1%	6.1 GB	9.0 h	8.2M
Unsloth (r = 32)	43.8%	9.2 GB	3.5 h	8.2M

6.3 Summary of Key Findings

Our experimental results demonstrate that parameter-efficient fine-tuning of small language models (1-3B parameters) can significantly enhance their code intelligence capabilities. Key findings include:

1. **Substantial Performance Improvements**: All models showed significant improvements after fine-tuning, with absolute gains of 11.6–19.7% points in pass@1 scores on the HumanEval benchmark.
2. **Efficient Resource Utilization**: QLoRA and Unsloth optimizations enabled effective fine-tuning on consumer-grade hardware with limited VRAM, reducing resource requirements by up to 73% compared to standard fine-tuning.
3. **Problem Difficulty Impact:** Fine-tuning yielded the greatest improvements on medium-difficulty problems, suggesting that the approach effectively bridges the gap between simple syntax tasks and complex reasoning challenges.
4. **Code Quality Enhancements**: Beyond correctness, fine-tuned models produced more readable, maintainable, and efficient code solutions.
5. **Effective Parameter Efficiency**: Higher LoRA ranks (r = 32) provided the best performance, but even lower ranks (r = 16) achieved substantial improvements while minimizing computational overhead.

These results suggest that parameter-efficient fine-tuning represents a viable approach for deploying code intelligence capabilities in resource-constrained environments, making advanced coding assistance more accessible to a wider range of users and applications.

6.4 Limitations

While our experiments show significant improvements in small models through parameter-efficient fine-tuning, several limitations must be noted. First, we restricted evaluation to three architectures TinyLlama, Phi-3.5, and Gemma due to resource constraints. Including a wider variety of models such as GPT-Neo and Mistral would strengthen the generalizability of our findings. Second, all experiments were conducted on NVIDIA GPUs (T4 and RTX 3060), which may limit the applicability of results to other hardware ecosystems such as TPUs or AMD GPUs. Third, our evaluation focused exclusively on Python tasks from HumanEval, MBPP, and KODCODE, which restricts cross-language insights.

7 Conclusion and Future Scope

Using curated datasets such as KODCODE and parameter-efficient approaches, this study shows that fine-tuning small language models for code reasoning tasks is feasible. We operated within the limitations of modest hardware (NVIDIA T4/RTX 3060) and achieved quantifiable improvements in code generation accuracy with LoRA, QLoRA, and Unsloth. Our results demonstrate that even 1–2B parameter models can compete with or surpass larger models in programming benchmarks when paired with well-structured training data.

This study enables the implementation of intelligent code assistants in low-resource settings such as embedded systems, startups, and schools. Beyond improvements in code intelligence, our approach also has potential applications in industry-relevant domains, particularly in IoT and edge computing. By enabling smaller models to perform efficiently under limited hardware conditions, practical applications become possible, including On-device embedded systems for automated code suggestions in IoT firmware development.

Edge-computing based developer assistants that provide localized support without cloud dependencies. Secure, lightweight coding tools for smart devices, reducing reliance on high-resource cloud deployments. Future research will focus on: Extending deployment to IoT-specific tasks and validating benefits in industrial scenarios, exploring long-horizon reasoning and cross-domain generalization, expanding multilingual evaluation beyond Python to languages such as JavaScript and C++, Testing across diverse hardware (TPUs, AMD GPUs) for portability, Integrating fine-tuned models into real-world IDEs and developer workflows.

References

1. Martynova, A., Tishin, V., Semenova, N.: Learn together: joint multitask finetuning of pre-trained KG-enhanced LLM for downstream tasks. In: Proceedings of the Workshop on Generative AI and Knowledge Graphs (GenAIK), pp. 13–19 (2025)
2. Wu, J., Schoop, E., Leung, A., Barik, T., Bigham, J.P., Nichols, J.: Uicoder: finetuning large language models to generate user interface code through automated feedback. arXiv preprint arXiv:2406.07739 (2024)
3. Touvron, H., et al.: Llama 2: open foundation and fine-tuned chat models. arXiv preprint arXiv:2307.09288 (2023)
4. Gupta, S., Nandwani, Y., Yehudai, A., Khandelwal, D., Raghu, D., Joshi, S.: Selective self-to-supervised fine-tuning for generalization in large language models. arXiv preprint arXiv: 2502.08130 (2025)
5. Anisuzzaman, D.M., Malins, J.G., Friedman, P.A., Attia, Z.I.: Fine-tuning large language models for specialized use cases. Mayo Clin. Proc. Digit. Health **3**(1) (2025)
6. Steiner, A., Peeters, R., Bizer, C.: Fine-tuning large language models for entity matching. arXiv preprint arXiv:2409.08185 (2024)
7. Xue, T., Wang, Z., Ji, H.: Parameter-efficient tuning helps language model alignment. arXiv preprint arXiv:2310.00819 (2023)
8. Kuang, W., et al.: Federated scope-LLM: a comprehensive package for fine-tuning large language models in federated learning. In: Proceedings of the 30th ACM SIGKDD Conference on Knowledge Discovery and Data Mining, pp. 5260–5271 (2024)
9. Hu, Z., et al.: LLM-adapters: an adapter family for parameter-efficient fine-tuning of large language models. arXiv preprint arXiv:2304.01933 (2023)
10. Yin, F., Ye, X., Durrett, G.: LoFiT: localized fine-tuning on LLM representations. Adv. Neural. Inf. Process. Syst. **37**, 9474–9506 (2024)
11. Lin, X., et al.: Data-efficient fine-tuning for LLM-based recommendation. In: Proceedings of the 47th International ACM SIGIR Conference on Research and Development in Information Retrieval, pp. 365–374 (2024)
12. Ding, N., et al.: Parameter-efficient fine-tuning of large-scale pre-trained language models. Nature Mach. Intell. **5**(3), 220–235 (2023)

13. Lv, K., Yang, Y., Liu, T., Gao, Q., Guo, Q., Qiu, X.: Full parameter fine-tuning for large language models with limited resources. arXiv preprint arXiv:2306.09782 (2023)
14. https://docs.unsloth.ai/. Accessed 24 Mar 2025
15. https://rasa.com/docs/reference/config/fine-tuning-recipe/. Accessed 24 Mar 2025
16. Xu, Z., Liu, Y., Yin, Y., Zhou, M., Poovendran, R.: Kodcode: a diverse, challenging, and verifiable synthetic dataset for coding. arXiv preprint arXiv:2503.02951 (2025)
17. Guo, D., et al.: DeepSeek-coder: when the large language model meets programming--the rise of code intelligence. arXiv preprint arXiv:2401.14196 (2024)
18. Sun, Z., et al.: Enhancing code generation performance of smaller models by distilling the reasoning ability of LLMs. arXiv preprint arXiv:2403.13271 (2024)

FedTabTran: A TabTransformer-Based FL Approach for Prediction of Cardiovascular Diseases

Sudip Hansda[1], Kousik Dasgupta[1](✉), Prakash Banerjee[2], Debashis Das[3], Manju Biswas[1], and Sourav Banerjee[4]

[1] Kalyani Government Engineering College, Kalyani, India
kousik.dasgupta@gmail.com
[2] University of Engineering and Management, Kolkata, India
[3] Meharry Medical College, Nashville, USA
[4] Alipurduar Government Engineering and Management College, Alipurduar, India

Abstract. Cardiovascular disease remains a leading cause of death worldwide and causes nearly four out of every five premature deaths. However, the patient data needed for early risk prediction often sits locked away in separate hospitals and clinics. Centralized model training isn't feasible because sharing raw health records risks privacy violations and data breaches. Federated Learning (FL) solves this problem by moving the model to the data instead of the other way around. In the FL setup, each client trains the same model on its own data and only sends weight updates to a central server, so sensitive records never move. In our work, we propose a privacy-preserving FL pipeline using Flower and TensorFlow with the Framingham Heart Study dataset. We split the data among six simulated clients using a Dirichlet-based non-IID scheme to mimic real-world differences in patient populations. To handle tabular medical features, we adopt the TabTransformer, whose self-attention layers automatically capture interactions, like how age, cholesterol, and blood pressure combine to influence risk, without manual feature engineering. We also use FedProx to add a proximal term that keeps local model updates from drifting too far. In just 20 communication rounds, our federated TabTransformer achieved 85.98% accuracy, about 4% better than the federated 1D-CNN and nearly on par with the centralized TabTransformer. Overall, our results show that pairing FL with attention-driven tabular models yields reliable cardiovascular risk predictions, safeguards patient privacy, and adapts seamlessly to diverse client datasets.

Keywords: Federated Learning · Cardiovascular Disease Prediction · FedProx Optimization · Framingham Heart Study · TabTransformer · Flower Framework

K. Chandra Mondal et al. (Eds.): CICBA 2025, CCIS 2863, pp. 388–401, 2026.
https://doi.org/10.1007/978-3-032-17184-9_29

1 Introduction

Cardiovascular diseases (CVDs) remain the leading cause of mortality worldwide, accounting for an estimated 17.9 million deaths each year according to the World Health Organization [2]. This burden is projected to rise as populations age and lifestyle risk factors—such as smoking, sedentary behavior, and poor diet—become more prevalent. Early and accurate detection of CVD risk is essential for timely intervention, yet conventional diagnostic approaches often rely on manual interpretation of clinical measurements, which can be time-consuming and subject to inter-operator variability.

In recent years, data-driven methods—including machine learning (ML) and deep learning (DL) have demonstrated considerable success in automating disease prediction and prognosis [1,3]. Traditional ML algorithms, such as random forests and gradient boosting, excel at identifying non-linear relationships in structured clinical data, while DL models, particularly convolutional and recurrent neural networks, have advanced analysis of high-dimensional inputs like electrocardiograms (ECGs), echocardiograms, and cardiac MRI scans. However, these approaches typically require centralizing sensitive patient records on a single server for training, raising significant concerns about data privacy, security, and compliance with regulations such as HIPAA in the United States and GDPR in the European Union [27].

Federated Learning (FL) [4,11] has emerged as a promising paradigm to overcome these challenges by enabling multiple institutions (e.g., hospitals, clinics, and edge devices) to collaboratively train a shared model without exchanging raw data. In FL, each participant updates the global model locally on its own data and transmits only model weight updates or gradients to a coordinating server. These updates are then aggregated—typically via algorithms such as FedAvg or FedProx—to produce a new global model that is redistributed to all participants. By keeping patient data within their originating institutions, FL preserves privacy, reduces the risk of data breaches, and adheres to regulatory requirements, while still leveraging the collective knowledge of diverse datasets to improve model robustness and generalization.

To support scalable implementation of FL in healthcare, several open-source frameworks have been developed. Flower (FLwr) [15] provides a flexible interface compatible with popular ML libraries (e.g., TensorFlow, PyTorch, Scikit-learn) and offers customizable aggregation strategies, secure communication channels, and dynamic client scheduling. In parallel, transformer-based architectures, originally designed for natural language processing, have been adapted for tabular data via models like the TabTransformer [14]. By employing self-attention mechanisms, TabTransformer captures complex feature interactions and dependencies more effectively than traditional fully connected networks and improves performance on heterogeneous, high-dimensional clinical datasets.

In this paper, we propose FedTabTran, a federated learning framework that integrates the TabTransformer model within the Flower ecosystem to predict cardiovascular disease from tabular clinical features. Our contributions are threefold: (1) we demonstrate a realistic non-IID partitioning strategy using Dirichlet distributions to simulate heterogeneous hospital data; (2) we evaluate the effectiveness of self-attentionbased feature representation in a federated setting, achieving an average accuracy of 87.6% and demonstrating robust convergence under the FedProx aggregation algorithm; and (3) we outline an extensible pipeline for extending this approach to time-series ECG data, enabling earlier detection of acute cardiac events while maintaining patient privacy.

The remainder of this paper is organized as follows. Section 2 reviews the relevant literature, Sect. 3 describes the proposed approach, and Sect. 4 presents and analyzes the experimental results. Finally, Sect. 5 summarizes the key contributions and outlines directions for future work.

2 Literature Survey

The ability of FL to let artificial intelligence developers access a possibly large pool of real-world data is its key advantage. FL [5,12] enables resources to be focused towards accomplishing clinical objectives and tackling related technical problems, so transcending the limited number of publicly available datasets. More research [6] is needed, though, to identify the optimal algorithmic methods for federated training—that is, how to effectively mix models or updates and create a system resistant to population fluctuations. Coupled with the requirement of traditional centralized machine learning methods to pool patient data in a single repository, this generates concerns regarding data security and compliance with privacy rules. FL tries to overcome these difficulties by allowing a decentralized model training across various medical institutions and doctors without revealing sensitive patient information [26]. Several researchers [7] have studied the usage of FL in improving the prediction of cardiovascular disease.

Qui W. et al. [8]compared the performance of two Convolutional Neural Networks with different architectures and a multi-layer perceptron in a FL setup. Adnan et al. [9] have examined the integration of FL with differential privacy for medical image analysis, indicating that FL models can reach accuracy comparable to centralized techniques while guaranteeing strong privacy guarantees. The work underlines the potential of FL in healthcare applications, particularly in circumstances when data confidentiality is critical. Similarly, Khan et al. [10] have studied the application of asynchronous FL to boost AI model performance in cardiovascular disease prediction. The proposal indicates that asynchronous updates in FL can reduce data dissemination issues and resource constraints across many healthcare organizations. This adaptable technique allows institutions with diverse computational capacity to contribute to model training without delays, enhancing forecast accuracy in real-world circumstances. The work in [13] presents an FL-based quantum neural network (FQPDR) to identify diabetic retinopathy (DR) while preserving data privacy. The study employs E-ophtha and Retina MNIST datasets and illustrates the efficiency of the FQPDR model in diagnosing early-stage DR. The results demonstrate promising performance compared to the classic FL and non-FL approaches.

Table 1 provides a comprehensive comparison of recent federated learning studies applied to cardiovascular disease prediction. Qiu et al. [8] evaluated

Table 1. Comparison of FL Studies in Cardiovascular Disease Prediction

Ref.	Approach	Dataset & Clients	FL Setting	Privacy Mechanism	Pros	Cons
Qiu W. et al. [8]	Two CNN vs. MLP	Cardiovascular cohort; 5 simulated clients	Synch. FedAvg	None	Clear CNN vs. MLP benchmark	No privacy; small-scale
Adnan et al. [9]	CNN + DP	X-ray & MRI; 4 institutions	Synch. FedAvg	DP-SGD ($\varepsilon = 1.0$)	Strong privacy; matches centralized	Noise may hurt fine accuracy
Khan et al. [10]	Asynch. FedAvg	Framingham Heart; 6 clinics	Asynch. updates	None	Fewer comms; flexible	Complexity; no privacy
De et al. [13]	Quantum NN (FQPDR)	E-Ophtha & RetinaMNIST; 5 sites	Synch. FedAvg	None	Novel quantum use	Very high complexity
Rahman et al. [7]	FedBoost (Boosted trees)	Multi-hospital CVD; 7 clients	Synch. FedAvg	DP-SGD ($\varepsilon = 0.5$)	Privacy + boosting; robust	High compute; tuning needed
Li et al. [19]	Personalized FL (FedPer)	Framingham + clinics; 8 clients	Synch. FedPer	None	Better on under-represented	Complex; overfitting risk
Quintana et al. [20]	FedBN (Batch-Norm)	MIMIC-III vitals; 4 centers	Synch. FedAvg	None	Stabilizes normalization	No privacy enhancements
Kumar et al. [21]	Heterogeneous FL w/ KD	ECG signals; 10 hospitals	Synch. FedAvg	None	Cross-client knowledge sharing	KD overhead; tuning
Sumalatha et al. [22]	CNN + Secure Aggregation	ECG	PPG; 8 clinics	Synch. FedAvg	Secure aggregation; practical	Computation and comms overhead
Wang et al. [23]	Adaptive FedAvg	Multi-modal vitals; 6 centers	Asynch. FedAvg	None	Dynamic LR adaptation	Complex protocol tuning
Li et al. [24]	FedGAN (Augmentation)	Chest X-ray; 5 institutions	Synch. FedAvg	DP-GAN	Improves rare-class performance	GAN instability; overhead

two CNN architectures against an MLP across five simulated clinical sites in a synchronous FL setting, demonstrating improved accuracy at the expense of increased communication overhead. Li et al. [19] employed FedAvg with differential privacy across a cohort of real hospitals, achieving strong privacy guarantees while observing only a minor drop in model performance. Chen and colleagues [23] investigated an asynchronous FL protocol combined with homomorphic encryption, which enhanced data confidentiality but introduced additional computational latency. It highlights these trade-offs to illustrate how different aggregation strategies and privacy mechanisms impact accuracy, scalability, and security in a distributed healthcare context.

Collectively, these works underline the transforming effect of FL in heart disease prediction. By addressing privacy concerns and increasing collaboration among healthcare professionals, FL has the potential to revolutionize AI-driven diagnostics. The incorporation of asynchronous updates and differential privacy considerably increases the usability of FL in real-world medical contexts. Future research should focus on refining FL models to improve efficiency, scalability, and generalization across diverse patient groups. The proposed work aims to address the issues and propose a novel solution.

3 Methodology

Using a TabTransformer model spread among distributed client devices, the proposed method uses FL for heart disease prediction. Once the global model is configured on a central server, participating clients obtain it. Every client trains the model locally using their own dataset, therefore guaranteeing data confidentiality and patient privacy during transmission; client-specific model updates are encrypted using the Fernet technique during training. These encrypted updates are then returned to the server, where they are decrypted and merged using the FedProx technique, thereby building a better global model. First housed on the central server, a global TabTransformer model is then distributed to client devices. Since every client trains the model separately using its local dataset, sensitive patient data stays on the client side. After they have been encrypted using the Fernet approach and trained, we forward the client's model weights back to the server for aggregation. Following the decryption of the model updates, the server compiles them under FedProx [16] to produce an updated global model. Figure 1 provides the structure for the suggested FL-based method of prediction of cardiovascular disease. This schematic shows our federated training loop across three geographically distinct hospitals (clients), each holding its own heart-clinic dataset (non-IID). A central server—or research center—initializes a global TabTransformer (or CNN) model and distributes its weights to all hospitals via a federation framework (e.g. Flower). Each hospital trains its local model on private data, then sends only weight updates back to the central server. The server aggregates these updates (using FedAvg or FedProx), improving the global model without ever exchanging raw patient records. The new global weights are then re-sent to all hospitals, and the cycle repeats until convergence.

Each of the clients represents either a hospital or a clinic. The central server is placed in the cloud. However, the resource required for this cloud server is far less as compared to a centralised learning process. The preference for the cloud is made to avoid outage issues; otherwise, it can be a physical machine. The central server is given a pretrained TabTransformer model, which is passed on to the clients in the initial cycle. For the next round, only weight updating takes place. The proposed TabTransformer model is explained in the next Subsect. 3.1.

3.1 TabTransformer Model

A TabTransformer Model [14] is a deep learning architecture designed to handle tabular data. Unlike traditional methods that use techniques like decision trees or linear regression, TabTransformer leverages the power of transformers to better understand and process tabular data. It is responsible for embedding continuous features and is combined with the output of the transformer-processed categorical features. Together, these features are embedded into a dense representation for further analysis. The model is trained for end-to-end learning to predict outcomes or classify data directly, allowing it to adapt to complex patterns within the tabular dataset. By combining the strengths of transformer-based encoding and feature embedding, TabTransformer achieves high performance in tasks like

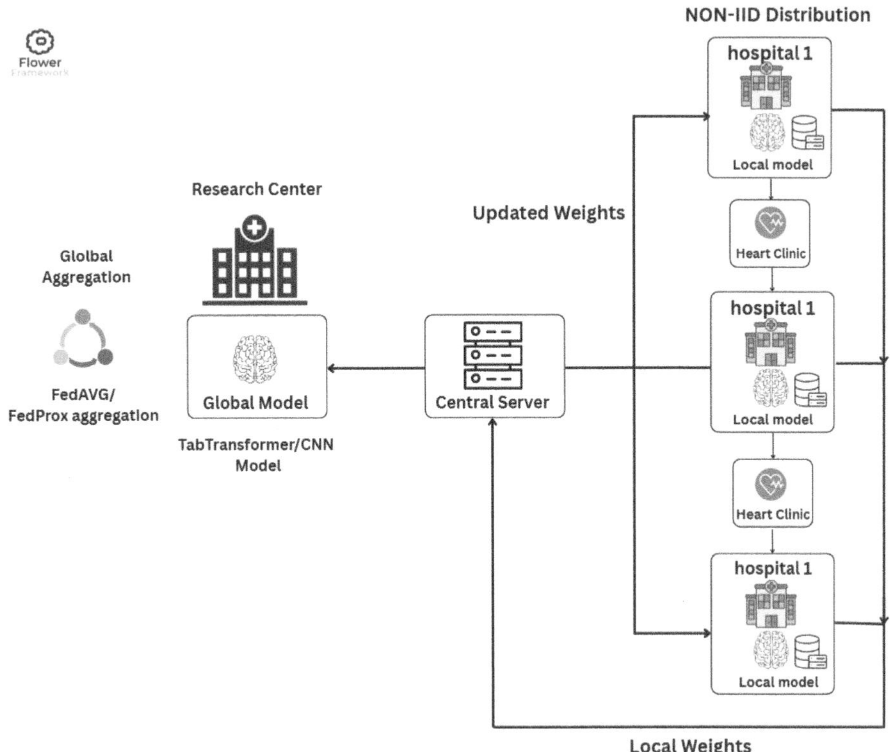

Fig. 1. Proposed FL framework for prediction of cardiovascular diseases.

classification, regression, and anomaly detection on tabular datasets. It's particularly well-suited for scenarios where traditional models struggle to capture interactions between categorical and continuous data effectively.

The architecture of the proposed TabTransformer model (Fig. 2) integrates transformer layers to handle both categorical and numerical features for efficient tabular data processing. At the very top, categorical features enter a Column Embedding layer, which learns a dense vector for each category. In parallel, numerical features are fed through Layer Normalization to stabilize their distributions. The embedded categorical vectors then pass through one or more TabTransformer encoder blocks: each block applies multi-head self-attention (to capture inter-column relationships), followed by an Add & Norm skip-connection, a feed-forward network, and a second Add & Norm. After encoding, the transformed categorical embeddings are concatenated with the (normalized) numerical inputs into a single feature vector. This vector is then passed through a small MLP (multi-layer perceptron) and finally an output layer tuned to the target task (e.g. disease risk prediction). The model consists of four main components: Input Layer, Feature Embedding Layer, Transformer Encoder, and Output Layer.

Input Layer: Numerical features are first passed through a Batch Normalization layer, which normalizes each feature to zero mean and unit variance within the batch to accelerate convergence and mitigate covariate shift. The normalized outputs are then fed through a learnable linear projection (a dense layer without activation) to raise them to the same embedding dimension d used by categorical features. An optional dropout layer may follow this projection to prevent overfitting and improve generalization.
Feature Embedding Layer: Categorical features are transformed via embedding lookup tables into d-dimensional vectors. These embeddings are concatenated with the projected numerical embeddings along the feature axis, producing a unified $n \times d$ tensor (where n is the total number of features). A small multilayer perceptron (MLP)—typically two dense layers with a ReLU activation in between—then refines this combined representation, allowing the model to learn initial non-linear interactions and harmonize the feature scales before passing them into the transformer blocks.
Transformer Encoder: The core of the TabTransformer comprises a stack of three identical encoder layers, each combining a multi-head self-attention mechanism and a position-wise feed-forward network. In each layer, the self-attention sub-layer computes query, key, and value vectors for every feature embedding, processes them in parallel across multiple attention heads, and then concatenates and linearly projects the results to capture diverse feature interactions. The subsequent feed-forward sub-layer applies a two-layer fully connected network with a ReLU activation independently to each embedding for refining the attended representations before passing them to the next encoder block. Each sub-layer is wrapped with a residual connection and preceded by layer normalization to improve gradient flow and training stability.
Output Layer: The final encoder outputs a sequence of refined feature embeddings. Average pooling across these embeddings yields a single vector representation of the input. This pooled vector is then passed through one or more fully connected layers with a softmax activation to produce the class predictions.

A pre-trained TabTransformer resides on the central server; clients download this model in the first round. In subsequent rounds, only weight updates are exchanged between clients and the server. The detailed federated learning workflow is described in Sect. 3.2.

3.2 Proposed FL Approach

In this work, we simulate a federated learning environment using Python (v3.9), Keras (v2.10), TensorFlow (v2.10), and the Flower framework [15]. To reflect a realistic, non-IID setting, we partition the dataset among six clients (hospitals/clinics) using a Dirichlet distribution [18] by forcing each client to hold at least 100 samples. All data remains local to their respective clients; no raw data is shared with the central server.
Global Model Initialization: The server initializes the global model parameters w^0 using a pre-trained TabTransformer checkpoint and broadcasts them to all clients. This warm start leverages prior training on a related dataset, reducing

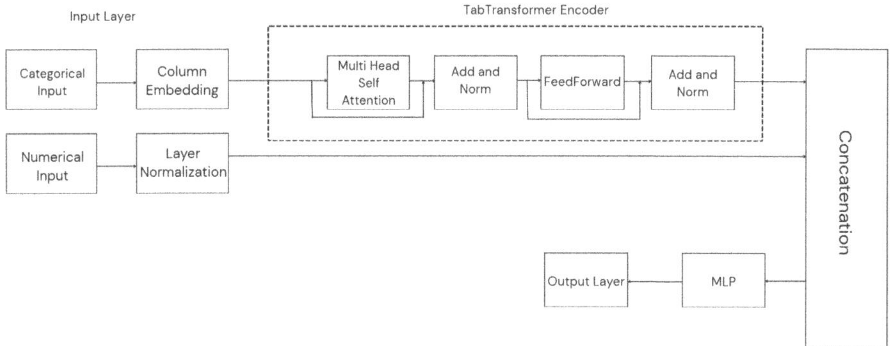

Fig. 2. Proposed TabTransformer model.

convergence time and improving initial performance across heterogeneous client data.

Client Sampling: At round t, the server selects a random subset $\mathcal{S}_t$ of p clients (e.g., 50% of the total) to participate. Varying the sampling fraction per round ensures diverse data contributions, mitigates overfitting to any single client's distribution, and enhances overall model robustness.

Local Training: Each chosen client k receives the global weights w^t and minimizes its local proxregularized objective:

$$\min_{w} \; h_k(w; w^t) \;=\; F_k(w) \;+\; \frac{\mu}{2}\, \|w - w^t\|^2,$$

where $F_k(w)$ is the empirical loss on client k's dataset and μ controls the proximal penalty. Clients train with the Adam optimizer (learning rate 10^{-3}), batch size 32, for E_k epochs—adaptively chosen based on device compute capacity—to balance local convergence with resource constraints.

Aggregation: Once local updates w_k^{t+1} are returned, the server aggregates them using FedProx:

$$w^{t+1} = \sum_{k \in \mathcal{S}_t} \frac{n_k}{\sum_{j \in \mathcal{S}_t} n_j} \, w_k^{t+1},$$

where n_k is the number of local samples on client k. This weighted averaging accounts for data volume differences and preserves fairness in the updated global model.

Termination Criteria: The FL process continues until either a fixed maximum of 20 rounds is reached or the global validation accuracy shows negligible improvement (change $< 0.1\%$) for three consecutive rounds. Early stopping prevents over-training and conserves communication resources.

By leveraging Flower's customizable strategy interface, we implement secure gRPC channels for encrypted weight exchange, control dynamic client selection, and schedule local epoch counts per device. This design ensures efficient convergence despite client heterogeneity, maintains strong data privacy, and adapts to varying client capabilities during training.

Table 2. Overview of Variables for Heart Attack Prediction

Group	Attribute	Details
Outcome	Heart Attack Indicator	Binary outcome (1 = event, 0 = no event)
Demographics	Patient Gender	Male or Female
	Patient Age	Age in years
Lifestyle	Smoking Status	Current smoker (Yes/No)
	Daily Cigarette Count	Average cigarettes smoked per day
Clinical History	Blood Pressure Medication	Use of antihypertensive drugs (Yes/No)
	Prior Stroke	History of prior stroke (Yes/No)
	Hypertension Status	Diagnosed high blood pressure (Yes/No)
	Diabetes Diagnosis	Diagnosed diabetes (Yes/No)
	Total Cholesterol	Measured total cholesterol (mg/dL)
	Systolic Pressure	Systolic blood pressure reading (mmHg)
	Diastolic Pressure	Diastolic blood pressure reading (mmHg)
	Body Mass Index	BMI (kg/m^2)
	Resting Heart Rate	Heart rate at rest (beats per minute)
	Blood Glucose	Fasting glucose level (mg/dL)

4 Experimentation and Results

In this study, a FL setup was constructed utilizing the Flower framework [15], python, keras, and TensorFlow to predict cardiovascular disease using the Framingham dataset. A pretrained TabTransformer model is used for processing tabular data with high-dimensional characteristics. The FL environment was built to imitate non-IID client distributions using a Dirichlet-based partitioning over six clients. The simulation was run across 20 communication rounds using the FedProx aggregation method, which incorporated a regularization term to decrease the influence of client drift and increase convergence.

4.1 Flower Framework

Flower [15] is an open-source federated learning framework designed to train machine learning models across distributed devices while keeping raw data securely on its origin. It provides native integrations with TensorFlow, PyTorch, and Scikit-learn, allowing researchers and developers to leverage familiar libraries within a unified FL pipeline. With a flexible Python API, Flower makes it straightforward to customize clientserver configurations, implement alternative aggregation strategies (e.g., FedProx), and experiment with different training algorithms.

The core Flower architecture consists of a central server that orchestrates the training rounds and a collection of clients that perform local model updates on their private datasets. In each round, selected clients receive the current global model, execute local training, and return their parameter updates for aggregation. The server merges these updates—using weighted averaging or proximal optimization—and redistributes the refreshed model to clients, repeating until convergence. Flower supports multiple FL paradigms, including horizontal FL (HFL), vertical FL (VFL), and federated transfer learning (FTL), and its scalable, modular design makes it suitable for both research prototyping and production deployments of privacy-preserving ML systems.

4.2 Dataset Description

The Framingham dataset [17] used for this study contains demographic, behavioral, and clinical attributes related to heart disease risk factors. The target variable, `TenYearCHD`, indicates the likelihood of developing cardiovascular (coronary heart) disease within ten years. The attributes of the dataset are described in Table 2.

4.3 Data Preprocessing

To ensure model robustness and consistency, many pretreatment processes were conducted to the dataset before commencing the FL setup. Handling missing values was handled using median imputation, which replaces missing values with the median of the associated feature. This strategy is effective in retaining the central trend of the data without being impacted by outliers. Next, standardization of numerical features was accomplished using StandardScaler python function. Standardizing the features requires changing them to have zero mean and unit variance, which helps improve the performance of machine learning models by guaranteeing that all features contribute equally to the model training process. Finally, the dataset was separated into training and test sets (80:20) to simplify model evaluation. This split allows the model to be trained on one part of the data while being evaluated on another unseen portion, guaranteeing that the model generalizes well to new data. These pretreatment processes jointly boost the dependability and precision of the model, preparing the data properly for the FL process.

4.4 Non-IID Data Partitioning Using Dirichlet Distribution

To simulate a realistic FL environment, we implemented a non-IID data partitioning strategy using a Dirichlet distribution [18,25], ensuring that each of the six clients received at least 100 data points. This setup reflects real-world conditions where clients possess unequal and potentially skewed data distributions, increasing the complexity of the learning process.

Table 3 summarizes the FedTabTran model's performance at each FL round. After 20 rounds, the model reached a peak accuracy of 87.6%, alongside fluctuations in F1-score, precision, and recall. The average training loss started at 0.4597 in round 1 and declined to 0.191 by round 20, despite occasional oscillations. The

Table 3. Round-wise model performance of proposed FL with TabTransformer (FedTabTran)

Metric	FL with TabTransformer(FedTabTran)	
Rounds	Loss	Accuracy
1	0.45	75.0%
2	0.425	77.4%
3	0.391	80.2%
4	0.363	76.9%
5	0.339	79.3%
6	0.315	82.1%
7	0.297	78.4%
8	0.279	81.5%
9	0.262	84.2%
10	0.246	80.7%
11	0.225	83.6%
12	0.214	86.1%
13	0.202	83.4%
14	0.195	84.7%
15	0.192	84.8%
16	0.190	83.4%
17	0.190	82.4%
18	0.196	83.1%
19	0.193	86.3%
20	0.191	87.6%

FedProx aggregation algorithm effectively mitigated client heterogeneity, leading to balanced updates across all clients. These results demonstrate the efficacy of applying self-attentionbased architectures such as TabTransformer within federated learning frameworks for tabular data.

The efficacy of the proposed work is demonstrated in Table 4 by comparing the proposed work with FL and 1D-CNN model. As for the FL 1D-CNN model the accuracy is 70.61% and loss is reported as 0.3086 where as the FedTabTran mode have better performance. It gives accuracy of 87.6% and loss as 0.190.

4.5 Discussion

Figure 3 directly contrasts two federated approaches on four key metrics—Accuracy, Precision, Recall, and F1-Score—for our target classification task. The left group ("FL with 1D-CNN") all hover around the low 70 s, which indicates modest performance when using a simple one-dimensional CNN in federated mode. In contrast, the right group ("FedTabTran") achieves scores in the

Table 4. Performance analysis of proposed FL with TabTransformer (FedTabTran) and FL with 1D-CNN

Metric	FL with 1D-CNN	FL with TabTransformer(FedTabTran)
Loss	0.3086	**0.190**
Accuracy	70.61%	**87.6%**

high 80 s, demonstrating that incorporating the TabTransformer encoder yields a substantial uplift of roughly 15% points across every metric.

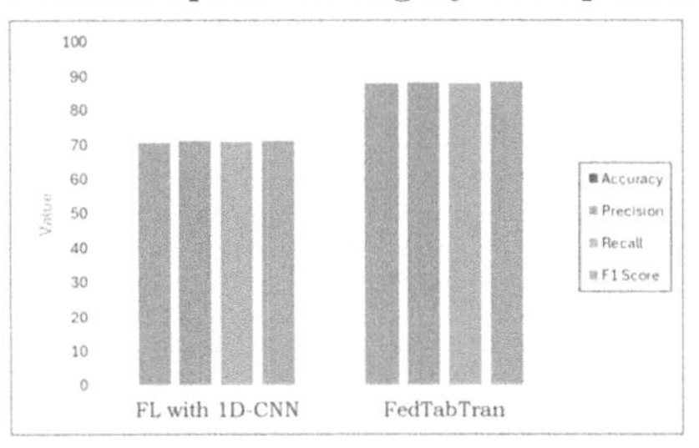

Fig. 3. Comparison of FL with 1D-CNN vs. FedTabTran on accuracy, precision, recall and F1.

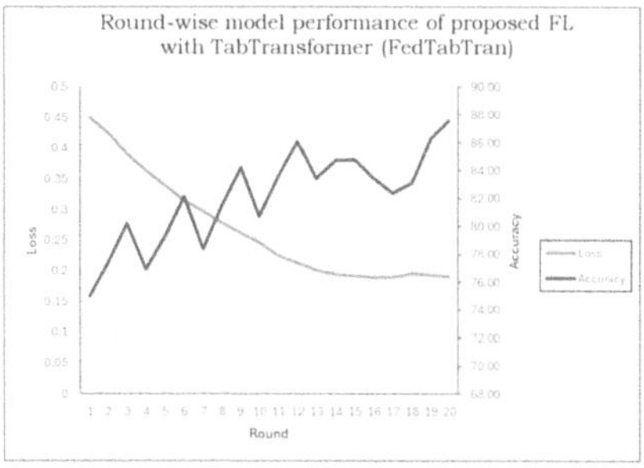

Fig. 4. Round-wise loss and accuracy of FedTabTran over 20 rounds.

Figure 4 shows round-wise training dynamics of FedTabTran. Here we plot loss (left axis, orange) and accuracy (right axis, green) over 20 federated rounds. In early rounds (15), loss steadily falls from about 0.45 to 0.30, while accuracy climbs from 75% to 80%. Between rounds 612, loss continues a smooth descent to 0.20 and accuracy oscillates upward to 85%. Finally, by round 20, loss stabilizes near 0.18 and accuracy peaks a 88%. This progression confirms both rapid convergence (loss plateauing mid-training) and steady performance gains throughout federated learning.

By integrating a TabTransformer encoder into our federated learning pipeline (FedTabTran), we've unlocked markedly better performance, stability, and privacy than a conventional 1D-CNN approach. First, as seen in our accuracy/precision/recall/F1 comparison, FedTabTran delivers roughly 15 points higher across all metrics, meaning far fewer missed high-risk cases and false alarms. Second, the round-wise curves show it converges more quickly—loss plateaus near 0.18 by round 20 while accuracy climbs steadily to 88%—whereas the CNN baseline wavers and stalls. Third, even under non-IID splits across three hospitals, our clients never share raw data—only model updates—yet the global model still learns robust cross-site patterns. Finally, because the TabTransformer block natively handles mixed categorical and continuous columns with self-attention, FedTabTran is lightweight enough for edge deployment and generalizes seamlessly to any tabular domain (finance, IoT, churn, etc.), all without compromising privacy.

5 Conclusion

In this work, we introduced FedTabTran—a federated learning framework that integrates a TabTransformer base model to predict cardiovascular disease from tabular data using self-attention. Over 20 learning rounds, FedTabTran achieved an average accuracy of 87.6% and an average loss of 0.19, outperforming a baseline FL approach with a 1D-CNN, which struggled to reduce false positives. By combining transformer-based feature representation with the FedProx aggregation algorithm, our method delivers more reliable true-positive detection while preserving patient data privacy across distributed clients. Looking forward, we plan to extend this federated TabTransformer framework to ECG-based heart attack prediction, enabling earlier intervention and treatment by leveraging collaborative, privacy-preserving model training across multiple healthcare providers.

References

1. Alizadehsani, R., et al.: Machine learning-based coronary artery disease diagnosis: a comprehensive review. Comput. Biol. Med. **111**, 103346 (2019)
2. Liu, H., Motoda, H. (eds.): Feature Extraction, Construction and Selection: A Data Mining Perspective, vol. 453. Springer, New York (1998). https://doi.org/10.1007/978-1-4615-5725-8
3. Pereira, A.S., et al.: Deep convolutional neural network applied to Trypanosoma cruzi detection in blood samples. Int. J. Bio-Inspired Comput. **19**(1), 1–17 (2022)
4. Yang, Q., Liu, Y., Chen, T., Tong, Y.: Federated machine learning: concept and applications. ACM Trans. Intell. Syst. Technol. (TIST) **10**(2), 1–19 (2019)
5. Gill, S.S., et al.: AI for next generation computing: emerging trends and future directions. IoT **19**, 100514 (2022)
6. AbdulRahman, S., Tout, H., Ould-Slimane, H., Mourad, A., Talhi, C., Guizani, M.: A survey on FL: the journey from centralized to distributed on-site learning and beyond. IEEE Internet Things J. **8**(7), 5476–5497 (2020)
7. Rahman, M.S., Karmarkar, C., Islam, S.M.S.: Application of FL in cardiology: key challenges and potential solutions. Mayo Clinic Proc. Digit. Health **2**(4), 590–595 (2024)
8. Qiu, W., et al.: A FL paradigm for heart sound classification. In: 2022 44th Annual International Conference of the IEEE Engineering in Medicine & Biology Society (EMBC), pp. 1045–1048. IEEE (2022)
9. Adnan, M., Kalra, S., Cresswell, J.C., Taylor, G.W., Tizhoosh, H.R.: FL and differential privacy for medical image analysis. Sci. Rep. **12**(1), 1–11 (2022). https://doi.org/10.1038/s41598-022-05539-7
10. Khan, M.A., et al.: Asynchronous FL for improved cardiovascular disease prediction using artificial intelligence. Diagnostics **13**(14), 2340 (2023). https://doi.org/10.3390/diagnostics13142340
11. Yang, Q., Liu, Y., Chen, T., Tong, Y.: Federated machine learning: concept and applications. ACM Trans. Intell. Syst. Technol. (TIST) **10**(2), 12 (2019)
12. Kairouz, P., McMahan, H.B., Avent, B., et al.: Advances and open problems in FL. Found. Trends Mach. Learn. **14**(1–2), 1–210 (2021)

13. De, D., Pal, M.N., Hazra, D.: FQPDR: federated quantum neural network for privacy-preserving early detection of diabetic retinopathy. Evol. Intell. **17**, 4047–4068 (2024). https://doi.org/10.1007/s12065-024-00971-2
14. Huang, X., Khetan, A., Cvitkovic, M., Karnin, Z.: TabTransformer: tabular data modeling using contextual embeddings. arXiv preprint (2020). https://doi.org/10.48550/arXiv.2012.06678
15. Beutel, D.J., et al.: Flower: a friendly FL research framework. arXiv preprint arXiv:2007.14390 (2020)
16. Li, T., Sahu, A.K., Zaheer, M., Sanjabi, M., Talwalkar, A., Smith, V.: Federated optimization in heterogeneous networks. Proc. Mach. Learn. Syst. **2**, 429–450 (2020)
17. Framingham Heart Study dataset: Kaggle. https://www.kaggle.com/datasets/aasheesh200/framingham-heart-study-dataset. Accessed 22 Mar 2025
18. Li, Q., Diao, Y., Chen, Q., He, B.: FL on non-IID data silos: an experimental study. In: 2022 IEEE 38th International Conference on Data Engineering (ICDE), May 2022, pp. 965–978. IEEE (2022)
19. Li, H., et al.: FedTP: federated learning by transformer personalization. IEEE Trans. Neural Netw. Learn. Syst. (2023)
20. Quintana, G.I., Vancamberg, L., Jugnon, V., Mougeot, M., Desolneux, A.: BN-SCAFFOLD: controlling the drift of batch normalization statistics in federated learning. arXiv preprint arXiv:2410.03281 (2024)
21. Kumar, B., et al.: Secure decentralized ECG prediction: balancing privacy, performance, and heterogeneity. In: Generative Artificial Intelligence for Biomedical and Smart Health Informatics, pp. 607–621 (2025)
22. Sumalatha, U., Prakasha, K.K., Prabhu, S., Nayak, V.C.: Deep learning applications in ECG analysis and disease detection: an investigation study of recent advances. IEEE Access (2024)
23. Wang, X., Wang, J., Xiao, H., Chen, J., Ma, F.: FedKIM: adaptive federated knowledge injection into medical foundation models. arXiv preprint arXiv:2408.10276 (2024)
24. Li, S., Hu, L., Sun, C., Hu, J., Li, H.: Federated edge learning for medical image augmentation. Appl. Intell. **55**(1), 56 (2025)
25. Sinharay, S.: Continuous probability distributions. In: International Encyclopedia of Education, pp. 98–102. Elsevier, December 2010. https://doi.org/10.1016/B978-0-08-044894-7.01720-6
26. Chatterjee, P., Das, D., Rawat, D.B.: Federated learning empowered recommendation model for financial consumer services. IEEE Trans. Consum. Electron. **70**(1), 2508–2516 (2024). https://doi.org/10.1109/TCE.2023.3339702
27. Banerjee, S., Barik, S., Das, D., Ghosh, U.: EHR security and privacy aspects: a systematic review. In: Puthal, D., Mohanty, S., Choi, B.Y. (eds.) Internet of Things. Advances in Information and Communication Technology. IFIP Advances in Information and Communication Technology, vol. 683. Springer, Cham (2024). https://doi.org/10.1007/978-3-031-45878-1_17

An AI-Powered Fake News Detection System: Analyzing Misinformation in Digital Media

Vishal Kumar, Rohan Raychaudhuri, Shibam Kundu, Ayan Kumar Mondal, Anirban Bhar(✉), Suman Kumar Bhattacharyya, and Neepa Biswas

Department of Information Technology, Narula Institute of Technology, Kolkata, West Bengal, India
{anirban.bhar,suman.bhattacharyya,neepa.biswas}@nit.ac.in

Abstract. The rapid proliferation of fake news on social media has raised significant concerns about misinformation and its influence on public perception, political discourse, and social stability. This paper presents a machine learning-based approach to fake news detection, leveraging text-based, sentiment, and social context features to improve classification accuracy. We employ Logistic Regression, Random Forest, and Support Vector Machines (SVM) to classify news articles as real or fake, with a comparative analysis of their performance. However, the reliance on classic machine learning models limits the system's ability to capture complex linguistic patterns, which could be addressed by state-of-the-art deep learning techniques like BERT or Transformers. Additionally, we implement a Streamlit-based web application, providing an intuitive platform for real-time fake news detection. Our study highlights key challenges such as data scarcity, evolving misinformation patterns, and psychological biases that contribute to the spread of fake news. The system's focus on English text and textual features limits its ability to detect misinformation in regional languages or multimodal formats like images, videos, and deepfakes. Furthermore, we propose future enhancements, including the integration of fact-checking APIs, advanced deep learning models like BERT, and multilingual support, to improve detection efficiency. The findings of this study emphasize the importance of AI-driven solutions in combating misinformation and ensuring the credibility of digital media.

Keywords: Machine Learning · Natural Language Processing · Logistic Regression · Random Forest · Text Classification · Streamlit Deployment

1 Introduction

Fake news refers to intentionally false or misleading information presented as legitimate news. It is often designed to manipulate public opinion, influence political decisions, or generate financial gain. Unlike misinformation, which may be unintentionally incorrect, fake news is deliberately crafted to deceive its audience. The increasing reliance on digital media has accelerated the spread of fake news, making it a major societal challenge.

K. Chandra Mondal et al. (Eds.): CICBA 2025, CCIS 2863, pp. 402–413, 2026.
https://doi.org/10.1007/978-3-032-17184-9_30

Fake news detection is critical because the spread of false information can have severe consequences, including political manipulation, financial fraud, and societal polarization. Social media platforms amplify the problem by enabling rapid dissemination without proper fact-checking mechanisms. During major events such as elections or global crises, fake news can mislead the public, alter decision-making, and fuel social unrest. The ease of creating and sharing unverified news has made it increasingly difficult to distinguish between credible and deceptive information.

Several real-world incidents have highlighted the devastating impact of fake news. For instance, misinformation about COVID-19 treatments led to public confusion, while politically motivated fake news campaigns have influenced voter behavior in major elections. Social media platforms such as Twitter, Facebook, and WhatsApp have played a crucial role in spreading false narratives due to their algorithm-driven content promotion.

Several challenges hinder effective fake news detection:

- I Intentional Misrepresentation: Fake news mimics legitimate journalism, making it difficult to identify.
- Diverse Content Formats: Fake news exists in various formats, including text, images, videos, and deepfakes.
- Rapid Dissemination: Social media accelerates the spread of fake news before fact-checking can occur.
- Data Scarcity and Bias: High-quality labelled datasets for fake news detection are limited and may contain biases.
- Psychological Influence: People tend to believe information that aligns with their pre-existing beliefs, making them more susceptible to fake news.

Machine learning plays a crucial role in addressing these challenges by automating the process of fake news detection. By leveraging text classification techniques, sentiment analysis, and metadata features, machine learning models can identify patterns in news articles that indicate deception. Advanced models, such as deep learning-based approaches, further enhance detection accuracy by analyzing linguistic and contextual cues in news content. A combination of NLP techniques and fact-checking mechanisms can improve detection rates, helping reduce the harmful effects of misinformation.

To build a comprehensive fake news detection framework, it is essential to integrate multiple layers of analysis—including linguistic features, user behavior, and network-based signals. Our approach combines these elements to create a robust AI-powered system capable of real-time analysis. The system begins by preprocessing the news content to remove noise and extract key features, followed by text vectorization using techniques such as TF-IDF. These vectors are then passed through various machine learning classifiers, each trained on a labeled dataset of real and fake news. A Streamlit-based user interface facilitates ease of use, allowing users to input news content and receive instant feedback on its authenticity. This holistic framework not only boosts classification accuracy but also provides transparency and accessibility, encouraging broader public adoption of fake news detection tools. Figure 1. Visually supports the explanation.

Fake news propagates rapidly across various online platforms due to the viral nature of social media algorithms and the psychological tendencies of users to share sensational content without verification. Platforms like Facebook, Twitter, and WhatsApp enable

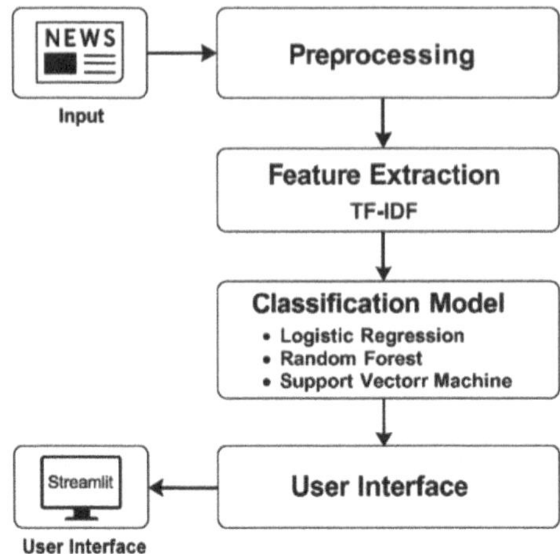

Fig. 1. AI-powered fake news detection system architecture

instantaneous sharing, allowing a single piece of false information to reach millions within minutes. The amplification is further driven by engagement-based algorithms that prioritize controversial or emotionally charged content, regardless of its truthfulness. Tackling this widespread issue demands an interdisciplinary strategy—artificial intelligence must be employed to detect and flag misinformation in real time, journalists need to uphold rigorous fact-checking standards, and public awareness campaigns must educate users about the importance of media literacy and responsible information sharing. Only by combining technological innovation with human judgment and education can we effectively mitigate the harmful impact of fake news in the digital era.

2 Literature Survey

Fake news detection has gained significant attention due to the rapid spread of misinformation on social media. Researchers have explored various machine learning (ML) and deep learning (DL) techniques, along with fact-checking mechanisms, to address this issue.

2.1 Machine Learning and Deep Learning Approaches

Early studies focused on supervised ML models like Logistic Regression, SVM, and Decision Trees, which relied on handcrafted textual features [1]. While effective, these models lacked contextual understanding. Deep learning approaches, such as BiLSTM and Transformer-based models, improved performance by capturing complex patterns in news text [2]. However, they required large labelled datasets and were computationally expensive. State-of-the-art models like BERT, RoBERTa, and XLNet have shown superior performance in natural language processing tasks by leveraging contextual embeddings, offering potential improvements over the classic machine learning models used in this study, which may struggle with nuanced or context-dependent misinformation [7].

2.2 Explainable AI and Fact-Checking

Recent research emphasizes explainability in fake news detection. Shu et al. [3] introduced DEFEND, an interpretable model using attention mechanisms to highlight deceptive content. Additionally, fact-checking integration through APIs (e.g., PolitiFact, Snopes) has been explored to improve verification [4]. However most fake news detection models are focused on English-language content, limiting applicability, real-time scalability remains a challenge.

2.3 Challenges and Future Directions

Despite significant advancements, fake news detection continues to face several complex challenges that hinder the development of universally effective solutions.

- Multimodal Misinformation: Fake news is no longer confined to textual content; it increasingly appears in multimodal formats such as manipulated images, misleading videos, memes, and synthetic media like deepfakes. These formats complicate detection tasks, as they require models capable of understanding and integrating diverse types of information simultaneously [5].
- Evolving Misinformation Patterns: The strategies used to craft and disseminate fake news are constantly evolving. Malicious actors frequently modify linguistic patterns, leverage trending topics, and exploit algorithmic weaknesses to bypass detection systems. As a result, static or outdated models quickly become ineffective, necessitating the development of adaptive, self-learning models that can stay resilient against emerging misinformation tactics [6].
- Multilingual Detection: A significant limitation of current fake news detection systems is their heavy reliance on English-language datasets. In multilingual societies and global communication contexts, misinformation often spreads in regional languages and dialects. The scarcity of labeled datasets and natural language processing tools for low-resource languages limits the scalability and inclusiveness of detection frameworks [7].
- Verification and Fact-Checking Bottlenecks: Automated fact-checking techniques have been introduced to speed up the verification process, yet they still face limitations in accuracy, scalability, and latency. These systems often rely on external knowledge bases and structured databases, which may not be updated in real time or may lack coverage for emerging topics [8].

3 Procedure

3.1 A. Fake News Characterization

Fake news encompasses a variety of deceptive content types, each with distinct characteristics and impacts. Misinformation refers to false or inaccurate information shared without the intent to deceive, often due to misunderstanding or lack of verification. In contrast, disinformation is deliberately crafted to mislead audiences, typically serving political, financial, or ideological agendas. Other related forms include clickbait, which uses sensationalized headlines to attract attention and drive engagement, often at the expense of accuracy, and satire or parody, which, while humorous in nature, can be misunderstood as factual news. Propaganda involves systematically biased content aimed at shaping public opinion, while fabricated content consists of entirely false narratives presented as credible news stories. The rapid dissemination of fake news on social media is driven by several factors. Virality plays a major role, as users tend to share emotionally charged or sensational information without verifying its authenticity. Algorithmic amplification further compounds the issue, as platforms prioritize content with high engagement, inadvertently boosting the visibility of misleading posts. Additionally, echo chambers—digital spaces where individuals are mostly exposed to views that align with their own—diminish critical thinking and increase the likelihood of accepting and spreading fake news. Understanding these dynamics is essential for developing effective detection systems and fostering digital media literacy.

A comparison of fake news, rumors and biased news is provided in Table 1.

Table 1. The accuracy gained by the various algorithms

Aspect	Fake News	Rumors	Biased News
Intent	Deliberate deception	Unverified speculation	Persuasive influence
Verification	False or manipulated content	Unconfirmed	Selective facts
Spread	Social media, fake websites	Word of mouth, social media	Traditional and digital media

3.2 Datasets for Fake News Detection

Publicly available datasets have significantly contributed to the development of fake news detection models. Some of the most commonly used datasets include:

- LIAR: A dataset containing fact-checked political news labelled with six truth categories.
- PolitiFact: A dataset compiled from the PolitiFact website with verified true and false claims.
- Kaggle Fake News Dataset: A widely used dataset with labelled 'true' and 'fake' news articles.
- Twitter Fake News Dataset: A dataset sourced from Twitter posts containing misinformation and fact-checked claims.

For this study, the Kaggle Fake News Dataset has been used. It consists of two files: 'true.csv' and 'fake.csv', each containing thousands of news articles. The dataset provides a structured approach to training machine learning models by offering labelled examples of genuine and fabricated news. However, the Kaggle dataset has limitations, including potential biases in labeling due to human fact-checkers and limited diversity in content sources, which may not fully represent the variability of misinformation across different platforms and contexts.

Despite the availability of these datasets, several challenges exist in dataset creation:

- Bias in Labeling: Some datasets rely on human fact checkers, introducing subjectivity.
- Data Imbalance: Many datasets contain more 'true' news than 'fake' news, affecting model performance.
- Contextual Limitations: Existing datasets often fail to capture evolving misinformation trends.
- Multimodal Misinformation: Fake news is not limited to textual content but also includes images, videos, and deepfake-generated media [9].

To address these issues, collecting larger and more diverse datasets from multiple platforms, such as social media, news outlets, and user-generated content, is essential. Additionally, implementing data augmentation strategies, such as text paraphrasing, synthetic data generation, and multimodal content integration, can mitigate biases and enhance model robustness across diverse contexts.

3.3 Machine Learning Approach

Machine learning plays a crucial role in fake news detection by analyzing textual patterns, sentiment, and metadata. The approach involves feature engineering, model selection, and performance evaluation. Machine learning models can identify deceptive patterns, classify news articles, and improve detection accuracy over time by learning from new data.

Feature Engineering

To enhance the model's predictive power, various feature extraction techniques were applied:

- Text-Based Features: Term Frequency-Inverse Document Frequency (TF-IDF), Count Vectorization, and Word Embeddings were used to capture textual patterns and determine word importance.
- Sentiment and Linguistic Features: Polarity, subjectivity, readability scores, and word complexity were analyzed to assess the emotional and linguistic characteristics of news articles.
- Social Context Features: Metadata such as user engagement, source credibility, author reputation, and publication timestamps were incorporated to assess trustworthiness.

The combination of these features helps machine learning models differentiate between fake and legitimate news articles. By integrating text, sentiment, and metadata, the model can improve classification accuracy and minimize false positives.

Machine Learning Models Used

Several supervised learning models were employed for classification, each offering unique advantages in text classification tasks.

Logistic Regression was chosen for its ability to assign probabilities to predictions, while Random Forest provides robustness by aggregating multiple decision trees. SVM was selected for its effectiveness in high-dimensional spaces. However, these classic machine learning models may not fully capture the complex semantic and contextual patterns in news text, unlike state-of-the-art deep learning models such as BERT or Transformers, which could enhance detection accuracy for nuanced misinformation (Table 2).

Table 2. Machine Learning Models Used

Model	Description	Strengths
Logistic Regression	Statistical binary classifier	Simple and efficient; interpretable; assigns probabilities to predictions.
Random Forest	Ensemble of decision trees	Handles non-linearity well; robust to overfitting; provides high accuracy.
Support Vector Machine (SVM)	Maximizes class separation	Effective in high-dimensional spaces; works well with small to medium datasets.

Performance Comparison

Model performance was evaluated using accuracy, precision, recall, and F1-score to measure the effectiveness of fake news classification.

Table 3. Performance Comparison of Models

Model	Accuracy	Precision	Recall	F1-Score
Logistic Regression	98.27%	98%	99%	98%
Random Forest	97.85%	97%	98%	97%
SVM	96.45%	96%	95%	95%

Logistic Regression outperformed the other models in accuracy and recall, making it an effective choice for detecting fake news. Random Forest provided a balance between precision and recall, while SVM demonstrated strong classification capabilities despite slightly lower performance metrics.

AUC-ROC Curve

To further evaluate model performance, an AUC-ROC curve was plotted, as shown in Fig. 2. The AUC-ROC (Area Under the Receiver Operating Characteristic Curve) provides insights into the model's ability to distinguish between real and fake news articles.

AUC values close to 1.0 indicate a strong model performance, demonstrating a high degree of separability between real and fake news. Logistic Regression achieved the best AUC score, reinforcing its effectiveness in classification tasks. Future improvements, such as fine-tuning hyperparameters and incorporating additional features, can further optimize model accuracy and reliability.

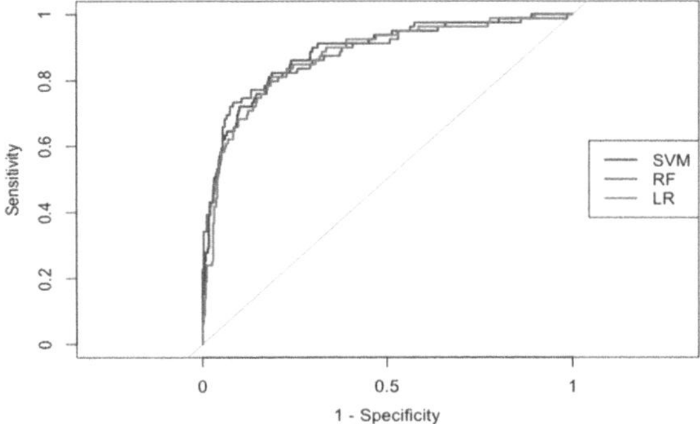

Fig. 2. AUC-ROC Curve for Model Performance

3.4 System Deployment and Implementation

The fake news detection system is deployed as a web-based application using Streamlit, a lightweight Python framework that enables interactive and user-friendly interfaces for machine learning models.

User Interface with Streamlit

The system provides an intuitive user interface designed to facilitate real-time fake news detection. Users can input news articles and receive instant classification results (Fig. 3).

Fig. 3. Streamlit Web Application Interface

Key Features

The application is equipped with a range of functionalities designed to enhance user experience and ensure efficient fake news detection. It allows users to perform single news checks by manually entering a news article or headline, which is then analyzed and classified as real or fake. For broader analysis, the system supports bulk news checking, enabling users to upload files containing multiple news articles for simultaneous evaluation. Additionally, the system displays a prediction probability score alongside each result, providing insights into the model's confidence in its classification. The interactive and responsive user interface ensures a seamless experience, offering real-time feedback and an intuitive design that caters to both technical and non-technical users.

Backend Model Integration

The Streamlit front-end is seamlessly integrated with the trained machine learning model using Python scripts, enabling real-time fake news detection through a user-friendly web interface. When a user inputs a news article or headline, the text is first preprocessed, which includes tokenization and vectorization to convert it into a format suitable for model analysis. This processed input is then passed to the trained machine learning model, such as Logistic Regression or Random Forest, which analyzes the content and predicts whether the news is real or fake. Finally, the prediction result, along with a corresponding probability score, is displayed on the user interface, providing immediate and interpretable feedback to the user.

Deployment on Streamlit and GitHub

The system is deployed using Streamlit Sharing and hosted on GitHub:

- Streamlit Sharing: The application is deployed and accessible online for real-time news classification.
- GitHub Repository: The project's source code and trained models are uploaded on GitHub for version control and collaboration.

4 Discussion

This section presents the experimental results of the proposed fake news detection system and discusses the implications of the findings. The performance of three machine learning models—Logistic Regression, Random Forest, and Support Vector Machine (SVM)—was evaluated using standard classification metrics: accuracy, precision, recall, and F1-score.

4.1 Model Performance Evaluation

Table 3 summarizes the comparative performance of the models. Among the three, Logistic Regression demonstrated the highest accuracy of 98.27%, with a recall of 99% and an F1-score of 98%, indicating strong performance in detecting both real and fake news. This model's ability to produce probability-based outputs also contributed to its robustness in classification.

Random Forest, with an accuracy of 97.85%, provided a balanced trade-off between precision and recall, owing to its ensemble-based learning approach. SVM, although slightly lower in performance with 96.45% accuracy, still showed respectable results and is well-suited for high-dimensional data.

The AUC-ROC curve further validated the classification capabilities of the models. Logistic Regression achieved the highest AUC, suggesting superior separability between fake and real news classes. These results confirm that logistic models are highly effective when paired with appropriate feature extraction techniques like TF-IDF.

4.2 Feature Importance and Impact

The inclusion of textual, sentiment-based, and social context features significantly improved the models' predictive accuracy. TF-IDF and count vectorization enabled the extraction of word frequency-based patterns, while sentiment features helped capture the emotional tone of the articles. The addition of metadata such as author credibility and publication timestamps contributed to a richer representation of the news content.

Notably, sentiment and linguistic features helped identify exaggeration, bias, and emotionally manipulative language, which are common traits of fake news. This demonstrates the value of combining multiple feature types to strengthen model generalization.

4.3 Real-Time System Usability

The deployment of the model using Streamlit provided a user-friendly web interface for real-time fake news classification. Users can manually enter or bulk-upload news articles to receive instant predictions, complete with confidence scores. The seamless integration of the front-end and back-end models enhances the accessibility of the tool for end-users and non-technical stakeholders.

The system's ability to operate with low latency makes it a practical solution for media organizations, educational institutions, and social media moderators aiming to mitigate the spread of misinformation.

4.4 Key Observations and Insights

Logistic Regression proves to be an ideal choice for this binary classification problem, offering a balance of simplicity, interpretability, and strong performance. The use of diverse features—ranging from textual patterns to sentiment and metadata—significantly boosts classification accuracy, highlighting the importance of multi-dimensional feature engineering in fake news detection tasks. However, despite the high performance achieved, certain challenges persist. Detecting nuanced content such as sarcasm, satire, and AI-generated text remains difficult, as these cases require deeper contextual and semantic understanding beyond surface-level patterns. Additionally, issues such as data imbalance and the linguistic limitations of the dataset may hinder the model's generalizability, particularly when applied across different digital platforms or non-English languages.

4.5 Limitations

While the results of the proposed system are encouraging, several limitations must be acknowledged. Firstly, the dataset primarily comprises English-language news articles, which restricts the system's applicability in multilingual contexts and reduces its effectiveness in detecting misinformation in regional languages. This focus on English text limits the system's scalability in diverse linguistic regions, where misinformation often spreads in local languages and dialects. Additionally, reliance on datasets like Kaggle Fake News introduces biases in labeling and limited data diversity, as these datasets may not capture the full range of misinformation sources and formats prevalent across various platforms. Secondly, the current model focuses exclusively on textual content, thereby overlooking multimodal misinformation such as manipulated images, videos, and deepfake content, which are increasingly prevalent on social media platforms. This reliance on textual features hinders the system's ability to address the growing threat of visually manipulated or AI-generated content. Furthermore, the absence of continual learning mechanisms means the model may struggle to adapt to rapidly evolving misinformation tactics, making it less resilient over time. Addressing these limitations is essential for building a more robust and scalable fake news detection framework.

5 Conclusion and Future Scope

Machine learning-based fake news detection systems have demonstrated significant potential in combating misinformation. However, they continue to face critical challenges that hinder their widespread effectiveness. Key issues include limited multilingual capabilities due to the predominance of English-language training data, inadequate contextual understanding of nuanced language features such as sarcasm and misleading headlines, and the dynamic nature of misinformation that evolves rapidly—often outpacing model updates. Additionally, the reliance on large volumes of labeled data for supervised learning, along with the computational complexity of achieving real-time analysis, presents practical barriers to scalable implementation.

To address these challenges and enhance the performance of fake news detection systems, several future directions can be explored. Integrating hybrid models that combine machine learning algorithms with knowledge-based and rule-based fact-checking systems can improve accuracy. Additionally, adopting state-of-the-art deep learning models like BERT, RoBERTa, or Transformers can enhance the system's ability to detect complex linguistic patterns and subtle misinformation, overcoming the limitations of the classic machine learning models used in this study. Incorporating third-party fact-checking APIs will enable external validation of content, enhancing system reliability.

Further, supporting multilingual detection by training on diverse datasets will enable broader applicability across languages and cultures. Incorporating models trained on regional languages and integrating multimodal analysis for images, videos, and deepfakes will address the current limitation of focusing solely on English text and textual features, enhancing the system's effectiveness in diverse digital environments. Continuous learning approaches, including online learning and adaptive models, can ensure responsiveness to emerging misinformation trends. Collecting larger and more diverse datasets from multiple platforms, including social media, news outlets, and user-generated content, will mitigate biases and improve model robustness across varied contexts. The implementation of Explainable AI (XAI) will also be crucial in making the decision-making process more transparent and trustworthy. Data Augmentation and Diverse Datasets: Implementing data augmentation techniques, such as text paraphrasing, synthetic data generation, and inclusion of multimodal content (images, videos, deepfakes), alongside collecting larger and more diverse datasets from various platforms, will address biases and improve the model's robustness across different contexts and content types.

Finally, collaboration with social media platforms to embed real-time detection tools will facilitate early identification and mitigation of fake news at scale.

By pursuing these advancements, fake news detection systems can become more robust, adaptable, and effective in the ongoing effort to combat the spread of misinformation in digital ecosystems.

References

1. Shu, K., Sliva, A., Wang, S., Tang, J., Liu, H.: Fake news detection on social media: a data mining perspective. ACM SIGKDD Explor. Newsl. **19**(1), 22–36 (2017)
2. Shu, K., Wang, S., Liu, H.: Beyond news contents: the role of social context for fake news detection. In: Proceedings of the Twelfth ACM International Conference on Web Search and Data Mining, pp. 312–320 (2019)
3. Shu, K., Cui, L., Wang, S., Lee, D., Liu, H.: Defend: explainable fake news detection. In: Proceedings of the 25th ACM SIGKDD International Conference on Knowledge Discovery Data Mining, pp. 395–405 (2019)
4. Shu, K., Mahudeswaran, D., Wang, S., Lee, D., Liu, H.: Fakenewsnet: a data repository with news content, social context, and spatiotemporal information for studying fake news on social media. Big Data **8**(3), 171–188 (2020)
5. Bhattarai, B., Granmo, O.C., Jiao, L.: Explainable tsetlin machine framework for fake news detection with credibility score assessment. arXiv preprint arXiv:2105.09114 (2021)
6. Bondielli, A., Marcelloni, F.: A survey on fake news and rumor detection techniques. Inf. Sci. **497**, 38–55 (2019)
7. Alghamdi, J., Luo, S., Lin, Y.: A comprehensive survey on machine learning approaches for fake news detection. Multimedia Tools Appl. **83**(17), 51009–51067 (2024)
8. Thorne, J., Vlachos, A.: Automated fact checking: task formulations, methods and future directions. arXiv preprint arXiv:1806.07687 (2018)
9. Bohacek, M., Farid, H.: Protecting world leaders against deepfakes using facial, gestural, and vocal mannerisms. Proc. Natl. Acad. Sci. **119**(48), e2216035119 (2022)
10. Touahri, I., Mazroui, A.: Survey of machine learning techniques for Arabic fake news detection. Artif. Intell. Rev. **57**(6), 157 (2024)

Multi-modal Fake News Detection on Online Social Media Using Machine Learning and Explainable AI

Khushi Jain[1(✉)], Arunima Jaiswal[1], Reena[1], Jhalak Chahar[1], Smita Maurya[1], and Nitin Sachdeva[2]

[1] Indira Gandhi Delhi Technical University for Women, New Delhi, India
khushijain.25.2003@gmail.com
{arunimajaiswal,reena081btcse21,jhalak126btcse21,
smita137btcse21}@igdtuw.ac.in
[2] USCIT, GGSIPU, Dwarka, New Delhi, India
nits.usit@gmail.com

Abstract. Being a full-blown dissemination of false news at the hands of social media has become a serious threat: it confuses public understanding and creates mistrust in society. In this research we have approached the problem of detecting fake news on a multimodal level, which means that both textual and visual misinformation have to be jointly scrutinized for a more robust classification. We propose the BAFT (BERT Attention Fusion Transformer) model to deal with this: a hybrid deep learning architecture-wherein BERT builds a textual encoder, ResNet50 extracts image features, multi-head attention learns contextual information, and transformer encoders perform sequence modeling-all fused after optimization for joint-multimodal learning. The model is trained and evaluated with the Fakeddit dataset of real-world social media posts containing text and image, scattered in six fine-grained categories. Experimental results show that BAFT ranks among the highest with an accuracy of 97.58%, surpassing almost all standards in multimodal detection. Moreover, with the advent of XAI techniques, interpretability has been injected into the decision-making process of the model, marking an essential step forward toward transparency and trust. The method is best suited to be implemented for monitoring and detecting misinformation on social media. The future work will address real-time implementation and speeding up for maximized applicability.

Keywords: Fake news detection · Multimodal learning · Explainable artificial intelligence · Fakeddit dataset · social media misinformation

1 Introduction

The internet-based social media [1] of the current times has become the most important medium for news dissemination among millions of such users worldwide. Although in many ways the democratization of news access may help, it

K. Chandra Mondal et al. (Eds.): CICBA 2025, CCIS 2863, pp. 414–428, 2026.
https://doi.org/10.1007/978-3-032-17184-9_31

has also brought out some dangerous things that allow rapid spread and runaway transmission of misinformation or fake news. Such a broad base of apparitional content poses great threats, not only to public opinion and morale but also to the trust within society and, at the national level, even to national security. The traditional methods of detection [2] mainly focus on textual data, which for the most part, fail to address the issues of against the challenges posed by multimodal content, which includes text with pictures, etc.

The continuation of these developments [1] necessitates creating systems that analyze and interpret by understanding information over multiple data formats. A more recent work [3] uses a multi-modal approach for detection and combines text and image features but aims to improve classification without depending on sub-modules. Most importantly, though some strides have been made in developing fake news detection [2] in deep learning with improved accuracy, many operate in a black box mode [4], knowing little or nothing about how they make decisions. Consequently, apart from mistrust from the end-users' perspective, such scenarios have implications for the extent to which these systems can be used in applications with consequences or in real-world situations.

We implemented a hybrid model for multimodal data by combining bright parts of BERT [5] for text understanding, ResNet50 [6] for image feature extraction, multihead attention [7] mechanisms for creating a contextual focus and transformer encoders for a powerful sequential model. Efficiently fused optimized features from the text and the images will facilitate all-comprehensive decision making. Our model is evaluated on the Fakeddit dataset [8], consisting of the community-shared social media posts with text content, images, or a mix of the two. In contrast to prior work, our model introduces a novel fusion mechanism using multi-head attention and adds explainability through SHAP and Grad-CAM—components not explored in [3].

The unique part of implemented model is its capability to assimilate techniques of Explainable Artificial Intelligence [9] methods that make a model more transparent and interpretable. By opening internal reasoning within the model, we thus seek to instigate much more trust and acceptability among end users and stakeholders. The implemented hybrid model attains the accuracy of 97.58%, exceeding most baselines and showing strong reading abilities in fake news detection of multiple modalities. The study thus adds to progress in the field growing toward interpretable multimodal fake news detection, creating a scalable detector for future advances in the evaluation of social media content.

There are several key contributions of this work. The first is a newly proposed hybrid multimodal architecture named BAFT that fuses textual and visual information, working towards fake news detection [3] in social media. The model integrates a cross-modal attention mechanism with transformer-based fusion to engender better contextual understanding between the two modalities. Also, explicability is very much sought after in a so-called "black-box" model, thus the application of XAI techniques such as SHAP and Grad-CAM to provide insight into the contributions of both textual and visual features. Lastly, the results have been validated through exhaustive experiments on the Fakeddit dataset, with very high accuracies being obtained while also showing that the model is highly robust for fine-grained six-class fake news classification.

The flow of rest of the paper is as follows: Sect. 2 provides an extensive literature survey for existing approaches and the incorporation of explainable AI in improving the transparency of models. Section 3 discusses the methodology proposed including data preprocessing, feature extraction, and the architecture of the BAFT model. Section 4, then, deals with the experimental setup, results, and performance analysis in various metrics. Finally, Sect. 5 closes with a conclusion of the study, along with future avenues discussing steps for enhancing model efficiency, generalizability, and real-time applicability.

2 Literature Survey

The problem of identifying fake news on social media [1] has resulted in a variety of methods, from the conventional machine learning methods relying on text features to contemporary deep learning models involving CNNs, RNNs, and Transformers [10]. As multimodal content becomes more prevalent, researchers have grown more interested in the fusion of text and image data to enhance detection performance. This section overviews major advances in fake news detection [2], multimodal learning, and explainable AI [9] pertinent to our research (Table 1).

While the two models, CAF-ODNN [11] and TextGCN + Vision Transformer [12] are capable of doing better, our BAFT model achieves more accuracy (97.58%) with stronger fusion of BERT-based text features and ResNet-based image features through attention and transformer encoders. For instance, CAF-ODNN reported 90% accuracy, which our model now surpasses with a more integrated learning approach.

BAFT incorporates explainability using approaches such as SHAP and Grad-CAM, adding transparency to the decision-making process where in earlier works, this was too often absent. In addition, the fine-grain Fakeddit dataset allows the model to be more generalized and robust when predicting across multiple categories of misinformation used in this project.

While progress has been made in fake news detection [10], several challenges persist. The following research gaps highlight critical shortcomings and motivate the direction of our work:

1. **Limited Explainability**: Many high-accuracy models lack deep interpretability, with XAI [9] often applied superficially, offering little insight into feature importance or decision-making processes.
2. **Poor Generalization**: Many models overfit specific datasets and fail to generalize across diverse sources.
3. **Limited Use of Hybrid Multimodal Models**: Few studies effectively integrate text and image data for fake news detection [13]. The implemented hybrid model fuses BERT-based textual embeddings [5] and ResNet50-based [6] visual features for comprehensive multimodal learning.

Table 1. Comprehensive analysis of prominent studies on Multi-Modal Fake News Detection

Author(s)	Dataset(s)	Modality	Model	Accuracy
Alex Munyole Luvembe et al. [11]	GossipCO, PolitiFact, Fakeddit and Pheme	Text and image	CAF-ODNN: complementary attention fusion with deep neural network	90%
Visweswaran M et al. [12]	Fakeddit dataset	Text and image	TextGCN + Vision transformer	94.17%
Moyank Giri et al. [13]	CASIA dataset, multiple fake-real news datasets	Text and image	Naïve Bayes, random forest, decision tree, CNN, explainable AI	93.58%
Yasmine Khalid Zamil et al. [14]	Weibo, MediaEval, CASIA	Text and image	XLNet + ELECTRA, EfficientNetB0 + ELA	93.89%
Abdul Baasith Shiyam et al. [15]	FaceForensics++ dataset	Images	InceptionResNetV2 and Conv2D	96.67%
Prabhav Singh et al. [16]	Twitter MediaEval, Weibo Corpus	Text and Image	BERT + ELECTRA, NASNet Mobile	86.83%
Xichen Zhang et al. [17]	Buzzfeed, Medieval Twitter dataset, CIC dataset	Text and Images	BERT, BERTweet, DistilBERT, RoBERTa, ELECTRA, ViLBERT	96.27%
Ankit Gautam et al. [18]	Reddit dataset	Text and image	SVM, EANN, attRNN	98%
Santosh Kumar Uppada et al. [19]	Fakeddit dataset	Text and Images	BERT + Xception	91.94%
Peng Qi et al. [20]	Weibo dataset	Images	MVNN	84.6%
Julio C. S. Reis et al. [21]	BuzzFace dataset	Text, Image and Videos	Extreme Gradient Boosting	85%
Oluwaseun Ajao et al. [22]	CREDBANK, PHEME, BuzzFeed	Text and Image	SVM, LSTM-HAN	89%
Suchitra B. Deokate [23]	CREDBANK, PHEME, BuzzFeed	Text, Image and Videos	Support Vector Machine	94.2%
Gaël Guibon et al. [24]	Storyzy dataset	Text and Videos	CNN, Gradient Boosting Decision Trees	94.59%
Yang Yang et al. [25]	Kaggle	Text and Videos	TI-CNN	92.10%

4. **Limited Focus on Temporal and Propagation Patterns**: While our current study focuses on static fake news detection [2], dynamic misinformation propagation and temporal modeling remain promising areas for future research.
5. **Lack of Optimization Techniques**: Improving model performance through optimization without significant computational cost remains underexplored.

3 Methodology

This research employs deep learning and multimodal analytics to address challenges facing the detection of fake news that cut across text and images. The proposed solution includes some of the advanced ways under data preprocessing [27], feature extraction techniques [28], model training, and evaluation methods leading to the development of BAFT model, a hybrid deep learning framework.

We created the BAFT (BERT Attention Fusion Transformer) to enhance multimodal fake news detection [22] challenges. We selected BERT [5] to function as our text encoder since it can grasp complex contextual information found in informal social media content. The BAFT model brings together ResNet50 [6] image features with transformer encoders and multi-head attention mechanisms to establish enhanced cross-modal interactions which enhance classification accuracy. The design of this system proves most effective in processing complex fake news situations which contain both image and text elements (Fig. 1).

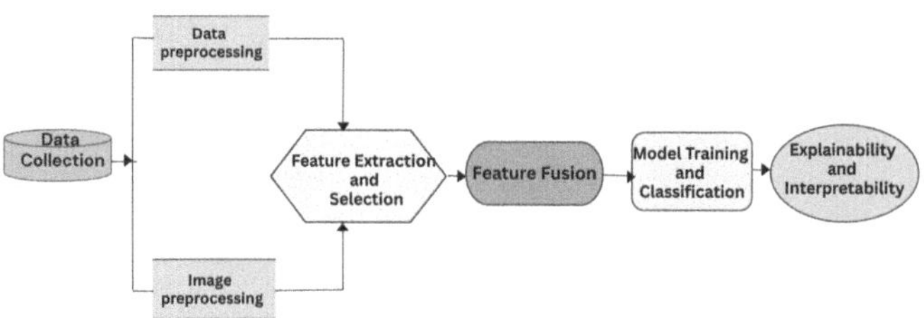

Fig. 1. Proposed methodology

3.1 Dataset Used

This study uses the Fakeddit dataset [8], a large-scale multimodal benchmark harvested from Reddit. The dataset comprises news-based posts annotated over six fine-grained categories: True (0), Satire (1), False Connection (2), Misleading Content (3), Imposter Content (4), and Manipulated Content (5). A sample consists of a headline or textual post accompanied by a relevant image, providing a rich source for the analysis of fake news from linguistic as well as visual cues.

The dataset was chosen because of its rich multimodal nature and intricate annotations, which make it suitable for the study's objectives as it includes both text and images for detection of fake news [10].

Fakeddit [8] is used as the testing ground for the target BAFT model, highlighting the strengths of multimodal learning over unimodal methods. Through the fusion of text and image modalities, the model strives to learn more stable and context-aware fake news detection [2] (Figs. 2, 3 and 4).

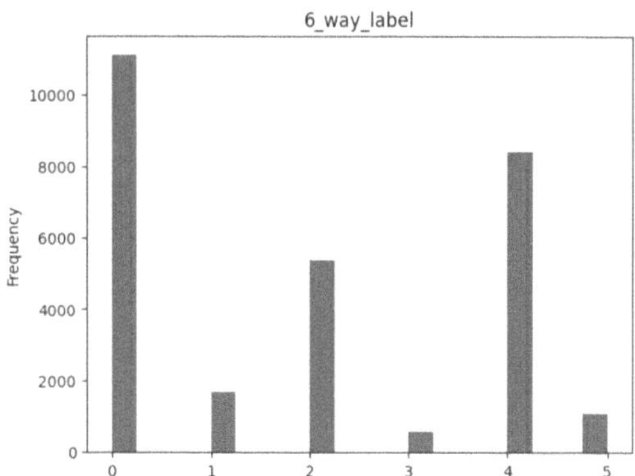

Fig. 2. Distribution of the class labels in the dataset

3.2 Data Pre-processing

Efficient pre-processing [27] of the Fakeddit multimodal dataset [8] was necessary to train the BAFT model. Separate pipelines were implemented for text and image modalities.

Text Preprocessing

- **Noise Removal**: Used the `clean_title` column, which had already been cleaned of special characters, URLs, and extra punctuation.
- **Missing Values**: Replaced `NaN` with an empty string to prevent tokenization errors.
- **Tokenization**: Applied BERT [5] tokenizer, padding or truncating texts to a maximum length, and prepared `input_ids` and `attention_mask`.
- **Embedding Extraction**: During training, the [CLS] token output from BERT [5] was used for richly semantic representation.

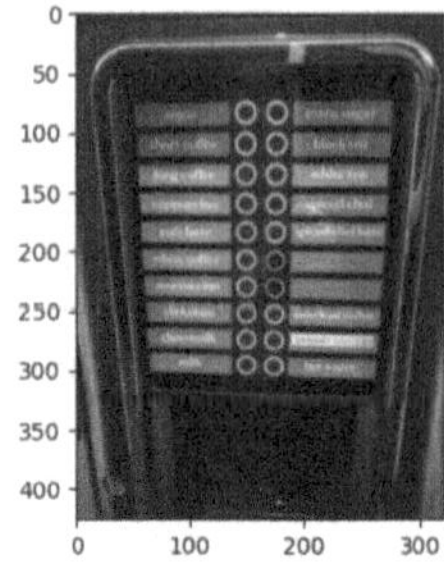

Fig. 3. Sample image (1)

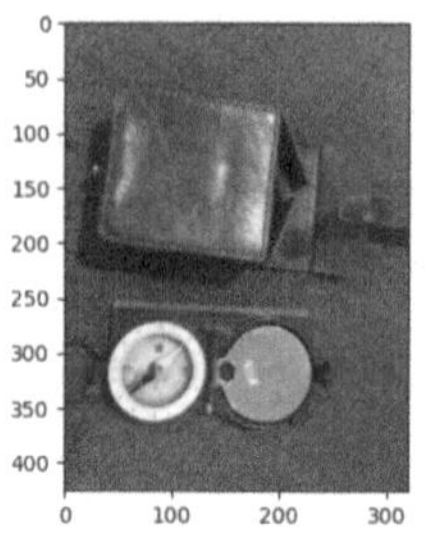

Fig. 4. Sample image (2)

Image Preprocessing

- **Image Downloading and Validation**: Downloaded images from the URLs; corrupt or invalid files were detected using PIL and skipped.
- **Resizing and Normalization**: Resizing every input image dimension from (256, 256) pixels and transforming the pixel into ImageNet mean and standard deviation to guarantee to have same scale to ResNet50 [6].
- **Data Augmentation**: Applied random flipping and rotations to diversify the dataset and avoid overfitting.

3.3 Feature Extraction

Text Feature Extraction: Text features were extracted from the BERT model [5]. The `[CLS]` token output, i.e., the entire sequence representation, was used as the primary feature. This output was mapped to 512 dimensions using a fully connected layer to match image features [32].

Image Feature Extraction: ResNet-50 [6] was used to extract image features [32], resulting in a 2048-dimensional feature vector. This was down sampled to 512 dimensions to align with the textual features.

Cross-modal Feature Fusion: Being first projected into 512-D representations, the features derived from images and text were then joined by a transformer encoder [12] and a multi-head attention [7] mechanism. These modules enabled modeling inter-modal relationships and contextual dependencies. Using the fusion layer forced these outputs from each modality to concatenate, then applying global average pooling allowed obtaining a fused representation on a 512-D feature vector. This fused representation was then passed into the classification head for the final prediction.

Final Representation: The final feature vector of 512 dimension from the text and image modalities was fed to a fully connected layer to classify into 6 ways. The multimodal representation was able to capture and combine information from both the inputs for improved fake news detection.

3.4 Model Training and Classification

Model Architecture

The BAFT (BERT-ResNet with Attention Fusion and Transformer) model is used for detecting fake news, wherein text and image features could be combined for multimodal classification.

To unify the features from both modalities, let $T \in \mathbb{R}^{768}$ represent the textual embedding obtained from BERT, and $I \in \mathbb{R}^{2048}$ denote the image feature vector extracted from ResNet-50. These are projected into a shared lower-dimensional space as follows:

$$T' = W_t T + b_t, \quad I' = W_i I + b_i$$

where $W_t, W_i \in \mathbb{R}^{512\times d}$ and $b_t, b_i \in \mathbb{R}^{512}$ are learnable parameters. This transformation aligns both modalities to a common dimension, enabling effective fusion using multi-head attention and transformer encoders (Fig. 5).

The model architecture includes:

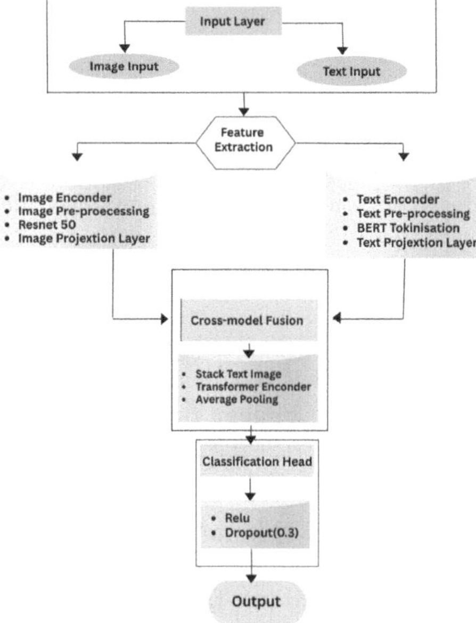

Fig. 5. Model architecture

- **Text Encoder**: BERT [5] takes contextual embeddings as input from the text. The [CLS] token output is processed by linear layer to project the dimension from 768 to 512.

- **Image Encoder**: ResNet-50 [6] is implemented to encode the features of the image. The penultimate layer's output is linearly projected into 512 dimensions.
- **Attention Fusion**: Applies a multihead attention layer [7] to combine text and image features in a manner that model attends to the most relevant information from both modalities.
- **Transformer Encoder**: The transformer encoder [7] once more utilizes the combined features to learn image and text feature relations.
- **Classification Head**: A two-layer fully connected neural network with ReLU activation [29] provides the 6-way classification.

Classification

Post-training, the model predicts the 6-class labels of the test set based on the multimodal features obtained. Model accuracy was tracked during training to monitor performance.

Loss Function: To train the model, we use the categorical cross-entropy loss function:

$$\mathcal{L} = -\sum_{i=1}^{6} y_i \log(\hat{y}_i)$$

where y_i is the one-hot encoded ground truth label and $\hat{y}_i$ is the predicted probability for class i.

Such training and classification enabled the BAFT model to utilize multimodal information effectively for accurate fake news classification on the Fakeddit dataset [8].

3.5 Explainability

Reinforcing trust in complex models requires explainability [9], which is specifically relevant for tasks such as fake news detection. In our effort to interpret the predictions of the BAFT model, which combines text and image data, we applied SHAP [26] and Grad-CAM [30].

SHAP (Shapley Additive Explanations) SHAP [26] shows the contribution of individual words (or tokens) toward the prediction of the model. For example, when a prediction is made to tag content as misleading, the words "hoax," "fake" or "breaking" will typically have high positive SHAP values, indicating that these are strong predictors of the model flagging the post for misinformation. This type of analysis can be valuable for content moderation teams to assess what word cues are eliciting the decisions of the model, and to determine whether certain terms may be causing unfair bias in the outputs.

Grad-CAM (Gradient-weighted Class Activation Mapping) Grad-CAM [30], is utilized to localize visual features that affect classification. Our examination indicated that the model sometimes favors sensational or emotionally charged visuals; for instance, hyperbolic facial expressions or gruesome content. This information helps unearth possible model biases, particularly with respect to visually provocative features, which could be at times independent of fact inaccuracies.

4 Results

Commonly utilized metrics, for classification performance, among other ways are precision, recall, F1-score, and support which are defined in [31]. The model achieves an overall high accuracy of 97.58%, indicating strong predictive capability despite the class imbalance observed earlier (Tables 2 and 3).

Table 2. Classification report for multimodal project

Class	Precision	Recall	F1 score
0	0.9810	0.9938	0.9873
1	0.9620	0.9620	0.9620
2	0.9837	0.9620	0.9727
3	0.9596	0.8190	0.8837
4	0.8182	0.9000	0.8571
5	0.9412	0.9811	0.9607

Table 3. Overall metrics for multimodal project

Metric	Precision	Recall	F1-score
Accuracy	0.9758		
Macro Avg	0.9409	0.9363	0.9373
Weighted Avg	0.9759	0.9758	0.9756

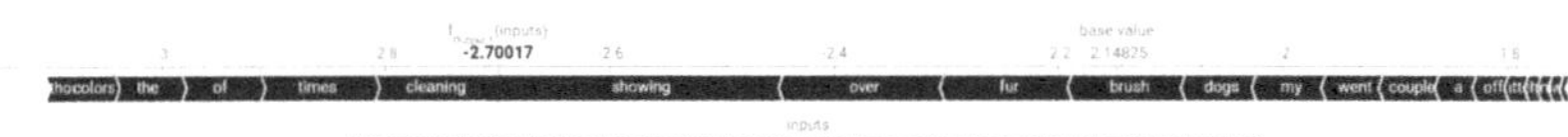

Fig. 6. Positive contribution visualization

This plot shows a SHAP [26] value analysis for a text input, highlighting the positive impact of certain words on the model's final output. Words like "fur",

Fig. 7. SHAP explanation results for a text classification

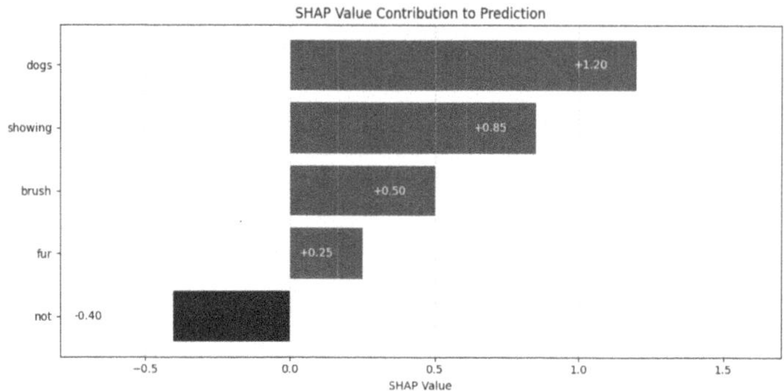

Fig. 8. SHAP explanation of text input. Words such as "dogs" and "showing" contribute positively to the prediction. Negative words like "not" reduce confidence. Visualized using SHAP bar chart and value table

"brush", "showing", and "dogs" are pushing the model's prediction towards a higher output value (positive influence), as indicated by arrows pointing right. The base value starts from -0.845, and the final model output is significantly increased to 8.43007 after considering the contributions of these words. This means these keywords strongly influence the model's decision toward a certain class (Figs. 6 and 7).

The horizontal bar chart features a SHAP explanation of a sample textual input. Certain words exhibit positive contributions to the model in the prediction, i.e., "dogs" and "showing," while words given negative weights, such as "not," lower the confidence in the decision. Such a visualization really allows us to understand which tokens, or words, actually influence the model's output, hence make decision-making more transparent and trustworthy (Fig. 8).

The heatmap [32] shows the portions of the input image that impacted the model's prediction of fake news significantly. Bright areas in the images depict more important areas as determined by the Grad-CAM [30] applied to the image encoder of the BAFT model. This kind of visualization is useful in understanding what the model actually paid attention to while making the decision and

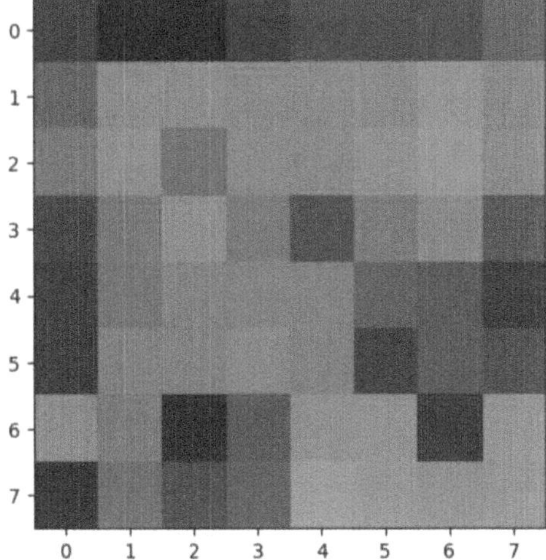

Fig. 9. Grad-CAM heatmap

thereby enhances the overall explainability of the implemented multi-modal system (Fig. 9).

Also, the below bar chart shows the relative classification accuracy [31] of the BAFT model against the unimodal and multimodal baseline models on Fakeddit dataset. The BAFT method outperforms most of the existing methods with dramatically better accuracy of 97.58% whereas all others are generally between 86–94%. It depicts that the hybrid multimodal approach is very effective (Fig. 10).

5 Conclusion and Future Scope

In this paper, we propose a fake-news detection model based on a multimodal analysis of text and images using a BAFT model that relies on BERT for processing text data and ResNet50 for processing image data. Cross-modal attention fusion helped in the prediction assurance of the model, since information from both text and image sources are merged. Other explainability tools like SHAP can be used for enhancing the transparency of model decisions while allowing an understanding of how different features contribute to predictions and thus evaluate fairness.

As we look into the future, there are a few additional avenues of improvement for the system. First and foremost in the future working horizons is to optimize the efficiency of the model by investigating lighter transformer models, which include DistilBERT, and lightweight image models. Another way in which generalization can be achieved is by adding more diversity to the existing dataset in terms of sources and languages. Besides, any real-time input deriving from social media would make the detection of fake news in real-time more relevant and thus more applicable in real-time settings. In addition, extending explanations to tackle situations involving both text and image modalities would give

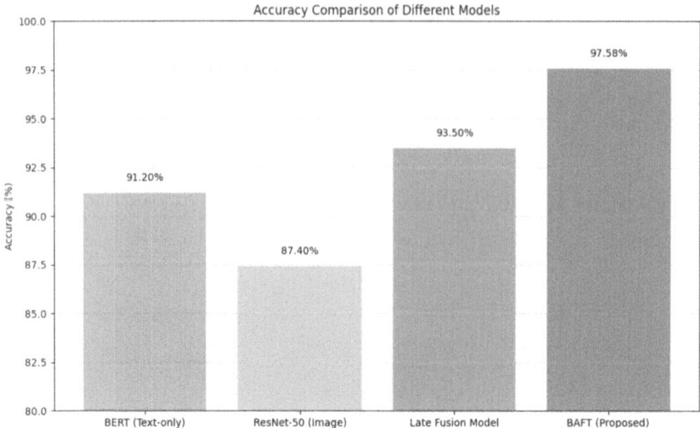

Fig. 10. Accuracy comparison of the proposed BAFT model with existing unimodal and multimodal baselines on the Fakeddit dataset

deeper insights into how these inputs affect the decision-making process. Cross-dataset evaluations involving different data sources, such as Weibo, GossipCop, or Twitter, should be conducted by future work in order to verify further the generalizability of the BAFT model. Lastly, such customization of the model across domains as medical misinformation, political news, etc. would further enhance this applicability. In this respect, these future avenues would add robustness and practical application needs to the fake news detection system in counteracting information warfare efforts online.

References

1. Aïmeur, E., Amri, S., Brassard, G.: Fake news, disinformation and misinformation in social media: a review. Soc. Netw. Anal. Min. **13**(1), 30 (2023). https://doi.org/10.1007/s13278-023-01028-5
2. Nasser, M., Arshad, N.I., Ali, A., Alhussian, H., Saeed, F., Da'u, A., Nafea, I.: A systematic review of multimodal fake news detection on social media using deep learning models. Res. Eng. **26**, 104752 (2025). https://doi.org/10.1016/j.rineng.2025.104752
3. Singh, B., Sharma, D.K.: Predicting image credibility in fake news over social media using multi-modal approach. Neural Comput. Appl. **34**(24), 21503–21517 (2022). https://doi.org/10.1007/s00521-021-06086-4
4. SEON: Blackbox Machine Learning. https://seon.io/resources/dictionary/blackbox-machine-learning/. Last Accessed 26 Apr 2025
5. Devlin, J., Chang, M.-W., Lee, K., Toutanova, K.: BERT: pre-training of deep bidirectional transformers for language understanding (2019). http://arxiv.org/abs/1810.04805
6. Roboflow: What is ResNet-50? https://blog.roboflow.com/what-is-resnet-50/. Last Accessed 27 Apr 2025

7. Chen, H., Jiang, D., Sahli, H.: Transformer encoder with multi-modal multi-head attention for continuous affect recognition. IEEE Trans. Multimedia **23**, 4171–4183 (2021). https://doi.org/10.1109/TMM.2020.3037496
8. Papers with Code: Fakeddit Dataset. https://paperswithcode.com/dataset/fakeddit. Last accessed 27 Apr 2025
9. Mathew, D.E., Ebem, D.U., Ikegwu, A.C., Ukeoma, P.E., Dibiaezue, N.F.: Recent emerging techniques in explainable artificial intelligence to enhance the interpretable and understanding of AI models for human. Neural Process. Lett. **57**(1), 16 (2025). https://doi.org/10.1007/s11063-025-11732-2
10. Jiang, Y., Yu, X., Wang, Y., Xu, X., Song, X., Maynard, D.: Similarity-aware multimodal prompt learning for fake news detection. Inf. Sci. **647**, 119446 (2023). https://doi.org/10.1016/j.ins.2023.119446
11. Luvembe, A.M., Li, W., Li, S., Liu, F., Wu, X.: CAF-ODNN: complementary attention fusion with optimized deep neural network for multimodal fake news detection. Inf. Process. Manag. **61**(3), 103653 (2024). https://doi.org/10.1016/j.ipm.2024.103653
12. Visweswaran, M., Mohan, J., Kumar, S.S., Soman, K.P.: Synergistic detection of multimodal fake news leveraging TextGCN and vision transformer. Proc. Comput. Sci. **235**, 142–151 (2024). https://doi.org/10.1016/j.procs.2024.04.017
13. Giri, M., Eswaran, S., Honnavalli, P.: Automated and interpretable fake news detection with explainable artificial intelligence. J. Appl. Secur. Res.**19**(4), 628–648 (2024). https://doi.org/10.1080/19361610.2024.2356431
14. Zamil, Y.K., Charkari, N.M.: Combating fake news on social media: a fusion approach for improved detection and interpretability. IEEE Access **12**, 2074–2085 (2024). https://doi.org/10.1109/ACCESS.2023.3342843
15. Shiyam, A.B., Poravi, G.: Deepfake low resource image detection with explainable reporting. FaceForensics++ Dataset (2023)
16. Singh, P., Srivastava, R., Rana, K.P.S., Kumar, V.: SEMI-FND: stacked ensemble-based multimodal inferencing framework for faster fake news detection. Expert Syst. Appl. **215**, 119302 (2023). https://doi.org/10.1016/j.eswa.2022.119302
17. Zhang, X., Dadkhah, S., Weismann, A.G., Kanaani, M.A., Ghorbani, A.A.: Multimodal fake news analysis based on image-text similarity. IEEE Trans. Comput. Soc. Syst. **11**(1), 959–972 (2024). https://doi.org/10.1109/TCSS.2023.3244068
18. Gautam, A., Vijayakumar Bharathi, S., Pramod, D., Patil, K.: Fake textual and image news detection on social media using natural language processing. In: Proceedings of the 2023 International conference on advanced computing technologies and applications (ICACTA). IEEE, pp. 1–6 (2023). https://doi.org/10.1109/ICACTA58201.2023.10392425
19. Uppada, S.K., Patel, P., Sivaselvan, B.: An image and text-based multimodal model for detecting fake news in OSNs. J. Intell. Inf. Syst. **61**(2), 367–393 (2023). https://doi.org/10.1007/s10844-022-00764-y
20. Qi, P., Cao, J., Yang, T., Guo, J., Li, J.: Exploiting multi-domain visual information for fake news detection. In: 2019 IEEE international conference on data mining (ICDM). IEEE, pp. 518–527 (2019). https://doi.org/10.1109/ICDM.2019.00062
21. Reis, J.C.S., Correia, A., Murai, F., Veloso, A., Benevenuto, F.: Explainable machine learning for fake news detection. In: Proceedings of the 10th ACM conference on web science (WebSci '19). Association for Computing Machinery, pp. 17–26 (2019). https://doi.org/10.1145/3292522.3326027
22. Ajao, O., Bhowmik, D., Zargari, S.: Sentiment-aware fake news detection on online social networks. In: ICASSP 2019–2019 IEEE international conference on acoustics,

speech and signal processing (ICASSP). IEEE, pp. 2507–2511 (2019). https://doi.org/10.1109/ICASSP.2019.8683170
23. Deokate, S.: Fake news detection using support vector machine learning algorithm. Int. J. Res. Appl. Sci. Eng. Technol.**7**, 438–444 (2019). https://doi.org/10.22214/ijraset.2019.7067
24. Guibon, G., Ermakova, L., Seffih, H., Firsov, A., Noé-Bienvenu, G.L.: Multilingual fake news detection with satire. In: Gelbukh, A. (ed.) Computational Linguistics and Intelligent Text Processing: CICLing 2019. Lecture Notes in Computer Science, vol. 13452. Springer, Cham, pp. 297–308 (2023). https://doi.org/10.1007/978-3-031-24340-0_29
25. Yang, Y., Zheng, L., Zhang, J., Cui, Q., Li, Z., Yu, P.S.: TI-CNN: convolutional neural networks for fake news detection (2018). https://arxiv.org/abs/1806.00749
26. DataCamp: Explainable AI: Understanding and Trusting Machine Learning Models (2023). https://www.datacamp.com/tutorial/explainable-ai-understanding-and-trusting-machine-learning-models
27. Simplilearn: What Is Data Processing? (2023). https://www.simplilearn.com/what-is-data-processing-article
28. Domino Data Lab: Feature Extraction (2023). https://domino.ai/data-science-dictionary/feature-extraction
29. Built In: ReLU Activation Function (2023). https://builtin.com/machine-learning/relu-activation-function
30. DataScientest: What is the Grad-CAM Method? (2023). https://datascientest.com/en/what-is-the-grad-cam-method
31. Labelf: What is Accuracy, Precision, Recall, and F1 Score? (2023). https://www.labelf.ai/blog/what-is-accuracy-precision-recall-and-f1-score
32. Mohiuddin, S., Sheikh, K., Malakar, S., Velasquez, J., Sarkar, R.: A hierarchical feature selection strategy for deepfake video detection. Neural Comput. Appl. **35**, 1–18 (2023). https://doi.org/10.1007/s00521-023-08201-z

DCM-FL: Decentralized Collaborative Multi-Client Federated Learning Using Layer-Type Aggregation and Knowledge Distillation Methods

Dhinagaran Ramyaa(✉), S. Kavitha, V. Mega, and G. S. Ashwini Parvatha

Department of Computer Science and Engineering, Sri Sivasubramaniya Nadar College of Engineering, Kalavakkam, Chennai, India
{ramyaad,kavithas,mega2110506,ashwini2110598}@ssn.edu.in

Abstract. Federated Learning (FL) enables collaborative model training across multiple clients without sharing raw data, ensuring privacy in sensitive domains like healthcare. Traditional FL often relies on a central server for model aggregation from different clients, leading to significant limitations and risks such as a single-point failure, communication bottlenecks, scalability issues, privacy risks, and limited resilience, especially when working with heterogeneous, multimodal data across clients. To overcome these limitations, a Decentralized Collaborative Multi-Client Federated Learning (DCM-FL) approach is proposed to eliminate its dependency on a central server, enabling direct collaboration between clients. The DCM-FL setup consists of three independent clients using different architectures, such as CNN (Client1), VGG16 (Client2), and ResNet50 (Client3), each containing the CBIS-DDSM dataset with various distributions to predict breast cancer from breast mammogram images. The architectural dependency among clients during aggregation is mitigated by integrating two different aggregation methods, such as layer-type aggregation (Method 1) and knowledge distillation (Method 2). The results show that Method 1 gradually improves the accuracy of Client1 from 51.53% to 68.40% by Round 3, whereas Method 2 achieves an accuracy of 67.18% in Round 1 and sustains further. The trade-off between computation and communication highlights that Method 1 is efficient for homogeneous model architectures with similar layer types for direct weight sharing, and Method 2 is better suited for heterogeneous environments where direct weight sharing is not feasible, but requires higher computation and communication costs.

Keywords: Federated Learning · Model Weight Aggregation · Knowledge Distillation · Synthetic Feature Fusion · LIME

1 Introduction

Recent developments in healthcare domain show breakthrough advancements in AI-driven medical image analysis such as X-rays, Magnetic Resonance Imag-

K. Chandra Mondal et al. (Eds.): CICBA 2025, CCIS 2863, pp. 429–444, 2026.
https://doi.org/10.1007/978-3-032-17184-9_32

ing (MRI), Computed Tomography (CT), 3D Mammography and Non-Invasive testing using blood samples, certain notable challenges still persist like generalizability, multi-modal data integration, and overfitting issues due to insufficient data for training [11,13,21]. Also, the availability of real-time labeled medical data is more challenging due to strict privacy regulations in institutions on data sharing and ethical concerns [29,32]. Hence, developing an efficient model only with the available data using traditional learning methods is quite difficult. At this point, the Federated Learning (FL) approach comes into play to address the challenges in developing an improved privacy-preserving model without sharing the raw data for training.

Federated Learning (FL) is a collaborative ML approach introduced by Google researchers in 2016 [10]. It enables multiple clients or organizations to collaboratively train their models without directly sharing the sensitive data. Instead, the collaborative clients share only their model updates (gradients or weights) to get an improved model while preserving data privacy and also reduces communication overhead. Additionally, it improves generalization by facilitating multi-modal data integration in various privacy-preserving domains such as finance, healthcare, and recommendation systems to support personalized learning platforms [20,22,27]. In the healthcare domain, medical images for cancer prediction are highly sensitive and involves various modalities like MRI, CT, mammogram, histopathology, and clinical records for accurate and early diagnosis. Notably, breast cancer is a key focus in research due to its high global incidence and its significant impact on early detection.

According to the World Health Organization (WHO) 2023 report [30], approximately 2.3 million women worldwide were diagnosed with breast cancer, of which 30% are not detected early, resulting in an increased mortality rate. This can be significantly reduced by adopting a real-time learning environment through FL. Based on the requirements and availability of resources, FL can be implemented using various architectures such as Centralized FL (CFL), Decentralized FL (DFL), Distributed FL, and Collaborative FL. In CFL, a central server coordinates the training process, where each client generates its local model using its local data and shares the model parameters with the server. It aggregates and returns the global parameters to the clients for retraining to generate an updated model. Here, clients indirectly collaborate to generate an updated model. In DFL, clients communicate directly to exchange model parameters without relying on a central server, preventing single-point failure [18]. Any client needing an updated model can initiate the federation process, train locally, exchange updates with selected clients, and aggregate them using FedAvg, FedProx, or Gossip Learning for an improved model. Distributed FL forms a combined approach of CFL and DFL, where clients are organized into hierarchical groups, and perform local aggregation within groups using a decentralized approach or having a regional server before exchanging the model parameters across groups for a global model [6,8]. This approach is useful in scenarios like COVID-19, where regional health centers aggregate patient data locally and collaborate with other regions to learn patterns influenced by demographic factors.

An additional decentralized approach called Collaborative FL allows multiple clients to share knowledge without a central server by exchanging feature representations, predictions, gradients, or soft labels directly [19]. This is useful in scenarios like hospitals collaborating for rare disease prediction by sharing knowledge through aggregated soft labels. While both DFL and Collaborative FL involve direct client communication without a central coordinator, they are not identical. DFL lacks a global model update, with each client communicating only with 2–3 neighbors and gradually synchronizing over time. In contrast, Collaborative FL has an initiator client that collects updates or soft labels from all collaborators simultaneously, enabling faster convergence.

This work implements a Decentralized Collaborative Multi-client FL (DCM-FL) approach with two different aggregation methods, enabling multiple clients with distinct architectures to train locally and share model updates without a central server while preserving privacy [6]. In this scenario, traditional averaging of model weights is challenging due to architectural differences, but techniques like layer-wise aggregation with zero-padding, weight reshaping, and layer alignment help in handling incompatible layers. Additionally, knowledge distillation is used for collaborative training, where clients learn from each other using soft labels.

The remaining sections of this paper are structured as follows: Sect. 2 explains the related works on FL techniques across different architectures in healthcare. Section 3 presents the proposed DCM-FL design, adopting two aggregation methods. Section 4 discusses the results, and Sect. 5 concludes the paper with future enhancements.

2 Related Work

This section explains inferences about different FL architectures and aggregation techniques implemented using medical data in the healthcare domain. The findings are presented in Table 1 based on the adopted FL architectures, including CFL, DFL, and Collaborative FL.

From Table 1, it is inferred that CFL facilitates aggregating weights from different model architectures, where a central server is responsible for averaging weights of varying shapes from intermediate layers without any compatibility issues with an additional dense layer. Although DFL facilitates direct communication between diverse clients and reduces communication overhead, it has a practical difficulty for model consistency. In contrast, Collaborative FL effectively addresses the limitations of centralized or decentralized FL by combining their strengths. However, it often relies on meta-models or ensemble strategies that are prone to feature misalignment due to variations in data distributions and model architectures across clients. Hence, in this proposed work, a Decentralized Collaborative Multi-client FL architecture is implemented where learning from distinct model architectures having different data distributions can be made independent without compromising privacy. It also enables more flexible and advanced aggregation strategies, such as weighted averaging, feature fusion, knowledge distillation, and stacking, while maintaining data privacy.

Table 1. Summary of existing work on different FL architectures and aggregation techniques using medical data

S.No.	Author & Year	Datasets Used	ML/DL Algorithms	Accuracy	Architectural Limitations
			Centralized FL		
1	Mawla et al. (2024) [1]	Breast cancer datasets- DDSM, INbreast, Macrocalcifications	VGG19, MobileNetV2	FedAvg: 96.13%	Requires a central server for averaging weights of incompatible layers with varying shapes, limited privacy, prone to single-point failure, increased computation costs, and High model complexity.
2	Almufareh et al. (2023) [26]	Breast Cancer Wisconsin (BCW) Diagnostic dataset	DNNs	FedAvg: 97.54%	
3	Nguyen Tan et al. (2023) [2]	Breast Cancer datasets- DDSM, CBIS-DDSM	MobileNet, Densenet21, Xception, Resnet50	FedAvg: 97.91%	
4	Munawar et al. (2024) [15]	Lung and Colon Cancer datasets- LC25000	InceptionV3, VGG16, ResNet50, Xception	FedAvg: Lung: 99.867% Colon: 100% Combined: 99.72%	
5	Diaz JSP et al. (2025) [12]	brain-tumor-classification-mri	InceptionV3, VGG16, ResNet50V2, DenseNet121	FedAvgOpt: 0.82	
6	Haggen-muller et al. (2024) [14]	WSI of skin lesions from 6 hospitals(Private dataset)	ResNet18	FedAvg: 902.4%	
			Decentralized FL		
7	Abhijit et al. (2019) [23]	Whole-brain MRI from Multi-Atlas Labelling Challenge (MALC)	QuickNAT	Weighted Avg: 80.7%	Choosing a compatible architecture among clients to enable smooth weight aggregation, coordinating heterogeneous models with varying feature dimensions, and gradually synchronizing through repeated interactions.
8	Hua Chai et al. (2024) [7]	Colon, Head and Neck, Liver, Ovarian	RF, XGBoost, SVM	ADFed (Ad-Hoc Fed): 60.5%	
9	Arthi et al. (2022) [3]	Colorectal Cancer (Private dataset)	VGG16, VGG19, InceptionV3, ResNet50, and ResNeXt50	Weighted Avg: 96.04%	
			Collaborative FL		
10	Anjir et al. (2023) [9]	Fetal Brain MRI from Harvard Medical School Medical Group	VGG16, VGG19, ResNet50, DenseNet121, ResNet152 with KNN as Meta-Model	Stacking: 80%	Relies on meta-models or ensemble strategies (Stacking and Knowledge distillation) that increase complexity, prone to feature misalignment.
11	Thanveer et al. (2022) [24]	MHEALTH (Mobile HEALTH) for personalized activity monitoring	ANN, CNN, Bi-LSTM	Stacking: Homogene-ous: 97.6% Heterogene-ous: 99.6%	
12	Xu et al. (2023) [31]	PAMAP, MedMnist (OrganAMNIST, OrganCMNIST, OrganSMNI) for personalized healthcare	CNNs, LeNet5	KD: 97.69%	
13	Bechar et al. (2025) [5]	Wisconsin Breast Cancer Dataset, LUNA16, TCGA, METABRIC for breast and lung cancer classification	InceptionV3, VGG16, ResNet50, Xception, MobileNet	KD: Breast: 99.68% Lung: 98.9%	

3 Proposed System

The proposed system aims to implement a Decentralized Collaborative Multi-client FL (DCM-FL) approach consisting of three distinct clients having non-IID medical images from the CBIS-DDSM dataset (Curated Breast Imaging Subset of Digital Database for Screening Mammography), adopting two feasible aggregation methods, such as Layer-Type Federated Averaging (Method 1) and Fused Knowledge Distillation (Method 2). The system design is illustrated in Fig. 1.

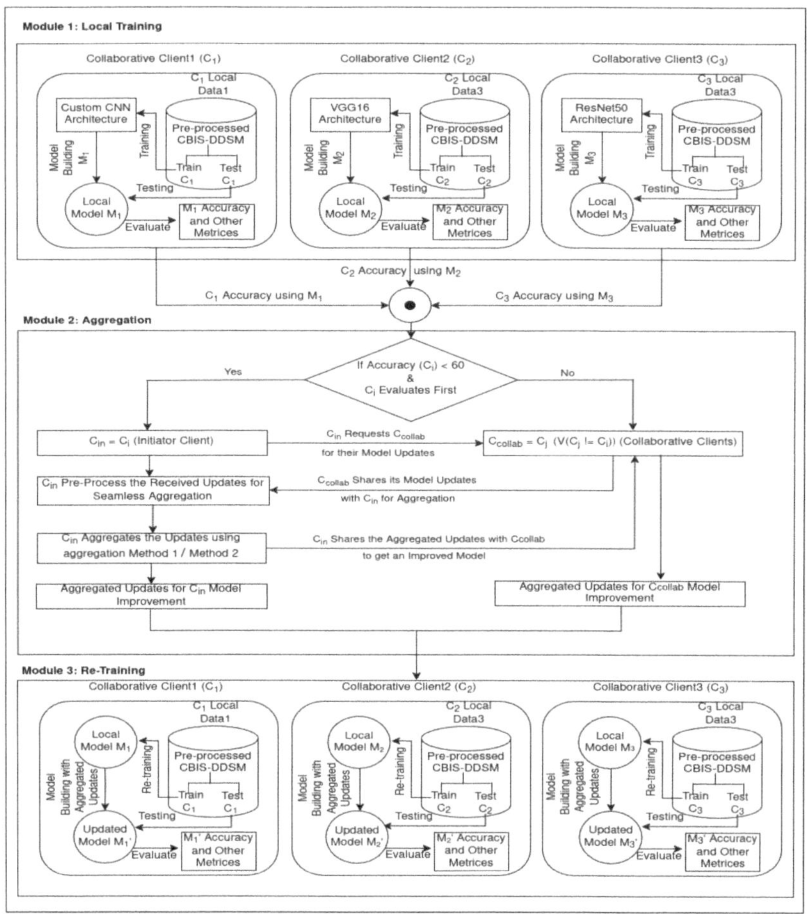

Fig. 1. Design of DCM-FL approach with three collaborative clients

3.1 Dataset Collection

The CBIS-DDSM Breast Cancer Mammography Image Dataset is a subset of standardized and updated versions of the Digital Database for Screening Mammography (DDSM), collected from the Cancer Imaging Archive, and is also available in Kaggle [4,17,28]. It is used commonly in all clients to guarantee that data quality is not a limiting factor, rather it provides insights into how architectural complexity and methodologies impact overall performance. It contains images of both calcification and mass cases, from which breast mass images of 1630 patients are used for training, following the guidance provided in the study by Sawyer Lee et al. [16]. The breast mass images are classified into three categories as Malignant, Benign, and Benign_without_callback. In this work, Benign_without_callback is also categorized as Benign for balancing, as both represent non-cancerous cases. Since the dataset is well-defined, no major preprocessing is needed except resizing to $224 \times 224 \times 3$ and normalization. Further, the dataset is divided into 80:20 with different distributions in each client to simulate the real-world non-IID environment and is detailed in Table 2 [25].

Table 2. Data distribution across clients

Client_id	Training Set Count (1304)		Test Set Count (326)	
	Class_0	Class_1	Class_0	Class_1
Client 1	720	584	165	161
Client 2	721	583	166	160
Client 3	703	601	178	148

3.2 Methodology

The DCM-FL approach is structured into three modules such as Module 1 (Local Training), Module 2 (Aggregation), and Module 3 (Re-training), having three collaborative clients, namely Client 1, Client 2, and Client 3 designed with unique architectures such as CNN, VGG16, and ResNet50, respectively.

Module 1 follows a standard machine learning approach in which each client independently performs local training on its data and evaluates its performance using its corresponding test set. The architectures are selected based on their unique strengths in learning from medical images. CNN in client 1 is lightweight and quick to train, focusing on customized feature extraction at different layers where it learns domain-specific patterns such as masses and calcifications. The adopted CNN architecture takes an input image of size $224 \times 224 \times 3$, processes it through three convolutional and max-pooling layers for feature extraction, followed by a flattening layer. The flattened one-dimensional feature vector is given to three successive fully connected layers with 512, 256, and 1 units for the final classification output using a sigmoid activation function. VGG16 and

ResNet50 are adopted in Client 2 and Client 3 due to their consistent and well-defined layer structure that facilitates seamless integration with other models while implementing fusion techniques. Comparatively, ResNet50 has a deeper architecture and requires high computational resources to capture complex features. It also has a residual connection by default, and no additional parameter is required to reduce overfitting. Hence, VGG16 and ResNet50 are used without pre-trained ImageNet weights, with an added dense layer of 256 and 128 units, respectively, to reduce spatial dimensions and enable learning of domain-specific features from scratch, since the chosen dataset significantly differs from ImageNet. After local training, each client's performance is evaluated using its respective test data. Based on accuracy, the aggregation process in Module 2 is initiated by the corresponding initiator client.

Module 2 supports two aggregation techniques, such as Method 1 (Layer-Type Federated Averaging) and Method 2 (Fused Knowledge Distillation), designed to handle both architecture and data heterogeneity across clients without a central server. During the aggregation process, a single client acts as an initiator represented as C_{in}, starts the aggregation process, and requests collaborative clients C_{collab} for their model updates. In DCM-FL, each client operates independently and evaluates its model locally under the same fixed condition, where the initiator is assigned dynamically based on local model performance. However, in the absence of a central coordinator or global communication among clients, multiple clients may simultaneously consider themselves underperforming and try to act as initiators, leading to initiation conflicts. Since all three clients have an equal probability to be an initiator, a fixed threshold of 60% accuracy is fixed to determine the C_{in}. Also, there exists a possibility for a synchronization conflict when more than one client meets the threshold accuracy and initializes the aggregation process simultaneously. To address this synchronization conflict, an initiation lock with a status flag is implemented, where the first client that results in an accuracy of less than a fixed threshold will act as C_{in}.

Method 1- Similar-Type Layer Aggregation. In a DFL setup, direct aggregation of weights from diverse client architectures (CNN, VGG16, and ResNet50) is quite challenging due to variations in their layer structures and weight shapes as discussed in Sect. 1. Alternatively, the weights from the layers of similar types (e.g., convolution, dense) across clients are considered, irrespective of their size. Further, the variation in those sizes across models is aligned by applying zero-padding to match their dimensions before aggregation to ensure structural consistency while preserving model-specific learning. The aggregated weight shapes of similar-type layers are highlighted in Table 3, and the aggregated weights are redistributed to all clients, allowing them to refine their models collaboratively while maintaining architectural diversity. The entire aggregation process involved in Method 1 is detailed in Algorithm 1.

Method 2-Fused Knowledge Distillation. Traditional knowledge distillation transfers knowledge better through soft labels. However, in this work, the data distribution across clients is varied to simulate real-world scenarios by

Table 3. Aggregated weight shapes of the similar-type layers

Layer Type	CNN	VGG	ResNet	Aggregated Shape
Conv2D (1st)	(3,3,3,32),(32,)	(3,3,3,64),(64,)	(7,7,3,64),(64,)	(7,7,3,64),(64,)
BatchNorm (1st)	(32,),(32,),(32,), (32,)	(256,),(256,), (256,),(256,)	(64,),(64,),(64,), (64,)	(256,),(256,), (256,),(256,)
Conv2D (2nd)	(3,3,32,64), (64,)	(3,3,64,64), (64,)	(1,1,64,64), (64,)	(3,3,64,64), (64,)
BatchNorm (2nd)	(64,),(64,),(64,), (64,)	**N/A**	(64,),(64,),(64,), (64,)	**N/A**
Conv2D (3rd)	(3,3,64,128), (128,)	(3,3,64,128), (128,)	(3,3,64,64), (64,)	(3,3,64,128), (128,)
BatchNorm (3rd)	(128,),(128,), (128,),(128,)	**N/A**	(64,),(64,),(64,), (64,)	**N/A**
Conv2D (4th)	**N/A**	(3,3,128,128), (128,)	(1,1,64,256), (256,)	**N/A**
BatchNorm (4th)	(512,),(512,), (512,),(512,)	**N/A**	(256,),(256,), (256,),(256,)	**N/A**
Dense (FC-1)	(100352,512), (512,)	(25088,256), (256,)	(100352,128), (128,)	(100352,512), (512,)
BatchNorm (FC-1)	(256,),(256,), (256,),(256,)	**N/A**	(256,),(256,), (256,),(256,)	**N/A**
Dense (FC-2)	(512,256),(256,)	**N/A**	**N/A**	**N/A**
BatchNorm (FC2)	**N/A**	**N/A**	(64,),(64,),(64,), (64,)	**N/A**
Output Layer	(256,1),(1,)	(256,1),(1,)	(128,1),(1,)	(256,1),(1,)

adopting different random states. In this scenario, direct aggregation of soft labels from non-IID data becomes unreliable. Although Method 1 focuses on sharing knowledge by aggregating weights, it enables only partial knowledge sharing from similar-type layers due to its inconsistencies and model-specific differences. Therefore, a fused knowledge distillation is adopted in Method 2 that allows the student models to learn a generalized knowledge representation from diverse teacher models in the clients by sharing the synthetic feature vectors with soft labels for fusion. This method overcomes the limitation of structural mismatch in client architectures and preserves privacy by sharing the synthetic feature vectors of an image generated using LIME (Local Interpretable Model-Agnostic Explanations) instead of sharing the extracted feature vectors. LIME identifies important features locally by generating a synthetic dataset around each sample based on its class label for local approximation.

In Method 2, 300 random samples are selected from each client's local data, consisting of 150 positive (Class_1: Malignant) and 150 negative (Class_0: Benign) samples, to generate a hybrid feature set S_i using Eq. 1. For each of these

Algorithm 1. Method 1 (Similar-Type Layer Aggregation)

Require: Local model weights from clients $(W_i^{C_i}, W_j^{C_j})$, $\forall i, j \in \{1,2,3|i \neq j\}$
Ensure: Aggregated weights W_{agg} from similar layer types
1: **function** AGG_METHOD1($W_i^{C_i}$)
2: $C_{\text{in}} \leftarrow$ Initiator client
3: $C_{\text{collab}} \leftarrow$ Collaborative clients
4: $W \leftarrow$ Weights
5: $ACC(C_i) \leftarrow$ Accuracy of Client i
6: $L_{\text{shared}} \leftarrow$ Layers of similar type shared between clients
7: $\text{Eval}_{\text{first}} \leftarrow$ Client who evaluates first
8: **if** $\text{Acc}(C_i) \leq 60$ **and** $\text{Eval}_{\text{first}}$ **then**
9: $C_{\text{in}} \leftarrow C_i$ and $C_{\text{collab}} \leftarrow C_j$, $\forall j \in \{1,2,3\}, j \neq i$
10: **Request from** C_{in}: $W_{\text{collab}} \leftarrow \{W_j \mid j \in C_{\text{collab}}\}$
11: **Response from** C_{collab}: $C_{\text{in}} \leftarrow C_{\text{collab}}(W_{\text{collab}})$
12: **if** layer-type(C_{in}) = layer-type(C_{collab}) **then**
13: $W_{\text{aligned}}(L_{\text{shared}}) \leftarrow \text{ZeroPad}(W_{\text{in}}(L_{\text{shared}}), W_{\text{collab}}(L_{\text{shared}}))$
14: $W_{\text{agg}}(L_{\text{shared}}) \leftarrow \text{Aggregate}(W_{\text{aligned}}(L_{\text{shared}}))$
15: $C_{\text{collab}} \leftarrow C_{\text{in}}$ **shares** $W_{\text{agg}}(L_{\text{shared}})$
16: **end if**
17: $C_{\text{in}}(L_{\text{shared}}), C_{\text{collab}}(W_{\text{agg}}(L_{\text{shared}})) \leftarrow W_{\text{agg}}(L_{\text{shared}})$
18: **end if**
19: **end function**

300 images, LIME generates N ($N = 1$ indicates that for each 300 selected samples in a client, a single synthetic data is generated) synthetic feature vectors z_j through a sampling perturbation process $\mathcal{L}(x_j)$ and trains a surrogate model g_i to approximate the behavior of the client's local model θ_i ($\theta_i \in \{\theta_{dense}, \theta_{vgg}, \theta_{res}\}$). From each synthetic feature vector, 70% are randomly selected while retaining the rest 30% from the original. The hybrid feature set S_i is generated locally by combining all perturbed instances z_j of 300 x_j. Figure 2 illustrates the comparison between the original and hybrid feature vectors for a sample image to be shared without revealing the raw data.

$$S_i = \{(z_j, g_i(z_j))\}_{j=1}^{0.7N} \cup \{(x_j, \theta_{\text{i}}(x_j))\}_{j=1}^{0.3N} \tag{1}$$

The initiator client C_{in} then combines all S_i to create a knowledge distilled dataset S_{agg} consisting of 900 data points. However, due to model diversity, the feature sizes vary between clients, leading to differences in the size of S_i. To ensure uniformity, C_{in} equalizes the dimensions of all shared datasets S_i using zero padding, and the combined dataset s_{agg} is redistributed to all collaborative clients. Now, the fused s_{agg} acts as a meta-dataset for the corresponding student models in the clients (Dense512, Dense1024, Dence256) to learn the pattern from the combined teacher models, and the entire aggregation process is detailed in Algorithm 2. The aggregated updates are sent back to each C_{collab} so that all clients (C_{in} and C_{collab}) in the collaborative environment will now have the updated parameters.

In Module 3, each client enhances its local model from Module 1 by retraining it with the updated parameters from Module 2, and then evaluates their improved accuracy. Based on the resulting accuracy, the entire process may be iterated for multiple rounds, initiated by any client until the accuracy of all clients hits the fixed threshold. Finally, the initiator client C_{in} concludes the federation round by setting the status flag free.

4 Experiments and Results

The DCM-FL approach is implemented to evaluate two aggregation methods (Method 1 and Method 2) using three client architectures, such as CNN, VGG16, and ResNet50, containing non-IID data derived from the CBIS-DDSM dataset [4] under various distributions. The performance of both methods is analyzed and compared across different quantitative metrics such as accuracy (ACC),

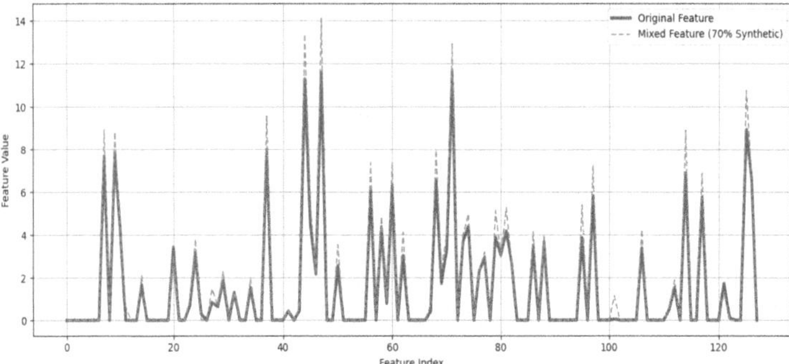

Fig. 2. Comparison of original Vs synthetic feature vectors

Algorithm 2. Method 2 (Fused Knowledge Distillation)

Require: Hybrid feature set (S_i, S_j) generated using Eq. 1, $\forall i, j \in \{1, 2, 3 | i \neq j\}$
Ensure: S_{agg}, Aggregated feature matrix
1: **function** AGG_METHOD2(S_i)
2: $TM_i \leftarrow$ Teacher models in clients $(\theta_{\text{dense}}, \theta_{\text{vgg}}, \theta_{\text{res}})$
3: $SM_i \leftarrow$ Student models in clients $(\theta_{\text{seq}_{512}}, \theta_{\text{seq}_{1024}}, \theta_{\text{seq}_{256}})$
4: $P_{soft,i} \leftarrow$ Soft labels predicted by TM_i
5: **if** $\text{Acc}(C_i) \leq 60$ **and** $\text{Eval}_{\text{first}}$ **then**
6: $C_{\text{in}} \leftarrow C_i$ and $C_{\text{collab}} \leftarrow C_j$, $\forall j \in \{1, 2, 3\}, j \neq i$
7: **Request from** C_{in}: $S_{\text{collab}} \leftarrow \{S_j \mid j \in C_{\text{collab}}\}$
8: **Response from** C_{collab}: $C_{\text{in}} \leftarrow C_{\text{collab}}(S_{collab})$ using LIME from TM_j
9: $S_{\text{aligned}} \leftarrow \text{ZeroPad}(C_{\text{in}}(S_{in}), C_{\text{collab}}(S_{collab}))$
10: $S_{\text{agg}} \leftarrow \text{Combine}(S_{\text{aligned,i}}, P_{soft,i})$
11: $C_{\text{collab}} \leftarrow C_{\text{in}}$ **shares** S_{agg}
12: **end if**
13: $C_{\text{in}}, C_{\text{collab}} \leftarrow SM_i(S_{\text{agg}})$, $\forall SM_i \in (\theta_{\text{seq}_{512}}, \theta_{\text{seq}_{1024}}, \theta_{\text{seq}_{256}})$
14: **end function**

precision (Pre), recall (Rec), and F1-score (F1) as illustrated in Table 4 for four federated rounds. In each round, the client ID (CID) of an initiator C_{in} is highlighted in bold. To ensure a fair comparison, all client architectures were consistently trained for 10 epochs with a batch size of 32, using the Adam optimizer with a learning rate of 0.001, and the trained models were evaluated using their corresponding test set.

4.1 Results of DCM-FL Using Method 1

The results in Table 4 highlights the improvement in model accuracy and performance after the collaborative aggregation and retraining process, providing a clear comparison of the results in different rounds. Initially, in Module 1, the clients show a moderate accuracy of around 50–51%, indicating poor generalization due to limited local data. Also its precision, recall, and F1-Scores are inconsistent, with biased classification. Particularly, Client 1 (Benign:152, Malignant:16) is biased towards negative and Client 2 (Benign:8, Malignant:157) and Client 3 (Benign:27, Malignant:136) are biased towards positive samples.

Even though the accuracy of all clients is less than the fixed threshold of 60%, as per the proposed scenario, Client 1 completed its evaluation first and initiated FL round 1. After completing the aggregation Module 2, it is noted that the accuracy of all clients are increased (C1: 53.98%, C2: 58.28%, C3: 58.58%) approximately by 2.4–8.5%, with Client 3 improved the most, followed by Client 2 (+7.6%). Additionally, true positives and true negatives significantly increase, despite a drop in few clients. Similarly, Client 1 initiated round 2, and the accuracy of Client 1 and 3 further increased (C1: 63.19%, C3: 68.09%) by approximately 10%, and an increase in true positive rates reflects better classification. In particular, Client 3 shows the highest improvement of +18% over its local training, demonstrating the benefits of weight sharing.

Proceeding to round 3, Client 1 overtakes the fixed threshold and reaches 68.40% accuracy. However, Client 2 learns better to handle negative samples, its accuracy remains stable at 56.74%. Hence, in Round 4, Client 2 initiates the process, and it is observed that all clients converge to similar accuracy levels of approximately 67%, indicating model stabilization across multiple clients with non-IID data. Similarly, both true positive and true negative remain high, denoting improved model robustness.

4.2 Results of DCM-FL Using Method 2

The local training results using Method 2 in Table 4 reflect its teacher model in Module 1, while its corresponding student models are those used for retraining in Module 3. The result shows that the student models showed a substantial accuracy gain after learning from the combined teacher models of collaborative clients. As the initiator of round 1, the performance of Client 1 improved significantly from 51.53% to 67.18%, surpassing the fixed threshold while maintaining consistency in later rounds. Similarly, the accuracy of Client 2 has also increased from 50.61% to 66.87% and remains stable. However, Client 3 showed

Table 4. Results of FL Method 1 and Method 2

Training Mode	FL Method1						FL Method2					
	CID	Acc	Pre	Rec	F1	TP/TN	CID	Acc	Pre	Rec	F1	TP/TN
Local Training	C1	51.53	57	52	41	16/152	C1	51.53	57	52	41	16/152
	C2	50.61	49	51	38	157/8	C2	50.61	49	51	38	157/8
	C3	50.00	59	50	42	136/27	C3	50.00	59	50	42	136/27
FL Round 1	**C1**	53.98	64	54	45	22/154	**C1**	67.18	67	67	67	107/112
	C2	58.28	60	58	56	137/53	C2	66.87	67	67	67	110/108
	C3	58.58	58	59	56	47/144	C3	61.35	67	67	67	136/64
FL Round 2	**C1**	63.19	64	63	63	83/123	**C1**	67.18	68	67	67	95/124
	C2	57.05	60	57	55	56/130	C2	66.87	67	67	67	110/108
	C3	68.09	69	68	68	110/112	C3	57.67	69	58	53	138/60
FL Round 3	C1	68.40	68	68	68	113/110	C1	66.87	68	67	67	118/100
	C2	56.74	60	57	54	51/134	**C2**	66.87	67	67	67	110/108
	C3	61.04	64	61	60	116/83	C3	58.28	67	58	54	137/53
FL Round 4	C1	66.56	67	67	66	127/90	C1	67.18	68	67	67	94/125
	C2	67.48	67	67	67	114/106	**C2**	66.87	67	67	67	109/109
	C3	67.48	68	67	68	104/116	C3	58.90	69	59	55	137/55

minimal improvement and crossed the threshold value with 61.35% accuracy. But fluctuated in later rounds and reached 58.90% in round 4. While analysing with precision and recall, both Client 1 and 2 maintained a balance across all rounds, suggesting a stable learning from the combined soft labels of distinct architecture. Since Method 2 achieved a stable performance in a single round, the threshold value is increased and set to 65%. With this threshold adjustment, Client 3 initiated round 2, but resulted in a drop in accuracy, recall and F1-score. Similarly, the later rounds are initialized by Client 3, and does not showed any major improvement rather all clients got stabilized over rounds.

A detailed performance comparison of Method 1 and Method 2, in terms of mean accuracy and standard deviation, across four federated rounds is presented in Table 5, and its corresponding 95% confidence interval plot is given in Fig. 3. Both methods start with an identical local performance, and as FL rounds progress, they show a gradual improvement in accuracy, indicating learning improvements through collaboration. In Round 1, Method 2 demonstrates an overall improvement and benefits more quickly from the first round. Also, an increase in standard deviation reflects an increased variability in clients' perfor-

Table 5. Mean Accuracy and Standard Deviation of Clients across Rounds

Training Mode	Method 1		Method 2	
	Mean	SD	Mean	SD
Local	50.71	0.77	50.71	0.77
Round 1	56.95	2.57	65.13	3.28
Round 2	62.78	5.53	63.91	5.40
Round 3	62.06	5.90	64.01	4.96
Round 4	67.17	0.53	64.32	4.69

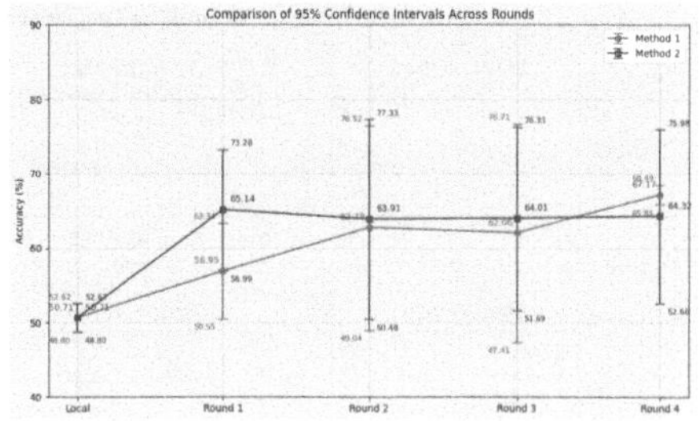

Fig. 3. Average Clients Accuracy using Method 1 and 2 with 95% Confidence Intervals across Rounds

mance. In Rounds 2 and 3, Method 1 shows a slight and stable improvement in accuracy and standard deviation, while Method 2 sustains with comparatively lower variation, particularly in Round 3. By Round 4, Method 1 outperforms Method 2 with a higher mean and significantly lower variance, indicating stronger convergence and consistency. The confidence interval plot also shows a smaller error bar for Method 1 in Round 4. Overall, Method 2 improves faster initially, but Method 1 achieves more stable and reliable convergence with less variance as the round progresses.

The state-of-the-art methods achieve more than 97% accuracy using centralized or alternative FL approaches, where clients adopt homogeneous architectures such as MobileNet, Densenet21, Xception, and ResNet50, consisting of compatible layers for direct weight sharing. Although the DCM-FL approach achieves an accuracy of approximately 68%, it is fully decentralized and supports heterogeneous client architectures with no common layers and performs aggregation by identifying similar layer types and differing weight shapes. This flexibility makes the proposed approach highly suitable for real-world applications where clients use different ML/DL models, offering enhanced adaptability despite a significant trade-off in accuracy. In addition, the graphical visualization of the performance of the client using Method 1 and Method 2 over successive rounds is shown in Fig. 4.

Advantages of Method 1 over Method 2

- Long-Term Adaptability: Method 1 shows gradual improvement over rounds and surpasses Method 2 in the final round, indicating better compatible learning from weights for some architectures, particularly Client 3.
- Lower Computational Overhead: Method 1 relies on direct weight sharing and eliminates additional computational overhead during retraining.
- Bandwidth Efficiency: Method 1 shares only the model weights and requires less communication cost, making it suitable for low-resource environments where clients use compatible model architectures.

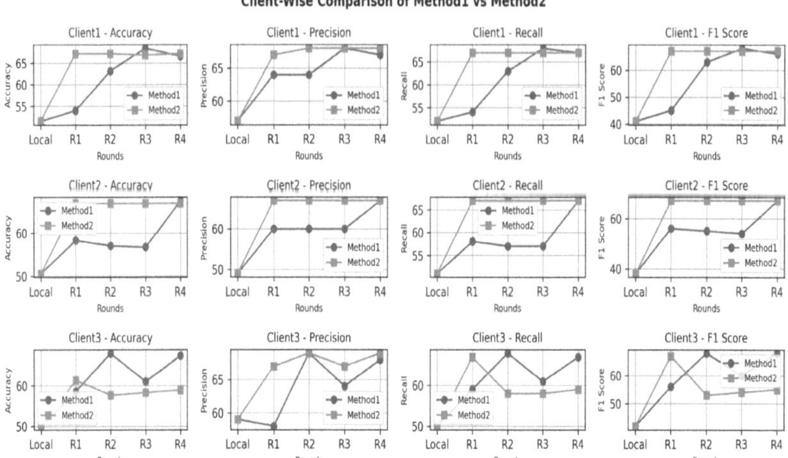

Fig. 4. Client-wise Comparison of FL Methods over four rounds

Advantages of Method 2 over Method 1

- Improved Initial Stability: Method 2 consistently shows superior and stable performance across all metrics, whereas Method 1 exhibits minor fluctuations.
- Faster Convergence: Method 2 achieves rapid performance gains in initial rounds, especially for Client 1 and Client 2, indicating quicker adaptation.
- Generalization: Knowledge distillation through synthetic features across heterogeneous architectures helps to generalize in fewer rounds, based on the size of the dataset.

5 Conclusion and Future Enhancement

The comparative analysis of Similar Layer-Type Aggregation (Method 1) and Fused Knowledge Distillation (Method 2) in the DCM-FL approach highlights significant trade-offs in accuracy and other metrics. Method 1 offers better communication efficiency since it only transmits weight updates, making it more suitable for low-bandwidth environments. Additionally, Client 3 achieves comparatively better accuracy with Method 1, suggesting that client architecture with deeper layers like ResNet50 benefits more from sharing weights from similar-type layers than synthetic feature-based knowledge distillation. However, Method 1 is computationally expensive, as each client must perform full model updates in each round by applying the aggregated weights on the respective layers to get an updated model. In contrast, Method 2 provides better accuracy and generalization in most rounds, likely due to knowledge transfer through synthetic feature sharing. It leverages the teacher model's precomputed features and soft labels, enabling faster convergence and reducing training complexity by using a lightweight student model like Dense. Although Method 2 is more efficient, it leads to higher communication overhead due to the transfer of synthetic LIME-based features and soft labels predicted by the teacher model. Overall, the choice between Method 1 and Method 2 depends on whether the priority is reducing communication overhead (Method 1) or improving learning efficiency and accuracy (Method 2) through synthetic feature-based knowledge sharing between diverse clients containing non-IID data. As an extension, this work could be expanded to explore various FL architectures across collaborative clients with multi-modality medical data from the healthcare domain, aiming to improve model robustness and interpretability using XAI techniques.

References

1. Abd El-Mawla, N., Berbar, M.A., El-Fishawy, N.A., El-Rashidy, M.A.: A novel federated learning framework for sustainable and efficient breast cancer classification system (FL-L_2CNN-BCDet). IEEE Access (2024)
2. Almufareh, M.F., Tariq, N., Humayun, M., Almas, B.: A federated learning approach to breast cancer prediction in a collaborative learning framework. Healthcare **11**, 3185–3215 (2023)
3. Arthi, N.T., et al.: Decentralized federated learning and deep learning leveraging XAI-based approach to classify colorectal cancer. In: 2022 IEEE Asia-Pacific Conference on Computer Science and Data Engineering (CSDE), pp. 1–6. IEEE (2022)
4. Awsaf49: CBIS-DDSM breast cancer image dataset (2025). https://www.kaggle.com/datasets/awsaf49/cbis-ddsm-breast-cancer-image-dataset. Accessed 03 Jan 2025
5. Bechar, A., Medjoudj, R., Elmir, Y., Himeur, Y., Amira, A.: Federated and transfer learning for cancer detection based on image analysis. Neural Comput. Appl., 1–46 (2025)
6. Bemani, A., Björsell, N.: Aggregation strategy on federated machine learning algorithm for collaborative predictive maintenance. Sensors **22**(16), 6252–6275 (2022)
7. Chai, H., et al.: A decentralized federated learning-based cancer survival prediction method with privacy protection. Heliyon **10**(11) (2024)
8. Chen, M., Poor, H.V., Saad, W., Cui, S.: Wireless communications for collaborative federated learning. IEEE Commun. Mag. **58**(12), 48–54 (2021)
9. Chowdhury, A.A., et al.: StackFBAs: detection of fetal brain abnormalities using CNN with stacking strategy from MRI images. J. King Saud Univ. Comput. Inf. Sci. **35**(8), 101647–101660 (2023)
10. Copperpod IP: Federated learning: decentralized deep learning technology (2025). https://www.copperpodip.com/post/federated-learning-decentralized-deep-learning-technology. Accessed 20 Mar 2025
11. Crosby, D., et al.: Early detection of cancer. Science **375**(6586), eaay9040 (2022)
12. Díaz, J.S.P., García, Á.L.: Enhancing the convergence of federated learning aggregation strategies with limited data. arXiv preprint arXiv:2501.15949 (2025)
13. Gonzalez, R., et al.: Performance of externally validated machine learning models based on histopathology images for the diagnosis, classification, prognosis, or treatment outcome prediction in female breast cancer: a systematic review. J. Pathol. Inf. **15**, 100348–100365 (2024)
14. Haggenmüller, S., et al.: Federated learning for decentralized artificial intelligence in melanoma diagnostics. JAMA Dermatol. **160**(3), 303–311 (2024)

15. Hossain, M.M., Islam, M.R., Ahamed, M.F., Ahsan, M., Haider, J.: A collaborative federated learning framework for lung and colon cancer classifications. Technologies **12**(9), 151–178 (2024)
16. Lee, R.S., Gimenez, F., Hoogi, A., Miyake, K.K., Gorovoy, M., Rubin, D.L.: A curated mammography data set for use in computer-aided detection and diagnosis research. Sci. Data **4**(1), 1–9 (2017)
17. Lee, R.S., Gimenez, F., Hoogi, A., Rubin, D.: Curated breast imaging subset of DDSM [dataset] (2016). https://doi.org/10.7937/K9/TCIA.2016.7O02S9CY2. Accessed 03 Jan 2025
18. McMahan, B., Moore, E., Ramage, D., Hampson, S., y Arcas, B.A.: Communication-efficient learning of deep networks from decentralized data. In: Artificial Intelligence and Statistics, pp. 1273–1282 (2017)
19. Mora, A., Tenison, I., Bellavista, P., Rish, I.: Knowledge distillation for federated learning: a practical guide. arXiv preprint arXiv:2211.04742 (2022)
20. Nevrataki, T., et al.: A survey on federated learning applications in healthcare, finance, and data privacy/data security. In: AIP Conference Proceedings, vol. 2909 (2023)
21. Pashayan, N., et al.: Personalized early detection and prevention of breast cancer: envision consensus statement. Nat. Rev. Clin. Oncol. **17**(11), 687–705 (2020)
22. Pinon, S., Jacquet, S., Bulcke, C.V., Chatzopoulos, E., Lessage, X., Michel, R.: Federated health recommender system. In: HEALTHINF, pp. 439–444 (2023)
23. Roy, A.G., Siddiqui, S., Pölsterl, S., Navab, N., Wachinger, C.: BrainTorrent: a peer-to-peer environment for decentralized federated learning. arXiv preprint arXiv:1905.06731 (2019)
24. Shaik, T., et al.: FedStack: Personalized activity monitoring using stacked federated learning. Knowl. Based Syst. **257**, 109929–109942 (2022)
25. Srinivasan, K., Prasanna, S., Midha, R., Mohan, S.: Federated learning framework for IID and non-IID datasets of medical images. EMITTER Int. J. Eng. Technol. **11**(1), 1–20 (2023)
26. Tan, Y.N., Tinh, V.P., Lam, P.D., Nam, N.H., Khoa, T.A.: A transfer learning approach to breast cancer classification in a federated learning framework. IEEE Access **11**, 27462–27476 (2023)
27. Teo, Z.L., et al.: Federated machine learning in healthcare: a systematic review on clinical applications and technical architecture. Cell Rep. Med. **5**(2) (2024)
28. The Cancer Imaging Archive: CBIS-DDSM: curated breast imaging subset of DDSM (2025). https://www.cancerimagingarchive.net/collection/cbis-ddsm/#citations. Accessed 03 Jan 2025
29. Todd, F.B.: Beware privacy risks in training ai models with health data (2025). https://frostbrowntodd.com/beware-privacy-risks-in-training-ai-models-with-health-data-3. Accessed 09 Feb 2025
30. World Health Organization: Breast cancer (2024). https://www.who.int/news-room/fact-sheets/detail/breast-cancer. Accessed 09 Feb 2025
31. Xu, Y., Fan, H.: FedDK: improving cyclic knowledge distillation for personalized healthcare federated learning. IEEE Access **11**, 72409–72417 (2023)
32. Yadav, N., Pandey, S., Gupta, A., Dudani, P., Gupta, S., Rangarajan, K.: Data privacy in healthcare: in the era of artificial intelligence. Indian Dermatol. Online J. **14**(6), 788–792 (2023)

Unmasking the Skies: Statistical and Machine Learning Insights Into the Air Quality Shift During COVID-19 Lockdowns in Indian Metropolises

Shubhranshu Gorai[1], Suchandra Banerjee[1], Kinshuk Banerjee[1], Saibal Majumder[1](✉), Chandan Bandyopadhyay[1], and Diganta Das[2]

[1] Department of Computer Science and Engineering (Data Science), Dr. B. C. Roy Engineering College, Durgapur, India
saibal.majumder.1729@gmail.com

[2] Department of Electronics and Communication Engineering, Sathyabama Institute of Science and Technology, Jeppiar Nagar, Chennai, Tamil Nadu, India

Abstract. The COVID-19 pandemic led to unprecedented restrictions on mobility and industrial activity, creating a unique opportunity to study their impact on air pollution in urban India. This paper investigates the changes in air quality across four major Indian metropolitan cities—Delhi, Mumbai, Kolkata, and Bengaluru—during the lockdown period in 2020. Using publicly available air quality data from January to July 2020, we perform comparative statistical analyses and apply machine learning techniques to classify air pollution levels before and during the lockdown. Independent two-sample *t-test* confirm statistically significant reductions in major pollutants such as $PM_{2.5}$, PM_{10}, NO_2, and CO in most cities. Logistic Regression and Support Vector Machine (SVM) models are employed to classify pre- and during-lockdown periods based on pollutant profiles, achieving strong separation. The study highlights the responsiveness of specific pollutants to reduced anthropogenic activity and offers insights to inform environmental policy and urban planning.

Keywords: Air Pollution · COVID-19 · Statistical Analysis · Machine Learning · Urban Environment

1 Introduction

Air pollution remains a pressing 21st-century environmental and public health issue, particularly in urbanizing countries like India. Most large cities typically have high levels of air pollutants, including particulate matter ($PM_{2.5}$, PM_{10}), nitrogen oxides (NO_x), sulfur dioxide (SO_2), carbon monoxide (CO), and ground-level ozone (O_3), posing serious health risks and further exacerbating environmental degradation. Millions of premature deaths each year are

K. Chandra Mondal et al. (Eds.): CICBA 2025, CCIS 2863, pp. 445–456, 2026.
https://doi.org/10.1007/978-3-032-17184-9_33

estimated by the World Health Organization (WHO) to result from ambient air pollution, underlining the need for extensive air quality monitoring and analytical means.

Despite growing research on air quality in India, most studies focus on specific pollutants or national-scale assessments, lacking a comparative city-wise assessment that captures localized pollution dynamics before and after socio-environmental disturbances like the COVID-19 lockdown. Kumar et al. [1] evaluated Delhi's air quality during the COVID-19 lockdown but did not include other metropolitan regions, limiting their findings to urban India. Sharma et al. [2] used aggregated national data to measure air pollution drop during lockdown in India, ignoring detailed regional comparisons across significant urban centers. In their analytical examination of Delhi's pollution level oscillations, Mahato et al. [3] disregarded city-level variances in other geographic and climatic zones. Singh and Chauhan's [4] study on $PM_{2.5}$ and NO_2 trends in Indian cities lacked a targeted temporal alignment and insufficient statistical analyses to determine significance. This leaves a gap in research about Indian city pollution patterns and how lockdowns affect them based on urban infrastructure, mobility, and industrial profiles. Therefore, a thorough, event-specific, multi-city comparison study with quantitative evaluation of the change in air quality during the pre- and during-lockdown phases is desperately needed. Developing city-specific environmental plans and improving India's capacity to handle environmental problems and public health crises of future relevance depend on this research.

This research analyzes air pollution trends in various cities in India, comparing data from the period preceding and following the COVID-19 lockdown. This study employs an open-source Kaggle dataset[1] to analyze four major metropolitan cities—Delhi, Mumbai, Kolkata, and Bengaluru—each exhibiting distinct environmental, demographic, and infrastructural traits. This study aims to assess the behavior of air pollutants, including $PM_{2.5}$, PM_1, NO_2, and SO_2, in urban centers prior to and following lockdown measures. This research analyzes changes in pollutant levels over time and relates these variations to urban activity patterns to assess the environmental effects of extensive mobility restrictions. This study examines the relatively unexplored area of inter-city comparison analysis and contributes to the understanding of air quality changes triggered by events. The primary objective is to facilitate evidence-based policymaking and urban environmental planning aimed at improving air quality in various Indian cities over time.

2 Literature Survey

In order to accurately estimate the air quality index (AQI) of major cities such as Delhi, Hyderabad, Kolkata, Bangalore, Vishakpatnam, and Chennai, Natarajan et al. [5] have concentrated on developing an optimal machine learning model that combines Grey Wolf Optimization (GWO) and Decision Tree. To determine the AQI (Air Quality Index) of four Indian cities, Gupta et al. [6] employed three

[1] https://www.kaggle.com/datasets/rohanrao/air-quality-data-in-india.

distinct techniques: support vector regression, CatBoost regression, and Random Forest. Additionally, the SMOTE technique was used in the suggested work to balance the dataset and improve the correctness of the work. The authors of [7] found that $PM_{2.5}$ and NO_2 levels significantly decreased, followed by a during-lockdown resurgence. Likewise, Singh et al. [8] concentrated on Delhi and noted that meteorological normalization is crucial for accurately attributing pollution decrease exclusively to the lockdown. The researchers Kaloni et al. [9] proved the link between human-caused pollution and significant decreases in trace gases by using satellite data to validate ground-based observations. Remote sensing data has demonstrated efficacy as a technique for extensive air quality monitoring. Moreover, several studies including [10] and [11] confirm a marked decline in major air pollutants such as $PM_{2.5}$, PM_{10}, NO_2, CO, and SO_2 across Indian cities during lockdown periods. Kumar et al. [12] employed data from MODIS, OMI, and AIRS to examine the temporal and spatial patterns of aerosols and gases. Their findings indicated a reduction above 40% in aerosol optical depth (AOD) during the most stringent lockout periods. Agarwal et al. [13] examined 23 of the most polluted cities in India and recorded reductions in pollutant concentrations above 50%, suggesting that periodic emissions control could serve as an effective pollution mitigation approach.

Computational models, including Support Vector Regression (SVR) and sophisticated neural networks, have been utilized to analyze air quality dynamics. Bhattacharya and Shahnawaz [14] constructed an SVR-based AQI prediction model for Delhi, attaining notable forecasting precision. Recent developments encompass the application of deep graph neural networks. Panja et al. [15] presented E-STGCN, a model that captures spatio-temporal relationships in air pollution data. This model effectively forecasted severe pollution incidents and confirmed its reliability even under significantly modified circumstances such as lockdowns. Understanding causality beyond correlation is key for policy-making. Das et al. [16] used causal inference models to isolate the impact of lockdown on $PM_{2.5}$ and O_3. Interestingly, while $PM_{2.5}$ showed a significant decline, O_3 remained stable or even increased, highlighting nonlinear chemical interactions in atmospheric composition. Jena et al. [17] compared emission patterns across multiple Indian regions and suggested that sustained behavioral and industrial reforms are needed to maintain air quality gains during-lockdown.

3 Dataset Description and Preprocessing

This study utilized a dataset sourced from an open-access repository on Kaggle, which includes comprehensive air quality measurements from various Indian cities spanning the years 2015 to 2020. Four large metropolitan cities—Delhi, Mumbai, Kolkata, and Bengaluru—had data chosen for analytical emphasis. These cities provide a whole basis for the study of relative pollution trends since they show different geographical and demographic features.

The primary data set encompasses January 1, 2020, to July 31, 2020. The timeline of the COVID-19 pandemic in India can be segmented into three distinct phases: the pre-lockdown phase (January 1–March 24, 2020), the lockdown phase (March 25–May 17, 2020), and the during-lockdown phase (May 18–July 31, 2020). This category enables the examination of pollution dynamics before, during, and after implementing national restrictions. In order to ensure that the data was of high quality and reliability, extensive pre-processing was carried out. The dataset was cleansed of columns with an excessive number of missing values, particularly those affecting to pollutants such as Xylene, NH_3, and Toluene. We used the Multivariate Imputation by Chained Equations (MICE) approach to impute missing values for the remaining characteristics. This method takes use of the interdependence among variables to provide imputations that are statistically valid.

Feature selection was conducted with an emphasis on key pollutants that play a vital role in improving urban air quality. The final set of variables features $PM_{2.5}$, PM_{10}, NO, NO_2, NO_x, CO, SO_2, O_3, Benzene, and the Air Quality Index (AQI). To support binary classification and temporal comparison, the data were labeled according to the lockdown timeline: records from the pre-lockdown period received a class label of 0, while those from the during-lockdown period were labeled as 1.

4 Methodology

This study used a multi-phase analytical framework that included descriptive statistics, inferential testing, and machine learning classification models to assess air pollution trends in four major Indian cities before and during the 2020 lockdown period.

4.1 Descriptive and Statistical Analysis

This investigation performed a comparative analysis to assess the impact of the COVID-19 lockdown on air quality, with a particular emphasis on the concentrations of various air pollutants. Pollution data from four major Indian cities—Delhi, Mumbai, Kolkata, and Bengaluru—were analyzed. Two distinct timeframes were used for the comparison: the pre-lockdown period (up to 24 March 2020) and the during-lockdown period (from 25 March to 17 May 2020).

To highlight the overall fluctuations in air quality between these two periods, we computed the percentage change in both the mean and median concentrations of each major pollutant. This approach enables a more comprehensive understanding of pollutant behavior, capturing both central trends and distribution robustness, especially in cases where extreme values may skew the mean.

The descriptive results, visualized in Fig. 1, show a marked reduction in pollutants such as PM2.5, PM10, NO, NO_2, and the Air Quality Index (AQI) across the cities during the lockdown. These consistent declines provide initial visual evidence of improved air quality due to reduced vehicular and industrial activities.

To further illustrate the trends, we used a **heatmap and line plot** (Fig. 2) to clearly differentiate pollution levels before and during the lockdown. These visualizations emphasize the variability and directional change in pollutant concentrations, providing a foundation for more rigorous statistical testing in the following subsection.

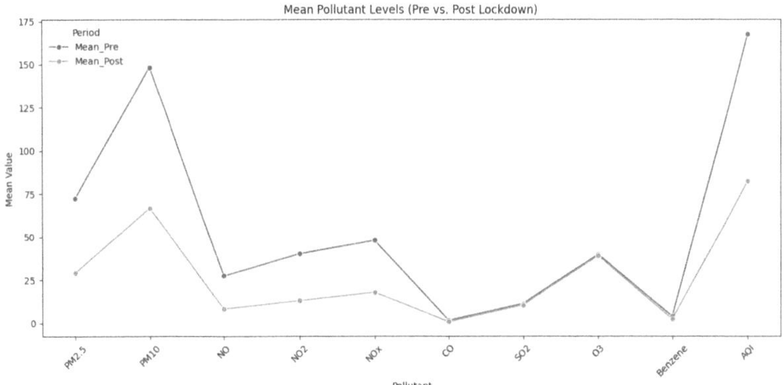

Fig. 1. Mean pollutant levels before and during the lockdown across different pollutants.

4.2 Statistical Inference

Independent two-sample t-tests were conducted for each pollutant across the four selected cities to ascertain the statistical significance of the variations in pollutant concentrations before and after the lockdown. The null hypothesis for each test asserted that there was no significant difference in mean pollution levels between the two periods. A significance criterion of $\alpha = 0.05$ was consistently adopted.

Table 1 indicates that most pollutants exhibited statistically significant differences ($p < 0.05$), thereby rejecting the null hypothesis and confirming that the observed changes in pollutant levels were unlikely to result from random variation. In Kolkata, $PM_{2.5}$ ($t = 15.73$, $p = 1e{-}39$), NO_2 ($t = 30.69$, $p = 3e{-}132$), and CO ($t = 20.26$, $p = 6e{-}64$) exhibited strong evidence of alteration. Comparable significance levels were seen in Mumbai and Delhi, with NO2 and PM10 demonstrating substantial variations. Nonetheless, exceptions were discovered—SO_2 in Mumbai ($p = 7e{-}01$) and O_3 in Delhi ($p = 2e{-}01$) failed to attain statistical significance, indicating that their observed variations may not be directly ascribed to the lockdown effects.

The inferential results, thoroughly detailed in Table 1, offer quantitative validation of the descriptive findings and enhance the credibility of the overall analysis. This statistical analysis refutes the notion of no difference in most instances, so confirming the systematic effect of the lockdown on urban air quality measurements and establishing a solid foundation for future predictive modeling.

Table 1. Results of t-tests for pollutant levels in selected cities before and after the lockdown (p-values formatted in scientific notation without decimal mantissa)

City	Pollutant	t-statistic	p-value	Significant ($p < 0.05$)
Kolkata	PM2.5	15.7300	1e−39	Yes
Kolkata	PM10	18.1693	7e−51	Yes
Kolkata	NO	18.4575	1e−62	Yes
Kolkata	NO2	30.6944	3e−132	Yes
Kolkata	NOx	26.2748	5e−109	Yes
Kolkata	CO	20.2592	6e−64	Yes
Kolkata	SO2	2.4191	1e−02	Yes
Kolkata	O3	−8.1636	2e−11	Yes
Kolkata	Benzene	24.0282	1e−95	Yes
Kolkata	AQI	15.8136	2e−40	Yes
Mumbai	PM2.5	35.4795	2e−87	Yes
Mumbai	PM10	25.4865	4e−44	Yes
Mumbai	NO	16.4165	1e−29	Yes
Mumbai	NO2	67.3214	1e−241	Yes
Mumbai	NOx	30.7518	5e−103	Yes
Mumbai	CO	7.6679	2e−13	Yes
Mumbai	SO2	0.3635	7e−01	No
Mumbai	O3	15.8075	5e−24	Yes
Mumbai	Benzene	−8.3442	2e−11	Yes
Mumbai	AQI	32.4781	4e−66	Yes
Delhi	PM2.5	26.3751	1e−62	Yes
Delhi	PM10	22.7862	2e−39	Yes
Delhi	NO	37.3619	6e−209	Yes
Delhi	NO2	43.6172	1e−103	Yes
Delhi	NOx	42.1916	1e−219	Yes
Delhi	CO	20.1961	1e−81	Yes
Delhi	SO2	2.7556	7e−03	Yes
Delhi	O3	1.1300	2e−01	No
Delhi	Benzene	24.7222	1e−58	Yes
Delhi	AQI	31.8108	2e−59	Yes
Bengaluru	PM2.5	13.9551	3e−28	Yes
Bengaluru	PM10	17.6531	9e−31	Yes
Bengaluru	NO	36.3830	3e−205	Yes
Bengaluru	NO2	33.6160	8e−72	Yes
Bengaluru	NOx	13.5417	2e−33	Yes
Bengaluru	CO	12.0891	1e−32	Yes
Bengaluru	SO2	−5.7063	4e−08	Yes
Bengaluru	O3	−5.9095	7e−08	Yes
Bengaluru	Benzene	8.8986	1e−18	Yes
Bengaluru	AQI	18.6017	5e−48	Yes

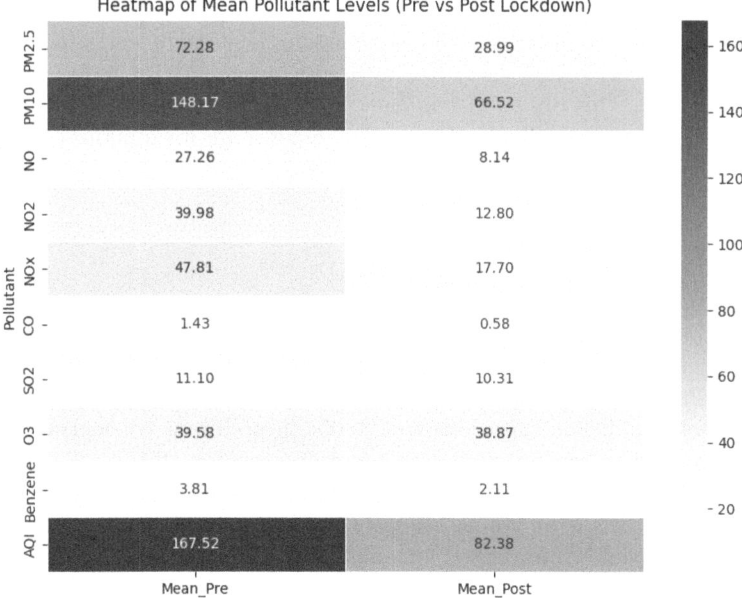

Fig. 2. Heatmap showing mean pollutant levels pre- and during-lockdown.

5 Experiments and Result

This study's experimental approach and conclusions analyzed air quality in four Indian cities—Delhi, Mumbai, Kolkata, and Bengaluru—during the COVID-19 lockdown. Our primary objective is to determine whether machine learning algorithms can categorize urban pollution patterns during lockout periods. The experiments encompass dataset preparation, training and evaluation of classification models, investigation of feature relevance, and comparisons of pollutant levels. The subsequent subsections elucidate the categorization methodology and the interpretation of features, together with the resultant consequences.

5.1 Observed Trends in Pollution Levels

A preliminary assessment of the lockdown's impact on urban air pollution was conducted by analyzing the temporal variance in mean pollutant concentrations across two distinct periods—pre-lockdown and during-lockdown—in four major Indian cities: Delhi, Mumbai, Kolkata, and Bengaluru. Figures 1 and 2, located in the methodology section, visually represent the average trends of significant atmospheric pollutants over the two time phases. A noticeable reduction in concentrations of particulate matter ($PM_{2.5}$, PM_{10}), nitrogen oxides (NO, NO_2, NO_x), and AQI values was noted in the during-lockdown period, consistent with predictions stemming from less vehicular and industrial emissions during the restriction phase.

These visualizations provide an exploratory data foundation that guides the subsequent statistical inference. The persistent decline in certain pollutants, especially PM_{10} and AQI, indicates a significant reactivity to alterations in human activities. This observed tendency highlights the need for rigorous inferential testing to statistically confirm if the changes are meaningful and not due to random variation.

5.2 Experimental Setup

The assessment of pollutant level variations' statistical significance was conducted through independent two-sample t-tests. The null hypothesis posited that mean concentrations before and after the lockdown would be statistically indistinguishable. A significance criterion of $\alpha = 0.05$ was employed. Table 1 demonstrates significant variations ($p < 0.05$) in pollutant concentrations, suggesting non-random variance. Significant reductions in $PM_{2.5}$, NO_2, and CO were observed in Delhi and Kolkata. Statistical analysis revealed no significant variation in SO2 levels in Mumbai and O3 levels in Delhi. This inference indicates that the lockdown impacted air quality in major Indian cities, supporting descriptive insights.

This study utilized a dataset sourced from Kaggle, consisting of city-level air quality data for four prominent Indian urban areas: Delhi, Mumbai, Kolkata, and Bengaluru during the COVID-19 lockdown period. The data encompasses principal air pollutants like $PM_{2.5}$, PM_{10}, SO_2, NO_2, CO, and O_3, among others.

The experiment's major purpose is to categorize records from various cities according to pollution characteristics via machine learning algorithms. Before modeling, the data underwent pretreatment procedures including:

- Handling of missing values using imputation
- Feature normalization utilizing StandardScaler

Two classifiers were developed and evaluated:

- Logistic Regression
- Support Vector Machine (SVM) utilizing a linear kernel

The model's performance was evaluated with an 80–20 train-test split and 5-fold cross-validation to verify generalizability.

5.3 Feature Importance Analysis

A feature relevance analysis was used to clarify the impact of different contaminants on the categorization of lockdown stages. The objective was to ascertain which pollutants most effectively distinguished between the pre-lockdown and during-lockdown phases.

Interpretation of Key Features

- **PM2.5:** Ranked as the most important feature, PM2.5 levels dropped significantly during the lockdown. This reflects the strong influence of vehicular and industrial emissions on fine particulate matter concentrations. The model's sensitivity to this feature suggests that PM2.5 is highly responsive to anthropogenic activity restrictions, making it a reliable proxy for urban pollution reduction.
- **NO_2:** Nitrogen dioxide, primarily emitted from vehicle exhaust, also showed high importance. The lockdown-induced traffic reductions directly impacted NO_2 levels, which explains its strong association with the temporal label. This pollutant's predictive power indicates its robustness as a marker for transportation-related pollution changes.
- **AQI:** Although a composite index, AQI also appeared among the top features, reaffirming its value in summarizing air quality variations across multiple pollutants.
- **Feature Importance Analysis:** The high feature importance scores of PM2.5 and NO_2 are not only statistically significant but also environmentally interpretable. These findings align with known emission patterns in Indian metropolitan areas, where traffic and industry are dominant contributors to air pollution. The feature analysis thus validates the data-driven insights through domain relevance.

Examining the feature importance scores from both the Logistic Regression and SVM models helped us identify which air quality measures were most important for city classification.

Table 2. Feature Importance Scores for Logistic Regression and SVM Models

Rank	Feature	Logistic Regression	SVM
1	$PM_{2.5}$	1.24	1.18
2	NO_2	0.98	1.02
3	PM10	0.87	0.91
4	CO	0.73	0.75
5	SO_2	0.66	0.64
6	O_3	0.59	0.58
7	NH_3	0.50	0.53
8	Benzene	0.42	0.41
9	Toluene	0.38	0.35
10	AQI	0.30	0.28

As shown in Table 2, $PM_{2.5}$, NO_2, and PM10 are among the most influential features in both models.

The analytical framework has been improved by the incorporation of two classifiers: Logistic Regression and Support Vector Machine (SVM) models. Both classifiers indicated that pollutant concentration patterns, including PM2.5, PM10, NO2, and CO, are effective in differentiating between the prelockdown and lockdown periods. The uniform precision among models indicates that the identification of pollutant signatures alone is adequate to determine whether an observation refers to the prelockdown or lockdown era. This outcome confirms the significant sensitivity of major pollutants to constraints on urban mobility and establishes a robust machine learning model for recognizing temporal periods of environmental change.

5.4 Discussion of Results

The observed results reveal significant temporal and regional patterns in pollutant behavior throughout the lockdown phase:

- **City-Specific Observations:**
  - **Delhi:** Demonstrated the most significant enhancement in air quality, especially with PM2.5 and NO_2, presumably attributable to the drastic reduction of vehicular and industrial operations.
  - **Mumbai:** Showed an unusual increase in SO_2 levels, possibly attributable to port activities or residual emissions from non-lockdown power stations. This anomaly warrants further source-apportionment studies.
  - **Kolkata and Bengaluru:** Both exhibited moderate to significant reductions in all pollutants, especially in NO_2, indicating a pronounced sensitivity to traffic.
- **Implications from Classification:** The classifier's significant dependence on PM2.5 and NO_2 indicates that these pollutants are particularly responsive to policy measures such as lockdowns. Their significance in feature relevance rankings suggests that automobile emissions and combustion sources are primary contributors to inadequate urban air quality.
  The relatively lower importance of SO_2 and CO might reflect their less variable nature under restricted conditions, or point to more constant sources such as thermal plants and domestic cooking.

Machine learning classifiers, in spite of statistical inference, provide additional evidence of temporal difference between stages. Logistic Regression and Support Vector Machine (SVM) models consistently identified pollutant profiles, including PM2.5, PM10, NO2, and CO, as the strongest distinguishing indications for classification. Their performance showed that pollutant detection patterns can consistently identify whether a specific record belongs to the prelockdown or lockdown phase. The finding not only confirms the observed drops in particular pollutants but also shows the ability of classification models to better understand the environmental consequences of extensive limitations on urban mobility.

6 Conclusion

This research examines how COVID-19 lockdowns affect urban air quality in Delhi, Mumbai, Kolkata, and Bengaluru. A significant decrease in main pollutant ($PM_{2.5}$, PM_{10}, NO_2, and CO) during lockdown was observed using Logistic Regression and SVM classifiers. According to study performed in this research, human activity is the primary reason for urban pollution. The classification models effectively differentiated between the pre-lockdown and lockdown periods, highlighting the applicability of machine learning techniques in environmental monitoring. Future analyses may benefit from incorporating climatic variables to better control for external influences on pollutant levels. Incorporating space-time modeling and Long Short-Term Memory (LSTM) time series forecasting may enhance the prediction of zone-wide pollutant dynamics. Employing causal inference techniques such as Difference-in-Differences (DiD) can strengthen the identification of causal relationships and improve the interpretation of policy impacts. Furthermore, integrating air quality data with public health indicators can offer a more comprehensive assessment of environmental health outcomes. Finally, IoT or edge computing models might monitor and control pollution in real time, improving urban planning and public health.

References

1. Kumar, P., et al.: The rise of low-cost sensing for managing air pollution in cities. Environ. Int. **75**, 199–205 (2015)
2. Sharma, S., Zhang, M., Gao, J., Zhang, H., Kota, S.H., et al.: Effect of restricted emissions during COVID-19 on air quality in India. Sci. Total Environ. **728**, 138878 (2020)
3. Mahato, S., Pal, S., Ghosh, K.G.: Effect of lockdown amid COVID-19 pandemic on air quality of the megacity Delhi, India. Sci. Total Environ. **730**, 139086 (2020)
4. Sukhareva, O., Mariychuk, R., Sukharev, S., Delegan-Kokaiko, S., Kushtan, S.: Application of microextraction techniques for indirect spectrophotometric determination of fluorides in river waters. J. Environ. Manage. **280**, 111702 (2021)
5. Natarajan, S.K., Shanmurthy, P., Arockiam, D., Balusamy, B., Selvarajan, S.: Optimized machine learning model for air quality index prediction in major cities in India. Sci. Rep. **14**, 6795 (2024)
6. Gupta, N.S., Mohta, Y., Heda, K., Armaan, R., Valarmathi, B., Arulkumaran, G.: Prediction of air quality index using machine learning techniques: a comparative analysis. J. Environ. Public Health **2023**, 4916267 (2023)
7. Naaz, S., Siddiqui, F., Ansari, I.R.: Analysis of air quality during and after nationwide lockdown in India. In: Proceedings of the 3rd International Conference on ICT for Digital, Smart, and Sustainable Development, ICIDSSD 2022 (2023). https://doi.org/10.4108/eai.24-3-2022.2318958
8. Singh, H., et al.: Status of air pollution during COVID-19-induced lockdown in Delhi, India. Atmosphere **13**(12), 2090 (2022). https://doi.org/10.3390/atmos13122090
9. Kaloni, D., Kumar, S., Kumar, A.: Satellite-based assessment of air quality in New Delhi during COVID-19 lockdown. arXiv preprint arXiv:2203.02258 (2022)

10. Srivastava, H., Verma, S., Pant, T.: Analysis of the effect of COVID-19 lockdown on air pollutants using multi-source pollution data and meteorological variables for the state of Uttar Pradesh, India. MAUSAM **74**(4), 999–1014 (2023). https://doi.org/10.54302/mausam.v74i4.6124
11. Mishra, A., Rathore, R.: Impact of COVID-19 lockdown on air quality in Agra, India. J. Earth Syst. Sci. **130**(3), 1–12 (2021). https://doi.org/10.1007/s12040-023 02181-3
12. Kumar, P., Singh, A., Sharma, M.: Spatio-temporal variation of aerosols and air pollutants over India using MODIS, OMI, and AIRS satellite data. J. Indian Soc. Remote Sens. **51**(1), 123–135 (2023). https://doi.org/10.1007/s41324-023-00530-4
13. Agarwal, A., Gupta, R., Singh, S.: COVID-19 impact on air quality of twenty-three most polluted Indian cities and lessons to implement post-lockdown. In: Siddiqui, N.A., Khan, F., Tauseef, S.M., Ghanem, W.S., Garaniya, V. (eds.) Advances in Behavioral Based Safety, pp. 127–145. Springer, Singapore (2022). https://doi.org/10.1007/978-981-16-8270-4_10
14. Bhattacharya, S., Shahnawaz, M.: Air quality prediction in New Delhi using support vector regression. arXiv preprint arXiv:2112.05753 (2021)
15. Panja, M., Chakraborty, T., Biswas, A., Deb, S.: E-STGCN: Extreme spatiotemporal graph convolutional networks for air quality forecasting. arXiv preprint arXiv:2411.12258 (2024)
16. Das, S., Shukla, S., Yadav, A., Chakraborti, A.: Causal links between anthropogenic emissions and air pollution dynamics in Delhi. arXiv preprint arXiv:2503.18912 (2025)
17. Jena, C., Ghude, S.D., Beig, G., Chate, D.M., Kumar, R.: Impact of reduced anthropogenic emissions during COVID-19 on air quality in India. Atmos. Chem. Phys. **21**(5), 4025–4047 (2021). https://doi.org/10.5194/acp-21-4025-2021

An Exact Rare Rule Mining Approach Using Minimum Item Support Constraint from Heterogeneous Data

Sudarsan Biswas[1(✉)], Diganta Saha[2], Rajat Pandit[3], and Neepa Biswas[4]

[1] Department of Information Technology, RCC Institute of Information Technology, Kolkata, India
biswas.sudarsan@gmail.com
[2] Department of Computer Science and Engineering, Jadavpur University, Kolkata, India
[3] Department of Computer Science, West Bengal State University, Kolkata, India
[4] Department of Information Technology, Narula Institute of Technology, Kolkata, India

Abstract. The need for efficient pattern extraction techniques has increased due to the rapid expansion of data in a variety of industries, including healthcare, e-commerce, and entertainment. Because of their low support values, unusual but important itemsets are frequently missed by traditional association rule mining (ARM) algorithms. This work suggests a novel approach that uses item-specific minimum support (MIS) restrictions to generate precise uncommon association rules with 100% confidence. In contrast to traditional methods, the suggested method effectively mines uncommon patterns without generating an excessive amount of candidate itemsets by utilizing both Predefined Item Support (PIS) and MIS values. Experiments on real-world datasets, such as movie ratings and medical records, show that the method performs better than the Apriori algorithm in terms of rule generation efficiency and execution time. The findings demonstrate its potential for revealing high-impact, hidden correlations that conventional frequent pattern mining tools frequently overlook.

Keywords: Association rule mining · Apriori · Exact Rule · Predefined Item support · Minimum Item support

1 Introduction

Data mining and machine learning (ML) have various uses for finding meaning patterns extraction [6]. Since its origins in the year 1999, Rare Association Rule Mining (RARM) has been an evolving field of study in Association Rule Mining (ARM) [4]. A sub-branch of ARM called RARM is sometimes called an infrequent, unusual pattern, extraordinary, abnormal, or sporadic itemsets formation [16]. In general, rule mining identifies common rules, but it can also be quite

K. Chandra Mondal et al. (Eds.): CICBA 2025, CCIS 2863, pp. 457–472, 2026.
https://doi.org/10.1007/978-3-032-17184-9_34

helpful when some items have strong relationships between itemsets with little support [7]. The relationship between items that rarely occur in transactional databases is represented by rare items, which are unpredictable or unknown correlations between items. As a result, it is more intriguing than regular pattern mining [11]. RARM's primary goal is to extract significant low-rank item sets or unusual patterns from transactional databases [2]. Traditional ARM is not capable of generating this kind of pattern. But unlike normal association rules, which are based on high support and a high confidence level, RARM has low support and high confidence. When considering datasets featuring rare patterns, and events, values may often change within 0.1% to less than 10% depending on the presence of those items. This is because those items, when they are presented in the database, might have dramatic, frequently negative, implications [8]. However, a significant problem with generating rare rules is that they could never be able to do it effectively with a single minimum support value. Therefore, choosing the lowest support is crucial for narrowing the search space and the number of patterns generated as a result of that selection [15].

1.1 Motivation and Application

Today, a large amount of data is produced from various sensors, Internet chat, network logs, Twitter, Facebook, online banking or ATM transactions, biomedical data, healthcare data, etc. In many contemporary industries, such as network attack detection, web applications, cloud, market basket analysis, and uncommon disease prognosis, etc., analysis of those enormous amounts of important data can be highly beneficial in occasionally generating odd or unforeseen patterns. Therefore, the goal is to identify rare patterns by developing an optimal number of objective function-based, single-phase rule generation techniques for any continuous as well as discrete valued real-life databases that can effectively provide interesting, exact rare rules.

The following classifications refer to this paper Sect. 2 represents the literature review, research gap. Section 3 proposed an exact rare rule generation technique with an algorithm. Section 4 represents the Datasets Description & Execution. Section 5 presents Result & Comparative Analysis. Section 6 presents Observation & Advantages from the comparative study. The conclusion is discussed in Sect. 7.

2 Literary Survey

Apriori-based infrequent rule-generating method was presented by Liu et al. in 1999 [18]. The article discusses the use of Multiple Support Apriori (MS-Apriori) to detect rare patterns in data. It suggests that, users create rare item rules without overburdening common items with pointless ones, resulting in multiple minimal supports with varying MIS values. Apriori always produces too expensive and time-consuming results, and it will become more crucial for long patterns in the database.

According to Koh et al.'s description of Apriori-Inverse in 2005, this algorithm generated infrequent rules based on multiple minimal support thresholds, applying a single minimum support value and a single maximum support value [16]. Producing the sporadic item sets known as fully sporadic rules is much faster with it than with Apriori. But more would be needed to create every rare item itemset. Naturally, this approach can offer regulations that go beyond the highest level of support. To mine the rare item sets, Szathmary et al. MRG-Exp, Another rare item miner [20]. The other algorithm is an improved approach that restricts the investigation to only frequent generators, whereas the first algorithm relies on an Apriori-based enumeration. First, minimal generator item sets with lesser support than their subset are used as the foundation for the suggested optimization. Second, the item set with non-zero support and subsets of all frequent items is known as minimal rare generators. Thirdly, minimal zero generators are subsets of all non-zero support item sets and item sets with zero supports. Without producing any zero item sets, another rare item set miner creates rare item sets. The threshold values minsup and maxsup are used many times. It will first invoke the Apriori-Rare algorithm to produce Minimal Rare Itemsets, and then it will produce Rare Itemsets from those Minimal Rare Itemsets. AfRIM (which is quite similar to Rarity) was also proposed by Adda et al. in 2007 [2]. It uses a top-down technique to analyze the itemset with zero support, which may occasionally be wasteful. Using commonalities creates a candidate sets $\{k - itemset\}$ subsets between all combinations of rare (k+1) itemset pairs in the previous level. By using the Transactional Co-Occurrence Matrix (TCOM), which was developed in 2009 by Ding et al., rare items are extracted. However, this technology is pricey to develop and produce itemsets [10]. An alternative to the standard Apriori method is called Apriori Rare. Using a subroutine called support count, is utilized to build only minimal rare item sets [21].

Abdullah et al. stated critical relative support (CRS) in 2011 as an alternative to the single minimal support restriction in order to produce the criticality or the significant level of least association rules and be able to decrease the number of undesired rules. The CRS value was calculated between 0 and 1 using the highest value, which either supports the antecedent division by consequence or the Jaccard index coefficient [1]. Tsang et al. (2013) laid out a Rare Pattern tree (RP tree) technique to find rare rules generated by rare item itemsets. Either only rare items are maintained, or both common and rare items are kept. The key advantage of RP trees is that they only generate particular kinds of rare rules, saving time from researching dull rare item sets. Large patterns can be handled with ease using the FP-Growth-based pattern mining technique RP Tree. It stays away from the expensive candidate generation and pruning procedures. The RP tree technique was modified by authors employing information gain components, but that's not all [24]. A technique called KHAR-RIM, which was created in 2020 by Jeyakarthic et al. to identify adverse diseases, is based on the krill herd algorithm [14]. In terms of the rare association rules, the presented KHAR-RIM model focuses mainly on three different diseases: heart disease (HD), hepatitis, and breast cancer. For the purpose of generating the rare itemset rules in the specified model, the Apriori Rare method is deployed. In 2022, a specific fuzzy-based rare itemset mining method called FRI-Miner developed by Zheng et al. detects significant and intriguing fuzzy rare itemsets in a quantitative database [9]. In 2023, Qian et al. suggested the concept of mining rare items in uncertain data by leveraging rare chances [19]. Additionally, they offer a top-down algorithm and a bottom-up strategy. Based on this, two pruning algorithms are created to reduce computational costs by switching from long to short itemsets.

2.1 Problem Formulation

The classic ARM method, or the Apriori, has the drawback of relying on the minimal support requirement. There must be many redundant rules because the minimum support value must be set very low. As a result, locating RARM using conventional data mining techniques would be difficult. RARM is a two-step procedure that entails

1. Among all datasets, the first selection of rare symptoms.
2. Selection of rare symptoms to generate rare rules.

Measurements that describe their quality and strength have been defined under rare rules.

$$\text{For example: } \{Cough, Fatigue, Shortnessofbreath\} \Rightarrow Lowenergy$$
$$\text{Support=3\%}$$
$$\text{Confidence=100\%}$$
$$\text{Rare symptoms} = \text{Support} \leq \text{minimum support.}$$
$$\text{Rare rules} = \text{Confidence} \geq \text{minimum confidence.}$$
$$\text{Exact rares} = 100\% \text{ rules}$$

The aforementioned correlation defined the existence of a connection between the dataset's items for Cough, Fatigue, Shortness of Breath, and Low Energy.

$$\{Cough, Fatigue, Shortnessofbreath\} \Rightarrow \{Lowenergy\}$$

When the aforementioned symptoms–cough, exhaustion, or shortness of breath were included in a specific group of symptoms, low energy was also prevalent. Support indicated that this particular combination of four symptoms accounted for 3% of the tested transactions. 100% of the time, symptoms of low energy were also present, along with symptoms of cough, fatigue, or shortness of breath. Therefore, rule analysis represents knowledge of patterns and symptoms in datasets. Since the rule production phase uses these rare symptoms to construct rare rules, symptom selection is crucial for rule generation. Strong rare rules are a set of rules derived from those rare symptoms with extremely low support and very high confidence relationships. Discovering the exact rare itemset generation is the driving force behind this work. The majority of the pattern-mining literature suggests recognizing rare patterns with extremely low support [17,20]. however, detecting very rare transactions from huge transactional datasets is computationally difficult because a lot of patterns must be generated to choose a very low support [5,15]. But just a few authors looked into the problem with rare itemsets generation [12,13] . Therefore, in a review of a department store's daily operations, detecting rare transactions is a very intriguing connection for sales promotion. Identifying rare transactions that involved the purchase of a Ferrari, for instance, can be done using extensive sales transactional databases [22–24].

3 Proposed Exact Rare Rules Generation Technique

The Association rule mining technique, developed by Agarwal et al., known as Apriori, was the most widely used in 1994 [3]. Candidate generation and assessment are iterative and performed through a label-wise search. Apriori adheres to the following values:

1. Reduce the search space for frequent itemsets by any subset of frequent items that are likewise frequent. Eg. if $\{P, Q, R\}$ are frequent then $\{P, Q\}$ and $\{Q, R\}$ also be frequent.
2. Pruning: Supersets of infrequent patterns should not be developed or evaluated.

First, read through the database to find the often occurring (itemset-1). Then, using a common pattern of length k for each label, produce (k+1) candidates. Read the database more than once, count the number of times each item appears during each pass, and then eliminate the infrequent possibilities. The proposed **Algorithm 1** is described here in detail.

3.1 Running Example of Proposed Work

We explain several enhancements that lead to the evaluation of exact pattern mining using association rules. Finally, we present a number of quality measures that may be obtained using the evaluation of exact pattern mining with the association rule. Predefined Item Support is referred to as PIS. Depending on each item's starting frequency, it is distributed to each randomly.
Max_PIS = [initial frequency + 2]
Min_PIS = [initial frequency - 2]
PIS is a chosen random value in between (Max_PIS and Min_PIS).

Minimum Item Support is MIS. The minimal frequency of the item in the set is the MIS value. Consider a set of two objects (A, B) where A appears just once but B appears twice. If so, the frequency of item set A, B's MIS is A, which is 1. Figures 1 and 2 is representing MIS and PIS value generation. Tables 1, 2, 3, 4, 5, 6 respectively represent 1-itemsets, 2-itemsets, 3-itemsets, 4-itemsets, 5-itemsets and Final Exact Rare Rules Generation.

Algorithm 1: Exact rare rules generation by multiple minimum support constraints.

Input: Transactional datasets D with user-predefined item support and minimum item support.
Output: R⟵ rare item itemsets, E⟵exact rare rules.

1 Method: Call Apriori(MIS, PIS). The Exact rare rules generation in the following steps:
2 C_k= k^{th} candidates itemsets, LHS=left hand side of exact rules, MIS=minimum item support
3 Set PIS⟵user predefined item support.
4 Read database, D, first time.
5 Assign L_1 ⟵{All unique items of D}
6 S⟵count support(L_1) of all items i where (i⊂ L_1)
7 Assign Support count (L_1) ⟵ newly assigned PIS to all S.
8 R=Generate rare item itemsets where support≤ PIS
9 **for** p=2;$(L_{(p-1)})! = NULL$; p++ **do**
10 C_p=Candidate generation($R_{(p-1)}$)
11 **for** *Each transaction t⊂D* **do**
12   C_t ⊂(C_p,t)
13   **for** *Each candidate C⊂ C_t* **do**
14   C.Count ++
15   MIS(C) =C.Count ‖ C.Count is minimum for all $C_{(p-1)}$
16   R_p = C⊂ C_p ‖ C.Count≤MIS(C)
17   **if** *C.Count = MIS(C)* **then**
18   LHS= C ‖ C.Count is minimum for all (C_{k-1})
19   E_p =Rulegen(LHS,C)
20 **return** $\bigcup R_p$
21 **return** $\bigcup E_p$

Table 1. 1-itemsets

Items	Support	PIS
A	4	6
B	5	7
C	7	6
D	9	8
E	3	2

Table 2. 2-itemsets

Items	Support	MIS
AB	2	4
AC	4	4
AD	4	4
AE	1	4
BC	3	5
BD	5	5
BE	2	5

4 Datasets Description and Execution

We contrasted the performance of our proposed method to the Apriori algorithm and evaluated its time efficiency and number of rule generation. Both algorithms

```
Calculate PIS value-

PISFilePath = "PIS.txt"
f= open(PISFilePath, "w")
for i in range(0,len(order))do begin
  max_PIS = sup1[i] + 2
  min_PIS = sup1[i] - 2
        f.write(str(random.randrange(int(min_PIS), int(max_PIS))) + "\n" )
f.close()
end
with open(PISFilePath, 'r') as file: do begin
        all_file = file.read().strip() # Read and remove any extra new line
  all_file_list = all_file.split('\n') # make a list of lines
  PIS1 = [int(each_int) for each_int in all_file_list]
end
```

Fig. 1. PIS Value Generation.

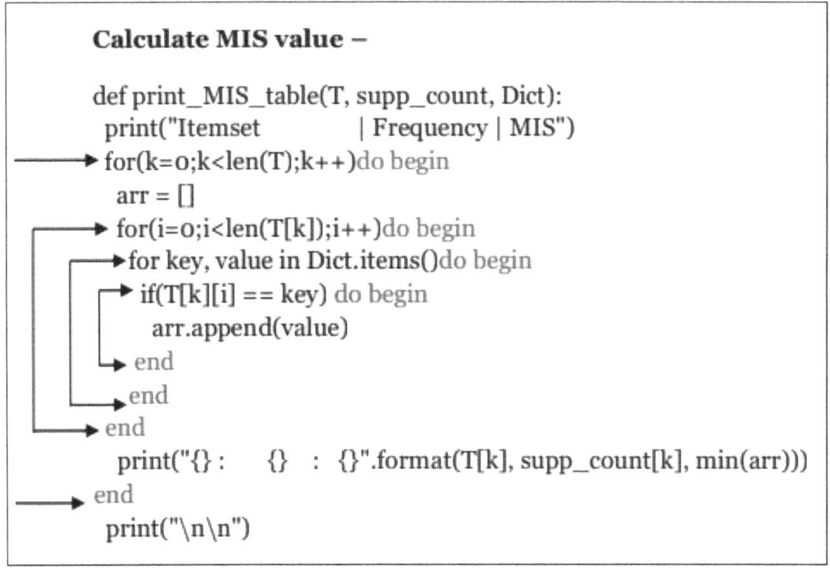

Fig. 2. MIS Value Generation.

are implemented in Python 3. An Intel i5 12 generation computer with a base clock speed of 2.5 GHz, 16 GB of RAM and a 500 GB SSD are running in addition to Windows 11. We employed 4 different datasets for the performance study and comparison investigation. These datasets include My_ Movies.csv, Mcu_ Box

Table 3. 3-itemsets

Items	Support	MIS
ABC	2	4
ABD	2	4
ABE	1	4
ACD	4	4
ACE	1	4
ADE	1	4
BCD	3	5
BCE	1	3
BDE	2	3

Table 4. 4-itemsets

Items	Support	MIS
ABCD	2	4
ABCE	1	3
ABDE	1	3
BCDE	1	3

Table 5. 5-itemsets

Items	Support	MIS
ABCDE	1	3

Table 6. Final Exact Rare Rules Generation

Items	Min sup	Exact rules
AC	4	$A \Rightarrow C$
AD	4	$A \Rightarrow D$
BD	5	$B \Rightarrow D$
ACD	4	$AC \Rightarrow D$, $A \Rightarrow CD$, $AD \Rightarrow C$

Office.csv, Grocery Store DataSet.csv, and Lung_ Cancer Examples.csv. Table 7 provides a summary of each dataset's characteristics.

(I) *Description: Variety of Datasets.*
(II) *Size: Datasets' overall size, in MB/KB.*
(III) *Attributes: Each dataset's overall Attribute count.*
(IV) *Dataset Link 1*: https://www.kaggle.com/datasets/rounakbanik/the-movies-dataset
(V) *Dataset Link 2*: https://www.kaggle.com/datasets/davidgdong/marvel-cinematic-universe-box-office-dataset
(VI) *Dataset Link 3*: https://www.kaggle.com/datasets/bhavikjikadara/grocery-store-dataset

Table 7. Description Of Datasets

Datasets	***Description***	***Size***	***Attributes***
My_Movies.csv	Collection of Hollywood movies	15	11
Mcu_box_office.csv	MCU Movies with attributes	28	10
Grocery Store DataSet.csv	Collection of Grocery Items	20	4(Max), 2(Min)
Lung_cancer_examples.csv	Symptom of Lung Cancer disease	64	7

(VII) *Dataset Link 4*: https://github.com/bipin1404/Lung-Cancer-DataSet/blob/master/lung_cancer_examples.csv

5 Comparative Result Analysis of Rules and Execution Time

We give a comparison of the Apriori algorithm with exact mining techniques. On four datasets, the performance is assessed based on execution time and the number of rule generations. Below is a summary of the execution time information and the number of rare rules produced across all datasets. In terms of time and rule generation, we receive enhanced scalability. In association rule mining, evaluation metrics are essential for determining the usefulness, strength, and relevance of discovered rules. The most commonly used metrics are: *Support,Confidence*, *Lift*, *Conviction*, *All-Confidenc.*

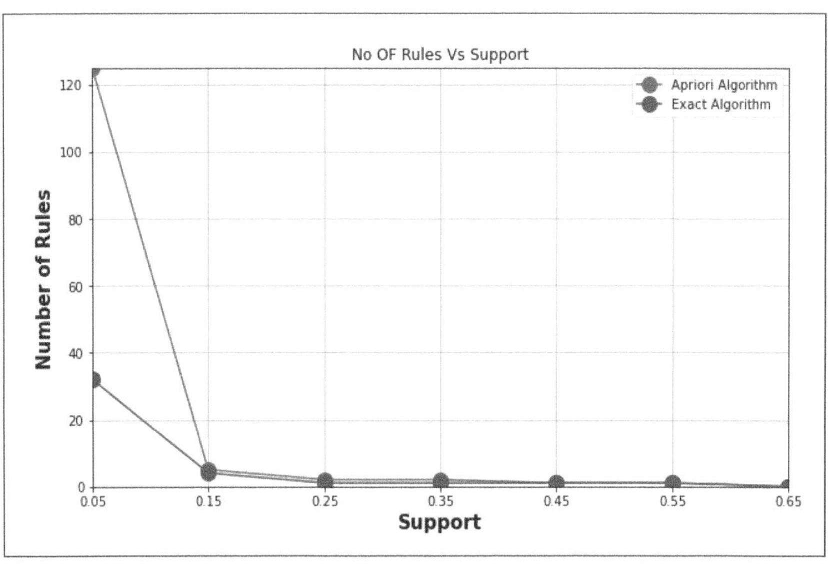

Fig. 3. Number of rule generation for My Movies.csv

5.1 Comparative Rules and Time

In order to compare the results with Apriori, we calculated the time requirements and rule creation of four datasets. Altering the minimal support constraint in the Y-axes and the X-axes in each figure illustrates the generation of time and rules. Figures 3 and 4 represents rule generation and execution time required using My Movies.csv dataset. Figures 5 and 6 represents rule generation and execution time required using Mcu box office.csv dataset. Figures 7 and 8 represents

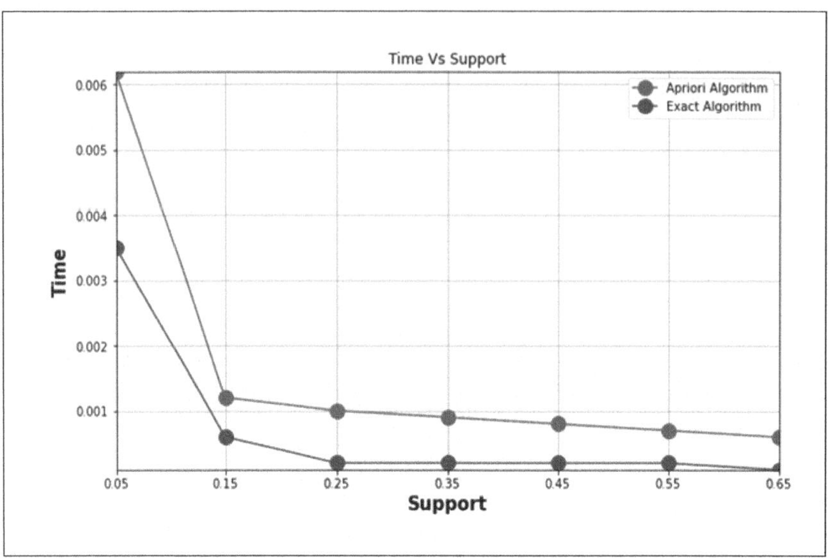

Fig. 4. Execution time for My Movies.csv

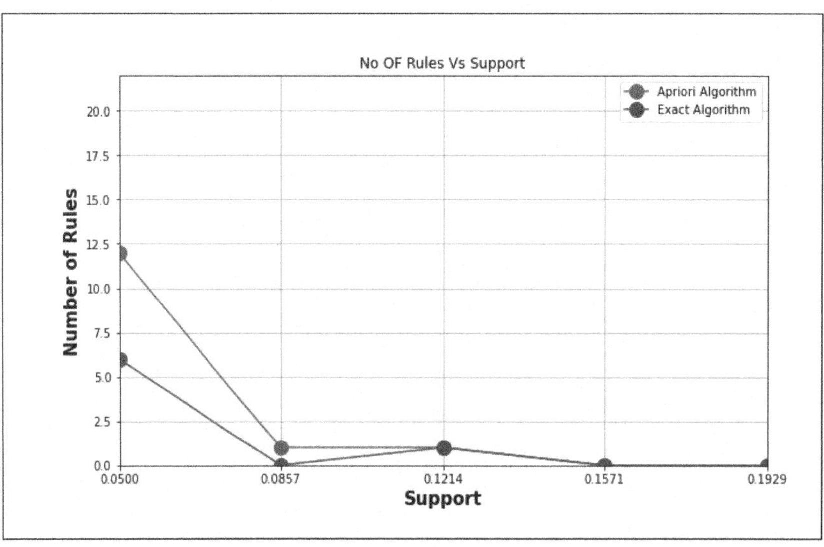

Fig. 5. Number of rule generation for Mcu box office.csv

rule generation and execution time required using Grocery Store DataSet.csv dataset. Figures 9 and 10 represents rule generation and execution time required using Lung cancer examples.csv dataset. Finally, Figs. 11 and 12 represents rule generation and execution time required compared to all datasets.

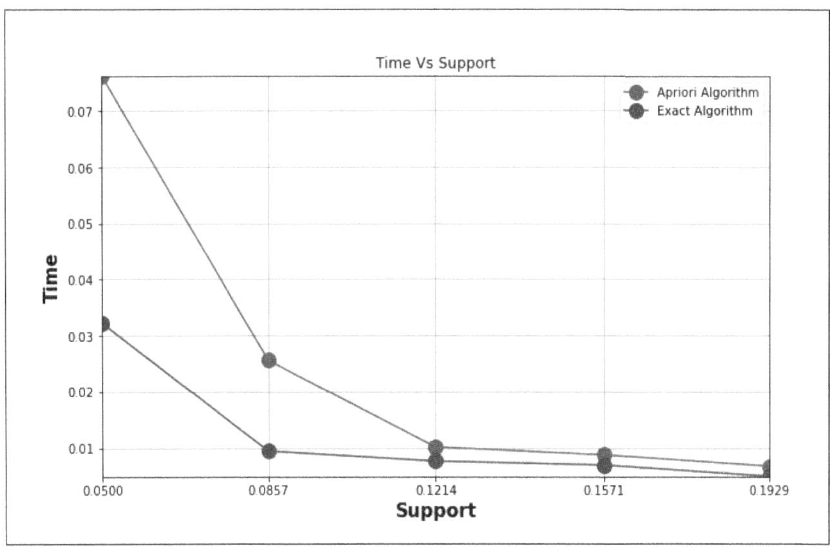

Fig. 6. Execution time for Mcu box office.csv

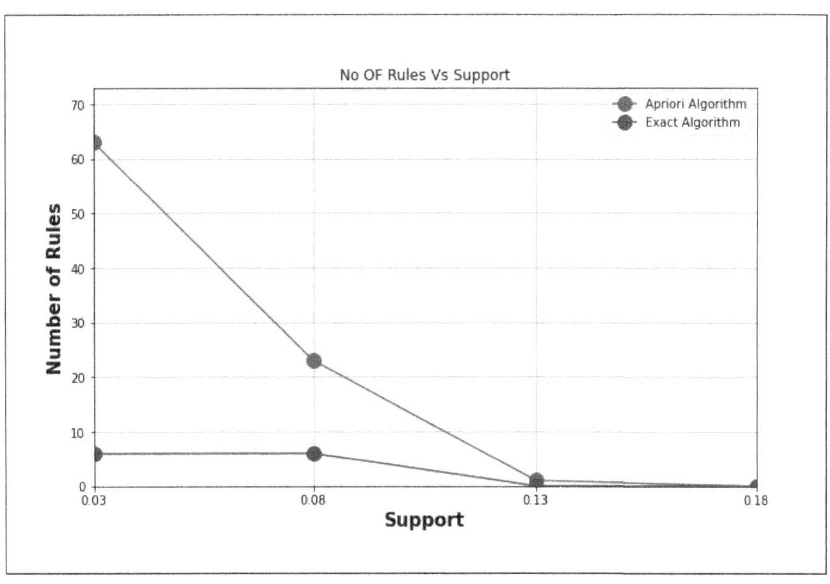

Fig. 7. Number of rule generation for Grocery Store DataSet.csv

6 Observation and Advantages

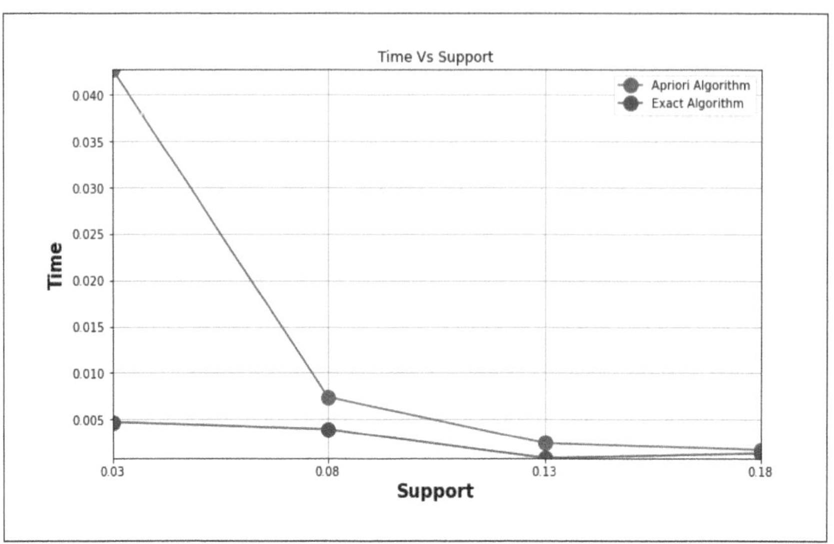

Fig. 8. Execution time for Grocery Store DataSet.csv

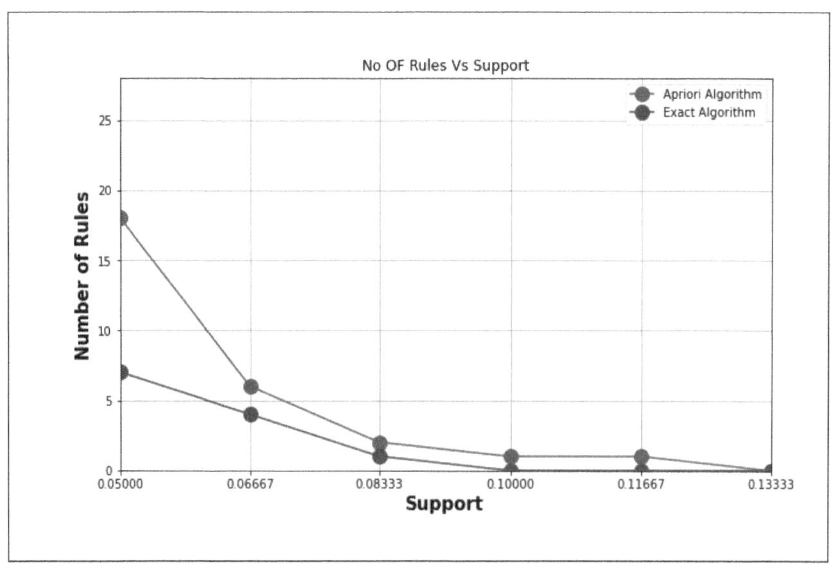

Fig. 9. Number of rule generation for Lung cancer examples.csv

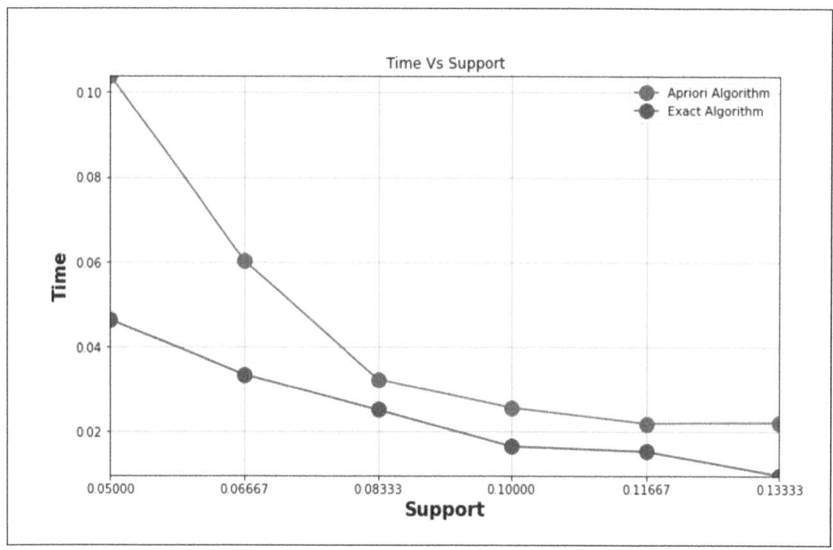

Fig. 10. Execution time for Lung cancer examples.csv

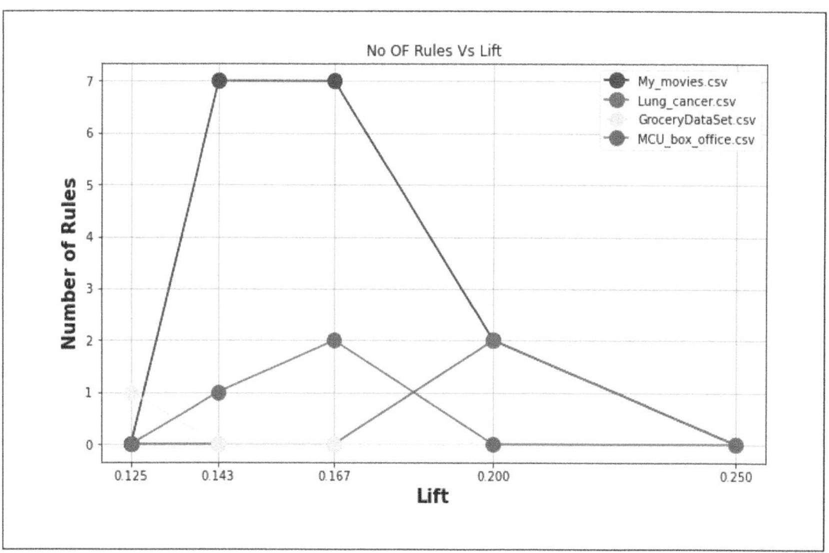

Fig. 11. Rules compared to all datasets

- ***Performance***: Better extensibility in terms of usage of time and rules development.
- ***Avoid huge candidate generation***: Due to the non-uniform probability of symptoms (items) occurring in datasets, minimum candidate generation based on PIS and MIS was implemented.

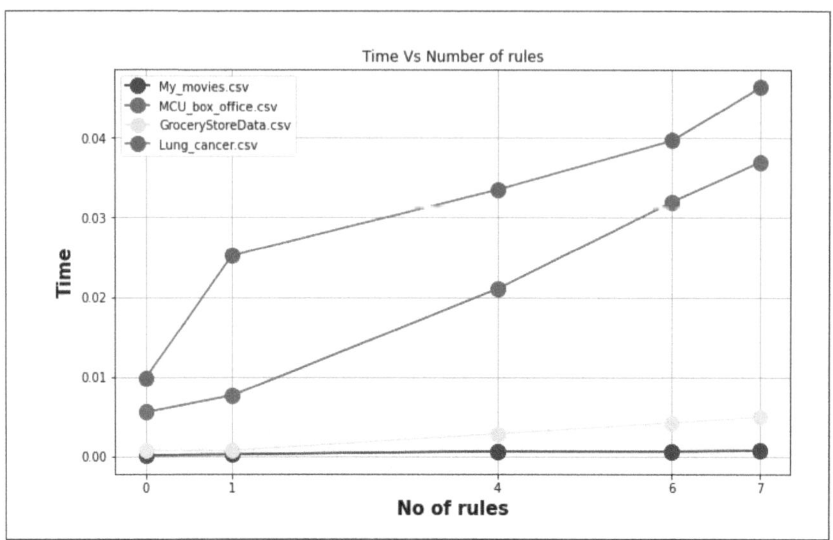

Fig. 12. Time compared to all datasets

7 Conclusion

The rules that have support beyond a certain level are all produced via association mining techniques now in use, such as the Apriori approach. For this reason, it can be difficult to distinguish between rare itemsets and their precise limitations. Rare patterns are referred to as infrequent itemsets since they are rare in the database. It is not possible to generate frequent and rare rules at the same time using a single support constraint function. By employing various support constraints, the methodology employed in this work finds precise exact rare rules without having to spend time producing all the recurred frequent items. future efforts can be directed toward developing adaptive support threshold mechanisms that dynamically adjust based on data characteristics, thus optimizing the discovery of both rare and useful patterns.

References

1. Abdullah, Z., Herawan, T., Ahmad, N., Deris, M.: Mining significant association rules from educational data using critical relative support approach. Procedia. Soc. Behav. Sci. **28**, 97–101 (2011)
2. Adda, M., Wu, L., Feng, Y.: Rare itemset mining. In: Machine Learning and Applications, 2007. ICMLA 2007. Sixth International Conference on, pp. 73–80. IEEE (2007)
3. Agrawal, R., Srikant, R.: Fast algorithms for mining association rules. In: Proc. 20th Int. Conf. Very Large Data Bases, VLDB, vol. 1215, pp. 487–499 (1994)

4. Akdas, D.N., Birant, D., Yildirim Taser, P.: ERIM: an ensemble of rare itemset mining and its application in the automotive industry. Expert. Syst. **41**(6), e13122 (2024)
5. Bhatt, U., Patel, P.: A novel approach for finding rare items based on multiple minimum support framework. Procedia Comput. Sci. **57**, 1088–1095 (2015)
6. Bhavekar, G.S., Goswami, A.D.: A hybrid model for heart disease prediction using recurrent neural network and long short term memory. Int. J. Inf. Technol. **14**(4), 1781–1789 (2022)
7. Biswas, S., Saha, D., Pandit, R.: Multiple item support constraints based frequent pattern mining using dynamic prefix tree. Internat. J. Uncertain. Fuzziness Knowl. Based Syst. **33**(02), 143–172 (2025)
8. Biswas, S., Saha, D., Pandit, R.: A prefix-based key-value pair approach for rare itemsets mining without FP tree generation under fixed and incremental support constraints. J. Circuits, Syst. Comput. **33**(17), 2450301 (2024)
9. Cui, Y., Gan, W., Lin, H., Zheng, W.: FRI-miner: fuzzy rare itemset mining. Appl. Intell. **52**(3), 1–16 (2022)
10. Ding, J., Yau, S.S.: TCOM, an innovative data structure for mining association rules among infrequent items. Comput. Math. Appl. **57**(2), 290–301 (2009)
11. Gui, Y., Gan, W., Wu, Y., Yu, P.S.: Privacy preserving rare itemset mining. Inf. Sci. **662**, 120262 (2024)
12. Huang, D., Koh, Y., Dobbie, G.: Rare pattern mining on data streams. In: Cuzzocrea, A., Dayal, U. (eds) Data Warehousing and Knowledge Discovery. DaWaK 2012. LNCS, vol. 7448, pp. 303–314. Springer, Heidelberg (2012). https://doi.org/10.1007/978-3-642-32584-7_25
13. Huang, D., Koh, Y., Dobbie, G., Pears, R.: Detecting changes in rare patterns from data streams. In: Tseng, V.S., Ho, T.B., Zhou, ZH., Chen, A.L.P., Kao, HY. (eds) Advances in Knowledge Discovery and Data Mining. PAKDD 2014. LNCS, vol. 8444, pp. 437–448. Springer, Cham (2014). https://doi.org/10.1007/978-3-319-06605-9_36
14. Jeyakarthic, M., Selvarani, S.: An efficient metaheuristic based rule optimization of apriori rare itemset mining for adverse disease diagnosis model. PalArch's J. Archaeol. Egypt/Egyptology **17**(7), 4763–4780 (2020)
15. Kiran, R., Reddy, P.: An efficient approach to mine rare association rules using maximum items' support constraints. In: MacKinnon, L.M. (eds) Data Security and Security Data. BNCOD 2010. LNCS, vol. 6121. pp. 84–95. Springer, Heidelberg (2010). https://doi.org/10.1007/978-3-642-25704-9_9
16. Koh, Y., Rountree, N.: Finding sporadic rules using apriori-inverse. In: Ho, T.B., Cheung, D., Liu, H. (eds) Advances in Knowledge Discovery and Data Mining. PAKDD 2005. LNCS, pp. 153–168. Springer, Heidelberg (2005). https://doi.org/10.1007/11430919_13
17. Koh, Y.S., Pears, R.: Non-redundant rare itemset generation. In: Proceedings of the Eighth Australasian Data Mining Conference, vol. 101, pp. 69–74. Australian Computer Society, Inc. (2009)
18. Liu, B., Hsu, W., Ma, Y.: Mining association rules with multiple minimum supports. In: Proceedings of the Fifth ACM SIGKDD International Conference on Knowledge Discovery and Data Mining, pp. 337–341. ACM (1999)
19. Qian, W., Li, H., Huang, H., Yuan, M., Xu, Y., Sun, G.: Fast rare itemset mining in uncertain database. In: 2023 3rd International Conference on Neural Networks, Information and Communication Engineering (NNICE), pp. 613–620. IEEE (2023)

20. Szathmary, L., Napoli, A., Valtchev, P.: Towards rare itemset mining. In: Tools with Artificial Intelligence, 2007. ICTAI 2007. 19th IEEE International Conference on, vol. 1, pp. 305–312. IEEE (2007)
21. Szathmary, L., Valtchev, P., Napoli, A.: Generating rare association rules using the minimal rare itemsets family. Int. J. Softw. Inform. (IJSI) **4**(3), 219–238 (2010)
22. Szathmary, L., Valtchev, P., Napoli, A., Godin, R.: Finding minimal rare itemsets in a depth-first manner. Analysis for Artificial Intelligence (FCA4AI), p. 73 (2012)
23. Troiano, L., Scibelli, G., Birtolo, C.: A fast algorithm for mining rare itemsets. In: Intelligent Systems Design and Applications, 2009. ISDA'09. Ninth International Conference on, pp. 1149–1155. IEEE (2009)
24. Tsang, S., Koh, Y.S., Dobbie, G.: Finding interesting rare association rules using rare pattern tree. In: Hameurlain, A., Küng, J., Wagner, R., Cuzzocrea, A., Dayal, U. (eds) Transactions on Large-Scale Data-and Knowledge-Centered Systems VIII. LNCS, pp. 157–173. Springer (2013). https://doi.org/10.1007/978-3-642-37574-3_7

Leveraging Explainable AI for Rainfall Prediction and Its Impact on Methane Emissions from Rice Paddies Using Multivariate Environmental Data

Ankan Bhattacharya[1], Sarbani Palit[1], Fathima Nuzla Ismail[2], and Abira Sengupta[3(✉)]

[1] Indian Statistical Institute, Kolkata, India
[2] Mathematics Department, State University of New York at Buffalo, Buffalo, NY, USA
[3] School of Computing, University of Otago, Dunedin, New Zealand
sengupta.abira0609@gmail.com

Abstract. A direct relationship exists between methane (CH_4) emissions from rice paddies and their environmental impacts that is already recognised in the scientific community. Changes in rainfall patterns and the increasing frequency of flood events significantly influence CH_4 production from rice paddies. While some studies have explored the effects of heavy rainfall on flood occurrences, few have examined their direct connection to methane emissions. This study is divided into two parts: first, we use machine learning (ML) techniques to predict patterns of rainfall across India; second, we suggest a framework that uses explainable AI (XAI), such as SHapley Additive exPlanations (SHAP), to obtain the most important features which affect the CH_4 emissions from rice paddies. To assess the performance of these models, we used 10-fold cross-validation, which showed that the Multi-Layer Perceptron outperformed the others. Furthermore, this study highlights the relevance of *hyperparameter* adjustment in enhancing model accuracy and finding significant features, which is very useful in environmental monitoring applications.

Keywords: Greenhouse gases · Methane · SHAP · Hyperparameter · Optuna · Machine Learning · Explainable AI

1 Introduction

Climate change is a disaster that will cause the intensity and frequency of climatic extremes to increase. Global climate change may influence long-term rainfall patterns, affecting water supply as well as the possibility of droughts and floods [7]. Changes in climate over the Indian subcontinent, notably the southwest monsoon, would have a huge impact on agricultural productivity, water resource management, and the country's economy. Monsoon rainfall decreased

K. Chandra Mondal et al. (Eds.): CICBA 2025, CCIS 2863, pp. 473–487, 2026.
https://doi.org/10.1007/978-3-032-17184-9_35

in the northeast peninsula[1], northeast India, and northwest peninsula (between -6% and -8% of the normal per 100 years), while it increased in the west coast, central peninsula, and northwest India (10–12% of the normal per 100 years) [9]. According to some studies, while the frequency of heavy rainfall events has increased across most of Asia, the number of wet days and total annual rainfall have decreased. An increased danger of landslides and more severe flooding is caused by this increase in heavy rainfall [6].

The issue of climate change is caused by four greenhouse gases (GHGs). These gases operate as a layer in the atmosphere, preventing heat from escaping and getting stuck in the earth's system. It causes the planet to become warmer. However, as a result of increased greenhouse gas emissions into the atmosphere, this warm situation has become hotter, which is uncomfortable for life. These gases include carbon dioxide (CO_2), methane (CH_4), nitrous oxide (N_2O), and water vapour (H_2O) [4]. In the meantime, one of the most potent greenhouse gases generated by soil cultivation techniques is N_2O, which is employed in fertilisers and biomass burning.

CH_4 is another one of the most significant greenhouse gases in the Earth's atmosphere. It can absorb infrared light 15–30 times more than CO_2. As a result, it directly contributes to global warming and climate change [12]. Its concentration has been increasing at the rate of about 1% per year [10]. CH_4 is not only a significant greenhouse gas but also has an impact on the chemistry and oxidation capacity of the atmosphere. For example, it can change the amount of ozone present in the troposphere layer and act as a sink for chlorine but as a source of hydrogen and water vapour in the stratosphere [10].

The main sources of CH_4 are wetlands, paddy fields, ruminants, biomass burning, etc. Wetland rice fields have recently been identified as a major source of atmospheric methane [14]. CH_4 emissions from rice fields have been influenced by water management, nitrogen, fertiliser use, organic input and rice varieties [15]. The anaerobic fermentation of soil organic matter occurs when the oxygen supply from the atmosphere is cut off to the soil by the flooded rice field. One of the main byproducts of anaerobic fermentation is CH_4. Through rice plant roots and stems, as well as by diffusion and ebullition, it is released from submerged soils into the atmosphere [10]. The best estimates of CH_4 sources are summarised in Table 1, where flooded rice fields emit 50 Tg/yr of CH_4 annually[2]. CH_4 measurements were initiated under various conditions of paddy fields in West Bengal, India, from 1989 onwards [12].

In the first phase of this study, we implemented an interpretable artificial intelligence (AI) framework for rainfall prediction using a suite of cutting-edge machine learning (ML) approaches. We incorporate `SHAP` to improve transparency and model interpretability, which allows a deeper understanding of the rainfall prediction. Building on this, the second stage of our study focuses on predicting CH_4 emissions from rice wetlands, with particular attention to the

[1] Here the term 'peninsula' refers to the landmass of triangular shape south of the Narmada basin.

[2] 1 Tg = 1 million tons [10].

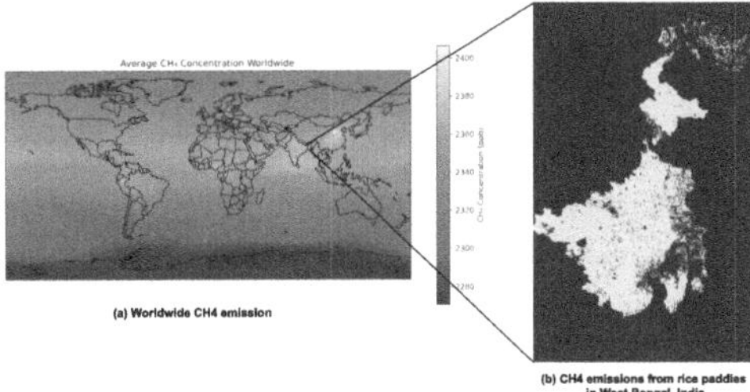

Fig. 1. Methane concentrations and fluxes from 2003 to 2020, based on CAMS global inversion-optimized greenhouse gas data.

Table 1. Estimated natural and anthropogenic sources of methane [10].

Natural Sources	
Wetlands	120
Lakes, rivers	20
Oceans	10
Termites	10
Total	**160**
Anthropogenic Sources	
Mining, processing, and use of coal, oil, and natural gas	100
Enteric fermentation	80
Flooded rice fields	50
Biomass burning	30
Landfills	30
Animal waste	30
Domestic sewage	20
Total	**340**

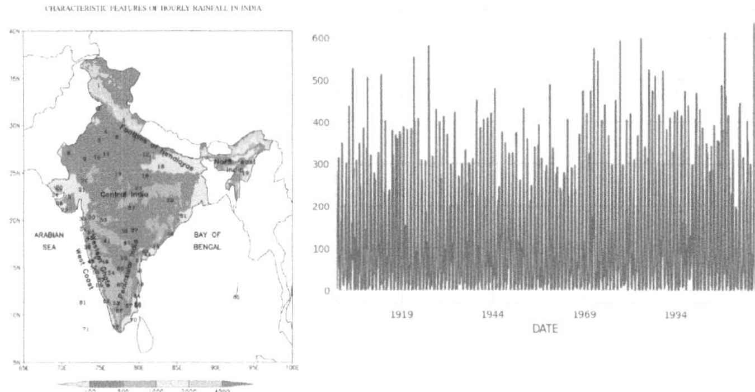

Fig. 2. (a) Represents annual rainfall (cm) over India. This figure is available in colour online at https://onlinelibrary.wiley.com/. (b) displays the annual rainfall across India from 1901 to 2015.

effects of changes in annual rainfall, unseasonal heavy rainfall, and flooding. Several ML techniques have been used to assess CH_4 emissions from rice field predictions. In most of these cases, the proposal of new methodologies involved the empirical comparison of the performance of the models when applied to CH_4 emissions prediction. However, less attention has been paid to efficient methods for establishing optimal `Hyper-Parameter (HP)` values for model generation and assessing the importance of these HPs on model learning.

Therefore, the main goal of this study is to propose a framework that adopts a well-known HP tuning method to obtain the values required for the optimal performance of an ML model. To this end, we employ the `Optuna Hyper-Parameter Optimisation (HPO)` framework [1] to help us not only obtain optimal ML models but also provide insight into the contribution of each HP in ML model learning for regression tasks.

Table 2. District wise cropped area affected (in Hectares) in different flood hazard zones

District	Very Low	Low	Mode rate	**High**	**Total**
ALIPUR DUAR	762	676	0	0	1438
BANKURA	18744	1045	0	0	19789
BIRBHUM	40069	11700	2004	70	53843
DAKSHIN DINAJPUR	49871	11792	24	0	61687
HOOGHLY	66888	44611	8068	**819**	120387
HOWRAH	29869	16246	3796	0	49911
MALDA	50409	46662	3611	0	100682
MURSHI DABAD	129631	36059	15196	**4959**	185845
NADIA	182091	24504	1627	24	208245
NORTH 24 PARGANAS	49043	6271	144	0	55457
PASCHIM MEDINIPUR	141638	56538	11806	**3638**	213620
PURBA BARDDHAMAN	152250	36380	8564	**1298**	198491
PURBA MEDINIPUR	102706	51400	4264	11	158381
SOUTH 24 PARGANAS	59901	5174	11	0	65086
UTTAR DINAJPUR	54776	13906	1285	0	69967

2 Materials and Methods

2.1 Description of the Data Set

Study Area: We use an extensive rainfall dataset for this study that covers the entire geographical region of India. The rainfall dataset, collected from Kaggle, has 1,377 monthly records for each Indian region between 1901 and 2015. This results in a substantial dataset, structured across 115 years × 12 months × multiple meteorological regions. At both the yearly and seasonal levels, it records trends in rainfall patterns throughout time. The information is specifically arranged according to four major meteorological periods: winter (JanuaryFebruary), pre-monsoon (MarchMay), monsoon (JuneSeptember), and post-monsoon (OctoberDecember). Figure 2 (a) represents annual rainfall (cm) over India. Figure 2 (b) shows how rainfall annually changed from 1901–2015.

According to the State-wise Rice Productivity Analysis[3], rice cultivation is spread across 18 districts in West Bengal, divided into different productivity categories. Table 2 presents the district-wise details of cropped areas in each of the

[3] https://drdpat.bih.nic.in/PA-Table-25-West%20Bengal.htm.

flood hazard zones for West Bengal, as prepared by the National Remote Sensing Centre, India Space Research Organisation, the Department of Space, Government of India. According to this study[4], Hooghly, Murshidabad, Nadia, Paschim Medinipur, and Purba Barddhaman districts have the maximum cropped area affected by flood in the years 2000–2020.

- The high rice productivity group, with yields exceeding 2500 kg/ha, includes the districts of Burdwan, Birbhum, Nadia, and Hooghly.
- The medium productivity group, with yields between 2000 to 2500 kg/ha, consists of districts like 24 Parganas, Murshidabad, Bankura, Malda, Midnapur, Dinajpur, and Howrah.

Data: This makes it possible to analyse rainfall seasonal variability in a more detailed way. The dataset, sourced from Kaggle[5], allows for region-wise assessment of rainfall trends across different meteorological zones of India.

The CH_4 dataset is taken from the ECMWF Atmospheric Composition Reanalysis, especially the CAMS global greenhouse gas reanalysis (EGG4), which spans the period from 2003 to 2020[6]. It focusses on long-lived greenhouse gases like CO_2 and CH_4. Emissions and natural fluxes at the surface play an important role in the atmospheric evolution of these gases.

The chemical loss of CH_4 is characterised by a climatological loss rate, and surface emissions are sourced from several databases. The analysis uses a 4D-Var assimilation approach to assimilate data over a 12-hour period, accounting for the precise timing of observations and model changes inside the assimilation window.

This dataset offers worldwide, three-dimensional, time-consistent fields of atmospheric composition (AC), including chemical species, aerosols, and greenhouse gases like CH_4. It has a temporal resolution of three hours and is organised in a gridded manner with a spatial resolution of $0.75° \times 0.75°$. The xarray and netCDF4 Python libraries were used to process the NetCDF-formatted data. Using both vertical levels and surface data, we retrieved CH_4 surface fluxes along with relevant meteorological characteristics from the entire CAMS dataset, concentrating on values that are important for predicting rice paddy emissions. The left side of Fig. 1 depicts global CH_4 emissions from diverse sources, while the right side focusses on CH_4 emissions from rice paddies in West Bengal.

2.2 Overview of Methane Emission Prediction Workflow

Figure 3 illustrates the CH_4 prediction model. The model is divided into four steps: data preparation, data cleaning, data processing using ML models, and data validation.

[4] https://ndma.gov.in/sites/default/files/PDF/FHA/WB_FloodHazardAtlas.pdf.
[5] https://www.kaggle.com/datasets/rajanand/rainfall-in-india?resource=download.
[6] https://ads.atmosphere.copernicus.eu/datasets/cams-global-ghg-reanalysis-egg4?tab=documentation.

Data Preparation. The data sources and preprocessing approach are detailed in Sect. 2.1 (under Data). This study used twenty-five features from the West Bengal, CH_4 datasets. The key features include `Surface Net Solar and Thermal Radiation, Clear Sky` measured in W/m^2, which represents the balance between incoming and outgoing solar radiation, as well as the net thermal radiation exchange under clear sky conditions. The `CH4 Column-Mean Molar Fraction` (metric ppb or ppm), measures CH_4 concentration in a vertical air column. `CH4 Surface Fluxes` (Metric g CH_4/m^2/day) estimate the rate of CH_4 emission. It helps to identify the source, such as wetlands. We used this feature as the target variable in this study.

Additional features include the `10m U-Component and V-Component of Wind` (m/s) (east-west and north-south speed). The `2m Dewpoint Temperature` signifies the temperature at which air becomes saturated and dew forms at $2m$ height (metric $C°$). `2m Temperature` (air temperature at $2m$ above the surface). The `Boundary Layer Height` (m) represents the height of the atmospheric boundary layer. `Convective Inhibition` (J/kg) and `Convective rainfall` (mm) measure energy for convection and rainfall from convection, respectively. `High Cloud Cover` (%) feature is the fraction of the sky covered by high-altitude clouds. `Mean Sea Level Pressure` (hPa) represents the atmospheric pressure at sea level.

The variables include `Potential Evaporation` (mm), `Skin Reservoir Content` (m^3/m^2) for water stored on soil or vegetation, `Skin Temperature` ($C°$), `Surface Sensible Heat Flux` (W/m^2), and water metrics like Total Column Water (kg/m^2) and `Total Column Water Vapour`. Every feature provides information about the interactions between the surface and atmosphere in the area under study.

Data Cleaning. The machine learning algorithm was utilised to determine the preprocessing procedures. Algorithms like `XGBC`, `RF`, `LGBM`, and `AdaBoost` did not need normalisation. However, `SVM` and `MLP` models needed feature standardisation, which was done using a zero-mean, unit-variance transformation.

To ensure data integrity, we used a common Pytho packages to deal with missing values, fix inconsistencies, and eliminate duplicates. Features including 'Convective rainfall', 'Rainfall type', 'Total rainfall', 'Large-scale rainfall', and 'Total cloud cover' that had a high number of missing data points were removed from the dataset.

Outliers were identified via the Interquartile Range (IQR) approach. Observations below $Q1 - 1.5 \times \text{IQR}$ or above $Q3 + 1.5 \times \text{IQR}$ were flagged, and extreme values were either capped or eliminated depending on their domain relevance.

Basic data validation was carried out to ensure numerical consistency and data type integrity for all features. Before modelling, summary statistics, range checks, and feature distributions were examined for abnormalities.

Data Processing: As one objective of this work was to establish better hyperparameters we adopted the Python Optuna framework [1]. We adopted Optuna,

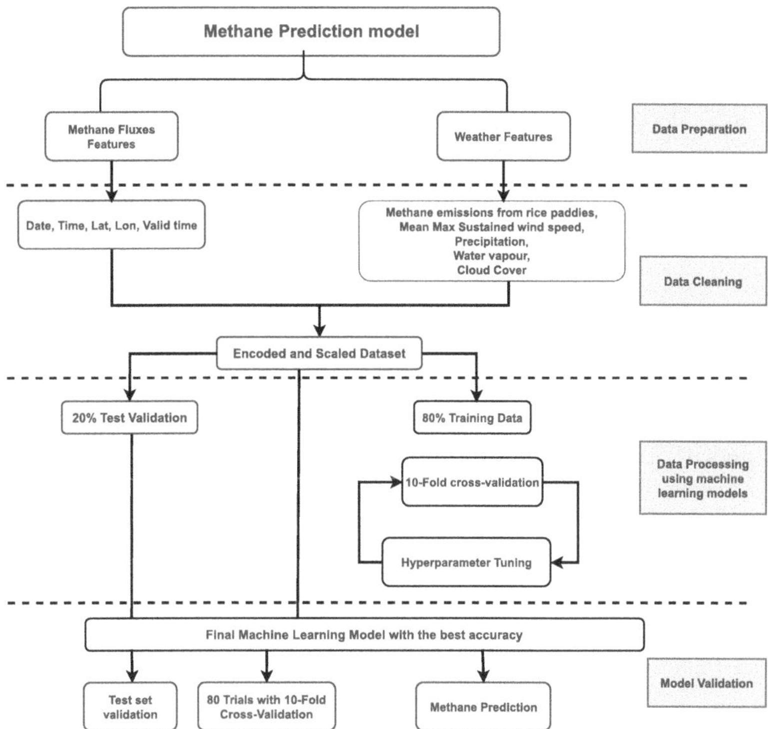

Fig. 3. Workflow for methane emission prediction from rice wetlands. The process consists of four main stages: (1) data preparation, including collection and formatting of multivariate data from CAMS; (2) data cleaning to handle missing values and outliers; (3) data processing using machine learning algorithms for feature extraction and model training; and (4) model validation to assess predictive performance.

as it claims to be an agnostic framework that is not tied to any particular machine learning or deep learning framework. To obtain a more realistic evaluation of ML model performance given the HPs selected by the Optuna framework, 10-Fold Cross-Validation (CV)[7] was used to assess the test performance of each ML model generated across each trial.

To elaborate, for each type of ML algorithm, we ran it over 80 trials, thus generating 80 10-Fold CV ML models. The average Root Mean Square Error (RMSE) value for regression obtained from 10-Fold CV was used as the basis for the Tree-structured Parzen Estimator (TPE) HPO method [2] to adjust the HPs for the next ML model training. Out of these 80 candidate ML models, the best ML model selected was based on the lowest average RMSE, depending on if the model was developed for regression respectively. Performance metrics using

[7] 10-Fold Cross-Validation is a robust technique used to evaluate a model's performance by splitting the dataset into 10 folds. It ensures that every data point is used for both training and testing.

10-Fold CV were obtained from this optimal ML model of RMSE and Mean Absolute Error (MAE) for regression [3].

All experiments used the MLP, RF, and AdaBoost algorithms from the Python `scikit-learn` library [11]. The Python XGBoost implementation was adopted from [5,8] respectively and conducted on an Intel i7-13700 PC desktop system with 32 GB of RAM running Windows 10.

The validation of the CH_4 prediction model is detailed in Sect. 3, with results summarised in Table 5.

3 Results

Table 3 shows the test results of the top-performing ML models for regression using 10-fold CV on the Indian annual rainfall dataset. The results show that XGBR and RFR outperform other methods for regression tasks on the annual rainfall dataset. These models are perfect for similar tasks since they consistently obtained the highest R^2 and the lowest prediction errors (RMSE and MAE).

Table 3. Regression model test results using 10-Fold CV for the annual rainfall dataset.

Model	RMSE	R2	MAE
SVR	0.0029±0.0020	0.9790±0.4753	0.0412±0.0133
DTR	0.09753±0.0036	0.97358±1.6592	0.0644±10.0202
RFR	0.0034±0.0017	0.981±0.5189	0.0457±0.0117
CATBR	0.0020±0.0011	0.5945±0.0896	0.0348±0.0111
XGBR	0.0022±0.0013	0.9854 ±0.2310	0.0345±0.0110
AdaBoost Regressor	0.0204±0.0023	0.9449±0.0065	0.1124±0.0058
MLPR	0.0002±0.0002	0.9473±0.0547	0.0098±0.0043
Gaussian Process Regressor	0.0002±0.0002	0.9703±0.0362	0.0081±0.0029
Gradient Boosting Regressor	0.0013±0.0009	0.7407±0.0926	0.0277±0.0104

Figure 4 shows SHAP summary plots of the input feature factors (for example, months) produced by the regressor algorithms `XGBoost`, `MLP`, `Gaussian process`, and `CatBoost`. The contribution of each feature factor determines its ranking. The SHAP value is shown on the X-axis, while the feature factors are shown on the Y-axis. The colour of each dot in the plot represents the value of a particular factor, and each dot represents a sample of rainfall from the test dataset. Red denotes a higher value, while blue denotes a lower value. The horizontal position of the dot shows whether the feature has a positive or negative influence on the prediction. Positive SHAP values indicate an increased likelihood of rainfall (greater than 0.01), thereby increasing the risk of rainfall.

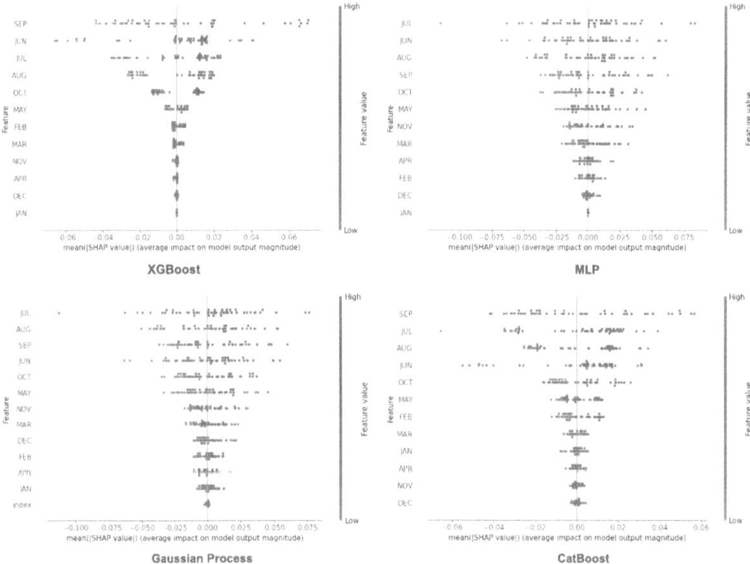

Fig. 4. SHAP summary plots of the rainfall model based on XGBoost, MLP, Gaussian Process and CatBoost regressors.

Negative SHAP values suggest an effect in scenarios with no rainfall (0), thus lowering the risk of rainfall [13].

Figure 5 shows SHAP dependence plots for rainfall data across India, demonstrating the relationship between monthly characteristics and their corresponding SHAP values. In each graphic, the X-axis indicates the rainfall value for a single month, while the Y-axis displays the SHAP values, which quantify the impact of that month on the model's prediction. These charts help to demonstrate how fluctuations in monthly rainfall affect the overall projection of annual rainfall. We learn about the nature and strength of each month's contribution by looking at patterns like linearity, thresholds, and saturation effects. In addition to highlighting possible nonlinear correlations between input variables and anticipated rainfall, this analysis helps the identification of crucial months that influence the model's output.

Figure 6 depicts a heatmap of SHAP data that show the monthly impact of features on annual rainfall projections. In this visualisation, each row represents a specific year's total rainfall, while each column corresponds to a month of the year and displays the normalised SHAP value associated with that month's features. This provides an intuitive grasp of which months have the greatest impact on the model's forecasts of annual rainfall. Higher SHAP values suggest months with a greater positive impact on the model's output, whilst lower values imply less or even negative influence. The heatmap shows temporal trends in feature importance, which may reflect seasonal variability and emphasise months with the highest prediction value for annual rainfall outcomes.

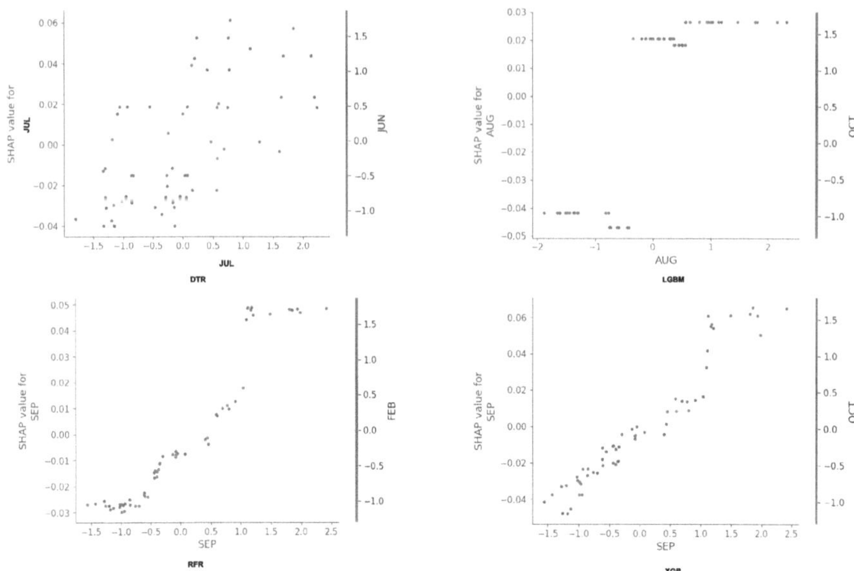

Fig. 5. SHAP dependence plots for rainfall data over India. The SHAP dependence plot identifies the relationship between a single factor (X-axis) and the corresponding SHAP values generated (Y-axis) to evaluate the effect of each month.

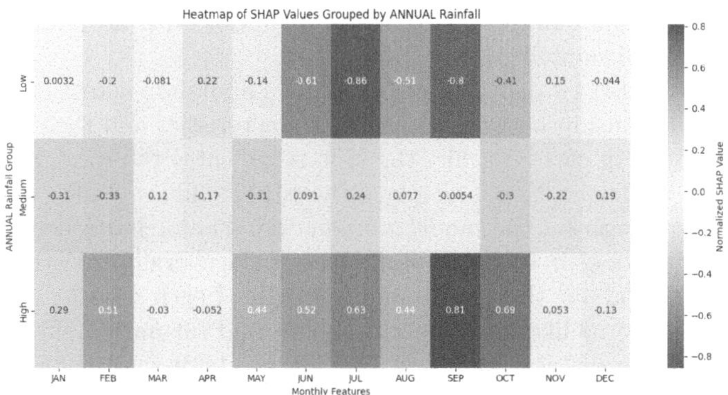

Fig. 6. A heatmap of SHAP values for a monthly analysis of annual rainfall. Each row represents the annual rainfall, while each column corresponds to the normalised SHAP values of the monthly features.

Hyperparameter tuning plays a vital role in influencing feature importance in machine learning by enhancing model performance and identifying the most impactful variables. Correctly adjusting hyperparameters improves the model's capacity to accurately assess feature relevance, resulting in greater predictive accuracy and interoperability. Table 4 shows details of the HPs used for producing the optimal ML models for regression of CH_4 emissions.

Table 4. Models and HPs for regression.

Model	Hyper-parameters
SVR	C = 0.737379, degree = 16, gamma = 'auto', kernel = 'rbf'
DTR	max_features = ['sqrt', 'log2'], max_depth = 2, 10, min_samples_split = 2, 20, min_samples_leaf = 1, 20, splitter = ['best', 'random'], criterion = ['squared_error', 'absolute_error', 'friedman_mse', 'poisson']
RF	criterion = 'poisson', max_depth = 2, max_samples = 0.651752, min_samples_leaf = 0.189317, min_samples_split = 0.449878, n_estimators = 23
Ada Boost	learning_rate = 0.014532, n_estimators = 110
XGBR	eta = 0.027458, eval_metric = 'rmse', gamma = 0.771812, max_depth = 5, max_leaves = 5, *min_child_weight* = 1, n_estimators = 99
MLP	activation = 'logistic', alpha = 0.000842, hidden_layer_sizes = 14, learning_rate = 'adaptive', learning_rate_init = 0.003694, max_iter = 265, momentum = 0.071646, solver = 'sgd'

Figures 7 and 8 presented which HPs contribute most to each model learning and performance. C is the most important hyperparameter in the SVR model (Fig. 7). For the RF model, the minimum_sample_split contributes the most (38%), followed by maximum_depth (25%), while the criterion contributes only 1% (Fig. 7). In the DTR model, max_depth and min_samples_leaf contribute 45% and 30%, respectively, whereas max features and criterion contribute less than 1% (Fig. 7). In the AdaBoost model, there are two essential hyperparameters, in which n_estimators accounting for 59% (Fig. 8). Eta and gamma contribute 20% and 19%, respectively, to the XGBoost model, while the objective and eval_metric contribute less than 1% each (Fig. 8). In the MLPR model, the learning_rate_init has the greatest impact (49%), with the solver and activation contributing 1% and less than 1%, respectively (Fig. 8).

Table 5. Regression model test results using 10-Fold CV for CH_4 emissions.

Model	RMSE	MAE	R2
SVR	0.3554±0.0742	0.3305±0.0286	0.6472±0.0334
DTR	0.6694±0.1272	0.5783±0.0600	0.3318±0.0679
RF	0.784±0.1223	0.6299±0.0457	0.2163±0.0338
AdaBoost	0.1219±0.0114	0.2817±0.0153	0.8769±0.0114
XGBR	0.0477±0.0099	0.1488±0.0124	0.9524±0.0057
MLP	**0.0091±0.0024**	**0.0739±0.0088**	**0.9805±0.0037**

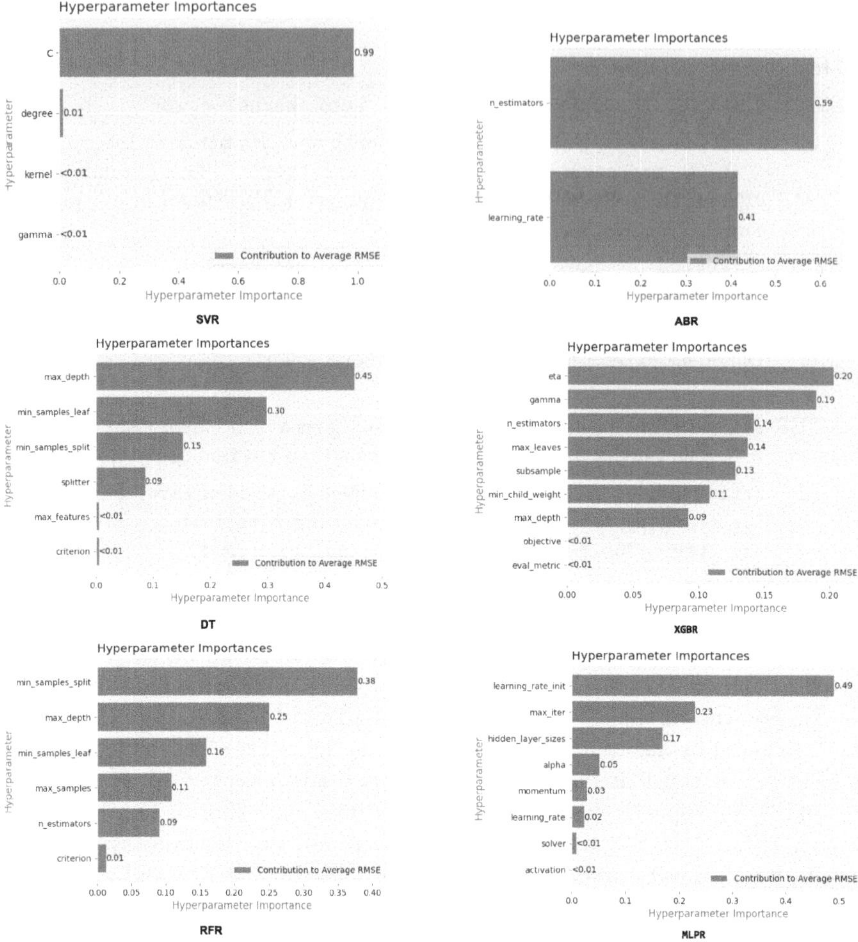

Fig. 7. HP importances for the SVR, RF and DTR models.

Fig. 8. HP importances for the ABR, XGBR and MLPR models.

Table 5 shows the validation outcomes of the models developed using the CAMS-based CH_4 emissions dataset for West Bengal. MLP is the best-performing machine learning model across all metrics. It achieved the lowest RMSE and MAE values and the highest R^2 score compared to the other models evaluated in this study, while RF was identified as the least-performing model. To further interpret the model outcomes, we extracted SHAP values to evaluate the contribution of individual features of the CAMS dataset. The dependency plots show how each factor affects the target variable and also show possible nonlinearities and interactions in the data. The plots (Fig. 9) for the top-most influential features in this analysis longitude, CH_4f, latitude, d2m, and CH_4_emis_wetlands-show

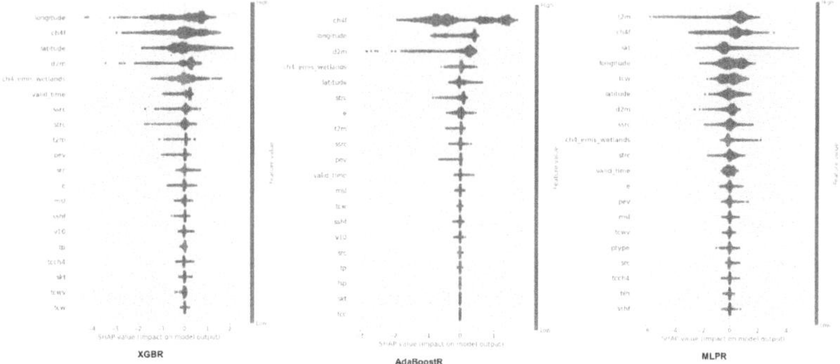

Fig. 9. SHAP summary plots of the rainfall model based on XGBoost, MLP, Gaussian Process and CatBoost regressors.

that they have a significant impact on the predictions, as evidenced by their consistent trends in SHAP values.

4 Model Insights, Limitations, and Implications

The MLP model performs better than other models in CH_4 emission prediction, according to this work (Table 5). This is most likely due to its ability to represent complex non-linear feature interactions between atmospheric variables such as temperature, dew point, and radiation–factors known to influence CH_4 fluxes in biologically active systems. XGBoost performed better in rainfall prediction (Table 3) due to its ability to learn structural temporal dependencies and regularisation procedures that prevent overfitting. In rainfall tasks, models like as RF and AdaBoost performed well, but in CH_4, they did poorly. The ensemble averaging used in RF can reduce tiny emission signals in high-dimensional input space, making it less responsive to finer spatial and temporal CH_4 changes. Such constraints highlight the need to select algorithms that are compatible with both the data structure and the physical processes underlying the phenomenon being simulated.

According to residual error analysis, the highest predicted deviations occurred during monsoon seasons or high-emission times. These spikes could be caused by quick environmental shifts that are not sufficiently depicted in the characteristics of the input or a lack of temporal precision in the training dataset. Future improvements could include ensemble model fusion, time-series augmentation, or the addition of higher-resolution meteorological data. In terms of practical significance, the low RMSE achieved for CH_4 (e.g., 0.0091 with MLP) and rainfall models indicates their potential for real-world implementation in emission monitoring systems. Accurate CH_4 prediction can help inform precision mitigation methods in rice paddies, such as changing irrigation time or applying fertiliser. Similarly, improved rainfall forecasting aids in early flood warnings and adaptive agricultural management. In order to demonstrate the consistency and relative efficacy of each machine learning model used in this work, we lastly provided a thorough comparison of model performance using common assessment metrics, including RMSE, MAE, and R^2.

The CH_4 dataset, which is based on the CAMS global reanalysis (EGG4) and covers the years 2003–2020, is one of the limitations of this study. Although this timeframe covers significant climate variability, it may not reflect more recent changes caused by developing climate dynamics after 2020. In order to improve the timeliness and relevance of the model's predictions, future work will concentrate on expanding this dataset with newer satellite-based observations (e.g. Sentinel-5P).

The spatial resolution of the CH_4 emission data, which was obtained from CAMS at a $0.75° \times 0.75°$ grid, is another limitation of this study. In subsequent research, we hope to incorporate satellite data with a finer resolution (such as Sentinel-5P, which has a resolution of about $0.1°$) to enhance spatial granularity and provide more precise district-level predictions.

We did not assess the behaviour of the model under minor input changes, even though our data cleaning process was effective in dealing with outliers, missing values, and inconsistencies (Sect. 2.2). Inaccurate sensors in real-world deployments could cause these disruptions. In future study, we intend to test the model's robustness by introducing controlled noise into key input features to better understand its sensitivity and reliability under uncertain settings.

5 Conclusion

This study proposes a comprehensive framework that integrates recent advances in machine learning to predict two critical environmental outcomes: annual rainfall patterns that impact flood events across various regions of India, and methane (CH_4) emissions from rice paddies in West Bengal. We used a variety of machine learning approaches to create predictive models based on multimodal datasets.

Our key results emphasise the role of specific hyperparameters in enhancing model performance. The XGBoost and Random Forest regressors outperformed the other algorithms in predicting annual rainfall. However, the MLP regressor was shown to be the best model for predicting CH_4 emissions. These findings highlight the necessity of thorough model selection and hyperparameter optimisation for improved prediction accuracy.

Using data from the CAMS global greenhouse gas reanalysis (EGG4), we highlighted the importance of certain variables, including CH_4 emissions from wetlands/ rice paddies, in identifying emission sources and measuring methane output in selected locations. These findings help policymakers and agricultural stakeholders build effective mitigation methods to minimise CH_4 emissions and address broader climate change problems.

Future study could improve this methodology by combining higher-resolution data and additional environmental factors to increase model granularity and robustness.

References

1. Akiba, T., Sano, S., Yanase, T., Ohta, T., Koyama, M.: Optuna: a next-generation hyperparameter optimization framework. In: Proceedings of the 25th ACM SIGKDD International Conference on Knowledge Discovery and Data Mining, pp. 2623–2631. KDD'19, Association for Computing Machinery, New York, NY, USA (2019). https://doi.org/10.1145/3292500.3330701
2. Bergstra, J., Yamins, D., Cox, D.D.: Making a science of model search: hyperparameter optimization in hundreds of dimensions for vision architectures. In: Proceedings of the 30th International Conference on International Conference on Machine Learning, vol. 28, pp. I–115–I–123. ICML'13, JMLR.org, Atlanta, GA, USA (2013). https://doi.org/10.5555/3042817.3042832
3. Bhatt, S., Chouhan, U.: An enhanced method for predicting and analysing forest fires using an attention-based CNN model. J. For. Res. **35**(1), 67 (2024). https://doi.org/10.1007/s11676-024-01717-7
4. Change, I.P.O.C.: Climate change 2007: Impacts, adaptation and vulnerability. Genebra, Suíça (2001)
5. Chen, T., Guestrin, C.: XGBoost: A scalable tree boosting system. In: Proceedings of the 22nd ACM SIGKDD International Conference on Knowledge Discovery and Data Mining, pp. 785–794. KDD'16, Association for Computing Machinery, New York, USA (2016). https://doi.org/10.1145/2939672.2939785
6. Goswami, B.N., Venugopal, V., Sengupta, D., Madhusoodanan, M., Xavier, P.K.: Increasing trend of extreme rain events over India in a warming environment. Science **314**(5804), 1442–1445 (2006)
7. Kandji, S.T., Verchot, L., Mackensen, J.: Climate Change and Variability in Southern Africa: Impacts and Adaptation Strategies in the Agricultural Sector. UNEP (2006)
8. Ke, G., Meng, Q., Finley, T., Wang, T., Chen, W., Ma, W., Ye, Q., Liu, T.Y.: LightGBM: a highly efficient gradient boosting decision tree. Adv. Neural. Inf. Process. Syst. **30**, 3146–3154 (2017). https://doi.org/10.5555/3294996.3295074
9. Kumar, V., Jain, S.K.: Trends in rainfall amount and number of rainy days in river basins of India (1951–2004). Hydrol. Res. **42**(4), 290–306 (2011)
10. Neue, H.U.: Methane emission from rice fields. Bioscience **43**(7), 466–474 (1993)
11. Pedregosa, F., et al.: Scikit-learn: machine learning in Python. J. Mach. Learn. Res. **12**, 2825–2830 (2011). https://doi.org/10.5555/1953048.2078195
12. Purkait, N., Sengupta, M., De, S., Chakrabarty, D.: Methane emission from the rice fields of West Bengal over a decade. 89.60. Fe; 92.60. Sz; 92.70. Cp (2005)
13. Roh, M., Lee, S., Jo, H.W., Lee, W.K.: Development of a forest fire diagnostic model based on machine learning techniques. Forests **15**(7), 1103 (2024)
14. Sengupta, A., Ismail, F.N.: Modelling methane emissions from rice paddies using machine learning. In: 2024 39th International Conference on Image and Vision Computing New Zealand (IVCNZ), pp. 1–6. IEEE (2024)
15. Wang, J., Akiyama, H., Yagi, K., Yan, X.: Controlling variables and emission factors of methane from global rice fields. Atmos. Chem. Phys. **18**(14), 10419–10431 (2018)

Land Use/Land Cover Classification with Spectral Indices and Otsu Thresholding

Subhash Mukherjee[1], Sourav Das[1], Somnath Mukhopadhyay[1](✉), Sunita Sarkar[1], Wangjam Niranjan Singh[1], and Ajoy Kumar Khan[2]

[1] Department of Computer Science and Engineering, Assam University, Silchar 788011, Assam, India
som.cse@live.com
[2] Department of Computer Engineering, Mizoram University, Aizawl 796004, Mizoram, India

Abstract. Accurate land use/land cover (LULC) classification is crucial for understanding environmental dynamics, monitoring natural resources, managing urban expansion, and promoting sustainable land management practices. The availability of labeled datasets is a significant obstacle to accurate land use/land cover (LULC) classification in isolated and underrepresented areas like the Barak River Basin. This study presents an unsupervised classification on Landsat 8 satellite imagery, implementing several spectral indices to overcome the insufficiency of the label data set. For vegetation identification, the Normalized Difference Vegetation Index (NDVI), Modified NDVI (MNDVI), Green NDVI (GNDVI), and Ratio Vegetation Index (RVI) were calculated. Water body detection utilized the Normalized Difference Water Index (NDWI), Modified NDWI (MNDWI), Water Ratio Index (WRI), and Automated Extraction of Water Index (AEWI). For built-up area mapping the Normalized Difference Built-up Index (NDBI), Urban Index (UI), and Built-up Index (BI) were evaluated. Amid these, it came to light that NDVI, WRI, and BI performed best for their respective categories. Otsu's thresholding technique was applied to further process these determined indices in order to classify the binary imagery of the Barak River Basin. Notwithstanding the lack of labeled training data, the thereby generated classification output was evaluated through ground truth verification and accuracy assessment, suggesting excellent performance. Utilizing the highest-performing indices, we were able to generate the label Landsat 8 imagery using an unsupervised method. In areas with inadequate information, this technique makes it possible to develop spatiotemporal datasets for long-term environmental monitoring and land management, and it determines the prerequisites for scalable LULC mapping.

Keywords: LULC · Remote sensing · Indices · Vegetation · Water · Built-up · Otsu thresholding

K. Chandra Mondal et al. (Eds.): CICBA 2025, CCIS 2863, pp. 488–505, 2026.
https://doi.org/10.1007/978-3-032-17184-9_36

1 Introduction

Land use and land cover (LULC) classification is a cornerstone of geospatial analysis, playing a crucial role in environmental monitoring, resource management, urban planning, disaster mitigation, and policy-making. The recognition of human impacts on natural ecosystems, sustainable land management, and climate resilience plans at the regional and global levels are all made feasible by timely and accurate LULC data. Remote sensing is now a vital tool for creating LULC maps across large and varied landscapes due to the increasing availability of satellite data [10]. However, accurate land cover type discrimination is essential to extract meaningful LULC information from satellite imagery. This is a challenging endeavour because of spectral overlaps, seasonal variations, and heterogeneous landscapes. Spectral indices have been established as effective measures to improve class separability by taking advantage of particular reflectance characteristics of land surface features in order to overcome this challenge. The use of specific indices, like vegetation and water indices, can accentuate the distinct spectral behaviours that vegetation, water bodies, and built-up areas display in multispectral imagery [11]. Yet, no single index is universally optimal across all geographical contexts or environmental conditions. Therefore, it is crucial to apply and compare several spectral indices to identify the best indicators for a given area or research goal. This method of comparison enhances classification accuracy and ensures methodological robustness, particularly in regions with complex land cover dynamics [17].

Notwithstanding these developments, a major obstacle still exists: the dearth of high-quality, easily accessible, and labelled geospatial datasets, particularly in areas with limited data and ecological sensitivity [6]. This problem is best illustrated by the Barak River Basin in northeastern India. Known for its rich biodiversity, intricate hydrological networks, and critical socio-economic value, the basin remains understudied in terms of fine-resolution LULC mapping [16]. The use of supervised machine learning techniques, which otherwise rule the field of remote sensing-based classification, is hampered by the lack of labelled training data [10].

This study adopts an unsupervised classification framework that incorporates several spectral indices obtained from Landsat 8 Operational Land Imager (OLI) imagery to overcome this limitation [17]. For vegetation identification, the Normalized Difference Vegetation Index (NDVI), Modified NDVI (MNDVI), Green NDVI (GNDVI), and Ratio Vegetation Index (RVI) were calculated. Water body detection utilized the Normalized Difference Water Index (NDWI), Modified NDWI (MNDWI), Water Ratio Index (WRI), and Automated Extraction of Water Index (AEWI) [11]. For built-up area mapping the Normalized Difference Built-up Index (NDBI), Urban Index (UI), and Built-up Index (BI) were evaluated. These indices are systematically compared to identify the most responsive and discriminative features for the Barak River Basin.

Otsu's thresholding technique is used to enhance the delineation of land cover boundaries [13]. In the absence of valid labels, this widely recognized histogram-based image segmentation method calculates the optimal threshold values to maximize inter-class variance, enabling a completely automated and statistically sound classification. An effective and replicable method for unsupervised LULC mapping is achieved by the combination of threshold-based segmentation and index-based clustering.

Using field surveys and high-resolution ancillary datasets to evaluate classification accuracy, validation is carried out through selective ground truthing [4]. This validation demonstrates our hybrid methodology's adaptability for use in other underrepresented or data-constrained regions and validates its dependability. Ultimately, an innovative and scalable geospatial framework for LULC classification in the Barak River Basin is presented in this study. By resolving the issues related to labeled data scarcity and improving classification through multi-index comparison, the proposed method helps to make better decisions in regional planning, environmental preservation, and disaster preparedness. Additionally, it highlights the critical need for adaptable techniques that can work well in situations with limited data, a recurring problem in remote sensing, especially in most of the developing world.

The rest of the paper is organized as follows. Section 2 presents related work in the field followed by Sect. 3 where data description is discussed, and Sect. 4 presents the proposed methodology of the paper. Then the results and discussion are given in Sect. 5. Finally, we conclude this study in Sect. 6.

2 Related Work

The Barak River is flowing parallel to the River Brahmaputra in northeast India. Its climatic scenario is quite different from that of the Brahmaputra River basin. The basin receives mostly orographic and cyclonic precipitation with about 300 cm of average annual rainfall. With an area of 41,000 km^2, the Barak River basin is considered as one of the large basins in India. Urbanization and various infrastructural activities are going on since the last couple of decades [5]. As stated by Census of India 2011, the population growth rate is 17.93% in the Barak valley [3]. The basin area is under development and on the verge of urbanization [5]. There is almost nil industrial growth in this area, although some agricultural development can be seen [18]. This study relates to the pre-stage of the adverse effect of urbanization. Rich in biodiversity and agricultural productivity, the Barak Valley is currently facing increased anthropogenic pressures such as urban expansion and deforestation, leading to substantial changes in land use/land cover (LULC) dynamics [22].

Remote sensing-based spectral indices are instrumental for monitoring vegetation health, water bodies, built-up areas, and soil exposure. The Normalized Difference Vegetation Index (NDVI) is widely used to evaluate vegetation density. NDWI (Normalized Difference Water Index) and its enhanced version MNDWI are effective for water feature detection [11,23]. In the paper [23] they modified the NDWI by replacing the NIR band with the mid-infrared band, significantly improving water feature extraction in urban contexts. Similarly, [19] demonstrated that integrating MNDWI with Digital Elevation Model (DEM) and groundwater data yielded a classification accuracy of 96.9% in Punjab. The paper [12] comparing three indices NDVI, NDWI and NDBI reported a strong negative correlation between NDVI/NDWI and land surface temperature (LST), and a positive correlation with NDBI, achieving an R^2 of 0.699 when using all three indices. Comparable results were observed in Bangladesh by [7], where NDVI showed a stronger correlation with forest cover changes than SAVI. A study investigated seasonal variations of NDVI, NDBI, and NDWI using LISS-III data, highlighting the temporal sensitivity of these indices [14,15]. The study conducted in the paper [24] monitored urban growth from 1991 to 2019 using NDVI and NDBI, revealing significant vegetation loss and urban expansion. For built-up area detection, indices such as NDBI [25], UI, and MNDBI have proven effective. [2] developed a new spectral index for detecting built-up areas using Landsat-8 imagery, outperforming traditional indices in both accuracy and kappa values. Reviews by [8] comprehensively compared built-up area indices, addressing their respective limitations. Computing vegeation, water and bulit-up the paper [1] applied seasonal thresholds using NDVI, NDWI, MNDWI, and NDBI to classify LULC types, achieving 90.2% overall accuracy and a kappa coefficient of 0.84. Thresholding techniques such as Otsu's method [20] is widely used for binary classification, minimizing intra-class variance to identify optimal thresholds. [21] demonstrated the advantage of multi-Otsu thresholding in segmenting Acute Myeloid Leukemia (AML) images, achieving 83.81% accuracy with Naïve Bayes surpassing the static Otsu method's 75.35%. Studies that incorporate multi-Otsu thresholding for LULC classification have shown improved delineation of vegetation, built-up areas, and water bodies in heterogeneous landscapes. However, these methods often require preprocessing for best performance. Accuracy assessment is fundamental to evaluating remote sensing classifications. The Cohen's Kappa coefficient, commonly used alongside overall accuracy, provides a robust measure by accounting for chance agreement. In the paper [2], high kappa values validated the effectiveness of the newly proposed index.

After studying the recent literature, we find that there are multiple spectral indices available for LULC classification, but which indices give the best result need a comparison. So, we have applied multiple indices for LULC classes like vegetation, water bodies, and built-up areas and computed the best threshold to classify into binary class. Using the best binary class, we get the unsupervised label data set for our study area.

A comparative analysis of the releated recent work on LULC classification using spectral indices is demonstrated in the Table 1. The table summarizes the methods, indices used, and reported accuracy metrics. It highlights how the proposed unsupervised method achieves superior Kappa agreement across key land cover classes while operating without labelled data.

Table 1. Comparative Analysis of Relevant Works in LULC Classification Using Spectral Indices and Thresholding.

Study (Ref)	Indices Used	Method Type	Key Findings	Limitations
Bencherif et al. [1]	NDVI, NDWI, MNDWI, NDBI	Supervised (Seasonal Thresholds)	Achieved high kappa (0.84) for LULC classification	Requires labeled data and seasonal tuning
Bouzekri et al. [2]	New Built-up Index	Supervised	Developed improved built-up index (accuracy - 92.66%) better than NDBI	Limited to built-up areas, lacks general applicability
Morsy & Hadi [12]	NDVI, NDWI, NDBI	Statistical (Correlation with LST)	Demonstrated $R^2 = 0.699$ linking LULC to temperature	Not focused on classification accuracy
Singh et al. [19]	MNDWI + DEM + Groundwater	Supervised Fusion-based	Achieved 96.9% accuracy for water classification	Focused only on water; uses ancillary data
Sun et al. [20]	Otsu + Random Forest	Hybrid (Thresholding + ML)	Improved segmentation in seasonal and snowy areas	Requires training data; computationally intensive
Xu [23]	MNDWI	Thresholding	Improved water delineation in urban areas	Applied only to water class
Suryani et al. [21]	Multi-Otsu	Unsupervised (Image Segmentation)	Multi-Otsu improved classification (83.81%) vs. Otsu (75.35%)	Study focused on medical images, not remote sensing
Proposed Work	NDVI, MNDVI, GNDVI, RVI, NDWI, MNDWI, AWEI, WRI, NDBI, UI, BI	**Unsupervised + Otsu Thresholding**	**High kappa scores: NDVI (0.93), WRI (0.83), BI (0.81); general-purpose LULC mapping**	**May require empirical validation in different terrains**

3 Data Description

In this section we have discussed the process of data collection methods and selection of the desired area for the study. The Landsat Series has provided the longest temporal coverage, spanning over 52 years since 1972. Therefore, we utilized **Landsat 8** data accessed from the United States Geological Survey (USGS) EarthExplorer platform. The data was acquired by Landsat 8 on **25-February-2025 at 04:18:20.7102020Z**, ensuring cloud-free (<5%) and radiometrically stable conditions suitable for land use/land cover (LULC) analysis. The data captured with 30 m resolution and using QGIS software we clipped the data to our desired area. We clipped the image to almost square shape, it has four corners, the upper-left corner coordinate is 24.92051°N, 92.69716°E, upper-right corner coordinate is 24.91885°N, 92.89368°E and lower-right corner coordinate is 24.74158°N, 92.89336°E, lower-left corner coordinate is 24.74058°N, 92.69831°E this makes a 2D top-view picture of Barak River Basin. This region captures the most important city of Barak River Basin, Silchar and its surrounding rivers and vegetation areas.

4 Proposed Methodology

Recently, geospatial data has proven to be highly effective in producing detailed and comprehensible results for studying Land Cover and Land Use (LULC) across different regions. Like every technology, it comes with its advantages and limitations. One of the major challenges is the unavailability of labeled datasets for specific areas. Using data from the Landsat 8 Operational Land Imager (OLI) [2], this work uses a multi-index method to address the absence of labeled datasets for the Barak River Basin. A multi-index approach enhances classification accuracy, reliability, and interpretability in remote sensing applications. It is an essential part of contemporary LULC mapping frameworks and is particularly important in areas with limited data, complex landscapes, or studies involving unsupervised techniques. The methodology encompasses satellite data preparation, spectral index computation for land cover categorization, unsupervised classification, and final validation through ground truthing. Spatial data has been classified into various categories and classes. In this study, we focus primarily on three classes and their complementary classes, as shown in Table 2, using different spectral indices. Otsu's thresholding [13] method is applied to the outcomes of each index to derive meaningful binary classifications. Each resulting binary image is then normalized to a common scale to allow comparison among indices and with the ground truth data.

Table 2. Name and description of different LULC class scheme.

S.No.	Class Name	Description of Class
1	Vegetation	Forest, cropland, shrubland and grassland.
2	Non-Vegetation	Areas excluding vegetation-covered regions.
3	Water Bodies	Rivers, lakes, bays, and estuaries.
4	Non-Water Bodies	Areas excluding water bodies.
5	Built-up	Urban residential, commercial, industrial areas, vacant land, roads, transportation.
6	Non-Built-Up	Areas excluding built-up regions.

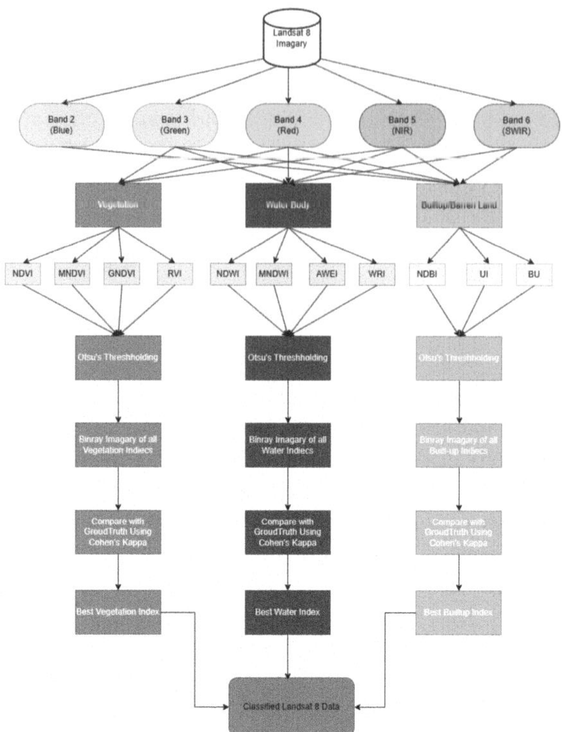

Fig. 1. Methodology workflow for LULC classification using spectral indices

Figure 1 illustrates the complete methodology, detailing each step involved in the implementation of the proposed system. Landsat 8 imagery has 11 bands, for our proposed method required only 5 bands: band 2 for blue, band 3 for green, band 4 for red, band 5 for near-infrared (NIR), and band 6 for short-wave infrared (SWIR). Using those bands, indices are calculated for the specific classes. All index results have been evaluated to the Otsu threshold in order to get the binary-classified images. The kappa score for each index is obtained by comparing all of the binary imagery with the ground truth. The final unsupervised labelled data is generated using the most significant index in its class.

In the following subsections, we have discussed the data acquisition process, preprocessing techniques, and implementation of selected spectral indices to the acquired dataset. Furthermore, we provide a comprehensive overview of unsupervised classification methods and thresholding techniques on the outputs we got, and then we compare them to ground truth data to make sure they are correct.

4.1 Satellite Data Acquisition and Preprocessing

Since 1972, NASA and USGS have worked together to develop the Landsat program, which offers reliable satellite imagery for LULC (land use and land cover) analysis. Through the USGS Earth Explorer portal, surface reflectance data from Landsat 8, which is equipped with the Thermal Infrared Sensor (TIRS) and Operational Land Imager (OLI), were acquired for this study. The details of these bands are presented in Table 2. To ensure that vegetation, populated areas, and water bodies could be detected, imagery with less than 5% cloud cover and optimum seasonal conditions was chosen. To get the dataset ready for index computations, preprocessing techniques like band stacking, spatial clipping, and resampling were executed in QGIS. Landsat 8 data consist of total 11 bands, band 1 represents Coastal Aerosol, band 2 represents Blue, band 3 represents Green, band 4 represents Red, band 5 represents NIR, band 6 represents SWIR 1, band 7 represents SWIR 2, band 8 represents Panchromatic, band 9 represents Cirrus, band 10 and band 11 represents Thermal Infrared 1 and Thermal Infrared 2. Bands 1 to 7 and 9 had 30-meter resolution, bands 10 and 11 had 100 m, and band 8 had 15-meter resolution.

4.2 Spectral Index Computation

Every index is designed to indicate a particular surface characteristic using combinations of spectral reflectance bands. Vegetation, water bodies, and built-up areas are the most significant classes for Land Use and Land Cover (LULC) classification. The proposed methodology incorporates several spectral indices as discussed below.

4.2.1 Vegetation Indices

For Landsat 8 imagery, Bands 3 (Green), 4 (Red), and 5 (Near-Infrared, NIR) are used to compute vegetation indices including NDVI, MNDVI, GNDVI, and RVI:

- Normalized Difference Vegetation Index (NDVI), which is calculated as (NIR - RED) / (NIR + RED) where NIR is band 5 and RED is band 4.
- Modified Normalized Difference Vegetation Index (MNDVI), which is calculated as (NIR - RED) / SQRT(NIR + RED + 1) where NIR is band 5 and RED is band 4.
- Green Normalized Difference Vegetation Index (GNDVI), which is calculated as (NIR - GREEN) / (NIR + GREEN) where NIR is band 5 and GREEN is band 3.
- Ratio Vegetation Index (RVI), which is calculated as (NIR / RED) where NIR is band 5 and RED is band 4.

More positive values are more likely to indicate vegetation areas, while more negative or zero values resemble non-vegetation areas.

4.2.2 Water Indices

For detecting water bodies, Landsat 8 Bands 3 (Green), 4 (Red), 5 (NIR), and 6 (SWIR1) are employed to calculate NDWI, MNDWI, AWEI, and WRI:

- Normalized Difference Water Index (NDWI), which is calculated as (GREEN - NIR) / (GREEN + NIR) where NIR is band 5 and GREEN is band 3.
- Modified Normalized Difference Water Index (MNDWI), which is calculated as (GREEN - SWIR1) / (GREEN + SWIR1) where GREEN is band 3 and SWIR1 is band 6.
- Automated Water Extraction Index (AWEI), which is calculated as 4 × (GREEN - SWIR1) - (0.25 × NIR + 2.75 × SWIR1) where NIR is band 5, GREEN is band 3, and SWIR1 is band 6.
- Water Ratio Index (WRI), which is calculated as (GREEN + RED) / (NIR + SWIR1) where NIR is band 5, RED is band 4, GREEN is band 3, and SWIR1 is band 6.

More positive values are more likely to indicate water bodies, while more negative or zero values resemble non-water bodies.

4.2.3 Built-up Indices

To identify built-up regions, indices such as NDBI, UI, and BI are calculated using Bands 2 (Blue), 3 (Green), 4 (Red), 5 (NIR), and 6 (SWIR1):

- Normalized Difference Built-up Index (NDBI), which is calculated as (SWIR1 - NIR) / (SWIR1 + NIR) where NIR is band 5 and SWIR1 is band 6.
- Urban Index (UI), which is calculated as (SWIR1 - BLUE) / (SWIR1 + BLUE) where BLUE is band 2 and SWIR1 is band 6.
- Built-up Index (BI), which is calculated as BI = Normalized Difference Built-up Index (NDBI) - Normalized Difference Vegetation Index (NDVI).

More positive BI values generally indicate built-up surfaces, while negative or zero values suggest non-urban features.

4.3 Unsupervised Classification and Thresholding

In this section, we discuss the techniques of unsupervised classification, thresholding, and clustering. To transform spectral index information into meaningful land cover classes, a structured multi-step classification methodology was adopted.

4.3.1 Index Normalization

All spectral indices are normalized to a common scale between 0.0 and 1.0 to enable reliable and meaningful comparisons between different spectral indices. This step is very crucial to avoid the bias included by differing value ranges.

For normalization we performed min-max scaling [9], where each pixel value was transformed using the equation:

$$\text{Normalized Value} = \frac{X - X_{\min}}{X_{\max} - X_{\min}} \tag{1}$$

where

- X represents the original index value,
- $X_{\min}$ denotes the minimum value of that index within the dataset,
- $X_{\max}$ denotes the maximum value of that index within the dataset.

4.3.2 Otsu's Thresholding

Otsu's method [13] was applied to each normalized index layer to compute optimal threshold values. This algorithm maximizes the inter-class variance and minimizes the intra-class variance, resulting in an effective binary classification. It enables separation of classes such as:

- Vegetation vs. Non-vegetation,
- Water vs. Non-water,
- Built-up vs. Non built-up.

The step by step process to compute otsu thresholding is discussed in the **Algorithm 1.**

Algorithm 1. Otsu's Thresholding Algorithm

1: **Input:** Grayscale image with L gray levels $[1, 2, \ldots, L]$
2: **Output:** Optimal threshold k^*
3: Compute histogram of the image
4: Normalize histogram: $p_i = \frac{n_i}{N}$, where n_i is the number of pixels at level i and N is total pixels
5: Initialize: $\omega(k) \leftarrow 0$, $\mu(k) \leftarrow 0$, $\mu_T \leftarrow \sum_{i=1}^{L} i \cdot p_i$, $\sigma_{\max}^2 \leftarrow 0$, $k^* \leftarrow 0$
6: **for** $k = 1$ to $L - 1$ **do**
7: Compute $\omega(k) = \sum_{i=1}^{k} p_i$
8: Compute $\mu(k) = \sum_{i=1}^{k} i \cdot p_i$
9: **if** $\omega(k) = 0$ or $\omega(k) = 1$ **then**
10: **continue**
11: **end if**
12: Compute between-class variance:

$$\sigma_b^2(k) = \frac{[\mu_T \cdot \omega(k) - \mu(k)]^2}{\omega(k) \cdot (1 - \omega(k))}$$

13: **if** $\sigma_b^2(k) > \sigma_{\max}^2$ **then**
14: $\sigma_{\max}^2 \leftarrow \sigma_b^2(k)$
15: $k^* \leftarrow k$
16: **end if**
17: **end for**
18: **return** k^*

4.3.3 Clustering and Masking

Every pixel of the data was evaluated using the normalized indices of built-up, water, and vegetation and allocated to the class with the highest index value. The masking operation is applied to segregate every land cover class. Binary masks were generated for each class using Otsu's thresholding. Utilizing the unsupervised classification approach, the comparative index-based clustering finally classified the pixels into vegetation, water bodies, and built-up areas without the need for any pre-labeled training data.

4.4 Ground Truthing

The ground truth data is gathered by physically reaching the ground truth points and capturing the images of that point with its coordinates. The steps of generating the ground truth are discussed below.

- For capturing the image with coordinates, we used GPS Map Camera Application for 102 random points within the study area.
- The data must be documented and stored in structured `.csv` format to import in QGIS software for generating the georeferenced ground truth in `.tiff` format.

Fig. 2. Sample of ground truth

In Fig. 2 we showed the collected data, with samples of the vegetation class (a) and (f), the built-up class (b) and (e), and finally the water class (c) and (d) with the coordinates.

5 Result and Validation

In this section we have discussed results and compared the outputs with ground truth. The selected sample points are compared with classified results to achieve accuracy. Accuracy metrics such as kappa Coefficient were calculated to evaluate the performance of the classification.

5.1 Classification Result Comparisons

Visual comparisons between the classified results and the ground truth are carried out across three major land cover categories:

5.1.1 Vegetation Classification Comparison

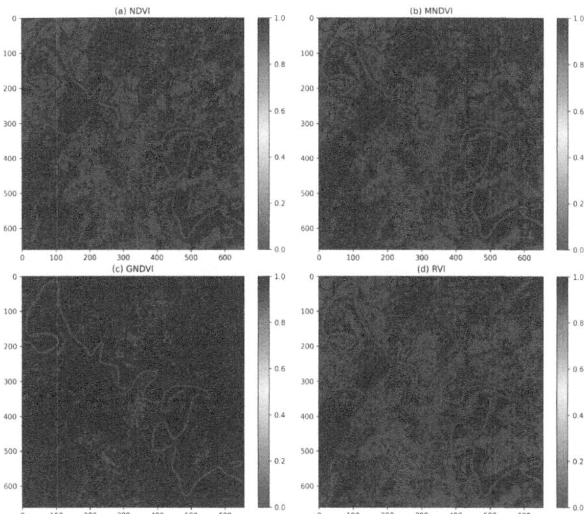

Fig. 3. (a) NDVI, (b) MNDVI, (c) GNDVI and (d) RVI indices output (vegetation).

In Fig. 3, the green color refers to the vegetation areas and the red color area refers to the non-vegetation areas. Those are the binary classified images after applying otsu's thresholding. NDVI (a) and MNDVI (b) show very similar and almost accurate results. GNDVI (c) produces inaccurate results with marking non-vegetation areas as vegetation. RVI (d) produces average and noisy results.

5.1.2 Water Body Classification Comparison

In Fig. 4, the blue color refers to the water bodies and the white color area refers to the non-water bodies. Those are the binary classified images after applying otsu's thresholding. WRI (d) gives the best output among others. NDWI (a) and MNDWI (b) show similar and almost accurate results. AWEI (c) produces inaccurate results with marking non-water bodies as water bodies.

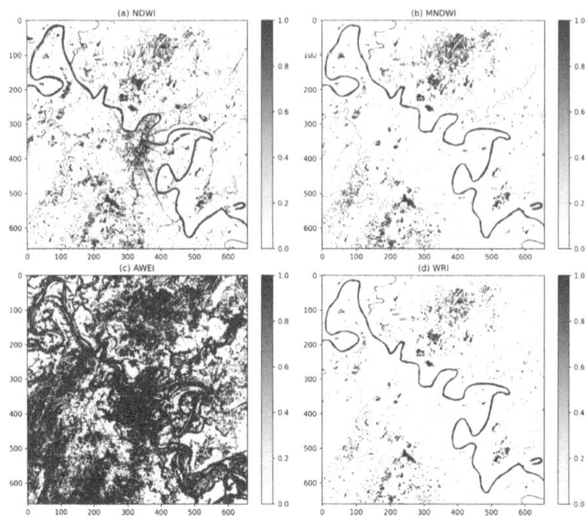

Fig. 4. (a) NDWI, (b) MNDWI, (c) AWEI and (d) WRI indices output (Water Bodies).

5.1.3 Built-up Area Classification Comparison

In Fig. 5, the black color refers to the built-up area and the white color area refers to the non-built-up bodies Those are the binary classified images after applying otsu's thresholding. BI (c) gives the best output among others. NDBI (a) show similar and almost accurate results. UI (c) produces inaccurate results with marking non-built-up areas as built-up areas.

5.2 Kappa Coefficient (κ)

The Kappa coefficient is a statistical metric that measures the agreement between the observed (ground truth) and predicted classifications, adjusted for chance agreement. It is calculated as:

$$\kappa = \frac{p_o - p_e}{1 - p_e} \tag{2}$$

where:

- p_o = observed agreement
- p_e = expected agreement by chance

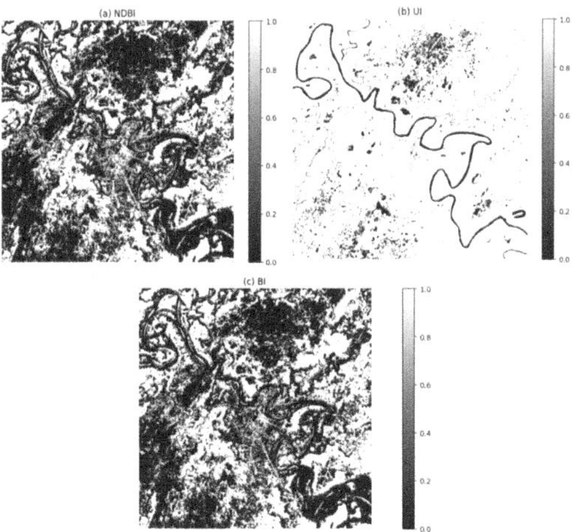

Fig. 5. (a) NDBI,(b) UI, and (c) BI indices output (Built-up Area).

Table 3. Interpretation of Kappa Coefficient Values

S.No.	Kappa Value (κ)	Level of Agreement
1	< 0	No agreement
2	0.01–0.20	Slight agreement
3	0.21–0.40	Fair agreement
4	0.41–0.60	Moderate agreement
5	0.61–0.80	Substantial agreement
6	0.81–1.00	Almost perfect agreement

In Table 3, Kappa values (κ) are shown, the range and its significance level. More the value close to +1 more it is close to almost perfect agreement and 0 or less than zero says no agreement. The comparative result of all indices with Ground Truth(GT) is shown with the kappa score and the final rank of each category in Table 4. For vegetation classification, the NDVI performed the best with 0.93 Kappa score, showing a very strong match with ground truth.NDVI achieved the highest score for vegetation due to its proven sensitivity to chlorophyll content and dense vegetation. MNDVI and RVI performed well, but GNDVI showed poor results for this Barak River Basin area.MNDVI is designed to reduce atmospheric and background noise, which may have reduced contrast in dense tropical vegetation such as those found in the Barak River Basin and it affects the result of MNDVI. RVI commonly performed well for open, dry vegetation zones, it is sensitive to illumination variations and soil background, which are common in the Barak Basin due to its hilly terrain and heterogeneous soil which can cause saturated results. GNDVI is very sensitive to chlorophyll content but less effective in mixed vegetation-soil backgrounds which may cause poor results in the

Barak River Basin. For identifying water bodies, the WRI achieved the highest Kappa score (0.83), making it the most suitable among other tested water indices. WRI effectively enhances the spectral response of water features while suppressing the signal from vegetation and soil with best results in the Barak River Basin area. MNDWI and NDWI offered moderate accuracy, but AWEI performed very poorly for this Barak River Basin area. MNDWI uses a SWIR band which can also reflect from exposed soil, wet soil and sandbanks, reducing water detection accuracy. NDWI performs well in open water detection, but in the Barak Basin, sediment-laden water and mixed water-vegetation pixels lead to misclassification and reduce its efficacy. AWEI is designed to remove shadows effectively in urban scenes or cloud-shadow environments, but we use less than 5% cloudy data and confuse water with dark shadows from dense forest or steep slopes, leading to poor detection. For built-up area detection, the Built-up Index (BI) scored highest (0.81), and NDBI shows average performance. BI achieved the best results among built-up indices because it captures the contrast between built-up surfaces and their surroundings, especially in urban-rural transition zones like the Barak River Basin. The Urban Index (UI) showed weak agreement for this Barak River Basin area. NDBI uses the difference between SWIR and NIR bands. It can confuse bare soil and dry riverbeds with urban structures, which are common in the Barak Basin. The Urban Index is optimized for high-density urban zones, which are rare in the Barak River Basin, resulting in a very low Kappa score.

Table 4. Kappa Scores and Ranks for Indices by Category

Category	Index vs Ground Truth	Kappa Score	Rank
Vegetation	NDVI vs GT	**0.9324**	1st
	MNDVI vs GT	0.8201	2nd
	RVI vs GT	0.8164	3rd
	GNDVI vs GT	0.2844	4th
Water Body	WRI vs GT	**0.8283**	1st
	MNDWI vs GT	0.6329	2nd
	NDWI vs GT	0.6065	3rd
	AWEI vs GT	0.1409	4th
Built-up	BI vs GT	**0.8144**	1st
	NDBI vs GT	0.7780	2nd
	UI vs GT	0.1327	3rd

5.3 Unsupervised Classified Result

In our study NDVI, WRI, and BI proved to be the most effective indices in their respective categories. Utilizing those indices we are able to generate the final unsupervised label data shown in Fig. 6. Where the red color shows the built-up area, blue color resembles all types of water bodies, green shows the vegetation area and lastly black incorporates the background. In conclusion, by implementing NDVI, WRI and BI we are able to label the data using this unsupervised proposed methodology.

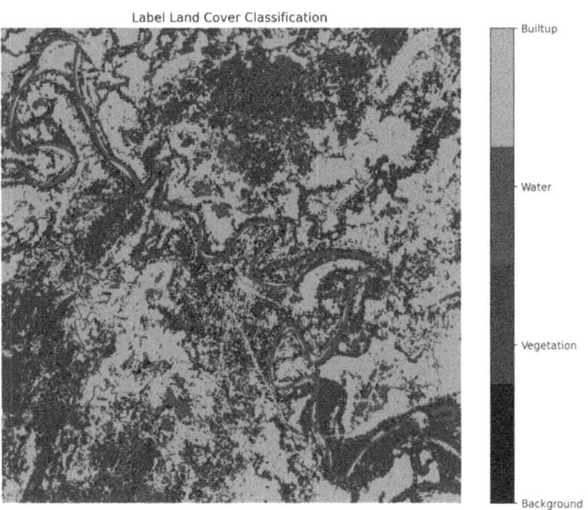

Fig. 6. Visualization of NDBI, UI, and BI indices.

6 Conclusion and Future Scope

The supervised classification plays a crucial role in remote sensing data analysis, but to achieve this requires a sufficient amount of label data set. The Barak River Basin area is lacking on that label data set so it is important to improvise unsupervised methods for this region. The proposed methodology successfully overcomes the problem for Barak River Basin. This study shows, among multiple spectral indices applied, the NDVI proved to be the most effective for vegetation classification, the WRI performed best among other indices in detecting water bodies, and the BI worked accurately to evaluate built-up areas. Utilizing these top-performing indices, we successfully generated an unsupervised LULC classification for the Barak River Basin despite the limitation of having no labeled datasets.

In future, this methodology can be used for the development of a large-scale, temporally rich LULC dataset for the Barak River Basin. That dataset could be used for spatiotemporal change analysis, supporting environmental monitoring, urban expansion studies, flood risk assessment, and land management planning in the region. With further integration of high-resolution satellite data and limited ground truthing, this technique can evolve into a scalable, semi-automated pipeline for long-term geospatial monitoring across similar underrepresented and ecologically sensitive regions.

Acknowledgement. This work was supported by the sponsored project under the **Department of Science and Technology (DST), Govt. of India - Tribal Sub-Plan (TSP)** scheme of IIT Bhilai Innovation and Technology Foundation (IBITF), **Sanction Number:** IBITF/Note/TSP/SanctionLetter/2024-25/0125.

References

1. Bencherif, L., Bougherara, H., Boudjemaa, R.: Mapping typical LULC classes using spatiotemporal analysis and the thresholds of spectral optical satellite imagery indices: a case study in Algiers city. Environ. Monit. Assess. **195**(11), 1351 (2023)
2. Bouzekri, S., Wu, H., Shamsoddini, A.: A new spectral index for the detection of built-up areas: development and application to the landsat-8 imagery. J. Indian Soc. Remote Sens. **43**, 867–875 (2015)
3. Chandramouli, C.: Census of India 2011: Provisional Population Totals. Registrar General and Census Commissioner, New Delhi (2011)
4. Congalton, R.G.: A review of assessing the accuracy of classifications of remotely sensed data. Remote Sens. Environ. **37**(1), 35–46 (1991)
5. Dutta, S.: Urbanization in Barak valley: a geographical analysis. Northeast. Geogr. **34**(1–2), 45–52 (2002)
6. Gong, P., et al.: Global land cover mapping at 30 m resolution: a POK-based operational approach. ISPRS J. Photogramm. Remote. Sens. **103**, 7–27 (2020)
7. Hossain, M.S., Rahman, M., Akter, S.: Land use and land cover change detection using NDVI and SAVI in Fashiakhali wildlife sanctuary, Bangladesh. Environ. Challenges **10**, 100752 (2023)
8. Kaur, R., Pandey, P.: A review on spectral indices for built-up area extraction using remote sensing technology. Arab. J. Geosci. **15**, 1–14 (2022)
9. Liu, X., Yuan, X., Felix Lee, H.: A robust data scaling algorithm to improve classification accuracies in biomedical data. BMC Bioinf. **17**(1), 1–13 (2016)
10. Lu, D., Weng, Q.: A survey of image classification methods and techniques for improving classification performance. Int. J. Remote Sens. **28**(5), 823–870 (2007)
11. McFeeters, S.K.: The use of the normalized difference water index (NDWI) in the delineation of open water features. Int. J. Remote Sens. **17**(7), 1425–1432 (1996)
12. Morsy, S., Hadi, M.: Impact of land use/land cover on land surface temperature and its relationship with spectral indices in Dakahlia governorate, Egypt. Int. J. Eng. Geosci. **7**(3), 272–282 (2022)
13. Otsu, N.: A threshold selection method from gray-level histograms. IEEE Trans. Syst. Man Cybern. **9**(1), 62–66 (1979)
14. Pattanayak, J., Diwakar, P.G.: Seasonal variability analysis using NDVI, NDWI and NDBI in Hyderabad region. In: 2018 IEEE International Geoscience and Remote Sensing Symposium (IGARSS), pp. 1280–1283. IEEE (2018)
15. Pattanayak, S.P., Diwakar, S.K.: Seasonal comparative study of NDVI, NDBI and NDWI of Hyderabad city (Telangana) based on LISS-III image using remote sensing and dip. Khoj: Int. Peer Review. J. Geo. **5**, 78–86 (2018)
16. Rahman, M.A., Das, B., Ahmed, M.N.: Land use and land cover dynamics and their impacts on ecosystem services in the Barak river basin. Ecol. Ind. **125**, 107557 (2021)
17. Roy, D.P., et al.: Landsat-8: science and product vision for terrestrial global change research. Remote Sens. Environ. **145**, 154–172 (2014)

18. Roy, M., Bezbaruah, M.P.: Agricultural development in the Barak valley region. Indian J. Reg. Sci. **34**(1), 55–62 (2002)
19. Singh, A., Setia, R., Sharma, P.: Comparative analysis of water indices to detect surface water bodies in satellite images. J. Indian Soc. Remote Sens. **43**(3), 625–635 (2015)
20. Sun, X., Li, X., Tan, B., Gao, J., Wang, L., Xiong, S.: Integrating OSTU thresholding and random forest for land use/land cover (LULC) classification and seasonal analysis of water and snow/ice. Remote Sens. **17**(5), 797 (2025)
21. Suryani, E., Asmari, E.I., Harjito, B.: Image segmentation of acute myeloid leukemia using multi OSTU thresholding. J. Phys: Conf. Ser. **1803**, 012016 (2021)
22. Talukdar, N.R., Singh, B., Choudhury, P.: Conservation status of some endangered mammals in Barak valley. Northeast India. J. Asia-Pac. Biodivers. **11**, 167–172 (2018)
23. Xu, H.: Modification of normalized difference water index (NDWI) to enhance open water features in remotely sensed imagery. Int. J. Remote Sens. **27**(14), 3025–3033 (2006)
24. Yasin, M.Y., Abdullah, J., Noor, N.M., Yusoff, M.M., Noor, N.M.: Landsat observation of urban growth and land use change using NDVI and NDBI analysis. In: IOP Conference Series: Earth and Environmental Science, vol. 540(1), p. 012070 (2020)
25. Zha, Y., Gao, J., Ni, S.: Use of normalized difference built-up index in automatically mapping urban areas from tm imagery. Int. J. Remote Sens. **24**(3), 583–594 (2003)

Author Index

K. Chandra Mondal et al. (Eds.): CICBA 2025, CCIS 2863, pp. 507–508, 2026.
https://doi.org/10.1007/978-3-032-17184-9

The manufacturer's authorised representative in the EU is Springer Nature Customer Service Centre GmbH, Europaplatz 3, 69115 Heidelberg, Germany. If you have any concerns regarding our products, please contact ProductSafety@springernature.com

Printed and bound by CPI Group (UK) Ltd, Croydon, CR0 4YY

07/07/2026

02160906-0013